Gunnar Myrdal
and America's Conscience

The Fred W. Morrison
Series in Southern Studies

Gunnar Myrdal
and America's Conscience

Social Engineering and

Racial Liberalism, 1938–1987

Walter A. Jackson

The

University

of North

Carolina Press

Chapel Hill

and London

The paper in this book meets the guidelines for permanence and durability
of the Committee on Production Guidelines for Book Longevity of the Council
on Library Resources.

94 93 92 91 90   5 4 3 2 1

Library of Congress Cataloging-in-Publication Data
Jackson, Walter A.
   Gunnar Myrdal and America's conscience : social engineering and
racial liberalism, 1938–1987 / by Walter A. Jackson.
      p.   cm.—(Fred W. Morrison series in Southern studies)
   Includes bibliographical references.
   ISBN 0-8078-1911-5 (alk. paper)
      1. United States—Social conditions—1933–1945.   2. United States—
Social conditions—1945–   3. Myrdal, Gunnar, 1898–   American
dilemma.   4. Race discrimination—United States—History—20th
century.   I. Title.   II. Series.
HN57.J246   1990
306'.0973—dc20   90-12015
[0904]   CIP

To the memory of my mother
and for my father

Contents

Illustrations

Preface

In a life that spanned most of the twentieth century, Gunnar Myrdal contributed ideas to many of the century's major political, economic, and social debates. As a young economist in the late 1920s, he shocked the older generation of Swedish neoclassicists with a daring critique of political biases in neoclassical economics. In the 1930s Myrdal was one of the architects of the Swedish welfare state, proposing new policies concerning economic planning, birth control, women's rights, child care, public housing, and agricultural modernization. During the Second World War, he was a critic of Nazi ideology, urging Swedes to remain faithful to democratic ideals and to resist Nazi propaganda. As a United Nations official from 1947 to 1957, Myrdal played a prominent role in planning the economic reconstruction of Europe and advocated détente before it was in vogue in Washington or Moscow. From the mid-1950s until his death in 1987, he directed inquiries into poverty in the Third World, studied the problems of Western welfare states, and spoke out against United States policy in Vietnam. Together with his wife, the diplomat and Nobel laureate Alva Myrdal, he championed nuclear disarmament.

Gunnar Myrdal is best known in the United States for his book *An American Dilemma: The Negro Problem and Modern Democracy*, one of the most influential works of social science ever written in America. This fourteen-hundred-page study, published in 1944, established a liberal orthodoxy on black-white relations and remained the most important study of the race issue until the middle of the 1960s. As the civil rights movement gained momentum, many educated white Americans turned to Myrdal's book in an effort to understand the effects of white racism on Afro-American life. Activists, educators, ministers, and social workers referred to *An American Dilemma* in campaigns against segregation and discrimination. A generation of college students read it as a textbook in social science courses. Most significantly, Chief Justice Earl Warren cited *An American Dilemma* in the Supreme Court's *Brown v. Board of Education* decision to support the view that segregated schools were inherently unequal.[1]

Myrdal turned the conventional wisdom of white Americans on its head by arguing that the "Negro problem" was really a "white man's problem," a massive social problem of national dimensions caused by white racial discrimination. In analyzing "America's greatest failure," he developed a new interpretation of American race relations that would strongly influence postwar racial liberalism. At a time when the Roosevelt administration avoided the issue of civil rights, Myrdal argued that the federal government had to take action to end racial discrimination and to establish equality of economic opportunity. In an era when most American social scientists sought to practice their craft on the model of the natural sciences, eschewing discussions of morality and viewing social engineering as beyond the scope of their work, Myrdal combined appeals to morality with advocacy of ambitious programs of social engineering. He saw racial discrimination as an irrational aberration from a fundamentally egalitarian tradition of American life and believed that educational efforts would substantially reduce white prejudice. In addition, Myrdal took a strongly assimilationist position on black culture, emphasizing the strategic importance of blacks acquiring the cultural characteristics deemed valuable by white Americans.

While many liberals of the 1930s had concentrated on bettering the economic condition of blacks, Myrdal emphasized the psychological and moral dimensions of the race issue. The central argument of *An American Dilemma* was that white Americans experienced a profound psychological conflict concerning blacks: on the one hand, whites believed in an "American Creed" of democracy and equality of opportunity; on the other hand, they held prejudices against blacks.[2] The idea that Americans were not living up to their democratic principles on the race issue had been a commonplace assertion, perhaps even a cliché, in the rhetoric of civil rights advocates. But Myrdal did not merely argue that the contradiction existed; he insisted that white Americans experienced it as a mental conflict. In addition, he argued that this conflict between creed and practice occurred in the American legal system, federal bureaucracy, political parties, labor unions, corporations, and voluntary organizations. Segregation and disfranchisement were sanctioned by law in many states, yet American blacks could appeal to Constitutional guarantees of equality in pressing their case before the Congress, the Supreme Court, and the federal agencies. Myrdal was optimistic that eventually the American creed would win out, because he recognized that the United States would have to confront the race issue in a new global context. White Americans, in his view, would be forced to bring their racial practices into conformity with their creed because of increasingly militant black protest together with the international embarrassment that segregation caused the United States.[3] Myrdal focused attention on the reduction of prejudice among individual whites and argued that better-educated whites were more sympathetic to black demands than white workers.[4] In examining Afro-American culture, he stressed the destructive effects of white racial oppression and argued that in those areas in which black culture differed from white culture, it was a "distorted development, or a pathological condition, of the general American culture."[5]

Although these ideas would become widespread among American intellectuals in the 1950s and 1960s, reviewers of many persuasions saw *An American Dilemma* as a bold and strikingly original book when it appeared in 1944. The sociologist Robert S. Lynd compared Myrdal's work to the classic interpretations of American culture of Alexis de Tocqueville and James Bryce.[6] Black intellectuals such as W. E. B. Du Bois and E. Franklin Frazier applauded its forthright assault on racial inequality.[7] White southern reviewers were less enthusiastic, but most expressed admiration for Myrdal's exhaustive investigation, even if they thought that the Swedish interloper misunderstood certain features of the race issue in the South.[8]

American readers were particularly impressed by the fact that when Gunnar Myrdal began his research in the fall of 1938 he knew practically nothing about black Americans. He had come to the United States at the invitation of the Carnegie Corporation of New York, a private philanthropic foundation. In his foreword to *An American Dilemma*, Carnegie president Frederick Keppel offered an explanation for the foundation's selection of a Swedish economist to conduct a broad survey of American race relations. According to Keppel, former secretary of war Newton D. Baker, a Carnegie trustee, had suggested that the corporation sponsor a study of black Americans to gain a better understanding of how to distribute its funds. Because the race issue was so "charged with emotion" in the United States, Keppel explained, the foundation decided to invite a foreign scholar from a country "with no background or traditions of imperialism which might lessen the confidence of Negroes in the United States as to the complete impartiality of its findings." With these criteria in mind, Keppel claimed, the corporation had approached Gunnar Myrdal, a professor of economics at the University of Stockholm, economic advisor to the Swedish government, and member of the upper house of the Swedish parliament. To assist the foreign scholar in his research, the foundation had provided a staff of American social scientists selected by Myrdal.[9]

Although Baker and Keppel were only dimly aware of conditions among black Americans, they commissioned a major study precisely at a point of rapid social change in American race relations. The years from 1935, when Baker called for an investigation of the "Negro problem," to 1944, when *An American Dilemma* was published, comprised nearly a decade of economic, social, and political upheaval among Afro-Americans. The Great Depression pushed thousands of southern black tenant farmers off the land and into the cities of the North and South, where they faced conditions of high unemployment, limited relief, and overcrowded housing. Yet the race issue did not attain the high profile in political and intellectual discussions that it would enjoy in the 1960s. The political response of the New Deal was ambivalent, reflecting the conflicting interests of its diverse constituencies: wealthy southern landowners, poor farmers, industrial unionists, and northern blacks. Civil rights organizations, radicals, and reformers differed sharply in their strategies for opposing racial inequality, which ranged from the interracial unionism of the Communists to the civil libertarianism of the NAACP. American social scientists who wrote about race relations were also divided into several schools of thought with widely divergent interpretations.

This book investigates how Gunnar Myrdal came to write *An American Dilemma* and why it exerted such a powerful influence on American thought and public policy concerning black Americans. To address these issues, I offer, first, a detailed analysis of the relationship between the Carnegie Corporation and the Myrdal study and examine the ways in which the foundation influenced Myrdal's approach. Keppel's account of the origins of the study, which omitted several highly significant details, has led to considerable speculation about the politics of the Myrdal project. While some scholars have accepted Keppel's account uncritically,[10] others have viewed Myrdal primarily as a mouthpiece for American capitalism.[11] Yet another group of writers has argued that Myrdal merely summarized the work of American social scientists concerning race relations.[12] In an effort to understand the interaction between the foundation and this major social science research project, I analyze the legacy of the donor, the structure of the foundation and its policies concerning black Americans, and the motives of Baker and Keppel. I also ask to what extent the foundation shaped the questions being investigated, the assumptions behind the study, and the networks of scholars and reformers who worked with Myrdal. But an author may come to conclusions that are quite different from the views of officials of the sponsoring foundation, and it is also important to ask how Myrdal interpreted the role of foreign observer of American race relations and what values he brought to the study. An independent thinker with extraordinary energy and fierce determination, Myrdal was neither a docile servant of American elites nor a mere imitator of American social science.

Scholars who have written about *An American Dilemma* have given little attention to Myrdal's career prior to 1938. And yet the political, moral, and intellectual commitments that informed his research on Afro-Americans had their roots in his early life and work as an economist and political figure in Sweden. Born in rural Dalarna province in 1898, Myrdal spent his earliest childhood and several summers of his youth in a remote rural hamlet where his ancestors had farmed for three hundred years. His father was an ambitious man who left farming, moved the family to Stockholm, and rose to become a successful building contractor. Myrdal's mother was never comfortable with this upward mobility, however, and her outlook remained rooted in the religious, moralistic culture of rural Dalarna. As a young man, Myrdal lost his Lutheran faith but found a substitute in the secular, rationalistic philosophy of the Enlightenment, with its promise of using scientific knowledge for human betterment. A brilliant outsider at the University of Stockholm, he struggled to win academic honors and to gain acceptance from teachers and peers. In the years from 1918 to 1932, Myrdal's political and economic thought moved rapidly through three phases. As a university student, he was something of an "intellectual aristocrat," influenced by the Nietzschean ideal of the superman, and he proposed a "party of the intelligent," a meritocracy of brilliant men from all classes who would manipulate the masses and provide rational direction for Sweden in the new world of universal suffrage. In the mid-1920s, Myrdal embraced the European liberalism* of his mentor, the neoclassical

---

* The term "liberal" has different meanings in Europe and America in the twentieth century. In Chapter 2, and in other references to Swedish politics and thought, the term refers to an ideology that opposes government intervention in the free market while

economist Gustav Cassel, who taught him that the free market was the most efficient means of diffusing prosperity to the largest number of people. In 1931, Myrdal joined the Social Democratic party, and he soon emerged as one of the party's leading intellectuals, contributing ideas to the creation of the Swedish welfare state.

This last and most important transition reflected the influence of his wife, Alva Reimer Myrdal, who had grown up in a Social Democratic family and exerted a powerful influence on her husband toward a greater concern for social reform and equality. Gunnar Myrdal's decision to become a Social Democrat also emerged, ironically, out of his experiences as a Rockefeller Foundation Fellow in the United States in 1929–30. The spectacular collapse of the American economy and the inability of neoclassical economics to prescribe an effective cure for it turned Myrdal toward an interest in social engineering,[13] institutional economics, and interdisciplinary social science research. Both Gunnar and Alva Myrdal thought that much American social science research in the 1920s was too narrow and technical, and they found most American intellectuals to be cynical and politically apathetic. The Myrdals drew their inspiration from the legacy of the Progressive movement in social science, especially the work of John R. Commons and John Dewey, and they resonated to the Progressive generation's rationalism, optimism, moralism, and commitment to social engineering.

On returning to Sweden, Gunnar Myrdal swiftly rose to prominence as a member of the Stockholm school of economics and was appointed to the chair of economics at the University of Stockholm at the age of thirty-five. As an economic advisor to Social Democratic governments and as a member of the upper house of the Swedish parliament, he was deeply involved with social engineering and planning for the welfare state. Though his outlook remained elitist in many respects, he threw himself into the struggle to eliminate poverty and to provide a secure foundation of economic prosperity for Swedish democracy. On royal commissions and parliamentary committees, he developed skills in the politics of consensus, and he often argued to Swedish conservatives that they should adopt reforms as preventive or "prophylactic" measures so that social problems would not become unmanageable later. Myrdal was an unusual social engineer because he maintained that social scientists should state explicitly the value premises that they bring to a particular investigation, and he held that, in a democracy, social scientists should attempt, in so far as possible, to draw their value premises from the general beliefs and values of the people. Yet he retained a faith that social science experts could lead the people to a life based on rational, scientific princi-

---

supporting universal suffrage, the right of the individual to equal justice before the law, and parliamentary government. In chapters dealing with the United States, I analyze the process through which civil rights was incorporated into the tradition of "liberal" reform coming out of the New Deal, in which an active federal government engaged in planning and intervened in the economy to create jobs.

ples, and he confidently recommended a wide range of policies of social engineering that included communal housing, day care, improvements in the status of women, and eugenics.

By the time Myrdal began his investigation of black Americans in the fall of 1938, American social scientists had produced a significant body of research on race relations, but, for the most part, this research did not directly address questions of public policy or social reform, though of course it contained political assumptions and biases. Most professional sociologists, anthropologists, and psychologists who wrote about race relations held that social science research should be value neutral. Some of these men and women thought that it was appropriate for social scientists to sign petitions or advocate political positions in their roles as citizens, but in their scholarly publications, they generally refrained from discussing the political implications of their findings. This stance was part of an effort to establish the "scientific" status of the various social science disciplines and to make them independent of both reformers and the government. Robert Park and other social scientists of the 1920s and 1930s sought to distance themselves both from the moralistic reformers of the Progressive Era who had spun out grand designs for "social control" and from the racists of the 1920s who sought to use social science studies of ethnic differences to support immigration restriction and eugenic legislation. The avoidance of political involvement by social scientists who wrote about black-white relations was reinforced by the attitude of most New Deal administrators that the race issue was "too hot to handle." Although Franklin Roosevelt relied on a "Brains Trust" of economists and although various New Deal agencies employed social scientists, no significant policy-oriented studies of Afro-Americans had been published under government sponsorship when Myrdal began his work.[14]

American social scientists had destroyed an important scientific rationale for segregation by discrediting the idea of innate racial differences in intelligence. Yet the triumph of "environmentalism" did not mean that social scientists had reached any clear consensus in explaining the causes of racial prejudice, the nature of Afro-American culture, or the ease with which racial attitudes could be changed by state action or popular education. The 1930s yielded a number of meticulous case studies of race relations in particular communities and a variety of methodologies for the study of race and ethnicity. These included the Chicago school of sociology, Donald Young's comparative analysis of "minority peoples," Melville Herskovits's anthropological study of African influences on black Americans, John Dollard's "caste and class" approach, Howard Odum's southern regional sociology, W. E. B. Du Bois's interdisciplinary studies of Afro-American culture, and the work of Ralph Bunche and other young radicals at Howard University.

Myrdal perceived his invitation from the Carnegie Corporation as a semiofficial appointment to write a major interpretation of the American "Negro problem" that might serve both as a source of information for the educated citizen and as a guide for policymakers. When he began his study in 1938, he soon realized that the economic, social, and political future of Afro-Americans was uncertain. Government policy on civil rights, economic planning, and social welfare was very much up for grabs, with groups both inside and outside the Roosevelt administration contending for influence. As he visited the rural areas of the South and the ghettos of northern cities, he recognized that most educated white Americans had no conception of the enormous dimensions of black poverty or the complexity of patterns of racial discrimination. Driven by a sense of moral urgency and an ambitious vision of social engineering, Myrdal traveled through the United States, interviewing Americans of all political persuasions: black communists, interracial activists, corporate executives, members of Roosevelt's cabinet, and southern conservatives.

With a quarter of a million dollars from the Carnegie Corporation, Myrdal selected a staff of American collaborators representing all the important schools of thought on race relations in American social science as well as the major civil rights and reform organizations, thus bringing together scholars and reformers who rarely talked to each other. The scale of the Myrdal study dwarfed all previous investigations of race relations, and social scientists and civil rights leaders believed that the future direction of foundation activities in the field would be strongly influenced by Myrdal's conclusions. Each of the collaborators wrote a summary of the literature in his or her area of research or a monographic study of some more limited topic, which he or she was then free to publish independently. The Myrdal project thus became a battleground in miniature, a microcosm of the larger intellectual and political struggles among American social scientists and reformers concerning the future of Afro-Americans. But Myrdal remained firmly in control of the enterprise, reading and evaluating his collaborators' reports and shaping his own interpretation.

World War II was crucial to Myrdal's conceptualization of the issue of race relations. The central argument of *An American Dilemma* took shape in 1940–41 as Myrdal attempted to analyze American race relations while he moved back and forth between the United States and Sweden. He interrupted his study of the American race question to return home for ten months after the German invasion of Denmark and Norway in April 1940 because he believed that Sweden would soon be attacked and wanted to be in Stockholm during the national crisis. Once back in Sweden, however, he found his native land confronting a difficult "moral dilemma" about the politics of neutrality. Both Gunnar and Alva Myrdal were deeply disturbed by government censorship of newspapers critical of Nazi Germany, self-censorship by the Swedish press, and a tendency of many Swedish officials and intellectuals toward accommodation of Germany. In their book *Kontakt med Amerika* (1941), the Myrdals argued that their countrymen needed something like the American creed, a formulation of democratic principles and civil liberties clearly understood by the citizenry, so that Swedes would know what the nation stood for. Such a creed, in the Myrdals' view, would enable Swedes to reject Nazi propaganda and would form a basis for popular resistance if the German army should occupy the country. American institutions, though deeply flawed by racial inequality, seemed to rest on a solid foundation of broad popular support for democratic procedures and civil liberties. However nebulous the American creed would seem to a later generation of critics, it appeared to Gunnar Myrdal to be a powerful weapon against fascism in Europe and a potential source of leverage against racial oppression in the United States.

Returning to the United States in March 1941, Myrdal began writing *An American Dilemma*, which he called his "war work." At a time when Americans were acutely conscious of the nation's professed values, Myrdal counterposed the American creed to Nazi ideology and offered a symbolic framework that helped to legitimate the struggle of Afro-Americans for civil rights. He reintroduced into social science discussions of race relations a conception of the race issue as a moral question, an idea that had always been present in popular writings by civil rights advocates but which most social scientists of the 1920s and 1930s had rejected in favor of more "scientific" and ostensibly "value-free" approaches to the study of social behavior. Myrdal's "moral dilemma" thesis and his championing of the rights of the individual also helped to make his social engineering more palatable in a nation in which many intellectuals of the 1930s had associated social engineering with fascism and Stalinism. His advocacy of social engineering met with a more favorable reception in 1944 than it would have ten years earlier because many American social scientists were involved in government work during the war. *An American Dilemma* was more than a wartime tract, however. Myrdal saw more clearly than most American social scientists that civil rights was reemerging as a national political issue, and he offered educated white Americans a new way of conceptualizing and understanding the race question as well as a sense of the urgency of the situation. A broad-ranging and original investigation, *An American Dilemma* represented a major rethinking of the race issue in American society and politics, and it would remain the leading work in the field for twenty years.

In this book I focus on Gunnar Myrdal as a political intellectual moving between two cultures and confronting the American conscience on the issue of race. I also consider Myrdal's ideas about American politics and culture from his first visit in 1929 to his death in 1987. In *Gunnar Myrdal and Black-White Relations*, which was published as this book neared completion, David Southern examines in much greater detail the influence of *An American Dilemma* on intellectuals, politicians, judges, and civil rights activists from 1944 to 1969.[15] The present study treats the reception more briefly and does not attempt to address internal developments in each of the social science disciplines that Myrdal's work influenced. Instead, it explores only the major issues in the debates about black-white relations in the years from the book's publication to the middle of the 1960s. During that time, Myrdal's study strongly influenced intellectuals and policymakers and played a crucial role in establishing a liberal orthodoxy around the ideas of integration, equal opportunity within the private economy, educational campaigns to reduce prejudice, and social engineering to repair the "damage" of racial discrimination and to enable blacks to assimilate to white culture. As the black movement turned more radical after the passage of the 1965 Voting Rights Act, each of those tenets of racial liberalism was questioned both within the academy and among political activists. The liberal orthodoxy took on a life of its own, independent of Gunnar Myrdal, who lived in Europe and India from 1942 to 1973 and did not participate actively in debates about American race relations. He remained a bold, creative, and iconoclastic scholar, applying his skills as a social engineer to problems of poverty in the Third World and reform in Western welfare states, and his solutions to social and political problems in other countries were often more radical than the ideas he had expounded in *An American Dilemma*. His 1963 book on the American economy, *Challenge to Affluence*, was an attempt to move the debate on poverty in the United States beyond the limits of conventional liberalism. In that study, Myrdal warned of the growth of an underclass left out of the affluent society, advocated education and training programs for the poor, proposed a range of welfare reforms, and emphasized the need for the poor to become organized politically. He also broke with his own history of top-down social engineering and advocated the decentralization of many government functions, though he was vague about how this would be carried out. Yet when Myrdal returned to the United States in 1973 to commence work on "An American Dilemma Revisited," he proved unable to follow up on the innovative ideas of *Challenge to Affluence*, and he did not move very far beyond the liberal orthodoxy he had created on black-white relations thirty years earlier. Dismayed by the continuing poverty of America's underclass and the growing conservatism of the nation's politics, Myrdal clung to his role of moral critic of racial inequality but offered few concrete proposals for lessening racial discrimination or increasing the power and standard of living of the black poor. He remained a staunch assimilationist in an era when many American intellectuals embraced cultural pluralism or Afro-American nationalism. Though he saw little political support for the ambitious programs of social engineering that he favored, Myrdal nevertheless sought, during the last years of his life, to appeal to America's conscience in an effort to eliminate poverty and the remaining barriers to racial equality.

It is a pleasure to be able to thank some of the many people who have generously helped me in tracking Gunnar Myrdal's career in the United States and Sweden and in formulating my ideas for this book. I owe an especially great debt to my undergraduate teachers at Duke University: Anne Firor Scott, who set high standards for the study of American social history; Harold T. Parker, who sparked my interest in intellectual history and biography; and Syd Nathans, who taught me Southern history and has been a source of critical analysis, wit, and warm encouragement for many years. My dissertation advisor, Donald Fleming of Harvard University, shared his extraordinary knowledge of American and European intellectual history and listened patiently to many versions of this study as it evolved from an analysis of the study of Afro-Americans in the social sciences to an investigation of Gunnar Myrdal. His enthusiasm for new ideas, tolerance of differing viewpoints, and steadfast support of his students make him a remarkable teacher.

I am especially grateful to the W. E. B. Du Bois Institute of Harvard University for a dissertation fellowship. Preston Williams, the former director, and Fath Davis Ruffins, the former administrator, made every effort to facilitate my research. The Charles Warren Center, the Rockefeller Archive Center, and the National Endowment for the Humanities supported travel to archives. During my two and a half years on the faculty of the University of Odense, Denmark, I was fortunate to receive travel grants from the Faculty Research Council and the Danish Social Science Research Council. North Carolina State University's Faculty Research Council has generously supported my visits to archives as well. A summer stipend from the National Endowment for the Humanities and a Mellon Faculty Fellowship at Stanford University made it possible for me to complete the project.

Many archivists and reference librarians have answered innumerable queries. Roberta Selleck of Harvard University, William Fredlund of Stanford, Cynthia Levine of North Carolina State, Cynthia Adams and Harry McKown of the University of North Carolina at Chapel Hill, and Bengt Rur and Kerstin Abukhanfusa of Riksarkivet in Stockholm aided my research. Stellan Andersson of the Arbetarrörelsens Arkiv guided me in using the vast collections of Gunnar and Alva Myrdal, answered many questions, and commented in detail on three of my chapters. I am greatly indebted to him and to Klaus Misgeld for making my months of research in the Myrdal papers such a pleasant experience.

I would like to thank the many people who granted me interviews, most of whom I have mentioned in the Essay on Sources. I am grateful to Sissela Bok, Leslie Dunbar, and the late Arthur Raper for sharing letters from their personal files as well. It is impossible for me to name all the people who have offered advice, criticism, and encouragement in the course of my work. I would like to express my appreciation to the following scholars who commented on portions of the manuscript: Jean-Christophe Agnew, Mitchell Ash, Jeff Biddle, Alan Brinkley, Alex Charns, Liz Cohen, Carl Degler, John S. Gilkeson, Jr., David Gilmartin, Rudolph Haerle, Jr., David Hollinger, David Howard-Pitney, the late Nathan Huggins, Tom Jackson, David M. Kennedy, Tony LaVopa, Doris Linder, Thomas F. Pettigrew, Robert Proctor, Roy Rosenzweig, Bruce Schulman, Franklin Scott, Edward Shils, Daniel J. Singal, Peter Stansky, George W. Stocking, Jr., Paul Streeten, Steven Vincent, and Cornel West. I am especially grateful to those who commented on drafts of the entire manuscript: Fred W. Anderson, Robert Cummings, George Fredrickson, Joan T. Mark, Syd Nathans, Gail W. O'Brien, Daryl Scott, John David Smith, and Morton Sosna. Any errors that remain are entirely my responsibility.

My colleague Gordon Newby initiated me into the mysteries of word processing, restrained me from acts of Luddism, and provided calm encouragement in moments of technologically driven despair. Iris Tillman Hill and Lewis Bateman of the University of North Carolina Press offered wise counsel on turning a dissertation into a book. Grant Barnes, Stewart Fisher, Patricia Hill, and Lee Lourdeaux gave unfailing moral support.

Finally, I should acknowledge the help of the late Gunnar Myrdal, whose belief that we need to know more about the value premises of social scientists led him to open his professional correspondence to scholars during his lifetime. If our oral history sessions often turned into debates about Afro-American culture and strategies for social change, it was because he cared to know what the younger generation of Americans thought about racism, poverty, and war. Though we often disagreed, my own intellectual horizon was greatly broadened by my attempt to understand his wide-ranging work. Myrdal was a man driven by a desire to change society and was not content merely to study it. His spirit of activism remains a challenge. "Your country's in a hell of a mess now," he told me the last time I saw him. "I'm not going to be around to do anything about it, but you will."

Raleigh, North Carolina
August 28, 1989

Gunnar Myrdal
and America's Conscience

Introduction
The Race Issue in the 1930s

For the great majority of white Americans in the 1930s, civil rights was not an issue of immediate concern. White southerners generally thought that the "Negro problem" had been solved in the period between 1890 and World War I, when the southern states had disfranchised blacks and erected a system of rigid segregation laws. The moral and legal validity of this system was rarely questioned by the region's political leaders and journalists. Outside the South, white Americans still considered the "Negro problem" to be a southern problem, and they had only a very limited idea of the conditions of blacks in the North. Yet fundamental changes were occurring in American race relations. From 1935 to 1937, Frederick Keppel would try to comprehend these developments as he groped his way toward commissioning a Carnegie study of the American race question. And from 1938 to 1940, Gunnar Myrdal would investigate the economic, social, and political changes in race relations and would seek to shape a new consensus on the issue.

The Great Depression created unprecedented levels of deprivation among Afro-Americans in the cities of the North and South and triggered a crisis in southern agriculture with far-reaching consequences for American race relations. Rising militance among black Americans also thrust the issues of antilynching and race discrimination before Congress and the American public. The New Deal, in responding to these issues, provided more economic aid to Afro-Americans than any previous administration but failed to solve the problems of southern rural poverty, urban black unemployment, and the denial of civil rights.

The Depression had a catastrophic impact on blacks, who occupied the lowest-paid jobs as unskilled laborers in the cities and as tenant farmers in the rural South. At the depth of the Depression in 1932, unemployment among blacks in New York, Philadelphia, Chicago, and Detroit stood at 40 to 50 percent. Two million Afro-Americans were on relief when Franklin D. Roosevelt assumed the presidency. Blacks were usually the first to be fired when employers cut their work force, and in the South, whites pushed blacks out of jobs they had traditionally held as garbage collectors, street cleaners, hotel workers, and railroad brakemen.[1] Local governments were often unable to provide relief to the massive population of unemployed people in the early years of the Depression. In southern communities, public and private relief agencies openly discriminated against blacks. Hunger and malnutrition were common among Afro-Americans in all sections of the country, and the Depression placed families of both races under great pressure. Housing in the urban ghettos, already substandard, was inadequate for the continued influx of rural blacks. Evictions and breadlines were common in many black neighborhoods.

In the South, where 75 percent of Afro-Americans lived, the Depression set in motion a series of economic changes that would transform the region, weakening the tenant farming system and creating a vast population of uprooted rural people of both races. Since Reconstruction, tenant farming had been one of the major distinguishing characteristics of southern agriculture. The terms of land tenure varied widely and included renting, sharecropping, and wage labor, but the system as a whole had the effect of keeping the majority of black southerners in conditions of appalling poverty and dependence upon landowners and merchants. Economic powerlessness had its counterpart in the political sphere, since most southern blacks were denied the right to vote. Segregation laws and the widespread use of extralegal violence completed the pattern of rigid racial subordination.

Rural poverty afflicted white southerners as well as blacks. Southern agriculture suffered from poor farming methods, an inadequate credit system, the boll weevil, generally low cotton prices, and natural disasters. From the 1890s to the 1930s, increasing numbers of white farmers were forced into tenancy. While much of the nation experienced prosperity during the 1920s, the South endured an agricultural depression, and in 1929, the average per capita income in the South was $368, compared with $703 for the nation.[2] Despite national prosperity, real wages of farm laborers in the South were no higher in 1929 than they had been in 1890. The gap between southern and northern wages for farm labor was greater in 1929 than it had been in 1914.[3] By 1930, tenant farmers accounted for one quarter of the South's population and half of its farmers. Tenant families included about 8.5 million people, 5.5 million whites and more than 3 million blacks in a southern rural population of 18 million. Their birthrate was the highest of any group in the country, and many of these rural southerners were illiterate, lived in inadequate housing, and suffered from diseases such as malaria, pellagra, and rickets.[4]

The Great Depression had a devastating effect on the rural South, worsening the already desperate condition of the tenant farmers. Thousands of rural families were uprooted and destitute, and neither local governments nor private charities were able to provide adequate relief. Those who managed to stay on the land struggled to survive as the price of cotton fell to six cents per pound.[5] One study of two rural counties in Georgia indicated that the income of black farm families declined by 30 to 50 percent from 1927 to 1934.[6]

The Roosevelt administration, which took office in March 1933, moved decisively to stimulate an economic recovery but exercised extreme caution in responding to the needs of Afro-Americans. During the first six months of the New Deal, more than two hundred thousand dispossessed rural families of both races received federal relief in the cotton-growing areas of the South.[7] New Deal programs such as the Public Works Administration, the Civilian Conservation Corps (CCC), the Works Progress Administration (WPA), and the National Youth Administration (NYA) provided jobs for thousands of unemployed blacks as well as whites. Never before had the federal government provided economic aid for Afro-Americans on such a large scale. Yet blacks often faced segregation and discrimination in New Deal programs. Local relief administrators in the South made it more difficult for blacks to receive assistance and offered blacks smaller benefits than whites. During the first year of the New Deal, blacks comprised only 5 percent of the youth employed by the CCC and less than 1 percent of the payroll of the Tennessee Valley Authority.[8] Segregation in New Deal programs was not limited to the South. CCC camps were segregated in other parts of the country, and the Federal Housing Administration built segregated projects in the North.[9] The Social Security Act did not cover workers in agriculture or domestic service, occupations in which blacks were concentrated. Not surprisingly, some black leaders labeled the New Deal a "raw deal" and feared that the government would encourage the spread of segregation from the South to the North.[10]

The New Deal was never committed to a systematic attack on poverty, in part because of the political clout of businessmen and southern farmers who needed a low-wage labor force. Though he reluctantly embraced deficit spending, FDR was basically a fiscal conservative, and as an advocate of federalism, he insisted that the states take responsibility for direct relief after 1935. A crazy-quilt pattern of federal and state agencies with overlapping authority resulted from the complexities of the legislative process and executive bureaucracy, and an optimistic belief prevailed among New Dealers that such agencies were only temporary expedients until the private sector could hire the unemployed.[11] In this context, it is not surprising that there was no coordinated federal strategy to solve the problem of black unemployment. In 1935, nearly one-third of the black population was on relief, and in 1937, 23 percent of urban black men were unemployed.[12] A study of Chicago found that, as late as 1939, half of the black families in the city were dependent upon some type of government aid for their subsistence.[13] In the late 1930s, unemployment among blacks was twice that of whites, and blacks were more likely to stay on the relief rolls for longer periods of time.[14] To social workers and other observers, it appeared increasingly likely that the long-term unemployed would become a class of permanent relief clients.[15]

The Roosevelt administration's agriculture policy led to the displacement of thousands of tenant farmers in the South. The Agricultural Adjustment Act of 1933 had as its primary aim the reduction of acreage, and its authors did not intend to effect changes in the distribution of landholdings or in landlord-tenant relations. But as landowners took acreage out of production, they dismissed some of their tenants. The increasing use of tractors in cotton farming resulted in further reductions in the number of tenant farmers. Large landowners were also able to take advantage of the allotment payments and technological innovations to increase the size of their land holdings.[16]

These developments provoked a vigorous protest from the Southern Tenant Farmers' Union, an interracial organization, as well as demands in Congress for aid for tenant farmers. The black sociologist Charles S. Johnson joined with white reformers Edwin Embree and Will Alexander to write *The Collapse of Cotton Tenancy* (1935), which helped to focus public attention on the problem. By 1937, sharecroppers had become an important subject for American writers and photographers such as Norman Thomas, Howard Kester, Erskine Caldwell, and Margaret Bourke-White. Though these observers often focused their attention on poor whites, they did make the American public more aware of the larger crisis in southern agriculture.[17] In response to these pressures, Roosevelt issued an executive order in 1935 creating the Resettlement Administration (RA), which established communities to aid displaced farmers. Two years later he signed into law the Bankhead-Jones Farm Tenant Act, which transformed the RA into the Farm Security Administration (FSA). Under the leadership of Will Alexander, the FSA made rehabilitation loans to farmers to upgrade their livestock, equipment, and supplies as well as loans to tenants who wished to purchase farms.[18] But these efforts were too little and too late. Between 1935 and 1940, the number of tenant farmers in the South declined by 25 percent.[19] There were 192,000 fewer black tenants in 1940 than there had been in 1930. The FSA was able to provide purchase and resettlement loans to only 3,400 blacks.[20]

As thousands of black farm families were driven off the land in the late 1930s, few industrial jobs opened up for blacks in the South. Between 1929 and 1939 there was virtually no net growth in industrial jobs in the region.[21] Blacks were usually the first to be fired when a factory laid off workers. In tobacco manufacturing, for example, blacks comprised 67.9 percent of the work force in 1930 but only 54.7 percent in 1940.[22] The textile industry remained virtually all white in the South. Because of this dismal job market in the South, more than four hundred thousand Afro-Americans migrated from the South to the rest of the country during the 1930s, increasing the black population of the North by 25 percent and swelling the ranks of the unemployed.[23]

In August 1938, two months before Gunnar Myrdal began his investigation, Roosevelt's National Emergency Council (NEC) issued a report on economic conditions of the South. In a letter introducing the report, Roosevelt declared that the South was "the Nation's No. 1 economic problem." Moving beyond the sharecropper issue, the report addressed a wide range of problems in the region's economy and argued that the South's problems were inextricably intertwined with the welfare of the rest of the nation. The low purchasing power of the southern poor, the authors maintained, retarded the economic growth of the rest of the country. The NEC claimed that "the South is the Nation's greatest untapped market and the market in which American business can expand most easily" and warned that "northern producers and distributors are losing profits and northern workers are losing work because the South cannot afford to buy their goods."[24] The authors observed that the South's excess population was moving to other parts of the country and that the migrants would take with them such problems as illiteracy and poor health.[25]

Although Roosevelt raised these issues of southern poverty and its consequences for the rest of the nation, the political context of the late 1930s made it impossible for the federal government to intervene decisively to provide employment, education, health care, and housing for the South's rural poor. Nor did the New Deal assist displaced tenant farmers in moving to other parts of the country. Migrants had an especially difficult time in receiving relief, and black migrants faced the most hostile reaction from local authorities.[26] By 1938 FDR was struggling to muster the support in Congress that he needed for more modest assaults on southern problems through minimum wage laws, the FSA, the WPA, and the NYA. Increasingly, conservative southern Democrats joined with Republicans to block new measures and obstruct the operation of some of the existing New Deal agencies. Roosevelt sought to purge anti–New Deal Democrats in the primary elections of 1938, but his candidates lost key Senate races in Georgia and South Carolina. Southern conservatives managed to portray the NEC's report as an attack on the South.

Roosevelt never supported civil rights legislation, nor did he make any vigorous attempts to combat discrimination in New Deal programs. In his career prior to the presidency, he had shown no interest in black issues, and he made no mention of civil rights in the campaign of 1932.[27] Once in office, he gave first priority to his program for economic recovery, for which he needed the support of southern Democrats in Congress. FDR did allow a small number of liberal New Deal administrators to work quietly to provide a greater share of economic benefits to blacks, and he appointed more Afro-Americans to administrative positions than any previous president. In the late 1930s his wife, Eleanor, emerged as a major spokesperson for the cause of civil rights—not always with her husband's approval. On the whole, though, FDR remained aloof from struggles over racial discrimination within his administration, a stance that worked to the disadvantage of blacks because they were one of the least powerful groups in American politics while the white South was a major element in the New Deal coalition. Only a small fraction of his time was devoted to the problems of Afro-Americans.

Despite President Roosevelt's caution on the race issue, a group of white racial liberals did emerge within the administration. Interior Secretary Harold Ickes, who had been president of the Chicago chapter of the National Association for the Advancement of Colored People (NAACP), saw that blacks received a substantial share of jobs in the Public Works Administration and fought discrimination in other New Deal agencies. Will Alexander, who headed the FSA after a long career as an interracial reformer in the South, was an important advocate within the administration for blacks. Under his leadership, the FSA employed a higher percentage of black supervisors than any other government agency.[28] Another white southern liberal, Aubrey Williams, served as deputy director of the WPA from 1935 to 1938 and head of the NYA from 1938 to 1943. Williams made the NYA the government agency that most actively aided blacks.[29]

These racial liberals generally took an economic approach to the race issue. The

Depression, in their view, was a national catastrophe that united Americans of all racial and ethnic groups in a common struggle for national recovery. They regarded the New Deal as a turning point in American history that marked the end of laissez-faire individualism and the beginning of a recognition by most citizens of the economic interdependence of all groups and the need for a strong federal government to plan for the common welfare. The greatest needs of Afro-Americans, they believed, were the same needs of many white Americans: relief, jobs, housing, education, and social security. Thus Ickes contended that the "Negro problem merges into and becomes inseparable from the greater problem of American citizens generally, who are at or below the line in decency and comfort from those who are not." Though morally opposed to segregation, these white New Dealers believed that any direct assault on the Jim Crow system in the South was doomed to failure, and they advised blacks to concentrate on the attainable goal of economic progress and to postpone the challenge to segregation. They assumed that the causes of racial prejudice were economic, and they believed that white racial discrimination would diminish as whites rose out of poverty and as blacks improved their educational and social standards.[30]

These cautious steps toward federal concern for the economic and social welfare of Afro-Americans were possible because northern blacks joined the New Deal coalition. A decisive shift in voting behavior came in the congressional elections of 1934, when a majority of black voters switched their allegiance from the Republican to the Democratic party. Two years later, Roosevelt won the votes of 76 percent of northern blacks in his reelection. Despite FDR's refusal to endorse civil rights measures, the unprecedented federal economic aid to blacks was enough to shake their seventy-year loyalty to the party of Lincoln.[31] As northern blacks became a significant interest group within the Democratic party, many northern Democratic politicians endorsed antilynching legislation and embraced the rhetoric, if not the substance, of racial equality. Blacks, who had been a politically marginal group since the end of Reconstruction, began to find allies among urban liberals and in the labor movement. The greatly expanded role of the federal government raised the expectations of Afro-Americans and led them to demand more from the New Deal.

During the Depression years the black protest movement grew more militant than ever before: activism accelerated on many fronts in the South as well as in the North. From the celebrated cases of the Scottsboro youths and Angelo Herndon to the more mundane business of grass-roots organizing, Afro-Americans struggled against racism in government, corporations, and labor unions. Yet there was a significant division of opinion among black leaders about both tactics and goals. The NAACP remained the largest civil rights organization, growing from twenty-one thousand members in 1929 to fifty-four thousand ten years later.[32] With a membership consisting primarily of middle-class blacks, the NAACP pursued a long-term strategy of litigation aimed at overturning Jim Crow laws, lobbied in Congress for an antilynching bill, and appealed to the conscience of white Americans to support civil rights. At the beginning of the 1930s, the association came under intense criticism from a number of young black intellectuals for being elitist and out of touch with the black masses. The economist Abram Harris chaired an NAACP committee in 1934–35 that urged the association to alter its approach and to work to build an interracial labor movement as the main thrust of the black struggle. In response to Harris's report, the NAACP leadership accepted, in principle, the idea of developing an economic program to advance the welfare of poor blacks. The organization gave some support to unions that welcomed black members and sought to influence New Deal administrators to oppose discrimination against Afro-Americans, but the antilynching crusade remained the focus of the NAACP's program in the 1930s.[33]

The campaign for a federal antilynching bill emerged as the civil rights issue with the highest public profile from 1935 to 1938. NAACP executive secretary Walter White, who had investigated lynchings in the South, made the issue a personal crusade and lobbied both on Capitol Hill and with the White House. No previous civil rights bill had ever received such an extensive lobbying campaign. Church leaders, labor leaders, liberal organizations, radical groups, writers, intellectuals, and entertainers all called upon the president and Congress to pass the Wagner-Costigan antilynching bill. President Roosevelt condemned the practice of lynching and indicated his sympathy for the aims of the bill but declined to endorse the proposed legislation. "I did not choose the tools with which I must work," he told Walter White, "Had I been permitted to choose them I would have selected quite different ones. But I've got to get legislation passed by Congress to save America. The Southerners by reason of the seniority rule in Congress are chairman or occupy strategic places on most of the Senate and House committees. If I come out for the antilynching bill now, they will block every bill I ask Congress to pass to keep America from collapsing. I just can't take that risk."[34]

In 1937, after a brutal lynching in Mississippi, the House of Representatives passed an antilynching bill by a vote of 277-120. When the measure was debated in the Senate the following year, a filibuster by southern senators prevented the bill from coming up for a vote. Southern conservatives had won after a long and bitter fight, but the NAACP had succeeded in dramatizing the issue of racial injustice by focusing on the most hideous expression of southern racism.[35]

The traditional civil rights organizations also received a persistent prodding from the Communist party, which made substantial gains among blacks by publicizing the Scottsboro case and organizing unemployed councils and relief-bureau sit-ins. While most white reformers avoided the issue of segregation and shunned the appearance of social equality, Communists insisted upon a policy of militant interracialism in all party activities. The Communist party was also one of the few organizations that took black intellectuals seriously and gave them prominent exposure in party activities. After 1935, the party pursued a Popular Front strategy that emphasized the formation of a broad coalition with liberals to oppose fascism. In this context, Communists participated actively in the National Negro

Congress, an organization begun in 1935 that included Ralph Bunche, John P. Davis, A. Philip Randolph, and other militants who were dissatisfied with the civil libertarian strategy of the NAACP. Embracing liberals and socialists as well as Communists, the congress sought to build a mass organization among Afro-Americans in support of an interracial working-class movement. The congress supported the organization of black workers by the Congress of Industrial Organizations (CIO), lobbied in support of antilynching legislation, and linked the struggle against racial discrimination at home to the international fight against fascism in Europe. Despite its ambitious goals and strident rhetoric, the congress never achieved a mass following, and it eventually splintered after the Nazi-Soviet Pact of 1939. But when Myrdal began his research in 1938, the congress still claimed the loyalty of many black activists and exerted pressure on the NAACP from the Left.[36]

The 1930s saw the beginnings of a change in organized labor's response to civil rights. Prior to the New Deal, blacks were excluded from most craft unions in the American Federation of Labor (AFL). But in 1933–34 the United Mine Workers and the International Ladies' Garment Workers' Union began to recruit blacks in organizing drives. A. Philip Randolph, taking advantage of New Deal legislation, achieved recognition of the predominantly black Brotherhood of Sleeping Car Porters in 1935. The Southern Tenant Farmers' Union signed up thousands of blacks in the most antiunion section of the nation. Most significantly, the CIO, which broke off from the AFL in 1935, recruited Afro-Americans in unprecedented numbers in such industries as steel, automobiles, and meatpacking. Through its political organizing and financial contributions, the CIO became a major interest group within the Democratic party, strengthened the urban liberal wing of the party, and supported antilynching and other civil rights goals.[37]

Gunnar Myrdal would encounter a mood of rising militance among Afro-Americans even as the nation faced a political stalemate on civil rights. Afro-American protest was more vigorous than ever before, and many black intellectuals were calling for radical changes in American institutions. The CIO's organizing drives enrolled thousands of black workers and strengthened support for civil rights within the Democratic party, while northern white liberals and leftists spoke out on civil rights and condemned lynching, racial discrimination, and disfranchisement as un-American. And in the South, there were stirrings of change, as the Southern Tenant Farmers' Union reached a peak of thirty-one thousand members, the CIO began organizing workers in southern industries, and liberals formed the Southern Conference on Human Welfare and launched a campaign against the poll tax. Though historians now date the decline of the New Deal from the Court-packing fight of 1937, many liberals whom Myrdal met in 1938–39 optimistically forecast a continuation of reform. They saw the defeat of the antilynching bill and the failure of FDR's attempt to purge conservative senators as merely temporary setbacks and believed that a liberalized Democratic party in the South would help to revitalize the New Deal.

These optimistic expectations would collide with some harsh realities of power. After the 1938 elections, a conservative coalition of Republicans and southern Democrats dominated Congress, crushing antilynching legislation and chipping away at liberal agencies such as the WPA and NYA. Southern Democrats complained that their party had been taken over by northern liberals, and they objected not only to the antilynching bill but also to minimum-wage legislation, public housing, fair labor standards legislation, and expansion of the WPA. The newly formed House Un-American Activities Committee, chaired by Martin Dies of Texas, harassed racial liberals in the administration.[38]

In this unpromising situation, Gunnar Myrdal would seek to find a formula that would compel white Americans to address the issues of civil rights and black poverty. Because blacks possessed little political power, the New Deal faced no immediate political consequences from its failure to act on these concerns. Most policymakers, moreover, were unaware of the scale of black deprivation and the extent to which the "Negro problem" was a national, not merely a southern, issue. But Myrdal, as one of the architects of the Swedish welfare state, would come to see racial discrimination and black poverty as serious, long-term problems that undermined the general welfare of the society. To a generation acutely conscious of the nation's image, he would stress the glaring contradiction between America's claims to be a democratic society and its practice of racial discrimination.

1

Finding a Tocqueville

Although fundamental changes in the economic, social, and political status of blacks occurred in the 1930s, American elites were only vaguely aware of these developments. The poverty of Afro-Americans in the South, the continued migration of blacks to the North, and the high rates of black unemployment in all parts of the country rarely made the headlines. While the Scottsboro case and the fight for an antilynching bill were reported in the national press, most white leaders in business, education, and the professions remained ignorant of the growth of a more militant political movement among Afro-Americans and the radicalization of a generation of black intellectuals. The planning structure of the New Deal ignored blacks for the most part, and few economists studied the dynamics of racial discrimination or offered policy suggestions for combating black unemployment.

During the first three decades of the century, American philanthropic foundations had come to play a significant role as planning agencies, undertaking studies of subjects that neither government nor corporations chose to support. These large, tax-exempt foundations constituted a new sphere of private power, and Americans debated the issue of whose interest the foundations served.[1] Though these philanthropic organizations sought to bring expert opinion to bear on social problems in the 1930s, most of them remained locked into the assumptions of an earlier era with respect to black-white relations. Several of the foundations had invested substantial sums in a complex strategy of improving southern black education within the separate and unequal framework of segregation. Though the foundations gave significant resources for the education of black southerners, their policies often helped to perpetuate the system of racial inequality.[2] In their conceptualization of black education, moreover, many foundation officials in the 1930s retained traces of an imperial mentality and perceived a similarity between the education of Afro-Americans in the South and the education and development of colonial peoples in Africa and Asia. As the president and one of the trustees of the Carnegie Corporation grew concerned about America's "Negro problem" in the middle and late 1930s, they were caught between a desire to draw upon expert knowledge to plan for a more just future for blacks and impulses deeply rooted in the racism of the nation's past.

Frederick Keppel and the Carnegie Corporation

The institution that would bring Gunnar Myrdal to the United States was the creation of one of America's most flamboyant and inventive millionaires. Andrew Carnegie, born in Scotland in 1835, had immigrated to the United States as a boy and had risen to become the master of the steel industry and one of the world's wealthiest men. In 1889, Carnegie had shocked his fellow millionaires by declaring that it was a disgrace to die rich. According to Carnegie's Gospel of Wealth, it was the duty of the rich man, after providing moderately for himself and his family, to distribute the bulk of his fortune during his own lifetime for the public good. He should "consider all surplus revenues which come to him simply as trust funds which he is called upon to administer . . .—the man of wealth thus becoming the mere trustee and agent for his poorer brethren, bringing to their service his superior wisdom, experience, and ability to administer, doing for them better than they would or could do for themselves."[3] Carnegie threw himself into the task of distributing his wealth with the same flair and determination that he had brought to the business world. He built libraries and supported programs for adult education, provided churches with organs and cities with music halls, endowed scientific research institutes, and supported a pension plan for college teachers.

Carnegie also thrust himself into the arena of international diplomacy and attempted to mediate between the German kaiser and the British government in 1907. He was strongly interested in the arbitration of international conflict, and he gave the money for the construction of the Peace Palace at The Hague.[4] An enthusiastic champion of American institutions, Carnegie sought to encourage his native Britain to adopt a republican form of government, even going so far as to propose that Britain and Canada should become part of a Reunited States, with the capital in Washington, as part of a grand design of "race imperialism" based on his belief in the superiority of the English-speaking peoples.[5]

By the age of seventy-five, however, Carnegie had tired of his efforts to supervise personally the distribution of his wealth. He was besieged by applicants and found it difficult to apply a consistent doctrine of "scientific philanthropy." Although he had given away $180 million, he had nearly as much left and found himself in danger of dying rich and thus disgraced. His lawyer Elihu Root suggested that Carnegie create a foundation and assign most of his remaining wealth to it. Carnegie did this in November 1911 by establishing the Carnegie Corporation of New York "to promote the advancement and diffusion of knowledge." He gave it an endowment of $125 million, making it the largest philanthropic organization in the world. Although Carnegie had championed many causes, he decided not to limit his trustees to any narrow set of concerns. Writing with the reformed spelling with which he hoped to modernize the English language, Carnegie explained his purpose to his trustees:

My desire is that the work which I hav been carrying on, or similar beneficial work, shall continue during this and future generations. Conditions upon the erth inevitably change; hence no wise man will bind Trustees forever to certain paths, causes or institutions. I disclaim any intention of doing so. On the contrary, I giv my Trustees full authority to change policy or causes hitherto aided, from time to time, when this, in their opinion, has become necessary or desirable. They shall best conform to my wishes by using their own judgment. . . . My chief happiness as I write these lines lies in the thot that, even after I pass away, the welth that came to me to administer as a sacred trust for the good of my fellow men is to continue to benefit humanity for generations untold, under your devoted and sympathetic guidance and that of your successors, who cannot fail to be able and good men.[6]

The board of trustees consisted of the presidents of the five smaller, more specialized foundations which Carnegie had previously established as well as his three secretaries. Carnegie himself served as the first president of the corporation and ran it from his home at 2 East Ninety-first Street in Manhattan until he became ill in 1915. He remained titular president until his death in 1919 and was succeeded by James R. Angell, who resigned in 1921 to become president of Yale University.[7]

The task of shaping the Carnegie Corporation as a modern American institution fell to Frederick P. Keppel, who was president of the foundation from 1923 to 1941. A man who moved easily in academic, philanthropic, and corporate circles, Keppel assumed the presidency of the corporation after holding a variety of administrative posts. Born on Staten Island in 1875, he was the son of an Anglo-Irish immigrant who had established a prosperous business as an art dealer in New York. Keppel attended public schools in Yonkers and worked in his father's firm before enrolling in Columbia University, from which he received an undergraduate degree. After working for the publishing company of Harper & Brothers, he became a university administrator and served as dean of Columbia College from 1910 to 1917. During the First World War, Keppel was appointed assistant secretary of war under Newton D. Baker, with whom he formed a close friendship. In the War Department, Keppel was responsible for dealing with problems of morale, vocational education, and recreation. After the war, he was director of foreign operations for the American Red Cross and served as the American representative of the International Chamber of Commerce in Paris. Keppel returned to the United States in 1922 and was briefly secretary of the Plan of New York before his election as president of the Carnegie Corporation. He was married to Helen Tracy Brown, a niece of Mrs. J. P. Morgan, and they lived in Montrose, New York, in northern Westchester County.[8]

During the 1920s, Keppel eased the foundation out from under the shadow of its famous donor and established it as an independent institution. While Andrew Carnegie had been brash, opinionated, and eccentric, Keppel established a reputation for moderation, learning, and tact. Several of Carnegie's enthusiasms lived on under Keppel's regime. Adult education and the arts were major passions for both men. Aiding education in the British Empire and Dominions remained a charter obligation, though Keppel's deferential consultations with British officials replaced Carnegie's personal ventures in international arbitration. When Keppel assumed the presidency, a sizable proportion of the corporation's funds had already been committed to several large projects, a situation that would limit Keppel's flexibility throughout the 1920s and early 1930s.[9]

With patience and diplomacy, Keppel gradually wrested control of the foundation from the trustees who had been close associates of Andrew Carnegie. Keppel had inherited an anomalous situation in which the majority of the trustees were presidents of the smaller Carnegie foundations that applied to the corporation for additional funds. He was forced to deal with these people both as grantees and as bosses. But a charter reform at the time Keppel took office provided that the board should be enlarged and that a majority of the trustees should be persons who were not officers of other Carnegie foundations. Keppel gradually added to the board leading businessmen, lawyers, and university presidents whom he knew personally. In this way the Carnegie board gained such members as Newton Baker, Wall Street lawyer Nicholas Kelly, and AT&T vice-president Arthur W. Page. The board members closest to Keppel were lawyer Henry James, the son of the philosopher William James, and Russell Leffingwell, Keppel's boyhood friend and a partner of J. P. Morgan & Co. Keppel thus transformed the Carnegie board from a parochial group that had formed around an industrial magnate to a cross section of the American establishment. The change of trustees also allowed Keppel the freedom to develop a more active role for the foundation.[10]

Keppel became an articulate spokesman for the foundation through his books, lectures, and annual reports. He saw the foundation as an agent of innovation, which should identify neglected areas of research, initiate experimental programs, and move into areas of public concern where governments and industry could not act. In order to allow for flexibility in foundation policies, he sought to prevent the foundation from committing its resources to long-term projects. Instead, he believed that the foundation should continually change the emphasis of its programs, responding to new ideas and new opportunities in society. Keppel argued that the foundation should not interfere with the research of grantees nor should it use conditional grants to force policy changes in recipient institutions. He differed from other "philanthropoids" of his day in his skepticism that philanthropy, social science, or public policy could be made exact sciences.[11]

A major theme of Keppel's administration was the importance of the foundation supporting the exceptional individual. He believed that the foundation should actively look for scholars to undertake research projects that it thought valuable, and he was fond of quoting Andrew Carnegie's maxim: "Find the exceptional man and, having found him, give him a free hand."[12] For Keppel, nurturing the research of exceptional men took precedence over building institutions. One of his favorite stories involved a conversation he had allegedly overheard at the Century Club between two university presidents who had come to New York seeking foundation money. One advised the other: "If you want to build a racetrack, go to Rockefeller. But if you want to buy a racehorse, go to Carnegie."[13]

Keppel sought to keep a certain distance between the foundation and the federal government. He had never been active in party politics, and as foundation president, he assumed a stance of nonpartisanship and a diplomatic caution in discussing controversial issues. His political attitudes had been formed at the turn of the century, and like many progressives, he believed that most men of good will could agree on what constitutes the public interest. He assumed that there was an underlying harmony of interests in the polity, rather than fundamental conflict, and he believed one of the key functions of the foundation to be facilitating education and communication among different groups. Keppel's experience in Washington during the First World War had strengthened his sense of vocation as a public servant but had not left him with a thirst for political power. Instead, he came out of the experience with an abiding distrust of the federal government and of large bureaucracies in general. He acknowledged the need for planning and the coordination of efforts to solve problems, but his speeches stressed the importance of voluntarism, public-spiritedness, and an informed citizenry. Like most foundation officials of his day, Keppel assumed that elites, working through private foundations, could act on behalf of the public interest. He was not an active social reformer, and he never publicly challenged corporate power. Although Keppel voted for Franklin Roosevelt in 1932 and 1936, his relations with the New Deal were not close, and he was privately critical of the extent of the expansion of the federal government under the New Deal. Keppel strove to live up to his ideal of the disinterested public servant and saw his role as that of a steward of a great public trust. Serving the public interest meant, for Keppel, that the foundation should innovate but should not stray too far from the mainstream of American politics.[14]

Informality was the hallmark of Keppel's administration of the Carnegie Corporation. He prided himself on conducting foundation business with a personal touch, and he ran the foundation as a one-man show, receiving a large number of grant applicants in his office. His associates praised his "buoyancy of spirit," "vivacity," and zest for meeting people, hearing new ideas, and launching new projects.[15] While the Rockefeller Foundation expanded into a large bureaucracy with staffs specializing in medicine, social science, education, and other fields, Keppel employed only a small staff.[16] He worked intuitively in developing foundation programs, and his erratic personal style was something of an anomaly in an age of increasing specialization and bureacratization. His assistant John M. Russell remarked that "FPK never approached a problem in a conventional way. His way was original, and hence interesting and creative." Russell observed that "it was sometimes difficult for the legal or academic person to appreciate him fully," because Keppel "had too much of the artist in his makeup."[17] The trustee Henry

James thought that Keppel's "chief limitation" was an "inability to rationalize and formulate his policies." When pressed to define his policies, Keppel told James, "I have to play by ear and proceed by 'hunch.' I can't work otherwise; it's the only way I can work." James saw Keppel's genius as essentially "cooperative": "He lubricated, and facilitated, and fostered. He was a wise patron who supported and encouraged with rare discernment."[18]

From day to day, Keppel was compelled to respond to a dizzying array of requests that came to his desk from all corners of the globe. Applicants entreated him to send a telescope to South Africa, preserve Maori art in New Zealand, aid education in the United States, and support thousands of other causes. Keppel had little time for reading specialized scholarly journals, but he consulted constantly a wide circle of friends and acquaintances. He followed no orderly procedure of referring proposals in a certain field to experts in that field: Keppel picked the brains of people who came into his office to apply for grants, and he liked to sound out his friends among New York professional, business, and academic men at the Century Club, where he often had lunch. Keppel also had weekly luncheons downtown with Leffingwell and other former "wartime public servants" in the New York financial community. In the academic world he remained in contact with former colleagues at Columbia and sometimes turned for advice to the American Council of Learned Societies and the Social Science Research Council. Keppel regularly visited London to consult British officials and scholars and traveled throughout the British Empire and Dominions to meet with political and educational leaders. He was also in touch with the world of diplomacy and international relations through his ties with the Carnegie Endowment for International Peace, the Council on Foreign Relations, and the Institute for Pacific Relations.[19]

Although Keppel developed proposals in an informal way, he presented his ideas forcefully to the Carnegie trustees, and he rarely encountered any serious opposition from the board. Keppel privately discussed with his staff the importance of having "foundation-broken trustees" who could overcome narrow concerns and think in terms of broader public goals.[20] These foundation-broken trustees were also responsive to the concerns of the foundation's president, who managed the agenda and controlled the flow of information at the infrequent trustee meetings. The trustees were rarely concerned with the details of corporation policy. As Leffingwell put it, "when all the talk was over, and the subject fully debated, the Board pretty generally did what Fred said."[21] Reminiscing about the Carnegie Corporation in later years, Gunnar Myrdal would recall that "Keppel was running this as his little play-toy together with his friends. It was very human."[22]

During the Depression, requests for foundation assistance increased exponentially, and appeals from all quarters were submitted as urgent. Since he continued to meet with many applicants himself, Keppel felt the pressure of these new demands. Thomas Jesse Jones of the Phelps-Stokes Fund complimented Keppel on hiring a tactful young assistant who could "throw beggars out of his office and make them feel that they are landing on a feather bed!" Jones acknowledged that Keppel possessed "a good deal of the same skill," but Jones feared that in such hard times "you may require an especially strong coat of mail."[23] In addition to these private tribulations, the foundations faced more serious public criticism for failing to respond actively to the national economic crisis. Keppel believed that the foundations had to maintain their primary commitment to the world of education and research rather than expend their resources on short-term humanitarian or relief programs, and he evinced little interest in social welfare issues, even during the depths of the Depression. He argued that if the foundations did not support basic research in the humanities and sciences, no one else would. In addressing the nation's political and economic problems, Keppel thought that the foundations had to proceed with caution. Tax-exempt foundations could not engage in politics or advocate specific legislation, and they had to contend with public suspicion of philanthropic institutions that had been founded by "robber barons." Furthermore, Keppel sought to maintain an independent role for the foundation and to avoid too close an involvement with the federal government. In his annual report of 1935, Keppel reminded his readers that the foundation, as a corporate entity, could not act politically, even in a time of crisis. He lamented that the current crisis had thrown "our leaders far to the left or to the right, and we find men and women, equally sincere and usually equally angry, walking as far apart as the width of the road will permit." Under such circumstances, Keppel contended, "for our endowed foundation as such to take sides upon any question which is *sub judice* would be contrary to public policy." He suggested, however, that when a consensus began to emerge in place of the ideologically charged atmosphere of that time, the foundation could work with those in the center, "good citizens, who are well informed, and neither angry nor excited."[24]

Keppel also believed that foundation support for the humanities helped to keep alive a spirit of philosophical inquiry, freedom of thought, and tolerance in an era in which many in Europe were turning to totalitarian ideas. "On street corners and in their homes," he warned, "men are talking an impossible language, the language of dialectical materialism, and in a large part of Europe men are putting on colored shirts and making gestures in the interest of a philosophic concept, the totalitarian state." Keppel thought that the appeal of totalitarian movements came from their providing "something in which men can believe." Americans should remember, he warned, "that if men are not taught good philosophies, they are pretty sure to turn to bad ones."[25]

Newton Baker's Proposal

On October 24, 1935, the Carnegie board of trustees met in the walnut-paneled boardroom at the corporation's headquarters at 522 Fifth Avenue and routinely approved appropriations for several southern black colleges that the foundation had been aiding for a number of years. Then Newton D. Baker asked for the floor. A short, bespectacled, soft-spoken man of sixty-four, Baker was the only one of the trustees with political experience in dealing with the race issue. He suggested that aiding southern Negro education should not be the corporation's only approach to the problems of Negroes and that the corporation should concern itself with the condition of blacks in northern cities. Baker was not intimately acquainted with the economic and social conditions of blacks. But he served on the boards of several local charities in Cleveland, and he had recently seen a study conducted by one of these organizations that revealed appalling poverty, unemployment, family breakups, and crime among Cleveland's black population. From other sources as well, he had learned about the desperate situation of blacks in northern cities, the inability of private charitable groups to cope with these problems, and the danger of mounting racial tensions. Yet his own racial attitudes and political philosophy were such that he lacked a clear sense of what should be done about the "Negro problem."[26]

Like most Democratic politicians in the North, Baker had generally avoided taking part in public discussions of black issues during his long career in politics. Born in Martinsburg, West Virginia, in 1871, he was the son of a country doctor who had fought in the Confederate army as one of Jeb Stuart's cavalrymen. After undergraduate study at Johns Hopkins University and law school at Washington and Lee University, Baker established a law practice in Cleveland, Ohio, in 1899. He entered city politics as a disciple of progressive mayor Tom Johnson and rose to become city solicitor. Baker was elected mayor of Cleveland and held office from 1912 to 1916, gaining a reputation as a champion of efficient public services and municipal ownership of utilities.[27]

Woodrow Wilson had appointed Baker secretary of war in 1916, and the following year Baker assumed responsibility for the mobilization of a vast conscript army during World War I. One of the issues that he faced was the role of blacks in the Army. Baker, in keeping with Wilson administration policy, organized black soldiers in segregated units and declared that "there is no intention on the part of the War Department to undertake at this time to settle the so-called race question."[28] In response to pressure from black leaders, however, he commissioned black officers in unprecedented numbers and appointed as a special assistant Emmett Scott, an accommodationist black leader who had served as Booker T. Washington's secretary at Tuskegee Institute. Although he did little to combat widespread mistreatment and abuse of black soldiers, Baker did state his opposition to racial "discrimination" and helped to persuade Wilson to issue a statement condemning lynching.[29]

During the 1920s Baker devoted himself to the practice of law and represented corporate clients in several industries. He was a director of several major corporations and served on the boards of many charitable and voluntary organizations. His political interest during the 1920s was focused on advocacy of United States membership in the League of Nations and the World Court.[30] In 1932 Baker was the choice of many influential conservative and centrist Democrats for the presidential nomination.[31]

With the coming of the New Deal, Baker found himself out of sympathy with Franklin D. Roosevelt's expansion of the power of the federal government. He considered the Tennessee Valley Authority "palpably unconstitutional" and thought that the National Recovery Administration was "headed toward the establishment of a permanent control of industry from Washington."[32] Publicly, he lamented the "decay of self-reliance" and feared that Americans "are willing to surrender the adventure of striving, and are willing to be content to accept, as the best we can get, a sort of secure equality in a State which does all our planning and thinking and providing for us."[33] Privately, he made scathing remarks about FDR. In a letter to one of the Carnegie Corporation trustees, he wrote that Roosevelt's failings seemed "to proceed from a sort of juvenile immaturity of mind rather than to be the gross vices they would be in a more grown up person. I hope it is not a jest in bad taste, but I confess it has seemed to me that the fact that he could get *infantile* paralysis at fifty has seemed to me significant. . . . His swings to the extreme left go much farther and constitute a much deeper menace than he is at all aware of."[34]

Baker's opposition to new federal programs did not diminish his support for relief measures by local governments and voluntary organizations, however. As early as December 1932, he had written an article in the *New York Times* calling on local governments to assist the "homeless wanderers," principally young people, who moved from city to city as hoboes and vagrants. Baker warned that Americans should learn from the experience of Russia with its *bezprizorni*, groups of vagabond youths that sprang up after the overthrow of the czar in 1917 and eventually numbered 2–3 million young people. "This army of children, many of them as young as 10 years, terrorized whole villages and cities and became known for their murders, robberies and other acts of violence," Baker wrote. In contrast, the average American transient of the Depression was a "normal boy" whose goal is "a chance to work." Baker asked his readers if America could "afford to permit permanent injury to the character of this generation of youth."[35] On October 1, 1935, Baker assumed the chairmanship of the American Council on Education to investigate problems of youth unemployment and the adequacy of public education. In his work with this commission, Baker supported a project for the study of Negro youth. Financed by a $110,000 grant from the General Education Board (GEB), the project eventually resulted in a series of books on black youth by social scientists Charles S. Johnson, E. Franklin Frazier, W. Lloyd Warner, Ira DeA. Reid, Allison Davis, and John Dollard.[36]

Baker had long been concerned about the need to reduce ethnic conflict, which he saw as a dangerous and divisive force in American society. He had had to respond to intergroup tension as mayor of a multiethnic city, as secretary of war at a time when many immigrant groups were suspected of disloyalty, and as a national figure in the Democratic party during the 1920s when the party was riven by Protestant-Catholic divisions. As a leading internationalist who followed European affairs, he knew of the role of national and ethnic antagonisms in sparking World War I, and in the early 1930s he viewed the rise of Nazism and fascism with increasing concern. In 1928 Baker had been one of the founders of the National Conference of Jews and Christians (NCJC) (later to be called the National Conference of Christians and Jews), and he served as one of the national cochairmen of the organization in the 1930s.[37] Baker's work with the NCJC was partly motivated by a conservative desire to hold American society together so that politics, education, and business could function normally. Yet, as racism grew in Germany in the 1930s, he was inexorably led into a rhetoric of liberalism, making public attacks on "racial and religious prejudice" and "discrimination" as incompatible with the "American way." He contrasted "foolish philosophies like the recently discovered Aryan man" with the ideas of the Declaration of Independence. "If I could have my prayer for America," he wrote, "I would pray that the time should come when all through the world—wherever there is any prejudice of the disfiguring and corroding kind, whenever men hate each other . . . because of religious or racial difference, or wherever injustice is practiced—men would again look to America."[38]

In August 1935, two months before he requested that the Carnegie Corporation make a Negro study, Baker chaired a week-long Institute of Human Relations in Williamstown, Massachusetts, sponsored by the NCJC. Although the conference was primarily concerned with intergroup tolerance among Protestants, Catholics, and Jews, Baker also presided over a session concerning race relations. Two papers read at the session highlighted the desperate condition of black Americans during the Depression and the growing radicalism of the younger generation of black intellectuals. Ira DeA. Reid, a young black sociologist, argued that northern blacks had organized themselves into a political pressure group capable of taking reprisals against either political party. He credited "left wing political groups" with "making the Negro more keenly alive and vocal about the general social problems of which his maladjustment is but a symptom" and claimed that a younger generation of black leaders was connecting their race's struggle to broader economic and social issues. Reid observed that "drastic cuts" in philanthropic funds for Negro institutions had been a "serious blow," but that this loss of support would lead to a "new independence" for black institutions. He added that "within the last five years, Negro groups have openly refused certain foundation aid because they disagreed with the spirit of the givers." Reid concluded that the times required something more than "these gracious gestures of racial good will at which we in America have become expert." Like many of the young black intellectuals of the 1930s, he issued a radical call for "fundamental programming for altering the social conditions that permit the exploitation of the twelve million American Negroes and millions of American whites that a few chosen ones might pay sur-taxes on their incomes."[39]

At the same session, Oswald Garrison Villard, editor of the *Nation* and a longtime board member of the NAACP, invoked the memory of Wendell Phillips in a fiery speech concerning the desperate condition of blacks in New York City. Villard was then vice-chairman of Mayor Fiorello LaGuardia's committee to investigate the causes of the Harlem riot of March 1935. He told the assembly that the investigation had found 60 percent unemployment in Harlem, serious overcrowding in housing and public schools, discrimination against blacks by city officials, and police brutality. Villard also reported that an alarming increase in female-headed households led to "juvenile depravity" and a high incidence of sexual experience among teenage girls.[40] Baker did not respond to Reid's paper or Villard's speech. He coedited a book entitled *The American Way* that blandly summarized the conference and only briefly mentioned black issues. It contained toned-down, two-sentence summaries of Reid's and Villard's comments.[41]

Baker's main source of knowledge about the condition of urban blacks was his work as a member of the boards of various charitable associations in Cleveland. The Depression had overwhelmed the efforts of voluntary organizations to provide relief for the poor, and the black population was the group hardest hit. From conversations with social workers, teachers, and city officials, Baker became aware of the high percentage of unemployment among urban blacks, inadequate housing, and the potentiality of race conflict. Ten months prior to his suggestion of a Negro study, he had written Carnegie Corporation secretary Robert Lester concerning the danger of racial conflict in public housing projects in Cleveland. The problem, in his view, developed because black migrants from the South "brought with them their habits, which were better adapted to cabin life in the palmetto swamps than they were to the sanitary and hygienic needs of congested life in an industrial city." He predicted racial conflicts between whites and "untidy" blacks "who will not live happily together in these socialized structures."[42]

In proposing a Carnegie study of urban blacks, Baker was not recommending any specific policy changes with regard to civil rights. Despite his public denunciations of prejudice and discrimination, he remained skeptical of the capacity of most blacks for education beyond a basic level. In a letter to Keppel in December 1935, Baker criticized a U.S. Office of Education report, *Fundamentals in the Education of Negroes*, that contained the recommendations of a conference of black and white educators called by Interior Secretary Harold Ickes in 1934. The conference report advocated the "principle of the single standard" in education and condemned inequalities in educational facilities for white and black children. The members of the conference listed among their immediate educational objectives and ideals the "discouragement of and opposition to the extension of segregated schools."[43]

Baker suggested to Keppel that political pressures from black members of the conference committee had prevented an examination of the "biological questions" involved in Negro education. He stressed the importance of encouraging practical education and self-reliance among blacks. Though public schools were generally funded from local tax resources, Baker thought that the black community should be required to furnish labor or funds for the construction of their schools to prove that they really wanted education for their children. Baker's chief objection to the report was its advocacy of "education for education's sake" instead of teaching black children "the wisdom of life." He continued:

> I think anybody who has read *Anthony Adverse* will share my feeling of unlimited amazement at the courage of the white people in this country who received the slaves from slave ships and undertook to make useful laborers of them. How many white civilizations could have dared to receive so many wild savages, who were practically uncaged animals, and spread them around over their farms in contact with their own families passes human comprehension. What has been done for the Negro in a hundred years is an unparalleled achievement and nothing but a theoretical democratic impatience can make us critical of it, though, of course, much more remains to be done.
>
> My own criticism of this report, however, is chiefly that it does not provide any way in which the Negro people can be made to work for their own education. It all proceeds on the theory of a system being provided for them without much effort or cooperation on their part. This, of course, is the theory of common school education in America, and yet with an infant race like the black people in this country, I feel very sure that education would mean more and be more helpful if its opportunity in some fashion could come in response to an aspiration and effort on their part. Rosenwald, I think, was profoundly right in his plan of Negro education in the South. As I understand it, he bought the material and the Negro men built the school houses. That made the school house something very much handsomer than a gift from a philanthropist.[44]

Shortly after Baker suggested that the Carnegie Corporation conduct a study of the "Negro problem" in northern cities, Keppel sent his assistant John M. Russell to Cleveland to study the work of the Neighborhood Association, a private group that sponsored cultural activities and educational programs in a black neighborhood. In April 1936 Russell filed a report that stressed the serious social problems of blacks in Cleveland. Baker wrote Keppel that Russell's report revealed a "dark and dangerous area" and speculated that "similar situations of like character exist in many northern industrial cities. . . . In the past," he recalled, "like neglect of like problems has resulted in such tragic episodes as the Springfield and East St. Louis riots. It may not be the duty of the Carnegie Corporation to try to solve this particular problem but surely it must be somebody's duty, and I suspect that it will have to be pioneered by one of the Foundations before it will have become sufficiently concrete to arouse official recognition and action."[45]

Baker was not to take any further initiatives in formulating the Carnegie Negro study, although Keppel would consult him on a few occasions. He had directed Keppel's attention to a major "social problem": the condition of blacks in northern cities. Baker felt that something should be done at the local level and by voluntary organizations, but he did not know what policies to propose. His own thinking about blacks was hedged about with contradictions. Baker had lived to see the "Negro problem" of his native region move North in alarming proportions. Troubled by the growth of fascism in Europe and by intolerance against Catholics and Jews at home, he publicly espoused the rhetoric of intergroup tolerance and supported an educational campaign against prejudice and discrimination. Yet he retained much of the paternalistic racism of his West Virginia upbringing and looked upon blacks as an "infant race" that needed guidance. He was disturbed by urban black poverty and by the danger of race riots and feared the consequences of a generation of young people growing up without work or a work ethic. Nevertheless, his philosophy of limited government condemned the federal employment programs of the New Deal. Baker died in 1937 and never met Gunnar Myrdal, but his own unresolved conflict between his general statements about "the American way" and his racial prejudices ironically anticipated the central argument of *An American Dilemma.*

Foundations and Black Americans

Keppel had great respect for Baker and agreed that the corporation needed more information about black Americans and a clearer set of guidelines for foundation policy in the area. As he considered Baker's suggestion, he became strongly enthusiastic about the idea of a study and felt that it was time for the corporation to "do more for the Negro."[46] He quietly sounded out friends and associates about the nature of American race relations and the persons most knowledgeable on the subject. Keppel had little previous involvement with black issues, and his ideas about race relations were not clearly formulated. He had worked with Emmett Scott in investigating racial incidents in the training camps during World War I, but he had not devoted a great deal of thought to the concerns of Afro-Americans since the war. The Carnegie Corporation had given a low priority to black issues before 1935, and its grants to black Americans were scattered among several organizations and educational institutions. With the onset of the Depression, demands upon the Carnegie Corporation from all quarters increased at the same time that its income from investments had diminished. Keppel thus had a practical interest in conducting a study that might help the foundation to determine its priorities in making grants to black organizations and institutions.[47]

The corporation's grants to blacks before 1935 had reflected Keppel's ad hoc but cautious approach to philanthropy. Andrew Carnegie had been an admirer of Booker T. Washington and had aided Hampton Institute and Tuskegee. Under Keppel's leadership, the corporation continued to award grants to those centers of industrial education but also supported black universities such as Atlanta and Fisk. During the 1920s and early 1930s the corporation had made small grants to the National Urban League, which Carnegie officials regarded as the most responsible of the black organizations. Yet in 1934, when the league was on the verge of bankruptcy, the Carnegie Corporation denied a request from the league for $5,000 "due to the unusual number of proposals before the Committee and the equally unusual bareness of the cupboard."[48] At the time of Newton Baker's suggestion for a study of American Negroes, both the NAACP and the Urban League were seeking money from the Carnegie Corporation to expand their programs during the Depression. NAACP secretary Walter White had informed Keppel in August 1935 that the NAACP was no longer limiting its activities to fighting racial discrimination but sought to attack economic problems that affected both whites and blacks.[49] Keppel was thus aware of new pressures on the foundations to move beyond the older view that saw education as the principal means of black advancement and to address the economic and social conditions of black Americans during the Depression.

Although the Carnegie Corporation aided black colleges in the South, it did not have the major stake in southern Negro education that the GEB, the Phelps-Stokes Fund, and the Julius Rosenwald Fund had. It was thus freer from pressure from southern white elites than any of those foundations. The Rockefeller-financed GEB was the largest and most influential of the foundations involved in southern education. Officials of the GEB had assiduously cultivated the good will of white southern moderates and reformers as part of a long-term strategy of improving southern education within the framework of legally mandated segregation. The GEB had begun its activities in 1902 and had worked with the Southern Education Board during the first two decades of the century to promote universal public education in the South. In a period when some southern politicians opposed any form of public education for blacks, the GEB had accepted a separate and inferior standard for Negro education.[50] Several GEB officials at the beginning of the century publicly reassured the white South that they opposed racial equality. Wallace Buttrick, secretary of the GEB, had told an audience in Tennessee in 1903, "The Negro is an inferior race. . . . The Anglo-Saxon is superior. There cannot be any question about that."[51] A cornerstone of GEB philosophy was the idea that educating the poor whites of the South would produce a more stable, prosperous, and tolerant society that would benefit blacks as well. The style of the GEB was low-key, and the foundation often worked behind the scenes to maintain the impression that the campaign for improved public education was a purely southern movement. Foundation officials realized that the combination of Yankee meddling, Rockefeller money, and Negro education made them a vulnerable target for Dixie demagogues.

After the First World War, public discussions of Negro inferiority were gradually dropped from foundation rhetoric, but the tradition of emphasis on industrial education for blacks and acquiescence in unequal schooling remained. In the 1920s and 1930s the GEB did provide substantial aid to black universities and colleges and fellowships for black teachers to earn higher degrees. These grants were of vital importance to financially threatened black colleges during the Depression, but this support was always made available within the context of larger sums appropriated by the foundation for southern white universities and scholars. From 1902 to 1960, the GEB appropriated over $62 million for black education from a total expenditure of approximately $324 million.[52]

The success of the GEB in stimulating southern states and school districts to spend more on education depended upon the foundation's ability to retain the cooperation of an elaborate network of southern white educators, clergy, moderate businessmen, and politicians. Such an approach required a cautious strategy on the race issue. Foundation officials such as Associate Director Jackson Davis concentrated on improving Negro schools and colleges and encouraging communication between white and black leaders through the Commission on Interracial Cooperation. GEB officials in this period maintained a discreet distance from the NAACP and avoided the issues of segregation, "social equality," and black disfranchisement.[53]

The Julius Rosenwald Fund was best known for building black schools in the South but was also active in supporting interracial conferences and social science investigations of black life. Initially it operated on premises similar to those of the GEB, but by the 1930s it had moved toward a more liberal program. Under the leadership of Edwin Embree, a white Kentuckian and former Rockefeller Foundation officer, the Rosenwald Fund established closer ties to the New Deal in the area of race relations than other foundations. It paid the salary of Clark Foreman, a white liberal who served as advisor on Negro affairs to Interior Secretary Harold Ickes. Foreman's prodding led to the appointment of economist Robert Weaver and several other young blacks who constituted an informal Black Cabinet to watch over black interests within the Roosevelt administration. The Rosenwald Fund also sponsored an investigation of southern agriculture by Will W. Alexander, Charles S. Johnson, and Embree, published as *The Collapse of Cotton Tenancy* (1935). This book influenced the establishment of the FSA, and Roosevelt appointed Alexander director of the agency.[54] Embree alienated some black leaders, however, by his interference in the internal affairs of black organizations. In an attempt to persuade the NAACP and the National Urban League to merge, he withheld grants from both organizations for ten years after 1933. Although the Rosenwald Fund gave fellowships to a wide range of black and southern white intellectuals, Embree was most closely identified with the economic reformism and program for interracial cooperation of Will Alexander and Charles S. Johnson.[55]

The Phelps-Stokes Fund was a small foundation specializing in Negro education. Its importance lay in its ability to influence the larger foundations and private donors to black colleges and schools. The fund's director, Thomas Jesse Jones, was a champion of the Tuskegee ideal of industrial education and looked with suspicion on black colleges that offered a traditional liberal arts education. In an influential report for the U.S. Bureau of Education in 1917, Jones had found most black colleges substandard and had suggested that Howard University should introduce a program in gardening and that Atlanta University should strengthen its agricultural department.[56] These proposals had drawn a stinging rebuke from W. E. B. Du Bois, who wrote in *The Crisis*, the NAACP magazine, that "the Negro who shows the slightest independence of thought or character is apt to be read out of all possible influence not only by the white South but by the philanthropic North."[57]

By 1931 Anson Phelps Stokes, president of the fund, had effected a rapprochement with Du Bois and was proposing an Encyclopedia of the Negro with Du Bois as editor. Stokes sought to persuade several foundations to appropriate a total of $250,000 for the project, and Keppel was considering the proposal in 1935 when Newton Baker made his suggestion for a Negro study. Keppel respected Du Bois as a scholar and writer, but the Carnegie Corporation had given Du Bois only minor assistance during his long career. In 1932 the Carnegie board had turned down an application for a $5,000 grant for *The Crisis* because of antagonism to Du Bois. In submitting the proposal to the trustees, Keppel had acknowledged that Du Bois "is not a popular man and is hard to get along with" but had added that he had "no hesitation in recommending a grant," observing that *The Crisis* was "without question the ablest publication by Negroes and for Negroes." The board had taken the unusual step of disregarding Keppel's recommendation, and Keppel had written to Du Bois's sponsors that "no fewer than three of the men on the Committee had run afoul of him one time or another, and while their adverse vote was quite sincere, I think it was inevitably influenced by that fact."[58] Nevertheless, two years later Keppel had arranged for the corporation to pay Du Bois $1,250 to aid in the completion of the manuscript of *Black Reconstruction in America*.[59] In the spring of 1935 Du Bois had asked the Carnegie Corporation for a grant to visit South Africa to study race relations, but his request was denied.[60]

The Encyclopedia of the Negro was projected as a major, multivolume publication to be edited by Du Bois and supervised by a board of leading black and white scholars and reformers. From the beginning, however, the enterprise was marred by conflict among scholars in the field. The black historian Carter G. Woodson thought that the project duplicated his own plans to publish an Encyclopedia Africana and denounced it as the Phelps-Stokes Fund's latest attempt at "Negro control." Social scientists such as Melville Herskovits and Donald Young feared that the presence of Stokes and other "uplifters" on the board would mean that the articles would lack a scientific character. They doubted whether Du Bois, after more than two decades of civil rights advocacy in the NAACP, was a suitable person to head an "objective" scholarly study of blacks. Herskovits conducted a letter-writing campaign behind the scenes in an effort to kill the encyclopedia project. Carnegie Corporation secretary Robert Lester, who attended some of the planning sessions, opposed support for the project because of the "tense" atmosphere between black and white participants. Alvin Johnson, editor of the *Encyclopedia of the Social Sciences*, told Keppel that he saw little scholarly merit and much bad management in the enterprise. Keppel would continue to consider funding the encyclopedia until 1941, but already by the middle of the 1930s he could see the difficulties in putting together a large, collaborative research project on black Americans.[61]

As he pondered Newton Baker's proposal in 1935 and 1936, Keppel had no coherent strategy on black issues. In contrast to the Rosenwald Fund, the Phelps-Stokes Fund, and the GEB, the Carnegie Corporation had largely ignored the South and had given only limited attention to black colleges and organizations. Keppel's informal, unsystematic approach to philanthropy meant that he decided on grants to black institutions without employing a staff of southern white advisors like the GEB. Although Baker and Arthur Page had been born in the South, no members of the Carnegie board resided in the South or considered themselves spokesmen for or representatives of the region, and Keppel did not turn to white southerners for advice on how to organize the study of blacks. On the other hand, Keppel's acquaintance with black leaders and intellectuals was also slight. He had not made any personal enemies by interfering with the operations of black institutions, nor was he identified with any particular faction of black leaders. Keppel remained aloof from various black groups and did not consult any blacks as he sought to set up his Negro study.

"Exceptional Men," Colonial Administrators, and Scandinavians

Following the Carnegie tradition, Keppel preferred to look for an "exceptional man" to conduct the Negro study instead of delegating the task to a committee or an existing organization in the field of race relations. Finding the right person for the project proved to be a lengthy process. In an after-dinner speech at the Andrew Carnegie centenary, Keppel had agonized about the difficulties the foundation experienced in attempting to carry out Mr. Carnegie's admonition to "find the exceptional man." "Shall we, ourselves, plod about like Diogenes with his lantern?" Keppel asked. "Shall we ask the universities and the independent institutes to pick him out, or pick her out? Shall we leave the selection to scholarly associates in the learned and professional societies, or turn to organizations which are neither academic nor purely professional? Or is there any satisfactory combination of these and perhaps other methods?"[62] Keppel would try all these methods and some hunches of his own in locating his exceptional man to study the American Negro.

In April 1936 Keppel unexpectedly received a grant proposal from Melville Herskovits for a major investigation of black cultures in West Africa, the Caribbean, and the United States. Herskovits, who was unaware of Baker's suggestion, sought support for fieldwork in West Africa, transcription of Haitian music, and publication of his completed monograph on Dahomey. These projects were part of his continuing research into the historical diffusion of culture from West Africa to the New World. Keppel referred this proposal to the psychologist Edward L. Thorndike, his close friend, former Columbia colleague, and neighbor in Montrose, New York. Thorndike had been one of Herskovits's teachers at Columbia, and he enthusiastically endorsed his former student as the best person in the country to undertake a Negro study. Keppel then checked with John Merriam of the Carnegie Institution of Washington, who was skeptical about the feasibility of Herskovits's research. When Robert Crane of the Social Science Research Council (SSRC) reported that Herskovits was hard to work with, Keppel began to look elsewhere.[63]

By the fall of 1936 Keppel had conceived of the idea of inviting a foreigner to conduct the study. This was not a new notion. In that same year, Bertram Schrieke, a Dutch colonial administrator who had served in the East Indies, published *Alien Americans*, a study of blacks and other minority groups in the United States undertaken at the request of the Julius Rosenwald Fund. Schrieke's investigation was a conservative study which attracted little attention, but his preface anticipated the rationale for the Myrdal study. The Dutch visitor wrote that "although the problems the [Rosenwald] Board wished me to study were entirely foreign to me, since I had never visited the United States nor had I ever met an American Negro, the Board regarded these handicaps as an advantage, as a guarantee of unbiassed opinion."[64] Keppel had read *Alien Americans* in April 1936 and recommended it to Newton Baker as "a very keen piece of work."[65] Herskovits, on the other hand, wrote a devastating review in the *Nation* which dismissed the book as superficial and impressionistic and suggested that Shrieke's background as a colonial official did not equip him to understand the American race issue.[66]

The Schrieke study was not the first instance of foundation-sponsored dialogue between colonial administrators and Americans concerned with black issues. The Phelps-Stokes Fund, the Carnegie Corporation, and the GEB shared in varying degrees the perception of the similarity between Negro education in the South and the education of colonial peoples, particularly in Africa. Under the leadership of Thomas Jesse Jones, the Phelps-Stokes Fund had worked aggressively since 1920 to export the Tuskegee model of politically safe industrial and agricultural education to Africa. The Phelps-Stokes Fund sent white specialists in Negro education from the American South to Africa to instruct colonial educators in the Tuskegee method. With aid from the Laura Spelman Rockefeller Memorial, it also sponsored visits to Hampton and Tuskegee by hundreds of British colonial administrators, missionaries, and educators in the 1920s and 1930s. In 1925, for example, an official of the Laura Spelman Rockefeller Memorial wrote to a visiting administrator from Kenya, "Our hope is that your observations may throw some light on the problems arising in working among backward communities where the process of assimilating European culture is just beginning in the negro groups."[67]

The Carnegie Corporation conducted educational activities in the British colonies of Africa and in South Africa as part of its charter obligation to aid the advancement of knowledge throughout the British Empire and Dominions. Although the Carnegie Corporation was less doctrinaire on African education than the Phelps-Stokes Fund, it supported Phelps-Stokes initiatives in transplanting the Jeanes teacher program from the black schools of the American South to the native reserves of East Africa. The Jeanes program was designed to direct African education away from the European model and toward agricultural education, sanitation, community development, and appreciation for African traditions. After Keppel visited the first Jeanes school in Kenya in 1927, he persuaded the Carnegie Corporation board to give $100,000 in support of Jeanes schools in various African colonies. The Carnegie Corporation also financed tours of southern black institutions by British missionaries involved in African agricultural work. It sent Jackson Davis of the GEB to Africa in 1935 to address an interterritorial Jeanes conference in Salisbury, Southern Rhodesia, and to study education, "native welfare," and race relations. As Keppel pondered Newton Baker's proposal for a study of American blacks, the Carnegie Corporation and the GEB were arranging a meeting of colonial administrators and white southern specialists in Negro education to be held at the University of North Carolina in 1937. The conference on "The Education of Negroes and the Native African" brought together directors of native education from British colonies in Africa and state agents for Negro education from the South.[68]

An explicit model for the American Negro study as Keppel conceived it was Lord Hailey's *An African Survey*, sponsored by the Carnegie Corporation and published in 1938. Lord Hailey, a former governor of the United Provinces in India, was completing a book while Keppel was searching for someone to study American blacks. The idea for Hailey's project had originated in discussions at the dining table of the country home of Lord Lothian, secretary of the Rhodes Trust. An African Research Survey committee, consisting of reforming colonial administrators, missionaries, and anthropologists, had met at Rhodes House in 1931 to discuss the impact of British commercial activity on African peoples. With support from the Carnegie Corporation, the committee commissioned Hailey's report. Hailey's sixteen-hundred-page survey of conditions in the African colonies took a reformist line within the context of British colonialism. He advocated the gradual introduction of self-government over a long period of time and argued that the British government should intervene to engineer economic and social development to precede political change. Although Hailey envisaged eventual independence, his modernizing mission provided a rationale for continued British presence in Africa. Neither Hailey nor his contemporaries in the Colonial Office foresaw the speed with which independence would come, but *An African Survey* and Hailey's subsequent writings were of major importance in shifting British policy toward greater emphasis on fostering economic development and social welfare in the colonies.[69]

Keppel initially did not conceive of the proposed study of American Negroes as a social science research project. He sought a statesmanlike figure, perhaps with colonial experience, who would travel around America for a year, assisted by a small staff, and write a report for the educated public concerning Negroes. In November 1936, Keppel came close to offering the job to Hendrik Mouw, a retired administrator of the Dutch colonial service in the East Indies.[70] Mouw had been recommended by J. T. Moll, a Dutch official whom Keppel and Baker knew through their work with the Institute for Pacific Relations. Moll explained Keppel's idea to Mouw in a letter:

> The Corporation is looking for a man perfectly free from sentimental and social bias and from political prejudice. I understand that in the U.S.A., this whole problem is interwoven with active and passive "charity," with political traditions, with dilettantism and hobby-riding to such an extent that the Board feels diffident of the probability of finding an American who would do justice to the subject in the sense which Dr. Keppel explained to me. Especially [Keppel] wants to get away from the point of view that "education" and "school instruction" can be the panacea, a conception which still has a remarkable hold on most people's mind, notwithstanding the disappointing results of the energy employed in this direction and of the big sums of money spent on schools, etc.[71]

Keppel wrote Moll that he would propose Mouw informally to his board and that he hoped for a favorable result.[72] He consulted Newton Baker, who approved of Mouw. But Keppel thought that it would be "prudent to see if there's anyone else on the horizon before closing with him [Mouw]."[73] He decided to write to the Dutch historian Johann Huizinga, who objected that Mouw was too conservative and lacked the breadth of vision necessary for scientific research.[74] Keppel also talked with Herskovits in December 1936 about commissioning Mouw or some other European to study American blacks, perhaps with the assistance of a committee of American social scientists who would provide advice and guidance. Keppel hinted that Herskovits might be asked to direct this committee of social scientists.[75]

Herskovits emphatically objected to a European from a country with a history of imperialism and argued that the conclusions of such a person would be discounted by American blacks. He advised Keppel that if the Carnegie Corporation decided to invite a European, they should look in Switzerland or Sweden. He suggested as possible choices Alfred Métraux, a Swiss anthropologist; William Rappard, a Swiss political scientist; and Gerhard Lindblohm, a Swedish anthropologist. Herskovits made it clear that he did not wish to participate in the project if it were to be "one of these *ad hoc* investigations such as Schrieke put on, with easy 'solutions.'" He proposed as members of the advisory committee two of his best friends: Donald Young, a white sociologist on the staff of the SSRC, and Abram Harris, a black economist at Howard University. Herskovits strongly urged that the American committee should include Negro members.[76]

Keppel dropped Hendrik Mouw from consideration, although he continued to investigate other candidates from European colonialist countries. On Herskovits's advice, he began consulting Donald Young. As a recognized authority on American minorities and an official of the Social Science Research Council, which served as an advisory agency to the foundations, Young emerged as an important advisor to Keppel during the formative stages of the Negro study. In January 1937, Young wrote a detailed memo that gave Keppel a new conception of the proposed project. Previously, Keppel had thought in terms of a European statesman who would spend a year in America and write a general report, aided by an advisory committee and a small staff that would collect data. Young proposed a more ambitious undertaking in which the foreign observer would spend three to five years in the United States. There would be an American director of a staff of social scientists, who would be hired to make independent studies of important topics regarding black Americans. These independent research projects could then be published separately from the main report.[77]

Young and Herskovits secretly collaborated on this proposal in the hope of turning what looked like a junket into a large project that would advance social science research on blacks. Both were skeptical that any European observer could master the literature on American race relations and say anything new. They saw this project as an opportunity to pry loose foundation dollars for American scholars to investigate neglected areas in Afro-American studies, such as linguistics, the economic status of the Negro, the historical relationship between African and Afro-American cultures, and fieldwork in several black communities concerning personality and cultural traits. With characteristic bluntness, Herskovits wrote Young that the purpose of their proposed advisory committee would be to "tell this European what was to be seen and give him the necessary documentation for this report." He added, "I really think it is our chance to do what we've been wanting to do, and to sketch in, with far greater support than we dreamed would be possible, the outlines of the longtime research we've planned."[78] Young expressed his hope that "between us we may be able to make something real out of what otherwise might easily turn into a sad affair."[79] Herskovits urged Young to press for the inclusion of Abram Harris on the advisory committee because "he is not only the best man I know to handle the economic aspects of the situation, and one with whom we could get on, but I think it would be extremely unfortunate if another study of the Negro was set up without any Negro being represented on it in a position of some importance."[80]

Regarding the selection of the foreign observer, Young cautioned Keppel that no European would be free of bias in studying American race relations. In addition to the colonial powers, Young noted that countries such as Germany and Hungary included "minority peoples" within their borders. He added that perhaps the Scandinavian countries were the most free of traditions of colonialism or the subjugation of ethnic minorities.[81] Young and Herskovits then waited nervously to see what Keppel would do next. As Young noted, the Carnegie president "takes something, fools around with it for a long, long time, and then sometimes something happens and sometimes it doesn't."[82]

Keppel was much impressed by Young's proposal and promised to give copies of it to the trustees.[83] Despite warnings from Young, Herskovits, and others that Europeans had their own biases on racial issues, Keppel remained convinced that the subject required a foreign observer. As a young administrator at Columbia, he had helped to arrange for a series of lectures by James Bryce, the English author of *The American Commonwealth*, and he hoped to find a man of comparable breadth of vision to tackle the race issue.[84] He continued the search throughout the spring and summer of 1937, considering Europeans from both colonialist and noncolonialist countries. Most of the prospective Tocquevilles were unaware that they were being considered. The most serious candidates besides Myrdal were Alfred Métraux, William Rappard, and Roy Forbes Harrod, a British economist. The list of personnel under consideration included several British colonial officials such as Lord Hailey and Sir Donald Cameron, the governor of Nigeria. It also included such diverse figures as Bronislaw Malinowski; W. W. Vaughn, the former headmaster of Rugby; and a Rev. J. H. Longenecker of Tennessee. Herskovits and Harris were mentioned as possible members of the advisory committee.[85]

The name of Karl Gunnar Myrdal, a thirty-eight-year-old Swedish economist, emerged late in the proceedings. Keppel's first memorandum on Myrdal is dated July 13, only a month before he was invited to undertake the study. Myrdal's name was suggested by Beardsley Ruml, an irrepressible social-scientist-turned-businessman who was then treasurer of R. H. Macy's department store.[86] Ruml played with great relish the role of idea man and behind-the-scenes coordinator among government agencies, corporations, universities, and foundations. He had received a Ph.D. in psychology from the University of Chicago in 1917, specializing in psychological testing. After serving during World War I on the War Department's Committee on the Classification of Personnel, Ruml became a member of a consulting firm that advised businesses on personnel matters. He entered the world of philanthropy in 1921 as an assistant to James R. Angell, Keppel's predecessor as president of the Carnegie Corporation. The following year Ruml was appointed director of the $80-million Laura Spelman Rockefeller Memorial. During his brief tenure as director of the memorial from 1922 to 1929, he did more than any other foundation executive to stimulate the development of empirical social science research, channeling millions of dollars into the development of research institutes at Chicago, Yale, Columbia, North Carolina, and other universities. The memorial also aided in the establishment of social science research institutes at several European centers including Stockholm University. Under Ruml's stewardship, the memorial funded black colleges in the South and was a mainstay of southern white racial moderates through its support for the Commission on Interracial Cooperation and for Howard Odum's Institute for Research in Social Science at the University of North Carolina. Ruml served as dean of the

Social Science Division of the University of Chicago from 1931 to 1933 and became treasurer of Macy's in 1934. Ruml was more liberal politically than Keppel and had close ties to New Dealers such as Charles Merriam and Frederic Delano of the National Resources Committee. He had been the originator of the domestic allotment plan which formed the basis of the New Deal's agriculture program. Appointed a director of the Federal Reserve Bank of New York in January 1937, Ruml was in touch with leading "spenders" in the Roosevelt administration and became an advocate of deficit spending to increase consumer purchasing power. He had met Gunnar Myrdal when Myrdal had been in the United states in 1929–30 as a Rockefeller Foundation Social Science Fellow and was familiar with the economic theory of Myrdal and other members of the Stockholm school. Their willingness to use planned deficits as a tool of fiscal policy was consistent with his own expansionary approach to the problem of economic recovery in the United States. Myrdal's work as a planner and social welfare innovator was also compatible with Ruml's political outlook.[87]

Myrdal had impressed other Rockefeller Foundation officials during his fellowship year when he visited several American universities, including Columbia, Wisconsin, and Chicago. In subsequent years, Rockefeller Foundation officers had followed his career and made grants to the social science research institute at Stockholm University of which he was first a staff member and then director. Myrdal had also served as an advisor to the Rockefeller Foundation and had evaluated grant applications from European scholars. As early as 1933, John Van Sickle of the foundation's European office had noted in a memo, "Myrdal is rapidly becoming the driving force in intellectual circles in Stockholm." Edmund E. Day, director of the Social Sciences Division of the Rockefeller Foundation, had written: "In granting Myrdal an SS fellowship, the Foundation placed its money on a winning horse! I wish we might register a larger proportion of such notable successes."[88]

Rockefeller officials admired in Myrdal not merely his brilliance as an economist but his effectiveness in applying social science research to legislation and public policy. Foundation officers in the 1930s cherished the ideal of a close connection between social science research and public policy. Tracy Kittredge of the Rockefeller Foundation wrote in 1935, "I know of no country where there has been so close a relation between research and application as in Sweden. The men who have been engaged on the various economic studies have at the same time been influential in the development of government projects of action based in many instances upon the results of the research. . . . The fact that Myrdal is the effective director of the research program of the Institute and the extent to which his activity is devoted to practical economic and social programs is a sufficient indication of this aspect of the Stockholm situation."[89]

A key memo that Keppel received from the former Rockefeller official Lawrence K. Frank stressed Myrdal's experience in conducting a series of social science studies that were used in Sweden "as a basis for legislation." Frank also described

Myrdal as "able, energetic and competent in the social field, well oriented psychiatrically and familiar with clinical methods and materials." He noted that the American sociologist W. I. Thomas, who had worked with Myrdal in Sweden on population research, "admires his work." On the final list of candidates, Keppel included a note that Myrdal "has worked on crime and disorders." Actually, criminology was a minor interest of Myrdal's, but the comment suggests that Keppel conceived of the study at this point within a "social problems" framework. When he ruled out Roy Harrod, Keppel noted Donald Young's comment that Harrod was a man without "proven ability to run a team." In choosing Myrdal, Keppel preferred an academic statesman with practical experience over a social scientist such as Alfred Métraux who wrote for a more limited scholarly audience and lacked political experience.[90]

Keppel's consultations with social scientists had led him to embrace a more sophisticated conception of the study and encouraged him to look for a European scholar from a nonimperialist country instead of a colonial administrator. In his final selection of Myrdal, however, he relied not on the advice of social scientists but on the recommendation of two former foundation officers, Ruml and Frank, who were familiar with the social sciences.[91] None of the trustees played a significant role in choosing Myrdal.[92] There is no evidence that any blacks or women were consulted at any point in the selection process.

The Carnegie president chose a Swedish Social Democrat with a strong commitment to social engineering and government intervention in the economy. Although Myrdal's political views were to the left of Keppel's and the Carnegie board members', there is no reason to suppose that Keppel knew that Myrdal favored deficit spending, planning for full employment, and extensive welfare programs. Myrdal's political activities in Sweden were not widely known in the United States in 1937. Keppel merely saw Myrdal as a distinguished scholar-statesman from a European country, highly respected by men whose word he trusted.[93]

On August 12, 1937, Keppel wrote to Myrdal inviting him to head the study. He explained that all of the American reformers and scholars interested in the race question were "influenced by emotional factors of one type or another, and many are also under the influence of earlier environmental conditions, family or community traditions of the abolition movement on the one hand or of the old regime of the South on the other." Keppel wrote that the Carnegie Corporation wanted "someone who would approach the situation with an entirely fresh mind. We have also thought that it would be wise to seek a man in a nonimperialistic country with no background of domination of one race over another." Keppel offered to provide Myrdal with a staff of experts who would be competent to investigate various aspects of Negro life, and he noted that the SSRC had agreed to act in an advisory role in the selection of these experts.[94]

Myrdal initially declined the invitation because of his responsibilities as an elected member of the upper house of the Swedish parliament.[95] But after discussing the matter with the ubiquitous Beardsley Ruml, who happened to be in Stockholm on a visit, Myrdal wrote Keppel that he wanted to reconsider the offer. Myrdal acknowledged that he had had little previous exposure to the study of racial issues, but he indicated a general sympathy for the "environmentalist" position on racial differences. "During my stay in the States in 1929–30 I found myself having a purely questioning attitude to the Negro problem," he wrote. "My general attitude to race problems . . . is that I am on the one hand inclined to keep very critical against the popular insistence on great biological difference in intellectual and moral qualities between races but on the other hand not apt *a priori* to postulate perfect parity."[96]

In choosing a man about whom he knew so little, Keppel had exposed himself to considerable risk. But Keppel's initial offer did not include a specific budget. Although he promised Myrdal a staff, the bulk of the funds for the project was not appropriated by the Carnegie board until after Myrdal had been in the United States for a year. Eventually the study would cost more than $300,000, a very high figure for a social science research project in that era.[97] Had Myrdal failed to impress Keppel during the early stages of the research, however, the Carnegie president could have cut the study off at a much lower level of funding. As it happened, the two men were to develop a strong working relationship: Keppel would give Myrdal a free hand in running the study and would support him in requests for additional funding from the Carnegie board. In addition, the Carnegie president possessed what his friend Russell Leffingwell called a gift of "perceptive, and almost imperceptible, guidance, correction, and encouragement" that would have a subtle influence in shaping the study and in buoying Myrdal's spirits through many adversities.[98]

Although there was an element of serendipity in Keppel's selection of Gunnar Myrdal to study American blacks, the project grew out of certain structural changes in race relations, philanthropic institutions, and in the social sciences. The migration of hundreds of thousands of blacks from the rural South to the cities of the North and their unemployment during the Depression led to suffering, social problems, and the danger of racial conflict, all of which worried Newton Baker. The New Deal was unwilling to face the race issue directly or to sponsor a major study of the "Negro problem" because of the fear of antagonizing southern members of Congress. Frederick Keppel, at the height of his power and influence as president of the Carnegie Corporation, believed that the foundation should innovate in areas in which corporations and governments feared to tread. Initially, he thought of importing a colonial administrator, an idea that reflected the imperial legacy of Andrew Carnegie as well as the attitude of several foundations that the education of black Americans and colonial peoples should proceed along similar principles. But the social sciences had grown in influence since the turn of the century, and Keppel felt compelled to consult Donald Young, an official of the SSRC, which served as an advisory body to the foundations, as well as other social scientists. American social scientists, moreover, had produced a considerable body of research on race relations since World War I. The notion of inviting a colonial official to study American blacks offended Young's sense of professionalism and commitment to the advancement of objective, specialized, social science investigation. Herskovits expressed similar views, warned Keppel that black scholars and white liberals would never accept the findings of a colonial administrator, and conspired to play a dominant role as director of an interracial research team of American social scientists in the proposed study. But if Keppel yielded some ground to the American social scientists in deference to their growing power over ideas about race relations, he remained stubbornly wedded to his idea of appointing a European scholar-statesman who would write a broad, interpretive book for the general reader that might be of some use to policymakers. Keppel may have been ignorant of Myrdal's political views, but his friends Ruml and Frank, who had helped to construct an elaborate Rockefeller network in Europe, assured him that Myrdal was a pragmatic social scientist whose studies helped to form the basis for Swedish legislation.

Paradoxically, because the Carnegie Corporation had largely ignored black issues, there would be few institutional checks and obstacles to Myrdal's intellectual freedom once the project got under way. The Swedish visitor would be able to chart a more liberal course on race relations because the Carnegie Corporation had no southern trustees, no elaborate educational programs that depended on the good will of southern white elites, and no staff of specialists on Negro education whose watchword was caution. Moreover, Keppel's elitism ironically opened the door to Myrdal's bold, policy-oriented racial liberalism because the foreign observer was not beholden to the American social science establishment, with its devotion to a narrowly defined concept of objectivity and its suspicion of policy-oriented investigations. Myrdal would not be required to submit his research procedures to peer review or to share the direction of the study with American scholars. Keppel had little knowledge of the social sciences or of black affairs, his procedures in setting up the Negro study were pervaded by what a later generation of scholars would call "institutional racism," and black scholars were given no power in shaping this important study of Afro-American life. Yet Keppel had no strong desire to support the status quo in the South, nor was he committed to a New Deal scenario of focusing on economic reforms and deferring action on civil rights. Given Keppel's disinclination to interfere with research, much would depend upon how Myrdal defined the role of foreign observer. The Carnegie tradition had been to support "exceptional men," and Keppel concluded that Gunnar Myrdal deserved the opportunity to write a major survey of the American "Negro problem."

2

Social Engineering and Prophylactic Reform

"I believe I was born abnormally curious," Gunnar Myrdal once boasted in looking back on his early childhood in the village of Solvarbo in the Swedish province of Dalarna. For more than three hundred years, his ancestors had lived in Gustaf's parish, where the Dalälven River winds gently through a broad valley on its course from Lake Siljan to the Baltic. In this land of surpassing natural beauty, they had struggled to claim a living from their small farms, worshiped at the parish church, and passed the long winter nights by recounting the legends and tales for which Dalarna is noted. These rich traditions stirred the imagination of the boy, even as social changes sweeping the province at the turn of the century piqued his curiosity.[1]

Dalarna was a poor, remote, mountainous region that for centuries had been isolated from the rest of Sweden. It was a land that had never known feudalism or occupation by a foreign power, and the Dalecarlians were proud of their fierce independence and democratic traditions. They liked to recall that in the sixteenth century the Swedish king Gustav Vasa, after being defeated by the Danes, took refuge in Dalarna, raised an army, and drove the invaders from the land. Through the centuries the Dalecarlian peasants often rebelled against the authority of the central government in Stockholm. To the rest of Sweden they were known for their hard work, stubborn temperament, religious piety, and traditional folklore.

In the late nineteenth century the traditional way of life in Dalarna was changing rapidly. The land could not support all the children of farm families, and many moved to Swedish cities, where they found work in factories, while others, including two of Gunnar Myrdal's uncles, emigrated to America. The railroad connected the mining areas of Dalarna to the rest of Sweden, and the telephone was introduced in Solvarbo in 1898, the year of Gunnar Myrdal's birth. The provincial cities of Falun and Säter grew as manufacturing supplemented agriculture, lumbering, and mining in Dalarna's economy. Dalarna was also the "burned-over district" of Sweden during these years, as evangelical sects broke away from the state church and set up mission houses in many villages. The temperance movement flourished, and socialism won some adherents among the Dalecarlians.[2]

Carl Adolf Pettersson, Myrdal's father, was an ambitious young man, born in 1876, who broke with the family tradition of farming and became a building contractor. Though he had only six years of schooling, he enrolled in a technical school in nearby Hedemora and began building houses in the region. On May 15, 1898, the twenty-two-year-old Pettersson married a nineteen-year-old woman from the village, Anna Sofia (Sofie) Karlsson, the daughter of the miller.[3] Six months and three weeks later, on December 6, 1898, Sofie gave birth to their first child, Karl Gunnar Pettersson. The Petterssons were away from home on that dark and cold winter night because Carl Adolf was building a railway depot in the village of Skattungbyn, near Orsa in north-central Dalarna. They were living in a small rented room next to the kitchen in Nissaper Jugga's cottage, on a mountainside looking out on a vast forest to the west. Sofie, a shy young woman who had scarcely been away from home before, worried about getting blood on the landlord's bed, so Carl Adolf fetched straw from the barn and spread it on the floor, where Gunnar was born.[4]

Gunnar spent his earliest childhood in Solvarbo, where the family lived in a new house that his father had built on his grandfather's farm. A path led from the house through a grove of birch trees to a sawmill, where his maternal grandfather worked. Fewer than a hundred families lived in the village, and the boy could wander from house to house seeing mainly relatives and family friends. There was no great inequality of wealth in Solvarbo. The village contained no manor houses of the nobility, and at the other end of the spectrum, there were only a few landless farm workers and loggers. Most families owned small farms where they grew wheat, rye, and oats, and wealth was measured more by the number of cows a family owned than by the size of their landholdings. The only structures other than private homes in the village were a cooperative store, a mission house, and a house belonging to the Good Templars, a temperance group. The parish church, built in 1752, was in the neighboring village of Gustaf's. Gunnar's family moved often during his childhood and youth; but they returned to Solvarbo for summer visits, and he retained a strong identification with the village and his kinfolk there.[5] He could look back on the village as a source of stability to compensate for the turbulence of his parents' home. Gunnar would always remain, in a sense, the village bright boy, astounding his elders with his precosity and "abnormal" curiosity and trying to impress his peers with his knowledge.

Though Carl Adolf Pettersson built a few homes in Solvarbo, there was not enough work for him in the village and surrounding area, and in 1902 he took the family to the nearby town of Falun, which offered an exciting prospect to his inquisitive son. To a small boy from a tiny village, this town of ten thousand people seemed like an enormous city, full of energy and activity. Gunnar liked to explore in the town, peeking in the windows of houses and wondering about the people who lived there: "How do they earn their living? Why do people become what they are? What are their families like? Why do they act as they do?"[6]

An even greater change came in 1905, when the restless Carl Adolf Pettersson moved the family to Stockholm and Gunnar was enrolled in elementary school. A stocky, aggressive, gregarious man with a mustache and goatee, Pettersson was

Anna Sofia "Sofie" Pettersson, Gunnar Myrdal's mother (courtesy Sissela Bok)

Carl Adolf Pettersson, Gunnar Myrdal's father (courtesy Sissela Bok)

successful as a contractor in the capital city, building apartment buildings and speculating in properties. His whole manner radiated energy and power, and he ruled the family as a patriarch. The Pettersson family lived in Stockholm and its suburbs through Gunnar's adolescent years, moving frequently as Carl Adolf would buy a house, fix it up, sell it, and move the family to another house. For the children, this meant changing schools often, adapting to new situations, and finding new friends. In addition to the strains of geographical and social mobility, problems developed between Gunnar's father and mother. A heavy drinker and womanizer, Carl Adolf often left Sofie at home with the children while he went out on the town with his business associates. Sofie was a gentle, soft-spoken, and religious woman who submitted to her domineering husband. A traditional housewife with little education, she did not share Carl Adolf's ambition for money and social distinction, and she resented having to move so often. Bitterly unhappy in her marriage, she complained tearfully to relatives and friends about her husband's drinking and womanizing, but divorce was out of the question for a religious woman of her generation. Sofie devoted herself to raising her four children, particularly her oldest son, Gunnar, who was always accorded special treatment as an unusually gifted child. She tried to instill in her children piety, traditional morality, a strong work ethic, and a sense of duty to the community. Sofie imparted to Gunnar an abiding moralism that would become more pronounced in the middle and later stages of his life and an emphasis on conscience as a guide to conduct.[7]

The Making of an Intellectual Aristocrat

For an upwardly mobile family that had money but not status, the education of the children was an important consideration, and Gunnar's parents encouraged him to do well in school. But this gifted child was something of a troublemaker. His grandmother declared that he could be so irritating that he would "make the boulders rock," a judgment in which his teachers concurred. Reminiscing on his childhood in later years, Gunnar suggested that he kept getting into trouble because he was always having to adjust to new schools and classmates and felt driven to stand out and attract attention. Problems at home undoubtedly contributed to his unruly behavior as well. He frequently neglected his homework, and recalled sitting in chapel at school every morning, holding his psalmbook in front of his face and praying: "Dear God, if you help me today, I'll do my homework for tomorrow." Divine intervention was not forthcoming, however; Gunnar kept getting mediocre grades, and his mother was called in by the teachers for conferences about his bad behavior. Then, at age fourteen, he injured his hip and had to miss school for several months. His academic grades and his conduct grade were poor enough to jeopardize his attending gymnasium, and his father was very angry that this gifted son might let down the family. During his time out from school,

Gunnar resolved to take his studies more seriously, and when he returned to school, his work improved. The hip injury kept him from excelling in sports, and he began to direct his enormous energy and competitiveness into academic work.[8]

During his teenage years, Gunnar had to learn greater self-control and had to assume more responsibility within the family. His mother turned to him, as the oldest son, to help the family in various difficult situations resulting from his father's drinking problem. Gunnar never broke openly with his father and outwardly played the role of the dutiful son, helping his father in later years with legal and business advice. Inwardly, however, he regarded Carl Adolf as as embarrassment and yearned to lead a different kind of life. Despite this conflict, Gunnar grew to resemble his father in his driving ambition, restless energy, contentious style, and insistence on deference from the rest of his family. Though he would embrace an optimistic worldview, there would always be an undercurrent of worry and occasional depression that was a legacy of these family problems, a sense that things could turn out badly if careful, rational planning did not succeed.[9]

In August 1914, as World War I erupted and Gunnar prepared to begin gymnasium, his father changed the children's surname to Myrdahl, the name of a farm owned by the family in Solvarbo.[10] Three years later, Gunnar would drop the *h*. Though a more distinctive name than Pettersson, it was hardly aristocratic: literally, it means "swamp-valley." With his new identity uneasily in place, Gunnar enrolled in the prestigious Norra Real gymnasium in Stockholm and was the first member of his family to undertake formal education beyond grammar school. He brought to this new milieu exceptional brilliance, an outgoing manner, and a competitiveness that masked an inner insecurity. Gunnar was an outsider in the world of the Stockholm bourgeoisie, and his fellow students sneered at him as a hick and considered the idea of an intellectual from Dalarna to be an oxymoron. But Gunnar was determined to prove them wrong. He gradually distanced himself from the democratic and religious values of Dalarna, cultivated a zealous rhetoric of public service, and sought to win acceptance from teachers and fellow students by embracing elitist views.

Gymnasium opened up a new world for Gunnar—a more optimistic and rational world than his parents' home. His teachers at Norra Real were learned men, several of them with doctorates, and he found the first of several academic father figures in his history teacher, John Lindqvist, who introduced him to the philosophy of the Enlightenment.[11] In a school essay, Myrdal praised Montesquieu, Diderot, and Voltaire for freeing men from religious dogma and furthering a more rational understanding of nature and society and greater tolerance. He mentioned Rousseau's attempt to replace religion with reason as a guide to moral conduct and regretfully noted that the mass of people were not then ready for such a transition. Though he discussed Montesquieu's admiration for the English Constitution and Voltaire's advocacy of enlightened despotism, he did not address the democratic strain in eighteenth-century French thought, nor did he mention the French Revolution or the ideals of liberty, equality, and fraternity. The lesson of

Gunnar Myrdal as a gymnasium student, 1915 (courtesy Arbetarrörelsens Arkiv, Stockholm)

the Enlightenment, for the young Myrdal, was that educated men could use reason to guide political development for the masses.[12]

In a 1917 school essay on Dalarna, Myrdal cast a backward glance at his native province and struggled with his ambivalent feelings of loyalty to its culture and ambition to be part of an educated urban elite that would shape Swedish politics. At times sentimental, at times ironic and satirical, the essay reflects both Myrdal's pride in the Dalecarlian tradition of stubborn independence and impudence toward authority and his desire to win the respect of his teachers as a cosmopolitan intellectual. The central issue that he examined was how Dalarna, the "heart of Sweden," known for the great patriotism of its people, could have become infected by popular movements imported from abroad: religious nonconformity, temperance, and socialism. He began with a proud account of how "the poor men of Dalarna" had come to the nation's aid "whenever freedom's cause called for a defender against foreign attack or domestic tyranny." The most prominent characteristic of the Dalecarlian, he averred, was a love of freedom and independence that stemmed from a society where "no castle stood overweening to raise its turrets to the sky." For a thousand years, the "democratic social structure" of the province had "shaped the farmers and timber-cutters, who said 'du' to everybody and who obeyed nobody except the law and the king, the latter only if his policies won approval and confidence." Candor was always the manner of speaking to the king, Myrdal reported. "With us, Sir, you are great, but against us, rather little," they had dared to write to the harsh King Gösta. Myrdal argued that this desire for independence "sometimes can go to excess and degenerate into contempt for and hatred of discipline and authority." But the Dalecarlian, he contended, cannot help being the way he is: "He is not meant to obey, . . . he is not meant to be a proletarian or cannon-fodder."[13]

The Dalecarlian's patriotism also rested on his passionate love of his birthplace, "the blue mountains and the deep forests, . . . Lake Siljan and the Dalälven," as well as a deep piety and devotion to the Swedish church, as evidenced by the "magnificent temples" erected in the region. "His own cottage could be dark and cramped, his bread could be mixed with bark, but the man of Dalarna would have a temple worthy of God." Another virtue of the traditional Dalecarlian was the capacity for hard work. "It is an acknowledged truth," Myrdal asserted, "that a barren land makes its inhabitants hard-working and persevering. . . . Experienced in hard work from his earliest childhood, the old man keeps going until the end to increase the size of his estate. . . . 'I don't take my pants off until I go to bed,' he answers if somebody tells him to rest in his old age." Poverty also made the Dalecarlians "Sweden's most intelligent" people, with a keen eye for business dealings.[14]

And yet among these virtuous and intelligent people "poisonous plants" had sprung up in the form of foreign-inspired popular movements. What had gone wrong? Myrdal asked. He suggested that the Dalecarlians of old had lived their own life in the mountains, which like a "Chinese wall" had left them "rather untouched by the outer world and its culture." He claimed that modern communications, especially the flow of letters and visitors back from America, had exposed the innocent Dalecarlians to religious sects, freemasonry, and socialism. These credulous farmers had been taken in by the mission houses, "where one is served both coffee and forgiveness of sins, and the 'pastor' in a simple and natural way, shows the children of God the short-cuts to heaven." Radical newspapers had stirred the excitable Dalecarlians because "the slogan and the strong expression are easy to remember." These modern popular movements had mobilized the same love of freedom that Gustav Vasa had awakened centuries before. "Contempt for authority" was the movements' "innermost driving force," Myrdal warned. "Both socialism and the temperance movement go so far as to declare the wants of the masses as law." Myrdal argued that "every step forward for these . . . popular movements means a decline of the inherited love of freedom, birthplace, and country" and concluded that "every patriot's wish must be that the subversive forces should not reach deeper than the surface, so that the folk soul's good powers should be able to awaken a reaction, a reversal which shall carry the old ideals and way of thinking to honor among the people of Dalarna."[15]

After this school essay, with its blend of romanticism about his birthplace and a craving for acceptance by his cosmopolitan teachers, Myrdal rarely discussed Dalarna in his writings. He would develop into a very self-consciously modern and forward-looking youth, eager to apply scientific ideas to social and political life. Though his political thought during his university years had an elitist cast, Myrdal would never lose a certain identification with the democratic political culture of Dalarna and the rebellious tradition of the farmers, and he would retain a certain impatience with the upper classes and a disdain for inherited social distinctions.

If Myrdal felt a conflict between his elitism and his affection for the ethos of his birthplace, so too did his newfound rationalism clash with the religious faith of his childhood. Though he was far from a pious young man, Myrdal had been steeped in the religious culture of Dalarna and thoroughly catechized in the Lutheran faith. He remained a nominal Christian throughout his gymnasium years and belonged to the Christian gymnasium movement. As a teenager, Gunnar was not sure if God existed but figured that since nothing bad could happen from believing in God, it was better to believe for the sake of security.[16] Nonetheless, he was deeply interested in the ideas of Charles Darwin and the German evolutionary biologist Ernst Haeckel. In a school essay on Darwin, he explored the concept of the survival of the fittest and pointed to the American Indians as an example of a people that had been overpowered by a superior civilization.[17] But while science seemed to offer exciting new possibilities for understanding human relations, he recognized that it could not supply moral values. Though Myrdal rejected much of Christian dogma and became an agnostic during his university years, he retained a deep sense of the importance of morality in public life. An extraordinarily ambitious youth, he nevertheless felt it necessary to convince his conscience that he was acting in the public interest.

During his gymnasium years, Gunnar Myrdal also read the work of the Swedish political thinker Rudolf Kjellén, a professor at Uppsala University and member of Parliament for the Conservative party. Kjellén was a nationalist who deprecated class conflict, distrusted the masses, and preached a doctrine of the subordination of the individual to the state. In contrast to Swedish liberals, who favored laissez-faire individualism, Kjellén argued that citizens had a moral duty to place the collective welfare of the nation above the pursuit of their individual or group self-interest. Social science, for Kjellén, was inherently a political enterprise: the scientist did not seek an objective detachment from politics in order to discover scientific laws of human behavior; he actively participated in politics to guide the nation-state's development. Though Myrdal would quickly move beyond Kjellén's conservative positions, the Uppsala professor's collectivist, interventionist vision would remain in Myrdal's mind as an alternative to the laissez-faire doctrines that he would learn from his academic mentor, the liberal economist Gustav Cassel. Kjellén's geopolitical realism would be one of several influences on the young Myrdal's writing as he attempted to develop his own political viewpoint.[18]

In a school essay entitled "Small Nations' Contributions to World History" (1917), Myrdal worried that the independence of Sweden and other small nations would be threatened by the Great War. This son of a building contractor used the metaphor of a building to describe the necessity for careful, long-range planning of Swedish political and economic development. In order to maintain the nation's independence and insure a prosperous future, it was necessary to "organize work nationally" so that the "component forces" worked together in the national interest. "First, it must be maintained that the state goes before the individual," Myrdal declared. Second, the work of reform must not be allowed to "degenerate" into a mere "experimentation" that would disrupt the normal functioning of the economy. Third, he contended that "democracy" was acceptable if it meant equality of opportunity, but if it meant an artificial "concocted equality," then it was harmful to the state and to the economy. The young conservative concluded that Sweden enjoyed a good geographical location, abundant natural resources, and good "folk material." If the nation planned carefully and the citizens worked together, Sweden could make a contribution to world history comparable to that of other "small nations," such as the Greeks, Romans, and Jews.[19]

Myrdal entered Stockholm University as a law student in 1918. Although his son had shown a talent for mathematics and science, Carl Adolf had wanted him to become a lawyer, and Gunnar was curious to know how law, politics, and society functioned. During the young man's first year at the university, class conflict in Sweden reached a crisis as the First World War drew to a close. The Bolshevik Revolution in Russia and the civil war between Reds and Whites in Finland sparked fears among the urban upper and middle classes that a revolution in Sweden was imminent among the working class, which was still unable to vote. A coalition government of Liberals and Social Democrats, under pressure from radical socialists, sought to secure passage of universal suffrage in the Swedish parliament. Conservatives resisted firmly until the collapse of the German and Austro-Hungarian empires in November, when it appeared that a revolutionary spirit was spreading through the continent. Fearing the worst, they conceded in December, and the Swedish parties reached an agreement which led to the passage of universal suffrage for men and women.[20]

In the midst of this tumultuous conflict, Gunnar Myrdal joined a small debating club formed by his close friend Fritz Thorén, the Fraternitas studiosorum Holmiae, which met in a back room of a modest Stockholm restaurant. An acquaintance, Gustaf Näsström, remembered Myrdal as an energetic debater, in "endless conversation" with his friends, "very loud-voiced and not exactly displeased with his own talents, full of paradoxical ideas, cheeky and cocky." But Myrdal "never tore down" an idea, Näsström recalled, "without having in his back pocket a program for building up anew." In this freewheeling atmosphere, the young men argued about politics and dreamed of leading a student renaissance that would awaken the idealism of the nation and redeem Sweden from the "philistinism" and "spiritual emptiness" of the age. In his first published work, a letter to the editor of the conservative Stockholm newspaper *Svenska Dagbladet*, Myrdal defended university students against the accusation that they were philistines who shared in the profiteer ethic that was thought to have infected the Swedish bourgeoisie during World War I. The young Myrdal, whose father had made money speculating during the war, regretted that some students had followed the example of shallow materialism set by many adults. In a romantic gesture, he implored his fellow students not to give in to the conformity and cultural "leveling" of the age, but to "assert their intellectual and moral superiority" and to "hope for and believe in . . . the future."[21]

In response to the dangers and opportunities raised by the passage of universal suffrage, Myrdal gave a provocative talk to the club on "The Masses and the Intelligence" in which he called for a "party of the intelligent" to direct Swedish politics in the coming era of mass politics. Though profoundly elitist, the speech was not a reflexive defense of government by wealthy industrialists and landowners. It was a proposal for rule by a meritocracy of talented men from all classes that would use new types of social control to replace the old village culture that had broken down under the impact of industrialization, urbanization, and mass literacy. Myrdal's party of the intelligent assigned a special role to youth, who would transcend the parochialism of the older generation of political leaders of all parties and rule in the public interest.[22] The speech reflected Myrdal's youthful infatuation with the Nietzschean idea of the superman, as well as his enthusiasm for Kjellén's ideas. His party of intelligence would make use of scientific techniques to manipulate and control the "irrational" masses.

"Democracy is a fact," Myrdal insisted to his student audience. Sweden was

Gunnar Myrdal as a student at the University of Stockholm, 1918
(courtesy Arbetarrörelsens Arkiv, Stockholm)

witnessing the culmination of a process of democratization that had begun a
century before, and all the "primary assumptions" of politics would be altered. In
particular it was "necessary to revise fundamentally the 'political technology,' the
science of how to win power." The masses, Myrdal argued, had historically been a
conservative and tradition-bound group in their political opinions, but with the

growth of mass literacy and the decline of religion, they had become increasingly "suggestible" and open to manipulation by demagogues.[23]

"Democratic politics are *stupid*," Myrdal declared, and voters lacked a sense of responsibility. The masses were "impervious to rational argument" and could only be influenced by politicians who made "intuitive appeals to emotion." The problem would get worse, he warned, with the enactment of women's suffrage, which would "increase the suggestibility [of the masses], lower the capacity for judgement—if that is possible," and perhaps add an "erotic coloring" to political discourse. The level of political leadership had sunk to the point that "every garrulous person with a sufficiently thick skin" had gone into politics. "Great aims [and] original thoughts" were actually hindrances in democratic politics; the ability to utter popular slogans and appeal to the irrational collective mind of the masses was what counted.[24]

Myrdal urged his audience not to accept this state of affairs and to form a "party of intelligence" to guide the nation. He admonished his fellow students to avoid the tendency of educated men in some other European countries to become weary of parliamentary politics and to transfer their "contempt for and hatred of the unsound directions within politics to politics itself." Myrdal decried the "tendency to egoistic individualism," the "turning away from public action," and the "intensification of the private" in contemporary Sweden. Conceding that the men of intelligence lacked a "strong feeling of community of interest," he contended nevertheless that as public policy became more irrational, educated men would be compelled to reach a consensus in order to offer a responsible alternative. He argued that the "unification of the men of intelligence" and their "rule in politics" was necessary. They needed to "unify themselves into a strong cultural class, in order to protect their interests, which to a great extent are also culture's and the land's." But the party of intelligence should not become the captive of any *economic* class or special interest. "Precisely because the intelligent can think and not be defenseless against mass suggestion," Myrdal maintained, "one can expect that the future party of intelligence shall have the ability to defend the national interest against selfishness and class-egoism."[25]

Anticipating an objection that his plan was impractical, Myrdal asserted that in order to influence the masses the "men of intelligence" would have to speak their language, "to translate the reasonable to the emotional, thought to slogan." He wrote that "the party [of intelligence] despises deeply the democratic principle but recognizes the driving idea [democracy] to be a powerful factor and is ready to work within this framework with suitable means." Myrdal acknowledged that the men of intelligence would have to be careful not to allow electoral sloganeering to damage their capacity for clear thought, but he firmly maintained that in the pursuit of intelligent government in the democratic era, "the end justifies the means."[26]

To those who might consider him "arrogant," Myrdal replied that "we young people are the future and it is youth's difficult privilege to think freely and presumptuously about things which belong to the future." He concluded by insisting that "the times demand a party of the intelligent, a party which on the basis of education and talent will fight the cultural battle against stupidity, selfishness, and class-egoism within Swedish politics." In a dramatic peroration, he exclaimed that, even if the battle should be hopeless, "Sweden's ancient legal culture is worth a fight. . . . It should not be buried in silence." If it falls, "then let it fall with a crashing thunder."[27]

The enfant terrible exaggerated his argument for the sake of debate with his fellow students on this occasion, but a strong element of elitism would remain in Myrdal's thought in the years ahead. Even after joining the Social Democrats in 1931, he would emerge as a strong advocate of social engineering and planning, working closely with intellectuals from other political parties on royal commissions and parliamentary committees. Like the young Walter Lippmann in the United States and Sidney and Beatrice Webb in Britain, Myrdal would combine an interest in social welfare with a belief that experts had a key role to play in shaping public policy and in stabilizing parliamentary democracy. The speech on "The Masses and the Intelligence" also anticipated a favorite rhetorical strategy that he would later term "prophylactic reform."[28] This consisted of making a moral argument to conservatives and centrists that the national interest required them to support a reform in order to stave off a much more radical alternative. The plan for the party of intelligence, with all its profoundly antidemocratic verbiage, was nonetheless a program for engagement with the new world of mass politics and an alternative both to last-ditch conservative resistance to universal suffrage and to cynical withdrawal from politics.[29]

Myrdal would stay aloof from politics during the 1920s, concentrating on his academic career, and he would never be identified publicly with the Conservative party or the ideas of Kjellén. He would, however, have a few opportunities to try out some of his ideas for manipulating the masses as a political advisor to his father, who was active in Conservative party politics. Though Carl Adolf Pettersson was financially successful, he never felt at home among the Stockholm bourgeoisie. He made enough money to buy and sell several farms, and the family always spent summers in the country, often in Solvarbo. Carl Adolf did not want to retire to the humble village of his birth, however. In 1922 he bought an estate in Toresund, Sörmland, southwest of Stockholm, where he and Sofie lived the last twelve years of his life. Addressed as "squire" by the local community, Pettersson involved himself in local politics as a champion of the Conservative farmers and took an interest in church and charitable affairs. As part of his quest for respectability, he persuaded Gunnar to write political articles for him, which he published under his name in local newspapers. In one such piece, Gunnar urged Swedish Conservatives to learn from their British counterparts, steal their slogan from their opponents, and proclaim themselves the party of "democracy and reform." The youthful ghostwriter advised the Conservatives that they would never get a majority of votes as long as their leaders all came from the upper class,

and he recommended that they recruit more ordinary citizens into party committees and make a special appeal to female voters.[30] With some help from his son,
Carl Adolf became known around Toresund as a man of sound politics, an
outspoken, contentious man, sure of the righteousness of his views and often
energetic enough to overcome all opposition. He was never really accepted by the
local elite, however, because of his lack of education, rustic manners, quarrelsome
temperament, and heavy drinking. Increasingly religious in his later years, he
remained an old-fashioned, hymn-singing, storytelling Dalecarlian.[31]

Gunnar's sense of filial duty did not interfere with his own search for a political
and intellectual viewpoint during the 1920s. He read widely in political, economic, and social scientific writings and moved gradually toward blending his
elitism with a commitment to social democracy. The change came in response to
new developments in his personal life as well as in reaction to political events.

Marriage to Alva and Apprenticeship to Cassel

On June 5, 1919, Gunnar Myrdal and two student friends who were cycling on
vacation in the province of Sörmland stopped at the farm of Albert Reimer's
family, near Eskilstuna, and spent the night in their barn. Early the next morning,
Mr. Reimer invited the boys to have coffee with the family. Gunnar was immediately attracted to seventeen-year-old Alva Reimer, a fair, slender, blonde young
woman with engaging blue eyes. She impressed him as self-confident and happy,
with a mischievous sense of humor and a remarkable intelligence. Alva was also
drawn to this lanky university student with light brown hair and playful blue eyes.
He seemed like the most extraordinary genius that had ever turned up in her rural
neighborhood, yet he was not stuffy like many educated people—he had an
irreverent sense of humor and an informal manner. The two erupted into an
intellectual talk-fest that touched on everything from the evolutionary biology of
Ernst Haeckel to the novels of Gerhard Hauptmann. After this experience, Gunnar
knew that he could not continue the bicycle trip. He stayed in the neighborhood
and met Alva a couple more times and then wrote a letter, inviting her to join him
and one of his friends, Gösta Lundberg, as they cycled through Dalarna. Much to
his amazement, she accepted. Her mother was away at a rest home, and she
deceived her father with a story of visiting a girlfriend for a few weeks.

The three young people biked along the Dalälven, and Gunnar and Lundberg
built a raft which they used on the river, enjoying the long and beautiful days of
midsummer. Gunnar showed Alva the cottage in Skattungbyn where he had been
born, and in many long conversations that lasted into the night they came to know
each other's hopes, ideals, and goals. He could not believe his good fortune in
having persuaded this beautiful young woman to join him. After several days, he
brought her to Solvarbo, where Gunnar introduced Alva to his parents, who were
vacationing in their native village, and to many of his relatives. It was only after he

Gunnar and Alva, *third and fourth from left*, shortly after they met, summer 1919 (courtesy Arbetarrörelsens Arkiv, Stockholm)

had introduced Alva to his family that he dared to touch her. Though he was a bold debater among his friends in the university, he was far less confident around women. After some hesitation, he lay his head against her knee, and she stroked his hair. The next day they made an excursion by boat from Gustafs to Falun. Afterward, he recalled, "I felt very unhappy for some reason, but I did not know why. But the next night I impulsively went into the room where Alva slept and kissed her. At that moment, the ice was broken, and we lived in a happy world of love."[32]

For Alva Reimer, the bicycle trip with Gunnar was a step into a richer, more stimulating milieu and an escape from the confining, provincial world of her family and Eskilstuna. Alva's intellectual attainments were the result of a tenacious struggle for an education. She was born in Uppsala on January 31, 1902, and her family moved several times before settling in Eskilstuna. Her father, Albert Reimer, was a master builder who later became a farmer. Unlike Gunnar's father, Albert was a practical idealist, a socialist, and an atheist who read Kropotkin and Rousseau and was active in the temperance and cooperative movements. Her mother, Lowa Reimer, was a homemaker who did not share her husband's radical views and berated him for not earning more money. Lowa had lost a sister and a brother to tuberculosis, and her fear of bacterial infection was so intense that she never kissed her children or grandchildren. "She was so dreadfully hygienic and everything had to be so perfect," Alva remembered. Lowa threw herself into housework with a vengeance. "Her ambition was clothes and food," Alva recalled. "It was so dominating. We children . . . understood very early that it was her lost professional dream. She should have become something. She taught herself to sew, . . . had enormous talent for needlework and should have become a milliner."[33] Although she admired her father's ideals, Alva considered her home a "really Strindbergesque family inferno," with the relationship between her parents marked by conflict and sexual repression. The oldest of five children, Alva knew at an early age that she wanted to be independent.[34]

When Alva finished grammar school, she had wanted to continue her education, but the gymnasium in Eskilstuna was for boys only. When she began to investigate gymnasium courses in other towns, she found that "Mamma was colossally opposed to it." Her daughter was not to leave home, and the family would not spend money sending a girl to gymnasium. Alva considered her mother's attitude to be "undoubtedly a mixture of protective instinct and jealousy." Thwarted in her efforts to get a higher education, Alva enrolled in a secretarial school and worked as a typist and stenographer, saving money for further schooling. Finally, when she was seventeen, her father took the initiative and organized private instruction for Alva and a group of young women who wished to take gymnasium courses. In 1922 she passed her qualifying exam and entered the University of Stockholm. Alva wanted to become a doctor, but her parents would not pay for the lengthy process of medical education because they expected her to get married rather than practice a profession. Thinking that she might become a librarian, she chose to study the subjects that interested her the most: the history of religion, Scandinavian languages, and the history of literature. Alva completed her studies in only two years and married Gunnar Myrdal in October 1924, shortly before receiving her undergraduate degree. Their wedding was a private ceremony with only two friends present as witnesses. Neither bride nor groom could bring themselves to invite their parents.[35]

Both Gunnar and Alva came from unhappy families, and they were determined to live their lives differently. Although Gunnar was not as radical as his wife, they shared a faith in the capacity of people to live according to modern, rational, scientific principles rather than myths, superstitions, and religious dogma. With their roots in rural Sweden, both of the Myrdals took a practical, optimistic approach to social questions. Since their nation had remained neutral in World War I, their optimism was not shaken by a direct or immediate experience of the carnage that decimated the young male population of their generation in other European countries. As a young man, Gunnar later admitted, he and others of his generation had "play[ed] with certain romantic feelings for Napoleon . . . and . . . indulge[d] in the pessimism of a Schopenhauer and in the aggressive egocentricity of a Nietzsche." But he and Alva remained, in essence, children of the Enlightenment. They would debate with each other liberal versus democratic socialist solutions to human problems, but neither of them was deeply affected by the fashionable, postwar pessimism and disillusionment or the cult of the irrational that gripped many young intellectuals in Britain, France, Italy, and Germany.[36]

After their marriage, the Myrdals resided in a small apartment at Roslagstorg in Stockholm. Gunnar had received his law degree in 1923 and served as a law clerk in the Stockholm municipal court. He had also served briefly as a magistrate in the town of Mariefred and as a public prosecutor in Norrsköping. But Gunnar found the routine practice of law boring and was deeply depressed and intellectually frustrated. He had always been good at mathematics, and with Alva's encouragement, he started to read economic literature in 1923 while practicing law. He soon took up the study of economics full-time under the direction of Professor Gustav Cassel at the University of Stockholm. In just seven years, Myrdal would establish an international reputation as an economist.[37]

Cassel was one of the leading neoclassical economists in the world and was especially noted for his general equilibrium theory of price formation and his study of monetary policy. Originally trained in mathematics, Cassel insisted that his students meet a high standard of technical rigor. His liberal political views had been formed in the late nineteenth century, when he had championed universal suffrage and the right of workers to collective bargaining. A newspaper columnist for many years as well as a professor, Cassel had a great influence on the economic thinking of a generation of Swedes. In public debates as well as in scholarly articles, he argued that the free market was the most efficient means of allocating goods and services and contended that economic planning led to dictatorship. A true nineteenth-century liberal, Cassel believed deeply in academic freedom, enjoyed lively debates with his students, and encouraged their intellectual independence.[38] He gathered about him a small circle of gifted students, four of whom would become leading figures in four different political parties: Gösta Bagge (Conservative), Nils Wohlin (Agrarian), Bertil Ohlin (Liberal), and Gunnar Myrdal (Social Democrat).[39]

Admission to Cassel's elite circle of students gave Gunnar Myrdal a sense of being chosen for leadership and recognized as what Swedes of that day called an "intellectual aristocrat." He respected his teacher's "optimistic rationalism and his hatred of intellectual authoritarianism," and he praised his breadth of vision. Cassel taught Myrdal "a healthy realism" and "a desire to avoid metaphysical speculation and to get down to facts and figures." The fledgling economist admired Cassel as a great scholar, active in Swedish intellectual and political life, who lectured abroad in German and English and gave advice to prominent figures in finance and politics. For Myrdal, Cassel was more than a professional mentor. The young man was drawn to Cassel's personal charm, sense of humor, warmth, and generosity. Myrdal cultivated a father-son relationship with his teacher, who took pride in the young man's accomplishments, and Gunnar and Alva grew close to Cassel and his wife, Johanna.[40] In 1927 Myrdal was awarded his doctorate for a thesis on price theory which built on Cassel's work and developed a new technique for understanding long-term fluctuations in prices. After this work, which won praise for its mathematical rigor, Myrdal would always be critical of static equilibrium models in economics and the other social sciences. His doctoral defense was a great triumph that marked his arrival in the academic world, and he celebrated his success with a luncheon for his professors and fellow students at the elegant Kronprinssen restaurant. Fearing embarrassment, he did not invite the bibulous Carl Adolf Pettersson or the simple Sofie to the luncheon. With strong support from Cassel, Gunnar Myrdal was appointed a docent in political economy at the University of Stockholm.[41]

Alva Myrdal had greater difficulty in launching a career. She did not hold an academic position in the 1920s but devoted herself to the study of psychology and read extensively in all of the social sciences, mastering much of the current literature in English, French, and German. Alva's interests had evolved from literature to psychology through her study of the work of I. A. Richards, an English literary critic who used psychological methods to study how readers from different social backgrounds experienced literature. In the late 1920s, she was fascinated by Freud's theories and wrote a paper on his methods of interpreting dreams.[42] Psychology was not yet an established subject taught in Swedish universities, but the absence of professional mentors and job opportunities did not deter Alva from entering the field, studying on her own, and developing an expertise in child psychology. In 1936 she would create a position for herself by founding a teacher training institute which she would direct until 1948. During the 1920s, her main source of intellectual stimulation was weekly gatherings that she organized at the Myrdals' apartment. Their guests included young economists, historians, architects, and scientists, many of whom would go on to distinguished careers. Their discussions, lubricated by large amounts of aquavit and whiskey, often lasted all night and usually focused on current political and social controversies. Alf Johansson, a close friend of the Myrdals who attended these sessions, remembered that while Gunnar was one of the most energetic and aggressive debaters in the group, Alva was generally more quiet, but her contributions were "clear, clever, and original." "She was not so eager to thrust herself forward," Johansson recalled, "she gave others understanding and support."[43]

Alva and Gunnar's talk-fests continued on study trips to England and Germany, when they shared the excitement of each other's intellectual explorations. As Alva read more deeply in psychology, they analyzed each other, their families, and the people around them. It was a time of intellectual growth for both of them. Yet for all its comradeship and intellectual excitement, it was not quite an equal relationship. Gunnar still yearned to be something of a superman. He believed that he was different from other people, that he had a special gift that he had to develop, which meant that he had to be free from the sort of practical concerns and social pleasantries that burdened most people. Gunnar liked to refer to himself as "asocial" and often said that he was not a "good person" like Alva. His pride was invested in his scholarly work, and like his father before him, he demanded support and help from those around him. Alva believed that Gunnar was a "genius" and saw it as her duty to help him, to be his "muse."[44] Though a very determined and independent person, Alva had been brought up in a home that stressed cooperation, not competition, and she did not feel the drive, as Gunnar did, to stand out from the crowd, to best others in debate. After the birth of their first child, Jan, in 1927, Alva assumed most of the responsibilities of child raising, while continuing her own self-directed study of psychology.

If Alva accepted a less than equal role within the marriage during the 1920s, she nonetheless had an enormous influence on her husband's intellectual and political development. When she met him in 1919, she recalled, he was a young "intellectual aristocrat," influenced by Nietzsche, among others. Alva, on the other hand, had been active in the Social Democratic youth movement and had an intensely moral view of the world as a struggle between good and evil. With her own values firmly anchored in the Social Democratic and cooperative movements, Alva exerted a steady, gravitational pull on her husband in the direction of greater concern for equality and issues of social welfare.[45] Several of their friends in the weekly discussion group were also deeply concerned about poverty and interested in social welfare reform and economic planning. Though the Myrdals were not politically active in the 1920s, both Alva and Gunnar shared a strong interest in political issues. By the mid-1920s, Gunnar's views, like Cassel's, were essentially liberal: individuals should enjoy an equal opportunity to attain wealth and power, and governments should not interfere with the free market. These ideas were, however, continually criticized both by Alva and by others in their circle who were concerned with the problems of the poor. As a psychologist with broad interests, Alva was dubious about some of the dogmas of neoclassical economics that her husband learned from Gustav Cassel.

Challenged by Alva's questions and criticisms and stimulated by a brilliant circle of young Swedes who delighted in debunking the received wisdom, Gunnar Myrdal developed into a most unconventional economist.[46] He was led toward a questioning of economic orthodoxies as he struggled to resolve a number of contradictions in his thought. Myrdal felt, first of all, a conflict between the democratic and antiauthoritarian culture of Dalarna and the elitism that he had embraced as a university student. Cassel's laissez-faire strictures were at odds with Myrdal's own temperament, which compelled him to intervene and to try to change things in the political sphere, a disposition that had been reinforced by his early reading of Kjellén and other conservative, nationalist thinkers. Third, though he had rebelled against his intensely moralistic upbringing, he could not quite let go of the habit of making moral judgments, and he wondered about the laissez-faire liberal postulate that the pursuit of economic self-interest led to the greatest human happiness. Finally, there was the question of how Freud's and Nietzsche's revelations about the irrational in human nature could be taken into account by the social scientist. How could one recover the heritage of the Enlightenment and subject the irrational in human behavior to scientific analysis so as to plan for a more rational future? Increasingly, Myrdal directed his attention to the hidden biases of economic theorists and the political assumptions that informed traditional economics. He was also curious about how psychology and sociology might contribute to interdisciplinary investigations of human behavior in the marketplace. And he wondered if economics might not become an instrument of political change.

In a series of lectures delivered at the University of Stockholm in the spring of 1928, Gunnar Myrdal advanced a daring critique of classical and neoclassical economics. Published two years later as *Vetenskap och politik i nationalekonomien* (*The Political Element in the Development of Economic Theory*), it was a book that challenged the very foundation of the sort of positivist economic science that Gustav Cassel and his colleagues and students practiced, and it would exert a strong influence on a generation of Swedish economists.[47]

Myrdal sought to expose the hidden value premises and political goals of economists through a study in the history of ideas. He regarded most of modern economics as "modified reminiscences of very old political thinking, conceived in days when a teleological meaning and a normative purpose were more openly a part of the subject-matter of economics." Myrdal did not argue that neoclassical economics was worthless, merely that its findings did not have the status of a natural science. Once value premises have been identified, he argued, economic theories can be seen for what they really are—constructs that approximate complex social, political, and economic reality. Myrdal sought to debunk the claims of economists such as Cassel who gave advice on public policy and presented their conclusions as the findings of science. These "quasi-scientific dogmas in the political sphere," he contended, "now serve as powerful obstructions to clear and realistic thinking in practical questions."[48]

Myrdal acknowledged the influence of Max Weber's insistence that economics must be kept value-free, and he cited Weber's critique of Marxism and of the German sociopolitical school of economists. With a touch of youthful arrogance, he labeled Weber's critique as "transcendental and based upon modern German logic." The young iconoclast observed that Weber had ignored classical and neoclassical economic theory, and he brushed aside the German thinker as "more of a sociologist and historian than an economic theorist." A more important influence on Myrdal was the Uppsala philosopher Axel Hägerstrom, whose motto, paraphrasing Cato, was "metaphysics must be destroyed." Though he never studied Hägerstrom in detail, Myrdal was impressed by the philosopher's assertion that "there are no values in the objective sense, only subjective valuations." For Hägerstrom, statements commonly believed to be moral truths were in fact associations between an idea and an emotion. The statements were perceived as true because they had been inculcated in children and supported by public opinion. Hägerstrom's critics labeled his theory "value-nihilism," but the Uppsala philosopher hoped that his critical analysis of valuations would lead to a more tolerant morality. In a study of the philosophy of law, Hägerstrom had argued that "normative and teleological notions" that originated in "primitive magic" were "still present in modern jurisprudence." And in a work called "The Social Teleology in Marxism," he had found elements of religious reasoning in the philosophy of dialectical materialism. Myrdal applied this type of analysis to neoclassical economics, arguing that these hidden "valuations" must be distinguished from mere perceptions of reality. According to Myrdal, these normative attitudes, which may be irrational, shape and influence economic theory.[49]

To the dismay of Cassel, Myrdal insisted that classical economics was clouded by metaphysical concepts. Adam Smith, in his view, had attributed theological significance to the operation of the price system. Most of the classical economists had based their reasoning upon a belief in natural law, and many had developed economic theories grounded in the assumptions of utilitarian psychology. Moreover, economists had glossed over conflicts of interest because their philosophical system assumed a harmony of interests. The pursuit of private economic interest was supposed to result in social harmony and to promote the welfare of all. "The theory of economic liberalism," he asserted, "is built upon this communistic fiction."[50] All economists, according to Myrdal, had confused their own valuations with fact and made policy recommendations based on these subjective judgments.

In his last chapter, "The Role of Politics in Economics," Myrdal attempted to sketch out a new type of economic research that would take account of the bias of the economist's valuations, incorporate the insights of psychology and sociology, and involve the economist in political change. He called for a "technology of economics" that would not take the existing legal order, institutions, and customs as given. The scope of economic inquiry would be greatly expanded, Myrdal suggested, if economists took institutional change into account. "All institutional factors which determine the structure of the market, indeed the whole economic system including its tax and social legislation, can be changed, if those interested in the change have enough political power."[51]

Myrdal insisted that "human actions are not solely motivated by economic interests." People are concerned about "social objectives" and "believe in ideals to which they want their society to conform." The Enlightenment and the French Revolution spread "new ideas of law and justice" that became as important to the labor movement as demands for higher wages.[52] Myrdal called for a "technology of economics" that was "not built upon economic interests, but upon social attitudes." He defined "attitude" as "the emotive disposition of an individual or a group to respond in certain ways to actual or potential situations." "Interests," he proclaimed, "are always blended with moral sentiment." Sometimes moral sentiment reinforced an attitude based on economic interest, but in other cases, people's moral feelings opposed or checked their economic interests. Myrdal, casting away all metaphysical conceptions, declared that there was no inherent moral order in the universe, no "logical connection between the valuations of individuals," and no "logical hierarchy dominated by ultimate axioms." "The desire to think of moral valuations as if they were logically coherent is a legacy from the days of the metaphysical systems," he declared.[53] The technology of economics, according to Myrdal, should "confine itself to empirically observable group attitudes." Thus a study of the working class or of farmers would examine the social psychology of those groups in evaluating their economic and political behavior. The economist making such a study should formulate his value premises "explicitly in concrete terms and relate them to the actual valuations of social groups." Only by acknowledging his value premises could an economist make a useful contribution to science and to political debate. Myrdal concluded that the economist must "renounce all pretensions to postulate universal laws and norms."[54]

In *The Political Element*, Myrdal thus took account of the manner in which scientific naturalism and ethical relativism had eroded the belief that a logical system of ethical values was rooted in natural law. From his reading of psychology and discussions with Alva and their circle of friends, he came to the view that much social behavior stemmed from irrational attitudes that often contradicted economic self-interest. In uncovering the hidden political agendas of the classical economists, he made a case that the separation of politics and economics was an artificial one, and that economists should address political questions without pretending that there is only one scientific answer. In calling for a technology of economics, Myrdal stopped short of advocating specific types of social engineering. He did note that Italian Fascists and Soviet Communists had achieved new kinds of social control over youth through indoctrination in public schools, and he alluded to the success of advertising and propaganda in shaping public opinion in various countries.[55] But he did not argue that economists should actually try to shape attitudes, only that they should consider in their studies how new technologies were making human attitudes ever more malleable. Myrdal's postulate that economists should state explicitly their value premises and relate them to the values of the population being studied would become fundamental to all his subsequent work.

In later years, Myrdal would remember that *The Political Element* "became from a personal viewpoint a catharsis, a way of liberating myself from all that I had picked up as a precocious school boy and later in high school."[56] He had discarded the conservatism of his father, the rhetoric of duty and public service he had cultivated in gymnasium, the romanticism of his university speeches, and the naive objectivism of Cassel. At the age of thirty, he had found his own voice as a scholar and had made an original contribution to economics by criticizing the giants of the field. Yet his analysis of the relativity of values carried with it implications that were bound to trouble a mind so rooted in the moralistic, religious culture of Sweden and the rationalistic vision of the Enlightenment. It was one thing to point out the hidden biases of one's elders and quite another to chart a new course for political economy in an era of economic convulsion and political upheaval. At the end of the 1920s, he still lacked a stable political viewpoint.[57] As Gunnar Myrdal sought to find a new approach for combining economics and politics, he would gain many insights into the possibilities for social engineering and multidisciplinary research during a journey to the United States.

First Visit to America, 1929–1930

A turning point in Gunnar and Alva Myrdal's lives came in 1929, when they were awarded Rockefeller Foundation fellowships for the 1929–30 academic year. Touted by Cassel as a brilliant prodigy, Gunnar had already begun to attain an international reputation as an economist,[58] and when he applied for the fellowship, he had made Alva's appointment as a Rockefeller Fellow a condition of his acceptance. The foundation selected both of them for the award, which was designed to introduce promising young Europeans to American scholarship. The United States was the scene of some of the most exciting and innovative research in the social sciences during the 1920s, but most Swedish scholars had little awareness of American intellectual life, and Swedish universities were organized along traditional lines, with few opportunities for interdisciplinary research. This situation had begun to change in 1926, when Gösta Bagge, an economist at the University of Stockholm and a Conservative party politician, landed a $50,000 grant from the Laura Spelman Rockefeller Memorial to support investigations of social and political issues in Sweden. As director of the University of Stockholm's Social Science Institute, Bagge led an investigation of wages in Sweden, with help from Gunnar Myrdal, Alf Johansson, Erik Lindahl, and other young economists. The Social Science Institute, which the Rockefeller Foundation continued to fund through the 1930s, emerged as the center of empirical social science research in the country and encouraged investigations that had practical applications for the Swedish government.[59] Bagge's Rockefeller connection would redound to the benefit of the Myrdals in the years ahead.

As they contemplated a year in America, Gunnar and Alva Myrdal faced one difficult decision, however. The fellowship required them to travel around the United States, visiting different universities, in order to meet with prominent scholars and to get in touch with the latest developments in American social science. The foundation did not provide sufficient funds for child care, however, and they had to decide what to do with their two-year-old son, Jan. Alva was reluctant to leave her child for a year when he was so young, but their pediatrician and various relatives thought that the boy would be better off with his grandparents in the country than he would be traveling around a foreign country. Gunnar was insistent that Jan should stay with Carl Adolf and Sofie at their manor house, with Alva's kinfolk nearby, and Alva went along with the idea, though she would later regard it as a great mistake.[60]

In October 1929 Gunnar and Alva arrived in New York, the first stop on their American tour, and met with officers of the Rockefeller Foundation and the SSRC, who provided them with letters of introduction to leading figures in their respective fields. Their itinerary began at Columbia University, where Gunnar talked with Wesley Mitchell and other institutional economists while Alva attended lectures on social psychology by Gardner Murphy and on child psychology by Charlotte Bühler. Their next stop was Washington, D.C., where Gunnar met economists in the government and at the Brookings Institute and completed the last chapter in his book *The Political Element in the Development of Economic Theory*. From Washington they took the train to Chicago, where Gunnar talked with economists Frank Knight and Jacob Viner, and both Gunnar and Alva met the sociologists William Fielding Ogburn and Ernest W. Burgess. Gunnar spent a week in Minneapolis with the Russian-born sociologist P. T. Sorokin, while Alva studied at a child welfare institute. After visiting relatives in Willmar, Minnesota, Gunnar went to the University of Wisconsin, where he struck up a friendship with the economist John R. Commons. When Gunnar's book on price theory won a prize in Sweden, the Myrdals used this windfall to buy a car, and they drove back to New York via a long, circuitous route that included Detroit, Toronto, Buffalo, Ithaca, and Boston.[61]

It was a year full of excitement, new experiences, and intellectual and political challenges for both of the Myrdals. From Columbia, Gunnar wrote Cassel that they were enjoying their status as "golden children": the Rockefeller Foundation officials opened doors to all the famous professors, and they were invited to receptions and asked to give lectures. The most amazing thing about the United States, Gunnar noted, was the way in which "Americans in all walks of life were trustingly asking [me] to tell them what was 'wrong with this country.'"[62] "Swedish science must have prestige abroad," Gunnar joked to Cassel, "otherwise I don't understand why all these people should have such a great interest in hearing the dumb things I say about this or that." But he quickly adjusted to the deference that Americans showed to visiting scholars from Europe and grew accustomed to "going around like a light from Nazareth with opinions ready on everything possible."[63] By the time he reached Chicago, he had perfected the art of public speaking, which consisted of talking "in a simple and easily-comprehensible way, as one would to very small children. A funny story in the beginning and thereafter a joke every three minutes. It comes as naturally as saliva when one eats starchy food." He remarked to Cassel that "Alva says that I have to get out of this country; otherwise my demagogic talents would be developed too much."[64]

The Myrdals found the Americans to be earnest, moralistic, and rather puritanical. Alva wrote Swedish friends that she had read Sinclair Lewis's *Elmer Gantry* and that it had seemed "so natural when I read it here that it was hardly funny."[65] Gunnar thought it "amusing to see . . . the whole of their public life developed out of the nonconformist religious society's customs and practices." "All people here are so serious," he wrote. American humor was entirely "good-hearted" and without a trace of satire. "Never have we so appreciated the element of mutual irony that permeates European cultural life." Gunnar confessed to Cassel: "In the beginning we almost got ourselves into trouble with our wicked tongues. Everyone took everything with such deadly seriousness. Now both Alva and I go around and smile piously. Sometimes we feel such a Satanic desire to break out of this whole freemasonry and begin to spew forth malice. But so far we have been able to hold our tongues."[66]

American intellectual and cultural life was working subtle changes on both of the Myrdals, however. From Columbia Gunnar wrote Cassel that he was attempting "to get a grip on 'the American trend of economics'" and was particularly trying to understand the institutionalist economists "who are so critical of our old [neoclassical] theory." Although he had pointed out biases in neoclassical theory in his Stockholm lectures a year and a half before, Myrdal still considered himself to be within the fold of neoclassicism and found American institutionalism vague and lacking in technical rigor. The basic tenet of institutionalism was that economics had to take into account the whole social system, all the social and political factors that influenced economic behavior. Institutionalism had been born in the Progressive Era and was closely associated with movements for social and political reform. Thorstein Veblen, the first institutionalist, who had used categories from anthropology to reveal some of the irrational behavior of the supposedly rational entrepreneurs, died in 1929. Myrdal met Wesley C. Mitchell of Columbia, the leading institutionalist on the East Coast, and the two argued past each other for more than an hour. Frustrated by this experience, the young Swedish visitor devised a set of "tricky questions" designed to expose the shallowness of the institutionalists' "reform generalizations" and "banalities."[67] After hurling these challenges at some of the younger institutionalists in debates, Myrdal helped to form the Econometric Society, which was conceived as a defense against the institutionalists.[68] Though he thought that he had done a creditable job of battling the Columbia institutionalists, many questions remained in his mind about the future of his own work.

Gunnar Myrdal informed Cassel that, after *The Political Element*, he did not plan to write anything else on general economic theory. His restless temperament, wide-ranging interests, practical concerns, and love of new experience and human interaction ill-suited him to the life of a pure theorist. While working in the British Museum the previous summer, Myrdal had decided that "I shall not—in the whole of my remaining life—sit and think over what Ricardo and Malthus meant by values, even though I am glad that I did it once." Instead, he resolved to "concern myself with something that has a more direct connection with human life."[69] Gunnar Myrdal's turn toward practical, interdisciplinary research was also influenced by Alva. Through her he met many more psychologists and sociologists than he otherwise would have, and her work brought her into contact with the applications of social scientific theories in schools, child guidance clinics, juvenile courts, parent education programs, and hospitals. During the year in America, Alva read broadly in social psychology and child psychology, studied behaviorism and depth psychology, and began work on a "theoretical critique of psychoanalysis."[70] She wrote Gunnar's sister that their experiences and readings in America gave a "new light" to their work. Gunnar's and her interests were growing closer, and they were making plans to work together on social science research projects when they returned to Sweden.[71]

The Myrdals caught only a brief glimpse of the issues of race and ethnicity and the American creed that would occupy Gunnar ten years later. At the University of Chicago, they talked with sociologists and gathered a few impressions of political corruption, the "hobo-problem," and the "mixture of races."[72] To the Swedish visitors, the juxtaposition of immigrants from so many different European countries was one of the most striking things about the United States, and they wondered what held the country together. Alva Myrdal visited many schools and observed civics classes in which "American" values were taught to children. Referring to these civics and "Americanization" classes, Gunnar declared that "next to Russia and Italy, the United States of America practices most consciously political indoctrination." "This may seem odd," he admitted, "for America is, in a sense, the most individualistic nation in the world." But because the United States had to absorb and assimilate immigrants from so many different countries, the educational system was designed to insure that "the young grow up with more uniform and standardized convictions and attitudes."[73]

In another context, however, Myrdal observed that political attitudes do not always determine behavior. When individuals are asked about their political beliefs, he noted, they often "use conventional and stereotyped stock phrases which may have little bearing on . . . behavior." As an example, he claimed that "American sociologists have found that people's declarations about their views on the Negro problem have very little to do with their conduct in daily life."[74] Myrdal did not systematically explore these contradictions during his Rockefeller year, but they would reemerge in a different light a decade later.

By the time he reached Madison, Gunnar Myrdal was much more receptive to institutional economics than he had been at the start of his year in America. The economics department at the University of Wisconsin was dominated by John R. Commons, the senior American institutional economist. At first, Myrdal confessed to Cassel, he found the old man "altogether dotty" and admitted that "his theoretical works seem rather curious to those who do not know him personally."[75] He joked that Commons "taught me bowling and endeavored to get me to understand the legal foundations of capitalism, the former with much greater success than the latter."[76] "But more and more," Myrdal wrote, "I have come to appreciate him, and when I leave, we shall part with a feeling of loss, which I believe is mutual."[77] The young visitor was impressed by the Wisconsin idea of directing academic research toward social reform, and he found the economists there "particularly sharp" on practical issues, "above all on the question of labor."[78] He also talked at great length with Wisconsin's agricultural economists and came to the conclusion that Sweden was on the verge of a great agricultural crisis resulting from the rationalization of agriculture, with massive unemployment of farmers and farm laborers.[79]

In the course of his year in America, Gunnar Myrdal formulated plans for an ambitious historical study of Swedish industrialization by a team of sociologists, economists, and statisticians.[80] From American social scientists he was learning the entrepreneurial skills necessary for organizing large, collaborative research projects. The institutional setting for this project would be Bagge's Social Science Institute at the University of Stockholm, and the funding, he hoped, would come from the Rockefeller Foundation. While in New York, he met the sociologists W. I. Thomas and Dorothy S. Thomas, who expressed an interest in conducting demographic research in Sweden in conjunction with this project. W. I. Thomas's stature in American sociology and his ties to the SSRC would enhance the project's appeal to the Rockefeller Foundation. In letters to Bagge, Myrdal passed on tips about the current priorities of the Rockefeller Foundation, and in letters to Cassel he maneuvered to become Cassel's successor as professor of economics at the University of Stockholm, the "professorship in the whole world" that he most aspired to hold.[81]

Gunnar Myrdal's transformation from a theoretically oriented, neoclassical economist into a reform-oriented, interdisciplinary academic entrepreneur took place against a setting of the stock market crash and the onset of the Great Depression. In January 1930 he wrote Cassel that "all of America is now the object of an especially intensive and cleverly organized prosperity propaganda," which "permeates the whole press, every article and every advertisement." "Large billboards alongside the railroad tracks and the highways show the American people in the form of a muscular valkyrie carrying the torch of civilization against the storm, with the caption: 'Nothing can stop the U.S.A. Forward on the road to prosperity.'" Businessmen, journalists, politicians, and ministers were all preaching the gospel: "consume and save." "Prosperity, prosperity, prosperity—it is trumpeted by loud-speakers and assaults you from electric signs," he reported. "You cannot get on an elevated train without being suddenly confronted along the way by a stern-looking chairman of some company who assures you that the country's economy is 'basically sound.'"[82] A large, continental nation with no internal tariff barriers and a minimum of government regulation of the economy, the United States was the one place in the world that most nearly approximated the free market advocated by Cassel and neoclassical economists. And yet the American economy proved to be a colossal failure in 1929–30. Billboards promoting prosperity were no help. Nor did Gunnar Myrdal have much advice to offer the Americans in his role as eminent European sage and lecturer.

Both Gunnar and Alva Myrdal experienced a "personal crisis" during their year in the United States.[83] They were appalled by the extremes of wealth and poverty, by the massive breakdown of the economy, and by the inability of the Hoover administration to respond decisively to the economic crisis. The Myrdals were also disturbed by the ineffectiveness of American intellectuals in the face of this national disaster. The social sciences in the United States were much more advanced and sophisticated than in Sweden and in many other European countries;

but social scientists had little impact on public policy, and most American intellectuals seemed to prefer debunking the dominant political and cultural ideas rather than engaging in constructive problem solving.[84] "People are so powerless," Gunnar Myrdal complained to Cassel. "All strivings are so powerless inside the gigantic machine . . . of business. No honorable person devotes himself to politics, and he would be ridiculously impractical if he did." Economists had an "obscure" and ineffective role, and most of them took refuge in "technical knowledge and specialization." They were optimistic about particular programs, but "when it comes to deeper cultural questions, there is no really honest and clear-sighted man who in his heart is an optimist." The Swedish visitor observed that "the prosperity-machine goes at full steam, the universities are all expanded, research is organized on a gigantic scale, masterpieces of literature and art are exploited and spread democratically—but the result cannot be anything other than civilized barbarism: Babbitry." Striking a note of cultural conservatism in deference to his mentor, he concluded this jeremiad by observing: "I have never had such a strong feeling for the old Biblical passage about the man who wins the whole world but loses his immortal soul."[85]

The young Swedish couple felt a strong bond with many Americans despite the pair's criticisms of American politics and culture.[86] The informality, spontaneity, and openness of the American people, the absence of rigidly demarcated class differences, the lively intellectual life, and above all, the willingness of a few American social scientists to think big and to propose ambitious plans of social engineering all left an impact on the young Swedes. The Myrdals, who had been apolitical in the 1920s, were determined to try to do in Sweden what had seemed impossible in the United States: to use social scientific knowledge to bring about social and economic reforms, "to do something beneficial for [our] own people," as Gunnar Myrdal put it in a letter to Cassel in January 1930.[87] Was it not possible, Gunnar wondered, to develop in Sweden something like the "Wisconsin idea" of Commons and other social scientists who studied social problems and contributed proposals to public policy debates? Alva resolved to put into practice in Sweden some of John Dewey's ideas for using education to strengthen democratic values in the society. The Myrdals thus embraced the legacy of Progressive social science—its moral energy, practical orientation, and commitment to social engineering—and disdained the narrow objectivism and pursuit of value-free science then in vogue among American social scientists. Even though they thought that many American intellectuals had lost their way since the Progressive Era and given in to pessimism and apathy, the Myrdals saw no reason why Swedes should follow suit.

The Myrdals delayed their return to Sweden for a year, however. Gunnar accepted an appointment as an assistant professor at the Graduate Institute for International Studies in Geneva, where he taught international economics during the 1930–31 academic year. His Rockefeller Foundation connection, together with Cassel's enthusiastic recommendation, helped him to get the position. Alva studied psychology at the Jean-Jacques Rousseau Institute and focused her investigations on Piaget's theory of child development. The new milieu did nothing to dim Gunnar's enthusiasm for importing American-style social science to Sweden. He corresponded with Bagge about arranging for the Rockefeller Foundation to bring the Thomases to Sweden and wrote to Ernst Wigforss, editor of the Social Democratic magazine *Tiden*, that Sweden really needed a journal like *Social Forces*, an interdisciplinary forum in which social scientists analyzed social problems and policy issues.[88]

During this year in Geneva, Gunnar Myrdal reflected on his experiences in America in an interpretive article for *Tiden*, in which he assessed the possibilities for political and economic change in the United States. Entitled "Socialism or Capitalism in America's Future?" the article is Myrdal's only published work on the United States prior to his acceptance, seven years later, of Keppel's invitation to head a study of the American race issue. Though it is primarily an analysis of the weakness of the American labor movement, the article is of broader importance as a statement of Myrdal's ideas about the American creed (or popular political ideology), race and ethnicity, and welfare capitalism. The piece is striking because of his pessimism about the American labor movement and his enthusiasm for reforms advocated by liberal businessmen. The article catches Myrdal's perceptions of America during his year as a Rockefeller Fellow just as he is moving into the Social Democratic orbit.

Addressing an audience of Swedish Social Democratic intellectuals, Myrdal posed the question of whether America was headed toward a stable equilibrium or toward catastrophe or revolution. "American capitalism," he wrote, was "the most magnificent realization of an abstract social scientific 'ideal type' that has ever existed." He found it to be "both fascinating and frightening with its rationalistic mystique, its planless effectiveness, and its mechanistically ruthless flexibility." But the "really curious thing" about American capitalism was that it lacked "the opposition which, according to Marx, is fundamental and necessary: *class struggle*." American workers, in Myrdal's view, were "deeply bourgeois in every sense of the word." Radical views were "extremely rare among the workers," who read only "scandal sheets . . . and, now and then, a patriotic biography of Lincoln." "If one is looking for subversive ideas," he suggested that "the chances of finding them are actually much greater among Jewish millionaires than in the slums." He maintained that "patriotic conservatism, capitalistic Americanism, spiced with hate and contempt for 'European' subversive dogmas, are not only Main Street's petit bourgeois froth and triumph, but also the slum's compensation for a sad and wretched daily life."[89]

American radicalism, according to Myrdal, was generally limited to small groups of intellectuals who had almost no contact with the masses. "With the exception of a few hundred enthusiasts with a more fantastic turn of mind, who sacrifice their lives in . . . fruitless agitating and organizing, these radical intellectuals keep their views to themselves and their congenial associates," he declared.

Political causes seemed "hopeless" to most intellectuals, and "intellectual radicalism . . . [generally] takes the form of an idle pessimism, which is in glaring
contrast to the average American's resourceful, but often misguided optimism."[90]

In explaining how American capitalism so successfully avoided radical opposition, Myrdal pointed first to American popular ideology, with its roots in the
Protestant Reformation and the Enlightenment. Drawing upon Max Weber's ideas,
he argued that America's religious puritanism was conducive to capitalist development, and that puritanism had spread through various denominations to become
a major force in American public life. Even the Catholic clergy had accommodated itself to the individualistic, practical, probusiness attitudes of American
Protestant culture. Closely connected to the Puritan tradition was the "natural
rights ideology" of the Declaration of Independence and the Constitution, which
was "deeply rooted in American popular thinking." In a phrase redolent of Veblen,
Myrdal wrote that on holidays and ceremonial occasions, Americans worshiped
the Constitution as "a fetish of an unmistakably religious nature." The actual
content of this fetish of natural rights theory was rather vague, however, and
depended upon the interpretation of the judiciary. Adapting Charles Beard's
analysis, Myrdal argued that the Constitution had given to the "ruling social
classes" a "flexible . . . tool, . . . with which they gradually could design an institutional system to suit their needs." The Constitution's "loose phrasing" had been
used "to fight the trade union movement" and "to hinder more effective antitrust
legislation." Though he would later argue, in *An American Dilemma*, that the
American creed enshrined in the Declaration of Independence and the Constitution was a dynamic force for equality and individual freedom, here he saw it as a
conservative force which gave the capitalist system a "moral sanction" that permitted it to grow "almost without any restraint."[91]

Another reason for the absence of a class-conscious labor movement was the
American party system, in which the two established parties made it difficult for a
workers' party, or other third parties, to establish themselves. To vote for a third
party often was seen as throwing away one's vote. The two established parties were
also effective in siphoning off the leaders of the working class by rewarding them
through the spoils system. Citing James Bryce's classic *The American Common-
wealth*, Myrdal concluded that corruption was widespread in American politics.
On his visit to Chicago, he had observed that "slum and Negro votes are bought to
a great extent, and whole sections of the city are ruled by powerful political bosses,
who are able to weave together both rich and . . . poor in a network of . . .
extremely suspect 'interests.'"[92]

Myrdal argued that the American labor movement was weak not only in
numbers but in "the spirit that makes a union movement in the West European
sense." The American labor movement was "a form of organization for the working-class aristocracy only . . . and it serves their purely private economic interest to
raise their income level." Its mentality was therefore "purely bourgeois." Citing the
work of Werner Sombart, Myrdal asserted that the American trade union move-

ment was "more of a vertical division than a horizontal one, more a splitting asunder of the working class into groups with their various interests than a welding together to common solidarity against the employer."[93]

A strong labor movement, in his view, depended upon a "feeling of solidarity" as the "living force" that propelled the movement. But such a feeling of solidarity was difficult to achieve in the United States because of the "throng of races" that comprised the working class. Myrdal noted that the "new immigrants" from southern and eastern Europe increased the religious, cultural, and linguistic divisions among the working class.[94] In discussing immigration restriction, he claimed that not only the American labor movement but "practically speaking, all of America stands united behind it." Echoing the views of Commons, he wrote that "the large cities actually could not absorb more Italians and south-east Europeans without the most serious social dangers."[95]

Barriers among European ethnic groups usually crumbled within a generation, according to Myrdal, but barriers between whites and blacks remained. He noted that large numbers of blacks had begun to move north during World War I and that they were generally excluded from trade unions. In his brief discussion of racial discrimination, Myrdal was not very hopeful. He stressed the psychological feeling of superiority that whites of all classes felt in comparing themselves with blacks, and he quoted a satirical article, "Our Greatest Gift to America," by the black journalist George Schuyler: "To have saved the nation from an enervating class system, such as exists everywhere else, by instead giving it a caste system based on race, which always stimulates the illusions and pretensions of mankind—is that not a contribution of which even we can be proud?"[96]

Except for the white-black division, Myrdal prophesied that the next generation of American workers would be more homogeneous because of the restriction of immigration, the intensive Americanization propaganda, and the tendency of radio and the automobile to "break down the walls around every particularism." The next generation would be "the labor movement's great chance" because of the possibility of a "homogeneous cultural base . . . for a radical labor movement."[97]

American capitalists were not likely to sit idly by and allow a radical workers' movement to win power, however. Myrdal observed a "change of psychological attitude" on the part of many businessmen who had become interested in welfare programs for children, the elderly, and the unemployed, as well as in other forms of "public social control." He quoted one businessman who told him that American capitalists did not intend to allow the emergence of European-style labor leaders who were "professional socialists." "Our ambition," he informed Myrdal, "is to ourselves be our workers' leaders" through company unionism and welfare capitalism.[98] The "driving force" of this shift in attitude by businessmen, according to Myrdal, was "the more intelligent people's clear perception that *if* [welfare reform] does not happen, doomsday approaches in the next generation." Myrdal predicted an era of public welfare reform during the next period of prosperity and wrote that he saw "in the whole country the beginnings of a new popular religion, which is socialistic capitalism in place of the old individualism." He declined to prophesy whether America would develop a radical workers' movement in the Western European sense or if American capitalism would carry through a "meaningful transformation" that would "dispel the social forces that otherwise would crystallize in the socialist workers' revolt." He concluded that "in a deeper sense" the result would be "socialistic" in either eventuality.[99]

The article "Socialism or Capitalism" is significant both as a barometer of Myrdal's shift from neoclassical economist to Social Democratic planner and as a harbinger of his ideas about the United States that would later be developed in *An American Dilemma*. He abhorred the wasteful and chaotic operation of unregulated capitalism and was appalled by the wretched living conditions of poor Americans in urban slums, but he doubted that a radical labor movement could successfully bring about change. His admiration for liberal businessmen led him to hope that American elites would support the development of welfare programs as an alternative to chaos or revolution. Myrdal believed that the ideological basis for this transition was being prepared through a fundamental change in popular thinking from old-fashioned individualism to "socialistic capitalism." Popular participation in decision making was of little interest to Myrdal; his primary concern was raising the standard of living of the poor, and his concept of socialism was basically a welfare state with a mixed economy. How race and ethnicity fit into the picture was not entirely clear. Viewing America from a Swedish perspective, Myrdal assumed that the labor movement could not succeed unless workers shared a common culture. He believed that culture was sufficiently plastic to allow for the assimilation of European immigrants within a generation, but he recognized that prejudice against blacks was more deeply rooted. He would not seriously consider that issue until his return to America seven years later.

Social Democratic Reform

Gunnar and Alva Myrdal returned to Stockholm in June 1931, just as the international Depression hit Sweden. Unemployment rose sharply from 32,000 in December 1930 to 89,000 in December 1931 and reached a peak of 187,000 in March 1933.[100] The country also faced a political crisis. Since the First World War, Swedish politics had been characterized by unstable factionalism, with no party or coalition of parties able to stay in power for more than two years. The Liberal government that was in office in 1931–32 was unable to reverse Sweden's slide into a Depression and was implicated in scandals. Some observers wondered if Sweden's parliamentary system could produce a government capable of restoring prosperity. In the midst of this crisis, Gunnar and Alva Myrdal joined the Social Democratic party and for the next seven years fought to create full employment and to establish many programs of the Swedish welfare state. Gunnar Myrdal's ambition to turn his knowledge of economics and the social sciences to practical ends at last was realized. The Social Democrats who were out of power at the onset of the depression, were Sweden's largest party and the only political party with any chance of initiating the kind of economic planning and welfare reform the Myrdals had come to support after their visit to the United States. Never deeply committed to socialist doctrine, Gunnar Myrdal was a pragmatic reformer who, had he been an American, might well have found a home in Franklin D. Roosevelt's New Deal. But the Liberals were a smaller and weaker party in Sweden, and Alva Myrdal was strongly committed to a democratic socialist vision of reform. Together the Myrdals threw themselves into Social Democratic politics. As intellectuals, they would be viewed with suspicion by some members of this labor party, but Gunnar could claim to be a farmer's son and trade on his Dalecarlian roots. In any case, respect for intellectuals was much greater among Swedes of that generation than among Americans. Per Albin Hansson, the Social Democratic leader, welcomed talented newcomers, and the young economist rapidly rose to a prominent position in the party.

Gunnar Myrdal sketched out his response to Sweden's economic and political crisis in a 1932 article, "The Dilemma of Social Policy," in which he argued for economic planning and social engineering in such fields as public housing and family policy. The essay, which was aimed at a broad audience of educated Swedes, provides a context for understanding Myrdal's turn to Social Democratic politics. Hoping to shape a consensus in support of the party's policies, Myrdal asserted that the Depression required a dramatic new departure in Swedish politics. His approach represented a radicalism from the top down, however, and a prescription for granting extensive power to experts to act in the public interest. Myrdal saw the early 1930s as a crucial period in Swedish history, a time when intervention by intellectuals could make a difference and avert an economic and political catastrophe.

The nation, Myrdal wrote, was beset by a "crisis of social policy," and Swedes faced a "deep-going moral dilemma" in deciding how to respond to it. As in his later work on black Americans, Myrdal did not use the term "dilemma" in its strict meaning of a choice between two equally unpleasant alternatives. Instead, he referred to a choice that Swedes had to make between following the older kind of social welfare policy that had grown out of nineteenth-century liberalism and adopting a new Social Democratic approach that represented a conceptual and ideological break with the past. He argued that prior to the world war, Swedish political parties had reached a consensus that social welfare measures were necessary. The roots of this consensus lay in the Enlightenment, in which people had broken with the "old, crass ideology of social status" and embraced a democratic spirit and recognition of the individual's "right to social happiness." During the nineteenth century, liberalism and socialism had developed as opposing ideologies, but their common roots in the Enlightenment provided a basis for a rapprochement by the end of the century and a mutual acceptance of the "social welfare ideology." John Stuart Mill's *Principles of Political Economy* (1848) had pointed the way for liberals, and the Northern and Western European Social Democrats' acceptance of parliamentary tactics and interest-group politics had represented a spirit of conciliation among socialists. Thus a "socialistically-softened liberalism and a liberally softened socialism" had converged in the social welfare ideology, so that one could actually belong to whatever political party one liked and still work for social welfare reforms. "We are all beginning to have similar viewpoints," Myrdal claimed, and this "common political ideology" meant that discussions of social policy had a "peculiar character of objectivity." Social questions "have come to be handled by experts: experts on unemployment, on the housing question, on prostitution, etc."[101]

Although elites had absorbed social welfare concerns into liberal ideology, they were beginning to balk at bearing the cost of these reforms, Myrdal claimed. Behind the common rhetoric of social welfare lay profound conflicts of interest and a struggle for power. Modern governments were faced with certain moral demands: that no one should suffer from hunger or a poor diet, that the sick should be cared for at no cost to themselves, that all children should have the same chance in life through free public education, and that every family should have decent housing. But all of these things cost money, and a crisis was at hand because the poor majority sought to use the democratic process to improve its standard of living at the expense of the upper classes. Liberals thus faced a "moral dilemma." According to Myrdal, they wanted to help the poor but their political ideology, rooted in classical economics, held that any aid to the unemployed beyond a subsistence dole would diminish their desire to seek work and would create more unemployment. Liberals were thus caught in a "conflict of conscience, because they have . . . to a great extent already accepted the theory of social equality's principle of justice." They began "to lose faith in the fundamental values on which [their] opinions are built," Myrdal asserted. "And nothing is so fundamental to an ideology as faith." Liberals no longer felt in command of the system, and with their ideology weakened at its moral foundation, they were beginning to doubt "the road of reform." He worried that, in the absence of a strong, unifying reform ideology, the danger of fascism or communism would grow more serious.[102]

Myrdal assured his readers that they had nothing to fear from a reform-minded Social Democratic party that wanted to preserve society. Sweden was not yet in the position of Germany, where, according to Myrdal, most working-class youths were embracing communism. But "all experts" agreed that a "*prophylactic social welfare policy*" was necessary, and to this end, the country required an "ideological renewal" of the social welfare concept. This new ideology should be "intellectually coolly rationalistic" where the old had been "more sentimental," and it should be too "technically oriented to lose itself in . . . impractical constructions." Myrdal did not want to romanticize the working class. Like Veblen, he thought that "the only group that should be romanticized" was the "engineers." In the present crisis the experts would only be able to find solutions to Sweden's problems by breaking with the conventional wisdom. Economists would have to "close the account books" of neoclassical economics and "cancel once and for all" the supposedly inviolable "economic principles." Architects would only be able to build low-cost housing for the urban poor if they had state subventions, because such construction could not be done on the free market. Social workers would need new welfare reforms to deal with the "maladjustment" and "social lag" of rural families adrift in the industrial cities. In conclusion, Myrdal conceded that developments in Sweden would be much affected by whatever happened in Germany and Russia and in the League of Nations. He emphasized the urgency of the situation by arguing that class conflict might reach a level of antagonism just as serious as the conflicts during the religious wars of the seventeenth century, but he held out the hope that "there are also, perhaps, the conditions for a new social-political compromise."[103]

The "Dilemma of Social Policy" article united all of the major themes of Gunnar Myrdal's early work, signaled the beginning of his career as a political activist, and developed some of the rhetorical strategies that he would employ in the years ahead. Myrdal's infatuation with technocratic social engineering was matched by his confidence that a popular consensus could be found to support the most scientific and rational approaches to social problems. Growing out of his book *The Political Element* was a concern to identify the moral foundations of political behavior and an interest in how political ideologies influence behavior. His assumption that his own moral concern about poverty was shared to a significant degree by elites led him to try the moral dilemma formula in an effort to gain political leverage from an alleged "conflict of conscience" among liberals. Finally, he believed that elites could be persuaded to support what he called "prophylactic reforms" if they realized that the alternative might be chaos or revolution.

The intended vehicle for these prophylactic reforms, the Swedish Social Democratic party, had attracted relatively few intellectuals to its ranks before the 1930s. Founded in 1889, it had taken a more pragmatic course than its counterparts in many other European countries. From its earliest days, the party had emphasized worker participation in economic and political decision making and public control over the market economy, education, and social welfare. The party had grown dramatically during the first two decades of the twentieth century, in pace with Sweden's rapid industrialization and the development of the labor movement. Under the leadership of Hjalmar Branting, the Social Democrats participated in a coalition with the Liberals from 1917 to 1920. After the introduction of universal suffrage, the Social Democrats emerged as Sweden's largest party, and in 1920 Branting became prime minister, heading the world's first socialist government to come to power through the parliamentary process. Branting's government was a minority government, however, as were two other Social Democratic governments during the 1920s. Neither the Social Democrats nor the three "bourgeois" parties—the Conservatives, the Liberals, and the Agrarians—was able to form lasting coalitions during the 1920s. From 1920 to 1932 Sweden had nine different governments with no regime in office for more than two years.[104]

Since they lacked a parliamentary majority, the Social Democratic governments of the 1920s pursued a strategy of gradual reform, but party leaders also believed that piecemeal reforms were contributing to a process of "socialization" in which the Swedish people were gradually learning to accept collective responsibility for directing industry and for providing for public welfare, a process that would culminate in socialism. In the early 1930s, the party leader, Per Albin Hansson, portrayed the Social Democrats as a "people's party" rather than a class-based workers' party and sought to win the votes of farmers and the middle class. Hansson spoke not about class struggle but about making Sweden a "home for all the people."[105] The economic crisis of 1931–32 was the Social Democrats' great opportunity, and in the election of September 1932 they won an impressive victory but were still a few votes short of an absolute majority in Parliament.

Again in office as a minority government, the Social Democrats presented in 1933 their crisis program, which would change the direction of Swedish politics. The government proposed to fight unemployment by appropriating 160 million kronor for emergency labor and another 40 million for other types of unemployment relief. The architect of this expansionary economic policy, a remarkable innovation in Swedish politics, was Ernst Wigforss, minister of finance in Hansson's cabinet and the Social Democrats' leading intellectual. During the 1920s, there had been a debate in Sweden about how to respond to the unemployment after World War I, and many Social Democrats had advocated greater public control over the marketplace. Wigforss had closely studied Swedish unemployment and had criticized the neoclassical idea that unemployment was the result of high wages and that only by lowering wages could unemployment be reduced. He argued, instead, that raising wages would increase purchasing power, stimulate consumption, and reduce unemployment.[106] Wigforss had been led to question neoclassical orthodoxy by his reading of Marx's prophecies of a capitalist crisis in which drastic wage reductions, massive unemployment, and underconsumption led to a final collapse of the capitalist system. But instead of waiting for this cataclysmic event, Wigforss sought to develop a policy that would reduce unemployment within the framework of the capitalist economy, and he was influenced in this endeavor by the work of both Swedish and British scholars as well as by the experiments of local governments controlled by Social Democrats.[107]

During the first decade of the century, the Swedish economist Knut Wicksell had argued that the government should extend credit to businesses during recessions to enable them to keep producing until prosperity returned, and he had urged the government to reduce unemployment through deficit-financed public works projects. Prior to the 1930s, no Swedish government had implemented Wicksell's policy proposals, but Wigforss and Swedish economists were aware of them. Meanwhile, the British Fabian socialists Sidney and Beatrice Webb had written a *Minority Report of the Poor Law Commission* of 1909, in which they called for public works programs during recessions together with unemployment insurance. Influenced both by Wicksell and the Webbs, Wigforss had written the

Gothenburg Program of 1919, a Social Democratic manifesto that insisted that citizens had a right to employment, that government had a duty to provide it when business could not, and that the Swedish government should therefore launch public works projects as a solution to postwar unemployment. During the 1920s, Wigforss had followed the debates on unemployment policy within the British Labor and Liberal parties and was aware of some of the early work of John Maynard Keynes.[108]

In the years immediately prior to the Social Democratic victory of 1932, a remarkable group of young Swedish economists had independently come to some of the same conclusions about the applicability of Wicksell's theories to the problem of unemployment during economic downturns.[109] Bertil Ohlin, who would later become the leader of the Liberal party, and Erik Lindahl, who was not identified with any political faction, were the major figures of the Stockholm school along with Gunnar Myrdal. The group also included Dag Hammarskjöld, Alf Johansson, Erik Lundberg, and Ingvar Svennilson.[110] They met regularly and read papers before the Economic Society in Stockholm, where the young economists defended their ideas against the criticisms of Cassel, Bagge, and other economists of the older generation.

With Wigforss as a mentor, Gunnar Myrdal quickly rose to become a leading economic advisor to the Social Democratic government. In January 1933 he achieved national recognition when his article "Business Cycles and Fiscal Economics" was appended to the government's proposed budget as a theoretical justification of the government's policies. Addressing a skeptical audience of nonsocialists, Myrdal argued in favor of a temporary expansion of public works to be financed by deficit spending. He insisted that such a measure would have a multiplier effect, stimulating the private sector to expand production and employment. When prosperity was restored, the public works projects could be phased out. Myrdal contended that reduction of government spending in a depression because of a decrease in revenue would simply worsen the instability of the economy. To those who objected that such a policy might undermine the soundness of the government's finances, Myrdal pointed out that deficit financing had been used in wartime and, more covertly, in peacetime as well, and he maintained that increased revenues after recovery would eliminate the deficit. Turning to the question of social welfare, Myrdal argued that it was more beneficial to the society to hire the unemployed for public works than to support them on relief. Society would receive improved roads, buildings, and other public works, as well as the benefit of maintaining the skills and morale of workers who would otherwise be on the dole. Myrdal concluded his article by suggesting that public works in the future should be planned over a number of years, with the government maintaining the flexibility to implement the projects during economic downturns.[111]

To win support for this crisis program, the Social Democrats made a deal with the Agrarian party, which had traditionally voted with the other nonsocialist, bourgeois parties. In exchange for Agrarian support for the public works projects, the Social Democrats agreed to endorse agricultural price supports and to impose an excise tax on margarine. With Agrarian support, the Social Democratic budget was passed by Parliament in May 1933. Unemployment declined from 187,000 in March to 139,000 in July 1933, then continued to fall dramatically to 21,000 in August 1936 and 9,600 in August 1937. To be sure, this success cannot be attributed to the "new economics" alone; recovery in the export sector had preceded the public works program of 1933.[112] But the government's success in overcoming the Depression laid the foundation for an era of remarkable stability in Swedish politics. Except for a three-month period in 1936, the Social Democrats continuously formed the government, sometimes in coalition, from 1932 to 1976.

As Gunnar Myrdal worked to combat unemployment and to build a consensus in favor of social welfare reforms, he was horrified by the development of Nazism in Germany. As students in the 1920s, Gunnar and Alva had spent several weeks reading at the Deutsche Bücherei in Kiel and had looked upon Weimar Germany as a land of cultural and intellectual sophistication. They returned to Kiel for three weeks in June and July 1933 and submitted a confidential report to the Rockefeller Foundation on the Nazi assault on academic freedom, including accounts of which professors had embraced the Nazi ideology and which would need foundation help in finding jobs in other countries. After a trip "filled to the brim with upsetting experiences," they returned to Sweden, which seemed like "a country forgotten by the devils."[113] The Myrdals were founding members of Kulturfront, a Swedish antifascist organization, and they aided refugees from Nazi Germany who fled to Sweden. If witnessing the American stock market crash had been a shock, observing the consolidation of Nazi rule was a chilling reminder of the possible consequences of a democratic government's failure to reduce unemployment and poverty.

Despite all of his political involvement in the early 1930s, Gunnar Myrdal produced a steady stream of scholarly publications, including historical and theoretical contributions as well as research focused on policy questions. His 1931 book *Monetary Equilibrium* built on the work of the Swedish economist Knut Wicksell and analyzed how expectations affected price formation. With his concepts of *ex-ante* and *ex-post*, Myrdal elucidated the difference between anticipated or planned savings in relation to investment and the actual investment after the fact. As in his doctoral dissertation, he sought to replace a static concept of equilibrium with a dynamic equilibrium that took account of historical change, expectations, and uncertainty.[114]

With support from the Rockefeller Foundation, Myrdal collaborated with Gösta Bagge on an ambitious, interdisciplinary research project on Swedish social and economic history that he had planned during his year in America. Myrdal arranged for the American sociologists W. I. Thomas and Dorothy Swaine Thomas to come to Sweden to take part in this interdisciplinary study. The Thomases, who became good friends with Gunnar and Alva Myrdal, sought to write a Scandinavian equivalent of W. I. Thomas's earlier book, *The Polish Peasant in Europe and America*, and they collected data on the migration of people from various Scandinavian countries to America. The Thomases and Gunnar Myrdal also investigated the relationship between psychiatry and criminology by examining the case study records maintained by Swedish psychiatric agencies. Myrdal and his research team assembled data on the Swedish population from 1830 to 1930 to study the migration of people from rural to urban areas as part of the process of industrialization, and Myrdal wrote *The Cost of Living in Sweden, 1830–1930*. As part of this large, Rockefeller-funded study, other Swedish scholars contributed monographs on the history of wages, interest rates, national income, and fertility rates during the same period.[115]

When Gustav Cassel retired in 1933, two of his students appeared to be strong candidates to become his successor as Lars Hjerta Professor of Economics at the University of Stockholm: Bertil Ohlin and Gunnar Myrdal. Ohlin was an economic advisor to the Liberal party, while Myrdal was, in Cassel's eyes, a "radical socialist." In many vigorous debates, Cassel had tried to dissuade Myrdal from his advocacy of economic planning, arguing that no planner was clever enough to foresee all the thousands of factors affecting a modern industrial economy and that the market would always be the most efficient way of allocating goods and services. Though dismayed by his student's apostasy, Cassel respected Myrdal's brilliance and, as a good nineteenth-century liberal, believed in academic freedom and the free marketplace of ideas. Ohlin, who held a professorship at the Stockholm Business School, declined to be a candidate for Cassel's chair, and Cassel threw his support to Myrdal. When Myrdal was installed, at age thirty-five, as the Lars Hjerta Professor, Cassel embraced his errant pupil and said: "You are the most dangerous man in Sweden, but I'm proud to have you as my successor."[116]

Sweden's "Population Crisis"

Gunnar Myrdal's most "dangerous" contribution to Swedish politics was yet to come, however. In the summer of 1934, Gunnar and Alva Myrdal rented a cabin in the mountains of Norway and wrote a book that would make the name Myrdal a household word in Sweden. At that time, Sweden had the lowest birthrate in Europe, and in *Kris i befolkningsfrågan* (Crisis in the population question), the Myrdals presented a Social Democratic program designed to reverse Sweden's declining birthrate. The population issue was the focus of the Myrdal's most celebrated attempt to use social engineering to rationalize and modernize Swedish society. Despite rapid urbanization and industrialization, many urban Swedes, in the Myrdals' view, suffered from a form of "cultural lag" and continued to apply older, rural values to family life. What was needed was a new, planned, socialist sense of community that was built on a broad, democratic foundation.

Alva Myrdal had become concerned about the population issue because of her interest in child development, parent education, and the feminist movement.[117] Gunnar Myrdal had written two chapters for *The Political Element* on Wicksell and the population problem, but had cut them out of the final version. When he had tried to publish them in *Tiden* in 1931, Wigforss had rejected them. Gunnar's interest in the population problem had quickened after he had investigated overcrowded, substandard housing of the urban working class and its impact on family life. He had been shocked to see how many working-class families in Stockholm lived in one- or two-room apartments.[118] The writing of *Kris i befolkningsfrågan*, with its bold vision of a new type of family life, came just six months after the death of Gunnar's father, Carl Adolf Pettersson.

As Allan Carlson has pointed out, the Myrdals met regularly during the early 1930s with a group of young radical architects that included Uno Åhren and Sven Markelius. These designers championed a functionalist movement that revolutionized Swedish architecture by constructing larger, more efficient, less expensive buildings. Modern skyscrapers, shorn of needless decoration, symbolized the triumph of a more rational way of life for the mass of people who would be freed of traditional attitudes by modern science. The Myrdals strongly resonated to the architects' modernizing program. Alva Myrdal collaborated with Markelius to develop plans for a collective house, a large apartment building that would allow a cooperative form of family life in which meals were prepared in a centralized kitchen and delivered by a dumb waiter to the apartments of families. The building would include a gym, reading rooms, lounges, and a nursery supervised by a scientifically trained staff. The collective house, which resembled plans drawn up by nineteenth-century utopian socialists such as Charles Fourier and by the American feminist Charlotte Perkins Gilman, was designed to free working women from some of the burdens of housework and to provide children with a healthier form of peer-group interaction.[119]

When the Myrdals focused their attention on the population problem in 1934, they came up with a radically new perspective. Sweden's declining birthrate had previously been an issue addressed by conservatives, who supported anticontraception laws, discouraged women from working outside the home, and played on nationalistic fears of Swedes dying out or being invaded by "inferior" immigrants. The Social Democrats, on the other hand, supported the individual's right to birth control information and devices and opposed pronatalist policies as an unwarranted intrusion by the state into the individual's private life. The Myrdals seized this traditionally conservative issue and used it to justify a broad range of social welfare policies designed to make it possible for couples who wanted children to have them.

The Myrdals began their book with a characteristic blending of morality and dire prophecy. The population issue, they declared, was "a question of individual conscience" but an issue that also touched problems of social welfare and the distribution of wealth. The birthrate had fallen catastrophically and would continue to decline, with a resulting economic slowdown. The Myrdals contended that the causes of the low birthrate were economic: unemployment, low wages, substandard housing, and the absence of child-care facilities. In the next generation, they predicted, the population issue would come to dominate social policy.[120] To avert economic catastrophe, Sweden had to find a way to increase the birthrate by 40 percent.[121]

In contrast to pronatalist advocates in Nazi Germany, the Myrdals rejected class, racial, religious, and ethnic distinctions in deciding which groups should have more children. All healthy Swedes, in their view, were equally desirable as parents.[122] The authors took pains to refute notions of hereditary differences in intelligence and temperament among the races and ethnic groups. "If Negroes in America or Jews in Poland exhibit certain average race characteristics in their behavior," they wrote, "it is to be explained, above all, by the fact that they have since childhood been treated in such a way that they are driven to react just as Negroes in America or Jews in Poland."[123] But this liberal environmentalism did not prevent the Myrdals from stressing cultural differences among European peoples. They rejected immigration as a solution to Sweden's population problem. The Myrdals considered immigration from other Scandinavian countries to be desirable and thought that Sweden should accept political refugees, but they feared that large numbers of working-class immigrants from outside Scandinavia would be difficult to assimilate. Swedish workers, they predicted, would oppose immigration just as the American workers had and would view any increase in worker immigration as an attempt by Swedish employers to decrease wages. Like most Swedes, the Myrdals believed that the country's democratic institutions and high standard of living had been possible in part because Sweden had avoided entangling alliances with non-Scandinavian countries and had stayed out of European wars since the Napoleonic period. Fearing that the presence of a minority population in Sweden might invite intervention from other European powers, the Myrdals argued that allowing large-scale immigration would risk importing to Sweden the "instability" of central Europe.[124]

The solution to Sweden's population problem, according to the Myrdals, was for Swedes to enjoy the economic security necessary to have more children. To this end they advocated the economic policies that Gunnar Myrdal had championed: national economic planning, full employment, and a redistribution of income sufficient to lift the lower class out of poverty. In addition they recommended policies that were more specifically designed to help families: tax deductions for families with children, government subventions for housing, free health care for children, free school lunches and textbooks, and free public day care centers.[125]

The Myrdals insisted that a Social Democratic population policy must not infringe on women's rights, and they rejected the conservative idea of restricting access to birth control information and devices. Though anticontraception laws were still on the books in Sweden, birth control was widely practiced by nearly all groups in the society, and illegal abortions were also widespread. Brushing aside religious objections to birth control, the Myrdals called for repeal of anticontraception laws so that parents would not have unwanted children. The authors also argued that the state should guarantee women's right to retain their jobs if they had children.[126]

Eugenics was another prophylactic reform advanced by the Myrdals as part of their population policy. They opposed any eugenic policy based on class, religion, or race, but argued that modern, industrial society demanded a higher quality of "human material" than life on the farm had required. Accordingly, it was necessary to face the difficult problem of how to "root out all types of physical and mental inferiority within the population, both the mentally retarded and the mentally ill, the genetically defective and persons of bad character."[127] To prevent the birth of children suffering from genetic defects, the state had the right to impose forced sterilization, and sterilization should be mandatory for persons incapable of making a rational decision.[128] The authors conceded that too little was known about the causes of schizophrenia to warrant compulsory sterilization, and they suggested that manic depression "does not so generally and not so unequivocally make the persons valueless." They insisted, however, that there were thousands of cases of persons with environmentally caused mental illnesses and social problems who would not make good parents. Such persons should be advised strongly by social workers and doctors to seek sterilization voluntarily, and the state should provide free sterilization, contraception, and abortion to such "undesirable parents." "Social medicine has here a field for missionary work of great importance," they concluded.[129]

The Myrdals envisaged radical changes in education as part of a democratic socialist transformation of society. They charged that Swedish schools perpetuated a "false individualism" and competitive ethic that was a legacy of nineteenth-century bourgeois liberal ideology. Instead of these obsolete values, they contended that the schools should teach children to be cooperative. The authors maintained that, in international circles, Swedes were viewed as "stiff," "formal," "boring," "timid," and "lacking in personal intensity and warmth." Because of the old-fashioned educational system, "Everything that is free and flowing in the human soul is hemmed in and twisted." Reflecting the influence of John Dewey, the Myrdals argued that schools should encourage spontaneity as well as democratic values. Schools also bore the responsibility of helping students to find work in accordance with their talents, not their parents' social class, and thus they would play a major role in Sweden's evolution toward a classless society.[130]

These changes in education had to be supplemented by important innovations in family life, the Myrdals insisted. Building upon Alva Myrdal's earlier work and borrowing language from Chicago sociology, the authors argued that the traditional patriarchal family of rural Sweden had broken down under the impact of industrialization and urbanization and was now in a state of "disorganization."[131] The industrial revolution had "burst apart the old unity of village, kin, and family;" had "made individuals more lonely;" and had "driven them to a heightened individualism in their social and moral attitudes."[132] Particularly distressing to the Myrdals was the way children were brought up in the small, modern families, a situation that they found "almost pathological." "That a modern adult should stay at home and devote herself to taking care of one or two children is utterly absurd," they wrote. Such patterns of family life led to overprotected children and unhappy marriages. Instead, parents needed to "free children more from ourselves" by putting them in day care centers where they would have more opportunities to interact with other children. The Myrdals argued that it was not inevitable that the modern family should drift toward "disintegration and sterility."[133] A new type of family, based on equality of the sexes and a greater sense of social responsibility, could be integrated into a democratic socialist society.

In their conclusion, the Myrdals returned to their interest in identifying fundamental values and in shaping public opinion. "History has never seen a balanced and harmonious society that was not grounded in secure values within a collective psychology," they wrote. The task for socialists was thus to educate the public to abandon older attitudes based on liberal individualism and to embrace more cooperative and egalitarian values. The Myrdals hoped to be able to shape a new national ideology in support of their population and social welfare policies, an ideology that would win support both from those on the left who supported welfare reforms and redistributive measures and from those on the right who were concerned about Sweden's declining birthrate. They acknowledged that their proposals were controversial, but they hoped that this new consensus would take hold among the younger generation of Swedes.[134]

Kris i befolkningsfrågan was a bestseller in 1935, and Gunnar and Alva Myrdal became celebrities overnight. Throughout the country, Swedes discussed the "population crisis" and debated whether the Myrdals' social welfare proposals would raise the birthrate. Gunnar and Alva Myrdal gave dozens of public lectures and debated their critics on the radio and in the popular press. The Swedish radio service organized a study course on the population problem with a handbook written by Gunnar Myrdal, and the issue was taken up by adult education groups and community forums. Apartment buildings for families with children, dubbed Myrdal houses, were built in Stockholm. Jokes about fertility abounded, and the Swedish language gained a new term for having sexual intercourse: to myrdal.[135]

When they wrote *Kris i befolkningsfrågan*, Gunnar and Alva Myrdal had only one child, their son Jan, who had been born in 1927. Alva had suffered a miscarriage in Geneva in 1930, and doctors had warned her against having more children.[136] But the Myrdals wanted a larger family, and they argued that Swedish families needed to have an average of three children if the nation was not to die out. Alva, with characteristic boldness, decided to disregard the doctors' advice and to try again. A daughter, Sissela, was born in 1934 while *Kris i befolkningsfrågan* was in press, and Alva continued to write articles about the population issue from her hospital bed. A second daughter, Kaj, was born in 1936, thus bringing the Myrdal family up to their recommended minimum standard.

The social welfare proposals advanced by the Myrdals in *Kris i befolkningsfrågan* drew fire from members of the bourgeois parties. In a series of newspaper articles, Gustav Cassel condemned their plans for redistributing income as "communistic." But the leaders of the nonsocialist parties agreed that there was indeed a population crisis and that something had to be done about it. Social Democratic leaders were initially cautious about abandoning their traditional neo-Malthusianism, but when the Myrdals' ideas proved to be popular, the party leaders adopted the population crisis as an issue for the 1936 elections. In May 1935, all the major parties agreed to the creation of a royal commission to study the population issue.[137]

Swedish royal commissions are appointed by the government to investigate a particular issue and include representatives of all political parties and of major interest groups. With the aid of a research staff, they write a report recommending legislation, which is often enacted into law by Parliament with few changes. Gunnar Myrdal was appointed to the Population Commission, which claimed a large portion of his time from June 1935 to June 1938. The commission was headed by Nils Wohlin, a member of the upper house of Parliament from the Agrarian party and Gustav Cassel's son-in-law. Myrdal worked hard to cultivate a close relationship with Wohlin, who reminded him of his own father in appearance and manner. As Allan Carlson has observed, Myrdal quickly emerged as the driving force on the Population Commission and was able to "set the terms of the debate" because of his enormous energy and intellectual power, his technical expertise, and his supervision of the research staff. As the work of the commission proceeded, he gradually won most of the members over to his ideas.[138] Gunnar Myrdal's work on the Population Commission would also be an important rehearsal for his study of the American race issue.

During the three years of its existence, the Population Commission recommended many of the reforms proposed in *Kris i befolkningsfrågan*. Gunnar Myrdal, who had been elected to the upper house in 1936 as a member for Dalarna, carried on the fight for these reforms in Parliament. With support from the Social Democratic leadership, Parliament approved legislation for constructing housing for families in urban areas. To encourage couples who wanted children, Parliament passed laws that provided subsidies for pregnant women, "marriage loans" to couples who could not otherwise afford to get married, aid to orphans and children of widows and disabled men, and an increase in the tax deduction granted to families with children. In addition, Parliament made it illegal for an employer to fire a woman or lessen her salary because of marriage, pregnancy, or childbirth. But these measures, important as they were, did not add up to the radical redistribution of income or fundamental change in child-rearing patterns that Gunnar and Alva Myrdal had advocated. In the spring of 1938, Prime Minister Hansson and the Social Democratic leadership decided that there must be a "reform pause" while Sweden built up its military defenses. As a result, commission proposals for free school meals and day care centers were stalled in Parliament.[139]

Gunnar Myrdal did not believe that there would be a general European war, but he recognized that there would be few opportunities for bold reforms in the immediate future. He continued to propose dramatic changes, however, in his last contribution to Swedish reform in the decade, the report of the Agriculture Commission in 1938. It was not in the national interest, he argued, for a large part of the rural population to live in poverty. But this son of Dalarna had no romanticism about rural life. His solution to rural poverty was not an increase in farm subsidies but greater migration to the cities, where Sweden had "unlimited possibilities for expansion" in its industries.[140] In this, as in other issues, Myrdal showed little sensitivity to the need that many people felt for a sense of community or attachment to place. His life, like his father's, had been marked by restless mobility, both geographical and social, and he sought to plan for thousands of Swedes a transition to a life based on rational, functional, scientific, and productive principles. With the reform pause on the way, however, he realized that social engineering and prophylactic reform would have to take a back seat to the politics of consensus and national unity.

It was in this context of frustration with Swedish politics that Gunnar Myrdal decided to accept the Carnegie Corporation's invitation to head a study of the American race issue. From 1932 to 1938 he had involved himself in political life as an economic planner, author, public speaker, member of royal commissions, member of Parliament, and director of the Bank of Sweden. Myrdal loved the excitement of political debate and the challenge of applying his expertise to problems of social engineering, but he was impatient with the day-to-day round of public duties, disliked the compromises necessary in parliamentary politics, and considered the Swedish bureaucracy a "cemetery of words and deeds." He lacked the self-discipline required to absorb criticisms from every direction and to reply with tact and diplomacy.[141] A strong individual with opinions on every subject, he found it unnatural to accept party discipline and to defer to older men that he regarded as intellectually inferior.

Egon Glesinger, an economist and close friend of the Myrdals, noted "the strength of Gunnar Myrdal's personality and his exceptional ability to create happiness and sorrow around him, simply by the intensity of his own feelings." Another close friend observed that Gunnar Myrdal could be incredibly generous, then exhibit a "mild sadism" with a sense of humor that was sometimes cruel.[142] Sissela Bok, the Myrdals' daughter, admired her father as a scholar but admitted that he was "deeply egocentric." "He could establish warm and immediate contact with people in a minute," she remembered, "and then quickly turn his attention elsewhere." Bok observed in her father "an inner insecurity that drove him to try to disparage everyone whom he saw as competitors." Gunnar Myrdal could not resist the temptation to prove himself brighter than everyone around him, and he brought to political debate a style that many found "aggressive" and "irritating." "It was as if he calculated this naughtiness," Bok wrote, "but at the same time did not understand its effect—as if he were just an unpredictable child when it came to dealing with other people."[143]

While many Swedish politicians and intellectuals resented Gunnar Myrdal and viewed him as an upstart from Dalarna and something of a bounder, American intellectuals would show more tolerance for his overweening ambition, his competitive nature, and his abrupt manner. Many American scholars of his generation were also ambitious and brilliant outsiders who had rebelled against various provincialisms, whether black, immigrant, or white Protestant, and who preferred open competition and freewheeling debate to the genteel norms of the older generation of academics.[144] Myrdal would later write that there was less envy in America than in Europe, that the less successful people do not hold the more successful back. "Luck, ability, and drive in others are more tolerated and less checked in America," he would note. "Climbing is more generally accepted." While he hoped that the United States would evolve into a society with a stronger labor movement, he appreciated the fact that "outstanding individuals are permitted to have wide space for their initiative according to the great American tradition."[145]

If Gunnar Myrdal often alienated politicians and academics that he viewed as competitors, he nonetheless possessed a contagious enthusiasm for ideas. "Gunnar's egocentricity was of an unusual kind," Bok recalled. "To be sure, he thought that the world revolved around him. But his world was so much more spacious than most other people's, so much richer in insight and possibilities, so much more complex."[146] He had an ability to draw people to him, especially younger scholars, to inspire them, and to demand and get an extraordinary amount of work out of them. Driven by an intense need for adulation, Gunnar was happiest when surrounded by a roomful of young intellectuals whom he could dazzle with his extraordinary brilliance. Though he had little time for nurturing students as individuals, they still flocked to his lectures at the university, fascinated by this enigmatic figure dressed in Brooks Brothers suits and elegant ties, his Swedish sprinkled with American expressions. They were intrigued by this Dalecarlian who had become an internationally known intellectual, this Social Democrat with a tough-minded, entrepreneurial style.[147]

Alva Myrdal felt her own set of frustrations, both with Swedish political and intellectual life and with problems closer to home, and the idea of spending two years in New York appealed to her as well. Although the population problem was, in many respects, more her issue than Gunnar's, the Social Democratic leadership had passed over her and named her husband to the Population Commission. Alva felt many demands on her time as she served as principal of a teacher training institute, participated in women's organizations and Social Democratic party affairs, and raised three children. By comparison to most Swedish couples of their generation, the Myrdals enjoyed a marriage based on a remarkable degree of equality. Gunnar took a strong public stand in favor of feminism in an era when it was hardly fashionable, and he supported Alva in her determination to pursue an active intellectual and political career. Indeed, he liked to brag about his wife's achievements. Yet, like many husbands before and after him, it was difficult for Gunnar to bring his behavior into line with his professed ideals. He had grown up in an upwardly mobile family with a domineering, ambitious father and a mother who devoted herself to caring for her children. His academic mentor, Gustav Cassel, was a charming, paternalistic, but egocentric professor whose family paid him great deference. Gunnar's work was the center of his life, and he put in long hours of work seven days a week. He had no hobbies, except for an occasional game of bridge, and his idea of a vacation was going away with Alva to a secluded rural retreat where both could work without the interruption of phone calls, official duties, or children. Although he thought that Swedes should have more of them, Gunnar found children puzzling and did not know quite what to do with them until they grew old enough to carry on an intellectual conversation. Absorbed in his work, he neglected to learn about traditionally feminine concerns like feeding babies and changing diapers, and he showed little interest in doing the things that other fathers did, such as reading stories to children or playing games with them.[148]

Alva felt tugged in three different directions. She had to respond to a demanding husband who deeply needed her as a lover, a source of emotional support, an intellectual companion, and a political ally. She had to forge her own career in a world hostile to ambitious women. And she had to find time to raise three small children. Inevitably, the children were cared for most of the time by servants, who were often young women from Alva's teacher training school. Reacting against her own mother's tendency to overprotect children, Alva wanted her children to grow up to be independent. She tried to give them a great deal of freedom and to encourage them to make their own decisions. But the Myrdal family, like many families with two strong-willed parents, was full of tensions. Jan grew into a rebellious child, while Sissela enjoyed a closer bond with her mother and learned to avoid provoking the wrath of her father, whom she viewed as an "absent-minded professor."[149]

Beset by all these demands on her time and emotional energy, Alva welcomed the idea of spending two years in New York, where she would be able to devote more time to intellectual pursuits and would be free of administrative duties. Her year in America in 1929–30 had been a formative experience in her professional development, and the prospect of renewing her dialogue with American psychologists and educators strongly appealed to her. Although the United States had its share of social and political problems, she found the intellectual life much more stimulating than Sweden's and the people much warmer than the inhabitants of what she liked to call "our frozen land."

Gunnar and Alva working at a desk specially built for them, in their futuristic house in a Stockholm suburb (courtesy Arbetarrörelsens Arkiv, Stockholm)

When Gunnar Myrdal received Keppel's letter, he and Alva and their children had recently moved into a new, futuristic, functionally designed villa that Sven Markelius had built for them. It was not a collective house for many families but instead a dwelling designed expressly for the remarkable Myrdal family. The house was so startlingly modern that people came to stare at it, and newspapers published articles about it. Perched on a hill in the Stockholm suburb of Bromma, the villa offered a commanding view of a large apple orchard. In its design, the house symbolized the Myrdals' commitment to a modern, forward-looking, scientific social engineering. Alva intended it as a spacious alternative to the "Strindberg-esque family inferno" she had grown up in; it was supposed to be a home that would offer possibilities both for family togetherness and for privacy for each person. The house consisted of a downstairs apartment that included bedrooms for each of the three children and for a children's nurse and maid, together with a kitchen, dining room, and large family room. The upstairs apartment for the adults included a large study that opened onto a terrace, plus a library and a bedroom. The library featured a large desk built so that Gunnar and Alva could work facing each other. In the bedroom, Alva installed an unusual feature that attracted considerable commentary in the press: a sliding wall that formed a partition between her bed and Gunnar's so that she could have a little peace and quiet when she needed it.[150]

The Myrdal family embarks for the United States to begin Gunnar's work on the American race issue, September, 1938. The children are, *left to right*, Kaj, Sissela, and Jan. (courtesy Arbetarrörelsens Arkiv, Stockholm)

For a Dalecarlian boy born in a humble cottage on a mountainside, Gunnar Myrdal had traveled far in thirty-eight years. But he was restless and ready for new challenges. His first reaction to Keppel's proposal was incredulity. "These Americans are crazy," he told Alva, and he cabled Keppel that he was grateful for the honor but he could not accept it because of his commitments in Sweden. But after discussing the matter with Beardsley Ruml, who was in Stockholm on a visit, Myrdal reconsidered. He liked Ruml and found him to be a "free-wheeling, risk-taking" American academic entrepreneur who was not afraid to use social science knowledge for ambitious planning. Then, he later recalled, "Alva and I were out one evening at a movie where they had the white doctors who were out fighting malaria somewhere in an undeveloped part of the world. Afterward we were obviously drinking too much coffee, and we were sitting up in the bed and I said to Alva, 'Perhaps we should do this thing at the end of our youth.' And the day afterwards I cabled Keppel: 'Prepared to discuss, etc., this problem.'"[151] A series of cables and letters followed, in which Myrdal negotiated for himself a salary commensurate with his "rather comfortable European upper class level [of income], with our own house, two servants, etc."[152]

Many of his friends thought it strange that Gunnar Myrdal should resign from various official positions and go to the United States for two years to study a subject as remote as American blacks. It was a big move for a two-career family with three small children. But the idea of heading a large study and applying his investigative skills to a major social problem in the United States greatly appealed to Gunnar's imagination. When Keppel offered Carnegie support for Alva to study education and child psychology at Columbia University, she agreed to the move.

In a letter to his friend Dorothy Swaine Thomas, Gunnar explained why he and Alva had decided to accept Keppel's extraordinary invitation: "One night we started to think seriously about our life. This was, after all, perhaps the last possibility to get free before we are old and absolutely stationary. Why not the Negro as well as anything else? I am longing [to get] back to disinterested work again, where I do not have my heart mortgaged, as in these Swedish things, where I am neutral and sceptical. So I took up discussion on the Negro plan."

After much correspondence, he and Keppel agreed that Gunnar would be able to bring "one of my own boys, Rickard Sterner," to America to work on the study. Gunnar obtained a two-year leave of absence from the university and Alva from her teacher training institute, but Gunnar had to resign from Parliament, from various commissions, and from the board of the Bank of Sweden. He reported: "Carnegie is under consideration of what we are giving up prepared to pay me on a rather high scale. We are going with the children and a Swedish nurse—just like Abraham and Sarah from the Holy Land. I shall work on the Negro—I will do nothing else: I shall think and dream of the Negro 24 hours a day, for I will really do a good job (Not like the Migration [study], which I always defrauded for other things). Alva, on her side, is getting time and freedom for her own academic work, which is a very important element of advantage."[153]

Gunnar Myrdal thus embarked for America in the hope that the Carnegie study of the "Negro problem" would offer an escape from political wrangling into "disinterested" social science research. He would soon discover that he had taken on the most demanding and controversial assignment of his career, a project that would test his political acumen as well as his research skills.

3

Encountering the
"Negro Problem"

On September 10, 1938, Gunnar Myrdal arrived in New York accompanied by Alva, their three children, the Swedish social statistician Richard Sterner and his wife, Margareta, and two young women from Alva's teacher training institute who looked after the Myrdals' children. They were met at the pier by Charles Dollard, Keppel's young assistant, who shepherded the group through customs and conducted the Myrdals to their apartment on Riverside Drive near Columbia University. Jan was enrolled in the Lincoln School, a private school on the cutting edge of the progressive education movement, while Sissela and Kaj attended kindergarten at Riverside Church. Alva participated in seminars on child psychology and education at Columbia and began work on a book in English about Swedish population policy.

Americans were fascinated by this Swedish couple that had accomplished so much in their youth. At thirty-six, Alva was a striking blond, fashionably dressed, quietly self-confident with a direct gaze and serious demeanor, always polite and seldom at a loss for words. Gunnar, at thirty-nine, was a dynamo with piercing blue eyes, a shock of light brown hair, and a mercurial temperament that alternated between playful banter and intense absorption in intellectual work. He was constantly erupting with ideas and questions about every aspect of American life. In New York, Washington, and other cities, the Myrdals moved in social circles that included social scientists, black intellectuals, politicians, diplomats, and European émigrés. To many American intellectuals and reformers, curious about the Swedish experiment in social democracy, the Myrdals seemed like oracles from a more advanced society who had been "over into the future" and had helped to make it work. Though Gunnar's time was largely devoted to his study of race relations, Alva accepted many speaking engagements from women's groups and discussed the Swedish welfare state and family policy. As they settled into their new life, both Gunnar and Alva felt liberated from the demands of all the committees they had served on and from the narrowness of the Swedish academic world. Life in the United States seemed to work a "personality transformation" on them, to broaden them as scholars, and to enlarge their sympathy and understanding of different groups of people; they also felt reinvigorated by the intellectual life in America and stimulated by the diversity of cultures in New York.[1]

For the next four years, Alva offered Gunnar intellectual stimulation and emotional support, but she did not participate directly in the Carnegie Negro study; thus her radical views on family policy and women's rights were not expressed in the study, as they had been in *Kris i befolkningsfrågan*. In addition, her emphasis on stimulating political participation at the grass roots and organizing reforms from below was not present as a counterweight to her husband's top-down social engineering.

Initial Impressions

Gunnar now turned his attention to the Negro study, about which he had only very general ideas. Few details of the study had been arranged in the initial exchange of correspondence between Keppel and Myrdal. Keppel had been relieved to find a European social scientist with experience in statecraft, and Myrdal had looked forward to applying his skills of social analysis and social engineering in the United States. How the study would be organized and in what manner Myrdal would collaborate with American scholars were to be determined after Myrdal's arrival. Before he came to America, Myrdal had insisted on having complete control over the planning of the entire study. Keppel agreed, and the two men had arranged to meet in May 1938 when Gunnar Myrdal was in the United States to deliver the Godkin Lectures at Harvard University. Keppel's notes from the meeting indicate that he had no overall conception of research strategy and little familiarity with the social science literature on blacks. The main points that Keppel listed for discussion were the Carnegie Corporation's activities in the past in aiding black colleges and current grant proposals from the Urban League, the NAACP, the Commission on Interracial Cooperation, and the Encyclopedia of the Negro. Keppel recommended a few books and articles dealing with black education and urged Myrdal to read Donald Young's memo of January 30, 1937, which outlined a plan for the study that envisaged a main report to be written by the foreign investigator and monographs to be prepared by American collaborators. During this visit, Keppel had introduced Myrdal to several of the Carnegie trustees, and Myrdal found that they were no more clear than Keppel on how he should approach the "Negro problem."[2]

When he returned to New York in September 1938, Gunnar Myrdal plunged into his study of American blacks with immense self-confidence and energy. He saw his role as an important one and, from the beginning, set out to write a major interpretive study of American civilization. He perceived his invitation from the Carnegie Corporation as a "semiofficial" commission to investigate a complicated social problem and to lay the groundwork for a more rational and democratic public policy.[3] In an era when senior American social scientists were hesitant to make policy recommendations about race relations, Myrdal proclaimed to his American friends that social engineering was "the supreme task of an accomplished social science."

Keppel postponed a formal announcement of Myrdal's appointment in order to give Myrdal and Sterner a chance to travel around the South to observe patterns of race relations without attracting publicity. It was Keppel's idea that they should have this firsthand exposure to the South before they read any of the literature on the American Negro. This was, after all, a time when American intellectuals were writing documentary studies based on travels designed to bring them close to the people. So the two Swedes set out on a two-month odyssey across the South from Virginia to Arkansas. Their guide on this trip was Jackson Davis, a fastidious and courtly Virginian who was a senior official of the Rockefeller-supported General Education Board. Davis was a cautious reformer who had come of age in the South during the turbulent period at the turn of the century, and he was a leading exponent of the GEB strategy of building up black education within the framework of segregation while cultivating the support of southern white moderates. Davis drove the two Swedes through the South in his Buick, making sure that they understood the southern white man's point of view about the "horrors of Reconstruction" and the need for proceeding slowly with racial change. Davis's key contacts on the trip were white officials in charge of Negro education in various states, and Myrdal's access to the black community was initially through black school principals and other professionals and through members of the Commission on Interracial Cooperation. Myrdal and Sterner soon grew distrustful of Davis's guidance and tired of hearing conservative, middle-class Negro spokesmen. They sought out sharecroppers, visited bars and nightclubs, and talked with blacks of all classes. They toured a tobacco factory and a textile mill, met sheriffs and a CIO organizer, attended black church services, and visited a resettlement project and many plantations and farms.

Myrdal also met a few social scientists in the field of race relations and did some preliminary talent scouting for his study. Jackson Davis's presence with Myrdal conveyed to southern scholars a message that this was an important study, commissioned by one foundation with the cooperation of another. In Chapel Hill, Myrdal talked with Howard Odum, the preeminent white southern sociologist, and met Odum's colleagues Rupert Vance and Guy B. Johnson. At Atlanta University, he conferred with W. E. B. Du Bois, then a professor of sociology after many years of work as a civil rights leader, and at Tuskegee Institute, he met the sociologist Monroe N. Work. Myrdal talked with southern liberals Jonathan Daniels and Frank Porter Graham in North Carolina and made some contacts among southern journalists, who gave him valuable behind-the-scenes information about the power structure in their communities. In November, he attended the Southern Conference on Human Welfare in Birmingham, a gathering of white and black reformers from throughout the region that seemed to promise an offensive to strengthen economic reforms, education, and unions in the region, in accordance with Roosevelt's declaration the previous summer that the South was "Economic Problem Number One."[4]

In the beginning, Myrdal thought that improving the efficiency of the southern economy was the key to the solution of the "Negro problem," and on the boat coming over, he had written Cassel that he understood that "my Negro-investigation in reality will be an analysis of the southern states' miserable economy."[5] Yet actually seeing the wretchedness of southern tenant farmers had been a shock. "When I traveled in the South," he wrote Cassel, "and saw these sick, undernourished masses of people and their depleted soil and poorly-conserved natural resources, I realized at once that the American economy was not operating at much more than fifty percent of its capacity."[6] "If America could get rid of the unemployment problem," he told the *Birmingham News*, the country would be richer than anyone could imagine."[7] To a modern, futuristic social engineer from Sweden, the South seemed hopelessly backward, but he thought that President Roosevelt had at least aroused in poor Americans a realization that a higher standard of living was possible, that action by the federal government could make a difference in their lives. Alva Myrdal went so far as to declare that the New Deal was "a social revolution of the same dimensions as the Russian experiment," but Gunnar was fully aware that the United States lagged far behind Sweden in reducing unemployment.[8] He believed that one of the most important goals of his study was to outline the kind of economic planning and social engineering that was needed to lift the southern masses from poverty. After visiting the South and talking with some American scholars, he also recognized that he was dealing with a complex cultural problem that he understood only dimly.[9]

The southern caste system was bewildering to the young Swede. In Birmingham, Davis took Myrdal and Sterner to a school assembly at a black high school, where they listened to a concert of Negro spirituals by the school's glee club. After this entertainment, the principal introduced Myrdal as a visiting Swedish educator and asked him to say a few words to the students. Myrdal delivered what he thought was a polite speech about American education, noting that the first Swedes who had come to America in the eighteenth century had been poor outcasts, but they had worked hard and their descendants now included powerful men in finance and government. His "gospel" was the "power of education," and he assured the young men and women that if they worked hard, they too could rise to become leaders in American society. Myrdal noticed that Davis and the white school officials behind him on the stage were looking uncomfortable, though he was not quite sure why, so he decided that he would end on a happy note and return the youngsters' hospitality by singing a Swedish folk song for them. It was the first time that a white person had ever sung for them, and the students erupted into a standing ovation and thronged around the podium to meet him, much to the annoyance and embarrassment of Davis and the school officials. As Sterner led him away to the hotel, the two Swedes puzzled over what had happened.[10]

Myrdal encountered another paradox during his southern trip when the news broke of the Nazi atrocities against Jews on Crystal Night, November 9, 1938. Southern newspapers condemned the Nazis for their murders, beatings, attacks on synagogues, and looting of Jewish homes and businesses, and all the educated white southerners that Myrdal met were outraged. When he pointed out that blacks in the South were still subject to lynching, and much more frequently, to other types of violence and intimidation, the whites replied, "But we do not say that these things are right!" They insisted that the Constitution, the Supreme Court, and public opinion were opposed to such practices and that racial violence was decreasing. Nevertheless, Myrdal wondered, as he traveled through the South, how strongly Americans in fact supported their constitutional guarantees of civil rights. Like many American intellectuals of the late 1930s, he worried that fascism could "happen here," and feared that if racial discrimination were allowed to spread, it could undermine the whole political and legal system.[11]

When he returned to New York from the southern journey, Jackson Davis gave a confidential report to the Carnegie Corporation that betrayed the anxieties of a southern gradualist reformer about the loquacious visitor from Sweden. Davis reported "some misgivings on the part of persons of both races which seemed to indicate that Myrdal's quick mind and remarkably successful work in Sweden made him jump to conclusions about southern problems, instead of keeping his mind open with a willingness to hear and appraise discussion by people most concerned with the several aspects of southern life." Davis considered it "necessary that he spend a considerable time in the South and make wide contacts in order to validate his study in the public mind. Otherwise, it would be discounted as an academic effort of a person unfamiliar with the history, traditions and general framework in which race relations and southern social problems must be worked out." Davis was encouraged, however, by Myrdal's remark "that he came back from his trip feeling that he knew nothing about the situation and that he wanted now to read and study and think through his own plans before taking any further steps in the field."[12] Keppel, who did not share Davis's commitment to a strategy of gradualist reform in the South, was not especially troubled by Davis's report.

Myrdal was fully aware that he had taken on an immense task. He returned from his southern trip feeling so overwhelmed by the enormity and complexity of America's racial problems that he doubted the wisdom of writing the book by himself and proposed to Keppel that he should coauthor the study with a commit-tee consisting of a white southerner, T. J. Woofter, Jr.; a white northerner, Donald Young; and a black, Charles S. Johnson. If the Carnegie president had wanted to insure a "safe" study that offended as few people as possible, this was a golden opportunity to nudge the project toward just such a result. But Keppel declined to accept this pragmatic solution, just as he had shrugged off Jackson Davis's warnings. Keppel had gone to considerable trouble to recruit a foreign observer, and he remained firmly wedded to the idea that Myrdal should write the main report by himself.[13] Myrdal accepted this decision and began organizing the project along the lines originally suggested by Donald Young: Myrdal would write a general book putting American race relations in a broad perspective, and several American social scientists would conduct independent research on specialized topics. Even though he gave up the idea of sharing authorship with a three-man committee, Myrdal continued to draw on his experience with royal commissions in setting up the study. He would recruit collaborators representing different points of view and let them debate methodological and political issues. But this would be a royal commission with a difference: Myrdal alone would control the content of the final report.[14]

Keppel and Myrdal formed a strong personal and professional friendship. Myrdal perceived the Carnegie president as a man much like Gustav Cassel, a "great liberal" in the European sense who was totally committed to academic freedom and confident that society would benefit from the free interplay of ideas. He cultivated a close relationship with Keppel, saw him as a mentor, and consulted with him on a wide range of issues. According to Myrdal, Keppel "thought Alva and I were a couple of young kids who were out to change the world, and he thought that was just great."[15] The young Swede who believed that business, labor, and the public could agree on prophylactic reforms as an alternative to violence or chaos reminded Keppel of his own youthful idealism and hopes during the Progressive Era. Keppel played the role of a patron fostering the research of a brilliant young man, and he provided constant encouragement and advice during the course of the study. But he was also somewhat in awe of Myrdal as a European professor and public figure who had resigned from the Swedish Parliament and a directorship of the Bank of Sweden to carry out this investigation for the Carnegie Corporation.[16] Though he never imposed his ideas on Myrdal, Keppel played an important role as a sounding board and gave Myrdal his reactions as a "layman-citizen." When his foreign observer returned from the South and reported on the poverty of blacks, the pervasiveness of discrimination, and the role of extralegal violence in maintaining the caste system, Keppel was genuinely shocked. The foundation president came to symbolize for Myrdal the educated white American who would take action on the civil rights issue if he just knew the facts.[17]

The study was run informally, as Keppel preferred. There was never a contract specifying how the research would be conducted. The project proceeded according to a gentlemen's understanding that Myrdal would direct his study and the corporation would supply the funding for the research staff and technical assistance. Keppel supported Myrdal in requests for additional funds from the Carnegie board, and he wrote to deans and university presidents asking that scholars be released from teaching duties to conduct research for the project. Again and again, Keppel used his prestige and influence to expedite matters. He wrote draft boards requesting deferments for young scholars on the study and pulled strings in Washington to get the Myrdals back and forth across the Atlantic during wartime. When Myrdal wanted data from the 1940 census, Keppel got it released before publication. When Myrdal wanted to know about the purchasing power of blacks, Keppel put him in touch with officials of advertising agencies, General Motors, and AT&T. Keppel acknowledged that turning a Swede loose on such a controversial subject had been risky, but he stood by him in spite of the fact that Myrdal was not as detached and unemotional as Keppel had originally hoped. The Carnegie president noted in a memo in May 1939 that his friend Edward L. Thorndike had met Myrdal and found him "an incurable romantic who won't give us what we expect, but what he gives us will be worth while."[18]

Myrdal was grateful for the freedom that Keppel allowed him in organizing the study, and he wrote to a Swedish friend, with a sense of relief, that the Carnegie Corporation had given him a "free hand" in running the study.[19] After three years of submitting to the formal procedure and compromises of royal commission and parliamentary work, Myrdal found it exhilarating to be able to establish a research project free of red tape. He could call on America's leading experts for advice and assistance, yet he alone was responsible for the final report. Organizing a major study of American race relations and proposing policies that would produce greater equality was a challenge that the social engineer could not resist, and he threw himself into the task with his customary energy and enthusiasm. Myrdal believed that intellectuals could make a difference in public policymaking; after all, he and a small group of young economists had defied economic orthodoxy to plan Sweden's recovery from the Depression, and he and Alva had stimulated a major debate on population policy that led to legislative changes. Racial inequality was a complex social phenomenon, but Myrdal was determined to try to help Americans face it and do something about it. As the Nazi regime broadcast racist propaganda to the rest of Europe, he realized that he was working on a problem with broad ramifications. "I am becoming more and more fascinated by this Negro study," he wrote to a Swedish colleague, "as I feel that I am coming down to certain fundamental features in the tragedy of humanity."[20]

An Absence of Consensus

After returning from his southern trip in November 1938, Myrdal immersed himself in the writings of American social scientists about black-white relations. As he read their work in the winter and spring of 1938 and 1939, he discovered that no consensus existed among the social scientists involved in the cultural and social study of black Americans. Social scientists were in general agreement that no proof existed of any hereditary differences in intelligence among the races, and most agreed that no hereditary differences in temperament existed. Among those who worked within an environmentalist framework, however, many disagreements remained. Social scientists disagreed about the causes of racial discrimination and the relative importance of psychological, social, and economic factors. They disagreed about the effectiveness of education and government action in inducing changes in racial attitudes and practices, and they differed on whether social scientists should intervene directly in the policymaking process. Most social scientists saw black culture as a variant of white culture, but some argued that blacks, especially in the rural South, had a distinct folk culture, perhaps with African roots. A variety of different research groups and methodologies for the study of black culture and social structure coexisted. These included the Chicago school of sociology, Donald Young's comparative analysis of minority groups, Howard Odum's regional sociology, Melville Herskovits's cultural anthropology, John Dollard's "caste and class" approach, W. E. B. Du Bois's interdisciplinary studies of black culture, Carter G. Woodson's Negro history movement, Charles S. Johnson's more liberal variant of Chicago sociology, and the cluster of young black radicals at Howard University.

Robert Park (1864–1944) was the senior American sociologist in the field of race and ethnicity when Myrdal arrived in the United States. The leading figure of the Chicago school of sociology, he had trained a generation of students and firmly established his department's preeminent position within American sociology during the 1920s and early 1930s. After his retirement from Chicago in 1934, he spent the last nine years of his life teaching at Fisk University in the social science department headed by his former student, Charles S. Johnson.[21] Park emphasized that race relations were dynamic, not static, and outlined a cycle of race relations whereby ethnic group interaction proceeds through four stages: competition, conflict, accommodation, and assimilation. He thus envisaged the eventual assimilation of blacks into American culture, but he saw such assimilation as a two-way process in which the minority group influenced the majority group as well as vice-versa. This lengthy, evolutionary movement toward assimilation would be marked by conflict, sometimes violent, between the races. Park disdained social engineering and argued that the social scientist should take a detached, objective approach to his subject. Racial change would come through the processes of conflict and accommodation between the races, he believed, not through government planning.[22] By the late 1930s, the Chicago Department of Sociology had begun to lose its preeminent position within the discipline, as Park's successors lacked the intellectual and personal cohesion to extend the influence of the Chicago school.[23] Nevertheless, Park and his students had produced the most significant body of research on race relations that Myrdal would confront.

Park's Chicago colleague, William Fielding Ogburn, though not a race relations specialist, was a powerful figure in the social sciences in the 1920s and 1930s, and his doctrine of scientific objectivism inhibited activism among sociologists in many fields. Ogburn was eager to distance sociology from its past associations with reform during the Progressive Era and to model the discipline on the natural sciences. In a 1929 address as president of the American Sociological Society, he declared that "sociology as a science is not interested in making the world a better place to live," even though individual sociologists as citizens might choose to take part in politics or charitable work. The future of the discipline, in Ogburn's vision, lay in quantification, and he averred that "a multiplication table should be reliable both for the Tory and the Communist." The "scientific sociologist" had little time for social theory or philosophy, which were usually "just a rationalization of wishes"; his concern was rather with the accumulation of knowledge by empirical methods. "It will be necessary," Ogburn warned, "to crush out emotion and to discipline the mind so strongly that the fanciful pleasures of intellectuality will have to be eschewed in the verification process; it will be desirable to taboo ethics and values (except in choosing problems); and it will be inevitable that we shall have to spend most of our time doing hard, dull, tedious, and routine tasks."[24] Ogburn's views were shared by a large school of "objectivists" in the interwar period, who looked upon this program as a way of insulating the social sciences from political influences and putting them on a firm, scientific footing.[25] Such an approach was also less threatening to powerful interest groups than the reform-oriented social science of the late nineteenth century and Progressive Era. Despite his strictures about objectivity, Ogburn served the Hoover administration as director of the President's Research Committee on Recent Social Trends and the New Deal as an advisor to the National Recovery Administration, the Resettlement Administration, and the National Resources Committee. A white southerner who had been educated in the North, Ogburn had repeatedly tried to obstruct E. Franklin Frazier's grant applications to the SSRC because he doubted Frazier's objectivity.[26] Though not an expert on Negro affairs, he would be tapped by Keppel to evaluate the manuscripts of Myrdal's collaborators.

Donald Young, a sociologist at the University of Pennsylvania, contributed a new perspective to the analysis of race and ethnicity with his *American Minority Peoples* (1932). Rejecting the race relations cycle of Park, Young drew upon methods of cultural anthropology to analyze the culture of various ethnic groups in American society and popularized the term *minority group*, which many social scientists embraced as a more appropriate category than *race* for analyzing social behavior.[27] By the late 1930s, Young's professional role had evolved from researcher to power broker, as he had accepted a position as research secretary on the staff of the SSRC. Like Park and Ogburn, he was committed to the goal of fostering value-free science and was skeptical of social engineering. His own empirical investigations had indicated that educational efforts and moral suasion had little impact on the ethnic prejudices of most people. Young thought that the foundations should spend less money on interracial reform efforts and more on sophisticated social science research on the social and cultural study of ethnic minorities. Though hostile to policy-oriented research, he was tolerant of scholars with different political views and methodologies as long as they produced what he considered objective scholarship. Young emerged as an important advisor to Myrdal, and he recommended scholars with a wide range of methodological approaches and political opinions.

Howard Odum (1884–1954) was the most distinguished southern white sociologist of the 1930s. Trained by G. Stanley Hall at Clark and by Franklin Giddings at Columbia, Odum adhered to the view that it was the duty of the social scientist to provide the public with analyses and policy recommendations concerning social problems. As chairman of the sociology department and director of the Institute for Research in Social Science at the University of North Carolina, Odum helped to develop a southern version of the Wisconsin idea of the state university's obligation to serve the people of the state. A skillful institution builder, Odum developed an outstanding graduate program and sent students to investigate social problems in various parts of the South. His influence extended throughout the region because of his scholarly and popular writings, his service as president of the Commission on Interracial Cooperation, and his close ties to the various Rockefeller philanthropies. Although he was not a major theorist within American sociology, he did play a national role as founder and editor of the *Journal of Social Forces*. During the 1930s, Odum concentrated on developing a regional sociology focused on the South and sought to foster planning for regional development, economic growth, improved social services, and better education. Waste of economic and human resources lay at the root of the South's problems, according to Odum. Yet he kept a certain distance from the New Deal, recognizing the growing unpopularity of Roosevelt among elite southerners.[28]

Ever mindful of the volatility of southern white public opinion, Odum treated the race issue with a caution developed through years of experience as a scholar working in a southern institution. By the 1930s, he had repudiated some of his earlier work and had rejected the idea of inherited differences between the races in intelligence and temperament. He perceived substantive differences between southern black folk culture and white culture while rejecting the idea that black culture retained extensive African influences. Continuing the Sumnerian tradition, Odum assumed that southern racial "folkways" would change very slowly. He strongly condemned lynching and worked to encourage interracial dialogue, but he declined to cooperate with the NAACP and considered integration an unmentionable topic in the South of the 1930s. A gradualist on the question of racial equality, Odum believed that the key to improving opportunities for blacks lay in encouraging economic growth and educational development within the framework of segregation in the South. On civil rights issues, Odum spoke softly, vaguely, or not at all.

John Dollard's *Caste and Class in a Southern Town* (1937) was the decade's most influential case study of race relations in a single community. Trained as a sociologist at Chicago under Ogburn, he conducted research in psychology at Yale's interdisciplinary Institute of Human Relations. Dollard initially sought to record the life histories of a few blacks in the town of Indianola, Mississippi, in order to study personality development. He decided instead to write a general study of caste and class structure in the community based on five months of observation in addition to his life history interviewing.[29] Dollard claimed that he did not wish to make value judgments about southern society. He attempted to identify his own biases as a "Yankee" and sought to be evenhanded in his treatment of the white South. "It must be clear," he wrote, "that we are not attempting to judge the relationships of whites and Negroes or to pronounce a verdict on the social situation from any point of supposed superiority." Dollard thought it "very likely that the emotional situation described herein could be re-created in any part of the country, if ample time were given and if the numbers of the two races were comparable to those in Southerntown."[30]

Writing within the psychoanalytic tradition, Dollard emphasized that the southern caste system afforded whites prestige and sexual gains as well as economic advantages over blacks. In his view, belief in white superiority was not an ephemeral attitude that could be dispelled easily by education; it was deeply rooted in narcissism and in the desire for deference.[31] He explored the complex of fears and repressed desires with which whites view interracial sex and argued that whites see any move toward social equality as a move toward "full sexual reciprocity between the castes."[32]

Dollard noted the contradiction between "national democratic mores" and "regional mores" regarding treatment of blacks, but he found that, instead of confronting this contradiction, most whites chose to take "the easier path of defense . . . which follows the fundamental psychic guide of avoiding painful perceptions." They rely on "defensive beliefs" and stereotypes of black inferiority to justify their caste position.[33] In contrast to the strongly entrenched psychological forces for maintaining the system of white supremacy, Dollard found the forces leading toward change rather weak. Although middle-class blacks bitterly resented discrimination and segregation, lower-class blacks derived certain psychological gains in the form of greater sexual freedom and avoidance of the inhibitions and repressions of middle-class values. Most lower-class blacks, in Dollard's view, were passive in their political attitudes and turned their aggression on each other rather than on the white man.[34] Focusing on the psychology of race relations, Dollard presented a picture of life in the Mississippi Delta as static and ignored the turmoil of the Depression, caused by evictions and population movements of uprooted sharecroppers. He did not believe it likely that the federal government would intervene in the South in civil rights issues, and he thought the American system of government too decentralized to muster the degree of force necessary to ensure southern compliance with civil rights laws. Although the caste system had a "feudal" character that conflicted with modern technological norms, Dollard did not see any imminent changes coming in the Deep South.[35]

While Dollard's book was the most celebrated work of the caste and class school, W. Lloyd Warner of the University of Chicago had also spelled out a "caste and class" methodology in an article in the *American Sociological Review* in 1937. Warner had obtained a grant from the WPA to study the black ghetto on the South Side of Chicago, and his students Horace Cayton and St. Clair Drake were engaged in research that would eventually be published as *Black Metropolis* in 1945. As Myrdal began his study, Allison Davis and Dollard were writing up the results of Davis's research on the life histories of southern black youth, which would be published as *Children of Bondage* in 1940, under the auspices of the

American Council on Education, as part of the American Youth Commission's series on Negro youth.[36]

In addition to using the life history interviewing methods of Dollard and Davis, social psychologists and sociologists developed experimental methods for testing the attitudes of Americans toward various racial and ethnic groups. Although W. E. B. Du Bois and W. I. Thomas had called attention to the issue of race prejudice at the beginning of the century, research on the subject did not really begin until the 1920s, when the debate over immigration restriction led to a heightened concern about reducing ethnic hostility in the United States. In a 1925 article, the Chicago-trained sociologist Emory Bogardus articulated his concept of social distance, which he measured by grading responses to a series of questions about various ethnic groups. Subjects were asked how they felt about intermarriage, social contact, and work with members of a particular group, and whether they would prohibit members of the group from immigrating to the United States. Of the major American ethnic groups, blacks were ranked at the bottom of the scale. Bogardus examined these issues in more depth in *Immigration and Race Attitudes* (1928), in which he observed that contact with members of a different racial, national, or religious group did not necessarily increase tolerance. The contact had to occur under favorable circumstances, or it might reinforce prejudice. Bruno Lasker's *Race Prejudice in Children* (1929), the first developmental study of ethnic hostility, recorded many expressions of prejudice toward various outgroups by children who were only five or six years old. Lasker concluded that the family, neighborhood, school, church, and the wider society all interacted to form and maintain racial and religious stereotypes. To reduce prejudice, reformers would have to change these institutions and to develop strategies for modifying the attitudes of individuals.[37]

In articles published in 1933 and 1935, Daniel Katz and Kenneth Braly examined the attitudes of Princeton undergraduates toward various racial, national, and religious groups and concluded that negative stereotypes did not depend upon personal contact. If a person's reference group condemned association with Jews or blacks, the person probably would conform to prejudiced norms of behavior, even though he might personally like individual Jews or blacks. Racial prejudice was not a function of individual personality disorder, but rather "a generalized set of stereotypes," remarkably consistent in all parts of the country. Eugene Horowitz's 1935 article, "The Development of Attitude toward the Negro," added more depressing statistics to the growing literature on racial hostility. Using a variety of new statistical techniques, the young psychologist tested the racial attitudes of white boys, from kindergarten through the eighth grade, in New York and the South, and found similar levels of prejudice against blacks in both parts of the country. Young children developed prejudices before they entered school, and attending an integrated school did not seem to lessen hostility. Neither living in an integrated neighborhood nor contact with a "nice" Negro appeared to reduce prejudice. The only bright spot in Horowitz's data came from a small group of Communist children tested in New York: the lower levels of prejudice recorded among these children suggested that parental training made a difference. On the eve of the Myrdal study, the literature on prejudice thus suggested that hostility to blacks remained strong in both the North and the South and that intervention to change racial attitudes was difficult and required simultaneous efforts in many institutions. Attitude research and public opinion surveys were in their infancy, and social psychologists were experimenting with new techniques to measure the subtle and elusive processes of stereotyping and the development of prejudice.[38]

Although a burgeoning literature of sociological case studies of southern communities and psychological investigations of racial attitudes developed in the 1930s, no political scientists had written important interpretive books on the effect of the New Deal on the politics of race. Paul Lewinson's *Race, Class, and Party* (1932) was the most recent survey of the politics of race in the South. Harold Gosnell's monograph, *Negro Politicians* (1935), dealt only with Chicago.[39] Similarly, no American economist had presented a broad-ranging overview of the effect of the New Deal on the southern economy and the fate of blacks in the northern economy. Sterling Spero and Abram Harris's *The Black Worker* (1931) antedated the New Deal, Harris's *The Negro as Capitalist* (1936) considered the devastating effect of the Depression on black business, and Horace Cayton and George Mitchell's *Black Workers and the New Unions* examined the role of blacks in the CIO.[40] This spotty economic literature was, of course, supplemented by the sociological work of Charles S. Johnson and the Odum school on southern tenant farmers.

Melville J. Herskovits (1895–1963), the leading American anthropologist specializing in Afro-American studies, challenged many of the assumptions of other social scientists in the field. A student of Franz Boas, he had been an important intellectual opponent of the myth of Nordic superiority during the 1920s and had published research in physical anthropology concerning American Negroes. In the late 1920s, Herskovits began investigating the historical diffusion of culture from West Africa to the Americas. Through field work in Surinam and Dahomey, he became convinced that there were significant cultural continuities between African and New World Negro cultures. Herskovits's most controversial assertion was his claim that blacks in the United States had developed a culture that retained African influences in speech patterns, religion, family life, music, food, and motor behavior. He further claimed that Afro-Americans had influenced white culture, particularly in the South. Herskovits's emphasis on the resilience of African culture patterns under both plantation slavery and urbanization ran counter to the Chicago school model of black culture as an isolated peasant culture that was gradually breaking down under the processes of education and urbanization. His political stance was liberal, and he strongly supported civil rights and integration and praised the interracial unionism of the CIO and the Southern Tenant Farmers' Union. But Herskovits was not a political activist, and he believed that his most important contribution lay in stating the conclusions of anthropological science about race and ethnicity, rather than in addressing policy questions in his scholarship. He thought that the foundations wasted money on interracial reform activities of the sort promoted by Odum and Charles S. Johnson. A professor of anthropology, Herskovits sought to develop an interdisciplinary, objective program of Afro-American studies that was concerned with long-range scientific research.[41]

Black social scientists did not enjoy the luxury of deciding whether to adopt a posture of detachment or one of advocacy. They were obliged to teach at black institutions and their research, for the most part, concerned racial issues. Although leading sociologists such as Charles S. Johnson and E. Franklin Frazier published in the *American Journal of Sociology* and other elite journals, black scholars wrote many opinion pieces for civil rights journals such as *The Crisis* and *Opportunity* and for black newspapers. Leading black social scientists devoted a substantial amount of their time to addressing an interdisciplinary audience of black intellectuals as well as the broader black reading public. Discrimination and institutional isolation combined with political commitment and a sense of social responsibility to foster a more activist stance among black social scientists. Sharp differences existed, however, among black scholars in their analyses of the dynamics of race relations, in their interpretations of black culture, and in their strategies for change.

W. E. B. Du Bois (1868–1963) was the senior Afro-American scholar when Myrdal arrived. Then seventy years old, Du Bois was professor of sociology at Atlanta University, where he had returned in 1934 after resigning from his position as editor of the NAACP journal *The Crisis*. Although he had made pioneering studies in the sociology of blacks in *The Philadelphia Negro* (1899) and the *Atlanta University Studies*, Du Bois was a peripheral figure in the social sciences in the late 1930s. His marginality was not only the result of racism and institutional isolation. He had spent twenty-four years outside the academy as an editor and civil rights leader, and his strident advocacy was considered unscientific in an age that so highly esteemed objectivity and value neutrality. Du Bois's literary and historical writings were seen as further evidence of amateurism and dilettantism by a generation of social scientists so keenly conscious of professionalism and disciplinary boundaries.[42]

Du Bois was also isolated politically from other Afro-American intellectuals in the period. In 1934–35 he had enunciated his "Negro Nation within the Nation" program designed to build black economic self-sufficiency. Du Bois had argued that blacks could not alter the reality of segregation during the Great Depression, that their best course lay in developing black consumer cooperatives and in improving black schools, hospitals, and other institutions. He did not reject integration as a long-term goal but thought that it would come only after blacks had increased their economic power, political unity, and self-respect. Du Bois's advocacy of building a separate black cooperative economy alienated him from

Walter White and the leadership of the NAACP, who continued to support integration. It also drew criticism from younger black radicals who called for interracial
unionism and condemned Du Bois for "black chauvinism."[43] In his analysis of
Afro-American culture, Du Bois was also at odds with many black thinkers of the
1930s. He noted continuities from West African cultures and emphasized the
distinctiveness of black folk culture in relation to white American culture.[44]

Carter G. Woodson (1875–1950) overcame great odds to establish himself as a
pioneering historian of black Americans. He was born into a poor family of ex-
slaves and worked as a coal miner in West Virginia before entering high school at
the age of twenty. After working his way through Berea College in Kentucky, he
earned a master's degree from the University of Chicago and a Ph.D. from Harvard. In 1915, Woodson founded the Association for the Study of Negro Life and
History, an organization that combined professionals and interested citizens in an
effort to encourage research in Negro history and the dissemination of that
research to the black reading public as well as to whites. As president of the
organization and editor of the *Journal of Negro History* for the next thirty-five years,
Woodson was largely responsible for creating the field of Negro history as a
scholarly specialization in an era when it was ignored by nearly all of the nation's
leading historians. Woodson published extensively on many aspects of black
history, gathered thousands of documents, and encouraged a generation of young
black historians. He painstakingly traced the history of black institutions and
sought to understand how Afro-Americans had defined their political, cultural,
and religious response to slavery and freedom. Like most historians of that day,
Woodson remained methodologically conservative, disregarding the trend toward
quantification in sociology and the anthropological concept of culture. He was,
however, one of the few scholars of his generation to examine the African background of the American Negro.[45]

A proud and rather lonely man, Woodson was without a university teaching
position for most of his career. Ignored by the foundations and scorned by most of
the white historians of his generation, Woodson became embittered as he grew
older. Single-mindedly dedicated to the study of Negro history, he kept a distance
from civil rights and reform organizations. He quarreled with Du Bois, and his
relations with many other black intellectuals were icy. Many of the younger
generation of radical black intellectuals dismissed him as a race chauvinist. White
and black scholars agreed that Woodson was hard to work with. Yet the research of
many of his contemporaries in history and the social sciences was greatly impoverished because they failed to examine and follow up his explorations in Afro-
American history.

Charles S. Johnson (1893–1956) was the black scholar most highly regarded in
foundation circles in the late 1930s. After studying with Robert Park at the
University of Chicago, Johnson had been the chief researcher and author of *The
Negro in Chicago*, a study of the 1919 Chicago race riot. From 1923 to 1928 he was
editor of the Urban League's journal *Opportunity*, in which he published many of

the writers of the Harlem Renaissance. In 1928 he was appointed chairman of the social science department at Fisk University. During the New Deal, Johnson undertook consulting and research work for various federal agencies and coauthored *The Collapse of Cotton Tenancy* (1935), which helped lead to the establishment of the FSA.[46] Johnson's most important work was *Shadow of the Plantation* (1934), a study of black tenant farm families in Macon County, Alabama. He dispassionately and meticulously analyzed the effects of the tenant farming system and catalogued the economic deprivation, disease, and poor educational facilities of rural blacks. Johnson discounted the importance of African cultural influences and described his subjects as rural "peasants" whose "backwardness" could be explained by their isolation from the American mainstream and by cultural lag. Although Johnson argued that the plantation system had left a heritage of apathy among rural blacks, he portrayed a more complex institutional life and a more vital folk culture than Dollard had seen or Myrdal would observe. In his interpretation of black family life, Johnson stressed the economic pressures making for early pregnancies and large families: "Every aspect of life urges to the earliest possible attainment of adulthood." He noted that, while southern black tenant farmers attached no great stigma to illegitimacy, similar patterns existed among peasants in various European countries.[47]

Like his mentor Robert Park, Johnson believed that assimilation would be the eventual result of a long-term process of racial conflict and accommodation. He differed from Park, however, in his willingness to advocate government planning and social reform. Although he was denounced by younger black radicals as a conservative, Johnson basically worked within the framework of reform offered by the New Deal while publishing studies that revealed the damaging effects of segregation. Deeply committed to building the social sciences at Fisk University, he played the role of interracial diplomat and cultivated the good will of southern white moderates and foundation executives.

Howard University was a center of radical thought among black scholars in the 1930s. When Myrdal began his study, Abram Harris was chairman of the economics department, Ralph Bunche headed the political science department, and E. Franklin Frazier chaired the sociology department. These young radicals reacted sharply against the "race chauvinism" of the older generation of black intellectuals such as Du Bois and Woodson and rejected the NAACP's traditional strategy of civil libertarianism and moral appeals to elite whites. In response to the Depression, they advocated interracial unionism as the strategy most likely to advance the mass of blacks and to diminish the causes of white hostility to blacks by lifting the lowest class of whites from poverty. Although none of these thinkers advanced an explicitly Marxist theory of race relations, all gave great weight to economic factors in explaining the historical development of racial inequality in the United States. Harris in particular argued that black capitalism benefited only the black bourgeoisie and asserted that Du Bois's program for a separate cooperative black economy was chimerical. Bunche, Harris, and Frazier condemned the New Deal as halfhearted reformism and envisaged some kind of social democratic solution to the United States' economic crisis.[48]

In their views of Afro-American culture, the Howard radicals adopted a strongly assimilationist stance. They held that the concept of race was a myth used by the white power structure to justify exploitation and manipulated by the black bourgeoisie to enhance their position within the black community. Bunche denied the existence of a distinctive Negro folk culture and claimed that "the Negro reflects the prominent characteristics of the section of the country and the class with which he is identified."[49] Frazier was a more thorough-going assimilationist than either Park or Charles Johnson. Where Park and Johnson saw assimilation as a distant prospect, Frazier emphasized that black migration to the cities was breaking down the older peasant culture and that blacks were adopting the values of white American culture. Frazier's classic study, The Negro Family in the United States, appeared in 1939 and strongly influenced Myrdal's conception of black culture and family life.[50]

Most of these specialists in race relations were pessimistic about the possibility of imminent changes in the racial status quo in the South, but they were pessimistic for different reasons. Park and Odum were influenced, in different theoretical frameworks, by the tradition of William Graham Sumner, and they thought that change in the mores of southern whites would be difficult and slow. Dollard's pessimism was based in Freudian psychology and in his idea that the caste system offered whites deeply rooted psychological gains. The young Howard radicals thought that race relations would not change without fundamental economic changes coming first and producing a class-conscious, interracial proletariat. Du Bois was counseling blacks to prepare for a long period of self-help in their struggle to attain equality.

In their analyses of Afro-American culture, Du Bois, Woodson, and Herskovits were among the few scholars who stressed the importance of African cultural influences. Park and Johnson saw rural black culture as a peasant culture that had its own strengths but that suffered from isolation and the damaging effects of the system of white supremacy. Bunche asserted that Negro culture consisted of varieties of white culture which had been damaged by segregation and discrimination.

On the question of the role of political activism in the social sciences, Park, Young, Dollard, and Herskovits avoided direct discussions of policy questions in their scholarship. While Johnson and Frazier sidestepped political issues in some of their articles in professional journals, both discussed policy questions in their contributions to popular journals: Johnson as a liberal, Frazier as a radical. The Odum school was policy oriented but of limited, regional influence. On the whole, the American social science establishment remained committed to an ideal of detachment from politics in the late 1930s, and this orientation tended to isolate black scholars further.

These social scientists who studied race relations were not necessarily addressing each other and were divided by discipline, politics, and race. Their voices were rarely heard by top policymakers in Washington or by the general white reading public. All wrote for national audiences within their respective disciplines; but Odum also spoke to a broader southern audience, and the black social scientists spoke to a broader black audience. Finding a consensus among these discordant voices was a daunting task even for so confident a social engineer as Gunnar Myrdal. Getting representatives of many of these points of view to work together on the same team would not be easy.

If Myrdal's vision of social engineering and policy-oriented social science was at odds with the view of the field's establishment, it nevertheless drew strength from some important trends in American politics and thought. According to one estimate, 2,500 social scientists were employed by the federal government by the end of the 1930s. To be sure, New Dealers such as the Chicago political scientist Charles Merriam insisted that these men and women were using their scientific training to carry out objective studies of economic, political, and social issues. The New Dealers portrayed their work as a process of applying scientific techniques to the solution of social problems, they avoided discussion of moral issues, and they especially shunned any appearance of overt meddling in the race issue in the South. Yet social scientists were conducting studies and advising administrators of government programs in such fields as agriculture, labor, housing, and unemployment relief. They were generating data on a scale unheard of ten years earlier. Critics inevitably asked to what end all this work was being done.[51]

In a series of lectures delivered at Princeton in the spring of 1938, Robert S. Lynd sharply challenged the objectivists' claim that an avoidance of policy questions insured value neutrality. Published the following year as *Knowledge for What?*, Lynd's lectures shook up the social science community and challenged scholars to use their research to bring about purposive social change in American society. He derided the objectivists' lack of theory and asserted that social scientists must have a goal toward which their research is directed. In his view, most social science research served the status quo, and most social investigators were piling up "mountains of data" but were not offering solutions to pressing problems.[52] The Chicago sociologist Louis Wirth, though less strident in his criticism of the objectivists, raised epistemological questions about objectivity in sociological research in an introduction to a 1936 translation of Karl Mannheim's *Ideology and Utopia*.[53]

John Dewey had articulated a concept of purposive social science a generation earlier, and he continued to challenge the positivists in the late 1930s with an alternative vision of social inquiry informed by democratic values and a respect for individual human rights. Dewey had greatly influenced Alva Myrdal's ideas, and both of the Myrdals continued to read his work. In 1939, as Gunnar was organizing his study of the race issue, Dewey published *Freedom and Culture*, in which he argued that social problems were fundamentally moral problems. In an era in which Hitler, Mussolini, and Stalin all engaged in different forms of social engineering, Dewey deplored the infatuation with technique, quantification, and abstract scientific models that social scientists of the era exhibited. Devoting much of his book to Jefferson and the importance of citizens learning democratic practices through participation in local government, he insisted that the "source of the American democratic tradition is moral—not technical, abstract, narrowly political nor materially utilitarian."[54] The social scientist, in Dewey's view, must choose the values that inform his study, and the value choices of the majority of the citizens must guide the uses of social engineering by the state. Dewey's views appealed to a growing number of American intellectuals, who favored an activist social science but worried about the implications of a social engineering detached from democratic control.

As Myrdal pondered the immense task he had taken on, he sought to build on the New Deal's efforts to use social engineering to alleviate problems of poverty and unemployment, but he tried to give a greater sense of direction and coherence to the efforts to attack Economic Problem Number One and its consequences. He attempted, moreover, to bring the black American back into the nation's discourse about poverty and inequality. Myrdal sought to relate the social science activism of some of the black scholars to the larger currents of reform in the intellectual community and in the nation. As he groped for a language that would accomplish these difficult goals and an explicit value premise to guide the investigation, he was drawn irresistibly to the "American state religion," the ideals of the Founding Fathers of which Dewey had written.

A Royal Commission for the "Negro Problem"

On January 28, 1939, four months after his arrival in the United States, Myrdal submitted to Keppel a lengthy memorandum that expressed, in tentative form, many of the value premises and ideas that would shape the book. He emphasized that his primary concern was the solution of contemporary racial problems and that this practical orientation would determine the direction of the study. The historical development of race relations would be included only to the extent that it was absolutely necessary to explain the contemporary situation. "*Practical significance*" would be the "guiding principle for the selection of topics" for investigation. Myrdal was most concerned with current trends in race relations and their implications for social and political programs.[55]

In this early memorandum, Myrdal did not stress the psychological and moral concerns that would dominate the introductory and concluding chapters of *An American Dilemma*. He did not mention the American creed, but he did emphasize that the project would be a study of the Negro "*via* a fresh attempt to reach an understanding of American culture and civilization as a whole."[56] The "Negro problem," in his view, could not be isolated from larger economic, social, and political problems. This approach assumed that black culture was basically determined by white, and Myrdal asserted that Negro culture should be judged by "objective evaluation in terms of accepted American standards." Viewing Afro-American culture from his perspective as a rational, secular, functionalist social engineer, he was struck by the "emotionalism" of the Negro church. He had taken his family to visit Father Divine's Kingdom in Harlem, where they had been seated among the "angels" near the podium. After this experience, Myrdal could only recommend that Afro-American religion be studied by the methods of abnormal psychology. Rejecting the perspective of Herskovits, Du Bois, and Woodson, he thought that African influences on black American culture were insignificant. Myrdal noted one marked difference between Negro culture and white culture: sexual behavior and family patterns, and he attributed that divergence to the heritage of slavery.[57]

Turning to black organizations, Myrdal argued that Negro protest movements were weak because of the absence of a strong labor movement in the United States and because of lynching and other forms of repression in the South. He found that the black elite did not identify its interests with those of the masses. From his rationalist perspective, Myrdal had little appreciation for the role of black institutions in providing Afro-Americans with a sense of symbolic identity and a sense of belonging. He raised the question of whether many Negro organizations, lodges, and churches served a "compensatory" function and kept the masses from forming a "fighting Negro front."[58]

Myrdal devoted a substantial portion of the memorandum to a discussion of economics, and his view of the future for rural southern blacks was pessimistic. The economic planner who had sought to improve the efficiency of the Swedish economy by encouraging small farmers to move to the cities perceived southern agriculture as an inefficient, unproductive, labor-intensive sector of the economy. But given the unwillingness of southern whites to provide industrial employment for blacks, he foresaw a disaster looming, as this surplus rural population had nowhere to go except the welfare rolls. In contrast to the moral and psychological focus of his later work, Myrdal gave great attention to economic "determinants" of black behavior. "The rural Negro's destiny," he wrote, "will . . . be determined chiefly by what happens to agriculture in the South, which is in turn dependent upon technical development in agriculture and the American and world market for agricultural products as well as upon American agricultural policy. The rural Negro is such a large proportion of the total Negro group in America that a study of the American Negro would be very incomplete if it did not embrace an investigation of this main economic determinant." Myrdal was skeptical of New Deal programs designed to reestablish family farms and felt that there was considerable romanticism in the South about the idea of forty acres and a mule. He predicted that technological development would continue to create a large surplus population among farm workers and wondered whether anything could be done to improve their standard of living "under the present political and institutional conditions of the rural South." Myrdal also claimed that there was considerable "wishful thinking" in the South on the subject of industrialization and that the growth of Southern industry could not proceed fast enough to provide jobs for the surplus rural population.[59]

In this lengthy memorandum, Myrdal expressed a strong commitment to social engineering but did not emphasize psychological and moral questions and did not discuss the American creed. He announced his intention to study the Negro within the framework of American civilization as a whole and to evaluate black culture by the standards of the general American culture. In response to suggestions from Donald Young and others, Myrdal had broadened his study beyond the economic sphere; but he still devoted considerable attention to the role of economic conditions in shaping the lives of black Americans, and he was pessimistic about the economic prospects of rural southern blacks. Myrdal sent copies of the memorandum to about fifty prominent scholars and experts in the field of race relations: social scientists such as Franz Boas, Robert Park, and Howard Odum; black civil rights leaders such as Walter White; and white reformers such as Will Alexander and Edwin Embree. Several of these people sent Myrdal comments on his memorandum, and this was the beginning of an elaborate process of consultation with social scientists and reformers.[60]

Many American social scientists initially doubted that a foreigner with no previous knowledge of American race relations could develop a significant new interpretation within the two-year period allotted for the Carnegie-Myrdal project. They viewed Keppel's idea of importing a foreign scholar as another foundation boondoggle that was all the more galling because it absorbed scarce research funds at a time when American social scientists had difficulty getting grants. During his first visits around the country, however, Myrdal impressed American scholars with his formidable intellect, quick grasp of the issues, and dedication to the task he had undertaken. Donald Young introduced Myrdal to Herskovits and Bunche and took them on a tour of Harlem nightclubs. During the excursion Myrdal and Herskovits debated the race issue so intensely that Bunche joked that "those boys just can't break down—they don't know how to relax."[61] After that evening, Bunche wrote Herskovits that "Myrdal impresses me as a real scholar and a hard worker. In addition, he seems to have the faculty of keen perception, so that he will not be easily duped."[62] Herskovits, though miffed that Keppel had not tapped him to head the study, agreed that Myrdal "is a keen person and I particularly like his critical sense."[63] After Du Bois met with Gunnar and Alva Myrdal in Atlanta in April, 1939, he remarked to Ira Reid, "My chief feeling is that he has bitten off a pretty big bite and is going to have a hell of a job in finishing it in two years; but it is on the whole well conceived."[64] Myrdal sought to win the cooperation of Howard Odum and other white southern liberals in a speech to a conference of the Commission on Interracial Cooperation in Atlanta in May. Adapting his message to his audience, he portrayed himself as a champion of "conservative reform" in Sweden and (with tongue in cheek) praised the slow, deliberate methods of royal commissions and parliamentary committees. Ralph

McGill reported that Myrdal "charmed" the delegates, and Odum wrote Keppel that Myrdal's "personality won them over." Odum emphasized that "everybody in Atlanta in the Commission on Interracial Cooperation two-day session was delighted with Dr. Myrdal."[65] Most of the American social scientists still resented the "pot of money"[66] that Carnegie had made available to the Swedish visitor, but they were beginning to respect Myrdal as a serious scholar and came to believe that his study would be influential.

In the spring of 1939, Myrdal began recruiting members of his research staff. His principal advisor on staffing was Donald Young, who was acquainted with many American social scientists through his work with the SSRC. Myrdal sought to establish a small nuclear staff of researchers who would work with him in New York. Most of the independent investigations would be assigned to scholars who would carry on their research at their own universities. None of the collaborators had any power to shape the project as a whole. Myrdal decided what tasks would be assigned to whom. Each collaborator conducted his or her investigation according to his or her own methodological preference, and each retained the right to publish his or her manuscript independently. When Myrdal later drew upon their research in writing *An American Dilemma*, he cited their manuscripts in the footnotes in the same way that he cited published sources.[67]

The Swedish investigator did not seek to develop a team of like-minded social scientists who would engage in a cooperative research program; he welcomed scholars representing a variety of methodologies in the study of race relations, gave them considerable independence in conducting their research, and enjoyed hearing conflicting points of view. Myrdal chose such a diverse group of collaborators in part because he valued individual excellence more than methodological uniformity. But he also wished to remain on good terms with the leading social scientists in the field of race relations, and he wanted them to feel that their views would be represented within his project. Myrdal did not ask for research memoranda from the most senior social scientists in the field of race relations, such as Park, Boas, or Odum. He felt that this was unnecessary, since they had written extensively in the area, and men of such age and stature might not have accepted his direction. He did, however, invite some of their students and junior colleagues to join the study.[68]

Myrdal chose collaborators from all of the leading centers of research on American race relations: the University of Chicago, the University of North Carolina, Atlanta University, Yale's Institute of Human Behavior, Howard University, Fisk University, and Columbia University. His first choice for deputy director of the study was Louis Wirth of Chicago, whom he greatly respected as a sociologist. Although Wirth declined because of teaching obligations, Myrdal visited with him frequently in Chicago and discussed the problem of establishing value premises for the study and other methodological questions. After Wirth passed up the post of deputy director, Myrdal turned to Guy B. Johnson, a close associate of Howard Odum at North Carolina. The other members of the nuclear staff were Myrdal's close friend Dorothy S. Thomas, a sociologist who had worked with him in Sweden; Ralph Bunche; Doxey Wilkerson, a sociologist from Howard; Paul Norgren, a Harvard-trained economist; and Richard Sterner.[69]

In addition, Myrdal hired thirty-one independent researchers to write monographs on various topics. These contributors included established scholars in the field of race relations as well as younger social scientists from major universities. Otto Klineberg, a Columbia University psychologist and student of Franz Boas, studied tests of Negro intelligence and personality and edited *Characteristics of the American Negro*. Charles S. Johnson wrote *Patterns of Negro Segregation* as a memo for Myrdal. The anthropologist M. F. Ashley-Montagu wrote a manuscript entitled "Origins, Composition and Physical Characteristics of the American Negro Population." Louis Wirth in collaboration with Herbert Goldhamer studied "The Hybrid and the Problem of Miscegenation." Edward Shils of the University of Chicago contributed a monograph on "The Basis of Social Stratification in Negro Society." In addition to Guy B. Johnson, three Southern white liberals wrote manuscripts: Arthur Raper, "Race and Class Pressures"; T. J. Woofter, Jr., "The Negro and Agricultural Policy"; and the historian Guion G. Johnson (Guy's wife), "A History of Racial Ideologies in the United States with Reference to the Negro."[70] Myrdal did not hire any conservatives or racists, but he did bring on board a broad contingent of reformers and radicals.

When he began selecting his collaborators in March 1939, Myrdal told an associate that "the whole project is now sympathetically viewed by all except the Chapel Hill group—which is politely antagonistic, probably through fear of competition."[71] The appointment of Guy Johnson as deputy director conciliated the Chapel Hill social scientists, and soon Johnson was helping Myrdal to bring other scholars into the study. Myrdal thought that Herskovits's "bias on the problem of African derivation of American Negro patterns" was "excessive," but he still invited Herskovits to write a monograph on Afro-American culture. As Guy Johnson noted, "It was much more important just to feel that he had got this man [Herskovits] to participate than to get what he was actually going to contribute to the study."[72] In May 1939 Myrdal wrote Johnson, "I went to see [John] Dollard and Allison Davis in New Haven. It was on the suggestion of Donald [Young] that I did this and principally to avoid a possible feeling of exclusion from our study. . . . Both of them seemed to me to be a little sectarian and doctrinal on certain points particularly the class and caste system." But he found Davis an "extremely able and high [sic] cultivated Negro social scientist" and hired him to write a monograph, "Negro Churches and Associations in the Lower South."[73]

In his effort to include a wide range of collaborators, Myrdal took great care to involve black scholars in the study. In a memo in March 1939, Charles Dollard noted that Myrdal explicitly reserved a place for a black on his nuclear staff: "Myrdal wants to gather around him here in New York a nuclear staff composed of one sociologist, one economist, one statistician, and one negro social scientist."[74] Myrdal decided that Ralph Bunche should have the Negro slot on the nuclear staff, and he wrote Keppel that Bunche "seems to be extraordinarily intelligent, open-minded and cooperative. . . . I think also, it would be a great advantage to have at least one Negro on the staff, who would serve as intimate contact with the Negro world."[75] But Myrdal soon moved beyond such tokenism and gave important assignments to a number of black researchers. At Donald Young's suggestion, he hired Charles S. Johnson, E. Franklin Frazier, and the poet and literary critic Sterling Brown to write monographs.[76] In addition, Myrdal sought out other black scholars representing a wide range of views. T. Arnold Hill of the Urban League wrote an analysis of questionnaires circulated by the league concerning Negro business, churches, lodges, and recreation. Ira DeA. Reid, a sociologist at Atlanta University, wrote "The Negro in the American Economic System."

Myrdal hired several younger blacks with socialist views. Bunche, Frazier, and Brown were part of a circle of young radical scholars at Howard University. Doxey Wilkerson and Lyonel Florant were both close to the Communist party, and Wilkerson joined the party in 1942. St. Clair Drake, who was active in left-wing protests in Chicago, authored a monograph, "Negro Churches and Associations of Chicago." These black radicals were hired because they possessed skills that were of value to the project and because Myrdal sought to attract the most talented black scholars, particularly of the younger generation. Frazier, Bunche, and Brown had established scholarly reputations. Drake was an experienced field worker in the urban ghetto who had worked with W. Lloyd Warner at the University of Chicago. Myrdal chose Wilkerson because of "his high qualification in his own field" and because neither Horace Mann Bond nor Charles H. Thompson were available to devote themselves full-time to a study of Negro education.[77]

When asked in later years why he hired so many young black radicals, Myrdal remarked, "It's very difficult to think of a Negro intellectual in that time who was not of a rather radical mind. Where in hell would you get them? It's not my choice. It's history's choice that the Negroes in the situation they were in, if they were intellectually advanced people, they were of course radical."[78] St. Clair Drake, who was brought into the study by Allison Davis for the research on black churches, observed, "The handing out of the assignments was partly to get data for Myrdal, but also it was to pacify these various sectors of potential criticism and opposition [competing social science approaches such as the Chicago school, caste and class, Marxism]. Therefore Davis was going to be given a slice and if he asked for a slice for me he could get it, and so on." Noting the dearth of research opportunities for black social scientists in the 1930s, Drake remembered that "when Myrdal comes in he puts them all on the payroll. Anybody who was willing to get on that payroll is on there."[79]

Another motive for employing these young radicals was explained in a memo by Myrdal's associate Samuel Stouffer: Myrdal believed that the radicals would be more aggressive than other scholars in ferreting out new information about American race relations. Stouffer noted that Myrdal "felt that it would be more valuable for him to get a radical and unconventional point of view, feeling that he could use this as a basis for asking questions of the more conservative and conventional persons and institutions and finally arriving at a better balanced picture than would have been possible if he had worked the other way around." According to Stouffer, Myrdal was influenced by the technique described by Myrdal's friend Russell Davenport of *Fortune* magazine. If *Fortune* wrote an article on a company, they began by collecting muckraking information from critics of the management. When *Fortune* confronted the management with these charges, the management usually revealed information that would otherwise have remained hidden.[80] In discussing Doxey Wilkerson's work on Negro education, Myrdal wrote Charles Dollard, "I need the radical Negro's point of view on the whole matter. The other point of view is easily accessible to me."[81]

During the process of assigning memoranda, Keppel suggested to Myrdal that Alain Locke and Du Bois "should not be left out of the picture." He proposed that Du Bois be asked to write a general memorandum on his conception of the "Negro problem." Keppel also noted that Locke had been educated in Europe and felt that Locke had "been very sympathetic toward the Carnegie Corporation for a number of years." But Myrdal decided against asking for monographs from Du Bois and Locke because they were senior figures who had already published substantially in the field of Negro studies.[82] In his search for talented blacks, Myrdal also overlooked another senior scholar, the irascible Carter G. Woodson, though he did attend a meeting of the Association for the Study of Negro Life and History. Myrdal regarded black history as a "waste field" and gave little attention to historical issues. His failure to establish a dialogue with Woodson or his students would have serious consequences. Myrdal depended upon the southern historian Guion Johnson for his history, and he failed to investigate carefully the growing literature that examined black institutions and portrayed Afro-Americans as historical actors rather than as the objects of white action.[83]

Scholars and university administrators were aware that Myrdal's findings would probably influence the future direction of foundation activities regarding blacks, and many were eager to cooperate with the project. Herskovits canceled a field trip to record the songs of blacks in the Sea Islands of Georgia in order to work on his manuscript for Myrdal. He wrote to the folklorist Lydia Parrish concerning the Myrdal project, "Because of its importance in determining the Foundation grant [*sic*] for future research in the field of Negro studies, it had absolutely to be made a first order of business."[84] Alain Locke thanked Herskovits for mentioning his name to Myrdal and added, "I will gladly cooperate if and when I hear from him."[85] Bunche informed Herskovits that "[Howard] university of course, has been eager enough for me to tie up with the Carnegie Study, for they hope thereby to establish a contact which will be profitable to them."[86]

Leaders of the NAACP, the National Urban League, and the Commission on Interracial Cooperation also assisted Myrdal in his investigation. All three organizations had received grants from the Carnegie Corporation, and they found that the corporation declined to consider new requests in the area of race relations until Myrdal had completed his study.[87] Walter White, national secretary of the NAACP, wrote dozens of letters to NAACP local branches asking for detailed information for Myrdal on issues such as police brutality, legal representation of blacks, and service of blacks on juries. He provided letters of introduction for Myrdal and Bunche to local NAACP officials.[88] Eugene Kinckle Jones of the Urban League told Charles Dollard that the league was "anxious to cooperate actively with Myrdal," and he opened the organization's records to scrutiny by Myrdal's staff.[89] The Commission on Interracial Cooperation "loaned" Myrdal their best investigator and field worker, Arthur Raper.

Civil rights activists realized how much was at stake. Roy Wilkins of the NAACP wrote to Walter White regarding the NAACP's cooperation with Myrdal: "As you have stated repeatedly, this survey probably will be the most important study of the Negro in the last 20 years. Unquestionably its findings will influence procedure along interracial lines for certainly the next ten years and perhaps longer."[90] Wilkins thought that Myrdal's study "would be used more or less as a Bible for Americans to guide them in their treatment of the Negro." He predicted that "the Carnegie report will be a guide for government use, for private enterprise and for public opinion in all walks of life." Wilkins stressed the importance of getting the NAACP's line across to Myrdal so that segregation would not spread from the South to the North.[91]

Myrdal's staff selection was a calculated attempt to involve representatives from the major schools of thought on race relations in American social science as well as members of leading reform groups. As Myrdal acknowledged to Keppel, "When we selected the collaborators we also had other qualities in mind than the ability to write well-balanced monographs."[92] In a period when foundation grants were scarce, Myrdal offered honoraria and research assistance and gave his collaborators substantial freedom in the conduct of their research and the right to publish their manuscripts independently. Guy Johnson observed that this inclusion of American scholars in the project was a crucial factor in producing a favorable response to Myrdal's book:

> In the beginning, I think the idea of trying to include as many important scholars as possible was simply a part of the whole business of the politics and public relations of the research. He wanted the work itself to be comprehensive and representative and he wanted its reception to be good and not be harmed by a lot of hurt feelings on the part of people who were left out. . . . He was thinking, you see, what happens when this is all done and there are important people who had nothing to do with it and who are now going to be commenting and reviewing. He was basically a politician . . . besides being a great scholar. . . . If you hadn't involved all these people and spent all this money and had a thousand names on the list of people that had helped, the reception might not have been as enthusiastic.[93]

After selecting his principal collaborators, Myrdal convened a small conference at Asbury Park, New Jersey, from April 23–28, 1939, to plan the study. The participants included four members of the nuclear staff: Guy Johnson, Ralph Bunche, Dorothy S. Thomas, and Richard Sterner. Donald Young, Charles S. Johnson, and Thomas J. Woofter, Jr., also attended. In a letter to Keppel written after the conference, Myrdal emphasized that the study would examine the opinions of blacks and whites about racial questions as well as the Negro's actual social, political, and economic status. He reaffirmed his intention to study race relations in terms of "the total American picture" and restated his commitment to "consider what changes are being or can be induced by education, legislation, interracial efforts, concerted action by Negro groups, etc."[94]

It was during the summer of 1939 that the idea of the "American state religion" assumed an important place in the study. Myrdal wrote a two-hundred-page "Memorandum on the Disposition of the Study on the American Negro," which outlined the entire project and provided guidelines for his collaborators. In considering values in social science, Myrdal expressed skepticism of social science research which purported to be objective and value-free, and he argued, as he had in the *Political Element in the Development of Economic Theory*, that most works of social science were full of biases which were simply unacknowledged. As an example, he pointed to naturalistic equilibrium models of social change which reinforced the status quo. Myrdal condemned "the common pattern of describing and analyzing a social process in terms of a 'change' from, or even a 'disturbance' in, an initial status of 'harmony' or 'balance,' which then, *via* 'maladjustments' approaches a new 'balance' or 'harmony.' It is clear that the very application of this conceptual apparatus opens the door wide for *any* kind of bias. These terms are value-loaded and, at the same time, indeterminate. . . . The question should be asked: 'balance' or 'harmony' in relation to what norm? 'Maladjustment' or 'adjustment' in relation to what telos? The answer to this question involves a whole sphere of valuations."[95]

Myrdal proposed that a social scientist should explicitly acknowledge his value premises. But if the social scientist was to be an effective social engineer, he had to select as his "instrumental norm" valuations that were held by a substantial proportion of the population. "Excluded from consideration," Myrdal wrote, "are to begin with all whimsical valuations and valuations which have not behind them a considerable number of citizens with a considerable actual or potential power."[96] For the Negro study, he chose as the value premise the American state religion consisting of "ideals of justice, equality, and freedom" expressed in the Declaration of Independence and the Constitution. Myrdal asked his staff to evaluate American race relations in terms of the "instrumental norm" of an "ideally working democracy," and he counseled his collaborators not to be discouraged if their evaluations seemed utopian, that practical political realities would be taken into consideration in forming his final conclusions. Myrdal stressed that "the whole work, finally, should be so pursued that the result should give the basis for what is the supreme task of an accomplished social science, namely rational planning of the 'induced changes.' "[97]

During his first visit to America ten years earlier, Myrdal had been impressed by the ease with which the courts could manipulate the Constitution to achieve probusiness results that were accepted by the public because of the "fetish" of Constitution worship. He and Alva had been amazed by the success of American elites in indoctrinating ordinary people with conservative political views through the public schools' civics classes and through Americanization classes for adults. In pondering the future of socialism in America, he had reported that American workers were deeply conservative and that they identified with American individualism through their uncritical celebration of the national tradition.[98] But if Myrdal was aware of how the American creed could be turned to conservative ends by elites so that it supported laissez-faire capitalism, he chose to ignore this in setting up the instrumental norm for the Negro study. In seeking to identify the struggle for civil rights with the American state religion, Myrdal was adopting a strategy used by the NAACP and other black protest groups, as well as by Popular Front radicals.

Although the American state religion had become the value premise of the study, Myrdal had not yet developed the idea that white Americans faced a moral dilemma or psychological conflict between their egalitarian beliefs and their racist practices. While the social engineer undoubtedly planned to point to the disparity between creed and deed in American political, economic, and social life, the "Memo on the Disposition of the Study" lacks the moral and ideological emphasis of the final book. The white American's conflict between prejudice and democratic values is only one of many social, political, and economic issues raised. Indeed, the memorandum devotes significant attention to the economic status of the Negro. Writing from an expansionary perspective, Myrdal observed, "Most important for the Negroes' fate up till now has been the general development of the American economy. Nearly everything in the Negro's future depends upon whether this frame will be an economy with ten million unemployed or an economy working up to nearly 100 percent capacity. It will also depend upon the degree of state-capitalism." He did hint at the direction of his thinking, however, in his conclusion to the "Memo on the Disposition of the Study": "Particularly the ideological influences on the American racial situation from the growing racial nationalism in Europe should be commented upon, as also the reaction in Europe and other parts of the world to the American way of dealing with the Negro population."[99]

In this long memorandum that provided guidelines for his collaborators, Myrdal articulated his major value premise but left many issues open. The collaborators were asked to contribute to a general study based upon the values of the American state religion and committed to economic and social planning, but Myrdal had not developed a central argument for his book at this point. The study was not focused upon moral or ideological questions and a large share of the research was to be devoted to an analysis of the southern economy. In the context of American politics, he put aside his Social Democratic goals of redistributing income and adapted his economic analysis to the realm of the possible in American politics. With Alva not participating in the study, Gunnar had shelved many of the radical ideas concerning family policy that had appeared in *Kris i befolknings-frågan*. By the late summer of 1939, he had signaled his support for civil rights and equality of economic opportunity for blacks, but he had not revealed a strategy for effecting the "induced changes" that he desired.

Having outlined the main questions and value premises for the study, Myrdal assembled the nuclear staff and research assistants in New York in the summer and fall of 1939. The Carnegie Corporation assumed responsibility for the practical administration of the study because Myrdal had no university affiliation in the United States and because Keppel wished to preserve Myrdal's status as an independent foreign observer who was not closely identified with any American institution or group of scholars. Instead of putting the study in a cloistered ivory tower, the foundation rented prime office space for Myrdal and his staff in the heart of Manhattan, on the forty-sixth floor of New York's new Chrysler Building, at Lexington Avenue and Forty-second Street, across the street from Grand Central Station. A monument to American capitalism, the Chrysler Building was one of the city's tallest skyscrapers, with eagle gargoyles resembling chrome hood ornaments protruding from the sixty-first floor. The entrepreneurial side of Gunnar Myrdal's personality would have ample scope for expression in his suite of fifteen offices plus a conference room. A visiting Swedish journalist noted that the secretaries were equipped with the latest in modern technology—electric adding machines—and the staff members looked more like young bank directors than professors. By the end of the project, Myrdal would reckon his retinue at "6 top staff members, 31 independent workers outside the staff, 36 assistants to the staff members and outside collaborators, and a corps of secretaries and typists."[100]

Although Myrdal tried to present the staff as a model of organized cerebration, their deliberations in fact were chaotic and marked by bickering. The staff did not function as a collective enterprise. Myrdal assigned research projects to individual staff members and generally discussed ideas with his collaborators on an informal, one-to-one basis. He felt that if he was to retain his status as the unbiased foreign scholar, he had to define his own viewpoint and not be bound by any consensus of his American staff. He requested his collaborators' opinions on many subjects, including their concepts of an "ideally working democracy," but there were no formal staff discussions of the American creed or other subjects. Doxey Wilkerson recalled that "it was Myrdal and me . . . and Myrdal and Bunche, and Myrdal and Frazier, not a staff, collective, functioning together." Wilkerson remembered, "There were, of course, meetings of several of us together, but as a normal working operation, it wasn't a staff, planning, deciding: Myrdal did all of that and it was a matter of Myrdal assigning. . . . We all had our respective projects and dealt with Myrdal as such rather than sharing some of the basic ideas that would go into the book." "It was not a jolly company," Donald Young remembered, "Some of them just didn't mesh." Staff members complained that Myrdal was "bombastic" and opinionated. Guy Johnson supervised the day-to-day work of the staff while Myrdal traveled extensively around the country.[101]

Myrdal drove the staff hard, imposing unreasonable deadlines that required the memoranda to be researched and written within a few months. Charles Dollard saw Myrdal as "an enormously active, concerned, determined man—difficult as could be, but with great drive."[102] Myrdal had always driven himself at a ferocious pace and subordinated family and personal concerns to his work, and he expected the same kind of workaholic dedication from his associates. Inevitably, most of the staff members resented this pressure.[103] Bunche joked to Herskovits that "I am back on my slave routine for our Swedish Simon Legree now; he will be on my hands for most of next week." Bunche thought that working for Myrdal was a "valuable experience," but he felt that he was forced to do a "rush job" and wished that he could do his writing "without an ax over my head."[104] At one point, Donald Young told Myrdal frankly that "he had pushed his collaborators as hard as he could without precipitating a sit-down strike and that he'd be wise to lay off."[105] Myrdal admitted that he had become a "bossy bully," but he held firmly to his schedule because he did not want to be away from Sweden for more than two years.[106] He feared that if war broke out in Europe, he would be called home sooner, and if America went to war, his collaborators might be drawn into government service. Despite his limitations as a project director, Gunnar Myrdal did encourage his staff to be original and iconoclastic. "Let us be bold!" he wrote them in February 1940. Myrdal did not want it said that this was "just 'another' study of the Negro, or that we 'pulled our punches,'" and he called for "fundamental insights," "courageous" analyses, and "fresh and far-reaching proposals for social policy."[107]

On the Road

Although Myrdal had been a public official in Sweden and felt at ease among policymakers, he spent relatively little time in Washington. He admired Roosevelt and the New Deal but preferred to maintain a certain distance from federal government officials. This approach was designed to maintain his status as an independent foreign observer, and it also reflected the political reality that the race issue was to a great extent still a local and state issue at the end of the 1930s. Myrdal felt compelled to prove that he "knew the South" at first hand by conducting extensive interviewing in the region. Too close an identification with the New Deal might also have discredited Myrdal among younger blacks who were critical of Roosevelt's inaction on civil rights measures. Finally, as an irrepressible extrovert, Myrdal enjoyed talking with ordinary Americans across the country. The insatiable curiosity that had driven him since childhood impelled him into ghettos and into remote rural areas of the South in an effort to learn the attitudes of Americans about the race issue. Like many American writers of the 1930s, he sought to attain a closeness to experience through extensive travel and relished the "impetuous but temporary intimacy of the stranger."[108]

Myrdal did not conduct field work in any one community; with his thick Swedish accent and contentious temperament it was impossible for him to blend into the American scene. Instead he preferred to visit a wide range of urban and rural areas and to spend only a day or two—or a few hours—in each place. In an era when opinion surveys were in a primitive state of development, he relied heavily on his interviews for his sense of Americans' underlying racial attitudes. Myrdal drew on a wealth of experience in establishing rapport with Americans in different walks of life. With labor union members, he could say that he was a senator elected by a labor party; with businessmen, he could stress that he had been a director of the Bank of Sweden; with farmers, he could emphasize his rural roots; and with law enforcement officers, he could mention that he had been a magistrate in a police court. Myrdal was capable of projecting great warmth and appreciation for Americans' hospitality to foreign visitors, but he could quickly turn the tables and fire away with a line of aggressive questions.

Despite his great interest in methodological questions, Myrdal never systematically examined how his interviewing methods affected the responses that he got. He often did not tell Americans that he was studying the race issue and merely introduced himself as a Swedish educator traveling in the United States. Even so, his status as a foreign professor often evoked from Americans formal explanations of how the political system was supposed to work, rather than candid expressions of how it really operated. In conversation with a foreigner, Americans were inclined to stress the importance of American ideals more than they would have in ordinary, everyday conversations with other Americans. Myrdal sought to get at the attitudes behind the formal pronouncements through a variety of strategies. Sometimes he feigned ignorance. Arthur Raper, who traveled with Myrdal in the Deep South, described him as a brilliant interviewer and observed that Myrdal would explain to a southern sheriff that he was from Sweden and did not know anything about black people and would ask the sheriff to tell him what blacks were like. The sheriff, who would have been suspicious of the motives of any American interviewer asking such questions, would gladly oblige the foreign visitor by candidly providing a full inventory of his prejudices. On other occasions, Myrdal could not resist falling back on debating skills honed in years of legal education, college debating societies, academic conferences, and parliamentary debates. He liked to say controversial things in order to provoke a response. Guy Johnson noted that Myrdal liked to bait people into arguments and that the Swedish scholar assumed that "you don't get at their true feelings unless you get them disturbed a little and catch them off guard."[109]

One of Myrdal's most spirited interviews was with Mississippi senator Theodore Bilbo, whom he visited at the senator's office in Washington. Ostensibly a champion of poor whites, Bilbo had been a strong supporter of New Deal economic reforms but was principally known for introducing legislation that would forcibly remove American blacks to Africa. Myrdal began the interview by telling Bilbo that he had a "rather pessimistic view on the whole Negro problem in America." High unemployment, Myrdal suggested, was turning the "Negro problem" into a "relief problem," and blacks were becoming a "burden on the local and federal budgets." This opening statement created a common ground, and Bilbo replied that he completely agreed. The Mississippi senator declared that the federal wages and hours law, by raising wages in the South, made it possible for "the white man to grab the niggers' jobs," thus increasing black unemployment. Bilbo saw little economic future for blacks in the North because employers would not hire them and unions would not let them join; he therefore saw forced removal to Africa as the only answer.[110]

Bilbo noted, however, that his colonization plan had a second, "higher" motive, the preservation of the white race from the danger of miscegenation. When Myrdal protested that scientific studies indicated that miscegenation was decreasing, the old man shrieked that the increase in civil rights in the North was leading to greater interracial intercourse, because the "smart nigger wants white wives, and some of them have the idea that the outcome of it will be a yellow race of super-men." "Nothing less than the fear of death will keep the nigger from mongrelizing the white blood," the Senator insisted. After Bilbo went on at some length about the Negro's lack of sexual morals, Myrdal inquired whether poor whites were any different, since they too were trapped in poverty and ignorance. Bilbo indignantly replied that the morals of poor whites were "uncorrupted." He explained, "When the poor white man gets uncontrolled and wild he finds an outlet with some nigger woman. This practice results in the preservation of the morals of the white woman."[111]

Myrdal then tempted his host by suggesting that, instead of sending blacks back to Africa, it would be cheaper and easier simply to sterilize them or abort their pregnancies. Bilbo replied, "It is impossible; American opinion would never allow it; as long as the American Republic stands, it is not feasible; it goes against all our ideals and the sentiments of the people." He explained that, when he was governor of Mississippi, he had established an institution for "feeble-minded" whites and had gotten a law passed allowing for sterilization, but he had not dared to carry out the law because of public opinion.[112]

When Myrdal asked how Bilbo's bill to expel blacks to Africa would pass, since most southern Congressmen opposed it, the senator smiled and revealed his "secret" plan. Taking Myrdal into his confidence, he listed several obscure blacks who supported colonization and explained that he was raising the money to send "fifty young, educated Negroes from Harlem" on a "propaganda tour" around the country. "I am going to organize the niggers," Bilbo gloated. "We have several hundred local organizations already," he bragged, organized under different names, such as "the Peace Movement of Ethiopia, improvement organizations, etc." Bilbo promised to arrange a "march of a million niggers to Washington" and proclaimed that "they are going to stay there until every congressman will carry out my bill." After issuing a thundering denunciation of the antilynching bill, the senator excused himself to attend a committee meeting and left Myrdal with his secretary, who provided the Swedish visitor with a list of racist tracts and solemnly declared that Walter White's *The Fire in the Flint* was a "vicious" book that was "dangerous" and might lead blacks to "rebellion."[113]

In his interview with Bilbo, Myrdal alternately played the dumb Swede and tossed out tricky questions designed to get at his subject's underlying attitudes. This interview, and others like it, were important because they convinced Myrdal that even extreme racists in some measure adhered to the American creed. Bilbo's answer to the question about sterilization indicated that even he felt constrained to some extent by the values of the American creed and was not prepared to pervert the American legal system by practicing a fascist solution inside the United States. Blacks, in Bilbo's view, had to be thrust beyond the boundaries of the United States rather than treated in Nazi fashion at home.[114] Bilbo's comments, moreover, deepened Myrdal's impression that poor whites in the South were absolutely obsessed with the specter of miscegenation and that the idea of an interracial alliance of poor people of both races was not practical in the near future. Finally, Bilbo's tirades drove home to Myrdal the danger that the emphasis of Herskovits, Du Bois, and Woodson on the Africanness of the American Negro would play into the hands of Bilbo and other extreme racists. What Bilbo and his ilk seemed to fear most was the insistence of Walter White and other mainstream civil rights leaders that blacks wanted full constitutional rights and assimilation into American culture.

In an effort to get beyond official platitudes served up by safe and "responsible" Negro leaders, Myrdal made every effort to seek out a wide range of black political, labor, and business leaders. At times, this led to some bizarre adventures. The black sociologist Horace Cayton took Myrdal to meet the Detroit labor leader, political boss, and gangster J. Levitt Kelly. According to legend, Kelly had killed a white man in the small Alabama town in which he had grown up and had fled to the North. After working as a pimp in St. Louis, he moved to Detroit, where he rose to become the business manager for the Retail Clerks Association, an AFL union. As the political boss in his neighborhood, Kelly was able to shake down local businesses for "protection," and he also owned the slot machines and juke boxes in restaurants and ran a policy racket. Surrounded by bodyguards, he was a figure to be feared in the black section of Detroit.

Visiting Kelly at his office, Myrdal found him to be a nervous, excitable, energetic man surrounded by three beautiful secretaries who also served as mistresses. Myrdal began the interview by identifying himself as a labor senator from Sweden and calling him "Brother Kelly," whereupon "he laughed in my face to show that he was not deceived." When Myrdal asked how he persuaded blacks to vote for his candidates, the boss replied that he started rumors about the other side, and if anyone resisted, "I go to the man and say 'you realize that I have guns and that I have tough boys with me' and he loves his life." Kelly used similar tactics in labor organizing, threatening the life of employers who resisted, and bragged that "I am the man who can stop all deliveries. I can tell the teamsters' union that this restaurant is not going to get any supplies." The boss took Myrdal and Cayton to a bar and to a restaurant where obsequious managers and waiters kowtowed to him; then he discoursed at some length about how he was leading the proletariat in its struggle against the capitalists. When a Jewish couple that owned a small business in the neighborhood came into the restaurant, Kelly insulted them by saying he admired Hitler's treatment of the Jews as a way of showing Myrdal that even the whites in the neighborhood feared him. At the end of this evening, Myrdal reflected that he had never seen anything like this in his life and guessed that Kelly was "moulding his personality and behavior to the pattern of the white plantation boss in the South as he sees it." Was the deference of Kelly's followers a "hangover from slavery?" "I wonder if Herskovits perhaps sees an African inheritance in this very curious social relation between Kelly and all the other Negroes," Myrdal suggested. Finally, he doubted "that what Kelly is building up can ever be a foundation of a sound trade union movement."

Myrdal and Bunche

In spite of his abrasive personality, Myrdal managed to establish positive relationships with several of the younger black intellectuals. Virtually all of the black scholars were initially suspicious of the Swedish economist and resentful that the Carnegie Corporation should give such lavish funding to this supposedly unbiased outsider at a time when black social scientists earned low salaries and rarely won grants for their research. Yet a few young blacks admired Myrdal's intellectual intensity, his commitment to using social science to foster social change, and his willingness to argue vigorously with them for hours about strategies for black advancement. Myrdal may have been contentious, but he was not patronizing. Moreover, he did not limit his questions to the race issue; he wanted to know what his black friends thought about methodological issues in the social sciences, American domestic politics, and foreign policy. E. Franklin Frazier remarked that Myrdal's "objectivity was apparent from the beginning in his relations with Negroes. They were simply people to him, and their American characteristics impressed him more than their color or the texture of their hair." According to Frazier, Myrdal "could size up a Negro for what he was worth because he did not view him either with the pathetic attitude of most friendly white Americans or through the myths that have grown about Negroes in American life."[115] Kenneth B. Clark, a young graduate student in psychology at Columbia University who served as a research assistant on the study, agreed, recalling that Myrdal argued with him as an equal, despite his status as a graduate student. "He drove himself,"

Clark remembered. "He was enthusiastic, opinionated, but stimulatingly so, constantly searching for answers and usually the first to find them."[116] Clark insisted that "Gunnar wasn't socialized to racism as white Americans are."[117] Walter White found Myrdal to be a refreshing contrast to "stuffed-shirt" academics, someone with whom he could argue about political strategy and tactics.[118] Alva Myrdal was also an important asset in Gunnar's attempts to win the cooperation of black scholars and activists, and the Myrdals socialized with Bunche, Frazier, Sterling Brown, and White.[119]

Ralph Bunche was the American scholar closest to Myrdal. At first the young political scientist had been skeptical about this unbiased Swede with his "pot of money" from the foundation, but he quickly came to respect Myrdal, who gave him the important assignment of studying the political status of the Negro, the programs and tactics of black organizations, and Negro leadership, and provided him with funds for research assistants and extensive travel. If he could not direct the study himself, Bunche thought that at least he could present Myrdal with crucial documentation of voting discrimination in the South and perhaps persuade Myrdal to adopt his ideas about strategies for achieving racial equality. Bunche traveled in all parts of the country interviewing black politicians and civil rights activists, and he supervised field workers who gathered an unprecedented amount of information about black political activity in the South. When the president of the Chicago branch of the NAACP questioned him closely about the study and the uses to which the information would be put, Bunche explained why he had signed on with Myrdal. "Those of us engaged on the survey are entirely free to present the situation exactly as we see it and to propose suggestions and recommendations for improvement of Negro status," he wrote. "We feel that a frank appraisal of the position of the Negro minority in the United States at this time will constitute a striking document and one that should be extremely helpful to the Negro in his struggle for equality."[120]

Myrdal realized that most blacks would not speak candidly to a white man, and he greatly respected the judgment of Ralph Bunche, so he invited Bunche to accompany him on a long trip across the South in the fall of 1939. The two men grew closer as they drove through the South together, observing and analyzing the Jim Crow system. A Californian who had never had to submit to the etiquette of southern race relations, Bunche possessed an outgoing, frank, and direct manner that appealed to the Swedish scholar. Myrdal conceived of himself as an outsider from Dalarna, born in humble circumstances, who had overcome odds to become an important figure in Swedish intellectual and political life. The fact that Bunche, an equally brilliant, well-educated, and accomplished political scientist, was barred from rising to a comparable level of achievement in the United States symbolized to Myrdal the tragedy and irrationality of the color line. Although Jim Crow laws compelled the two collaborators to stay in different hotels and to eat in different restaurants, these inconveniences and indignities did not keep them from working closely together. Bunche spent most of his time with black political

Gunnar and Alva with Ralph Bunche, 1939 (courtesy Sissela Bok)

figures and community leaders, but he also interviewed sharecroppers, workers, and prisoners on chain gangs and was able to give Myrdal a fuller picture of black life. He brought Myrdal together with blacks in private meetings in funeral parlors and churches. At night, Bunche would come in through the back door to Myrdal's hotel, lugging his heavy dictaphone, and would sneak into Myrdal's hotel room, where he transcribed his recordings while the two scholars compared notes on their interviews in the black and white communities. Eventually Myrdal grew impatient with these racial restrictions and he and Bunche marched into a hotel dining room and ordered dinner. No one challenged them, perhaps because of Myrdal's foreign accent and imposing manner and Bunche's light skin color and unruffled behavior. On several subsequent occasions they violated the color bar. Bunche complained that Myrdal's audacity would get them lynched, but they managed to avoid serious confrontations with white racists.[121]

Their closest call came in Georgia, where Arthur Raper joined them on their tour. Myrdal was eager to meet Mrs. J. E. Andrews, editor of the *Georgia Women's*

World. A fanatical white supremacist, Mrs. Andrews had repeatedly claimed in her magazine that Raper had made his female students at Agnes Scott College available to black men, a charge that apparently rested upon the fact that Raper had once taken a sociology class on a field trip to Tuskegee Institute. Myrdal visited her at her home in Atlanta, and after listening to a long tirade about the evils of miscegenation and the lust of Negro men, he asked her if she was aware of psychological theories that people with such sexual phobias secretly desired that which they professed to abhor. At first Mrs. Andrews did not understand him, but when she realized that he was suggesting that she wanted to sleep with a black man, she flew into a rage, threw him out of her house, and shouted at him, "Remember your race! Remember your race!" She then called the police and had a warrant sworn out against Myrdal for indecent language. When Arthur Raper heard about the arrest warrant, he decided to spirit Myrdal and Bunche out of Georgia to Alabama. On their route out of the state, they noticed a car following them for several miles, but they were not sure if the car was in pursuit. Thereafter, Myrdal avoided Atlanta because of the danger that the warrant would be served.[122]

After the fracas with Mrs. Andrews, the two social investigators continued their journey across the Deep South until they reached New Orleans, where Myrdal explored some of the many nuances of race relations in that exotic city. Guided by Richard Babb Whitten, a local white man associated with the study, Myrdal visited a police precinct station and interviewed a police sergeant who bragged about running CIO organizers out of town. Myrdal asked about the organizers' constitutional rights, and the sergeant laughed and said they were communists and that the people of New Orleans did not want them there. When Myrdal inquired about police training, the sergeant said that the only training that the New Orleans police department had was in target practice. Myrdal and Whitten then stopped by a shop owned by a Jewish couple in a black neighborhood, where Myrdal examined their switchblades and bought a pair of brass knuckles and a blackjack as souvenirs. Asked about the parallels between Nazi treatment of the Jews and southern white behavior toward blacks, the proprietor said there was no similarity because the Jews were a superior people and the blacks an inferior race. Myrdal and Whitten then strolled down Rampart Street to the office of the *Louisiana Weekly*, a Negro newspaper, and talked with the editor, a Mr. Alexis, who was a graduate of Harvard with "iron-grey hair and eyes that had a sort of quizical and haughty mien." Myrdal baited him into an argument about black politics, and Alexis prophesied a coming struggle between communism and fascism in which the black masses would be the decisive factor on the side of communism, though he admitted that his own cynical philosophy was to "sit tight and not get out on the limb." The conversation turned to color gradations in the Negro community, passing, and interracial sex in New Orleans.[123]

Whitten and Myrdal ate dinner in the French Quarter, then walked to Canal Street, where they found a cab driver named Whitey whom Whitten knew as a man who would not mind having a black passenger in his cab. Whitey specialized in showing visitors the nightlife and was something of a specialist on the social pathologies of the city. Picking up Bunche that night, Whitey quickly warmed to the business of helping the "Docs" with their research and discoursed at some length on his knowledge of flagellants and esoterica involving bathtubs. Whitey had some difficulty persuading black prostitutes that his three passengers only wanted to ask them questions about their business. Most of the women feared that they were cops. One, after looking them over in the car, shook her head and said, "No, I ain't going to get in there, them is G-Men." Finally, they found two ladies who were willing to invite them to their room for an interview. Bunche and Myrdal bombarded them with questions about their life histories. When Myrdal asked whether the police ever interfered with their business, the women complained that they had more trouble with the police now that Huey Long was dead. Myrdal quizzed them at length about their knowledge of venereal disease and then started asking about their religious beliefs. At that point, both of the women got the idea that Myrdal was a preacher who was trying to reform them. As the Swedish visitor left, one of the women called out, "Doctor, before you try to save somebody else's soul, you better mind out for your own." Whitey took his three passengers to a segregated saloon in the French Quarter, where Bunche passed without difficulty and Myrdal chatted with a white prostitute. Their guide capped the evening's entertainment by taking them to a tawdry, second-story room to see an unusual oral sex show involving a bisexual male and a female prostitute, after which Bunche and Myrdal interviewed the young man about his experiences seducing Tulane boys. After this finale, Whitey drove the three home and, in a great demonstration of tolerance, shook hands with Bunche and wished them well in their efforts to "help people, white or colored."[124]

When he returned to his home in Washington, Bunche complained to a friend that Myrdal "thought he was on a lark, and I was always on the verge of being lynched because of his playful pranks." The young political scientist claimed that "we had to run for it a couple of times . . . and I was always running mentally from lynching-bent crackers."[125] Myrdal was so absorbed in testing and exploring the color line that he did not realize that his mischievous temperament, inquisitive spirit, and love of argument were endangering Bunche's life. Yet Bunche still felt an affection for his Swedish friend, who had become so deeply involved with an issue of social injustice so far from home. Moreover, Myrdal and the Carnegie Corporation opened doors for Bunche and enabled him to interview people who would normally be out of reach and to ask questions that black scholars were rarely able to put to elite whites.

In a two-hour conversation with Supreme Court Justice Hugo Black, Bunche pressed him on the future role of the Supreme Court in guaranteeing Negro rights. The liberal jurist allowed that the Court would have "some significance in pegging out new frontiers for groups whose rights were abused and in aiding them to move forward in their attempts to win their constitutional rights," but he cautioned that the Court "cannot change political opinion in the South." Black made the standard argument of southern New Dealers that the "core of the problem is economic" and that improvements in education, economic opportunity, and health care for poor people in the South would do more for blacks than immediately granting the right to vote to illiterate or semiliterate blacks. He advised Bunche that Negroes (pronounced Negras) should concentrate on these important economic issues and avoid more sensational issues that inflamed white opinion. Black nostalgically recalled his battles against the corporate interests in Alabama and in the Senate and rather lamely excused his early membership in the Klan by insisting that in northern Alabama it had been a "representative of the down-trodden," a "hang-over from Populism," and an enemy of the corporate interests. When Bunche asked him to prophesy the future of race relations in the South, the justice ironically replied that "no legislation can bring about over-night changes in the people's mores, nor can any decisions of the Supreme Court do so; history shows that such changes should come only gradually."[126]

Bunche encountered a more optimistic perspective when he called on Eleanor Roosevelt, who invited him to lunch on the south portico of the White House in May 1940 and answered a list of written questions about the civil rights issue. The First Lady's warmth, concern, and sense of humor "almost made me feel as much at home as though I were on 'U' Street," Bunche noted. He was struck by her intelligence and wrote that "I do not believe I have interviewed anyone about whose sincerity I am more impressed." Mrs. Roosevelt also argued that America's racial problems "can be most effectively attacked on the economic front" but mentioned "citizenship rights," equal educational opportunity, and justice in the courts. Like many white liberals of her day, she thought that "social equality ought to be crossed out of the equation because that is strictly a personal and individual matter." A considerable portion of the conversation was devoted to the war in Europe and the danger of a fascist movement growing in the United States. Mrs. Roosevelt feared that "conditions of racial intolerance in the country, and the disregard for law and authority in the South, are weaknesses upon which Nazi doctrines might well prey." She acknowledged that civil rights legislation and economic reforms faced determined opposition from the southern bloc in Congress but expressed the hope that "current international events might tend to impress the Congress with the necessity for making bold steps toward solution of our internal difficulties in order to present a united front against the Nazi menace."[127]

Among the social scientists with whom Myrdal worked, Bunche and Donald Young expressed two opposing points of view, the two poles against which the foreign scholar defined his position of liberal social engineering. Myrdal respected Young, who had been instrumental in helping him to recruit his staff, and Young had helped him to see, early on, that he was dealing with a complex cultural problem, not just a problem of the South's economy.[128] But he could not accept Young's pessimism about the effectiveness of state action in improving the status of blacks, and he saw the SSRC official as continuing the "do-nothing" tradition of William Graham Sumner. Myrdal found this point of view widespread in American sociology and devoted an appendix of *An American Dilemma* to a critique of Sumner's concepts of "folkways" and "mores" as inadequate explanations of "valuations" in a rapidly changing modern society. The Swedish scholar was particularly eager to defend social engineering against "fatalistic" theories in social science, and he was convinced that he was more in tune with the pragmatic, meliorist spirit of the American people than Young and his generation of American social scientists.[129]

Myrdal also considered Marxism to be a fatalistic theory, and he argued with Bunche and other young leftists about the most effective strategies for combating racial oppression. During their travels in the South, Bunche and Myrdal carried on a spirited debate about approaches to racial change. In *An American Dilemma*, Myrdal cited extensively Bunche's empirical data while criticizing his view that working-class solidarity was the only way to end race discrimination.[130] Though they often disagreed, Myrdal found Bunche's work compelling and provocative.

A democratic socialist formerly associated with the National Negro Congress, Bunche wrote a memorandum for the study entitled "Conceptions and Ideologies of the Negro Problem" in which he argued that the best strategy for American blacks lay in forging an alliance with the white working class. "If there is an ideology which offers any hope to the Negro," he wrote, "it would seem to be that which identifies his interests with the white workers of the nation." Bunche saw "encouraging evidence" that "even in the deep South, it is possible for working class and peasant whites to develop a consciousness of class and to subordinate racial prejudice to economic interest."[131] Much of this encouraging evidence came from the young field workers that Bunche employed to gather data on black political activity in the South. Although Bunche was strongly critical of the Communist party, his research assistant James Jackson, who was closely associated with the party, provided information on labor and radical activities that escaped the notice of most political scientists. Wilhelmina Jackson reported on a student-worker conference in Durham, North Carolina. Black southerners, traditionally viewed by social scientists as politically inert, emerge from Bunche's memoranda as militant, active, impatient with the status quo, and willing to join forces with progressive whites.[132]

Bunche doubted that blacks could attain full civil rights under the capitalist system: "That the full integration of the Negro population into the American society is the only rational approach, seems crystal clear. . . . But into just what sort of American society can this integration take place? Is there any real chance for it under a competitive capitalist economy? Can it transpire under conditions which keep the vast majority of the dominant white population in a position of permanent economic insecurity?"[133] If the poor of both races did not emerge from poverty, he warned that "the Negro may some day find himself marooned in a fascist world."[134] The young socialist strongly criticized the NAACP and depre-

Ralph Bunche, the American scholar closest to Gunnar Myrdal, ca. 1939–40
(courtesy Arbetarrörelsens Arkiv, Stockholm)

cated the "civil libertarian" approach to the black struggle. He asserted that "the political arm of the state cannot be divorced from the prevailing economic structure. Civil libertarianism is circumscribed by the dominant mores of the society. In the final analysis, whatever success it may have must depend upon its ability to elicit a sympathetic response to its appeals from among the influential elements in the white population."[135] Bunche argued that the Negro's "future status here will largely depend upon the political and economic course of the nation. This will prove even more vital to the Negro than his ability to 'develop' himself and to change white attitudes toward him."[136]

In pointing out the difficulty of changing white attitudes, Bunche took aim at what would become a central argument of Myrdal's book. He acknowledged the existence of something like an American creed but claimed that most people had no difficulty in rationalizing their prejudices. Bunche argued that most thinking is "largely 'reflex' and finds convenient streamlined expression through the 'pat response' and the conventionalized stereotype." Although every American learns slogans such as "land of the free" and "land of opportunity," these formulas do not have much effect upon actual social and political behavior. "There are no contradictions, no inconsistencies, too serious to be overcome by this sort of foolproof thinking," Bunche contended. "There can be no contradictions so long as one keeps the faith and utters the mumbo-jumbo of the gospel."[137] On this point, Bunche ironically repeated a point that Myrdal had made in *The Political Element in the Development of Economic Theory*, a book he could not have read because it had not yet been translated. Myrdal had ten years earlier pointed to studies by American sociologists that indicated that "conventional and stereotyped stock phrases . . . may have little bearing on our actual behavior" and had written that "people's declarations about their views on the Negro problem have very little to do with their conduct in daily life."[138] Yet in the late 1930s, Myrdal was eager, as a foreign observer, to ground his study in values that most Americans accepted, at least in theory. He did not commission an evaluation of the psychological mechanisms that white people used to evade their consciences on the race issue.

Ralph Bunche, the black intellectual closest to Myrdal, thus anticipated much of the Marxist critique of Myrdal's American creed thesis before the book was published. Myrdal found Bunche's three thousand manuscript pages of research on black political organizations and leaders brilliant and illuminating, but he attempted to compensate for his friend's left-wing bias by turning Bunche's memoranda over to other scholars and civil rights leaders for criticism.[139] To an extent, Myrdal agreed with Bunche's critique of the NAACP as elitist and ineffective, but he thought that all of the leading black organizations had a role to play in combating segregation and discrimination. In his opinion, Afro-Americans needed several organizations to attack racial discrimination and poverty on several fronts at once: the NAACP's legal strategy was necessary, along with the Urban League's attempts to persuade businessmen to hire more blacks, and the CIO's campaign for interracial unionism.[140] Although he began his research with the impression that improving the southern economy was the crucial first step toward bettering race relations, Myrdal soon realized that he was dealing with a compli- cated social and cultural problem as well, and he spurned any theory that the economic factor was more "basic" than any other factor. Throughout *An American Dilemma*, Myrdal would take pains to refute Marxist arguments, which he consid- ered deterministic and fatalistic. He emphatically rejected the idea that blacks could not make any progress until a strong interracial movement formed among workers. The Swedish observer saw no reason to modify the view he had formed on his first visit to the United States that American workers were sharply divided on racial and ethnic lines. In Myrdal's view, if the civil rights struggle had to await the formation of an interracial working-class alliance, it might wait forever.

Myrdal's experiences in both Sweden and America convinced him that most poor people were really quite conservative except on issues of immediate self- interest. The problem for the social engineer, in his view, was "first to lift the masses to security and education and then to work to make them liberal."[141] On the issue of an interracial working-class alliance, Myrdal felt that Bunche and other left-wing blacks did not grasp the depth of racism among white workers. In *An American Dilemma*, he would argue that "the Negro's friend—or the one who is least unfriendly—is still rather the upper class of white people, the people with economic and social security who are truly a 'noncompeting group.'" Regarding the competition of poor whites and blacks, Myrdal would invoke a Swedish proverb: "When the feed-box is empty, the horses will bite each other."[142]

While Bunche and Myrdal differed on questions of political strategy, they were in basic accord in their views of black culture. The young political scientist was not particularly interested in cultural issues and was deeply suspicious of Negro ideologies that exalted Afro-American culture and race pride. He charged that "such Negro intellectuals as Dr. Woodson, and loutish chauvinists such as Garvey, have set themselves to the task of creating a counter-irritant to the white concep- tion of the Negro." Bunche asserted that this line of thought "often tends to accentuate the antipodic division between the groups."[143] Like his colleague Franklin Frazier, Bunche emphasized the destructive effects of white racial dis- crimination and economic deprivation on black culture. Parting company with his friend Melville Herskovits, he declared that "'the Negro' is strictly a sociological phenomenon in this country, the product of a series of historical accidents, with his collective identification resting primarily upon the color of his skin, the texture of his hair, and most importantly, the white man's conception of him as a 'Negro.'"[144] Bunche thought that disfranchisement, discrimination, and poverty had prevented blacks from developing coherent political ideologies. "Most of these Negro ideologies," he lamented, "are characterized by an immaturity of thought, an uncertainty of approach and a vagueness in objectives." The "contrib- uting factors to this condition," according to Bunche, were "the peasant back- ground and psychology of the Negro and his resultant lack of institutional sophistication; together with the intellectual lag consequent upon the long years of servitude and denial of educational opportunity."[145]

Other Afro-American intellectuals associated with the study reinforced Myrdal's tendency to view black culture and institutions as essentially similar to their white counterparts but weakened by pathological elements resulting from racial oppression. Franklin Frazier, whose important book on the Negro family appeared just as the Myrdal study was getting under way, wrote a couple of short essays for Myrdal and served as a critic of the final manuscript of *An American Dilemma*. Frazier saw himself as a tough-minded student of race relations, developing an analysis of the destructive effects of racial discrimination and capitalism on the families and culture of Negro peasants in urban areas. In the late 1930s, he hoped that an interracial proletariat would create a new culture and politics to replace that which he saw breaking down. Allison Davis and St. Clair Drake, in their monographs on black churches and voluntary associations, portrayed those institutions as fiefdoms of a black middle class: backward-looking, beset with "cultural lag," and out of touch with the needs of the masses and the requirements of the black struggle.[146] Horace Cayton, who could have taught Myrdal much about the strategies for survival of poor blacks in the urban ghetto, failed to turn in a promised memorandum on the social structure of the Negro group, and in his role as Myrdal's tour guide, led Myrdal into a bizarre underworld normally beyond the ken of white scholars.[147] The black scholars around Myrdal thus reinforced the Swedish visitor's own perception that black Americans were culturally very much like white Americans, except that the group suffered from more "social pathologies" like broken families, crime, disease, and prostitution as a result of poverty and discrimination.

As American intellectuals worried about the possibility of fascism developing in the United States, many black intellectuals sought to stress the Negro's Americanism and feared any ideology that might single out blacks as scapegoats or play into the hands of racists like Bilbo. Alain Locke, who had always sought to balance his claims for the Negro's distinctiveness with an emphasis on the race's "contributions" to American culture, urged Myrdal to make the "dominant point of view" of his study "the interaction of Negro and white cultural factors and influences." In the ideological context of the late 1930s, Locke muted his own cultural pluralism and warned Myrdal that "the widespread notion of Negro culture as separate and sui generis is very unscientific and contrary to fact."[148] Locke, like most of the black intellectuals whom Myrdal knew, criticized Herskovits's "dogmatic obsession" with African influences on Afro-American culture.[149]Sterling Brown, the poet and Howard University English professor, socialized frequently with Gunnar and Alva Myrdal and entertained them by reading his poetry, reciting ballads, and playing blues records. Of all of Myrdal's collaborators, Brown had the most subtle understanding of Afro-American folklore and the traditions of resistance developed by blacks in the rural South. Unfortunately, this subtlety was lost on Gunnar

Myrdal, who never had much of an ear for music and was much more interested in politics than literature.[150] Brown's memorandum for Myrdal on Negro cultural achievements did not really explore the nuances of Afro-American folk culture. Preoccupied with other projects, Brown spent little time on his memorandum for Myrdal and produced a dull, superficial survey of blacks' contributions to mainstream American culture in entertainment, sports, and literature.[151] Since several of Myrdal's black collaborators turned in incomplete or weak memoranda, Ralph Bunche's three thousand manuscript pages would appear to Myrdal as the most complete and articulate statement by a black intellectual of the current goals and status of the race.

In addition to all these influences, Myrdal believed that, as a foreigner, he could see more clearly and objectively than most people in the United States how "American" blacks were in their political beliefs, religious behavior, institutions, and culture. Cultural differences that might have seemed significant to Americans appeared less striking to a Swede. He believed that European immigrants were assimilating rapidly into American culture, especially in the wake of the Immigration Restriction Act of 1924. While their cousins were madly killing each other in Europe, people from different European ethnic groups seemed to be forming a common identity as Americans and learning to get along. Myrdal also had many contacts with immigrants who had achieved success. His cousin, who had emigrated from Dalarna as a young man with little education, had worked his way through college and law school to become a lawyer with the Social Security Administration.[152] Myrdal's friends included immigrants such as Felix Frankfurter, who had risen to positions of prominence in American society. Since Myrdal traveled little in the Southwest or West and had little contact with Asians, Mexican immigrants, or Native Americans, blacks appeared to be the one ethnic group that was not assimilating rapidly into American culture and sharing in the economic opportunities available to other Americans. Were Negroes to be the great exception? he asked white Americans.

From his arrival in New York in September 1938 until his departure for Sweden in May 1940, Myrdal struggled intensely to understand—and to change—the American pattern of racial inequality. Though he had initially accepted Keppel's invitation as an intellectual challenge, a problem in social engineering far removed from his own experience, the study soon became much more than that. After Myrdal saw the desperate poverty of most Afro-Americans, the system of legalized segregation and discrimination, and the racial violence in the South, the research project became a challenge of the utmost personal importance to him. He demonstrated masterful skill in organizing a large social science research project. An experienced politician, he succeeded in forming a research team that included representatives from all of the major schools of thought on race relations within American social science. Quickly winning the confidence of Frederick Keppel, Myrdal expanded the scope of the study to a size almost unprecedented in social science research in the United States. If the interactions of the staff sometimes

Sterling Brown (ca. 1939–40) delighted the Myrdals with poetry, stories, and blues recordings (courtesy Arbetarrörelsens Arkiv, Stockholm)

seemed like a cacophony of divergent voices, Myrdal learned much by matching wits with his American collaborators, and he drew insights from many of them. Though he rejected Donald Young's political quietism, Young helped him to see that he was investigating a cultural issue as well as an economic problem and introduced him to many of his collaborators. Ralph Bunche produced crucial research memoranda on black politics and protest movements, and Frazier helped to shape Myrdal's perspective on the social pathologies of the black poor. While Myrdal disdained the gradualism of Howard Odum, he drew heavily upon the research of two of Odum's students: Raper's study of extralegal violence and Woofter's research on the southern economy. In informal discussions with Louis Wirth about methodology in the social sciences, Myrdal sharpened his commitment to making his value premises explicit and to using as an instrumental norm the American state religion. Even when he differed with his collaborators, such as Bunche, Young, Herskovits, and the caste and class school, Myrdal defined his own positions through vigorous debates with these American scholars.

Myrdal sought to engineer social change in accordance with his conception of America's democratic values, and his collaborators provided access to a broad range of data and opinions about race relations. Few social investigators have ever had access to so many corners of American society. As a Swedish senator, Myrdal was introduced to the U.S. Senate by Vice-President John Nance Garner and allowed to walk around on the floor of the Senate, where he talked with Harry Truman and Robert LaFollette, Jr. He had meetings with two members of Roosevelt's cabinet, Henry Wallace and Henry Morganthau, Jr. As an economist, he addressed the *Fortune* Round Table. But Myrdal also went to great lengths to seek out the poor and the dispossessed in an effort to understand the violence, repression, poverty, and social pathologies of black-white relations. He traveled the back roads of the South with Arthur Raper and Ralph Bunche, interviewing prisoners on chain gangs and the guards who watched over them, interrogating union organizers and a wizard of the Ku Klux Klan. Using black collaborators as contacts, he visited northern ghettos and interviewed black editors, politicians, businessmen, gangsters, and communists.

By the time Myrdal left for Sweden, he had planned a large research project based on the value premises of the American state religion and had commissioned memoranda on various subjects, but he had not yet formulated the problem of American race relations in the psychological and moral terms that would mark the introduction and conclusion of *An American Dilemma*. Since the moral dilemma thesis had not yet been developed, there was no empirical testing of that hypothesis by Myrdal's staff. From the fall of 1938 to the spring of 1940, Myrdal's efforts had been primarily directed toward investigating the scope of the economic problem in the South, identifying the potential sources of political change, and understanding the cultural complexity of black-white relations. The theme of the "Negro problem" as a problem "in the heart of the American" would emerge more fully when he contemplated American race relations from a different vantage point, neutral Sweden surrounded by Hitler's New Order of Europe.

4

My War Work

The threatening political situation in Europe was never far from Gunnar Myrdal's thoughts as he traveled through the small towns of the South and the ghettos of the North from the autumn of 1938 to the late summer of 1939. When he had left Sweden, Myrdal had believed that there would not be a second world war. Germany, in his view, lacked the resources to win a war, and Hitler would not dare to start one.[1] Still, Myrdal worried about what might happen to Sweden and whether he should be away during this difficult time. He and Alva constantly discussed European affairs with diplomats, politicians, journalists, intellectuals, and refugees. In February 1939 he wrote a Swedish friend: "We certainly feel very distressed about the whole world crisis and especially political relations in Europe. The American newspapers and magazines give a quicker, clearer, and more intensive survey of the course of events than the press in any other country. It is as though we are sitting in the orchestra seats of the world's theater. In the fall there were a few weeks when we could scarcely work because of anxiety over the world situation and especially the consequences for our homeland."[2]

After the German invasion of Poland in September 1939, Myrdal wrote to Ernst Wigforss, the finance minister and his closest friend in the Swedish cabinet, offering to return to Sweden if Prime Minister Per Albin Hansson wanted him for government service. He felt an obligation to complete his research on the American Negro, but he assured Wigforss that neither he nor Alva Myrdal wished to be "egotistical and forgetful of [our] duty as Swedish citizens." He wrote that "we have a dark feeling that we . . . do not have the right to stay away from the country in such difficult times. It is for us almost immoral that we should be fortunate enough to continue to work on constructive long-term problems." He insisted that "if Sweden is drawn into the war, we shall come home without an order upon first notice."[3]

Prime Minister Hansson did not order Gunnar Myrdal home, and the Swedish minister in Washington advised him to continue his research project on American blacks. Meanwhile, Alva Myrdal assumed a prominent role in the campaign to support Finland during the Soviet-Finnish Winter War of 1939–40. Although Sweden remained neutral during the war, eight thousand Swedes volunteered to fight for Finland, and Swedish organizations sent supplies to aid the Finns. The Myrdals strongly sympathized with Finland and saw the Soviet invasion of Finland as a grave threat to Swedish independence and to the neutrality of the other Scandinavian countries. Alva Myrdal joined with ex-president Herbert Hoover and other Americans in the campaign to raise money in the United States to aid Finland, and she made speeches on behalf of Finland's cause in cities across America.[4]

It was difficult for the Myrdals to get a clear picture of Swedish attitudes toward the war in 1939 and early 1940. Herbert Tingsten, a young Swedish political scientist and friend of the Myrdals, wrote them in December 1939 that he anticipated a Soviet or German invasion of Sweden. Tingsten explained that "here we now sit in fear of war and expect that everything is going to go to hell within some weeks or months. If this does happen, we thought that we would try to get to the USA. We will, of course, not leave before the dissolution sets in and we no longer can do anything useful." In the event of an invasion, Tingsten believed that he would be killed by either the Communists or the Nazis, and he sent the Myrdals money to put in their bank account in New York in case he should have to seek refuge in the United States. Tingsten emphasized that this precaution should be seen "not as a question of fleeing in advance but of a guarantee if one is forced to flee." "Perhaps you think this seems hysterical," he wrote, "but the fear here is tremendous. Like many others, we are obtaining poison and revolvers in case we should have to commit suicide." Tingsten insisted that these actions should not be seen as weakness. "The majority [of Swedes] would now want to participate directly in the war against Russia," he claimed, "if it were not clear that Hitler would then attack us and Finland would ultimately go down as a result."[5]

Gunnar Myrdal replied that he and Alva had been on the verge of returning to Sweden for six months, and he requested more information about the situation in the country. Countering Tingsten's pessimism, he affirmed his intention of returning home if Sweden should be attacked:

> We certainly don't want to stay out if Sweden is involved in the war. Personally we just don't like the idea of being refugees. Our feeling runs very definitely along these lines: farmers and workers can never be refugees. They have to stick to their country for better or worse. It is only the intellectuals who can run away. . . . Our primary reaction is that we want to be home. Of course it means a great disturbance of this big study which I am directing and I feel a certain loyalty also to my work; but that is in spite of everything a minor factor if we could be of any use in Sweden.[6]

In the spring of 1940 Gunnar Myrdal declined an opportunity to establish himself permanently in America when he was approached about a tenured position as professor of economics at Yale.[7] He was determined to return to Sweden by the fall of 1940, even though the future of his country remained uncertain. Finland had concluded peace negotiations ceding a substantial amount of territory to the Soviet Union, and Germany was at war with France and Britain. In despair, Myrdal wrote a Swedish friend, "Everything is terrible. The whole ideological basis for all of our interests and ideals seems to break down."[8]

"The World's Problem in Miniature"

As they followed the developments of the war in Europe and the American debates between isolationists and interventionists, both Alva and Gunnar Myrdal compared the strengths and weaknesses of democracy in Sweden and the United States and the capacity of both societies to resist pressures from dictatorships. For several years the Myrdals had been interested in the role of public opinion and ideological preparedness in resisting totalitarianism. The importance of propaganda in influencing opinion during World War I had been widely discussed on both sides of the Atlantic, and the Myrdals had observed the effectiveness of Nazi propaganda during the 1930s. In the spring of 1939, as American intellectuals debated whether American democracy was tough enough to stand up to totalitarianism, Gunnar Myrdal had been invited to give the Bronson Cutting lectures in Washington, D.C., which were published in *Survey Graphic* magazine under the title, "With Dictators as Neighbors." He had argued, before the outbreak of the war, that Sweden could not win a conventional military victory if it were invaded by Nazi Germany or the Soviet Union but that it could strengthen its "ideological defenses" by preserving individual liberty and democratic institutions. As long as the Swedish government was just, no disaffected minority would invite foreign intervention. The best defense for a small nation, he had claimed, was to strengthen its democratic practices so that any invasion would meet with determined resistance from an entire population.[9] Gunnar Myrdal had amplified this point in an interview with Marquis Childs in June 1939. Swedes would never accept totalitarianism, he had declared, and would continue to fight by every means possible, even if conquered by a dictatorial power. Myrdal had wondered if Americans were equally committed to preserving democracy and remarked that "perhaps your democracy began too early. You take it for granted. With us it began late and we are very conscious of the need to make it a workable way of life."[10]

By August 1939, Gunnar Myrdal's estimation of American political culture had risen as political conditions in Europe worsened. "We still believe in this culture," he wrote Gustav Cassel. "It will survive in a mainly democratic, liberal Western form, even if Europe 'goes to the dogs'; and in the next generation it will lead the Western civilization to heights not thought of yet." Myrdal confessed, "If we were Americans we should feel sorely tempted to become isolationists, to simply let Europe handle her own crises and war as best it can and build up America with a minimum of international obligations." Although he noted the strength of the isolationist impulse and the danger that it would dominate American foreign policy if the Republicans came to power, Myrdal predicted that the United States would get involved if war broke out in Europe because "the people are so full of religion and morals that they cannot let things take their course." He praised the climate of free discussion in the United States, the absence of censorship, and the critical discussion of foreign policy in the American press. Contrasting an essentially healthy American society with a troubled Europe, he observed that "here they still live in a land where people do not fear air raids and poison gas."[11]

That same month, Alva Myrdal addressed the issue of ideological preparedness in a lecture on "Education for Democracy in Sweden" at the Congress on Education for Democracy at Columbia University's Teachers' College. Taking up the question of how democracy was to survive in a world in which dictatorships were growing in strength, she insisted that education was crucial to "the fortifying of the survival value of democracy for tomorrow." Although she criticized the "formal and rigid" qualities of Swedish public schools, Alva Myrdal pointed to Swedish adult education programs as a model for America and praised the "high degree of civic activity and cultural participation in the Scandinavian countries." Always more radical than her husband, she argued that democracy is not an abstract theory to be handed down to the people by leaders or intellectuals, but a practice and a life-long process of learning in which ordinary citizens must participate. Sketching an idealized picture of Swedish social democracy, Alva Myrdal argued that workers and farmers developed skills of critical analysis in adult education programs, which they then applied by participating in political parties, labor unions, cooperatives, and women's organizations, and she insisted that "if education is to be for a working democracy, I believe that the masses are far more important than the leaders." She issued a challenge to Americans: "There is simply no chance for getting a thorough democracy in countries where citizens are passive—passive in the management of their local affairs, passive in their churches, passive in their organizations of business life, passive as consumers, passive in the arrangements on the labor market, passive in their own education."[12] At the Teachers' College symposium, Alva Myrdal also participated in a seminar on "Education and Minorities in a Democratic Society" in which the participants sought to apply the concept called "education for democracy" to the question of American minority groups. The participants concluded that "the democratic conception demands that these inequalities in educational opportunity be eliminated" and declared that it was the "peculiar responsibility of educators to support civil liberties in this critical period of our nation's life."[13]

From the fall of 1939 to the spring of 1940, Alva Myrdal wrote several articles for Swedish magazines in which she analyzed the strengths and weaknesses of American democracy and probed public opinion in the United States concerning the war in Europe. In November 1939, she described the American people's "righteous indignation" against fascism in spite of the fact that their material self-interest would seem to dictate an indifference to events in Europe. "I never thought that I should see a moral valuation grip people who could be comfortably indifferent," she remarked. Although the American people did not want their sons to go to war, they were not neutral in their attitudes toward the war, she observed, citing a *Fortune* poll that indicated that only 1 percent of Americans supported Nazi Germany. Alva Myrdal referred to the mental conflict that Americans experienced between their sympathy for the Allies and their commitment to a policy of neutrality as a "moral dilemma," a term that her husband had used a decade earlier in writing about Swedish welfare policy. She emphasized that American neutrality was based on the premise that England and France would win the war and suggested that if the Allies began to lose, American opinion would shift dramatically in favor of military intervention. In conclusion, she predicted that the "moral dilemma of neutrality" would become "more and more difficult" and contended that "the American people are writhing indecisively in agony over the problem of whether it shall be their duty to make the world's unhappiness their own."[14]

In probing American public opinion, Alva Myrdal also investigated the question of whether fascism was growing in the United States. Father Charles Coughlin, in her view, was interesting as a extreme example of a broader tendency in American culture to view the Old World as hopelessly corrupt. She compared his views to the early ideology of the Nazis because of his combination of anti-Semitism and hostility to capitalism, but she determined that his influence was limited to the urban Catholic masses in this largely Protestant nation.[15] The other potential source of fascism, according to Alva Myrdal, was the South. She characterized the southern states' "political and economic condition, with its great class inequalities, limitation of the right to vote, illiteracy, and racial persecution as a type of fascism." But she qualified this judgment to say that the South's "fascism" was "of the old-fashioned kind, which more properly is called feudalism." Alva Myrdal insisted that these reactionary tendencies in the South were growing weaker, that southerners did not hold up these conditions as an ideal, though they often used them as an excuse for racially prejudiced behavior. The tendencies toward fascism in the Coughlin movement and in the South were the exception rather than the rule, in her view. American opinion was strongly liberal and anti-Nazi.[16] In her 1939 articles, Alva Myrdal thus framed the conflict between fascism and democracy as an ideological and moral conflict, in which intellectuals and educators played a crucial role, and she optimistically predicted that democratic values would win out over class and racial inequality in America.

While Alva Myrdal lectured to women's and educational groups about Swedish social democracy and wrote articles for Swedish magazines about American foreign policy and domestic reform, Gunnar concentrated on his study of black Americans during the spring of 1940. He continued to prod his collaborators to complete their memoranda, and he kept up a punishing schedule of travel and interviewing, writing to Cassel that "no one in this era has seen America from the inside more than I have." As the Nazi armies advanced across Europe, Gunnar Myrdal came to believe that "in my investigation I have the world's problem in miniature: the whole aggression-complex and the circle of prejudices, violence, and poverty." "The race problem is even greater than the war," he concluded. "For the first time I can grasp the full reality of the whole colonial problem." Although Myrdal wanted to fulfill his obligation to serve Sweden during the war emergency, he confided to Cassel that he would concern himself with international problems after the war. "After the accumulated experiences of the world war and America's

Negro problem," he wrote, "I can never again really interest myself in the local problems of our little, idyllic land, if it survives. . . . I can never become really interested in practical problems other than those which affect the whole world."[17]

The news that Gunnar and Alva Myrdal had long dreaded came on April 9, 1940: German armies had invaded Denmark and Norway. The Myrdals, believing that Sweden would be the next target for Hitler's advancing armies, began making plans to return home. On Sunday, April 14, they walked through the Norwegian-American section of Brooklyn and found the whole community stunned and outraged. Bells rang for Norway in all the churches. People gathered around radios and discussed the invasion. They saw Norwegian seamen crying openly in a bar.[18] Gunnar Myrdal explained to an American colleague that "the most probable outcome of the present course of events, as far as Sweden is concerned, is that my country is going to be involved in a war against Germany within the next few weeks." "In such a case," he continued, "my services will probably be needed in Sweden or elsewhere for the rest of the European war." Myrdal acknowledged the "possibility that Sweden perhaps after a very short war will share the fate of Denmark and Norway and become a province of Germany." He concluded, "These are difficult words . . . to write for a Swede who has never reckoned on such an eventuality for his country and himself."[19] The Myrdals' decision to return home was definitely a joint one. Alva Myrdal wished to resume an active role in public life in Sweden during the national crisis, and she was prepared to take the three children back to Sweden without Gunnar if he should decide to stay in America to complete the Carnegie Negro study.[20] So Gunnar Myrdal wrote Keppel that, while it was "heart-breaking" for him to leave the Negro study, it was "the right thing to do in this catastrophe which has stricken the world."[21]

Frederick Keppel accepted with good grace Gunnar Myrdal's decision to return to Sweden. He appointed as acting director of the Negro study Samuel Stouffer, a sociologist from the University of Chicago and former student of William F. Ogburn, known for his statistical work. Richard Sterner was named as Stouffer's assistant. Keppel evidently considered a sociological quantifier to be the next best thing to a foreign observer in preserving an aura of objectivity for the study. He believed that the appointment of Stouffer and Sterner would "place the direction of the enterprise in the hands of competent persons not conspicuously identified with current controversies in the field." Stouffer's task was to ensure that Myrdal's collaborators turned in their monographs and memoranda as quickly as possible. Keppel hoped that Myrdal would come back to America to write the main report for the Negro study, but he set up a committee to evaluate the collaborators' manuscripts for publication in a series so that the corporation would have something to show for its efforts in the event that Myrdal did not return.[22]

As the Myrdals prepared for their departure, their friends wondered if they would ever see them again. A sense of shared danger strengthened the bonds between Myrdal and his American colleagues. Reflecting on his experiences with Gunnar Myrdal in the South, Ralph Bunche bade him an emotional farewell:

I like to think of you, Gunnar, as one of the truly great characters I have met in this life. It has been a pleasure to know you, to work and travel with you, and to count you as a valued friend. . . .

It is with the deepest feeling that I wish you well, Gunnar. I admire your courage, your conviction and your love for your people and country. I know that you and Alva are needed there and I understand the compelling motives behind your desire to return. . . . My personal regard for you both and my fear for your welfare are contrasted with my happiness at the knowledge that you are making this great sacrifice in order to strike vigorous blows in defense of freedom, democracy, and human decency. No other cause has ever been so vital to humanity, and when the opportunity arises here, as I think it will soon, I will be only too eager to put my shoulder to the same wheel.[23]

Some of the Myrdals' American friends pleaded with them to remain in the United States for the sake of their children's safety, but Alva replied that she and Gunnar would have a "guilty conscience" if Sweden should be conquered while they stayed in America. Melville and Frances Herskovits and other friends offered to take care of the Myrdals' children, but Alva declined these offers because she believed children should share the fate of their parents and native country.[24]

Both Alva and Gunnar Myrdal had a record of antifascist activities, and they realized that they might be interned in a concentration camp or killed if the German army invaded Sweden.[25] They knew that Social Democratic intellectuals with similar views had been imprisoned in Germany. Gunnar Myrdal took precautions by giving his close friend, the economist Arthur R. Burns, a list of prominent Americans, such as Keppel and Secretary of Agriculture Henry Wallace, who would try to exert pressure on the German government if the Myrdals should be detained. He also invented a code for sending messages to Burns from Europe, with such items as "Tell [Jacob] Viner my manuscript is ready"—meaning that Gunnar Myrdal was in prison. Preparing for the worst, Gunnar issued instructions to Burns on how to settle his financial affairs in the event of his death.[26]

It was not easy to find passage to Sweden at a time when nearly all of Europe was at war. Obtaining the necessary permissions took more than two weeks of frantic "wire-pulling," involving the Finnish and Swedish ministers in Washington and London, the British ambassador, the U.S. State Department, the Carnegie Corporation, and the British shipping minister, Arthur Salter, who was an old friend of the Myrdals as well as an advisor to the Carnegie Corporation. Diplomats were incredulous that this Swedish family wanted to sail back to a war zone at a time when thousands of European refugees were desperately trying to flee to America. After several additional days of agonizing delays, the Myrdal family sailed for Petsamo, Finland, on the *Mathilda Thordén*, a Finnish freighter.[27]

Once aboard, the Myrdals discovered that the *Mathilda Thordén* was carrying a cargo of dynamite packed in barrels on the deck, and they learned that the ship would pass near German mines off the coasts of Britain and Norway. During a storm the barrels of dynamite rolled around on the deck. When the ship sailed beyond radio contact with the United States, Gunnar and Alva knew that there was no turning back, that they were in the middle of the North Atlantic, beyond the safe world of America and headed toward a continent shaken loose from its old moorings. As the ship neared the British Isles, they listened to the radio, eager to hear about the fate of Norway and Sweden.[28]

The Myrdal family reached Petsamo safely, then traveled to Stockholm by plane and rail. On their return, they were interviewed by a reporter for *Dagens Nyheter*, a newspaper critical of the Social Democrats, who commented that the Myrdals had hurried home "in a half-panicked mood." Gunnar Myrdal seized the opportunity to predict that the United States eventually would enter the war because "the puritanical religion plays a great role 'over there' and world affairs are judged . . . as moral problems." Despite the government's neutrality policy, Americans were strongly anti-Hitler, and their political attitudes were pervaded by moral perceptions to an extent scarcely conceivable in Europe. But Myrdal failed to link this observation about American moralism to his research on the race issue. When asked about the "Negro question," he insisted that it was chiefly an economic problem and noted that unemployment was concentrated more and more among the Negro population, a situation with dangerous consequences for the whole nation.[29]

Gunnar and Alva Myrdal sent their children to live with relatives in Dalarna, where they would be safe if the German air force bombed Stockholm, and prepared to do their part in defending the country. As they walked around Stockholm, they found that an uneasy quiet had settled over the city. Alva's first impression was that "time had just stalled here," with "everybody looking as before and living as before." But suddenly she felt that "a new emptiness" lay underneath the surface. Although Swedes went calmly about their daily business, the Myrdals saw for the first time fortifications, sandbags and air-raid shelters in their capital. They were also shocked to discover that a few of their friends had turned into "outright nazis," though the majority still "walk[ed] upright."[30] Gunnar and Alva Myrdal called on officials in the government to offer their services, but neither was given an important post. Like the rest of their countrymen, the Myrdals waited to see what would happen next. "We had traveled home to a war, but the war did not come," they wrote. "Each day as the sun went up over the land in peace, we felt a happiness which gloomy news from the rest of the world and anxiety about the future could only prick at the edges. We had traveled home expecting duties, but no duties sought us."[31]

Sweden's strategic position in the spring and early summer of 1940 was extremely precarious. There was a possibility that the war in Norway would spill over onto Swedish territory as well as the danger that Hitler would simply decide to occupy Sweden to ensure total German domination of Scandinavia. In all probability, a German invasion would have overwhelmed Swedish defenses throughout most of the country in a matter of days.

Neutrality was the cornerstone of Swedish foreign policy. Since the Napoleonic era, Sweden had avoided involvement in European wars. During the First World War, all the Scandinavian countries had succeeded in maintaining their neutrality, but Hitler's blitzkrieg in the spring of 1940 created a radically different situation. After the fall of France in June 1940, Germany established military hegemony over the European continent. With their country encircled by German armies, the Swedish government pursued a policy of military mobilization and diplomatic accommodation designed to convince Hitler that an invasion of Sweden would not be worth the cost.[32] The question of how far to go in making concessions to German demands was an issue that bedeviled Sweden's neutrality policy from 1940 to 1943. Immediately after the invasion of Norway, the German government demanded rail transit rights across Sweden to reinforce German troops in Norway. The Swedish government at first refused to comply, but caved in under pressure and allowed more than two hundred German technicians and medical personnel to travel by rail through Sweden to the German garrison at Narvik. After the end of the fighting in Norway and the capitulation of France, Swedish representatives negotiated a transit agreement which allowed limited numbers of German troops to travel to and from Norway by Swedish railroads. Sweden also continued to trade with Germany during the war and exported iron ore and precision equipment, including ball bearings vital to the war effort.[33]

During the war, Sweden was ruled by a coalition government that included all of the major political parties except the Communists. Headed by the Social Democratic prime minister Per Albin Hansson, the government sought to foster a spirit of solidarity and to avoid divisive fights that might weaken national unity. In the wartime crisis, the government concluded that some forms of censorship were a political necessity. Throughout the war, the German minister in Stockholm filed repeated protests with the Swedish government concerning criticism of Germany in the Swedish press. Shortly after the German invasion of Denmark and Norway, Marshall Hermann Goering told a visiting Swedish delegation in Berlin that Hitler was personally annoyed at the attitude of the Swedish press. In the late summer and fall of 1940, the Swedish press became the hottest issue in German-Swedish relations. Swedish officials publicly and privately called on the newspapers to exercise restraint in their discussions of Germany. In September 1940 in response to strong German protests, the Swedish government confiscated issues of the *Göteborgs Handelstidning*, a major metropolitan daily newspaper. Foreign Minister Christian Gunther explained that the action was taken "to show that the government was not unfriendly to the Germans." The Swedish government had previously confiscated issues of several radical publications.[34]

Within the Swedish press, a considerable diversity of opinion existed in the summer and fall of 1940. Some newspapers argued that Sweden should accept the reality of German hegemony in Europe and accommodate the country's diplomacy and trade to the New Order. This accommodationist line sometimes included a critique of parliamentary democracy and demands for strengthening the power of the Swedish state. Other newspapers took an isolationist view that the Swedish government should take whatever practical steps were necessary to keep the country from being invaded and the press and public should avoid debate on foreign policy so as to give the government the broadest possible latitude. Another camp openly sympathized with Britain and held that the Nazi dictatorship would eventually collapse. These advocates of resistance called for a policy of strict neutrality, an active discussion of foreign policy, and a grounding of Swedish policies in ethical principles.[35] Gunnar and Alva Myrdal's sympathies were with this third point of view.

Life in wartime Sweden was frustrating for Gunnar Myrdal. He had interrupted a major research project in the United States to return home when his country was in danger, but there were severe limits to what he or anyone else could do in the face of German military might. Myrdal had given up his seat in Parliament, and he held neither an important government office nor a key position on a government commission in 1940. He had been away from Sweden for a year and a half—a long time in the tightly knit world of Swedish politics. Myrdal's introduction to political life had been in the early 1930s, an era of ambitious long-range planning and bold reform, and he felt out of place in a wartime situation that required crisis planning and reaction to events. His blunt and outspoken style was equally ill-suited to the coalition politics of the war years, in which caution and restraint were the virtues of the hour.[36] Shortly after his return to Stockholm, *Dagens Nyheter* ran an editorial cartoon that portrayed the king and the leaders of the coalition government in a comic posture aboard a bicycle built for fifteen. Gunnar Myrdal was depicted in a bib and baby clothes riding in a baby-seat at the tail end of the tandem bike.[37]

Facing a strong possibility of failure both in his study of American race relations and in his political career at home, Myrdal identified with Abraham Lincoln—"a man who still at 45 years of age could say of himself that he had failed in everything." "What would Lincoln's destiny have been if he had been born a Swede?" he wondered. After describing all the obstacles that Sweden's "more rigid," bureaucratized society would have placed in Lincoln's path, Myrdal still hoped that Swedes would be willing to listen to a man who, like Lincoln, possessed only "a burning sense of justice, a strong intellect, and a clever tongue."[38] He notified Keppel that he would have to stay in Sweden for several months. "I am under no delusion that I should be particularly indispensable at home," he wrote. "In the present course of events over here no single man or even group of men seem to mean much: destiny has its run." But, he explained, "The national life is under pressure and we in Sweden have to stick together. If even a few left, and for ever so good reasons, it would look like an attempt to escape and, what is worse, it might work into the hands of the defeatists." Myrdal insisted that he could not leave "as long as there is substantial risk of bombs being dropped here." He confided to his American mentor, "We are now under the acute pressure of the war of nerves. To say that we are anxious not only on behalf of ourselves but distressed for the sake of our whole western civilization is no exaggeration."[39]

In a letter to his close friend Richard Sterner, who had remained in America, Myrdal described the situation in Sweden after the fall of France and the end of the war in Norway: "The press is strangled. Nothing gets written against Germany. News is suppressed." He expressed his hope, however, that the Swedish government would soon allow a free press again. Myrdal declined to advise Sterner on whether he should return to Sweden but conceded that America might be a "more congenial milieu for a Swede of the 1930's than the changed homeland." He affirmed that he and Alva intended to stay in Sweden as long as "the values we have lived for have any future hope in the country: if one can fight for them. But if the country establishes itself as a little, happy Mecklenburg within the greater fatherland, we shall emigrate if we are then able to do so."[40] Myrdal complained to Samuel Stouffer that "Sweden is in the pocket of Germany and we have to behave. Life is doomed to be inactive and I hate it."[41] But inactivity was a condition utterly alien to Gunnar Myrdal's temperament, and he occupied himself during the tense months of the summer and fall of 1940 by advising Finance Minister Wigforss on economic planning, entering the debate on accommodation and press freedom, and formulating his ideas about American race relations in lectures at the University of Stockholm.

In Swedish politics, Myrdal supported the coalition government and concluded that the transit agreements with Germany, however objectionable morally, were politically unavoidable. He did, however, question some of the government's policies. On June 27, 1940, Myrdal met with Prime Minister Hansson and urged him to begin making preparations for a resistance movement in the event that Germany invaded Sweden. He suggested that the Landsorganisation, Sweden's trade union congress, should deposit money in foreign banks that could later be used to support a government-in-exile, and proposed that one of the cabinet ministers should be sent abroad to prepare the ground for such a refugee regime. Both Gunnar and Alva Myrdal believed that the local organizations of the trade unions and the Social Democratic party could form the infrastructure for a resistance movement if the country were occupied, and they thought that it was essential to begin the process of strengthening grass-roots organization and preparing the people ideologically to resist Nazism. Hansson dismissed these suggestion on the grounds that if word leaked out that the party was preparing for such a contingency, it might be interpreted as defeatism or lack of confidence in the Swedish army's defense preparations. This rejection did not deter Alva Myrdal, who circulated an unpublished memorandum to Social Democratic women's groups calling on the party to buy portable printing presses and radio transmitters that could be hidden in various parts of the country, ready for use by a resistance movement. In addition, she helped to develop adult education courses that would strengthen commitment to democratic principles and help people to understand the Nazis' propaganda techniques.[42] Gunnar Myrdal also staked out a strongly anti-Nazi position in Swedish political debates, warned that dictatorships might defeat the democratic nations in this war, and suggested that Swedes must be prepared to preserve their ideals of democracy and to carry on a resistance movement for decades, perhaps generations.[43] Yet the Myrdals did not go too far in their criticisms of government policies; their objections were phrased carefully so as not to alienate Hansson and the Social Democratic leadership. They did not throw in their lot with Ture Nerman, a dissident Social Democrat who served three months in prison for his vehement denunciations of Hitler in his weekly paper, *Trots allt!*[44]

From the beginning, Gunnar Myrdal was troubled by the Swedish government's restrictions on freedom of the press and by the danger to democratic institutions posed by too great an accommodation to Europe's New Order. In his first memo to Wigforss after returning from America, Myrdal complained that public opinion was "underfed" and called on the coalition government to explain its policies in a public document "which gives in clear relief the value premises, tendencies, plans, and aims." He urged that such a statement was "necessary first as a foundation for a more concrete and intelligent common discussion and for the formation of public opinion."[45] At the University of Stockholm, Myrdal circulated a paper to his colleagues in the social sciences and law calling attention to the erosion of civil liberties in Sweden since the beginning of the war. Writing just after the government had seized issues of the Gothenburg newspaper, he criticized the action as a violation of press freedom unprecedented in his generation and questioned the legal basis for other violations of individual rights, such as the opening of letters and the censorship of telegraph and telephone communications. Myrdal conceded that some extraordinary steps had to be taken in wartime to protect national security, but he was apprehensive that a series of legal changes made under exceptional circumstances would add up to a fundamental structural change in Swedish law in which the safeguards of civil liberties would be weakened. He feared a breakdown of the Swedish *rättstat*, the state that safeguards the freedom of the individual. "We must not let the legal system glide like a glacier, accommodating itself to the pressures of wind and weather," he warned. "The problem must be analyzed intellectually and that duty falls especially to the country's legal and political scientists." By directing attention to fundamental principles of democracy and civil rights, scholars could "make a contribution to the strengthening of the resistance power of the social principles . . . which can be assumed to be affirmed by practically all of our people."[46]

During the summer and fall of 1940, both Gunnar and Alva Myrdal concentrated on the issue of strengthening the "ideological defenses" of Swedish democracy. Alva Myrdal worked actively to stimulate an intellectual and ideological resistance to fascism, organizing forums for women's groups on topics such as "the war for democracy," the situation in occupied Norway, and help for refugees.[47] In contrast to official government propaganda, which was generally more hazy in calling on the citizenry to defend the Swedish way of life, the Myrdals explicitly linked the defense of the country to the preservation of democratic institutions and freedoms in Sweden. They believed that the Swedish people were basically democratic in their attitudes, but that some members of the "intellectual middle classes" waffled and the bureaucracy and government were sometimes out of touch with the people. It was the responsibility of Swedish intellectuals, in their view, to think clearly and to focus discussion on the principles that the country stood for. Even if the situation looked grim from a military point of view, intellectuals had the duty to continue their work of furthering free discussion and debate. Gunnar and Alva Myrdal's position thus paralleled Jean-Paul Sartre's observation about the responsibility of the French Resistance: "Because the Nazi poison was introduced into our thoughts, each accurate thought was a conquest."[48] In their efforts to counter Swedish attitudes of accommodation and defeatism, however, the Myrdals would engage in a fair amount of wishful thinking about both Sweden and America.

Contact with America

As they attempted to respond to the altered world of Swedish politics, Gunnar and Alva Myrdal reflected on their experiences in America and found that their admiration for the United States had increased substantially. During their first visit to the United States in 1929–30, they had felt a strong affection for the American people but had been sharply critical of the vast inequalities in American society and the lack of economic and social planning by the government. When they had returned in 1938, they had come as experts who had helped to create the Swedish welfare state, visitors from a more "advanced" society much admired by American liberals. Both had been sought after for speaking engagements and interviews, and Alva had lectured on Scandinavian democracy, education, and family policy while Gunnar had spoken about Swedish economic planning, farm policy, and royal commissions. Resuming life in wartime Sweden had been a shock. They had encountered not only a grave military emergency but also a society ridden with fear and pessimism, in which civil liberties were curtailed and some influential voices called for a policy of accommodation to Nazi Germany. In this context, the Myrdals came to view American democracy in a much more favorable light. Alva declared in a magazine article in July that the United States had experienced a "revolution" during the 1930s and was developing a social system more like Swedish social democracy, with the Social Security Act, farm subsidies, public housing, and improvements in public health and education. "The American people know," she insisted, "that if they are to be ready for world responsibilities, they must 'strengthen their social defenses' by quickly carrying out domestic reforms."[49] The Myrdals' admiration for the United States was controversial in Sweden, and Alva was assailed for being anti-German and for glossing over flaws in American society, such as the "Negro problem."[50] Alva and Gunnar Myrdal were concerned that most Swedes knew so little about the United States, and they decided to write a book about America for a Swedish audience, analyzing American society and government with comparisons to Sweden. Gunnar brought to the project his knowledge of American race relations, the South, the economy, the legal system, and American domestic politics, while Alva brought an expertise in social psychology and an involvement with American education, social welfare programs, women's groups, and Scandinavian-American relations. In the summer and fall of 1940, they synthesized various magazine articles, papers, and speeches into a book entitled *Kontakt med Amerika* (Contact with America), which was published in 1941.[51]

Kontakt was a resistance book designed to convince Swedish readers that the triumph of Hitler's vaunted New Order of Europe was not inevitable. The United States, which had not then entered the war, was portrayed as a source of hope for occupied Europe. Addressing a broad audience of Swedish readers, the Myrdals argued that a common belief in democracy and individual freedom united the peoples of Sweden and the United States. A central theme of *Kontakt* was the importance of strengthening Sweden's ideological preparedness. The Myrdals feared that Swedes were not as conscious of their liberties and rights as Americans were. Although they considered Sweden to be one of the most democratic societies in the world, they believed that Swedes needed to be vigilant about the erosion of their liberties, particularly in the area of government censorship of the press. As they looked back on their time in America, they were struck by the widespread knowledge among the American people of a U.S. citizen's rights under the Constitution. An ordinary American could explain his belief in the American creed of democracy, equality of opportunity, and individual freedom. But the Myrdals wondered whether Swedes had a belief system strong enough to resist pressures to refrain from criticizing Nazi Germany. They sought to make the Swedish people more conscious of their democratic traditions as a counterforce to defeatism and acquiescence in the inevitability of a Nazi-dominated Europe.

The authors began the book by recalling how they felt as they sat aboard a freighter filled with dynamite in the middle of the Atlantic on their way back to Sweden from the United States in May 1940. With their country surrounded by German armies, it looked as though everything they had believed in and worked for might be swept away: Swedish democracy, a social science based on free discussion, and the whole tradition of rationality and freedom of thought stemming from the Enlightenment. The Myrdals felt that many European intellectuals, by adhering to a fashionable pessimism after the First World War, had failed to offer a principled resistance to totalitarianism and had lost touch with the aspirations of ordinary people. They expressed pride in the contribution of Swedish social scientists to an enlightened and progressive program of social reform during the 1930s but wondered if Swedish intellectuals would have the strength to maintain traditions of free discussion and open criticism in wartime. As their boat approached its destination, the Myrdals feared "that we should have come home to a land that spiritually had given up."[52] In the midst of these dangers, they reflected on the importance of the United States as a strong, free, and fundamentally democratic nation that stood as a powerful alternative to Nazi Germany. Although their first loyalty was to Sweden, they felt at home in America as well. They considered the similarities between Sweden and the United States in their democratic institutions, reform traditions, and common heritage of the Enlightenment. And they remembered that one-third of the people of Swedish descent lived in the New World and would remain free even if Sweden went under. As the weeks passed during the summer of 1940 and the German invasion of Sweden that they had feared did not materialize, the authors came to believe that they could make a contribution to the Swedish citizens' understanding of their own society and the world by reporting on their "contact with America."[53]

After introducing the book on this personal note, the Myrdals devoted a chapter to the American creed. They conceded that "glaring inequalities and swift growth are what the observer first notices" in the United States but maintained that a common belief system helped to provide stability and unity in this heterogeneous and dynamic country:

> The secret is that America, ahead of every other country in the whole Western world, large or small, has a living system of expressed ideals for human cooperation which is unified, stable, and clearly formulated. The political belief system is not simply as among us, latent, unpracticed principles which—in degrees of compromise—find expression in the nation's laws and political order. Furthermore, the principles have been made conscious and articulate in all social levels. Every American has had them stamped in his consciousness. In America we referred to "the American Creed" . . . in our conversations with both the learned and the unlearned. . . . A poor farmer in Minnesota, an ordinary immigrant in Chicago, a Negro school teacher in the South can all give a full, satisfactory account of the Constitutional civil rights and freedoms of the citizen. Each of these people knows what the Constitution is and he knows which parts of it are important for him personally.[54]

The Myrdals contrasted this widespread knowledge of the American creed with the situation in Sweden, where a more legalistic and formalistic system of rights had developed without the public's becoming highly conscious of the fundamental moral norms of the society. A member of the Swedish parliament might be able to explain in detail the citizens' rights and freedoms, they averred, but an ordinary person could not.

The authors praised the American penchant for self-criticism and willingness to publicize America's ills to the world. Referring to Gunnar Myrdal's commission to study the "Negro problem," they inquired whether anyone could imagine "that the German Reich should have called in a foreign researcher to make an unbiased report on the country's most serious race problem—the Jewish question."[55]

Gunnar Myrdal recorded that he was traveling in the American South during the fall of 1938 when persecution of the Jews in Germany reached a new level of intensity. The southern newspapers all condemned the persecution. He recalled that he

> was very often together with the journalists in different places. They have a fine tradition in the South and often represented the top social knowledge and insight concerning both the local area and the nation. I often asked them how they could attack the persecution of the Jews in Germany so strongly since their own blacks and often many of the poor whites did not enjoy more security. The answer was, "But we do not say that what happens is right! That is the difference between America and Germany: here this state of affairs is against our ideals. The federal government and the Supreme Court strive openly and honestly to change this and the best people all over the nation as well. Few people dare to question the justice of these aims."[56]

Gunnar Myrdal then developed what would become the central argument of *An America Dilemma*: "The Negro problem, just like all other difficult social problems, is therefore in the first place a problem in the Americans' own heart. One can also say that it represents a conflict between a national ideology—which is described above—and dissimilar local ideologies which diverge from it. Both kinds are contained within the same American, and their conflict within his breast reflects the nation's perpetual ongoing moral and social development. The local ideologies correspond more directly to what one calls interests, as distinguished from ideals."[57] He asserted that this conflict between national ideals and local ideologies existed even within the mind of the most racist and reactionary southerner:

> The American Creed is alive deep down in every American, although often in conflict with other norms. When I traveled in the South and became intimately acquainted with the leader of the Ku Klux Klan, the Imperial Wizard Dr. Evans, and many other prominent and less prominent reactionaries in that part of America, which is very far from a democracy in a fuller sense, I used to carry out the following experiment. I chose the starting point in their strongly reactionary social viewpoint, containing among other things the acceptance of a static upper and lower class system of a caste nature among people. Then I led them up on the mountain of temptation through pointing out to them that society could be shaped after their own model more effectively and advantageously if they were ready to use modern scientific techniques of physical violence and psychological influence, as demonstrated by Nazism and fascism, instead of relying on cheap legal tricks, unorganized mob justice, and sometimes general social pressure. I never found more than one result of my experiment: They defended themselves

strongly and brought up from the bottom of their moral consciousness all of the American Creed. Their own actions could be excused but should by no means be made the rule, least of all for the nation.[58]

Gunnar Myrdal concluded from his interviews that "moral ideas really represent social forces, although unfortunately not the only ones and not always the strongest." He criticized the tendency of American social scientists to underestimate the social importance of moral ideals. "In America," he wrote,

> a rather extreme materialistic view of history has become dominant within social science, especially sociology, in the last generation. For our part, we consider this tendency to be the most questionable one-sidedness within an otherwise especially differentiated and excellent social research. It originated as a basically moral reaction against an earlier generation's one-sided idealism. Sociology developed in America as the writings of ministers and social reformers. It broke free, especially under Sumner and the Chicago School through studying with the utmost suspicion all the arguments containing morality. It gradually became the custom to explain exhaustively everything through generalizations about economic interests.

Myrdal noted the paradox of this intellectual skepticism about ideals in the midst of a strongly moralistic culture.[59]

The American creed was not simply a vague set of social norms, according to the Myrdals. It was deeply rooted in the ideas of the Enlightenment, anchored in the Constitution, and powerfully conveyed through the public school system and the pervasive moralism of the Protestant churches. Summarizing their view of the American creed, the Myrdals asserted that "there is scarcely any doubt that the national value system is continually increasing in influence. . . . The Supreme Court judges according to it. . . . Churches preach it. Schools teach it. A great part of the whole adult education activities are 'Americanization education.' "[60] The authors noted that Gunnar Myrdal had had the assignment of becoming an expert on America's social defects during the previous two years, when he had "lived in two separate worlds: the ruling white majority's world and the oppressed Negroes' world" and had seen the "disfiguring psychological marks on both the oppressed and oppressor." "He knows quite precisely how much more of wickedness, injustice, and weakness still remain in America than in Sweden," they acknowledged. "But he has also learned how much more there is of goodness, desire for justice, and magnificent strength." As foreign observers, the authors believed that they could see clearly that "the moral pulse beats much more strongly in the American civilization" than in most European cultures.[61]

The Myrdals arrived at this exaggerated notion of the importance of the American creed partly by listening to American intellectuals from the fall of 1938 to the spring of 1940. In response to the Great Depression, many writers had journeyed to the heartland of the United States in an effort to discover "authentic" American voices of protest, in contrast to foreign "isms."[62] During the period of the Popular Front from 1935 to 1939, intellectuals on the left had sought to anchor contemporary radicalism in the nation's democratic traditions, and Communist party spokesmen had embraced the slogan, "Communism is Twentieth-Century Americanism."[63] As Nazism, Fascism, and Soviet Communism grew more powerful in Europe, American liberals also endeavored to strengthen the "American democratic faith," to develop an American democratic ideology tough enough to stand up to totalitarianism. After the outbreak of World War II in Europe in September 1939, both interventionists and isolationists had framed their arguments in terms of preserving America's democratic values.[64]

The American creed thus meant different things to different intellectuals in the United States. To the Myrdals it meant, above all, civil rights, civil liberties, a free press, and democratic decision making. They argued that the creed was constantly being strengthened by forces in American politics, law, and religion, and that American public schools were spreading the democratic ideal throughout the society and creating a more democratic future for the nation. Alva Myrdal had visited many progressive schools and considered the ideas of John Dewey and his followers to be the cutting edge in American education. Education, in her view, was "America's most meaningful export to other lands" because of the "national tendency to take initiative, to think along new lines, and to experiment." In contrast to the educational systems under dictatorships, American education endeavored "*to liberate human energy*" and to create "richer and more complete possibilities for growth."[65] While Swedish teachers were often rigid and authoritarian, American educators cherished spontaneity in children and sought to foster independence and self-reliance. Alva Myrdal also praised American schools for bringing together children from many different ethnic and religious backgrounds and teaching them democratic values and skills of cooperation. She conceded that there were some horrid one-room schools in the rural areas of the South but maintained that they were the exception, not the rule. Most Americans, in her view, saw education as a mission, central to the goals of the society. Public schools were a laboratory for democratic social engineering and a powerful force for egalitarian social change.[66]

Another major theme of *Kontakt* was the idea that Franklin Delano Roosevelt had wrought a social revolution in the United States. Before the Great Depression, the Myrdals argued, America had come closer than any other country to approximating the nineteenth-century model of the purely liberal state (in the European sense) with a minimum of state intervention in the economy and a maximum of individual freedom. This laissez-faire liberalism was supported by the American creed in its emphasis on the rights and freedoms of the individual. The power of the federal government had been strictly limited in accordance with the nation's individualistic beliefs. But the stock market crash of 1929 and the long depression of the thirties drove Americans to reinterpret their ideals to allow for a greater acceptance of social responsibility.[67] This was "the greatest transformation . . . within the American social system since the revolution."[68] The Myrdals greatly admired Franklin Roosevelt as a "humanitarian pragmatist" who had begun to introduce planning into America's chaotic economy. They concluded that some New Deal programs had been hastily organized but contended that Roosevelt had at last given an opportunity to America's "brilliant men" by bringing experts to Washington. The New Deal had transformed a "negative radicalism" among muckraking intellectuals into a "positive radicalism."[69]

Although they acknowledged the existence of business opposition to the New Deal, the authors maintained that the majority of the American people were ready for a continuation of reform. Of particular significance was the fact that Roosevelt had awakened the nation's poorest one-third to demand change. The Myrdals contended that "Roosevelt and the New Deal, for the first time in American history, have taught the poor to start asking why they should be poor in this rich land, to demand their rights and to depend upon political means to win them. This is a lasting result of the Roosevelt regime. Roosevelt and his wife have through their radio talks and other political activities, played a decisive role in this political awakening."[70] Noting the importance of the Wagner Act in stimulating labor union organization, the authors expressed their hope that the labor move-ment would continue to advance under new, strong leadership—perhaps Sidney Hillman of the Textile Workers' Union or David Dubinsky of the International Ladies' Garment Workers' Union.[71]

The Myrdals predicted a realignment of political parties, as a result of which the Democrats would become a more thoroughgoing liberal party. As evidence of this trend, they cited FDR's appointment of liberal Republicans such as Wallace and Ickes to his cabinet, his cooperation with liberal Republican politicians such as La Guardia, and his attempts to purge conservative Democrats in the primary elec-tions of 1938. The authors concluded that "Roosevelt's longterm plan is obviously to transform . . . the Democratic Party to a clearly pro-reform people's party, to a left party in the European sense."[72] They anticipated that the South, the poorest section of the country, would become more liberal because of New Deal benefits; they expected that organized labor and a large part of organized farmers would continue to vote Democratic; and they observed that black voters were switching their allegiance from the Republican to the Democratic party. The Myrdals claimed that "the American Democratic Party resembles to a great extent our Social Democratic Party before the war, although it did not undergo a radical youth as a socialist labor party. Both are national reform-minded peoples' parties. Both include groups of people who are quite conservative. Both make room for a radical intellectual left wing which becomes the driving force ideologically."[73] In this rather strained comparison, the authors exaggerated the importance of intel-lectuals in both the Democratic party and the Swedish Social Democratic party and vastly overstated the "radicalism" of the New Deal. The Myrdals ended their discussion of the New Deal by remarking that ten years earlier they had thought

American politics so ridden with corruption and ineffectiveness that the only hope for change lay in a "new socialist labor party" that would gradually evolve into a "reformist people's party." But the New Deal had brought about change in a manner that grew out of American traditions and was not associated with European "isms." They concluded that "the honor for this result belongs almost entirely to one man, Franklin Delano Roosevelt, who now ascends to the first rank of America's historic folk heroes."[74]

Turning to the issue of foreign policy, the Myrdals assured their Swedish readers that American isolationism was "bankrupt." They admitted that isolationism had a long tradition in the United States and that Scandinavian-Americans in the Midwest had been among the staunchest isolationists, but they insisted that American public opinion had turned decisively toward sympathy for Britain and antagonism to the fascist dictatorships. They downplayed the importance of the machinations of Wall Street and of special interest groups and asserted that the question of American intervention in the war would be decided by public opinion. The Myrdals believed that moral concerns were most important in shaping public opinion about the European war.[75] Reiterating a point Alva had made a year earlier, the authors contended that Americans felt a moral dilemma in choosing between their traditional isolationism and their sense of justice: "The Americans have experienced the moral dilemmas of neutrality more deeply than any other people—because they are the most moralistic in outlook and because they are more secure and stronger." According to the Myrdals, the 1940 presidential election marked the end of isolationism. When the Republicans rejected isolationist candidates and nominated the internationalist Wendell Willkie, they strengthened the consensus behind Roosevelt's foreign policy. The Myrdals predicted that the United States would soon deliver war materiel to Britain without demanding payment or credit.[76]

Freedom of speech and freedom of the press were among the issues most strongly emphasized by the Myrdals in their comparisons between America and Sweden. At the beginning of the book, they noted that First Amendment rights were a cardinal point in the American creed. In their discussion of American individualism, the authors extolled the possibilities for free expression in the United States, contending that American culture did not attempt "to chisel away human diversity with convention's power." "The individual," they declared, "is nowhere as uninhibited and free from convention's pressure as in this land."[77] Pressure for conformity, in their view, was much stronger in Sweden, Denmark, Germany, and other European countries than in America. In reporting the results of a Roper poll of Americans' attitudes to free speech and the Bill of Rights, the Myrdals wondered "whether in Sweden five per cent of the population would answer 'yes' to freedom of speech if it had been formulated so absolutely according to the American tradition."[78] And in their analysis of the foreign policy consensus that had emerged during the Roosevelt-Willkie election, they pointedly instructed their Swedish readers that "this is national unity. It is the kind of 'unanimity' which, in a dangerous situation, can arise in a democracy, even though the press is completely free and the discussion heated. It does not depend on political pressure." It has its basis in the fundamental consensus of values in American life.[79]

After describing the free operation of the press in the United States, the Myrdals concluded that "Sweden clearly has not converted its leaders to the same respect for the press. Although there has been a great change for the better within the short time we have observed, the Swedish authorities still lack the confidence, interest and respect for the press which we found as a rule in America."[80] They argued that Swedes had lived in a stable and free society for so long that they tended to take for granted the fundamental principles of democracy. The Myrdals affirmed their respect for the Swedish Parliament but asserted that the absence of a strong consciousness of the first principles of democracy explained the Swedish public's toleration of press censorship.[81] A combination of government censorship and press self-censorship resulted in a "limitation and muffling" of certain types of news material as well as of analysis and discussion, according to the authors. They claimed that the Swedish public received very little accurate information about what was happening in the occupied countries and that "the whole area of social life in certain of the belligerent countries is likewise forbidden territory to the Swedish press and radio."[82] The danger that these journalistic shortcomings would mislead the public was obvious: "One draws the conclusion, for example, that concentration camps no longer exist because one has not read anything about them in the newspapers for a few years." Another danger was that many citizens would simply cease to believe anything they read in the newspapers. The Myrdals sarcastically observed that "it is certainly a serious defect in our intellectual preparedness that no efforts have been made to teach newspaper readers in Sweden the art of extracting a maximum of correct information from the Swedish press today."[83]

Despite these sharp criticisms of the Swedish press, Gunnar and Alva Myrdal acknowledged that Swedish intellectuals faced a "moral dilemma" in deciding how far to go in expressing their opinions while their country was threatened from without. This dilemma was an acute psychological burden for the political journalists who had to express themselves in print day after day. The Myrdals claimed that they could understand the position of those Swedish intellectuals who believed that more was to be gained by keeping quiet than by speaking out and thereby jeopardizing the nation's independence. But where did one draw the line with this kind of thinking? they asked. Was it not just a "weak rationalization" for "opportunism"? "What will happen to the nation's strength of resistance," the Myrdals wondered, "if the intellectual middle classes, who occupy all the key positions and are the nation's voice, give up?" "Our country may need martyrs instead," they declared. "It is perhaps not just soldiers who must be prepared to die in our defense. All must be prepared to lose at least income and position, influence and security, yes—even freedom."[84]

In their final chapter, "Sweden and Scandinavia," the authors expressed their solidarity with the people of Norway, Denmark, and Finland who lived under German or Soviet occupation. They contended that "it is wholly unreasonable to think of a continuation of our free life in Sweden after the war unless all of Scandinavia has been freed."[85] Living in America, they wrote, had given them a broader perspective on the cultural unity of the Nordic peoples and their common democratic heritage, and they expressed their hope that, after the war, Scandinavia and the United States would lead the way in the establishment of a peaceful and democratic world order.

Returning to their comparison of Sweden and the United States, the Myrdals affirmed that both societies were fundamentally democratic, but they reiterated their view that "no contrast between our two democracies stands out more clearly than this: that America is a long way from attaining the legal security which Sweden attained earlier, but on the other hand . . . the basic ideals of the legal system are more consciously held by the whole people. Sweden is more psychologically and ideologically unprepared for the strains of this troubled time, more helpless in this development than any other people we know."[86] It was time for Sweden to rediscover its own basic principles of democracy and freedom, the Myrdals emphasized. Legal scholars should turn their attention away from technicalities and study the principles which form the basis of the legal system. Organizations of workers, farmers, and consumers should concentrate on popular education in the principles of democracy as part of Sweden's "preparedness" against external threats.[87] Above all, Swedes should learn from the American creed and make the principles of democracy, justice, and freedom "holy national symbols for the people."[88]

To those among their compatriots who argued that Sweden should accommodate itself to Hitler's New Order of Europe, the Myrdals replied that Swedes should begin planning for a postwar world based on international cooperation, peace, and social justice. They entreated their readers to "strike down the darkening illusion that limits our spiritual horizon" and to dare to plan for a better world.[89] They proclaimed the need for an organization among nations that would have the power to guarantee disarmament and the enforcement of international laws. Foreseeing the decolonization process, they called for an international mandate system to guide the peoples of Africa to self-government. The authors confessed: "All this sounds terribly utopian in Sweden today. We know it. But we shall remember that these things are discussed as serious political problems in the belligerent countries and above all in America. Utopias are alive there. Here at home we must believe that some day other great events can be possible than the world catastrophes which dominated the last ten to twelve years."[90] In their peroration, the Myrdals warned that a national culture that did not care about the welfare of all mankind would become "narrow, greedy and heartless," and urged Swedes to join with Americans to inaugurate a new international order. "Our task," they declared, "is to reconcile millions of people with each other, to resolve conflicts between races and peoples, to uplift the weak, . . . to protect the strong

from the misfortune of aggression, to safeguard and organize international cooperation." The Myrdals predicted that the "intelligence" and "morality" of the
American people would soon be mobilized to support these humanitarian goals:
"America and Scandinavia . . . must take back responsibility for the old dream
of peace, freedom, reason, good will, law and order for all our people—for
humanity."[91]

Kontakt topped the Swedish bestseller list in the spring of 1941, and its authors
became known as the leading experts in Sweden on contemporary American
politics, economics, and culture. The Myrdals' argument that Swedes should
emulate certain aspects of American civic culture represented a sharp break with
the traditional condescending view of American culture among Swedish intellectuals. Copies of the book found their way across the border, and Norwegians read
it as a "resistance book" prophesying the end of Nazi supremacy.[92]

Writing *Kontakt* enabled Gunnar Myrdal to examine his experiences in America
and in Sweden and to make explicit the connection between the fight against
racism in America and the war against Nazism in Europe. Together with Alva
Myrdal, he formulated his version of the American creed, noted the absence of
such "holy national symbols" in Sweden, and explained how the creed was
institutionalized in the United States. Gunnar Myrdal saw the citizen's commitment to democratic values as absolutely vital to resistance to totalitarianism. His
nine months in Sweden gave him a strong sense that a nation's ideological
preparedness mattered, that it was important for a people to know what they were
defending. Ten years earlier, he had argued that the ideology of Americanism, as
taught in the public schools and in adult education classes, served to prop up the
system of unregulated capitalism.[93] Now he believed that the New Deal and
Americans' growing sense of their international responsibilities were leading to
a more socially responsible version of Americanism. The moralistic quality of
American culture, which had seemed puritanical and stifling to Myrdal in 1929,
emerged as a major strength of the United States in the context of the war.
American individualism, which had loomed as a major obstacle to reform in the
1920s, now appeared to be a sign of the culture's vitality. Though this shift in
Myrdal's thinking about American politics and culture took place in the context of
Sweden's precarious situation in 1940, it paralleled similar transitions in the
thought of many American intellectuals who were driven to celebrate America as
an alternative to the Nazi dictatorship.[94]

In formulating his psychological argument that Americans felt a mental conflict
between the values of their creed and their racial prejudices, Gunnar Myrdal took
one of many impressions from his interviews and gave it primacy in his analysis of
American race relations. His earlier emphasis on the problem of black unemployment gave way to a new psychological and moral interpretation in the context of
World War II. Alva Myrdal, as the coauthor of *Kontakt*, exerted a significant
influence on the shaping of this psychological, moral, and ideological interpretation of American racial conflict.

At a time when civil rights had been flagrantly violated in Germany and in the occupied countries and curtailed in Sweden, Gunnar Myrdal believed that the United States was moving resolutely in the opposite direction. He believed that the Supreme Court was gradually extending equal protection of the law to blacks and that the New Deal was a nascent social democratic movement. Myrdal expected a continued liberal advance after the war with realignment of political parties and renewed demands for reform from organized labor and the poor. His optimism was also a reaction against "realists" and pessimists in Sweden who expected a German victory and counseled accommodation to Germany. To believe in a democratic future, to plan for a postwar world based on international cooperation and racial justice was to assert an alternative to Hitler's well-publicized plans for a New Order.

In *Kontakt*, the Myrdals expressed their distaste for romantic nationalism and ethnic chauvinism. Sweden, in their view, was worth defending to the extent that it was a democracy that respected individual rights and a society that put into practice the universal values of the Enlightenment. They did not appeal to their readers' loyalty to Swedish culture or invoke a particularistic ideology that exalted the Swedes as a special people. In looking at American society, the authors most admired its ability to inspire in its ethnically diverse population a devotion to the universal principles of the American creed. While many Europeans looked upon Americans as naive, the Myrdals stressed that the United States had found a workable formula that allowed a heterogeneous continental nation to live in peace while Europe was destroying itself in a devastating war. In contrast to the usual view of the United States as a young nation, they asserted that American democracy was more than a century older than Sweden's and that Swedes had much to learn from America.

Gunnar Myrdal regarded all social questions as, at bottom, moral issues; the reference in *Kontakt* to the moral dilemma of Swedish neutrality exemplified this stance. He had long been interested in analyzing the moral values that informed social science and public policy, and in response to the challenge of Nazism, he focused his attention on the fundamental principles of government. As Myrdal looked at Sweden and America in 1940, he saw within each country a discrepancy between the basic ideals of the people and the reality of social conditions and government policies. He thought that both Sweden and America needed to bring their practice into conformity with the underlying principles of their people. According to Myrdal, a society that failed to anchor itself in laws that guarantee respect for basic human rights would "glide like a glacier," accommodating itself to political pressures.

Conflicts of Conscience

Through the summer and early fall of 1940, Gunnar Myrdal had remained uncertain whether he should return to the United States to complete his work on American race relations, and he seriously considered remaining in Sweden, giving priority to his responsibilities to his own country, and leaving the Negro study in the hands of Stouffer and his collaborators. But Richard Sterner kept up a steady stream of letters urging Myrdal not to forget his duty to write the main report for the Carnegie project.[95] As an old friend and a Swede, Sterner could speak more bluntly than Keppel, Stouffer, or the American collaborators. He reminded Myrdal that the Carnegie Corporation had "given you *carte blanche* to do precisely what you wanted with the investigation. That means that absolutely no one but you can complete the report as planned." Sterner added that "people here are actually tremendously excited about what you in your capacity as 'ace scientist' will say about the Negro question in general in case you find the occasion to come back and write a 'main report.' If that 'main report' does not come, there will be a very great disappointment."[96]

Sterner argued that Myrdal was out of place as a crisis planner in wartime Sweden. He insisted that "it is a complete mistake when you believe that you have more pressing duties at home. The only difference is that your patriotic duties have a stronger emotional attraction. But you are no warrior. Neither do you have any duty to serve as a political planner in a time when an idiot may guess better than a genius what may happen next week. Nor do I believe that you can be in a position to correct many administrative blunders." Sterner portrayed the Negro study as an opportunity for Myrdal to put his scholarly abilities to better use, and he stressed the long-term significance of the race question:

> Here you have, however, an assignment to fill of exceptional importance in the longer view. Perhaps it does not have such a great publicity-value at this time, but there is a chance that it will contribute in a decisive way to a future ideological reconstruction. I do not need to explain further to you, because you grasp surely better than I how a discussion of the Negro question can be recast so that it cuts into the actual basis of the ideological distress which the world suffers under. . . . Now one can see the deeper connections much clearer than was possible earlier.[97]

Myrdal had previously assured Samuel Stouffer that, despite the pressure of other duties in Sweden, "I am so definitely geared to the Negro problem that I cannot take any real interest in anything else, before my Negro-adventure is ended in an honest way."[98] Stouffer had taken on the herculean task of holding together a large study with which he had had no prior involvement and of supervising the completion of nearly fifty memoranda on various aspects of Afro-American life. The Chicago sociologist had put in sixteen-hour days, pleaded with collaborators to finish their memoranda, and threatened them with "loss of status in the eyes of the Carnegie Foundation and the public" if they failed to turn in their promised work.[99] Sterner's letters concerning the problems with the uncompleted study helped to remind Myrdal that his reputation as a scholar was at stake. He had created considerable disruption in this large study by returning to Sweden and was embarrassed to learn that many of the collaborators' memoranda had been "flops." He felt "only one dominant ambition: to come back and turn defeat into victory."[100] In November 1940, Myrdal wrote Keppel that he had decided to return to the United States early in 1941.[101]

Although Gunnar implored her to accompany him, Alva Myrdal decided to remain in Sweden several months longer, serving out the academic year as principal of the Social Pedagogical Institute. Gunnar Myrdal's departure was delayed for two months because the German government canceled his transit visa across Europe to Lisbon. He called on an acquaintance at the German legation in Stockholm, Dr. Werner Dankwort, to see if anything could be done about it. Dankwort told him that the German legation had complete dossiers on both of the Myrdals, knew of their hostility to Germany and the Nazi philosophy, and would therefore "do everything possible" to prevent him from going to the United States "to encourage the Americans in their attitude of hostility" to Germany. When Dankwort learned that the Myrdals had just completed a manuscript about America, he asked to see it and suggested that the matter of the transit visa might be reopened if he could see the manuscript before publication. Gunnar Myrdal exploded into rage at this attempt at censorship and blackmail, told Dankwort that Swedish economists such as Gustav Cassel had come to Germany's aid after the First World War when Germany was "despised by all the other nations of the world," and assured him that he and other Swedes would again come to the aid of the German people after the Nazi regime was defeated in the current war.[102] Myrdal then stormed out of the German legation and obtained a visa from his friend, the Soviet ambassador Alexandra Kollontai, to travel through the Soviet Union. When he said good-bye to the prime minister, Per Albin Hansson said to him: "You live in the great world and forget that we are a small country under great pressure." Myrdal managed to return to the United States via the trans-Siberian railroad and a flight from Japan to San Francisco, where he landed on March 6, 1941.[103]

Shortly after his return to New York, Myrdal made a speech designed to rebut assertions in the American press that Sweden's neutrality policy was really pro-German and to quash rumors of the growth of an indigenous Swedish Nazi movement like that of Quisling in Norway. Although he had been critical of some of the government's neutrality policies at home, he loyally portrayed Swedish policy in a favorable light before an American audience. Myrdal reassured Americans that Sweden was still a bastion of democracy and insisted, "The rumors spread in this country that the Nazi ideology is making inroads in Sweden are false." Swallowing his outrage over the government's censorship policies, he declared that "nobody who follows the Swedish press will deny that public discussion is free and unhampered." And he betrayed a certain defensiveness in insisting that "the American public must realize that we are doing our full part in defending democracy by defending ourselves."[104] Sweden's image in the United States would continue to decline, however, especially in the wake of the German invasion of the Soviet Union in June 1941, when the Swedish government allowed a German division to cross Swedish territory on its way from Norway to Russia. As he labored on *An American Dilemma* in 1941 and 1942, Myrdal had to contend with the fact that the American press often portrayed Sweden as a "vassal" of Germany.[105]

Gunnar Myrdal disappeared from the public eye after his speech in New York and devoted himself to intensive study of American race relations. After brief discussions with Keppel and Stouffer, he set off for the South to have a last look at Jim Crow. The Swedish observer checked into the Robert E. Lee Hotel in Jackson, Mississippi, where he pored over twenty thousand pages of manuscript reports that his collaborators had written on nearly every aspect of Afro-American life. Myrdal was disappointed in the quality of most of these memoranda. Some of the collaborators, thinking their leader would not return, had slackened in their efforts after he left for Sweden. Others had found it impossible to produce any original research or fresh analysis within the few months allotted by Myrdal's timetable. Myrdal was most impressed by Ralph Bunche's work on black politics and Arthur Raper's memorandum, "Race and Class Pressures," which contained many vivid accounts of extralegal violence in the South.[106]

After reading through the collaborators' manuscripts, Myrdal began to write the book at Dartmouth in the summer of 1941. He moved to Princeton in the fall and remained there for a year until the book was nearly finished. His vast staff had dispersed, and he had only two assistants, Richard Sterner and Arnold Rose, a young sociology graduate student from the University of Chicago whom Stouffer had brought on board while Myrdal had been in Sweden. They worked at a frantic pace and had little contact with other scholars. Sterner and Rose each prepared drafts of many of the chapters and critiqued Myrdal's work. Rose also did much of the editorial work, since Myrdal and Sterner were not writing in their native language.[107] In conceptualizing the book, Myrdal retained the moral, psychological, and ideological framework of *Kontakt med Amerika*. Although Sterner prepared eleven chapters on the role of blacks in the American economy that spelled out in grim detail the pervasiveness of discrimination, *An American Dilemma* would not focus on black unemployment to the extent that Myrdal had intended when he conducted his research from 1938 to 1940. After Pearl Harbor, the buildup of the armed forces and the defense industries would temporarily eliminate most black unemployment. Myrdal attempted, therefore, to take a long-term perspective, pointing to structural changes in economics, politics, law, migration, population, and international relations.

Gunnar Myrdal felt both an awesome sense of responsibility and a twinge of guilt over enjoying the privilege of carrying on his scholarly writing in America while much of the world was at war. He experienced an eerie sense of isolation in the cloistered campuses of Dartmouth and Princeton. "Sometimes it gives me a queer feeling," he wrote the rector of the University of Stockholm, "to be harnessed to a great scientific work with a perspective stretching over generations and centuries and concerning itself with the elemental factors in the human tragedy, while the rest of the world is crazily busy in the war and most of my colleagues the world over are drawn into short-range crisis administration problems."[108]

Though he felt a powerful commitment to his book, Gunnar Myrdal found it difficult to write without Alva. He wrote an introductory section of the book but confessed to Keppel that "I am afraid that I was a little crazy—for reasons which you now will understand—when I wrote it."[109] Gunnar and Alva had never before been separated for more than a couple of months, and he was lonely and depressed and needed her support and stimulation, her breadth of vision, her knowledge of psychology and sociology, and her sense of humor.[110] He had pressed her to accompany him when he had left Sweden in February 1941, but she had insisted on completing the academic year as principal of her teacher training institute, and she was reluctant to leave their three children. Jan was nearly fourteen, Sissela six, and Kaj four, and Alva knew that the children needed her. In letter after letter and in telegram after telegram, Gunnar demanded that she undertake the risky journey to America. Never one to underrate his own abilities, he believed that his book would play a crucial role in strengthening America's homefront and in defining the difference between its ideals and those of Nazi Germany, and he needed her help. Finally, Gunnar issued an ultimatum to his wife. Alva knew that if she did not go to America, there would be a divorce. And so Alva gave in to Gunnar's demand, putting her marriage ahead of her duty to her children, "but not without a nagging, tormented conscience and an inner feeling of indignation," she later wrote.[111] Gunnar's mother, Sofie, who had moved back to Dalarna to be near her kin after her husband's death, was summoned to Stockholm to look after the three children. Now sixty-two, Sofie embodied the world that Gunnar and Alva had striven so hard to leave behind, and she moved uneasily about the large, modern house that her son and daughter-in-law had built as a monument to their rational, scientific worldview.

In June, Alva obtained a visa to travel through Russia, as Gunnar had done in February, but just as she was about to depart, Hitler's armies invaded the Soviet Union. Gunnar was now beside himself with anxiety and depression. He wrote Charles S. Johnson, "Personally I am rather depressed at present as Alva was stopped two days before she was to leave by the Russians who cancelled her transit visa. But we are doing everything at present to clear up the matter and the Carnegie Corporation is stretching out its long tentacles. Let us hope that we may succeed."[112] Alva waited during the summer for a chance to leave Sweden. Finally, the British ambassador to Sweden secured passage for her aboard a secret British military plane, which flew from Sweden over occupied Norway to Scotland.

British planes flying this route were regularly shot down by German antiaircraft batteries in Norway, and Alva donned a parachute and oxygen mask for the flight, which proceeded without incident. In exchange for this favor from the British government, Alva spent a month in London writing articles about Britain for Swedish magazines and briefed British officials on the situation in Finland, which she had recently visited. But Alva still had difficulty getting a flight from Britain to the United States.

Frederick Keppel had never seen his young genius so depressed. He had advised Gunnar strongly against urging Alva to undertake the dangerous journey from Sweden to America. When Alva reached Britain, Gunnar approached him with some trepidation and asked "if now, when she is on her way anyhow and as return to Stockholm is at least as risky as a continuation to America, you would not feel free from a troubled conscience to lend me your very powerful help in obtaining a speedy continuation of her trip." Keppel used his influence in diplomatic circles to get Alva on a plane to Lisbon where she waited another month before getting a flight to the United States. She rejoined her husband in Princeton in October 1941.[113]

With Alva at his side, Gunnar Myrdal threw himself into writing his book with extraordinary energy and enthusiasm. If his mind was troubled over having put Alva through a dangerous passage to America, he suppressed these thoughts and concentrated on his book, which he believed to have global implications. On December 7, 1941, Gunnar was working in his office at Princeton when he heard of the Japanese attack on Pearl Harbor. He knew then that his book would have a greater significance for American public policy than he had imagined when he began the project in 1938. He would be free to frame his discussion of American race relations in terms of a global war for democracy. Reminiscing in later years on how the book came to be written, Myrdal recalled that the book gave his life a sense of moral purpose and commitment: "When I was sitting there in Princeton, which was a nice place, I thought about all the youngsters, all my friends in Europe, who were either in prison or killed in war. And here I was sitting and writing my book. It became my war work. And I think this meant much for what the book came to be."[114]

After a difficult period of juggling roles as scholar and politician, of balancing duties in Sweden and America, of enduring loneliness and anxiety about Alva, Gunnar Myrdal was able to concentrate his enormous energy on writing a scholarly book that he also saw as part of a worldwide fight for democracy. In Sweden, he had felt the sharp limitations on what he could do to oppose the Nazi threat to his own country. Now he had the opportunity to address a central ideological issue in the struggle between Nazism and democracy. *An American Dilemma*, like *Kontakt*, was an attempt to overcome the sense of impotence and irrelevance that he felt as a Swedish intellectual by making a vigorous effort to strengthen the ideological defenses against fascism. Within the space of a few months, he would write articles entitled "The Negro and America's Uneasy Conscience" and (in

Gunnar Myrdal writing *An American Dilemma*, Princeton, 1942 (courtesy Arbetarrörelsens Arkiv, Stockholm)

Swedish) "Neutrality and Our Conscience."[115] Both Swedes and Americans, in his view, faced a moral dilemma, a choice between following their consciences and ideals or giving in to an expedient but horrifically destructive alternative.

"The Limits of Optimism"

While Gunnar Myrdal was writing his book contrasting the American creed and Nazi racism, he was under surveillance by the Federal Bureau of Investigation as a suspected Nazi sympathizer. On June 12, 1941, an informant told an FBI agent in New York that a Swede named "Myrdal Gunnar," who was employed by the Julius Rosenwald Foundation, "is very definitely pro-nazi and is supposed to have made pro-Nazi utterances at various times." It took the bureau some months to track down this "Karl Gunnar Myrdal, with aliases Gunnar Myrdal, Mydal Gunnar." Agents in Chicago, Washington, Boston, New York, and Newark checked up on this mysterious Swede, interviewing officials at Dartmouth as well as neighbors and the postmaster in Princeton. The FBI discovered that he spoke in a "heavy German accent" and that the Myrdals "entertained Negroes often in their apartment" but found no conclusive evidence of "un-American activities." A Carnegie official, possibly corporation secretary Robert Lester, defended Myrdal in the strongest possible terms, declaring that he "was responsible more than any other man in Sweden for the rebirth of democracy in that country, was a bitter enemy of the Nazis, and was hated by them." The FBI closed the investigation in 1943.[116]

Defending their foreign observer against accusations of subversive activity was only one of many difficulties facing Carnegie officials in the final months of the Myrdal project. Frederick Keppel continued to advise the Negro study even after he retired as president of the Carnegie Corporation in 1941 and went to Washington to serve on the War Relief Control Board and the State Department's Board of Appeals on Visa Cases. Keppel had invested a great deal of time, energy, and foundation money in the Myrdal study. He had been forced to tackle the unexpected problems of getting the Myrdals back to Sweden, appointing a temporary director, and helping to arrange for Gunnar and Alva Myrdal to return to the United States. Keppel's personal affection for Gunnar Myrdal remained strong, however, and after American entry into the war, he came to perceive Myrdal's study as an important public document with a significance for the American war effort.[117] Keppel never attempted to censor the ideas of his foreign observer, but he and Charles Dollard did offer much advice about how Americans would react to Myrdal's judgments. The final stages of the Carnegie Negro study were marked by a process of negotiation between Myrdal and the two Carnegie officials, and the Swedish Tocqueville acknowledged his dependence upon Keppel for "fatherly advice" and added, "I rely on you as an old wise man."[118]

While Myrdal was immersed in writing his book, Keppel received the final reports of the manuscript committee that he had appointed to review the collaborators' memoranda for publication. Myrdal shrewdly declined to involve himself in the decisions on whether his colleagues' manuscripts should be published. That responsibility fell to a committee of three: sociologist William F. Ogburn of the University of Chicago, Shelby M. Harrison of the Russell Sage Foundation, and Donald Young. The committee relied heavily on the advice of Samuel Stouffer, who had supervised the completion of many of the memoranda. Keppel, Charles Dollard, Donald Young, and Stouffer considered appointing a black scholar to the committee but were unable to agree on a person that they thought would be acceptable to a majority of black social scientists. They decided that "to include a Negro would create more problems than it would solve" but agreed that the committee should be "at liberty to coopt a Negro scholar if it wished," an option that the committee declined to take.[119] With Keppel's approval, the committee made plans to publish nine monographs as part of a series on "The Negro in America," with the cost of publication underwritten by the Carnegie Corporation. Four books actually appeared in print: Melville Herskovits's *The Myth of the Negro Past*, Richard Sterner's *The Negro's Share*, Charles S. Johnson's *Patterns of Negro Segregation*, and a volume edited by Otto Klineberg entitled *Characteristics of the American Negro*. Five other manuscripts were provisionally accepted for publication: Guion G. Johnson's "American Ideologies and the Negro," Guy B. Johnson's "Negro Crime and Delinquency," Samuel Stouffer's and Harold Dorn's "Negro

Health, Population, and Migration," Sterling Brown's "Negro Art and Literature," and Ralph Bunche's "Negro Politics and Political Organizations." These five authors did not complete or revise the manuscripts by the committee's deadline, however, in several cases because of wartime responsibilities.[120]

The manuscript committee adopted more conventional political and intellectual standards than those of Gunnar Myrdal. As a veteran of royal commissions and parliamentary politics, Myrdal had made strenuous efforts to win the cooperation of black and radical scholars, but he did not want to silence them. He had been eager to hear their perspectives, get their insights, use their skills, and exploit their contacts, but he wanted to allow them the freedom to publish their research independently, either as part of a Carnegie-sponsored series or elsewhere. The manuscript committee members and Stouffer were less receptive to radical ideas and were inclined to insist upon a positivistic approach to social science. While the committee members were willing to publish Ralph Bunche's social democratic critique of black political organizations, they refused to publish a manuscript on adult education by the sociologist Bernhard Stern because the members believed that Stern's Marxist "bias" would detract from the objectivity of the series. Stouffer took the unusual step of sending Stern's manuscript out to nine readers. Richard Sterner, Louis Wirth, T. J. Woofter, Jr., and the sociologist Paul Lazarsfeld recommended in favor of publication with revisions. But Stouffer collected complaints about Stern's bias from Alain Locke, Chicago sociologist Ellsworth Faris, and three other readers.[121] The committee members and Stouffer objected on similar grounds to an uncompleted manuscript on black education by the Marxist sociologist Doxey Wilkerson, which Stouffer sent out to seven readers. Although Wilkerson's draft won praise from the black educator Horace Mann Bond and the white historian Merle Curti, it drew complaints of bias from southern white educators Jackson Davis and Louis R. Wilson.[122] After leaving the Carnegie Negro study, Wilkerson went to work as an organizer for the Communist party, and Stern was close to the party. Keppel, who had given Myrdal wide latitude in conducting his research, was equally willing to accept the politically centrist and methodologically conservative approach of the manuscript committee. In his report to the Carnegie trustees, he noted that a few manuscripts were rejected because of "what the committee deemed to be irremediable bias." Writing only a few days after A. Philip Randolph canceled his threatened March on Washington, Keppel explained that "the emotional climate of the United States has changed radically since the Study was inaugurated and . . . tension between minority and majority groups tends to rise in an emergency." Therefore, the committee made "every effort" to "insure that publications resulting from the Study are statements of fact rather than tracts." Keppel reassured the trustees that "insofar as possible, recommendations as to policy will be confined to Myrdal's own report."[123] The deliberations of the manuscript committee indicate that, in the absence of Gunnar Myrdal's prodding for the inclusion of black scholars beyond a level of tokenism and for the acceptance of diverse political viewpoints, the conventional political standards and institutional racism of the foundation and of the social science establishment quickly reappeared.

Keppel and Charles Dollard commented on the chapters of *An American Dilemma* as Myrdal and his two assistants wrote them. The only other people allowed to read the full unpublished manuscript were the sociologists Louis Wirth and E. Franklin Frazier.[124] Keppel and Dollard formed an important audience for Myrdal in addition to the social science community; both men had remained in close contact with Myrdal since the project's inception and had provided advice on staffing, research, and hundreds of practical details. Myrdal also used them as sounding boards for ideas as he developed them, regarding their comments on his manuscript as "the very best type of critiques from the viewpoint of the cultivated *layman-citizen*."[125] "When writing this book," he told Dollard, "I have had in mind God and my scientific conscience and such intelligent and respectable readers as you, Mr. Keppel, Fred Osborn and colleagues like Louis Wirth and Frazier."[126] Myrdal discovered that Keppel, who had known little about black Americans when he began the search for a scholar-statesman to study the "Negro problem" in 1935, was "shocked down to his bones" when he read the chapters on racial discrimination, poverty, and violence in the South.[127]

The Swedish scholar's discussion of the American creed and the moral dilemma of Americans had a special poignancy for Keppel as he read Myrdal's manuscript in 1942. As a member of the Board of Appeals on Visa Cases in Washington, Keppel was involved in the emotionally wrenching work of evaluating thousands of appeals from European refugees who had been denied entrance to the United States. Since the passage of the Immigration Restriction Act of 1924, the United States had used national quotas to limit severely the number of immigrants allowed into the country. Despite Nazi Germany's well-publicized persecution of Jews after 1933, American public opinion had remained hostile to a revision of refugee policy because of anti-Semitism and the fear of economic competition during the Depression. With the coming of World War II, the State Department slashed admission of refugees to 25 percent of quotas and erected a formidable three-tiered screening process, ostensibly designed to weed out enemy agents. A refugee seeking asylum in the United States faced scrutiny of his personal character, financial means, sponsorship by American citizens, and political beliefs. Potential immigrants born in one of the Axis countries or having relatives in one of those countries underwent especially strong scrutiny, and Communists and socialists were routinely barred because of their political convictions. Taken together, these policies constituted what the historian David Wyman has called a "paper wall," keeping out most Jewish refugees just as Hitler began his mass extermination of European Jews in 1941.[128]

The Board of Appeals on Visa Cases was the apex of the State Department's three-tiered structure, the final place of appeal for refugees. Keppel's boyhood friend, Morgan partner Russell Leffingwell, urged him to be vigilant in barring potential revolutionaries who might seek to slip into the United States as Lenin had entered Russia in 1917.[129] But Keppel managed to rise above the prejudices of his class and generation and to compile a record that was generous in the context of a very repressive institutional structure. Wyman observes that the former Carnegie president "worked hard to move the visa system away from excessive suspiciousness and toward the tradition of America as a haven for the oppressed." The board of appeals overturned about one-fourth of the negative decisions of the lower tribunals. Keppel pushed for policy changes designed to reduce the barriers facing refugees but enjoyed only limited success, as most of his superiors maintained a stony indifference to the fate of European Jews and other refugees.[130]

Reading the manuscript of *An American Dilemma* in his spare time, Keppel praised Myrdal's central argument, his grounding of the study in America's democratic values, and his conclusion that the United States now faced the race issue in a new international context. Keppel advised caution, however, on a couple of fronts. He thought that both (white) women and black men would be startled by a comparison that Myrdal drew between the oppression of the two groups, and he breathed a sigh of relief when Myrdal agreed to tuck the passage away in an appendix at the back of the book, thereby eviscerating the last remnant of the feminism of *Kris i befolkningsfrågan*.[131] Of greatest concern to Keppel and to Charles Dollard was the reaction of white southerners to the book. For a time they considered asking a white southerner to comment on the manuscript, but Myrdal vetoed all of the southern social scientists he had met, fearing that any of them would perceive the role of reader as that of a political representative of the South rather than that of an independent, critical scholar.[132] Keppel and Dollard then discussed with Myrdal the idea of approaching a southern intellectual such as Herbert Agar or W. J. Cash, oblivious to the fact that Cash had died the previous year.[133] In a memo to Walter Jessup, his successor as president of the Carnegie Corporation, Keppel expressed his fears that Myrdal's vigorous criticisms of the South and his lack of tact would alienate people whose opinions Myrdal sought to change:

> The real problem comes when we consider the southern whites. The liberals among them, who are already acutely disturbed by present conditions, will welcome the serious and comprehensive presentation of the situation, but they are in a small but growing minority. To the typical southerner, however, the whole matter is so charged with sentiment and emotion, is so confused by rationalizations of all sorts, that so bald and devastating a picture as Myrdal paints is bound to be a blow. Personally I feel that the blow is coming to them, in fact it is long overdue, but I feel also that we must be particularly careful as to the manner in which the blow is delivered. A phrase here and there could rouse men who might otherwise be of help to such fury that they would become incapable of finding any good whatever in the

report, and would work actively to prevent its exerting any influence in the south. The Swedes are not a particularly sensitive race, and Myrdal is a very clever Swede, who is quite capable of being clever at the wrong place. Wirth and Dollard and I have been on the alert to catch instances where this has happened, and Myrdal has been very generous in adopting the changes we have suggested. But we are none of us southerners, and the question arises whether, as a measure of insurance to the Corporation no less than in the interest of the report itself, it might not be wise to have someone of southern birth and background read the ms. with this question of southern suscepti-bilities constantly in mind.[134]

In the end, Carnegie officials and Myrdal failed to agree on a southern critic to read the manuscript before Myrdal returned to Sweden.

Myrdal, who would later be criticized for excessive optimism regarding the possibilities for racial change, conceded to Keppel that the book "does not give a flattering picture of the South" but insisted that he had emphasized the dynamic forces leading to changes in race relations. He assured Keppel that he had kept his advice "constantly in mind" when revising his chapters on southern politics, and "some qualifications have been the result." But Myrdal declared that "the task of making it acceptable to the South and at the same time truthful is impossible." "What I can do," he suggested, "is to stress the *dynamics*, the changes and the improvements, I have there now gone to the limits of optimism."[135] Myrdal realized that his criticisms of segregation and discrimination were well ahead of southern white opinion in 1942 and anticipated that "the short-time reaction from practically any Southerner must be defensive; so much of Southern chauvin-ism you have in every Southerner." Although he expected that "most Southerners will hit the ceiling," he suggested that "the effect of this might not be bad at all if we believe that truth and progress will [result from] facing problems." Sensing that he had pushed Keppel to the limits of his tolerance, Myrdal reassured him that a scholarly book of such length was unlikely to cause a public outcry.[136]

Keppel was pleased with the final manuscript and termed it "thoughtful, coura-geous and imaginative." He confided to Jessup his exasperation with Myrdal's lack of editorial ability, which resulted in a "sprawling, repetitive piece of work, far too long"; but he supposed that Myrdal's book "will take its place with such untidy but nevertheless very important books as 'The Golden Bough' and 'The Education of Henry Adams,' and that is a pretty honorable place." Keppel speculated, "The report will also have permanent value as the only bench mark upon which future studies and surveys can be based." He thought that the book would attract much attention because "the interest of all Americans in the Negro question has been definitely increased by the processes of building up an army and navy and by revolutionizing our industrial production under war conditions, which touch closely the problems of military and civilian morale." "Incidentally," he continued, "our record with our own most important minority group may prove to be an important factor in determining the degree of our national influence upon post-war adjustments and settlements."[137]

In selecting a black social scientist to criticize the manuscript, Myrdal narrowed the choice to Charles S. Johnson and E. Franklin Frazier and opted for the latter because "Frazier is definitely more of an individualist and less of a race symbol." Myrdal wanted a critical scholar for the job, not someone "inclined to feel himself as a representative of the race."[138] When he sent Frazier his chapters on the black community, Myrdal acknowledged that that section of the book was "the most difficult task in my entire work." Conceding that his discussion of the "Negro Community" was based mainly on Bunche's memorandum on black politics and on "my own observations and speculations," he implored Frazier to make "frank criticisms."[139]

Frazier admitted to Myrdal that he had initially been skeptical that a foreign observer would be able to say anything new about black Americans. But after reading Myrdal's drafts, he found that the Swedish scholar had critically examined many key assumptions in the social science literature on race relations. Indeed, Frazier concluded that the book "contains a lot of dynamite." He agreed with Myrdal that Sumner's concept of mores had led to much fatalistic thinking about American race relations, and he applauded Myrdal's advocacy of social engineering.[140] Frazier considered the timing of Myrdal's study fortunate and predicted that "certainly, as American social scientists participate in government planning they must abandon their fatalistic attitude."[141]

Myrdal did not emphasize the study of Afro-American culture, communities, and institutions in his book. Noting that several detailed community studies had been done, he considered it more important to write a broad study of American race relations and the dynamics of change. Myrdal thought that his collaborators had failed to generate any valuable new ideas in their memoranda on black churches, education, and culture. During his travels around the country, his own observations had been focused on the "power aspect" of black institutions: their role in the black protest movement rather than their other functions in the black community. Ralph Bunche's detailed memoranda also assessed black institutions in terms of their contributions to black political struggle. Therefore, Myrdal included chapters on "The Negro Church," "The Negro School," and "The Negro Press" in a section of the book primarily concerned with black politics and protest.[142]

The controversial section of the book, "The Negro Community," which contains the discussion "The Negro Community as a Pathological Form of an American Community," was not written by Gunnar Myrdal. Arnold Rose wrote it after Myrdal returned to Sweden in the fall of 1942. Myrdal regarded this section as a "residual part, which has to be filled, in order to make the book really 'comprehensive.'" He informed Keppel, "We have, however, a fresh approach which will throw new light on much: our value premise, that the American culture is 'highest' in America in the pragmatic sense that it is advantageous for Negroes as individuals and as a group to acquire so many traits as possible, which have positive value in the surrounding white culture. This disposes, for one thing, of the entire controversy about the Africanisms."[143] Frazier returned Rose's chapters without making any serious criticisms. Rose's treatment of the black family in chapter 43 ("Institutions") closely followed Frazier's own work, and Rose took Frazier's side in the controversy with Herskovits about African influences on black American culture. Frazier found chapter 44 "a very good analysis of the non-institutional aspects of the Negro community."[144] Keppel, however, complained to Louis Wirth that Rose's chapters struck "a patronizing and pitying tone about the Negroes which Myrdal himself has avoided, and which I think is very bad medicine."[145] Wirth agreed that "these two chapters together do not give a rounded picture of the Negro community."[146] Ironically, Keppel's and Wirth's objections anticipated the critiques that many black scholars would make twenty years later.

Early in September 1942, Gunnar Myrdal gave the nearly completed manuscript of *An American Dilemma* to Arnold Rose and prepared to embark for Sweden. Rose assumed the responsibility for editing and proofreading the manuscript as well as for writing "The Negro Community." It was a tremendous responsibility for a graduate student in his twenties, and Rose worked under incredible pressure to edit the manuscript and fill in gaps left by Myrdal.[147] In a final round of social engagements in Washington and New York, Gunnar and Alva Myrdal said farewell to the diverse group of friends they had made in America: black intellectuals at Howard University, diplomats from several countries, prominent New Dealers, foundation officials, and civil rights leaders. The Carnegie Corporation arranged a dinner for the Myrdals at Howard to help with the "public relations" of the book.[148]

Gunnar Myrdal's departure marked the end of his close association with two men who had followed the Negro study from beginning to end, Frederick Keppel and Charles Dollard. As he prepared to leave, he wrote Dollard, "You and I, in all the thousands of decisions we had to make in the course of this work, have never had a divided mind; I don't even recall a compromise between us."[149] Myrdal told Dollard of his regret that he had found it necessary to interrupt his work to return to Sweden in 1940–41. In the end, however, he felt that going home to struggle for maintaining democratic institutions in Sweden had preserved his status as a foreign observer of America—a posture that gave him critical distance and enabled him to make a more plausible case that he spoke for people throughout the world who expected the United States to live up to its democratic principles on the race issue. Myrdal wrote Dollard of how he had thrown himself into the work, putting aside all other concerns, such as the welfare of his family, to concentrate on his "war work":

As a Swede in a somewhat exposed public position, I should not have been able to carry out the work if I had not returned to Sweden in May, 1940; I

Gunnar Myrdal relaxing, Princeton, 1942 (courtesy Arbetarrörelsens Arkiv, Stockholm)

should not have been able to come back to the study if I had not left my children there as hostages. And if I did not return now after the work is finished to swim or sink with my own culture, I could not, as you well know, stand for the book. The book could not have been written by a refugee. Even the time I was away from the study was not lost entirely. I gained perspective and a fresh approach.[150]

Keppel expressed his deep gratitude to the man whom he had selected five years earlier for a difficult task. He wrote Myrdal that his study "was of such absorbing interest, and was one upon which I had risked my own reputation so definitely, that it has never been far from the front of my thoughts." He praised Myrdal's "energy, initiative, and resourcefulness" as well as his "magnanimity" and added, "in my pretty long experience I have never known anyone who received more advice and suggestions, and accepted them in better spirit." Keppel had groped for an understanding of the "Negro problem" from 1935 to 1937, as he had considered the possibility of inviting a colonial administrator to undertake the job. With some misgivings, he had given Myrdal broad latitude in conducting the study and had been shocked as he read Myrdal's chapters on the poverty of black Americans, the pervasiveness of discrimination throughout the nation, and the violence of the South. By 1942 he had concluded, like Myrdal, that the United

States needed to resort to social engineering to improve the status of blacks. Though he had initially been inclined to view blacks as passive recipients of charity, he now recognized that they were an increasingly militant group, capable of protesting and upsetting the status quo, and he accepted Myrdal's observation that the character of race relations in the United States would affect American diplomacy after the war. In his final letter to Myrdal, Keppel prophesied, "You can look forward to seeing the influence of your work grow from day to day and from year to year; you will constantly be consulted as to the significance of new developments over here, and your own mind will, I am sure, never cease to be creative." Looking back on the creation of the Negro study, he observed that "when the job was started we all knew it was important, but none of us could foresee how desperately important it would become for us in America to think straight about the Negro." "It may well be," Keppel concluded, "that in giving us the basis for straight thinking you have been making a major contribution to the World Peace which must come sooner or later, and may come sooner than we dare to hope today."[151] Keppel had planned to launch a publicity campaign, to send copies of the book to leading newspapers with a cover letter, and to arrange for a popular edition to be published after the war; but he did not live to carry out these plans.[152] Returning to New York from a meeting of the Board of Appeals on Visa Cases, he suffered a heart attack and died on September 8, 1943, while *An American Dilemma* was in press. Keppel's successors at the Carnegie Corporation in the 1940s and 1950s would not share his commitment to supporting research on black-white relations.

Democratic Internationalism or American Imperialism?

On his return to Stockholm in September 1942, Gunnar Myrdal plunged into a new round of duties, advising the Swedish government on economic policy and becoming the driving force on a commission charged with planning Sweden's postwar economy. The following year, the voters of Dalarna reelected him to the upper house of Parliament, a post that he assumed in January 1944. Alva Myrdal concentrated on trying to reform Sweden's educational system to make it less authoritarian and more democratic. But both Gunnar and Alva found reintegration into Swedish life difficult after spending most of the previous four years in America. Their plans for postwar Sweden were always part of a broader vision of international cooperation, and they maintained a wide acquaintance with intellectuals, journalists, and diplomats from many countries.[153] As Gunnar Myrdal looked ahead to the problem of reconstructing Europe after the war and considered the role of the United States in world affairs, he was forced to confront some of the latent contradictions between his posture as a liberal in America and his affiliation with the democratic socialist movement in Europe. As he examined further the American economy, domestic politics, and foreign policy, he would be compelled to abandon some of the optimism of *Kontakt med Amerika* and *An American Dilemma*.

Since the mid-1930s, Gunnar and Alva Myrdal had helped refugee intellectuals and Social Democratic exiles to find work in Sweden. After their exposure to the American race issue, the Myrdals argued for a generous refugee policy and pointed to the United States as an example of a nation in which people from many different countries could live together.[154] During the war, some two hundred thousand refugees came to Sweden, fleeing from Nazi Germany and German-occupied countries as well as from Finland and the Baltic states that had been overrun by Soviet armies in 1939–40. Refugees often encountered hostility from the police and from Swedes who feared the loss of their jobs to foreigners. Some were interned for short periods in labor camps and the Swedish border patrol denied entry to some refugees from Norway.[155]

Although foreign nationals were forbidden to engage in political activity in Sweden, a group of Norwegian Social Democrats formed a "study circle" in June 1942, while Gunnar and Alva Myrdal were in Princeton. In the ensuing months, the study circle came to include members from fourteen countries, was officially called the International Group of Democratic Socialists, and was dubbed by outsiders "Die Kleine Internationale." While the armies of their home countries were at war, the members of this small and obscure group met and boldly planned for peace and European reconstruction. In October 1942, Gunnar and Alva Myrdal and Richard Sterner joined the study circle and became mentors to several of its members, including the young German journalist Willy Brandt, who had lived in Norway and still held Norwegian citizenship, and the Austrian exile Bruno Kreisky.[156] Brandt regarded the Myrdals as an impressive duo; they both "radiated not only extraordinary intelligence but also a natural elegance." In contrast to many socialists he had known in other countries, the Myrdals were pragmatic, suspicious of Marxist orthodoxy, tolerant, and committed to democratic methods. Gunnar Myrdal made a lasting impression on Brandt by arguing that public control over industry was more important than the title of ownership; that the state could use tax, family, and social welfare policy to achieve greater equality; and that a mixed economy could be regulated to produce full employment. Kreisky also recalled that his experience in Sweden turned him from a "fatalistic," "old-Marxist" analysis that waited for a crisis of capitalism to produce the conditions for change to a more reformist approach that combined planning with a respect for individual freedom.[157]

The members of Die Kleine Internationale vigorously debated how the peace could be "won" and the tragic mistakes of the Treaty of Versailles avoided. While they held that responsibility for starting the war rested clearly with Nazi Germany, they agreed that the whole political and economic system of Europe had to be changed. Germany must be freed from Nazi influence and rebuilt on democratic socialist principles as part of a new, integrated, cooperative European community. The Stockholm group looked forward to a new international organization (replac-

Alva and Gunnar in Stockholm after their return to Sweden, autumn 1942
(courtesy Arbetarrörelsens Arkiv, Stockholm)

ing the League of Nations) that would lead in the rebuilding of war-torn lands,
supervise the decolonization process, and work for a new international order free
of race prejudice. Though most of the members of the Social Democratic group
were open to cooperating with the Soviet Union, they placed their greatest hopes
on the West. The ideals of the Atlantic Charter, though not an end in themselves,
offered a promising beginning for democratic socialists, and the British Labour

party's 1942 manifesto, "The Old World and the New Society," seemed to point toward a constructive approach to international cooperation and a just peace.[158]

Most Swedish and Central European Social Democrats knew little about the United States, and Gunnar Myrdal became an important interpreter of the emerging superpower during the war years. Shortly after his return to Stockholm in September 1942, he wrote another book about America, in which he informed the Swedes that the United States not only would win the war but would play a dominant role in world affairs after the war. In *Amerika mitt i världen* (America in the center of the world), published in 1943, he argued that Pearl Harbor had been a crucial turning point in the history of the United States: Americans now realized that they must take the lead in creating a stable, international economic and political order after the war. While Myrdal thought that "the American Century" had commenced, he hoped that it would unfold along the lines envisioned by Vice-President Henry Wallace as "The Century of the Common Man." Wallace, the "very probable successor to Roosevelt as the Democratic Party's presidential candidate in 1944," saw that a lasting peace depended upon greater economic opportunity for the poor in America, and on peaceful cooperation with the Soviet Union and economic aid to the nations of Africa, Asia, and Latin America. Since Wendell Willkie, "the Republican Party's leader," agreed that poverty, racial discrimination, and colonial oppression were the causes of war, a Republican victory in 1944 would not mean the abandonment of internationalism or a turning back from the social welfare policies of the New Deal.[159]

The United States, according to Myrdal, was experiencing a "technical revolution" comparable to what England went through at the beginning of the nineteenth century. After the war, "only the United States will have the conditions to utilize the new technical possibilities for mass production in all directions." Myrdal prophesied that "this industrial advance, together with Henry Wallace's political principles, should promise much for future peace in the world." Though he shared some of the traditional Swedish suspicion of Russia as an expansionistic power in the Baltic region, Myrdal hoped that American aid would encourage the Soviet Union to bring its practices more into line with its democratic rhetoric. He recommended that the United States assist in the rebuilding of Soviet industry to influence Russian policy in a peaceful and democratic direction and to create employment for American industry once wartime demand declined. Myrdal also saw American investment and development aid to Latin America, Africa, China, and India as a crucial element of world peace, and he thought that Sweden could contribute technical and administrative talent to the advancement of the economic and social systems of those countries. "Nothing less than the whole world can be our living space," he declared. "The American century with its bold democratic internationalism is therefore also our opportunity."[160] In a chapter that anticipated much of his subsequent career, Myrdal argued that economic nationalism had been one of the main causes of World War II and that an "internationalization of the world's economy" was needed to prevent a postwar depression and another cycle of poverty, aggression, and war. He called for an international organization that would regulate the world's economy, work for tariff reduction and the coordination of monetary policy, plan the rebuilding of the war-torn countries, and direct international investment and aid to the colonies as they became independent.[161]

Myrdal also insisted that world peace depended upon a diminution of racial antagonisms, both in the United States and throughout the world. Writing more bluntly about the American race issue than he had in *An American Dilemma*, he focused more on the structural changes in the economy, polity, and legal system leading toward racial equality than on the social psychology of racial conflict. Freed from the necessity of writing tactfully about the South, he charged that white southerners were gripped by "fear, uneasiness, and anxiety" over the criticisms of their institutions by the nation's leaders and warned that southerners would respond violently to the blacks' protest, agitation, and organizational activity. "Social and political reaction" was now "sweeping over the South," as whites closed ranks against "outside agitators," invoking traditions of the Civil War era. When he had finished the last chapter of *An American Dilemma* in August, he confessed, he had expected that "bloody conflicts" would soon break out in the South between whites and blacks. But Myrdal did not expect these riots to last long. No longer a strong power in the nation's politics, the South was itself one of the nation's economic and cultural problems. The North had the means to compel southern compliance and would do so through Congress, the courts, and presidential action. Myrdal bluntly declared that "it is crucially important . . . that the northern states take on the assignment of planning" and use their power to "reform the South's caste system." The "international consequences" of American racial discrimination "are the Negro protest's strongest argument today." Predicting the rapid industrialization of Asia, Africa, and Latin America, he argued that it would be a great advantage if the United States could send out to the developing world black American engineers, doctors, teachers, and agronomists. Preaching to his fellow Swedes as he had to Americans, Myrdal observed that whites were a shrinking percentage of the world's people and argued that "we must quickly seek a reconciliation with the colored people of the earth."[162]

By the spring of 1943, the Swedish government was willing to take Myrdal's pro-American views more seriously. The danger of a German invasion of Sweden had diminished after June 1941, when Hitler's armies had engaged the Russians on a two-thousand-mile front from the Arctic to the Black Sea. The Swedish government had begun to loosen restrictions on the press and had declined some German demands for troop transit across Swedish territory. After Rommel's defeat at El Alamein and the German debacle at Stalingrad, Sweden began to tilt toward the Allies. The transit of German soldiers across Swedish territory was stopped, and restrictions on the Swedish press were loosened. In the summer of 1943, the Swedish government decided to send Gunnar Myrdal on a diplomatic mission to the United States to study American economic planning for the postwar period.

That the Foreign Ministry would entrust a sensitive assignment to such an outspoken anti-Nazi was evidence that the Swedish government had concluded that the Allies would win the war and that they considered Myrdal the nation's foremost expert on the American economy. Accompanied by his former student Tore Browaldh, Myrdal visited the United States from August 28 to November 17, spending most of his time in Washington. It was not easy to represent Sweden abroad in this period. On the way over, Myrdal and Browaldh were stopped by the British border police in Scotland, who, in violation of the travelers' diplomatic immunity, forced them to take off all their clothes and confiscated some of their personal possessions. In Washington, they had a conference with Undersecretary of the Treasury Harry D. White, who insulted them, abruptly terminated the interview, and told them he would not talk to them until Sweden had been readmitted to the "family of nations." Myrdal's many contacts from his earlier visits proved invaluable, however, and he and Browaldh interviewed 350 political leaders, economists, social scientists, and journalists, including Henry Wallace and Wendell Willkie. Wallace introduced the visiting Swedish senator on the floor of the Senate, and Myrdal enjoyed "the privilege of the floor," making contacts among senators. Myrdal's friends in government gave him confidential reports on America's economic planning for the postwar period, and economists such as Alvin Hansen and Jacob Viner showed him the latest data and offered forecasts about the American economy after the war.[163] Since Alva was not along on the trip, Gunnar lacked her perspective on educational and social welfare institutions that seemed to offer promise of egalitarian reforms: his information would come from an elite of policymakers and intellectuals.

Myrdal was dismayed by what he heard from the American economists, many of whom predicted a postwar depression. Despite extensive planning for postwar reconversion to a peacetime economy, most economists thought that the United States would face serious unemployment and stagnation after the war. Equally disturbing were the signs that relations between the United States and the Soviet Union might sour after the defeat of Hitler. In an interview with Myrdal, Walter Lippmann predicted that Stalin would create a ring of Communist states in Eastern Europe and foresaw the possibility that the continent would be polarized between Communist and non-Communist blocs. Pollster Hadley Cantril showed Myrdal recent data that revealed continued suspicion of the Soviet ally on the part of the American people, and Myrdal guessed that there would be a dramatic swing of American opinion against Russia if Stalin violated the principles of the Atlantic Charter in Eastern Europe. The Swedish visitor was troubled by the vogue of "realist" thinking he encountered in Washington, which he considered to be out of phase with the essential idealism of the American people that he had noted in *Kontakt med Amerika, An American Dilemma,* and *Amerika mitt i världen.* Myrdal worried that this so-called realism would lead the United States to resort to a kind of imperialism after the war, imposing military solutions instead of working through international organizations. In his view, the new realism lacked the boldness and imagination necessary to create a new, cooperative international order that would ensure economic prosperity and protect the world against future wars. It was a self-defeating, cynical perspective, highly "unrealistic" and "full of illusions." Myrdal prophesied disaster if the United States decided to "play at the game of great power imperialism." "The only foreign policy that America can effectively participate in after the war," he insisted, "is a democratic international-ism."[164]

Chastened by his encounter with American policymakers, planners, and pun-dits, Myrdal returned to Stockholm and filed a report with the Foreign Ministry in which he predicted a serious recession or depression in the United States and Europe after the war. With the defeat of the Axis powers a virtual certainty, Myrdal the economist came to some different conclusions from Myrdal the social prophet and antifascist propagandist. He was now a social engineer with a different client, the Swedish government, and he had to make a realistic economic forecast that would guide Swedes in planning their own postwar economy. Myrdal also had to face some of the contradictions that he had ignored earlier between his social democratic vision of economic and social planning and his enthusiasm for America as an individualistic society that was liberal in the nineteenth-century European sense. The report and Myrdal's subsequent writings about the American economy reveal the extent to which the Swedish observer had softened his social democratic criticisms of American economic policy in *An American Dilemma* in order to keep the discussion "within the conservative reformist limits of average American economic discussion."[165] Myrdal informed the Foreign Ministry that the November 1942 election in the United States had brought to power an anti–New Deal majority in Congress, whose attacks on the Office of Price Administration were only the opening salvo in an assault on government economic planning. All of the New Deal agencies had their budgets slashed, New Dealers were being forced out of important leadership posts in government, and Henry Wallace had lost much of his power and influence and now fulfilled a "purely decorative function." Retreating from the optimistic conclusions of his earlier books, Myrdal declared that "in his heart and soul, the American is rather conservative, in spite of the radical direction of thought that Roosevelt and the New Deal introduced into American politics." For the average American, "'the American way of living' stands as a social ideal. When he looks to the future, it is not a radically reformed America that he wants to see, but a rather unchanged America." In August 1943, he observed, nearly 60 percent of the population told the pollsters that they were "satisfied with America as it was before the war."[166]

Armed with the latest data on the American economy, he presented a "cold-blooded and hard-boiled analysis" of the American economy to the National Economic Society of Sweden on March 9, 1944, just as reviewers were delivering the first round of accolades for *An American Dilemma*.[167] The United States, Myrdal warned his compatriots, was headed toward a serious postwar recession or depression because of its system of unregulated capitalism and its neglect of economic and social planning. He bluntly asserted that the New Deal, whatever its successes in the "social field," had failed to increase production and employment to 1929 levels and had left 10–12 million unemployed at the beginning of World War II. Assuming that an equally "negativistic" Congress would emerge from the 1944 election, Myrdal forecast a postwar recession because of declining demand for war materiel and the replacement of government management of the economy by so-called free enterprise. "In an unregulated capitalistic society," he lectured, "it seems that a boom must always have an end and lapse into crisis and depression." Myrdal noted that war production had accelerated the trend toward monopolization of industry and that big business was thriving under conditions of government regulation. Yet most businessmen, he protested, were oblivious to the need for continued government planning to avert a slump after the war.[168] Myrdal observed that American businessmen were as optimistic as they had been in the 1920s, but he submitted that this optimism derived more from wartime psychology than from careful analysis of economic trends. "In a country at war it is not patriotic to see the future otherwise than optimistically," he belatedly recognized. "Nobody wants to be a 'defeatist,' and this fact induces a mass suggestion which influences even expert opinion." Myrdal, on the other hand, expected mass unemployment, labor unrest, and a crisis of over-production in agriculture after the war's end. If millions of Americans should be unemployed, he lamented, "we must . . . contemplate that the race question may emerge in its most terrifying form," and he predicted "an epidemic of violence, sometimes expressed . . . in bloody fights on the part of labor."[169]

For his Swedish audience, Myrdal concluded that if the United States entered a postwar recession or depression, it would not be in a position to make extensive foreign loans and that international trade would decline.[170] He developed these arguments further in a book, *Varning för fredsoptimism* (Warning against postwar optimism), published in 1944. The book was never translated into English, and although Myrdal published an article in *The Atlantic Monthly* in which he offered pessimistic economic forecasts, his ideas did not ignite a major discussion in America.[171] Though he had warned of the danger of the United States playing the game of "great power imperialism," he did not foresee the levels to which American military spending would rise during the Cold War. Despite his pleas for massive American aid to reconstruct Europe, he did not imagine that a program on the scale of the Marshall Plan would be forthcoming. Nor did Myrdal predict the jump in domestic consumer spending at the end of the war. Myrdal's economic forecasts in 1944 and his candid reports to Swedes on American politics and society are worth noting because they indicate that he was not a hopelessly naive optimist, as many of his American critics would later charge. World War II brought a host of tumultuous, convulsive changes to the world's economic, political, and social systems, and Gunnar Myrdal sought to analyze those changes as they unfolded from month to month and from year to year. The swing to the right in American politics in November 1942 and the emergence of tensions between the United States and the Soviet Union were only two of many developments that he had not foreseen when he completed *An American Dilemma* in September 1942. But Myrdal had wisely refrained from tying his analysis of American race relations too closely to short-term developments in American politics and economics. Though his analysis of American culture and ideals in *An American Dilemma* would justly be criticized for its vagueness, he succeeded in providing a conceptual framework that would survive the vicissitudes of the war and offer a compelling challenge to Americans for another generation.

Myrdal and the July 20, 1944, Plot to Kill Hitler

While Gunnar Myrdal's vision was fixed on his plans for the postwar world and his hopes for international cooperation, he still watched with horror as the war continued in Europe and the destruction from bombing and "total war" vastly exceeded the wreckage of World War I. Though his work on postwar planning gave him a sense of preparing for a better world, the irrepressible Myrdal chafed against the restraints on a public figure of a neutral country and longed for more direct involvement in the struggle against Hitler. Stockholm was a fascinating observation point for watching the war and for gathering news about what was happening on both sides. Myrdal's friend John Scott, a correspondent for *Time* and *Life* magazines, observed, "In the feverish atmosphere of this neutral exchange center, political intrigue reached an amazing degree of complexity, and at every turn one found numbers of spies, suspicions, blonde agents, amateur military and political experts anxious to turn a dishonest penny, and vendors of photographs of everything from pornography to secret military installations." Diplomats from Allied and Axis countries passed by one another at the opera and in the dining room of the Grand Hotel, foreign journalists competed for the latest bits of military and diplomatic intelligence, and agents and double agents fed rumors of every imaginable sort.[172]

Both Alva and Gunnar Myrdal had maintained friendships with British and American diplomats since the early years of the war, and they had some contact with Allied intelligence agencies as well. Alva had briefed British officials on the situation in Scandinavia in 1941 while on her way from Sweden to the United States. During their time in Princeton in 1941 and 1942, Gunnar and Alva had advised the American Office of Strategic Services (OSS) and had made broadcasts to Sweden under the auspices of the Office of War Information.[173] In Stockholm from 1942 to 1945, the Myrdals were highly regarded by American and British diplomats because of their strong antifascist stand, and they were acquainted with R. Taylor Cole, the OSS officer at the American legation.[174] In addition, the Myrdals knew the Soviet ambassador to Sweden, Alexandra Kollontai, a seventy-four-year-old veteran of the Bolshevik Revolution, friend of Lenin, and author of books on feminism and sexual emancipation.[175] From their colleagues in Die

Kleine Internationale, Gunnar and Alva heard news of the resistance movements in Norway, Denmark, and Germany.

These disparate worlds would come together briefly in June 1944, when Gunnar Myrdal received a visit from Adam von Trott zu Solz, a brilliant young German diplomat who was a key member of the anti-Nazi Resistance movement. The son of the former Prussian minister of education, Trott had grown up on the family estate in Hesse and had attended the universities of Munich, Göttingen, and Berlin, receiving a law degree. After study as a Rhodes scholar at Oxford, he had written a doctoral dissertation on Hegel's political philosophy and international law at Göttingen and had spent a year in China studying East Asian politics. As a counselor in the German Foreign Ministry, Trott had conducted an audacious secret diplomacy, attempting to win support in Allied countries for the German Resistance movement. He had come to know Myrdal in America in the fall of 1939, when Trott had met with prominent Americans such as Reinhold Niebuhr, Roger Baldwin, Felix Frankfurter, and Eleanor Roosevelt before the United States entered the war. From 1940 to 1944, Trott's diplomatic duties carried him to Sweden, Switzerland, and Turkey, where he sought to make contact with Allied officials, and to occupied countries such as Holland, where he had friends in the Resistance movement. Again and again, his activities and his obvious lack of enthusiasm for the Nazi philosophy aroused the suspicion of his superiors, but Trott managed to survive many close calls through his extraordinary intelligence and charm and by virtue of his many friends and family connections in elite circles in Germany.[176]

Since Hitler's rise to power in 1933, individuals from many corners of German society had resisted the Nazi regime. Resistance cells included Communists, Social Democrats, conservative aristocrats, Jews, Catholics, and Protestants. But the group with the greatest chance of gaining physical access to Hitler in order to assassinate him was a circle of dissident military officers that included General Ludwig Beck and Colonel Claus Schenck Count von Stauffenberg. Various military leaders had plotted to overthrow Hitler since 1938, but plans had foundered in the face of Hitler's popularity with the German people, the difficulties in planning a coup d'état against a police state, and the unwillingness of Allied leaders to modify their demand for an unconditional surrender. Nevertheless, from 1941 to 1944 a conspiracy took shape that included some military leaders, conservative diplomats and civil servants, church leaders, and a few prominent Social Democrats. Adam von Trott zu Solz attended meetings of the group at Count Helmuth von Moltke's Kreisau estate, worked closely with Stauffenberg and military conspirators in Berlin, and attempted to win support abroad. By June 1944, Trott and most of the conspirators recognized that Germany would soon be occupied, but it was unclear how much of the country would be taken by the Soviets and how much by the British, French, and Americans. As long as the unconditional surrender formula held, Trott feared that German military leaders would have no incentive to risk their lives in support of a coup.[177]

Gunnar Myrdal had little sympathy for the idea of a coup d'état by a small clique of conservative military leaders and German nationalists, and in *Amerika mitt i världen*, he had bluntly warned that "a compromise peace with rebellious German generals and Junkers is unthinkable for the Americans." Myrdal had predicted that the American government would insist upon occupying Germany in order to root out Nazism and prevent the spread of Soviet Communism so that the United States would not be dragged into another world war in a few decades.[178] But when Trott called on him shortly after the Normandy landings, he informed Myrdal that the assassination and coup attempt was going ahead in any case, that the conspiracy included prominent Social Democrats such as the former Reichstag deputy Julius Leber, and that they were prepared to cooperate with the Soviet Union as well as with the United States and Britain. He asked Myrdal to arrange meetings with an American diplomat and with Kollontai. On June 23, Myrdal invited the German visitor to his office in the Riksdag, Sweden's parliament, which ironically was one of the few places where they could meet without the danger of interference from the Swedish police, and introduced him to John Scott, the *Time-Life* correspondent who also worked with the OSS. Like Myrdal and Trott, John Scott was an adventurous spirit, a risk taker, and an idealist. The son of the American socialist Scott Nearing, he had dropped out of the University of Wisconsin in 1931, trained as a welder, and moved to the Soviet Union, where he had worked for five years in the industrial city of Magnitogorsk. Disillusioned with many aspects of the Soviet system, he nonetheless had written with admiration about the Soviet people in his book *Behind the Urals* (1942). Signing on with Henry Luce's publications after he left the Soviet Union, Scott had been sent to Stockholm in 1943 to report on the Scandinavian countries.[179]

In his conversation with Scott, Adam von Trott pleaded with the American government to modify its unconditional surrender formula as an encouragement to the Resistance plot to overthrow the Nazi regime. He acknowledged that Germany would have to be occupied by the Allies but asked for an interval of several weeks between the overthrow of Nazi rule and the beginning of occupation. During this interval the Resistance would establish a non-Nazi government, demobilize the German armed forces, and try war criminals in German courts. Trott also requested that Germany be allowed to retain its 1936 borders and to preserve at least the outward form of national sovereignty. Myrdal recommended that the United States government give serious consideration to negotiating with the German Resistance.[180]

John Scott wrote a memorandum of the conversation, which Taylor Cole used as a basis for a cable sent under the American minister's signature to the secretary of state and the OSS in Washington. Cole and other officials at the American legation in Stockholm thought that the United States should consider negotiating with the German Resistance, and Myrdal's assurances that Trott was a sincere anti-Nazi helped to give him credibility in the eyes of the American diplomats in Stockholm.[181] By this point in the war, however, the United States was irreversibly committed to the unconditional surrender formula, and the State Department refused to negotiate with the German Resistance. Trott got a similar response when he spoke with an agent of the British Intelligence Service (MI6). During this same visit to Stockholm, the German diplomat met Willy Brandt, brought him greetings from his Social Democratic colleague Julius Leber, and asked him to arrange a meeting with Kollontai. Trott called off plans to meet with Kollontai, however, when he heard a rumor that there was a spy in the Soviet embassy. Having received no assurances from the Americans, the British, or the Soviets, Trott returned to Berlin, empty-handed, on July 3. His trip to Sweden was the last direct contact between a prominent figure of the German Resistance and Allied intelligence agencies before the attempted assassination of Hitler.[182]

Though denied Allied support, the conspirators decided to proceed because they believed that they, as Germans, had a responsibility to rid the world of the Nazi dictatorship. "It is now time that something is done," Stauffenberg said shortly before the attempt. "But he who has the courage to do something must do so in the knowledge that he will go down in German history as a traitor. If he does not do it, however, he will be a traitor to his own conscience."[183] On July 20, 1944, Stauffenberg exploded a bomb in Hitler's headquarters in East Prussia, narrowly missing the führer and igniting an abortive plot to seize control of the government and of military garrisons in Germany and France. Stauffenberg was shot in Berlin that night, and Adam von Trott zu Solz was apprehended five days later, tried in a Nazi court, subjected to gruesome torture, and hanged from a wire cord on August 26. Hitler had the torture and execution of the leading conspirators filmed so that he could watch it. Thousands of Germans were killed, imprisoned, and tortured in the orgy of revenge that Hitler unleashed in the wake of the assassination attempt.[184]

Myrdal seldom spoke about his contacts with the German Resistance, since he had overstepped the bounds of propriety for an elected official of a neutral state. He did acknowledge to Allen Dulles, the OSS official who had monitored the German Resistance from neutral Switzerland, that he "saw a lot of Adam von Trott during the war both in America and in Sweden." "I am afraid," he wrote, "that I belong to the many contacts of his which finally brought danger."[185]

On the evening of May 1, 1945, Gunnar Myrdal and Willy Brandt were addressing a Mayday rally of Stockholm Social Democrats and anti-Nazi refugees when someone handed Brandt a note containing the news that Hitler had committed suicide as Russian troops had reached Berlin. When the young German refugee made the announcement to the audience, he was met with "a deep silence" rather than applause or shouts of joy. "It was as if the people simply could not believe that the end had actually come," Brandt recalled. "And at the same time a question was almost physically present in the room: Hitler's dreadful challenge to all mankind—had it really ended in this way?" With the liberation of Denmark, however, Brandt observed an "ecstasy" that "shook Stockholm like a fever and reached its climax on the seventh of May." As the war in Europe officially ended, "the Swedes, allegedly cool and reserved, burst into a veritable frenzy of enthusiasm." But Brandt suggested, "Perhaps the rejoicing was so exuberant because many of them wanted to deafen the pangs of their conscience: the Norwegian and Danish brothers had suffered very much, they themselves had kept aloof from the struggle. They had been lucky, but shouldn't they have made some sacrifices too? Now one was rid of the dilemma once and for all; one could breathe freely again, in the truest sense of the word."[186]

The defeat of Nazi Germany brought an end to a tumultuous period in Gunnar Myrdal's life during which he had struggled to reconcile his duty as a citizen of a small, neutral nation with his intense desire to contribute to the fight against Nazism. He had sought to take a stand that was pragmatic enough to maintain his political career in Sweden yet effective in contributing to the anti-Nazi struggle, and the situation seemed to require some moral compromises. In 1940 Myrdal found the answer in his attempts to strengthen Sweden's "ideological defenses" in the face of government censorship and widespread accommodation of Hitler. Unable to do more in Sweden, he returned to the United States in 1941 and directed his enormous energy, intelligence, and political commitment into the writing of *An American Dilemma*, which appealed to Americans to live up to their ideals at a time when many of the democratic nations of the world counted on the United States for leadership. The moral, psychological, and ideological focus of the book stems in great measure from Myrdal's very personal perception of the strategic importance of a democratic creed in motivating people to resist Nazism. If the book's analysis of American culture and politics stressed American exceptionalism, it was because Myrdal believed that the United States was unique among the nations of the world in having an explicit national creed. His experiences during World War II deepened Gunnar Myrdal's commitment to human rights and gave him a global perspective that would inform his work for the rest of his life. Whether writing as a liberal in America or as a Social Democrat in Sweden, he sought to work with people of various nationalities in formulating ideas for a new "democratic internationalism" that would keep the peace, rebuild Europe, and aid the nations emerging from colonial rule. Through all these endeavors, Myrdal struggled to maintain his faith that democratic values and the scientific spirit of the Enlightenment would overcome the Nazi challenge and prevail over the manifold obstacles to economic and racial justice after the war. Myrdal's contributions to Sweden's economic planning would win him an appointment as minister of commerce in 1945, but he would be remembered in the United States for the optimistic, moralistic conclusions of *An American Dilemma*, which resonated powerfully with American intellectuals as World War II drew to a close.

5

An American Dilemma: The Text

In January 1944, Harper & Brothers published *An American Dilemma*, the product of four years of research and writing by Gunnar Myrdal and his collaborators. The reader who picked up this hefty volume was confronted with a text of more than a thousand pages, plus 10 appendixes and 250 pages of notes. Myrdal had constructed the book, however, so that the general reader or policy-maker could learn the essentials of his argument by reading part 1 and the concluding chapter, "America again at the Crossroads in the Negro Problem." In these chapters aimed at the "citizen-layman," Myrdal developed his argument concerning the American creed; analyzed the changing conditions of blacks resulting from education, migration, the New Deal, and World War II; and warned whites of the dangers that lay ahead if they ignored the "Negro problem." The remaining chapters constituted a detailed exploration of race relations and of Afro-American life. Although they summarized existing scholarship on some subjects, they also contained a wealth of insights and original observations. Myrdal recognized that many readers would not read the whole book and would consult certain chapters in encyclopedia fashion; he therefore repeated many of his key arguments throughout the book.[1] As Keppel privately noted, *An American Dilemma* is a "sprawling" and "repetitive" work that defies easy summarization.

In constructing his new liberal interpretation, Myrdal synthesized a vast litera-ture of scholarly monographs and articles as well as unpublished investigations by his collaborators and analyzed statistical data on every aspect of Afro-American life. No one had ever brought together such a comprehensive study of American race relations. In addition to making his argument about the conflict in the minds of white Americans, Myrdal presented a structural argument that a conflict be-tween the American creed and racial discrimination existed within American institutions. He presented the case against scientific theories of inherited differ-ences in intelligence and temperament among the races; he marshaled an enor-mous array of evidence to show discrimination in the economy, political system, and courts; he sketched a disturbing picture of the damage that segregation and racial discrimination inflicted on blacks; and he analyzed competing strategies within the black protest movement. Yet Myrdal did not merely echo the views of American scholars: he offered an essentially new interpretation rooted in his own experiences as a Swedish social scientist and policymaker. His judgments about the weaknesses of Afro-American and working-class movements in the United States were based on comparisons with labor, farm, and cooperative movements in the Scandinavian countries, and his critique of the denial of civil rights to blacks in the South was informed by his awareness of Hitler's destruction of constitutional government in Germany and the threats to the Swedish *rättstat* posed by the wartime emergency.

Myrdal reinvigorated two older traditions in American social science that had declined since the Progressive Era: social engineering and moral exhortation. He regarded social engineering as the "supreme task of social science."[2] Yet he saw his task in *An American Dilemma* as laying the analytical groundwork for new social policy rather than proposing particular legislation or outlining new policies in detail. Myrdal would make a number of general suggestions regarding public policy throughout the book, but in the wartime atmosphere of rapid social and political change, he preferred not to focus the book on a specific political program, which might soon be overtaken by events. Instead he assumed the mantle of Tocqueville and Bryce and wrote a broad interpretive study of American civilization "viewed in its implications for the most disadvantaged population group."[3]

Despite his advocacy of social engineering and his faith in modern social science, Myrdal in many ways preached an old-fashioned jeremiad to white Americans concerning the race issue. In chapter after chapter, he delineated in excruciating detail the damage that racial discrimination inflicted on black Americans and the cost to society as a whole of denying education, job training, and the rights of citizenship to a large minority. Myrdal pointed to the specter of race riots and protracted civil conflict if the nation did not move immediately to improve the status of Afro-Americans. More significantly, he was in a unique position, as a foreign observer, to warn Americans that they were not living up to their fundamental ideals, that they were in danger of failing to fulfill their cherished role of providing an example of democracy and liberty to the rest of the world. After pointing to the dire consequences if America did not change, Myrdal expressed his faith in the power of the American creed to vanquish white supremacy. Again and again, he squeezed the most optimistic interpretation possible out of the data he examined, stressing the dynamic forces in the society that were leading toward change. Though he wrote extensively about policy questions and urged the acceptance of "prophylactic" reforms, he always brought the race issue back to the moral choices of individuals. Steeped in the religious culture of rural Dalarna, Myrdal adopted—perhaps unconsciously—a rhetorical strategy that had been used extensively by abolitionists and by later, more secular, advocates of civil rights.[4] His moral exhortation would resonate powerfully with Americans during and after World War II, offering a compelling alternative to the antiseptic prose of most American social scientists, who, in their pursuit of value neutrality, had created an emotional distance between themselves and their subject.

In contrast to many American social scientists of the period, Myrdal bluntly and forcefully condemned racial oppression, particularly segregation and discrimination in the South. Totally absent from *An American Dilemma* was the vague rhetoric of racial adjustment, deference to southern white folkways, and silence or equivocation on the social equality issue that had characterized so many foundation-sponsored studies of black-white relations. Yet Myrdal did not engage in the kind of crude South-baiting that had awakened regional defensiveness in the past.[5] His status as a foreign observer, his emphasis on the American creed as a functioning part of the nation's culture, and his treatment of race relations in an international context during wartime allowed him to discuss the condition of blacks as a national problem and to avoid the appearance of singling out the South for censure.

The American Creed and Institutional Change

The foreword and preface to *An American Dilemma* were important in conferring on the work an aura of legitimacy and scientific objectivity. In a foreword written in December 1942, Frederick Keppel explained the Carnegie Corporation's decision to "import" a foreign observer, presented Myrdal's credentials as a scholar and public official, and offered the book as a comprehensive report on an issue related to the American war effort. He defended the foundation's decision to initiate broad and comprehensive studies of social problems and cited the report of Abraham Flexner's Committee on the Costs of Medical Care and Lord Hailey's *An African Survey* as precedents for the Myrdal project. To deflect any criticisms of foundation meddling in politics, he included a cautionary note that the foundation merely sought to "make the facts available and let them speak for themselves" and did not "undertake to instruct the public as to what to do about them."[6] This disingenuous claim was at odds with Myrdal's purpose of writing a new interpretation of American civilization and advocating social engineering, but Keppel was able to ask the reader's indulgence of Myrdal's unique perspective as a foreigner.

Anticipating criticism from white southerners, Keppel noted that the idea for the study had come from the late Newton D. Baker and mentioned that Baker was "the son of a Confederate officer." He gave a brief history of the project, conveniently omitting the early search for a colonial administrator and emphasizing the corporation's decision to look for a man with a "fresh mind" who came from a country "with no background or traditions of imperialism." Keppel argued that a close examination of the race issue was in the national interest because "the eyes of men of all races the world over are turned upon us to see how the people of the most powerful of the United Nations are dealing *at home* with a major problem of race relations." He concluded the foreword with a plea for scholarly criticism rather than emotional reactions to the book. Whatever private doubts he may have had about the book, Keppel stood by Myrdal publicly and threw the full weight of the Carnegie Corporation's prestige behind the study in an effort to insure that it received a fair hearing and in the hope that it would stimulate debate about an important public issue.[7]

Myrdal sought to overcome doubts about a foreigner's competence to investigate American race relations by listing in the preface the vast array of advisors and collaborators who had assisted him. His roster of advisors was a veritable who's who in American social science and included such names as Franz Boas, Ruth Benedict, Howard Odum, Robert Park, and W. I. Thomas—even though those luminaries had played only a minor role in the study. The listing of over one hundred American scholars who advised or participated in the study helped to create the appearance of a united front or consensus in support of Myrdal's liberal position on the race question. Myrdal also supplied the titles of the unpublished research memoranda written for the study and deposited in New York's Schomburg Library.[8] Returning to a theme he had broached in *Kontakt med Amerika*, Myrdal asserted that the very idea of inviting a foreigner to investigate one of the United States' most serious problems was "a new demonstration . . . of American moralism, rationalism, and optimism—and a demonstration of America's unfailing conviction of its basic soundness and strength." He expressed his regret that "the reading of this book must be somewhat of an ordeal to the good citizen" because "the Negro problem in America represents a moral lag in the development of the nation." But he contended that for the first time since Reconstruction the United States faced the possibility of a fundamental change in race relations, a change that would bring social practice closer to American ideals.[9]

In his introduction, Myrdal set out his central argument, that the "Negro problem" was an unresolved moral issue for Americans. He asserted that Americans were deeply moralistic by comparison with other Western peoples, and that most Americans felt uncomfortable about the contradiction between their egalitarian principles and their attitudes and behavior toward blacks. "The American Negro problem is a problem in the heart of the American," he wrote. "*It is there that the interracial tension has its focus. It is there that the decisive struggle goes on. This is the central viewpoint of this treatise. Though our study includes economic, social, and political race relations, at bottom our problem is the moral dilemma of the American— the conflict between his moral valuations on various levels of consciousness and generality.*" Myrdal defined the American dilemma as the conflict between the valuations of the American creed and the prejudices against blacks that arise from specific individual and local factors and situations. He held that each person carries within himself conflicting valuations. He maintained that "*there are no homogeneous 'attitudes' behind human behavior but a mesh of struggling inclinations, interests, and ideals, some held conscious and some suppressed for long intervals but all active in bending behavior in their direction.*" Myrdal distinguished between the "morally higher" valuations of the American creed, which enjoy "the sanction of religion and national legislation," and other valuations, commonly referred to as "irrational" or "prejudiced," which are "defended in terms of tradition, expediency, or utility."[10]

In outlining his methodology, Myrdal made it clear that social psychology would play an important part in the investigation. Although his comprehensive study would include "quantitative indices" of the "material conditions" of black life, he considered these less important than the analysis of the "doctrines and ideologies, valuations and beliefs, embedded in the minds of white and Negro Americans." Myrdal adopted W. I. Thomas's idea that "when people define situations as real, they *are* real," and he contended that "material facts in large measure are the product of what people think, feel and believe."[11]

The "Negro problem," according to Myrdal, was really a "white man's problem." He chose therefore to give primary attention in his book to "what goes on in the minds of white Americans." Since white Americans held "practically all the economic, social, and political power," they determined the Negro's "place." Myrdal insisted that there was already an extensive social science literature on the black community but that the attitudes and behavior of whites merited closer scrutiny. He insisted, "The Negro's entire life, and, consequently, also his opinions on the Negro problem, are, in the main, to be considered as secondary reactions to more primary pressures from the side of the dominant white majority."[12] Myrdal would face harsh criticism in the 1960s for his argument that Afro-American culture was primarily a "secondary reaction" to white hostility.[13] Most contemporary observers, however, would see Myrdal's focus on the "white man's problem" as a bold and innovative approach.[14] The race "problem," according to Myrdal, could not be explained primarily in terms of the Negroes' "backwardness," nor could it be blamed entirely on the prejudice of white southerners. "There are few liberals," he averred, "even in New England, who have not a well-furnished compartment of race prejudice, even if it is usually suppressed from conscious attention."[15] To educated white Americans, Myrdal said, in effect: "We have met the enemy and he is us."

The idea of a conflict between the American creed and racial discrimination was not new. Frederick Douglass had relentlessly indicted white Americans for refusing to extend the promise of the Declaration of Independence to blacks. In *The Souls of Black Folk*, Du Bois had contended that the "Negro Problem" was "a concrete test of the underlying principles of the great republic." Du Bois had found southern whites to be "deeply religious and intensely democratic," and he claimed that the color line was "a flat contradiction to their beliefs and professions."[16] Alain Locke, in *The New Negro*, had written that "an intelligent realization of the great discrepancy between the American social creed and social practice forces upon the Negro the taking of the moral advantage that is his."[17] Myrdal differed from these earlier writers, however, in asserting that the conflict caused an acute mental conflict in whites and that Afro-Americans were quickly acquiring the power to press their case aggressively before world opinion and to disrupt business-as-usual at home. Myrdal argued, moreover, that an *institutional* conflict existed in the political and legal system, as well as a conflict between the demands of a technologically advanced economy and the prescriptions of the caste system.

Though the value premises of the study were the principles to which Myrdal had been devoted as a Swedish Social Democratic policymaker, he presented them as having been taken entirely from the American creed. These value premises had been "selected from among those valuations actually observed as existing in the minds of the white and Negro Americans and tested as to their social and political relevance and significance." By stating his value premises explicitly, he hoped "to purge as far as possible the scientific investigation of distorting biases which are usually the result of hidden biases" and to "lay a logical basis for practical and political conclusions."[18] Myrdal thus refined a methodology he had advocated in *The Political Element in the Development of Economic Theory* and "Means and Ends in Political Economy."[19]

The concept of the American creed received detailed attention in Myrdal's first chapter. Restating a point he had made in *Kontakt med Amerika*, he contended that "America, compared to every other country in Western civilization, large or small, has the *most explicitly expressed* system of general ideals in reference to human interrelations. This body of ideals is more widely understood and appreciated than similar ideals are anywhere else."[20] As a foreigner, Myrdal found it "remark-able that a vast democracy with so many cultural disparities has been able to reach this unanimity of ideals and to elevate them supremely over the threshhold of popular perception." He pointed to the failure of fascism and Nazism to achieve such a success, despite their use of propaganda and violence.[21] Myrdal defined the "main norms" of the American creed as "the belief in equality and the rights to liberty." He saw the creed as part of a "humanistic liberalism" that had originated during the Enlightenment and found expression in the Declaration of Indepen-dence and the Constitution. Myrdal also stressed the contribution to the American creed of Protestant Christianity, especially the "lower class Protestant sects, split off from the Anglican church." English common law and the idea of a government "of laws and not of men" constituted a third source of the creed.[22]

In delineating his concept of the American creed, Myrdal occupied a middle ground between the progressive historians and the postwar "consensus school." He accepted, to a great extent, Charles Beard's interpretation of the Constitution as a conservative reaction against the democratic advances of the American Revo-lution, and he endorsed much of Vernon Parrington's portrayal of American history as a "conflict between the man and the dollar, between democracy and property." But Myrdal contended that the forces of democracy were winning the struggle against property and privilege and that the liberals had the American creed on their side. Although he was aware that conservatives also framed their arguments in constitutional terms, Myrdal generally ignored the ways in which elements of the American creed could be used to advocate laissez-faire or states' rights positions in opposition to New Deal programs or civil rights legislation. He considered the creed to be a coherent set of principles and rejected the idea of an inherent conflict between liberty and equality within the American political tradi-tion. In formulating his concept of the American creed, Myrdal drew upon Ralph Gabriel's idea of the "American democratic faith." But while Gabriel discussed the challenges to the democratic faith posed by the fashionable scientific naturalism and relativism of the 1930s, Myrdal emphasized the continuities between the Enlightenment and twentieth-century American political thought.[23]

In this first chapter, Myrdal made it clear that the American dilemma was not simply a psychological conflict in the minds of white people, but a complex institutional problem within the American legal system. As a lawyer and former magistrate, he was careful to note that the ideals of the creed were often disregarded in the day-to-day operation of the American law. He argued that Americans had "a relatively low degree of respect for law and order" and attributed this attitude to the "Jeffersonian distrust of government," the heritage of the frontier, and Thoreau's doctrine of the "higher law," which held that Americans should not obey "bad" laws. This "anarchistic tendency in America's legal culture" was also a reaction against a puritanical desire to overregulate behavior through such laws as prohibition of alcoholic beverages. The ordinary American, then, did not respect the authority of the state, the courts, or the police as much as a typical citizen in Britain or Scandinavia. Americans were less likely to participate in politics and more likely to take a fatalistic attitude toward government and the legal system. These tendencies, according to Myrdal, were important factors in understanding the American tolerance of southern "lawlessness" and the denial of civil rights to blacks. While acknowledging that the federal government had not been able to enforce compliance with Reconstruction statutes, antitrust laws, or prohibition, Myrdal nonetheless believed that the New Deal was moving the United States closer to something approaching the Swedish *rättstat*. Striking a note of conservative reform, he predicted that Americans would succeed in becoming a "law-abiding people" who would keep alive their "conservatism in fundamental principles." Two factors were of strategic importance: lawmaking must become a "task of scientific social engineering," and the administration of the law must be entrusted to a civil service that is "independent, legal, impartial, and efficient."[24] Myrdal thus assumed that the United States was moving toward an increasingly efficient, centralized system of laws and bureaucracy that would ultimately insist upon enforcement of civil rights legislation in all parts of the country. Americans would "conserve" their liberal principles by entrusting them to a Swedish-style bureaucracy.

Myrdal argued that most American intellectuals underestimated the strategic importance of the American creed in the struggle to improve the status of blacks. Returning to a theme in *Kontakt med Amerika*, he contrasted the idealism of the American people with the fatalism of American intellectuals. Myrdal referred to these intellectuals as "defeatists," a term he had applied to members of the Swedish intelligentsia who favored accommodation to Hitler's New Order rather than vigorous resistance and steadfast assertion of democratic principles.[25] Though he did not mention any names in this passage, Myrdal was criticizing the "do-nothing" approach of some of the senior, white social scientists such as Robert Park and Donald Young. At the same time, he condemned a similar fatalism that he detected among the younger generation of black scholars such as Ralph Bunche, Abram Harris, and Doxey Wilkerson. These black leftists, according to Myrdal, expressed "disbelief that much can be won by politics, legislation, and law suits, and have become inclined to set their hopes on what they conceive of as more fundamental changes of the economic structure." Myrdal saw himself as part of a generation of Swedish Social Democrats who, instead of waiting for the class struggle to reach a revolutionary point, cast aside Marxist dogma and made a coalition with a bourgeois party to win a parliamentary majority and lay the foundation for a welfare state. He had little patience with academic Marxists who, in his view, were unable to adapt to the exigencies of the American situation and advance a practical strategy of reform. Myrdal rejected as "superficial" Bunche's argument that white Americans merely pay "lip service" to the ideals of the American creed. "The American," Myrdal insisted, "is strongly and sincerely 'against sin,' even, and not least, his own sins." While "the true hypocrite sins in secret," Americans publicize their own imperfections to the world.[26]

Adapting W. F. Ogburn's concept of cultural lag to the realm of morality, Myrdal asserted that "from the point of view of the American Creed, the status accorded the Negro represents nothing more and nothing less than a century-long lag in public morals. In principle the Negro problem was settled long ago; in practice the solution is not effectuated. The Negro in America has not yet been given the elemental civil and political rights of formal democracy, including a fair opportunity to earn his living, upon which a general accord was already won when the American Creed was taking form." This "anachronism," according to Myrdal, "constitutes the contemporary 'problem' both to Negroes and to whites."[27] He suggested that increased agitation by blacks and their allies, together with sustained efforts to educate whites, would reduce this "lag in public morals" on the race issue.

Myrdal's redefinition of Ogburn's cultural lag is striking. As Ogburn conceived it, twentieth-century Americans were still trying to apply social and moral values formed in nineteenth-century rural and small-town society to the problems of modern urban-industrial life. The concept of cultural lag thus contained an implicit technological determinism: social values would, in time, catch up with modern technology and the demands of life in the metropolis.[28] Myrdal, however, argued that the United States was founded according to the ideals of the Enlightenment. Democracy and the scientific spirit worked hand in hand, and nineteenth-century American theories of racial inequality were an aberration from these first principles. According to Myrdal, modern scientific knowledge about race and the complexities of life in an urban-industrial society were rapidly undermining the rationale for the caste system. Americans—if they heeded the warnings of the Swedish Jeremiah—could recover their first principles and eliminate the moral lag and, at the same time, organize their modern, technologically advanced society on the only rational basis: individual merit rather than ascribed status. Myrdal thus wrapped both an appeal to morality and advocacy of social engineering in the mantle of the American creed and declared that both were essential if Americans were to conserve their original principles.

In describing mainstream American ideas, beliefs, and values, Myrdal rarely used the term *culture*. This is a notable omission because the culture concept had assumed a prominent place in American popular discourse as well as in anthropology and sociology in the 1930s.[29] It had never been an important category in Myrdal's earlier work, however, nor did the concept have such a central place in Swedish intellectual life. Though a great admirer of Franz Boas, Myrdal seems to have feared the conservative implications of the culture concept, associating it with Sumner's idea that the folkways and mores could not be changed by state action and with Park's and Odum's perceptions of cultural change in race relations as a long-term, gradual process.[30] He was aware that W. J. Cash had described a southern "cultural pattern" that stubbornly defied the homogenizing tendencies of American culture, and he profoundly disagreed with Herskovits's thesis that Afro-Americans maintained distinctive cultural patterns that resisted assimilation into the dominant culture. Since his early reading of Axel Hägerstrom, Myrdal had been convinced that valuations were the key to thought, and that if the social scientist could identify these fundamental attitudes, he would understand the wellsprings of behavior. By describing the average person's thought as an "unstable amalgam of conflicting valuations," he raised the possibility that the social engineer could selectively reinforce the "higher" valuations of the American creed, thus overcoming the "lower" valuations of prejudice.

Much of Myrdal's second chapter is an impressionistic account of his observations as a Swede traveling around the United States talking to Americans about race relations. The chapter's title, "Encountering the Negro Problem," suggests Ray Stannard Baker's *Following the Color Line*, a work Myrdal cited frequently. The chapter, like Baker's book, is an impressionistic account of American, particularly southern, race relations, and Myrdal preserves the "stranger in a strange land" tone of Baker's writing, thus emphasizing the irrationality of racial taboos in the eyes of a foreigner. The chapter allows the reader to see Myrdal as a provocative interviewer—upsetting the decorum of a southern, upper-class dinner party by questioning the conventional wisdom about blacks and provoking the wrath of a southern state official with rigorous questions about racial discrimination in wages and working conditions.[31] Myrdal emphasized how uncomfortable whites felt about discussing the "Negro problem," and he revealed some of the myriad strategies whites used for rationalizing prejudice and "explaining the problem away." Ridiculing the pretensions of southern whites who claimed to "know the Negro," he asserted that, in fact, whites were remarkably ignorant about the actual living conditions of blacks in their communities. Though racial prejudice was more salient in the South, Myrdal observed that most white northerners preferred that blacks stay in the South, fearing further additions to their welfare rolls.[32]

As a response to these racist attitudes, Myrdal advocated a publicity campaign about the situation of Afro-Americans and argued that "a great majority of white people in America would be prepared to give the Negro a substantially better deal if they knew the facts." He ignored the studies by Walter Lippmann, Harold Lasswell, and Thurman Arnold that explored the irrational elements in public opinion and pointed out some of the difficulties of educating the citizenry on an issue and mobilizing public opinion. Holding fast to his Enlightenment ideals, he declared that "*an educational offensive against racial intolerance, going deeper than the reiteration of the 'glittering generalities' in the nation's political creed, has never seriously been attempted in America.*"[33]

In his third chapter, "Facets of the Negro Problem," Myrdal argued that the hostility of whites to racial amalgamation made the status of blacks unique among American ethnic groups. The various immigrant groups were being assimilated into the dominant white American group, he concluded, but intermarriage with blacks was unacceptable to whites in both the North and the South. Because of this fundamental difference in the experiences of Afro-Americans and members of white ethnic minorities, Myrdal did not adopt a comparative framework such as Park's race relations cycle or Donald Young's analysis of American minorities. Thus Myrdal did not develop any general theories of ethnicity that could be applied to other groups.[34] But Myrdal was able to create a sense of moral urgency about the condition of black Americans precisely because he emphasized the uniqueness of American discrimination against blacks and the inability of Afro-Americans to overcome barriers that most white immigrant groups had surmounted.

When Myrdal compared the whites' phobias about intermarriage and social equality with the goals of blacks, he found some grounds for guarded optimism. From his interviews with whites, Myrdal constructed a "rank order of discriminations" which indicated that the taboo against intermarriage and sexual intercourse between black men and white women stood first in the whites' order of priorities. Rank two in the whites' scale consisted of a variety of measures designed to deny "social equality" in such areas as eating, drinking, dancing, and social intercourse generally. The third rank comprised segregation and discrimination in public facilities such as schools, churches, and transportation. Fourth was political disfranchisement. Fifth was "discrimination in law courts, by the police, and by other public servants." The sixth and final rank concerned economic discrimination: barriers to blacks getting jobs, buying land, securing credit, and obtaining relief and public assistance. In contrast to the white man's rank order of discriminations, Myrdal found that "*the Negro's own rank order is just about parallel, but inverse, to that of the white man.*" Blacks were most concerned with getting jobs. Justice in the courts and the right to vote were their next priorities. Marrying a white person was "of rather distant and doubtful interest" to most blacks.[35]

Though he saw economic advance as most important to blacks and least threatening to whites, Myrdal was skeptical that poor whites and blacks could form an effective class alliance. He offered the hypothesis that "*the lower class groups will, to a great extent, take care of keeping each other subdued*, thus relieving, to that extent, the higher classes of this otherwise painful task necessary to the

monopolization of the power and advantages." Myrdal observed that racial prejudice existed among all classes of whites but held that it was most "bitter, spiteful,
and relentless" among poor whites. Drawing upon John Dollard's Freudian interpretation, he asserted that poor whites felt enormous "frustration" at their situation, and that they displaced this "aggression" through racial prejudice. Since his
1931 article, "Socialism or Capitalism in America's Future?" Myrdal had seen
ethnic division as a major source of weakness in the American labor movement,
and he argued this point vigorously in *An American Dilemma*, taking issue with the
socialist strategy of his friend Ralph Bunche. To emphasize his point, he quoted a
Swedish proverb: "When the feed-box is empty, the horses will bite each other."[36]
Myrdal's political perspective had been developed in the Swedish Social Democratic party in the 1930s, a period in which intellectuals had played an unusually
strong leadership role in a workers' party during the struggle for a welfare state.
From this experience, he concluded that "in general, poor people are not radical
and not even liberal, though to have such political opinions would often be in
their interest." Focusing on poor whites in the United States, he declared that "the
problem for political liberalism . . . appears to be first to lift the masses to security
and education and then to work to make them liberal."[37]

By contending that lower-class groups kept each other subdued, Myrdal made a
structural argument that racial discrimination benefited the upper classes, even
though he thought that many individuals in the upper classes outside the South
were not consciously aware that they or their businesses profited from racial
discrimination. Discouraged by the prejudice of poor whites, he proclaimed that
"the Negro's friend—or the one who is least unfriendly—is still rather the upper
class of white people, the people with economic and social security who are truly a
'noncompeting group.'"[38] His experience in Sweden convinced him that elites
could be persuaded to embrace prophylactic reforms if they concluded that the
alternative was chaos or revolution. Myrdal hoped that by appealing to the
American creed and pointing out the obvious dangers of continued racial conflict,
he could reach some educated white Americans of the upper and middle classes,
people like Frederick Keppel who would be moved to action once they knew more
about the race issue. In addition, he glimpsed the possibility that more businessmen like Beardsley Ruml would come to see that the route to greater prosperity
lay in expanding the economy, increasing the purchasing power of the working
poor, and seeking new markets abroad. Keynesian economics, the welfare state,
and greater education would improve the productivity of the American economy
and make it possible for blacks to better their status as the income of whites also
rose. "In the end," Myrdal suggested, "the cost of raising the status of the Negro
may not involve any 'real costs' at all for society, but instead may result in great
'social gains' and actual savings for society."[39]

Myrdal reiterated the view he had expressed in *Kontakt med Amerika* that the
New Deal had "changed the whole configuration of the Negro problem" by its
willingness to "use the state as an instrument for induced social change." Though

many articles had been written in the 1930s about the impact of various New Deal agencies on Afro-Americans, Myrdal was the first social scientist to take a comprehensive look at the effect of the New Deal on the black struggle. Before the New Deal, he reported, the "Negro problem involved civil rights, education, charity, and little more." Under the new "welfare state," it included "housing, nutrition, medicine, education, relief and social security, wages and hours, working conditions, child and woman labor, and, lately, the armed forces and the war industries." "The Negro's share may be meager in all this new state activity," Myrdal conceded, "but he has been given a share. He has been given a broader and more variegated front to defend and from which to push forward."[40]

In contrast to Marxist scholars who assumed that one factor, the economic, was most basic in causing racial inequality, Myrdal assumed "a general interdependence between all the factors in the Negro problem." Borrowing a term from Charles S. Johnson,[41] he proposed a theory of the "vicious circle": "White prejudice and discrimination keep the Negro low in standards of living, health, education, manners and morals. This, in its turn, gives support to white prejudice. White prejudice and Negro standards thus mutually 'cause' each other. If things remain about as they are and have been, this means that the two forces happen to balance each other."[42] But Myrdal also set forth a "principle of cumulation," which posited that a change in one factor would set off a series of changes and move the whole social system in one direction or another. He suggested that if education could lessen white prejudice and discrimination, black social standards would rise. Myrdal also believed that an improvement in one aspect of the Negro's status, such as employment or political power, would lead to improvements in other aspects, such as housing and health standards. The Great Society programs of the 1960s would cast great doubt on the validity of the principle of cumulation as a general theory of racial change. To be sure, some Afro-Americans would be able to translate one benefit such as improved education or a better job into a series of other benefits that improved the quality of their lives. In other cases, however, targeting only one aspect of a system of structural racism would fail to help the black underclass. Liberals would discover, for example, that building new public housing projects in the inner city often brought little change unless there was a concerted effort to address simultaneously all of the interlocking problems of political powerlessness, jobs, education, and crime. To many liberals of the 1940s, however, Myrdal's principle of cumulation would seem to offer a way out of the impasse that arose from the New Deal's inability to address the civil rights issue directly. According to the principle of cumulation, local initiatives could make a difference, and federal programs could target one aspect of the race issue and start a cycle of improvement in the general condition of blacks.

Myrdal's language reified the issue of race relations and suggested that the various components of the race issue constituted an interlocking system susceptible to the planning of the social engineer. Economists are accustomed to working at a higher level of abstraction than other social scientists, to building complex models, and to arguing that, "other things being equal," x should follow from y. In devising the principle of cumulation, Myrdal took a concept from economic theory and transferred it to the realm of social and political change. According to Knut Wicksell's principle of cumulative causation, "if banks keep their loan rate of interest below the real rate of return on capital, they will encourage expansion of production and investment in plant and equipment. As a result, prices will rise and will continue to rise cumulatively, as long as the lending rate is kept below the real rate."[43] Applying this concept to American race relations, Myrdal assumed that complex social and cultural variables could be manipulated in the same manner as interest rates to yield a cumulative process of improvement in the status of blacks. Myrdal's language about the problem of managing social change in race relations is borrowed from fiscal and monetary theory. "As in the field of economic anti-depression policy," he wrote, "it matters a lot how the measures are proportioned and applied. The directing and proportioning of the measures is the task of social engineering."[44]

Myrdal thus concluded the first part of *An American Dilemma*—the section of the book aimed at the "lay" reader—by presenting a model of "dynamic causation" in which incremental changes could yield large results in the struggle against racial inequality. Though he had argued that American race relations could be seen as a moral dilemma, a psychological conflict in the minds of whites, Myrdal chose to emphasize the institutional side of the issue in his closing remarks to this introductory section. He pointed to American institutions as the places where changes in race relations might take place: churches, schools, universities, foundations, trade unions, voluntary associations, and the state. According to Myrdal, these institutions might bend to local pressures, but they were devoted to national ideals. "It is in these institutions that the American Creed has its instruments," he rhapsodized. "It plays upon them as on mighty organs. . . . Through these huge institutional structures, a constant pressure is brought to bear on race prejudice, counteracting the natural tendency for it to spread and become more intense." American institutions, he claimed, exerted "social controls" on white Americans, reinforcing their moral ideals of equality and fairness and discouraging prejudiced behavior.[45]

Race, Population, and Migration

After sketching out his argument concerning the conflict between American racial practices and national ideals, Myrdal turned to a more detailed analysis of race and American racial stereotypes. Returning to his touchstone, the Enlightenment, he asserted that modern biology supported the environmentalist and egalitarian ideas of the French philosophes and the American Founding Fathers. According to Myrdal, the philosophers of the Enlightenment emphasized environment, rather than heredity, in explaining human differences. The Lockean concept of the tabula rasa meant that "men were, on the whole, supposed to be similar; apparent differences were of cultural origin, and men could be changed through education." This descendant of a humble Dalarna family maintained that the environmentalism of the Enlightenment philosophers was an assault on European upper-class notions that the peasantry and urban proletariat were biologically inferior. In analyzing the American Founding Fathers, Myrdal acknowledged that the declaration that all men were "created equal" and endowed with natural rights "has to be understood in the moral sense that they were born equal as to human rights." He contended, however, that "the moral equality doctrine carried with it, even in America, a tendency toward a belief in biological equalitarianism. Among the educated classes, race prejudice was low in the generation around the Revolution."[46]

Antislavery sentiment, strong among the Revolutionary generation, waned after the invention of the cotton gin in 1794, according to Myrdal. The spread of a profitable slave system to the Southwest awakened a proslavery ideology that continued to influence southern white attitudes one hundred years later. Proslavery thinkers adhered to the American creed *as far as whites were concerned,*" but they introduced a "race dogma" of biological inequality to justify slavery. After the Civil War, Myrdal claimed, the theory of biological inequality was retained to support the caste system that replaced slavery, and race prejudice increased. In the years following Reconstruction, white northerners also needed the race dogma to justify their abandonment of support for civil rights. As white Americans North and South continued to believe in the American creed, it became all the more necessary for them to assert the biological inferiority of blacks in order to rationalize unequal treatment of the races. Myrdal argued that "the race dogma is nearly the only way out for a people so moralistically equalitarian, if it is not prepared to live up to its faith."[47] In the late nineteenth century, he maintained, American science came to support the race dogma originated by the proslavery apologists, and scientific theories of innate Negro inferiority held sway until the early part of the twentieth century, when Franz Boas and other critics began to undermine them. Research in the social sciences since the 1920s had led to a "veritable revolution in scientific thought on the racial characteristics of the Negro"—a revolution that substantiated the principles of the American creed.[48] Scientific environmentalism, in Myrdal's estimation, had so influenced educated Americans that it was no longer considered intellectually respectable to argue that blacks were genetically inferior.

Myrdal's history of racial beliefs thus allowed him to represent racial egalitarianism as the original American view and to treat the race dogma as a nineteenth-century doctrine, rooted in proslavery apologetics. By ignoring the colonial period, scanting social history, and focusing on the writings of the Founding Fathers, he erroneously associated the birth of the United States with racial egalitarianism and portrayed the ideology of white supremacy as a nineteenth-century aberration from a national tradition that was fundamentally democratic. Myrdal saw the environmentalist "revolution" of the 1920s and 1930s as highly significant because it deprived white Americans of a rationale for making an exception to the American creed in their treatment of blacks. By linking environmentalism to the American creed, Myrdal was able to present racial liberalism as an attempt to recover the nation's democratic heritage.

When he turned to the attitudes of ordinary white Americans in the 1930s, Myrdal had to admit that there was substantial evidence of widespread prejudice. His collaborator Eugene Horowitz submitted a memorandum that summarized recent studies of racial attitudes and concluded that prejudice had intensified during the depression of the 1930s and that "underprivileged" southern whites dealt with their frustrations by directing aggression toward blacks. But Myrdal thought that attitude research was in its infancy and that it had not yet registered the results of the wartime psychology and the return of prosperity. Given the rapid changes in the nation's life, he was more inclined to rely on his own interviewing than on the results of the studies of prejudice in the late 1930s.[49] Although he discerned hopeful signs among educated white Americans, Myrdal viewed the racial beliefs of "unsophisticated" whites as a tangle of negative stereotypes about blacks. He argued that "ordinary" white people believed in the Negro's biological inferiority because they made an incorrect deduction from the observation of the Negro's "inferior" social condition. They saw in their everyday experience evidence of the Negro's poverty, health problems, higher mortality rate, and lower "intelligence performance, manners, and morals," and they attributed these differences to biological causation.[50] Myrdal described a number of white stereotypes of black behavior, and he demonstrated that many of these beliefs served economic interests and fulfilled psychological needs of whites to feel superior. But Myrdal, in contrast to John Dollard, tended to ascribe prejudice to cognitive error rather than to narcissism and a deep-seated desire for deference. The Swedish visitor optimistically suggested, "The ordinary white American is an upright and honest fellow who tries to think straight and wants to be just to everybody. He does not consciously concoct his prejudices for a purpose."[51]

In addressing the practical question of how to reduce the prejudice of whites, Myrdal suggested that an actual improvement in "Negro status, Negro behavior, Negro characteristics" would lessen white bias to a degree.[52] Behind this proposal lay the assumption that black culture was essentially similar to white culture, and that white bias stemmed not from a perception of cultural differences but from an observation of the social inferiority of blacks according to white culture. Improvements in black education and health and a change in black characteristics toward the white norm would reduce white prejudice, in Myrdal's view. He did not accept Park's idea that a rise in the status of blacks would be seen as competition by whites and would intensify prejudice, at least temporarily.

Another of Myrdal's practical recommendations would have significant influence in shaping interracial work and social science research after the war. He suggested educational efforts "to rectify the ordinary white man's observations of

Negro characteristics and inform him of the specific mistakes he is making in ascribing them wholesale to inborn racial traits."[53] Myrdal held that the diffusion of scientific knowledge through popular literature, press, radio, school, and church would lead whites to a more rational understanding of blacks. The mind of white Americans, in his view, contained an unstable collection of conflicting valuations, and he thought that education would reduce prejudice and accentuate belief in the American creed. He admitted that most of the social science literature about racial stereotypes was impressionistic, and he urged American scholars to make the study of white prejudice an important research priority.[54]

Myrdal had risen to prominence in a society in which professors, teachers, and educated people generally enjoyed much greater deference from the public than their counterparts in the United States. He expected, therefore, that an educational campaign against prejudice would reduce the gap between the environmentalist beliefs of educated Americans and the prejudices of the masses of white people. Myrdal supposed that whites would be willing to give up what John Dollard called the psychological "gain" from feelings of racial superiority if they could understand that they would gain economically from the elimination of racial discrimination and the creation of a more productive society. He assumed that the discomfort that whites felt from holding two inconsistent sets of attitudes on the race issue would lead them to resolve their dilemma in favor of the American creed.

In a discussion of the concept of race, Myrdal essentially summarized the work of Boas and his students, noting that the term *Negro race* was a social rather than a biological category in North America. He observed that the term *race* was disappearing from scientific writings and was being replaced by "quantitative notions of the relative frequency of common ancestry and differentiating traits" among population groups. To speak of racial purity made little sense because the "white American race" contained people whose ancestry stemmed from many European nationalities and ethnic groups. Myrdal noted that there was great variability of traits among individuals in every population group and significant overlapping of traits between groups. The nineteenth-century concept of race as a fixed type had given way to a quantitative study of physical characteristics among groups of people.[55]

Pressing his case for environmentalism, Myrdal insisted that there were no significant cultural differences between American Negroes and whites and that racial prejudice alone kept blacks from fitting into American society. "Should America wake up one morning," he suggested, "with all knowledge about the African ancestry of part of its population and all memories of color caste absolutely forgotten and find all the outward physical characteristics of Negro people eradicated, but no change in their mental or moral characteristics, nothing we know about this group and other population groups in America would lead us to believe that the American Negro would not rapidly come to fit in as a 'well-adjusted ordinary American.'"[56]

Myrdal also marshaled an array of scientific evidence to disprove the notions that blacks were particularly susceptible to physical and mental diseases. He reviewed the literature on race and IQ and concluded that no differences in innate intelligence between whites and blacks had been proven. Citing the memoranda prepared for his study by Otto Klineberg, he argued that no evidence existed of innate racial differences in mental traits.[57] Although Myrdal's discussion of race and heredity did not break any new ground, it was a useful summary for the lay reader of two decades of research by American social scientists, and it provided much ammunition for the social activists and educators who combated racial stereotypes and racist myths. While some of the American scholars wrote for limited, professional audiences and did not stress the policy implications of the environmentalist revolution, the Swedish social engineer emphasized that the recent findings concerning race and heredity meant that there could be no justification of "*differential treatment in matters of public policy, such as in education, suffrage, and entrance to various sections of the labor market.*"[58]

From race, Myrdal turned to an analysis of population, examining issues very different from those that he and Alva had confronted eight years earlier in Sweden. He predicted a gradual increase in the percentage of the Negro population due to the restriction of immigration from Europe and a higher birth rate among blacks. Myrdal found that white and black Americans held starkly contrasting views on the optimum size of the Negro population: most whites wanted the black population to be as small as possible but were unwilling to resort to measures not sanctioned by the American creed to achieve that goal, while most blacks preferred that the Negro population grow as large as possible. Myrdal glimpsed a possible area of agreement in the desire of both white and black Americans "*in principle*" to improve the "quality" of the Negro population, and he argued that the American creed required equal provision of facilities in medicine, sanitation, nutrition, education, and other fields that affected the quality of the population.

Birth control, in Myrdal's view, offered another means of enhancing the quality of population for both blacks and whites. In a passage that would later become controversial, he set up as a straw man the idea of a policy of forced sterilization of the lowest stratum of blacks and whites. Myrdal then used the American creed to knock down the idea of forced sterilization and proposed birth control as the appropriate means of social engineering. He asserted that "there are in the South a great number of Negroes—as of whites—who are so destitute that from a general social point of view it would be highly desirable that they did not procreate. . . . The most direct way of meeting the problem, not taking account of the value premises in the American Creed, would be to sterilize them." Myrdal found, however, "that such proposals, if they are made at all, are almost as repugnant to the average white American in the South and the North as to the Negro."[59] He thus drew back from the idea of mandatory sterilization of "persons of bad character" that he and Alva had discussed in *Kris i befolkningsfrågan*. Though he continued to advance a vision of social engineering and to see the state as a parent, with experts making decisions traditionally left to individuals, he acknowledged that the American creed would tolerate forced sterilization only under limited circumstances. Since writing *Kris i befolkningsfrågan* about an ethnically homogeneous nation, Myrdal had had several years to observe the racially motivated eugenics policies of Nazi Germany, and he was not eager to entrust broader powers of mandatory sterilization to state governments in the American South. Nevertheless, he was so infatuated with social engineering that he could not resist the temptation to discuss forced sterilization, even though he rejected it as a policy option.

In arguing for birth control, Myrdal affirmed that "birth control facilities could be extended relatively more to Negroes than to whites, since Negroes are more concentrated in the lower income and education classes and since they now know less about modern techniques of birth control." He assumed that encouraging birth control would help to lessen the poverty of the black masses, prevent the spread of diseases, and reduce illegitimate births.[60] Myrdal's advocacy of birth control attracted criticism from Catholic reviewers in 1944, and his proposals for limiting the quantity and improving the "quality" of Negro births drew sharp rebukes from radical black scholars in the 1960s.

In his chapter on migration, Myrdal proclaimed that black migration to the North and West was, on the whole, a positive trend in race relations because it increased black economic opportunity, provided many blacks with a greater sense of freedom from caste restrictions, and augmented the Negro vote. He analyzed the "push" and "pull" factors that had impelled thousands of blacks northward since the great migration of World War I, and he pointed out that the migration had continued despite widespread black urban unemployment during the Depression.

One of the most significant policy recommendations in the book was Myrdal's suggestion that the federal government develop a migration policy of helping blacks move to areas where there were the most job opportunities. Noting that the federal government had established greater "public control of the labor market" during the war, he urged the creation of a "labor information service" as part of a program of postwar economic planning to avoid a recession. Myrdal was certain that the black exodus from the South would continue. A sharp decline in the number of jobs in southern agriculture together with the greater job opportunities, better relief benefits, and a higher political and social status in the North and West would induce many blacks to leave the South. Myrdal stressed that black migration was not the natural result of the play of market forces. He saw it as the result of a "complex of intentional policies" by federal and state governments in the areas of war industries, economic planning, welfare policies, and civil rights. Much of the future of American race relations, he predicted, would depend upon the government's effectiveness in planning for jobs and social services for the increasing numbers of blacks migrating to the cities of the North and West.[61]

Economics

Myrdal followed this discussion of the need for a federal migration policy with a long unit on economics, in which he sent a clear message to his white readers that the "Negro problem" was no longer a southern rural issue and that eventually all but a small minority of black Americans would have to be integrated into the nonagricultural economy of the United States. If blacks did not find industrial jobs, he warned, they would become a burden on the national economy as permanent relief clients. The economics section was the first comprehensive study of blacks in both the rural and industrial sectors of the American economy. Virtually a book within a book, it consisted of more than two hundred pages of analysis, supported by a wealth of statistical data assembled by Richard Sterner. Applying an institutionalist approach, Myrdal examined the economic status of blacks in the context of the entire society. His methodology was unorthodox for an economist because of its extensive treatment of the social and psychological causes of economic behavior. Using the American creed as his value premise, he made "discrimination" a central concept in the study. Focusing on discrimination and measuring economic behavior against a moral standard was, in itself, an unusual approach in the field of economics.

Although Myrdal was able to include some data on the beginning of the war boom, his economics section is primarily a portrait of the late 1930s, when black unemployment remained high despite New Deal recovery programs. He opened the discussion with a dramatic statement of the problem as a social pathology calling for a cure of social engineering:

> The economic situation of the Negroes in America is pathological. Except for a small minority enjoying upper or middle class status, the masses of American Negroes, in the rural South and in the segregated slum quarters in Southern and Northern cities, are destitute. They own little property; even their household goods are mostly inadequate and dilapidated. Their incomes are not only low but irregular. They thus live from day to day and have scant security for the future. Their entire culture and their individual interests and strivings are narrow.[62]

He insisted that the economic future of black Americans depended to a great extent on public policy. The problem for the social engineer was to decide where and how to intervene to break the vicious circle of black poverty, low social and educational standards among blacks, and white discrimination. Myrdal restated his hypothesis that a "primary change" in any one of those three factors would "bring changes in the other two and, through mutual interaction, move the whole system along in one direction or the other."[63]

Always conscious of the need to establish his value premises, Myrdal devoted most of his chapter called "Economic Inequality" to presenting a New Dealized version of the American creed as a sanction for economic planning and liberal social engineering. He acknowledged that the American creed was susceptible to many interpretations in the economic sphere, but he reiterated a central theme of *Kontakt med Amerika* in claiming that American economic liberalism was evolving gradually from "rugged individualism" toward ideals "of a more social type."[64] While Myrdal did not praise Franklin Roosevelt as effusively as he had in *Kontakt*, he nevertheless commended the New Deal's economic planning and social welfare programs. Citing Roosevelt's goal of establishing "freedom from want," Myrdal held that "*the American Creed is changing to include a decent living standard and a measure of economic security among the liberties and rights which are given this high moral sanction.*"[65]

In arguing that the American creed had been broadened to include the provision of a minimum standard of living for all citizens, Myrdal responded to the wartime rhetoric of President Roosevelt, Vice-President Wallace, and Wendell Willkie. Writing in 1941 and the first half of 1942, Myrdal ignored the defeat of much New Deal reform legislation at the hands of the conservative coalition in Congress since 1938 and failed to anticipate the Republican gains in the November 1942 congressional elections, which would lead to still more defeats for New Deal programs. He gauged the strength of the New Deal coalition to be so great that the United States would continue to move in the direction of greater social welfare benefits for its citizens.

With this social welfare version of the American creed established, Myrdal outlined the norms that he assumed ordinary Americans held "on the higher or national plane of the valuational sphere" with respect to the economic conditions of black people. These included, first, the idea that "*there is nothing wrong with economic inequality by itself.*" Myrdal noted that this norm would have the effect "of keeping our study within the conservative reformist limits of average American economic discussion." A second norm said to be held by the American people was the belief "*that no population group shall be allowed to fall under a certain minimum level of living.*" A third value premise was "*that Negroes shall be awarded equal opportunities.*" Myrdal saw equality of opportunity as an integral part of the American creed and pinpointed discrimination as the "key term" in his study of the economic status of blacks.[66]

Having established his value premises of combating discrimination and black poverty within the framework of American capitalism, Myrdal then asked what obstacles hindered the realization of these ideals. Here he discerned a significant difference between white attitudes in the North and South. Most northerners, according to Myrdal, were only vaguely aware of economic discrimination against blacks. To northerners, the Negro was "just an alien, felt to be particularly difficult to assimilate into the life of the community." In the South, however, economic discrimination was justified by an elaborate web of stereotypes of black mental and moral inferiority. Economic discrimination in the South, in Myrdal's view, was historically rooted in slavery.[67]

Myrdal's analysis of the southern plantation economy was heavily indebted to the work of several American scholars. Rupert Vance and T. J. Woofter, Jr., had written detailed studies of southern agriculture and landlord-tenant relations.[68] *The Collapse of Cotton Tenancy* (1935) by Will W. Alexander, Edwin Embree, and Charles S. Johnson had reached a broader audience with its succinct statement of the plight of the sharecropper.[69] Myrdal differed from these writers, however, in pushing race to the forefront of his discussion of the southern economy. The American scholars tended to deemphasize race in order to make the point that the decline of southern agriculture had created disastrous conditions for white and black tenants alike. In the political context of the 1930s, they thought it imprudent to stress the race issue and preferred to work for federal economic aid for farmers of both races and for planning for regional development. Myrdal's analysis, on the other hand, pointed to slavery and racism as the primary causes of the region's backwardness. He observed that a web of discriminatory practices made it extremely difficult for blacks to improve their economic status in either the rural areas or the cities, and he urged that federal intervention to end discrimination was necessary if government programs were to benefit blacks as well as whites.

To a generation of white Americans accustomed to viewing southern poverty as a general problem rather than a racial problem, Myrdal insisted that the tradition of slavery had remained "as a chief determinant of the South's economic life." The exploitation of tenant farmers—both white and black—was an "extension into the present of a modified slavery system." The South's economic backwardness could not be explained by lack of natural resources, the differential in freight rates, or the tariff. Nor was the absence of capital a sufficient explanation of southern poverty. In Myrdal's opinion, the causes of the South's backwardness lay in "the rigid institutional structure of the economic life of the region which, historically, is derived from slavery and, psychologically, is rooted in the minds of the people."[70]

In tracing the evolution of the tenant farming system, Myrdal stressed that racial discrimination and the heritage of slavery had stood as obstacles to economic innovation and progress. Indeed, he maintained that the caste system of the postbellum years was even more rigid than slavery because it barred blacks from jobs as artisans that they had held under slavery. Myrdal argued that the sharecropping system was not simply an economic consequence of the landowners' need for labor and of the freedmen's need for work. It also resulted from the planters' psychology of racist paternalism and their desire to maintain the political and social subordination of blacks.[71] Drawing upon the investigations of Woofter, Myrdal explained that the laws were designed to favor the landlord and that tenants had few possibilities for asserting their rights. The Swedish observer carried the argument farther than Woofter and most American scholars, however, when he insisted that the whole system rested upon extralegal violence and intimidation of tenants.[72]

Myrdal followed this historical survey with a summary of the contemporary effects of the plantation economy on southern society in general and on black farmers in particular. He noted that the tenant farming system encouraged soil erosion because of the planter tradition of disregard for the land and because of the tenants' lack of a stake in maintaining productivity. Overproduction of cotton resulted in part from the dependence of southern farmers on short-term credit. Inadequate banking and credit facilities were caused not only by the disruption of the Civil War and the low price of cotton but also by "the low plane of political life in the South and the lack of active desire and ability to create large-scale cooperative organizations."[73]

Another result of the southern plantation economy was the low level of landownership among blacks. Myrdal found that black landownership had been declining since 1920. He contended that slavery and its surrogate, the sharecropping system, had discouraged blacks from taking the initiative in economic matters and that blacks had difficulty in getting credit because of white belief in Negro inferiority. Myrdal also held that blacks' lack of legal security was a major obstacle to land ownership. Many southern rural blacks found that the safest course was to attach themselves to a white patron, who was usually their employer.[74] Myrdal summed up his case against the southern plantation system by stressing that the core of the problem lay in "the inherited paternalistic attitude on the part of the planters and the corresponding attitudes of dependence, carelessness, and lack of ambition on the part of the tenants." He concluded that "the plantation system . . . fails flagrantly to meet the standards of social and economic efficiency and justice."[75]

After sketching this dismal picture of the southern economy, Myrdal proceeded to argue that things would get worse—especially for rural blacks. Although he had praised the New Deal as a liberalizing force in the region, he observed that the Roosevelt administration did not have "a constructive long-range program for a reorganization of Southern agriculture."[76] The Agricultural Adjustment Act had resulted in the dismissal of hundreds of thousands of tenants because landowners had been paid for not growing crops. By reducing the labor force and increasing the landowners' supply of cash through allotment payments, the act had created an incentive to mechanization that eventually would further reduce the employment of rural blacks. Myrdal also predicted that competition from other cotton-producing countries would mean lower prices for southern cotton after the war.[77]

In response to these catastrophic conditions in southern agriculture, Myrdal urged a government policy of planned migration of displaced tenant farmers to urban areas with industrial jobs. He also called for vocational education programs to prepare black youth for industrial employment.[78] These policy recommendations differed from those which Alexander, Embree, and Johnson had offered nine years earlier. Myrdal commended the Farm Security Administration but argued that it lacked the political power and legal authority to help more than a small minority of tenants to become landowners.[79] He urged the federal government to protect the legal rights of tenants to organize unions and suggested that it would be difficult for the federal government to cope with the displacement problem "without having the farm workers organized and their interests and opinions articulated."[80] In the end, though, Myrdal thought that most blacks in the rural South would have to find industrial jobs in cities, either in the South or outside the region. He concluded, as he had in his studies of Swedish agriculture, that mechanization and improved farming techniques made the depopulation of rural districts inevitable.

In his chapter on nonagricultural employment of blacks, Myrdal warned his white readers that "eventually all Negroes, except for a small minority, will have to become integrated into the nonagricultural economy of America."[81] Whites in northern and western cities ultimately faced the stark choice of providing jobs for blacks or accepting blacks as relief clients. Myrdal sketched the history of job discrimination against Afro-Americans in northern cities, noting that blacks had made gains in employment during World War I and the 1920s only to encounter the devastating effects of the Depression. Citing the 1940 census, he claimed that in many northern cities only about one-half of black men had jobs, and he demonstrated that blacks did not improve their employment opportunities by staying in school longer.[82] In an appendix on the Negro wage earner, Myrdal synthesized the research of Herbert Northrup, Paul Norgren, Horace Cayton, and George Mitchell to document the discrimination against Afro-Americans in several major industries.[83]

Given this pervasive discrimination by white employers, many urban blacks sought to find work in black businesses or in professions that served the black community. Here again, Myrdal painted a grim portrait of limited job possibilities. He claimed that black-owned stores and restaurants were able to attract only about 5 to 10 percent of the total Negro trade. The rest went to white-owned businesses.[84] Myrdal found that real estate owners did not want to rent to black businessmen and that banks were reluctant to lend them money. In addition, black businessmen faced the usual problems of small entrepreneurs in competition with larger businesses. Myrdal surveyed the "Don't Buy Where You Can't Work" campaigns in which black organizations had boycotted stores in black neighborhoods that refused to hire blacks. He argued that these campaigns, even if successful, would make only a small dent in the black unemployment figures. Built upon the research of Abram Harris and Ira Reid, Myrdal's analysis was an implicit refutation of Du Bois's proposals for a separate black economy. Instead, he concluded that "the Negro's main concern must be to break down job segregation and job discrimination in the white economy."[85]

Myrdal found grounds for hope for black Americans in the expansion of the role of the federal government in the areas of education, housing, social security, and welfare. He pointed out that discrimination in the provision of public services was contrary to the American creed and to the Constitution, and he argued that growing federal involvement, NAACP lawsuits, and the black vote in the North would all contribute to a lessening of discrimination against blacks in education and in other public services. Myrdal enumerated New Deal contributions to black education such as Public Works Administration support for building new schools, WPA adult education programs, and the student aid program of the NYA. He did not raise the issue of integration but claimed that the southern states were gradually, though reluctantly, spending more money on black schools in response to legal and political pressures.[86]

In the area of housing, Myrdal urged urban areas to plan for an influx of black migrants, and he suggested that "race friction" might well result if no planning were done. He argued that "the issue of housing segregation will have to be faced squarely" but counseled different strategies for the South and the rest of the country. In the South, he suggested that "segregation will have to be accepted in the surveyable future, for the simple reason that local opposition against housing projects will otherwise be so strong that no projects can be built. . . . In the North, on the other hand, there is some chance that the evils of segregation can be removed by means of the gradual abolition of housing segregation itself."[87] On this, as on other policy issues, Myrdal proved willing to abandon the high ground of moral immediacy in order to embrace a pragmatic strategy for delivering needed resources to blacks. According to his principle of cumulation, an improvement in the black standard of living should set in motion a broader cycle of change, leading to eventual equality and desegregation.

Because of the disastrous decline of jobs in southern agriculture and in northern cities, public relief constituted "the one bright spot in the recent economic history of the Negro," according to Myrdal. Indeed, he found that relief had become "*one of the major Negro occupations . . . surpassed only by agriculture and possibly by domestic service.*"[88] Myrdal noted discrimination against blacks in relief services, however, particularly in the rural South. Turning to the issue of Social Security, he observed that the exclusion of agricultural and domestic workers from participation in the system meant that blacks were "'underrepresented' among recipients of benefits."[89] Myrdal's discussion of "The Negro in the Public Economy" thus pointed to many areas of discrimination. He maintained, however, that increased federal involvement created a trend toward greater equality, and according to his principle of cumulation, this trend might be significant if reinforced by other progressive trends in American life.

Myrdal confronted the reader with a depressing series of data on black-white differentials in income, consumption, and housing and concluded that the economic situation of Afro-Americans was "sinister." But he responded to these conditions by posing the social engineer's question: "*How would it be possible by a planned economic policy to increase Negro opportunities for employment?*"[90] His first suggestion was an educational campaign aimed at reducing the ignorance of northern whites about job discrimination. Myrdal held that most northern whites were opposed to economic discrimination "*as a general proposition*" and were often unaware of the extent to which they participated in it in concrete situations.[91] He believed that white workers in the North would be less prejudiced against blacks

after they had worked with blacks. In this context, Myrdal seriously underestimated the degree of racial prejudice among northern white workers and assumed
that greater contact between the races would lead to greater tolerance.

The Swedish visitor exaggerated the extent to which the federal government
was becoming involved in regulating the labor market. He insisted that "through
unionization and social legislation the labor market is increasingly coming under
the control of a formal regulation that will demand equality of opportunity." This
trend was "the great hope for the Negro at the present time" because "public
authority is compelled to side with him, in one way or another."[92] Myrdal argued
that New Deal labor legislation benefited black as well as white workers and that it
was strengthening America's trade union movement. Though prescient on many
other issues, he failed to foresee the postwar reaction against organized labor that
would lead to the Taft-Hartley Act rollback of some of the gains made by unions
under the New Deal. Myrdal predicted that the rapidly growing trade unions
would find themselves subject to federal regulation on civil rights after the war
and would feel political pressure to combat discrimination within their own
ranks.[93]

As part of a national employment strategy for blacks, Myrdal advocated a policy
of planned migration of Afro-Americans from the rural South to areas that could
provide jobs—particularly smaller cities in the North and West. He was guardedly
optimistic that, if the general unemployment level remained low, blacks would
improve their employment prospects in the North and West. In the South, on the
other hand, Myrdal saw "an entrenched and widespread popular theory that the
Negro should be held down in his 'place.' Discrimination in justice, politics,
education, and public service creates an atmosphere in which economic discrimination becomes natural or even necessary in order to prevent 'social equality.'"[94]

Myrdal concluded his unit on economics with an analysis of the effects of
World War II on the economic status of blacks. He believed that Afro-Americans
had reached a crucial juncture and had found their "strategic position strengthened not only because of the desperate scarcity of labor but also because of a
revitalization of the democratic Creed." In contrast to most white New Dealers and
southern liberals, Myrdal held that blacks could not afford to postpone agitation
for their rights until after the war. The time for raising these issues had arrived. In
surveying the wartime economy to mid-1942, Myrdal pointed to continued discrimination in war industries.[95] He noted that the president's committee on fair
employment practices lacked the power to punish industries for noncompliance
but observed that it had enjoyed some success in publicizing cases of discrimination. Myrdal also described the humiliation experienced by black servicemen
because of the discrimination and segregation in the army and navy. "There is no
point," he wrote, "in trying to divide the responsibility equally between both racial
groups or to characterize the incidents as exceptional. The white group has the
power, and hence, the responsibility."[96]

Looking ahead to the postwar era, Myrdal posed the question of the economic future of Afro-Americans. He concluded: "Of paramount importance will be the general level of employment. The Negroes' hope of becoming integrated into American industry is much greater if the American economy is geared to full utilization of its production forces. Should there be widespread unemployment for a protracted period, it will tend to be concentrated on the Negro." Myrdal put aside his doubts and assumed that government planning would avert a serious postwar depression, but he admonished Americans that "the Negro will have to be considered in this post-war planning work." He suggested that "there may be radical change ahead—both in the Negro's actual status and in ideologies affecting him."[97]

In spite of his detailed exposition of poverty, unemployment, and discrimination, Myrdal remained hopeful that the trends toward federal control of the labor market and unionization would work to the benefit of blacks. His policy recommendations centered on a federal migration policy, economic planning for full employment, and educational campaigns to encourage the hiring of blacks for nonagricultural jobs. But Myrdal failed to explain where the political and economic power to effect these changes would be found. Seeing American politics through the prism of his Swedish experience, he assumed that the New Deal was the first step toward greater political power for labor, the poor, and Afro-Americans. He did not observe that the political pendulum was swinging to the right, nor did he see that large corporations were expanding their influence in national politics through the spectacular growth of defense industries. Myrdal hoped that the trend toward government intervention in the economy together with the American democratic ethos would prove strong enough to force government planning for the integration of millions of poor, rural blacks into the life of the nation's cities. Myrdal did not envisage the development of what he would in later years term an "underclass" of unemployed urban blacks, nor did he grasp the role of urban blacks in providing a reserve labor force that kept wages down.[98] Looking back on *An American Dilemma* in 1973, he would write: "How could anyone in 1942 foresee that America would permit the stupendous and still continuing deterioration and ghettoization of its cities? And that this would happen in a country where, at the time, the science and art of city and regional planning were already so advanced?"[99] Actually Myrdal *had* foreseen the dangers of urban blacks becoming permanent relief clients, though he had not imagined the scale of the ghettos that would take shape. But his belief in the willingness of policymakers to take preventive measures and his faith in the power of the American creed had led him to assume that white Americans would heed his warnings and integrate blacks into the urban-industrial economy.

Politics, Justice, and Social Equality

In his analysis of southern politics, Myrdal acknowledged that white supremacy continued to reign without serious challenge as southern officials dug in their heels and truculently resisted any mention of civil rights and desegregation. He agreed with earlier observers that the issue of "white supremacy" versus "Negro domination" had "stifled" political discussion in the South and "retarded its economic, social, and cultural advance."[100] Beneath the surface, however, the Swedish scholar noticed other factors at work that were undermining the system that excluded blacks from political participation and denied them government benefits. The power of local officials in the South to discriminate against Negroes in all phases of life was being eroded gradually by the growth of federal and state government bureaucracies. Myrdal conceded that, historically, the United States differed from most European countries in its lack of an independent civil service to carry out government policies at the local level and that local government in the South had been particularly weak. (However much he complained about the Swedish bureaucracy when at home, he lamented its absence in the South.) But Myrdal assumed that the trends begun by the New Deal would lead to the development of a more impartial bureaucracy at the federal and state levels that would take some governmental decisions out of the hands of local courthouse cliques.[101]

Another factor of great significance was the Negro vote in the North, which served as "one of the strategic protections of the Negro people in American society." Myrdal suggested that "the Northern vote might become the instrument by which the Negroes can increasingly use the machinery of federal legislation and administration to tear down the walls of discrimination."[102] Drawing on the research memoranda of Ralph Bunche, he hailed the gradual increase in black voting in cities of the upper South and noted that thousands of black farmers voted in federally sponsored referenda required under the Agricultural Adjustment Act.[103]

Viewing southern politics in comparative perspective, Myrdal declared that southern conservatism was "a unique phenomenon in Western civilization in being married to an established pattern of *illegality*." While in most European countries the conservatives stood for "law and order," the American South presented "the unmatched political spectacle that the liberals are the party of law and order, while the conservatives are the habitual transgressors. *The party which works for change has the established law on its side, or rather, wants to enforce it, but has not the political power; the party which stands for the* status quo *has the power but not the law*."[104] He traced the tradition of "conservative illegality" from the Ku Klux Klan's activities under Reconstruction through the disfranchisement campaigns to contemporary violence and intimidation of blacks. Citing the work of Rupert Vance and W. J. Cash, he noted the survival of a frontier tradition and a pattern of vigilante action in the rural culture of the South.[105]

Myrdal followed Paul Lewinson in arguing that the one-party system based on white supremacy had removed substantive issues from southern politics to a great extent. Looking at America from a Swedish perspective, Myrdal held that the United States as a whole lacked the organized mass movements that were prominent in Scandinavia and in many other European countries: trade unions, farmers' organizations, and adult education associations. The southern masses were even more "inarticulate" and unorganized because of the "region's steadfast struggle to keep the Negro from participation."[106]

Although the South had a one-party system, Myrdal did not consider it a fascist system because of the absence of "the centralized organization of a fascist state." To a great extent, the region was a decentralized oligarchy, but its political philosophy was still the American creed. The oligarchs had to pay lip service to American democracy and to "appeal to the common white man as an equal and as the ultimate arbiter of political affairs."[107] In an era in which many American liberals worried that fascism could "happen here," Myrdal held that the South was not headed toward fascism precisely because conservative white southerners accepted "in principle" the American creed. He contended that "the Southern conservative white man's faith in American democracy, which he is certainly not living up to, and the Constitution, which he is circumventing, are living forces of decisive dynamic significance."[108]

One of the most original and perceptive parts of *An American Dilemma* was Myrdal's discussion of white southern liberalism. In his travels through the South with Jackson Davis, he had met many members of the Commission on Interracial Cooperation and had talked with liberal newspaper editors and reporters. He had also had extensive discussions with Howard Odum and other liberal university professors, and Guy and Guion Johnson had been members of his staff in New York. Myrdal saw the southern liberals as a small, upper-class group without much influence in the region. He wrote: "Southern liberalism . . . is beautiful and dignified. It preserves much of the philosophical grace of the mythical old aristocratic South. But until the New Deal came, it had no source of power. Even yet it does not have contact with, or support by, the masses. Social reform is now coming rapidly to the South, but it is coming mainly from Washington."[109] Except for a handful of elected officials and New Deal administrators, southern liberals were isolated men and women with no expectation of power or influence. Accordingly, they had learned "to stress the need for patience and to exalt the cautious approach, the slow change, the organic nature of social growth." The southern liberals were especially anxious that the southern white public should not be "enraged into resistance." Therefore the liberals had "developed the tactics of evading principles; of being very indirect in attacking problems; of cajoling, coaxing and luring the public into giving in on minor issues." Myrdal discovered that liberals camouflaged their criticisms of the South through an elaborate show of "regional patriotism." "In sectors other than those in which they happen to be interested at the moment," he wrote, "many Southern liberals lean over backwards to be conservative and so to avoid suspicion. . . . A stress on church and religion is generally such a front all over the South."[110]

Despite these criticisms, Myrdal held that the southern liberals could be effective leaders if "structural changes" should lead to the formation of a mass movement of farmers and workers: "The leaders for a truly progressive political movement in the South are there; the staff work for the battle is largely done. If Southern liberalism can recruit an army to lead, it will itself, as an ideological force, become one of the major factors of change in the South and in the nation."[111] Myrdal had repeatedly urged his friend Arthur Raper, the liberal interracial reformer, to run for governor of Georgia, and it had taken Raper several hours of argument to convince Myrdal that a man with his views would have no chance of being elected. The Swedish scholar never quite relinquished the idea that liberal intellectuals and newspaper editors were the natural leaders of the southern masses.[112] Such hopes revealed a fundamental elitism in Myrdal's political ideas, resulting from his experiences in Sweden, where he and other intellectuals had held important posts in Social Democratic governments and where public deference to intellectuals was much greater than in the United States.

Myrdal relied heavily upon the research memoranda of Ralph Bunche to present an account of disfranchisement and intimidation of blacks in the South. He brushed aside conservative southern myths about the alleged apathy of Negroes as voters by explaining the operation of the white primary; the poll tax; and property, educational, and character requirements for voting. Myrdal particularly emphasized the importance of "violence, terror, and intimidation" in keeping blacks from the polls, and he cited the research of Raper, Bunche, and Lewinson on such practices.[113]

After delineating the workings of the white supremacy system in grim detail, Myrdal concluded his politics section by suggesting that the system was breaking down. The key point of leverage, according to Myrdal, was the northern Negro vote. He assumed that blacks would continue to work within the two major political parties, pressuring the Democrats and Republicans for action on civil rights issues, and he expected that eventually the parties would realign on liberal-conservative lines, with most blacks supporting the liberal (presumably Democratic) party. Myrdal rejected the idea that any significant number of blacks would turn to Communism. Most Negroes, he claimed, realized that "*they have on their side the law of the land and the religion of the nation. . . . No social utopia can compete with the promises of the American Constitution and with the American Creed which it embodies.*"[114] Myrdal contended that the southern suffrage situation was unstable, and he predicted the abolition of the poll tax in all of the southern states. Improvements in Negro education, in his view, were eroding the legal effectiveness of the literacy and "understanding" tests, thus forcing southern whites to rely more on extralegal intimidation. Myrdal surmised that the Supreme Court was beginning to enforce compliance with the original spirit of the Fourteenth and Fifteenth Amendments, and he prophesied that the Court would declare the white primary unconstitutional. He predicted that additional support for civil rights would come from organized labor, which could not afford to alienate black workers by supporting the racial status quo in the South.

Finally, Myrdal argued that southern conservatives themselves should realize that their position on black disfranchisement was *"politically untenable for any length of time."* Alluding to suffrage and social reform questions in European history, he recalled that "political conservatives, who have been successful for any length of time, have always foreseen impending changes and have put through the needed reforms themselves in time. By following this tactic, they have been able to guard fundamental conservative interests even in the framing of the reforms. . . . They have kept the control and preserved a basis for the retention of their political power." Once again, Myrdal departed from the moral immediacy rhetoric of his introductory and concluding chapters and advocated what he considered to be a pragmatic strategy of piecemeal reform, urging southern conservatives to enfranchise blacks by stages, beginning with the "higher strata" of the black population. He warned that if this change were not *"planned* and *led* intelligently" in "the form of cautious, foresighted reforms," the result would be "unexpected, tumultuous, haphazard breaks, with mounting discords and anxieties in its wake."[115]

Myrdal thus drew on his experience as a social engineer, consensus politician, and advocate of prophylactic reform to argue that a program of gradual enfranchisement of southern blacks would serve the interests of the American public, blacks, labor, the legal system, and even southern conservatives. He raised the issue of disfranchisement and of discrimination in public services much more forcefully than most social scientists, New Deal officials, or white southern liberals of his day. Benefiting from Ralph Bunche's detailed studies of black political behavior, Myrdal offered a much more complex analysis of the politics of race than other social scientists, and he noticed dynamic forces leading to change that other observers missed. Yet he did not share Bunche's confidence in the possibility of a mass movement for economic and racial change in the South. Rejecting a one-factor approach that centered on economic change, Myrdal favored a strategy that coordinated various forces that tended to improve the conditions of blacks.[116] He saw the principal agents of change as the American creed, working itself out through the Supreme Court and government bureaucracy, and a new configuration of interest group power growing out of increased voting by blacks in the North and a shift in the stance of organized labor. Myrdal assumed that the United States was evolving toward a welfare state in which the federal government exercised greater power over many areas of life. In this context, the power of local officials in the South to discriminate would gradually diminish. Not willing to leave anyone out of the brokered, consensus solution, Myrdal offered southern conservatives the chance to participate in the planning for this change in the political status of southern blacks, and he warned them of the consequences if they did not take that chance.

In his discussion of justice, Myrdal followed a familiar formula employed in his earlier sections: a detailed account of discrimination against blacks in the South, an analysis of dynamic forces leading to an improvement in the status of blacks, and a prophecy of disaster if reforms were not carried out. Myrdal was by no means the first writer to emphasize extralegal violence in the South. The NAACP had publicized lynchings for three decades, and the Commission on Interracial Cooperation had organized white southerners to oppose lynchings. Yet Myrdal portrayed lynching as only the most spectacular example of the extralegal violence and intimidation that white southerners used to control blacks on a day-to-day basis. He asserted, moreover, that the southern legal system and patterns of extralegal violence and intimidation were closely intertwined in a structure of racial subjugation. As a former magistrate in a country with a tradition of central-ized administration of the law, Myrdal had worried about the threats to the Swedish *rättstat* posed by accommodation to the Nazis. Any departure from the rule of law had serious consequences for society as a whole, in his view, not just for the group victimized by the injustice. Southern "lawlessness" profoundly disturbed Myrdal, and he described it in language that was unusually blunt for social scientific writing:

> The Negro's person and property are practically subject to the whim of any white person who wishes to take advantage of him or to punish him for any real or fancied wrongdoing or "insult." A white man can steal from or maltreat a Negro in almost any way without fear of reprisal, because the Negro cannot claim the protection of the police or courts, and personal vengeance on the part of the offended Negro usually results in organized retaliation in the form of bodily injury (including lynching), home burning or banishment. Practically the only check on white maltreatment of Negroes is a rather vague and unformulated feeling on the part of Southern public opinion that a white man should not be "mean" to a Negro except when he "deserves" it.[117]

This structure of legal and extralegal controls over blacks had originated under slavery, Myrdal contended. The patrol system, the planter's freedom to discipline his slaves, and the white community's determination to band together to prevent black uprisings all had their counterparts in the modern South. Myrdal returned to an idea adumbrated in the politics section when he stressed the uniqueness of the American South's combination of conservatism and illegality.[118]

Ironically, in Myrdal's view, the *"extreme democracy"* of the American legal system, coexisting with the disfranchisement of blacks, was one of the chief forces undermining the legal rights of Negroes. In contrast to most European countries, where judges and minor public officials are appointed, the American tradition is to elect sheriffs, court clerks, and local and state judges. When blacks are dis-franchised, Myrdal pointed out, judges are influenced by local prejudices, juries are all white, and law enforcement officials become instruments for preserving white supremacy.[119]

Myrdal's experience as a magistrate in the Stockholm police court made him especially interested in the role of the police in the southern legal order. He asserted, "The Negro's most important public contact is with the policeman. He is the personification of white authority in the Negro community." Drawing upon the research of Arthur Raper, Myrdal detailed incidents of police brutality and police complicity in extralegal intimidation of blacks. He pointed to the low educational level of most southern policemen and called for the establishment of a police college in the South and the raising of educational standards for law enforcement officers.[120]

Although Myrdal contended that the judicial system in the South "represents a tremendous cultural lag in progressive twentieth century America," he described a number of "dynamic" forces that he thought were strengthening the trend toward an improvement in the justice available to blacks in southern courts. Foremost was the willingness of the Supreme Court to oppose the exclusion of blacks from juries and to censure other departures from "the principles of legal procedure." Myrdal believed that blacks would benefit from the steady improvement in standards of education and professional training for southern lawyers, and he held that advances in education among both white and black citizens would be reflected in higher standards in the courtroom. Myrdal saw a "decreasing provincialism of the region" resulting from urbanization and industrialization as well as from better education. He argued that the New Deal was bringing a new type of public official into contact with blacks: "educated and trained men and women whose primary interest is not simply to keep them in their place, but to advise them and help them to a better life. This will, in time, stand out as a social and spiritual revolution."[121] Myrdal assumed that a rational civil service bureaucracy and higher professional standards among policemen, lawyers, and judges would improve the chances of Afro-Americans for receiving justice in the courts, and he did not foresee the possibility that the legal system, even with higher professional standards, would continue to reflect inequalities of economic and political power.

Myrdal noted the activities of the NAACP and the Commission on Interracial Cooperation in opposing lynching and violence against blacks and observed that the northern press, the Negro press, and the southern white liberals all generated criticism of southern injustice. He argued that an increase in Negro voting in the South would lead to better treatment of blacks in the courts, and he recommended the establishment in the South of legal aid agencies insulated from local politics. "*In principle*," Myrdal maintained, "*the average white Southerner is no longer prepared to defend racial inequality of justice. . . .* White people must be taught to understand the damaging effects upon the whole society of a system of justice which is not equitable." The Swedish Jeremiah prophesied that the South would endure "severe race riots" unless "drastic action is taken."[122] Yet Myrdal never wavered in his faith that the forces of reason, order, and modernity would triumph in the South. As he had confided to Keppel, he had gone "to the limits of optimism" in stressing the dynamic forces in the South that were leading toward racial change.[123]

Myrdal followed his exhaustive analysis of the economic, political, and legal aspects of racial inequality with a unit on social inequality, in which he returned to themes he had raised impressionistically in his opening chapters. Adopting the ethnographic tone he had developed in that earlier section, he calmly cataloged southern racial conventions in a manner calculated to highlight their irrationality. "The live Negro body may be handled by the white physician," he drolly recorded, "but the dead one is handled only by the Negro undertaker."[124] Although Myrdal noted that segregation and discrimination preserved the political and economic power of the white elite in the South, he insisted that most whites in their everyday behavior did not consciously think about their self-interest in dealings with blacks. Instead, they were powerfully conditioned by the myths that white supremacy had historically instilled in white southerners. Foremost was the fear of black male sexuality, which lay at the root of the "no social equality" taboo. Myrdal invoked Paul Lewinson's humorous term, the "post-prandial non-sequitur," to denote the deadly serious southern fear that "if a Negro eats with a white man he is assumed to have the right to marry his daughter."[125]

White southern liberals, Myrdal lamented, almost universally conceded the right of the South to social segregation, even as they pressed for greater political, legal, and economic equality for blacks. Some northern white liberals like Eleanor Roosevelt also called on Afro-Americans to defer social equality until after they had made progress on the political and economic fronts. But could "social" life be exempted from the American creed? Myrdal asked. The Swedish observer reiterated his claim that the American creed was undergoing a transition from rugged individualism to a greater awareness of social interdependence and the rights of all citizens to equal opportunity. He questioned whether one group of citizens had the right to deprive others of their liberty and opportunity, and he noted that segregation laws required all whites to discriminate against blacks, whether they wanted to or not. Myrdal declared that segregation in public accommodations was not merely a matter of private social life but entailed a cost to black Americans in "cultural isolation, political and legal disabilities, and economic disadvantages, which are often much more important than the direct social discrimination." Referring to an issue that John Dewey had raised, Myrdal asked Americans to consider the kind of culture that was necessary to sustain democratic institutions. He conceded Lord Bryce's point that "good feeling and good manners cannot be imposed by statute," but he emphatically asserted that "the equalitarian, internally peaceful society, envisaged in the democratic Creed of this country, cannot exist when good feeling and good manners do not usually characterize the relations between members of the society."[126] This forthright declaration that the "social" sphere could not be exempted from the American creed would win Myrdal praise from many black reviewers.

In looking at how segregation might be ended, Myrdal celebrated the success of the NAACP's lawsuits and predicted that the legal campaign would "go from victory to victory." He suggested that if the Supreme Court began to require equal expenditures for black and white schools, the southern states would feel themselves in a financial squeeze and would have to reconsider their commitment to segregation. On the issue of housing, Myrdal lambasted the Federal Housing Administration for extending credit to blacks "only if they build or buy in Negro neighborhoods and to whites only if they build in white areas which are under covenant not to rent or sell to Negroes." He forecast a postwar housing boom, pointed to federal housing policy as a subject for immediate attention, and argued that segregated housing patterns would continue to spread if federal policies were not changed.[127]

Negro Politics, Culture, and Community

From the outset, Myrdal had argued that the American race issue was primarily a "white man's problem," that the status of blacks was defined largely by white political and economic oppression and by white prejudice and social discrimination. Yet he devoted over three hundred pages to examining Afro-American political leadership, protest organizations, institutions, class structure, and culture. Myrdal considered it his duty as an "objective" foreign observer to present in a dispassionate manner the devastating costs of racial discrimination, so as to find effective strategies for combating racial inequality. Strongly influenced by Bunche and Frazier, he stressed the warping effects of racial oppression on Negro personality and culture. Myrdal's analysis overemphasized the social pathologies in Negro life and failed to give adequate attention to many of the strengths of Afro-American culture portrayed by such contemporaries as Du Bois, Charles S. Johnson, and Herskovits. He sought to make the social and cultural condition of black Americans a political issue: he intended to rescue Negro studies from their status as a small academic subspecialty and to relate the lives of Afro-Americans to the mainstream of American politics and culture, thereby claiming a larger audience among white Americans. In doing so, he would distort Afro-American culture considerably by focusing excessively on the damage done by segregation and discrimination. Myrdal was an intensely political man with relatively little interest in aesthetic, cultural, and religious questions, and he assumed that the social and cultural life of blacks could be explained primarily by the denial of political power and economic opportunity. Despite the weaknesses of his cultural analysis, Myrdal did not portray blacks as essentially passive people: he found mounting anger in the black community and a wide range of protest movements and political ideologies. The central question he would ask as he surveyed the black community was, How could black anger be channeled into effective strategies of protest that would yield tangible results instead of the despair that so often came after the hopes of Afro-Americans were not fulfilled?

In examining the relationship between the black community and the rest of American society, Myrdal used the term *caste* to refer to the status of Afro-Americans, but he did not accept all the assumptions of the caste and class school. Myrdal's use of caste developed from his conception of Negro status as being determined by whites. If whites refused to intermarry with blacks, if they confronted blacks with insuperable social barriers that did not exist for white immigrant groups, then, Myrdal reasoned, the term *caste* was justified. Myrdal deployed the word *caste* to highlight the contradiction between the American ideology of open competition and the practice of excluding Afro-Americans from rising freely in the white class system. The Swedish Social Democrat swallowed whatever objections he had to the American economic system and declared that his value premise was "*the American ideal of free competition and full integration.*"[128] Myrdal was thus able to contrast the American ideology of open competition with American treatment of blacks by using a term that carried connotations of the static, hierarchical, tradition-bound social system of India. The concept of caste also enabled him to stress the social isolation of Afro-Americans and the extent to which blacks were forced to turn inward and create an elaborate class system of their own because of their exclusion from participation in the larger society. Myrdal invoked Du Bois's metaphor of Afro-Americans standing behind a plate-glass window, screaming about their condition, as white Americans passed by without hearing them.[129]

Myrdal's use of caste differed from that of John Dollard in one important sense: Myrdal saw dynamic forces at work in the South that promised to transform the caste system into a more egalitarian society if Afro-Americans and their white allies were able to apply pressure at critical points. He also took exception to the Warner school's use of the word *class*, with its emphasis on social intimacy among members of a class as the key to defining class membership. Myrdal's definition of class was more attentive to the upper class's monopoly of certain kinds of economic power, control of certain institutions, "*restriction of free competition*," and denial of "full social integration."[130] Yet, lest anyone think him too radical, he rejected the Marxist concept of class struggle as a "superficial and erroneous notion" and affirmed that in the analysis of race relations, a concept of caste struggle was more realistic.[131] The problem, then, became how Afro-Americans should mobilize their limited resources for this caste struggle.

In analyzing the weaknesses of black political organizations, Myrdal took care to place his discussion in the context of American political culture. Americans, he maintained, were highly individualistic and tended to defer to leaders rather than organize themselves at the grass roots. Reiterating the arguments he had made ten years earlier in his essay "Socialism or Capitalism in America's Future," Myrdal insisted that the masses in the United States did not form effective political movements because of ethnic fragmentation and the continual loss of leaders through social mobility. In comparing the United States with Sweden and other European countries, Myrdal found not only weak trade unions but also a virtual absence of working-class cooperatives, civic clubs, and adult education movements. The average citizen, he concluded, participated only intermittently in civic affairs, attending to politics only at election time.[132] Afro-Americans, in his view, exemplified this pattern of "mass passivity," albeit in "exaggerated" form.[133]

Myrdal surveyed a range of black leadership styles, beginning with the "accommodating leadership" that he saw as an outgrowth of the old master-servant relationship in the South. Since the days of slavery, he suggested, upper-class white southerners had sought to control blacks by appointing black leaders. By the mid-twentieth century, these leaders were black professionals rather than faithful house servants, but they still functioned as Uncle Toms. Their prestige in the black community derived from their ability to "talk to, and get things from, the whites." Myrdal observed that these upper-class black, accommodating leaders were often personally unpopular in the black community and that they often took on a dictatorial role toward their followers. Uneducated black clergymen, he found, might be more effective in speaking the language of the masses. But the accommodating leaders were seen as the only vehicle for approaching the white leadership.[134] These southern black leaders, according to Myrdal, had to accommodate the whites to a great extent or face violent retribution, and southern blacks expected their leaders to engage in a certain amount of Uncle Tomming. Yet the masses resented the leaders' kowtowing to whites. The leaders were thus "doomed to opportunism" and unable to articulate an effective political strategy for racial advancement.[135]

Drawing heavily on Ralph Bunche's monographs, Myrdal critically appraised various black protest movements, organizations, and ideologies. Like Bunche, he perceived much Negro protest as "shut in by caste" and "doomed to be introverted and self-consuming." He argued that many blacks suffered from an "inferiority complex," were frustrated and embittered over the refusal of white America to respond to their demands for justice, yet were unable to vent their rage publicly because of the danger of retribution. They therefore turned their anger inward, escaped into religion or "trivial" black social organizations, or took refuge in ideologies of race chauvinism. Myrdal generally accepted the view of Bunche and Frazier that black institutions were the fiefdoms of the Negro petit bourgeois elite, which used appeals to race solidarity as a means of securing the allegiance of the black masses, who might otherwise turn against them.[136] Like Bunche and Frazier, Myrdal was especially harsh in his evaluation of Afro-American nationalist currents of thought, chastising Carter G. Woodson's Negro History movement for inflating "mediocrities" into "great men" and placing ordinary cultural achievements on a "pinnacle." On Garvey, he quoted Bunche's judgment: "When the curtain dropped on the Garvey theatricals, the black man of America was exactly where Garvey had found him, though a little bit sadder, perhaps a bit poorer—if not wiser." Yet Garvey's brief success proved that it was possible to stir the Afro-American masses "if they are appealed to in an effective way." Garvey's popularity testified to the "basic unrest in the Negro community" and the profound "dissatisfaction" of blacks with the status quo. The question for Myrdal was how to tap that deep vein of anger and direct it into a pragmatic movement for civil rights, integration, and economic improvement.[137]

Myrdal was more encouraged by the success of the CIO in opening industrial unions to blacks, and he claimed that most Negro leaders now supported labor unions when the unions welcomed black members. He warned blacks, however, not to concentrate all their resources on an economic approach, as many of the radical black intellectuals had advocated. Reiterating his principle of cumulative causation, Myrdal argued that it was possible to intervene in the social system at any one of a number of strategic points and thereby move the whole system in the direction of racial equality.[138] This view led him to take exception to the view then widespread among black intellectuals that the black protest suffered from institutional rivalry and that all blacks needed to unify into one mass protest organization with one clear-cut program. Myrdal contended that the black protest was better served by several organizations, each of which was best suited to the particular function that it performed. The black movement could thus advance on several fronts simultaneously.[139]

The NAACP, in Myrdal's view, was doing a good job of challenging Jim Crow and disfranchisement in court, lobbying for antilynching legislation and economic reforms on Capitol Hill, and appealing to the conscience of educated white Americans through propaganda. He acknowledged, though, that the association was largely a middle-class organization and recommended that it appoint more working-class members to local boards and intensify efforts to reach the black masses through adult education programs and Swedish-style study circles and forums.[140] The black protest, in his view, also needed the work of the Urban League. Though he admitted that the league was often not forthright enough in support of labor unions, he praised the league's programs to help black migrants in urban areas and its efforts to combat job discrimination. Despite his reservations about white southern liberals, Myrdal even found some good things to say about the Commission on Interracial Cooperation, which he commended for its educational work against lynching. He did suggest, however, that the commission needed to make a greater effort to reach middle- and lower-class whites with its educational message.[141] Finally Myrdal was encouraged by the success of A. Philip Randolph's March on Washington movement, which was "something of a mass movement with the main backing from Negro workers, but has at the same time the backing of the established Negro organizations." He was impressed that, although it was a black-only movement, Randolph's organization had resisted the use of "racial emotionalism" as an appeal. Myrdal concluded that there was actually "*little friction and rivalry*" among the NAACP, Urban League, and Commission on Interracial Cooperation and that the three complemented each other in the struggle for racial justice. He surmised that Randolph's movement pointed the way toward a successful strategy of mass organization of blacks that also made pragmatic alliances with whites and appealed to the American creed.[142] Myrdal did not attempt to set priorities among the various strategies he endorsed, nor did he offer advice to Afro-Americans about how they should apportion their resources among the different organizations. He recognized that race relations were changing rapidly during the war, and he did not want to tie himself too closely to a particular set of tactics.

As we have seen, Myrdal's observations of black institutions during his travels around the country focused on the "power aspect": their role in the black protest movement rather than the other functions that they performed in the black community. His chapters on the Negro church, school, and press therefore concentrated on the political effectiveness of those institutions and did not present a more comprehensive or well-rounded evaluation of the organizations.[143] In his analysis of the black church, Myrdal underestimated the church as a source of political leadership, and he did not grasp the extent to which it gave coherence and meaning to the Afro-American community. As he would later acknowledge, he completely failed to predict the central role that the church would play in the civil rights movement.[144] This misunderstanding stemmed, in part, from his deep suspicion of religious emotion going back to his boyhood encounters with the Protestant evangelicals in the mission house in Solvarbo. Like the philosophes whom he so admired, Myrdal saw religious enthusiasm as something backward that humankind needed to jettison as it marched on to modernity. And when he had first observed Afro-American religious behavior on his trip to the South with Jackson Davis in 1938, he had found it so baffling that he recommended that it be studied by the methods of abnormal psychology.[145]

In tracing the history of the black church, Myrdal relied on an unpublished manuscript done for his study by Guy and Guion Johnson, who stressed the similarities between black religion and lower-class white southern evangelicalism, and he ignored the work of Woodson and Du Bois, who emphasized the uniqueness of the black church and its origins in the antebellum slave society.[146] Myrdal was also influenced by the younger generation of radical black intellectuals who saw the church as offering Afro-Americans otherworldly escapism that diverted them from political struggle. These young turks derogated the clergy as a poorly educated cadre of Uncle Toms and reproached blacks for wasting so much time, money, and energy on church activities. The ire of the radicals often stemmed from close personal exposure—St. Clair Drake was the son of a Garveyite minister and Frazier the son-in-law of a prominent Baptist clergyman—and they prophesied a diminution of the church's influence as the masses turned to an interracial class struggle. In addition to citing manuscripts by Drake and Allison Davis, Myrdal drew upon *The Negro's Church* by Benjamin Mays and J. W. Nicholson, which likewise criticized the black church but took a more reformist line. Influenced by modernist theology at the University of Chicago, Mays and Nicholson hoped for gradual improvements in the educational standards of the clergy and the evolution of the black church toward a social gospel mission.[147]

Synthesizing these critical perspectives, Myrdal lamented the "emotionalism" of the black church and judged it "inefficient and uninfluential" as an agency of social change. He deprecated the "uncouth manners" of the "jack-leg preachers" and declared that "the chief prerequisite for becoming a minister is traditionally not education, but a 'call' which is more often the manifestation of temporary hysteria or opportunistic self-inspiration than of deep soul-searching."[148] The Swedish rationalist viewed the Negro church as an egregious case of cultural lag. He discerned a few signs, however, of a "general process of acculturation" whereby the black clergy were becoming better educated and the church would develop into "a more efficient instrument for amelioration of the Negro's position." Still, he was even more encouraged by evidence that improvements in education would reduce "the relative importance of the church in the Negro community."[149]

If Myrdal could muster only guarded optimism about the black church, he was more sanguine about black schools and colleges as agencies of social change. He proclaimed that education—even in a Jim Crow system—was a destabilizing force that increased black dissatisfaction with the status quo and hastened blacks' assimilation of white American culture. Citing John Dewey, he noted the central place of education in American life as a vehicle of social mobility and a means of disseminating democratic values. Myrdal did not foresee a Supreme Court decision outlawing public school segregation in the near future. He did, however, predict that the NAACP's legal campaign would compel southern states to raise the salaries of black teachers and perhaps open the doors of graduate schools to blacks. Myrdal suggested a postwar federal program of constructing new schools for blacks in the South as a way of reducing expected unemployment as well as meeting an urgent social need, and he warned the North that it would continue to get "crude and untutored Negro immigrants from the South" if the educational level of black schools were not improved.[150]

Myrdal also looked to the black press as an important institution in the Negro protest and celebrated its "relentless criticism" of white racial discrimination. He grumbled about the "sensationalism" of black newspapers but allowed that white papers were just as bad. Myrdal embraced Frazier's view that the press was essentially controlled by the black upper class, which used an ideology of racial solidarity to "avert lower class hostility against themselves," but predicted that progress in black education and economic advances after the war would lead to increased circulation, which would enable the black press to improve its standards and become more responsive to the black population as a whole. Myrdal displayed, once again, his social democratic optimism that educated journalists, teachers, and professionals would act as responsible leaders and spokespersons for the masses and that they would provide a more disinterested type of leadership than that offered by the older black elite. In his view, Afro-Americans needed strong and militant institutions for the fight against segregation and discrimination, but eventually these institutions would disappear as integration and assimilation occurred.[151]

As we have seen, Myrdal delegated the writing of the unit on the Negro community to Arnold Rose because he conceived of it as a "residual part which has to be filled, in order to make the book really 'comprehensive.'"[152] As the senior author, Myrdal bore the responsibility for the chapters, which Rose wrote from an outline that Myrdal left behind after he returned to Sweden in September 1942. The two chapters are indeed residual in that they are compilations of various "social pathologies," only loosely tied together under the rubric "nonpolitical aspects of the Negro community."[153] Myrdal and Rose intended the chapters to be a tough-minded statement of the damage that segregation and racial discrimination had done to black Americans: they sought to provide a survey of social problems for policymakers and social engineers, and they also indulged in some moral exhortation designed to convince black readers of the need to put aside romantic illusions about the race and face the hard reality of rooting out social pathologies. Yet the portrait of Afro-American life is so bleak that the two chapters tend to contradict the optimistic tone of the previous unit, which argued that, despite segregation and discrimination, blacks were gradually and inexorably becoming a part of American culture. The Negro community unit also failed to address the issue of what held the black community together.

Myrdal and Rose insisted that the "melting pot" or "assimilation" was a "central element in the American Creed." Ignoring the work of such cultural pluralist thinkers as Randolph Bourne and Horace Kallen and disregarding the more subtle studies of immigrant acculturation by Robert Park and W. I. Thomas, they flatly asserted that assimilation was the goal of all ethnic groups in the United States. This stark assimilationism fit with some of the ideological pronouncements of black leaders during World War II, who emphasized the Negro's "American-ness" to show that blacks were not disloyal in wartime. Myrdal also believed that he, as a foreigner, could see more clearly than Americans of either race, just how "American" blacks really were in their culture and social life. Myrdal and Rose were keenly aware that the idea of a distinctive Negro culture could be used by white racists as an argument against integration and racial equality.[154]

For all of these reasons, therefore, Myrdal and Rose concluded that the Negro "imitates the dominant culture as he sees it and in so far as he can adopt it under his conditions of life. For the most part he is not proud of those things in which he differs from the white American." In a passage that would prove to be highly controversial, the authors declared:

> *In practically all its divergences, American Negro culture is not something independent of general American culture. It is a distorted development, or a pathological condition, of the general American culture.* The instability of the Negro family, the inadequacy of educational facilities for Negroes, the emotionalism

in the Negro church, the insufficiency and unwholesomeness of Negro recreational activity, the plethora of Negro sociable organizations, the narrowness of interests of the average Negro, the provincialism of his political speculation, the high Negro crime rate, the cultivation of the arts to the neglect of other fields, superstition, personality difficulties, and other characteristic traits are mainly forms of social pathology which, for the most part, are created by the caste pressures.

Myrdal and Rose admonished blacks to strive to fit into American culture and to eliminate cultural patterns that made them stand out. "*We assume,*" they wrote, "*that it is to the advantage of American Negroes as individuals and as a group to become assimilated into American culture, to acquire the traits held in esteem by the dominant white Americans.*" The authors sought to deflect criticisms from anthropologists by claiming that they were not making an "absolute" judgment that one culture was "higher" than another, only a pragmatic statement that in America individuals and groups had to embrace American culture.[155]

This rigid assimilationism led Myrdal into an ironic reversal of his conception of the normal and the pathological in family life. In *Kris i befolkningsfrågan*, the Myrdals had portrayed the modern nuclear family as "almost . . . pathological," an unstable "compromise" between the old agrarian patriarchal family and the new situation created by changing roles for women in the workplace. They had argued that the contemporary nuclear family was headed toward "disintegration and sterility." The Myrdals had concluded that "we must free children more from ourselves" and had urged the creation of publicly funded day care centers.[156] But Gunnar Myrdal sought to draw his value premises for *An American Dilemma* from the norms "actually observed as existing in the minds of the white and Negro Americans and tested as to their social and political relevance and significance."[157] Accordingly, Myrdal and Rose accepted the American urban nuclear family as the norm against which the black family was measured. The authors endorsed Frazier's conclusion that slavery was the primary cause of the greater "instability" found among black families and that the migration of rural blacks to the cities had heightened the "disorganization" and "demoralization" of many families.[158]

Black voluntary associations, according to Myrdal and Rose, also revealed a pattern of social pathology. Citing the work of Drake and Davis, the authors argued that because Afro-Americans were barred from politics, they squandered much time and resources on a plethora of lodges and other social organizations. The fact that such organizations continued to flourish among blacks while declining among whites was seen as yet another indication of cultural lag among blacks in adapting to modern American society.[159]

In the chapter "Non-Institutional Aspects of the Negro Community," Myrdal and Rose also cataloged "peculiarities" of Negro culture that whites found particularly striking. Although the intent of this analysis was to explain how these traits were rooted in the history of caste oppression rather than biology, the effect of the chapter was to highlight aspects of Afro-American social life that triggered white prejudice without really getting inside the black community and elucidating what Afro-American culture meant to black people. The authors suggested that blacks should strive to eliminate these peculiarities that hindered their assimilation of white culture. "Since the whites are the dominant group," they lectured, "it is important for Negroes to determine what whites find peculiar about their culture."[160] Myrdal and Rose then enumerated a series of white stereotypes: that blacks were aggressive or "bumptious"; that they were emotional or carefree; that they loved the "gaudy, the bizarre, and the ostentatious"; that they were secretive and superstitious; and that they could only speak in Negro dialect. After explaining how each of these peculiarities grew out of black adaptation to the caste system, the authors affirmed: "As more Negroes become educated and urbanized, it may be expected that they will lose their distinctive cultural traits and take over the dominant American patterns. . . . As the trend proceeds, and as there emerges a class of Negroes which is recognized by whites to have the same cultural traits as themselves, the Negro will be thought to be less 'peculiar' than he is now."[161] Cultural assimilation is thus a slow but inexorable tendency which, according to the principle of cumulation, could be expected to gradually lessen white prejudice. Myrdal and Rose concluded their superficial survey of Afro-American culture by presenting a roster of black celebrities and entertainers, drawn largely from Sterling Brown's manuscript "The Negro in American Culture." They allowed that the success of some blacks in the arts and in entertainment had helped many Negroes to find "a measure of self-confidence," but they warned against a "false pride in race." Never missing an opportunity to deprecate black separatism, the authors proclaimed that "Negro art will continue to be American because its creators are American and American influences continually mold it."[162]

In a sense, Ralph Bunche and Franklin Frazier won the battle to influence Myrdal. No other American social scientists had as great an impact on Myrdal's analysis of Afro-American politics, institutions, and culture. But Bunche and Frazier had criticized Afro-American elites, political organizations, institutions, and culture in the hope that a new socialist, interracial labor struggle would emerge from the tumultuous upheavals of the 1930s, bringing a new interracial culture in its wake. Instead, Myrdal's version of their critique led not to a process of socialist transformation but rather to a white perception of blacks as a people afflicted with social pathologies calling for the cure of social engineering and adjustment to the norms of white, middle-class society. Pervaded by cultural arrogance, the section on the Negro community would prove to be the weakest part of *An American Dilemma*.

Racial Justice in a Global Context

In a final chapter, "America Again at the Crossroads in the Negro Problem," Myrdal argued that the United States was on the verge of witnessing a historic change in race relations. Though many American social scientists in the 1930s had seen the southern caste system as essentially stable and unchanging, Myrdal emphasized dynamic forces leading to structural change. He predicted an early end to the "national compromise" that had lasted for two generations since Reconstruction, noting that the South could no longer count on northern acquiescence in Jim Crow. Myrdal summarized the political, social, and intellectual changes in race relations of the preceding decade: New Deal programs that delivered benefits to both blacks and whites, Supreme Court decisions on civil rights, unionization of many black workers, more aggressive black protest movements, and the declining respectability of racist theories among whites. He also warned of race riots if improvements in the status of blacks did not come at a faster rate.[163] In the conclusion, Myrdal linked the race issue to the war much more forcefully than he had in the earlier chapters. "There is bound to be a redefinition of the Negro's status as a result of this War," he declared. Emphasizing the importance of changes in valuations or beliefs, Myrdal suggested that whites would have increasing difficulty in defending segregation and discrimination while fighting a war against Nazi racism. Blacks would not hesitate to press their demands during wartime and they would have the American creed on their side.[164]

While American race relations were of strategic importance to the war effort, they would be even more significant in the postwar world that Myrdal envisioned. Foreseeing the international embarrassment that segregation would cause the United States when African and Asian nations gained independence, he argued that "it will be impossible to make and preserve a good peace without having built up the fullest trust and good will among the colored peoples" who would "be strong after the War" and would "become even stronger as time passes." Myrdal noted the higher birthrate among "colored" nations and predicted the rapid industrialization of "many backward countries." If the Western countries did not abandon white supremacy, he warned, eventually the "colored nations" might inflict "humiliation and subjugation" on the whites.[165] Myrdal informed his readers that American isolationism was "gone forever" and that the United States in the postwar era would have the "major responsibility for the manner in which humanity approaches the long era during which the white peoples will have to adjust to shrinkage while the colored are bound to expand in numbers, in the level of industrial civilization and in political power." He predicted the formation of an international organization like the League of Nations, before which American blacks could lodge complaints against segregation in the United States.[166] Though black nationalist thinkers since the nineteenth century had placed their hopes in a worldwide upsurge of people of color, few white Americans had listened. Myrdal's framing of the American race issue in a global economic and political context would be harder to ignore.

In his customary manner, Myrdal followed these warnings of potential violence and conflict with affirmations of the power of the American creed to meet the challenge, and his rhetoric appealed to the sense of awesome responsibility for world leadership that many Americans felt as the war drew to a close. "The Negro problem," he wrote, "is not only America's greatest failure but also America's incomparably great opportunity for the future." If America were to live up to its creed, it would be a stronger nation at home and its "prestige and power abroad would rise immensely." Appealing to the traditional idea of an American mission to the world, he suggested that if the nation embraced racial equality, "The century-old dream of American patriots, that America should give to the entire world its own freedoms and its own faith, would come true." "America," he insisted, "can demonstrate that justice, equality and cooperation are possible between white and colored people." Returning to the central theme of *Kontakt med Amerika*, Myrdal proclaimed: "This is what the world needs to believe. Mankind is sick of fear and disbelief, of pessimism and cynicism. It needs the youthful, moralistic optimism of America." For Myrdal, the quest for racial justice had an almost religious quality. If the United States lived up to its creed, he prophesied, "America would have a spiritual power many times stronger than all her financial and military resources—the power of the trust and support of all good people on earth."[167] Myrdal concluded his book by reaffirming the connection between social engineering and "the old American faith in human beings" that was the heritage of the eighteenth century. Social engineering, he declared, was the "supreme task of social science." "The world catastrophe places tremendous difficulties in our way and may shake our confidence to the depths," he admitted. "Yet we have today in social science a greater trust in the improvability of man and society than we have ever had since the Enlightenment."[168]

The writing of *An American Dilemma* required an enormous act of will as well as a mustering of Gunnar Myrdal's deep faith in the ideals of the Enlightenment. Throughout his lengthy study, he had sketched out in depressing detail the dimensions of American racial oppression in the economy, polity, legal system, society, and culture. Yet he had gone "to the limits of optimism" in stressing that the "dynamic forces" in America were strong enough to defeat white supremacy. Myrdal's testimony that America's response to the race question had a crucial impact on the fate of democracy in Europe and in the rest of the world gave to *An American Dilemma* a moral energy found in few works of social science. Fearing that the values to which he had dedicated his life were in danger of being overwhelmed by the Nazi conquest, he infused his writing with a moral "immediacy" that had not been present in the work of most American social scientists. Myrdal counseled Americans that this was no time for a "*defeatist attitude*"[169] with respect to civil rights, that if the nation could tap its deep wellspring of idealism and direct that energy into a program of constructive social engineering, it could eliminate "America's greatest failure."

In his conclusion, Myrdal blended an appeal to the American conscience with an analysis of the forces that promised to bring about structural changes in black-white relations. To be sure, the moral dilemma thesis rested on Myrdal's own interviewing and impressions rather than on a rigorous empirical testing of white racial attitudes. But *An American Dilemma* was much more than a study of the mental and emotional conflicts of whites, or a synthesis of the work of American scholars on the damage of segregation and discrimination to blacks. Though he did not summarize them in his conclusion, Myrdal made several policy suggestions for improving the status of blacks that were often overlooked both by his critics and by some of his admirers who focused exclusively on his moral appeals to individual whites. For the South, he advocated abolition of the poll tax, enfranchisement of southern blacks in stages, a federal program for constructing black schools, the establishment of a police college, the raising of educational standards for police officers, the creation of legal aid agencies insulated from local politics, and the organization of farm workers into unions. The Swedish social engineer called for government planning for full employment, birth control programs for the poor, federal planning for the migration of displaced tenant farmers from the rural South to urban areas, vocational education programs to aid these migrants in preparing for industrial jobs, and adult education courses to help them make up deficiencies caused by segregated schooling. Myrdal implicitly suggested that the Supreme Court require compliance with the Fourteenth Amendment's guarantee of equal protection of the law with respect to higher education and voting rights in the South, and he recommended the desegregation of public housing projects in the North and a nationwide educational campaign against prejudice. Finally, he made many suggestions as to how voluntary organizations and political pressure groups might modify their policies and tactics so as to work more effectively for racial justice.

These policy proposals were based on assumptions that the New Deal would renew its drive for economic reforms after the war, that a more moderate Republican Party would accept some of these reforms, and that the labor movement as well as black organizations would gain in strength, creating a new constellation of political power in the South and in the nation as a whole. In reality, however, Congress would have little interest in enacting costly programs designed to help blacks and other poor Americans climb out of poverty, and several of Myrdal's most important recommendations have never been followed. In the political context of the late 1940s and 1950s, public discussion would focus on Myrdal's theory of the "moral dilemma," his interest in the problem of white racial prejudice, and his attention to the "damage" that segregation and discrimination inflicted on black Americans.

6

The Study to
End All Studies

When *An American Dilemma* was published in January 1944, Americans knew that the Allies were winning the war and that the United States would emerge as the world's strongest power at the war's end. The radio and newspapers carried daily bulletins from distant fronts, giving Americans a global perspective they had never had before. In Italy, General Mark Clark's Fifth Army inched up the Apennines toward Rome, laying siege to one mountain garrison after another in the mud and snow of a severe winter. Dwight Eisenhower had just assumed command of Allied forces in Britain, where he began planning the cross-channel invasion while American and British bombers pounded targets in Hamburg, Berlin, Frankfurt, and Mannheim. On the eastern front, the Soviet army had reconquered 325,000 square miles of territory in the previous year, pushed the German army back to Vitebsk, and stood ready to strike into Poland. Allied progress in the Pacific theater was much less dramatic. But American marines had won a costly victory on Tarawa in the Gilbert Islands, Admiral Halsey had taken control of the northern Solomon Islands, and General Douglas MacArthur had captured Japanese bases in New Guinea. On the Asian mainland, American and British forces took the offensive in northern Burma in an attempt to open supply lines to Chiang Kai-Shek in China.[1]

The war brought a resurgence of national self-confidence as Americans responded to the attack on Pearl Harbor and to Nazi aggression with a determined effort to defeat the Axis powers. Many Americans saw the conflict as a war of ideas, a struggle for world domination between two systems with opposing ideologies. No one defined American war aims more eloquently than Franklin D. Roosevelt, who, in an address to Congress in January 1941, had affirmed that the United States looked forward to "a world founded upon four essential human freedoms": freedom of speech, freedom of religion, "freedom from want," and "freedom from fear." As the war progressed, freedom had become the central symbol in Roosevelt's oratory.[2] He promised in the Atlantic Charter to "respect the right of all peoples to choose the form of government under which they will live" and expressed his hope that "sovereign rights and self-government" would be "restored to those who have been forcibly deprived of them."[3] In the rhetoric of Roosevelt and other American leaders, the Allies' commitment to freedom was often contrasted to the Nazis' subjection of conquered peoples to "slavery."

The Race Issue in 1944

As Americans girded their ideological armor for the fight against fascism, segregation and racial discrimination were awkward facts that were increasingly difficult to ignore. Roosevelt heaped abuse upon Hitler's theories of the German master race and urged Americans not to allow ethnic differences to divide them. But he avoided the civil rights issue and tried to persuade black leaders that the nation's war effort required a postponement of their protest. The forcible relocation of Japanese-Americans into concentration camps was another conspicuous example of American racism, as were the racial stereotypes of the Japanese in the American press. Racism was also a factor as Americans looked toward a postwar peace settlement and contemplated the fate of Asian and African peoples. Though Roosevelt had promised to respect the right of all nations to self-government, he was reluctant to challenge Prime Minister Winston Churchill's plans to maintain the British Empire after the war.[4]

Other American political leaders were more audacious than the president in envisioning a new world after the war, however. Liberals in both political parties advocated a new global internationalism combining opposition to colonialism in Asia and Africa with support for civil rights at home. These liberal internationalists often argued that spreading American democratic values throughout the world was a moral imperative if peace and prosperity were to be assured. In 1943 Wendell Willkie, still the titular leader of the Republican party, published *One World*, an account of his trip around the globe in which he met with leaders in the Middle East, the Soviet Union, and China. Willkie reported a "reservoir of good will" toward the United States among the peoples of Asia but admonished Americans that they could not afford to alienate the millions of people in Asia, Africa, and Latin America by supporting European colonial empires. Turning to domestic affairs, he denounced "our imperialisms at home," particularly the exploitation of blacks, and argued that racial discrimination was a serious liability for the United States abroad.[5]

In his speeches in 1942 and 1943, Vice President Henry Wallace emerged as the preeminent spokesman for American liberalism and as a champion of internationalism, antiimperialism, and civil rights. A moralist strongly influenced by the Social Gospel movement, he saw the war as a "fight to the death between the free world and the slave world." Since the American Revolution, Wallace wrote, the people had moved forward on a "millenial and revolutionary march toward manifesting here on earth the dignity that is in every human soul." After the defeat of the Nazi "Satan," the world would enter "the century of the common man," in which the benefits of democracy, brotherhood, education, and industrial and agricultural progress would extend throughout the world.[6] Though Americans had failed to secure a lasting peace after World War I through shortsighted isolationism, Wallace argued that history had provided a "second chance" to establish a world order based on international cooperation, with a United Nations organization to resolve conflicts.[7] A strong proponent of government planning for postwar reconversion, Wallace's domestic program centered on a Keynesian strategy to create 60 million jobs, but he also spoke out in favor of civil rights. "We cannot plead for equality of opportunity for peoples everywhere and overlook the denial of the right to vote for millions of our own people," he told a labor meeting in Detroit in 1943. "Every citizen of the United States without regard to color or creed, whether he resides where he was born or whether he has moved to a great defense center or to a fighting front, is entitled to cast his vote."[8]

Both Willkie and Wallace had moved ahead of opinion in their respective parties during 1942 and 1943, and both paid for it: Republican voters spurned Willkie in the Wisconsin primary of April 1944, ending his quest for the presidential nomination, and Democratic urban bosses and southern conservatives successfully maneuvered to have Wallace dropped from the ticket at the Democratic convention in July. Yet both men played major roles in popularizing a new globalist liberalism that fused support for civil rights with the lofty rhetoric of internationalism. Their speeches and books spread these ideas to millions of white Americans—not simply to the readers of the *New Republic* and the *Nation* but to people in many walks of life. While most previous theorists of America's greatness had emphasized Manifest Destiny or the United States' racial or cultural superiority to other nations, Willkie and Wallace both warned that in order for the United States to play a great role in world affairs it had to set its own house in order on the issue of civil rights. They helped to establish a climate of opinion in which Myrdal's optimistic, moralistic approach to the race question seemed plausible to many educated white Americans.

Though he did not embrace the millenial vision of his vice president, Roosevelt delivered a dramatic affirmation of domestic liberalism in his state of the union address on January 11, 1944, just as *An American Dilemma* reached reviewers. In what one historian has called the "most radical speech of his life," the president proclaimed that achieving "freedom from want" required a "second Bill of Rights." "We have come to a clear realization," he asserted, "that *true* individual freedom cannot exist without economic security and independence." Roosevelt insisted that every citizen should enjoy the right to a "useful and remunerative job," "the right to earn enough to provide adequate food and clothing and recreation," "the right of every family to a decent home," and "the right to adequate protection from the economic fears of old age and sickness and accident and unemployment." To those standard goals of New Deal liberalism, the president added "the right to adequate medical care" and "the right to a good education."[9] These brave words raised the spirits of Roosevelt's supporters, who hoped for a continuation of the New Deal after the war, but they had little impact on the Congress, where the conservative coalition of Republicans and southern Democrats was firmly in control. The decline of the New Deal, which had begun with the Court-packing fight of 1937, had continued through 1941 as FDR had generally refrained from pushing new reforms in order to muster bipartisan support for America's military buildup and aid to Britain. In the November 1942 elections (shortly after Gunnar Myrdal had finished his book), Republicans had gained forty-six seats in the House and nine in the Senate, strengthening the conservative majority. In short order, Congress had abolished the Civilian Conservation Corps, the Works Progress Administration, the National Youth Administration, and the National Resources Planning Board, and had drastically reduced funding for the Farm Security Administration. Despite his bold rhetoric, FDR knew by January 1944 that the only reform that Congress would pass was the proposal to provide government support for veterans' education, the GI Bill of Rights.[10]

The character of American liberalism changed during the war in other important ways. Beginning in 1940, Roosevelt had brought hundreds of business executives to Washington to manage war production. As the scale of government expanded during the war, businessmen increasingly dominated the higher echelons of the bureaucracy at the expense of the New Deal reformers who had entered government service in the 1930s. Yet the businessmen, too, were changed by their experience in Washington. Prior to the war many, if not most, leading businessmen had viewed the Roosevelt administration as the enemy even though their firms often prospered under the New Deal. They had felt excluded from power and feared any new forms of government regulation. During the war, many businessmen had come to accept the fact that government would continue to play a large role in the economy, and they became much more adept at influencing government policy. This rapprochement between big business and government also led to a much wider acceptance of Keynesian economics by leading businessmen.[11] Faced with congressional opposition to New Deal agencies on the one hand and business acceptance of Keynesian economics on the other, many liberals after the war would conclude that it was futile to try to revive job training programs for the poor such as the NYA. Instead, they hoped that management of the economy on Keynesian principles would produce full employment, and they turned to new issues such as health insurance, federal aid to education, and civil rights.[12]

Roosevelt had tried repeatedly to defuse the civil rights issue, which threatened to blow apart his electoral coalition of southern whites, northern liberals, labor unions, and blacks. But it would not go away. The war years were a time of rapid social change for Afro-Americans, as the draft and war industries eliminated black unemployment and accelerated the migration of blacks from the rural South to the cities of the North, South, and West. Whether they served in the army or worked in defense plants, hundreds of thousands of Afro-Americans had new jobs, new neighbors, and higher expectations. The "caste system" of the South, which had seemed so enduring to John Dollard only seven years earlier, was now beginning to break down.[13] And in the cities of the North, discrimination by realtors and white homeowners meant that thousands of black newcomers were jammed into already crowded ghettos. The most galling indignity, however, was the continued segregation of the armed forces. Secretary of War Henry Stimson announced that the army could not function as a "sociological laboratory" in wartime and that any attempt to desegregate the army would destroy morale. Stimson also required blacks in segregated units to serve under white officers because "leadership is not imbedded in the negro race yet and to try to make commissioned officers lead men into battle—colored men—is only to work a disaster to both."[14]

On the homefront, the establishment of the Fair Employment Practices Committee (FEPC) had set an important precedent of recognition by the federal government of equal opportunity in employment as a civil right. The agency was able to use the authority of the federal government to censure employers who practiced racial discrimination, but it lacked the power to enforce compliance with its rulings. In a few industries, employers moved to promote black workers in response to FEPC pressure, but most companies evaded compliance. In December 1943, southern railroads had openly defied an FEPC order to stop discriminating against black workers, declaring that the FEPC was "wholly without Constitutional and legal jurisdiction." The episode prompted *Time* magazine to contend that race relations was the "hottest problem on Franklin Roosevelt's desk" and one that he could not avoid without offending either southern Democrats in Congress or black voters.[15]

Rank and file militancy among Afro-Americans increased during World War II to the point that it threatened to leave black leaders behind. In both the North and the South, many blacks were too angry over segregation and discrimination to suppress their protest in order to prove their loyalty to the nation.[16] In 1942 Roy Wilkins had written to Walter White, "It is a plain fact that no Negro leader with a constituency can face his members today and ask full support for the war in the light of the atmosphere the government has created." He conceded, "Some Negro educators who are responsible only to their boards or trustees might do so, but the heads of no organized groups would dare do so."[17] That same year, Will Alexander, Edwin Embree, and Charles S. Johnson warned the Rosenwald Fund that the black movement was heading in an increasingly "proletarian direction." Established leaders like White and A. Philip Randolph were in danger of losing out to "less responsible" leaders like Adam Clayton Powell, Jr.[18]

The *Pittsburgh Courier*, one of the largest black newspapers, expressed the sentiments of many Afro-Americans when it called for a fight for a Double V: victory over fascism and imperialism abroad and over racism at home. Editorialists in black newspapers complained that Roosevelt's rhetoric about the fight for freedom and democracy was just "words, words, words," and they demanded action by the federal government on civil rights.[19] The black press constantly reminded its readers of the absurdity of a segregated army fighting for freedom and of the many forms of discrimination to which black soldiers were subjected. Accounts of German POW's eating in American restaurants that denied service to black GI's vividly symbolized discrimination, as did reports of segregated blood banks maintained by the Red Cross. Black organizations continued to try a variety of strategies and tactics in pursuit of racial equality. Randolph's March on Washington movement had been a powerful lesson in what Afro-Americans could accomplish when unified behind a strategy of nonviolent mass demonstrations. The Congress of Racial Equality (CORE), an interracial organization founded in Chicago in 1942, successfully employed the tactic of nonviolent sit-ins to desegregate restaurants and theaters in Chicago, Denver, Baltimore, and other cities in northern, western, and border states. The NAACP remained the largest and most visible Negro organization, boosting its membership from 50,556 in 1940 to more than 450,000 in 1946, and Walter White kept up a barrage of public criticism of Jim Crow practices in the armed forces and in defense industries.[20] In the courts, Charles Houston led the NAACP's campaign against white supremacy and won a major victory in April 1944 when the Supreme Court in *Smith v. Allwright* ruled that the Democratic party in Texas could not prohibit blacks from voting in primary elections.

Even in the South, where black leaders faced the threat of violent retaliation, many spoke out against segregation. In April 1942, Jessie Daniel Ames, a white southern reformer, had invited a group of southern black leaders to make a statement to southern whites about race relations. Gordon Hancock, the black president of Virginia Union College, organized a conference of black leaders that met in Durham, North Carolina, in October 1942. The group included Charles S. Johnson of Fisk, Frederick D. Patterson of Tuskegee, Benjamin Mays of Morehouse College, Rufus E. Clement of Atlanta University, Horace Mann Bond of Fort Valley State College in Georgia, and P. B. Young, the editor of the *Norfolk Journal and Guide*. "We are fundamentally opposed to the principle and practice of compulsory segregation in our American society," the black spokesmen declared, and they focused their statement on job discrimination, lynching, unequal provision of public services, mistreatment of blacks by police, the poll tax, and white primaries. Though conciliatory in tone, the statement served notice to their white neighbors that southern blacks intended to press for rapid changes in the Jim Crow system.[21] The militant demands of black leaders reflected the mood of the black community generally. "It was as if some universal message had come through to the great mass of Negroes," Howard Odum observed with a touch of condescension, "urging them to dream new dreams and to protest against the old order."[22]

The black protest movement drew considerably more support from northern white liberals than it had before the war. In the late 1930s, most white liberals, North and South, had believed that the best strategy for improving the lives of black Americans lay in programs of economic assistance or job training such as the WPA, CCC, NYA, and the FSA. Civil rights and desegregation, they thought, could wait until a later stage of development when a better-educated and more prosperous black community would seem to be more worthy of these responsibilities and the lowest third of white southerners would have improved their economic and educational standards to the point that they would not offer such intransigent resistance to Negro rights. Events during World War II exposed the shallowness of this kind of thinking. The temporary elimination of unemployment meant that Afro-American leaders could focus their attention on civil rights and desegregation and make it clear to the nation that they would accept no substitutes for the fulfillment of these goals.

The rhetoric of America's leaders emphasized democratic values in contrast to fascism and a moral absolutism that would admit no compromise with the evil of Nazi ideology. In this context, advocacy of civil rights by Afro-Americans and their white liberal allies took on an "immediatist" character. Gradualist solutions to the race question lost legitimacy in the eyes of black Americans and northern white liberals. How could Americans temporize in the face of such a blatant moral evil as the denial of the right to vote and the compulsory segregation of blacks in so many areas of life in the South? liberals inquired. To many young Americans, the old southern arguments about states' rights sounded archaic in an era when the war effort required the subordination of local needs to the national interest. The American armed forces and war industries constituted the largest and most elaborately organized war machine in human history: here was social engineering on a vast scale exceeding anything that Americans had ever imagined. If thousands of farm boys could become fighter pilots and thousands of housewives could learn shipbuilding, was it really true that "stateways cannot change folkways," that the federal government could not ensure that southern blacks had the right to vote? The resurgence of national self-confidence, the "can-do" attitude with which Americans had tackled war production and pushed back the Axis powers in remote parts of the globe led many northern white liberals to conclude that the walls of segregation were not impregnable. Southern folkways would have to yield to the national interest, liberals insisted, even if it meant weakening the Democratic party in the South. No section of the United States was justified in resisting the moral imperative of extending to all citizens the rights that American GI's were defending at so great a cost. Howard Odum reported "an almost universal assumption on the part of the rest of the Nation that 'something must be done about' the South's treatment of the Negro." He claimed that 50 percent of the "articulate" journalists in the country saw segregation and discrimination as a moral evil that the federal government should eliminate immediately through legislation.[23] Surveying the change in attitude among northern politicians, Richard Polenberg has argued that "in the 1930s a man like George Norris could oppose an antilynching bill and still be counted a liberal in good standing," but by the war's end "support for civil rights had become an acid test of one's liberal credentials."[24] Yet northern liberals in Congress, though supportive of black equality in their rhetoric, were not yet willing to make civil rights a legislative priority. Only in response to mounting black pressure over the next twenty years would the issue move to the top of the domestic agenda. Nevertheless, Myrdal's book appeared precisely at a juncture at which many northern political leaders concluded that the South no longer could be allowed to handle its "Negro problem" as it saw fit.

Many white southerners were alarmed by the intensification of black protest activity during the war. To some, it seemed unpatriotic for a pressure group to take advantage of the national emergency (and attendant labor shortage) to press for improvements in the group's status. But more fundamentally, white southerners reacted viscerally against the break in the pattern of deferential behavior by blacks that they had known all their lives. Most white southerners saw racial tensions as a temporary wartime phenomenon; in fact, they were rooted in the vast economic and social changes that the war brought to the region.

Since the days of Henry Grady's New South movement in the 1880s, southern boosters had preached a gospel of industrialization as the means of delivering the region from its chronic poverty. Yet the South had remained predominantly rural, with per capita income half that of the rest of the country and industrial wage levels substantially lower. With the advent of World War II, southern congressmen used their seniority to ensure that the region got its "fair share" of defense contracts. Shipyards boomed from Virginia to Texas, aircraft plants moved into production, and oil refineries and chemical plants expanded operations. Wages rose significantly and the region became more economically interdependent with the rest of the nation. Rural southerners, white and black, crowded into southern cities in search of jobs in war industries, increasing the population of Charleston by 37 percent, Norfolk by 57 percent, and Mobile by 61 percent. Farm population declined by 20.4 percent from 1940 to 1945, and the mechanization of agriculture continued to increase.[25]

Uncle Sam also sent more Yankee soldiers to the South than at any time since the Civil War. Morton Sosna has estimated that "of the nearly 12.5 million men and women who entered the armed services during the war, at least half . . . saw service at a Southern air field, naval base, or army camp."[26] Their number included thousands of northern blacks who often had their first encounter with the Jim Crow system at segregated training camps in small southern towns. With such extraordinary movements of people within a rigidly segregated region, it is not surprising that rumors of black insurrections abounded, whites reported "uppity" behavior by their servants, and fights and other racial incidents broke out near training camps and defense plants. Throughout the South, it seemed to many observers that white racial attitudes were hardening, that whites were digging in and declaring that there would be no changes in the racial status quo. In Washington, southern senators and congressmen reacted to civil rights protests with intransigence, denounced the FEPC, and threatened to bolt the Democratic ticket in 1944.

The small band of southern liberals felt caught in the middle between the accelerating velocity of the black protest and the stiffening resistance of their fellow white southerners. "We seem to be almost back to the extreme abolitionists

and the extreme slaveholders in the lines of discussion," Jonathan Daniels wrote
Odum. "Between them, people like ourselves seem to be left in a sort of awareness and futility together."[27] Faced with the determination of the white South
to maintain the Jim Crow system, most southern liberals thought it imprudent
to criticize segregation openly. Instead they concentrated on improving black
schools within the separate-but-equal framework, encouraging industrial development and regional planning, and working quietly to diminish racial tensions.
Southern liberals also tended to regard blacks as junior partners in the struggle to
reform the South. In January 1943, Virginius Dabney, editor of the Richmond
Times-Dispatch, had delivered a stern lecture to blacks in an *Atlantic Monthly*
article entitled "Nearer and Nearer the Precipice." He blamed a "small group of
Negro agitators and another small group of white rabble-rousers" for creating a
situation that might easily lead to race riots. The militant tactics of Randolph and
the NAACP, the shrill rhetoric of the Negro press, and the black leaders' direct
assault on segregation all threatened to provoke a violent reaction in the South,
Dabney warned.[28] Odum, Mark Ethridge and other southern liberals agreed, but
recognized that they were becoming irrelevant in national discussions of civil
rights. The insistent criticism of segregation by black spokesmen shattered the
myth that regional economic development and improvement in the Jim Crow
educational system would be enough to ensure "harmonious race relations" and a
gradualist timetable of change.

In June 1943, the riot that Dabney had feared broke out, but it happened in
Detroit rather than in the South. Indeed it was very much the sort of tragedy that
Newton Baker had worried about back in 1935. A major center of defense
industries, Detroit had experienced a population increase of half a million from
1940 to 1943, including sixty thousand blacks. This influx of newcomers produced an extraordinary pressure on housing, especially in the ghetto where half of
the black population lived in substandard dwellings. The riot began on a hot
Sunday evening when one hundred thousand people, mostly black, jammed into
the Belle Isle municipal park. Groups of white and black teenagers clashed that
night, and a full-scale race riot developed over the next two days. White mobs
pulled blacks from streetcars and attacked blacks who entered their neighborhoods. Crowds of blacks smashed windows, looted stores, and beat up whites.
When it was all over, the rioting claimed the lives of twenty-five blacks and nine
whites, injured seven hundred people, and destroyed $2 million worth of prop-
erty.[29] The Detroit riot followed a four-day disturbance in Los Angeles, in which
white and Mexican-American youths had fought. And in August, another explosion of racial violence occurred in Harlem, leaving six blacks dead and three
hundred injured.

Many Americans feared that the riots in Detroit, Los Angeles, and New York
were harbingers of another wave of race riots that might erupt at the war's end, as
the "red summer" of 1919 had followed World War I. Concerned citizens demanded that President Roosevelt appoint a national committee on race relations

to investigate the causes of racial tensions and to recommend remedies. But FDR realized that such a presidential committee would itself become a center of controversy, since there was absolutely no prospect that black leaders and their northern white liberal allies would reach a compromise with white southern leaders about federal policy on civil rights. Instead of appointing a committee, Roosevelt asked Jonathan Daniels, then a special assistant at the White House, to collect information about race relations and to analyze what various government departments were doing to lessen conflict. Daniels understood that his job was to "keep the lid on" racial tensions that were simmering in many parts of the country, not to propose bold new advances in civil rights.[30]

An American Dilemma thus appeared at a time when white Americans, North and South, were beginning to recognize that black-white relations were a serious national problem. In one sense, the book served as the careful, national investigation of the race issue that Roosevelt was afraid to commission. When Myrdal had written the book from the spring of 1941 through the summer of 1942, it had been unclear how the race issue would develop during the war. By ignoring the cautionary suggestions of southern liberals and establishment figures and coming down on the side of civil rights leaders and their northern liberal allies, Myrdal had anticipated the direction in which American thought was moving. As many white Americans groped for an understanding of the condition of blacks, Myrdal's fourteen-hundred-page investigation provided an eye-opening survey of the devastating effects of segregation and discrimination on black people. Building on the work of American social scientists who had written for specialized, academic audiences, Myrdal presented race as an issue central to American culture and politics, a "problem in the heart of the American." Counterposing the American creed to Nazi ideology during World War II, he offered a symbolic framework that helped to legitimate the struggle for civil rights.

Myrdal's book played a major role in articulating and shaping a new racial liberalism for postwar America. While the rhetoric of Wallace and Willkie on civil rights had been of a vague and general character, *An American Dilemma* provided a detailed analysis of racial discrimination and an argument that intervention at a number of points by governments and private groups could break the vicious circle. Myrdal's appeal to morality and his advocacy of social engineering reinvigorated two older traditions in American thought that had fallen out of fashion among social scientists who studied race relations during the 1920s and 1930s. His confidence in American institutions led him to assert that the federal government could enforce compliance with civil rights laws in the South and ensure equality of opportunity in the private sector of the economy. Like many of the younger generation of American social scientists, Myrdal believed that blacks desired complete assimilation into the mainstream white culture and that distinctive patterns of Afro-American culture were a pathological vestige of slavery and segregation that would soon fade away. And Myrdal foresaw the global context in which Americans would confront the civil rights issue after the war. *An American*

Dilemma presented these ideas as the conclusions of a detached European observer with the implied endorsement of many leading American scholars and the imprimatur of a prominent foundation. To many readers, Myrdal's book appeared to throw the weight of European and American social science behind this new, moralistic, state-activist racial liberalism.

Acclaim in the National Press

Although Frederick Keppel had intended to initiate an extensive publicity campaign, *An American Dilemma* was published without great fanfare in January 1944. After Keppel died and Charles Dollard resigned to serve in the army, there was no one left at the Carnegie Corporation who had been closely involved with the Myrdal study. Ordway Tead, the book's editor at Harper & Brothers, doubted that such a long, scholarly treatise would sell and insisted that the Carnegie Corporation agree to cover any losses that Harper's might incur.[31] Tead's skepticism, together with the wartime paper shortage, resulted in a first printing of only twenty-five hundred copies, of which the Carnegie Corporation bought five hundred for distribution to notable people such as Eleanor Roosevelt and to newspaper columnists such as Walter Lippmann and Dorothy Thompson.[32] Harper's initially gave little promotion to *An American Dilemma*, but their advertisements did link the book to a popular theme: America's war against Hitler. One advertisement quoted a message of President Roosevelt to Congress concerning racial discrimination:

> We must guard against divisions among ourselves and among all other United Nations. We must be particularly vigilant against racial discrimination in any of its ugly forms. Hitler will try again to breed mistrust and suspicion between one individual and another, one group and another, one race and another, one government and another. He will try to use the same technique of falsehood and rumor mongering with which he divided France from Britain. He is trying to do this even now; but he will find a unity, a unity of will and purpose, against him, which will persevere until the destruction of all his black designs upon the freedom and people of the world.[33]

The publication of *An American Dilemma* did not create an immediate sensation. Reviewers for national magazines and major newspapers took their time in evaluating Myrdal's fourteen-hundred-page tome, and a trickle of favorable reviews appeared in the first two months after publication. On January 26, Lewis Gannett in the New York *Herald Tribune* likened *An American Dilemma* to "the classic works of De Tocqueville and Bryce" and declared that "the color problem in America has never before had so thorough a study."[34] Two weeks later, *Time* magazine picked up the Tocqueville-Bryce comparison and added that Myrdal's conclusions would "make U.S. citizens either nod or squirm."[35] In March the book drew favorable notices in two liberal magazines, the *New Republic* and *Survey Graphic*.[36] The *New York Times* did not run a review until April, but the review was an enthusiastic tribute by Frances Gaither, a southern novelist who marveled at the "overwhelming" scope of *An American Dilemma* and hailed it as "a book which nobody who tries to face the Negro problem with any honesty can afford to miss."[37] Also in April, the *Book of the Month Club News* termed Myrdal's book "the best single factual report on the American Negro. . . . It is a monumental book."[38] Several scholarly journals carried reviews of *An American Dilemma* in their spring issues, and Harper's ordered a second printing of twenty-three hundred copies for early May.[39]

Gunnar Myrdal's reputation grew steadily in 1944 and 1945 as reviewers for national magazines and major northern newspapers praised the book. These reviewers, who were mostly white northern intellectuals and journalists, generally accepted the moral dilemma thesis and urged white Americans to take up Myrdal's challenge to bring the nation's racial practices into conformity with the American creed. In his review for *Survey Graphic*, the Iowa-born journalist Harry Hansen argued that, like James Bryce in *The American Commonwealth*, Myrdal "offers us an opportunity to see ourselves in the mirror and to take heart from his conclusions." Just as Bryce had "found health in republican institutions" and had given Americans "reasons for confidence in democracy," Myrdal also had found grounds for believing that the United States would "live up to its dream" with respect to black Americans.[40] Albert Deutsch, writing in *P.M.*, welcomed *An American Dilemma* as a "veritable arsenal of indisputable scientific facts which blows to smithereens the hatemonger's cherished delusions of white supremacy." He found Myrdal's study "a devastating exposure of how the color line has thrown a deep shadow across the American creed."[41] The editors of the *New York News* cited Myrdal's study as evidence that "the Negro problem is one of the most acute facing this country," and they acknowledged that blacks faced severe discrimination in the North. Fearing that more race riots would occur, they declared that they knew of "no way in which this problem can be solved . . . without a complete change of attitude on the part of the white population."[42]

Robert S. Lynd, who had known Gunnar and Alva Myrdal since their first visit to the United States as Rockefeller Fellows, gave the book a major boost in the *Saturday Review*. The Columbia sociologist hailed *An American Dilemma* as "the most penetrating and important book on our contemporary American civilization that has been written" and greeted Myrdal's investigation as a triumphant vindication of the purposive social science he had championed in *Knowledge for What?* Applauding Myrdal's explicit statement of the value premises of the study, he exulted over the Swedish scholar's critique of American social science, which shunned "all value hypotheses and judgments lest its precious 'objectivity' become polluted by life." Like most liberals and radicals of the 1940s, Lynd accepted Myrdal's argument that Negro life was determined by white attitudes and behavior and that racial discrimination and segregation had fashioned a "prison for American genius." Despite his great admiration for the book, however, Lynd expressed polite skepticism about the foreign observer's optimistic view that the United States was ready for "large liberal advances through social legislation." Was it not possible, he asked, that Myrdal was "misreading the United States in terms of his more familiar Sweden" and underestimating the hostility of many Americans to an activist federal government? Lynd advocated a more chastened approach to reform, which recognized the power of conservative elites but worked "to build for the long term recovery of democracy." In conclusion, he quoted Myrdal's statement that in America, "political, social, and economic conditions gravitate toward equality." "I wonder," he mused.[43]

Reinhold Niebuhr, the nation's leading Protestant theologian, suggested that *An American Dilemma* should be a text for church-sponsored study groups and that every "thoughtful" American should own a copy. Niebuhr, who had moved from a socialist perspective to a liberal viewpoint, commended Myrdal for rejecting single-factor explanations of racial inequality and for portraying racial discrimination as a vicious circle. He agreed with Myrdal that the "vicious circle" could be "cut at a dozen different points and must be attacked from every angle, educational and political, economic and religious."[44]

In a long review essay in the *Contemporary Jewish Record*, Mordecai Grossman asserted that the "Negro problem" was perhaps America's most critical domestic issue. Although Grossman praised Myrdal's "monumental" book as an "indispensable" guide to the subject and summarized the Swedish scholar's findings at great length, he could not be as enthusiastic as Niebuhr about Myrdal's reliance upon "moral suasion, education and legislation as tactics for executing his strategy." The American creed, in his view, was not a coherent set of ideals that meant the same thing to all Americans. The ideal of liberty, for example, could mean to some people freedom to run their business without interference from government bureaucrats or labor unions. To others it might mean "states' rights" or "the 'right' to segregate, humiliate and discriminate" against black people. "Conscience," according to Grossman, "is only the consensus of the community's opinions operating through a particular individual. In the South one can feel righteous about one's devotion to 'white supremacy.'" Though he supported the use of moral suasion and education in the attempt to reduce prejudice, Grossman thought that the most effective approach was to reform the political and economic system to achieve "full utilization of our productive capacity" and "equitable distribution of the fruits of production." In a society of abundance and technological interdependence, it would be easier to wean people away from racial prejudices through a process of education. Grossman overlooked Myrdal's call for full employment and other policy proposals. His critique attracted little attention in 1944 but anticipated much of the subsequent criticism of the moral dilemma thesis.[45]

Henry Steele Commager, then an assistant professor of history at Columbia, endorsed Myrdal's interpretation of the American creed's powerful role in the nation's history. In a review for the *American Mercury*, Commager contended that the "principle of equality" had "worked like a ferment in the whole of American politics and society": "It hastened the attainment of manhood suffrage, and later of woman suffrage; it justified public education; it gave a powerful impulse to a liberal land policy." "If we continue to cherish it," Commager hoped, "we may expect that in time it will be applied even to the Negro question." But the young historian echoed Grossman's view that impoverished whites were unlikely to give up racial prejudices. Calling for a renewal of New Deal economic reform, he argued that "unless white men have jobs, Negroes will not have justice."[46]

Only one major national magazine assigned Myrdal's book to a black reviewer. The *New Republic* published a highly favorable evaluation by the novelist J. Saunders Redding, who accepted Myrdal's formulation of the race issue as a moral choice, a "problem in the heart of the American." Since the late nineteenth century, Redding noted, there had been a "stalemate" between the North and the South on the "moral issue" of Negro rights. "But with Gunnar Myrdal's book soberly plugging away at the issues and exposing the facts," he contended, "there can no longer be a stalemate." "In this time of momentous redefinition and change," Redding insisted that America faced a clear choice: "Either the American creed must prevail and the world sustain its hope in democracy, or the American deed must prevail and the faith in human goodness be destroyed."[47]

Redding's emphasis on the timeliness of *An American Dilemma* was underscored by an editorial on Negro rights in *Life* magazine in April 1944. *Life's* editors regarded racial conflict as "America's No. 1 social problem," a "great, uncured, self-inflicted wound" that was "aching violently, perhaps reaching a crisis." "Never before," they observed, "have Negroes been so outspokenly bitter about America's refusal to give them equal status in the Army, the Navy and industry, and never before have Negro leaders been so active on behalf of Negro rights." The editors viewed with alarm Adam Clayton Powell's campaign for a Harlem congressional seat on the slogan: "I will represent the Negro people first; I will represent after that all the other American people." Such militance, they explained, had aroused the white South "to a pitch of frenzied and unanimous resistance to change." Southerners were so riddled with fear on the race question that even a small step toward Negro rights, such as repeal of the poll tax, was perceived as a threat to the southern way of life. In this impasse, Americans were "lucky to have some very timely expert advice" from Gunnar Myrdal. Embracing Myrdal's thesis of a conflict between the American creed and racial practice, the editors maintained that "this makes us living liars—a psychotic case among the nations." The editors hoped that a way out of this dilemma might be found by focusing on the contrast that Myrdal drew between white Americans' "rank order of discrimination" and the goals of blacks. Thus whites might be most willing to give ground on the questions of equal economic opportunity, legal justice, and the vote—precisely the issues that were most important to blacks. On the other hand, the white South's greatest fear—racial intermarriage—was the issue of least importance to blacks, according to Myrdal's schema. The editors of *Life* concluded that the question of "social relations" between the races "does not call for a federal solution," but they warned white southerners that "the other three-quarters of the country cannot permit the South to disfranchise its Negroes forever."[48]

Life's willingness to censure the South on the voting rights issue is a striking illustration of the growing trend toward support for civil rights among northern white journalists and intellectuals. As the race issue gained a higher profile in the 1950s, *An American Dilemma* continued to provide ammunition for supporters of civil rights. Myrdal's flattering description of American ideals and his devastating and detailed exposure of the effects of segregation and discrimination on black Americans exerted a powerful influence on his northern white readers. Though social scientists debated Myrdal's methodology and conclusions in scholarly journals, the evaluation of *An American Dilemma* that went out to readers of leading national magazines and major newspapers was overwhelmingly positive, ensuring that the book would have a broad readership outside the academy. From the beginning of the enterprise, however, Myrdal had recognized that a favorable reception from black intellectuals would also be crucial to the book's success.

Afro-American and White Southern Reactions

At the time of the book's publication, most black reviewers were pleased with Myrdal's forthright assault on American racial inequality and his formulation of what had been called the "Negro problem" as really a white man's problem. Many black intellectuals were delighted that this "impartial" outsider was indicting white Americans for racial discrimination before the court of world opinion. Myrdal's focus on the conflict between the American creed and white supremacy fit well with the rhetorical strategy of most black leaders, who were then pointing to the hypocrisy of a nation that fought for freedom abroad and practiced segregation at home. In an era when moralistic rhetoric permeated the political culture, Myrdal's moral dilemma thesis seemed to offer a means of persuading white Americans to take a closer look at their racial prejudices and practices. While many high officials in the Roosevelt administration—including some erstwhile "friends of the Negro"—urged blacks to defer their protest until after the war, Myrdal recognized the moral legitimacy and urgency of the civil rights struggle. The Swedish scholar, moreover, provided massive documentation of the destructive effects of racial oppression on every area of Afro-American life, a message that most black intellectuals thought that whites needed to hear.

W. E. B. Du Bois, at seventy-six the dean of American Negro studies, acclaimed *An American Dilemma* as a "monumental and unrivaled study" and asserted that "never before in American history has a scholar so completely covered this field." In a review in *Phylon*, Du Bois showed no bitterness, even though the Carnegie-Myrdal study had eclipsed his Encyclopedia of the Negro project and soaked up scarce foundation dollars in a neglected field of research. He was pleased that

Myrdal had taken into account the role of "emotions, thoughts, opinions and ideals" and rejected the approach of many American positivists who produced fatalistic accounts of race relations in their attempt to model the social sciences on the natural sciences. Du Bois pointedly observed that Myrdal did not "appease the South" and quoted with obvious relish a passage in which Myrdal argued that "traditions of human exploitation" had "remained from slavery as a chief determinant of the South's economic life." Throughout his long career, Du Bois had written about the strength and resilience of Afro-American culture. Yet he chose not to comment on Myrdal's discussion of the social pathologies in black culture, preferring instead to emphasize the Swedish scholar's searing indictment of American racial inequality.[49]

Although he had been involved with the Carnegie-Myrdal study, E. Franklin Frazier wrote two highly favorable reviews of *An American Dilemma*. In the *American Journal of Sociology*, he embraced Myrdal's activist challenge to American social science and endorsed his critique of the "fatalism" and "laissez-faire bias" of much American scholarship on race relations. Like Du Bois, Frazier was delighted that a white scholar would attack the southern system of segregation and discrimination so bluntly. "Without the usual apologies and rationalizations," he observed, "the author makes clear the fact that in the South the supremacy and impersonality of the law do not exist so far as the Negro is concerned." Myrdal's refusal to blink at the issue of social equality and his insistence upon full equality for blacks in all spheres of life also set him apart from most American scholars, Frazier contended.[50]

Addressing the predominantly black readership of the NAACP journal *The Crisis*, Frazier concentrated more on Myrdal's analysis of the damage that white racial oppression had inflicted on Afro-American life and lauded Myrdal's objectivity and "freedom from the sentimentality and pathos" that led many white liberals to take a condescending attitude toward blacks:

> Dr. Myrdal recognized the Negro community for what it was—a pathological phenomenon in American life. . . . He recognized clearly that segregation kept the Negro in poverty and ignorance. Therefore, unlike many white Americans, he did not indulge in a lot of foolish talk about the peculiar "contributions" of the Negro and his deep "spirituality." . . . It is not surprising then that he did not indulge in over-rating the achievements of the Negroes and the ability and character of their leaders.[51]

Frazier concluded that "the present upsurge of the [Negro] masses" made it imperative that "every intelligent American" should read the book, especially "the intelligent Negro," who would "find a scientific Charter of his right to full participation in American democracy."

Horace Cayton and Richard Wright joined Frazier in commending Myrdal's exposition of the damage done to blacks by white racial discrimination. Both were radicals who, like Frazier, thought it more important to focus on the appalling effects of poverty and racial inequality on black people than to dwell on the virtues of the race. Both men assumed that a recognition, by the black and white publics, of the magnitude of the suffering of black Americans was a necessary step toward radical political change. Cayton considered the book "the most authoritative study we have on the problem" and quoted with approval Myrdal's statement, "The economic situation of the Negroes in America is pathological."[52] Richard Wright, who had broken with the Communist party during the war, recommended *An American Dilemma* in a newspaper column in the *New York Post*.[53] The following year, Wright praised Myrdal in his introduction to *Black Metropolis*, a social science study of blacks in Chicago written by Cayton and the anthropologist St. Clair Drake. Accepting Myrdal's argument that black culture was largely shaped by white racial discrimination, he declared that *Black Metropolis* "assumes that the Negro's present position in the United States results from the oppression of Negroes by white people, that the Negro's conduct, his personality, his culture, his entire life flow naturally and inevitably out of the conditions imposed upon him by white America. To that extent this book supplements and endorses the conclusions arrived at by Gunnar Myrdal in his *American Dilemma*, that monumental study of race relations in the United States."[54] Wright spoke privately about beginning "a project that would do for the inner personality, the subjective landscape of the Negro, what Gunnar Myrdal's *An American Dilemma* did for the external, social relations." Such an interpretation, he believed, would be "the single greatest moral weapon in our fight for social justice."[55] Wright's autobiography, *Black Boy*, which reached number one on the bestseller list in May 1945, was in many respects just that kind of exploration of the black psyche. His portrayal of relentless oppression in the South gave little attention to Afro-American political or cultural resistance. Thousands of white readers were shocked by *Black Boy*, and reviewers saw it as a companion piece to *An American Dilemma* in laying bare the full horror of what white America had done to blacks.[56]

Myrdal's forceful assault on American racial injustice received high marks from other black intellectuals. Charles H. Thompson, editor of the *Journal of Negro Education*, saw the book as a powerful statement of the kind of activist scholarship that his journal had promoted and a compelling critique of the "fatalistic" and "do nothing" bias of such writers as Sumner, Park, and Ogburn. The historian L. D. Reddick reviewed *An American Dilemma* in three periodicals: the Urban League's *Opportunity* magazine, the *Journal of Negro Education*, and *Science and Society*, a Marxist journal. To the predominantly black readership of *Opportunity*, Reddick recommended the book for its "outspoken frankness": "Myrdal calls things by their real names. Exploitation is exploitation, discrimination is discrimination, injustice is injustice. . . . This book is, in a word, the complete vindication of the case of the Negro for complete democracy."[57] Despite his admiration for Myrdal's work, Reddick briefly advanced three criticisms that later reviewers would develop in greater depth. He faulted the book's treatment of Negro history and culture;[58] he objected to Myrdal's use of the term *caste*, which he thought was inadequate to explain ethnic behavior in a dynamic, urban society; and he thought Myrdal unduly pessimistic about the possibility of black and white workers "uniting and struggling together toward common goals" through the CIO and other "broadly based movements."[59]

George Schuyler, the iconoclastic journalist whose satirical article Myrdal had admired back in 1929, lauded *An American Dilemma* in *Politics*, an independent magazine on the Left edited by Dwight Macdonald. Schuyler was deeply impressed by the scope of Myrdal's work, his list of prominent collaborators, and his objectivity. "Only a man from Mars," he proclaimed, "could have surveyed the idiocies of the so-called Negro problem with more impartiality." The Swedish diagnostician had discovered that "the American people are positively insane on the color question." Schuyler insisted that "there is no other word appropriate to describe the utter irrationality which dominates or terrorizes the vast majority of Americans." Racial prejudice was "like some fell malady eating malignantly into the bones, tissues, and cells of our social body, the while, with the optimism of tuberculars, we vociferously proclaim our virility and assert our confidence in our longevity." Schuyler contended that Myrdal, unlike most white American observers, recognized the deep anger among blacks and their determination to fight until they had "all the rights and privileges any other American enjoys."[60]

Carter G. Woodson did not actually review *An American Dilemma*, but he took a swipe at it in a review of Otto Klineberg's *Characteristics of the American Negro* in the *Journal of Negro History*. Myrdal had ignored this senior black historian during the research phase of the study and had criticized him in *An American Dilemma* for inflating the achievements of mediocre blacks in an effort to build race pride. In addition, Woodson was furious at the foundations for ignoring the work of his Association for the Study of Negro Life and History and supporting competing projects like Myrdal's. Woodson could have written a valuable critique of Myrdal's weak discussion of Afro-American history and culture, but he chose merely to issue a lofty dismissal of *An American Dilemma* as "the impressions of a foreigner of limited and infrequent contact with Negroes." Some months later, after Myrdal's study had drawn considerable attention in both scholarly and popular journals, Woodson had second thoughts. In a brief note in his journal, he still insisted that "the work contains practically nothing that a scholarly Negro living in the South does not know," but he admitted that the book was of some use in "focussing attention" of white people on the issue of racial injustice at a time when "we are talking so frequently about democracy and post-war reconstruction." The only strongly critical review by a black scholar published in 1944 or 1945 was Oliver Cox's Marxist critique, which will be considered in the section on the American Left. Ralph Ellison's famous review, which faulted Myrdal's analysis of Afro-American culture, was not published until 1964 and forms a crucial part of the discourse of the 1960s about Myrdal's ideas. The Swedish scholar's analysis of

Afro-American culture was not subjected to intensive criticism during the first round of reviewing.[61]

Myrdal's conclusions were disseminated to readers of black newspapers through a serialized synopsis of *An American Dilemma* by the historian Benjamin Quarles.[62] The Baltimore *Afro-American* called *An American Dilemma* the "finest scientific treatise on [the] race question" and predicted that it "will be quoted for the next quarter century."[63] Ben Burns, columnist for the *Chicago Defender*, expressed the amazement of many blacks that this bold indictment of American racial injustice could emanate from such an unlikely quarter. He surmised that the Carnegie Corporation had expected to find a foreign expert to produce a "dull, wheezy treatise" that would "gather dust" in a "far-off library corner." "But the Carnegie Board made one mistake in plotting its racial investigation," Burns averred. "It picked . . . Gunnar Myrdal to head the study." Myrdal had produced "some of the finest, enlightening prose ever written about the Negro." *An American Dilemma* would "stand for years as the best definitive, all-inclusive book on the Negro," and would serve as "a constant guide and reference point in the dire days to come." Burns concluded that "no thinking Negro should be without it."[64] Another black newspaper columnist, P. L. Prattis of the *Pittsburgh Courier*, offered even more extravagant praise for *An American Dilemma*. Declaring that the book "should be a Bible to every Negro," he advised his readers: "By all means, if you have the price of a fifth of good Scotch, forget about it and buy instead 'An American Dilemma,' written by Gunnar Myrdal, the distinguished and amazingly able Swedish sociologist, and published this week by Harper & Brothers. For the sake of all that's decent and worthwhile, buy the book, read it—and postpone the Scotch."[65]

Southern white reviewers were considerably less enthusiastic, though not as many "hit the ceiling" as Myrdal had anticipated. Liberal southerners faced their own dilemma as they pondered Myrdal's book. If they criticized it too severely, they might appear to be hostile to Negro rights, and their criticisms might even fan the flames of southern xenophobia and suspicion of outside agitators. On the other hand, nearly all believed that *An American Dilemma* rested on fundamental misconceptions about southern race relations. They considered Myrdal an optimist who assumed that by appealing to the morally "higher" valuation of the American creed, the nation could end segregation and discrimination. Most southern liberals doubted that the federal government could compel white southerners to accept desegregation of schools and public accommodations and feared that another Reconstruction would end in another bloody confrontation and ultimate failure. Though they favored equal voting rights, they considered it highly injudicious to raise the issue of social equality. Southern liberals also felt the situation slipping out of control. They believed that the continued growth of southern black education, the movement for interracial cooperation, and the New Deal programs that aided the southern economy were jeopardized by the aggressive demands of black leaders and the propensity of northern white liberals to indulge in moralistic chastising of the South. Myrdal, moreover, had unmasked some of the southern liberals' pretensions to leadership and had shown how impotent they really were.

Faced with these vexations, many southern intellectuals and journalists chose to ignore the book. Few southern newspapers published reviews of it. Virginius Dabney of the Richmond *Times-Dispatch* and Douglas Southall Freeman of the Richmond *News Leader* both gave *An American Dilemma* brief and lukewarm reviews.[66] John Temple Graves of the Birmingham *Age Herald* agreed with some of Myrdal's ideas but concluded that blacks could have "economic opportunity and equality before the law" only "if it were settled that the things having to do with segregation were not to be altered."[67] Gerald W. Johnson, a liberal journalist born in North Carolina, objected to the central argument of *An American Dilemma* in a review for the New York *Herald Tribune*. After serving up the usual encomiums to the foreign observer's brilliant achievement, he rejected Myrdal's moral dilemma thesis, lamenting that there was "precious little morality" involved in the South's view of the Negro. Johnson asked if Myrdal had not "flattered us so hugely with his American creed theory, as somewhat to obscure the true nature of the problem."[68]

Howard Odum, the South's most prominent social scientist, greeted *An American Dilemma* with polite skepticism in a review in *Social Forces*. With characteristic tact, Odum began by praising Myrdal's book as "the best thing that has been done on the Negro and is likely to be the best for a considerable time to come." As an advocate of regional planning, he welcomed Myrdal's critique of the laissez-faire bias of Sumner, Park, and Ogburn and his contribution to "purposive" social science. But Odum was clearly stung by Myrdal's portrayal of the "lack of courage" and ineffectuality of the southern liberals, and he reeled off a list of liberal accomplishments in the South since the turn of the century. He criticized Myrdal's weak grasp of southern history and his inadequate treatment of the bigoted mores of the poor whites. As a sobering reminder of the opposition that blacks faced, he quoted a "standard saying" among poor whites: "We ought to treat the Negro as we did the Indian, kill him if he doesn't behave" or "isolate him and give him what we want to." Ironically, Odum, who had written books on black folklore, was one of the few reviewers in 1944 to point to Myrdal's superficial understanding of the folk culture of southern blacks, but he did not develop his criticism in depth. In the end, Odum accepted the idea that the race issue was a moral question but assailed Myrdal for "moral isolationism"—singling out the race question as the one moral issue to be confronted in the South. For Odum, the "Negro problem" was inextricably intertwined with other economic and social problems in the region and could not be separated from this complex whole. Both morality and social engineering were appropriate components of social science, but in order for the social scientist to be effective, he had to plan for improvements in the South's economy, schools, public health, and welfare, and he needed a deeper understanding of the culture of both whites and blacks.[69]

Rupert B. Vance, Odum's colleague at Chapel Hill, reproached Myrdal for not presenting a specific political program for citizens who wanted to pressure the federal government to compel the South to grant civil rights to blacks. Writing in the *Virginia Quarterly Review*, he complained that, despite Myrdal's criticisms of the laissez-faire sociologists, the Swedish scholar did not offer a detailed analysis of how the United States was to get from its present imperfect situation to one of full compliance with the American creed. According to Vance, Myrdal had pointed to general trends in American politics, but in the end he was "an optimist without a program of meliorism." Vance argued that whites in the rest of the country were deeply prejudiced against blacks and had little interest in changing the status of blacks in the South. He asserted that Myrdal underestimated the strength of local government and states' rights within American federalism, and he predicted that after the war, the country would revert from "Planning to Normalcy," with an alliance of Republicans and southern Democrats in charge. Vance expressed puzzlement over what tactics "men of good will" should adopt on the issue of "racial adjustment" and wondered if Americans would know the answer even in a hundred years.[70]

Only one southern intellectual made a frontal assault on *An American Dilemma* in 1944. William Terry Couch, the director of the University of North Carolina Press, had established a reputation as a prominent southern liberal in the 1930s. At a time when university presses in all parts of the country shied away from controversial subjects, Couch had made the press a leading source of liberal thought in the region by publishing books on such topics as lynching, poverty, unions, mill villages, and public welfare. In 1942 he had asked Rayford W. Logan, a black historian at Howard University, to solicit essays from black leaders representing a broad spectrum of opinion on the topic, "What the Negro Wants." When Logan presented him with a manuscript the following year, Couch was stunned by the result. Fourteen black intellectuals—ranging from Frederick Patterson, the conservative president of Tuskegee Institute, to Doxey Wilkerson, then an official of the Communist party—agreed that the Negro wanted an end to segregation. Couch was deeply disturbed that the blacks seemed to demand an immediate dismantling of the Jim Crow system, a process that he thought would take fifty to a hundred years. After Logan refused to accept editorial changes and threatened a lawsuit, Couch decided to publish the book but added a publisher's introduction in which he expressed his own views on race relations.[71] Couch, strangely, did not criticize his black authors directly. He seems to have taken the condescending view that they were followers rather than originators of contemporary ideas of racial equality. Instead, he focused his critique on Myrdal's recently published book, which epitomized for him the errors of modern social science. The North Carolinian contended that Myrdal's concept of the American creed was based on a historically inaccurate understanding of the term *equality* as used by Jefferson and other Founding Fathers. Rejecting cultural relativism, he argued in favor of the cultural superiority of white civilization in America and predicted that it would be many years before blacks would reach the cultural level of whites. Though he declared himself in favor of removing many forms of racial discrimination, Couch insisted that the immediate integration of schools would be disastrous for both races. "No worse punishment for Negro children in the South could be imagined," he wrote, "than to send them to schools with white children."[72]

The letters of support that Couch received from fellow southerners suggest that *An American Dilemma* troubled white southern intellectuals much more than the handful of critical reviews would indicate. Gerald W. Johnson, who had blended praise with respectful criticism in his review of Myrdal's book, pronounced Couch's essay "the nimblest foot-work I have seen in a coon's age." Virginius Dabney and the Louisville editor Mark Ethridge privately commended Couch's blast at Myrdal, and the historian Fletcher Green considered the essay "one of the clearest and best statements of the problem I have ever read."[73]

Though Couch expressed views held by many white southerners, the really striking fact is that his essay did not ignite a public controversy in the South in 1944. Couch's friends may have lauded him privately, but they did not follow him into print to chastise Myrdal. Southern liberals, after all, had developed finely honed skills for muffling criticisms and containing controversies on racial issues within the bounds of genteel discourse. Myrdal's analysis of their political ineffectiveness had noted just that fact. With the South's leading intellectuals either silent or gently skeptical, southern editorial writers and politicians paid little attention to the Swedish critic. The only elected official to chastise Myrdal in the 1940s was Senator Theodore Bilbo, who had sparred with the visiting Swedish senator in his office in Washington in 1940. In his book *Take Your Choice: Separation or Mongrelization* (1947), the Mississippian fumed that Myrdal "treats the Southerner's fear of intermarriage as if it were emotional, silly, and unfounded." Citing Couch's critique, Bilbo insisted that the American ideas of democracy, freedom, and equality had been misinterpreted by the Swedish scoundrel, who wanted to turn the United States into a "land of mixbreeds [sic]."[74] But few southerners noticed Bilbo's fulminations. As Myrdal later observed, the book "passed by the whole reactionary South" at the time of publication, in part because "reactionaries didn't read long books."[75] Staunch segregationists would not launch a concerted attack on *An American Dilemma* until after its citation by Earl Warren in the Supreme Court's *Brown* decision ten years later. By then, the reputation of Myrdal's book as the definitive survey of the American race issue was well established.

The Reception in Scholarly Journals

Social scientists and historians writing in professional journals subjected *An American Dilemma* to more detailed methodological analysis than it received from reviewers for the major national magazines and the popular press. As we have seen, Robert Lynd gave the book a powerful endorsement in the *Saturday Review*, while Frazier praised it in the *American Journal of Sociology*, and Du Bois commended it in *Phylon*. On the other hand, Odum and Vance expressed serious doubts about Myrdal's central argument that most white Americans felt a moral dilemma on the race question, and they challenged his optimistic forecast that significant changes in race relations were imminent. Several of the reviews in scholarly journals had a "yes, but" quality: They acknowledged that *An American Dilemma* was an extraordinary achievement, but they raised questions about the moral dilemma argument or challenged Myrdal's methodology.

Frank Tannenbaum, a historian at Columbia University, brought to his reading of *An American Dilemma* a unique perspective as a student of both southern and Latin American race relations. In 1924 he had published *Darker Phases of the South*, a searching examination of southern racial and economic oppression that focused on the Ku Klux Klan, mill villages, prisons, sharecropping, and race relations.[76] In 1944 he was at work on a major comparative study of slavery and race relations in Latin America and the United States.[77] Tannenbaum began his review essay in the *Political Science Quarterly* with the assertion that *An American Dilemma* was "an important, perhaps a great, book" that deserved to be classed with the works of Tocqueville and Bryce. He accepted Myrdal's assimilationist assumptions, declaring that the Negro had become "culturally a European, a white man with a black face." On the basis of his research in Brazil, Venezuela, and Cuba, he predicted that eventually Afro-Americans in the United States would amalgamate with the white population and the distinction between "Negro and non-Negro" would become "a line difficult to draw."[78]

Tannenbaum endorsed Myrdal's claim that the New Deal had changed the whole configuration of race relations by creating a host of new federal programs from which blacks could not be excluded. But Tannenbaum went further and advanced an argument that liberals would often make in the 1950s and 1960s: that "industrialism" as well as the democratic political system was creating a society in which people were treated more uniformly in the marketplace, on the job, and in the distribution of public services. Racial prejudice, he asserted, was rooted in the isolated, impoverished rural areas of the South. Segregation was "not feasible, even if desired, in an industrial society, where the population is unstable, where population movement is fluid, and where skills are always changing in number and complexity." Overlooking the persistence of prejudice and discrimination in urban, industrial areas, Tannenbaum maintained that the industrialization of the South offered the most hope for improving the lives of the masses of poor blacks. If white southerners became more prosperous, he assumed, they would be less driven by fear and more willing to allow greater opportunities to blacks. Gradual economic change would thus be more effective than moralistic pleas for immediate racial justice. Appealing to the American creed would not work, Tannenbaum concluded: "The Southerner can be both a democrat and a practitioner of race discrimination in fact, even if he has a bad conscience over the matter." The only way to reduce prejudice was "by concentrating on other issues," particularly the expanding of economic opportunity through the industrialization of the South. And so, ironically, Tannenbaum, who had been one of the most vigorous northern critics of the South in the 1920s, ended up agreeing with the southern liberals. Seemingly unaware of the new mood of impatience among black Americans, he adhered to the purely economic approach to racial change that most northern liberals were then abandoning.[79]

While Tannenbaum found the moral dilemma thesis unpersuasive, another practitioner of comparative history rendered a different verdict. D. W. Brogan of Cambridge University, himself a "foreign observer" of American history and culture, pronounced An American Dilemma a "masterly" study and deemed Myrdal a worthy successor to Tocqueville. Writing in the Economic History Review, Brogan supported, on the basis of his own personal observations, Myrdal's claim that white Americans, particularly southerners, felt an emotional conflict between their professions of democratic values and their actual practice of racial discrimination. He maintained that if white Americans were as unambiguously prejudiced as white South Africans, they would not have had much difficulty in segregating and controlling the black minority. Brogan assented to Myrdal's view that it was precisely because racial discrimination was in conflict with American ideals that the United States had a "Negro problem." Though he recognized that the war had given the race issue a higher profile in America, he suggested that "international Communism" would continue to "exploit" the issue and prod Americans to live up to their creed. Like most reviewers, Brogan embraced Myrdal's assimilationist assumptions, and he included a patronizing reference to the Negro as "the problem child of the American culture" who was nonetheless "profoundly American" and eager to participate more fully in the culture.[80]

Harold Gosnell, who had written a book on black politicians in Chicago, applauded An American Dilemma in the American Political Science Review. Gosnell betrayed some irritation over the fact that he had not been invited to collaborate with Myrdal when he cited the high cost of the study and raised the question of "whether an all-American research staff could have done as well or better for the money." Yet he considered An American Dilemma "one of the best political commentaries on American life that has ever been written, because it places its discussion of politics in a well-rounded social science setting." As a political scientist, Gosnell focused not on Myrdal's psychological argument about the moral dilemma, but rather on his institutional argument that the American creed was firmly embedded in the Constitution and in the actual practices of American political life. He affirmed that Myrdal had succeeded in making "the Creed stand out as a living, dynamic influence." Gosnell also commended the Swedish visitor for pointing out that "many American social scientists, posing as scientists, have not really been as objective as they thought they were" and that laissez-faire assumptions were "as common among American sociologists as among American economists."[81]

Edward B. Reuter of the University of Iowa was just such a sociologist who had invested all his capital in the enterprise of "objective" and supposedly apolitical research on race relations. Trained at the University of Chicago, Reuter had written a study of the mulatto and a general survey of American race relations, both of which Myrdal criticized in *An American Dilemma*. Now at the end of his career, Reuter looked back on the previous twenty-five years as a heroic age in which the study of race relations had been wrested from biological determinists and shortsighted reformers and put on a firm scientific foundation. Like his mentor Robert Park, Reuter believed that sociologists were constructing a "natural history of group contacts" and developing a theory to explain the behavior of ethnic groups in contact with one another. "Until the natural history of race relations is worked out," he insisted, "efforts to mediate racial conflict cannot be expected to rise above the level of unenlightened good intentions."[82] Reuter saw *An American Dilemma* as a serious threat to the sociological undertaking to which he had devoted his life. In a review in *Phylon*, he objected to Myrdal's claim that social scientists who took a "naturalistic rather than a political point of view" were "defeatists" who furthered a "do-nothing" policy on the race question. Taking the offensive, Reuter charged that Myrdal, by explicitly stating his value premises and espousing social engineering, had "taken a theoretical position which, if consistently maintained, will determine the direction of the inquiry, determine the selection of topics, bias their presentation, and foretell the conclusions that the study will reach." He dismissed most of Myrdal's chapters as "encyclopedic and informational summaries" and contended that the book added little new information to the study of Afro-Americans. Myrdal had turned in such a "mediocre performance" under such "conspicuous circumstances" that Reuter fretted that the book might "adversely affect the prestige and influence of the social sciences." He concluded that Myrdal's moralizing and advocacy of social engineering had converted "what purports to be basic scientific research and analysis into practical and political investigations that end in vague historical prophecies rather than in tentative scientific generalizations."[83] It is striking how few Chicago-trained sociologists joined Reuter in attacking Myrdal. The many individuals of the Chicago school reacted as individuals and not as a coherent group. Frazier praised *An American Dilemma*, and Charles S. Johnson and Louis Wirth perceived no threat to the independence of social science in Myrdal's policy-oriented work. Everett Hughes, Herbert Blumer, E. L. Faris, and Edgar Thompson did not review the book.

Maurice Davie, a Yale sociologist in the tradition of William Graham Sumner,[84] rebuked Myrdal in the *Annals of the American Academy of Political and Social Science*. Some twenty years earlier during the debate on immigration restriction, Davie had affirmed that the nation's "best interests will be served by keeping the United States as far as possible a white man's country." Contending that nonwhite races were "unassimilable," he had recommended the total exclusion of immigrants from Africa and the West Indies "to stop the coming of blacks from those quarters."[85] In a 1936 book, *World Immigration*, Davie had abandoned overt racism, but he still advocated restricting immigration from the Western Hemisphere and wrote within the tradition of Sumnerian fatalism that Myrdal would deplore.[86] It is therefore not surprising that he found the moral dilemma thesis unpersuasive and argued that Myrdal was inclined to "overstress rationalism and moralism." Drawing on his long experience with the subject, Davie concluded that Myrdal "does not appear to realize how basic is the irrational in human motivation and behavior or how the ideal and the actual both exist in culture without creating undue conflict and troubled conscience."[87]

Kimball Young, a social psychologist at Queens College in New York, also expressed doubts about the moral dilemma argument. A Mormon who had grown up in Utah, Young was interested both in the role that ideals play in group behavior and in the issue of how minority groups function in America's heterogeneous society. Writing in the *American Sociological Review*, he suggested that Myrdal treated ideas and ideals as independent variables that were just as important in society as economic factors. In contrast, Young argued that "what really counts is the functioning combination of economic, political, and class technique or habits with ideas and values." The American creed, in other words, was not enough to induce change if it ran counter to deeply ingrained racial attitudes and economic and political forces. In examining Myrdal's advocacy of social engineering, he contended that the Swedish scholar had attempted to apply an approach formed in a small, homogeneous country to the more "complex" and "dynamic" society of the United States. Though he thought that American scholars should be challenged by Myrdal's combination of scholarship and advocacy, Young judged that "few among us can or may assume such multiple roles as he suggests."[88]

Two sociologists challenged Myrdal's critique of positivism. In an acerbic letter to the *American Sociological Review*, Gwynne Nettler of Reed College faulted the social engineer's imprecise usage of terms such as *valuation* and *science*. Nettler acknowledged that values enter into the selection of a problem for investigation but insisted that "it is possible to divorce consideration of what is from what should be." The archpositivist George Lundberg, professor of sociology at Bennington College, went after Myrdal in an article in the *American Journal of Sociology*. The son of Swedish immigrants, Lundberg had visited Myrdal in Stockholm in the 1930s and had read some of his early work in Swedish. Though he had started his career as a reformer, Lundberg, like so many other American sociologists of his generation, came to believe that a rigorous pursuit of objectivity on the model of the natural sciences was essential if sociologists were to reach an accurate understanding of social issues and overcome the public perception that they were "a tremendous conglomeration of uplifters, do-gooders, evangelists, and crackpots." He agreed with Myrdal that bias was present in any observer, whether in physics or sociology, but contended that a social or natural scientist could develop objective, scientific procedures for discovering the laws that regulate social or natural phenomena. Lundberg rejected Myrdal's argument that Park's naturalistic philosophy necessarily led to a do-nothing attitude, noting that physicians had to discover the causes of a disease before they could "do something" about it. The role of the scientist, in his view, was to "report the consequences and costs of alternate possible courses of action." If the sociologist wanted to do more in his role as citizen, that was permissible, but it was not a scientific action. Lundberg concluded his article by complaining that the public seemed more interested in following charismatic leaders than in listening to the scientific judgments of sociologists.[89]

The Divided Left

The most severe criticism of *An American Dilemma* in the 1940s came from scholars on the Left who thought that Myrdal had underestimated the economic causes of racial prejudice. During the Popular Front period of 1935–39, most intellectuals on the Left had not felt a need to choose between an economic approach to racial change and a conception of race as a moral or psychological issue. Indeed, socialist intellectuals simultaneously supported the interracial labor organizing of the CIO, appealed to Americans on moral grounds to end racial oppression, and sought to use American democratic traditions to build an anti-fascist ideology. One could hope for a socialist future and, at the same time, view racial prejudice as a psychological disorder which, if not treated, might lead to fascism. But Myrdal, a Social Democrat, threw down the gauntlet when he insisted that the economic factor was no more basic than other factors in causing racial inequality, and he challenged a fundamental assumption of Marxism when he argued that upper-class whites were "less unfriendly" than white workers to blacks.[90] Though Myrdal saw the growth of interracial CIO unions as an important advance, he argued that blacks should look for allies in all classes, and he focused on the struggle for equal opportunity within the capitalist system. As we have seen, Myrdal's strong indictment of American segregation and discrimination and his emphasis on the damage done to black Americans was enough to win him favorable reviews from a broad spectrum of liberal and radical scholars. In 1945 and 1946, however, several scholars on the Left challenged Myrdal's approach, and they did so in the context of the Communist party's declining influence among Afro-Americans.

Leo P. Crespi, an assistant professor of psychology at Princeton, took up this theme in an essay in the *Public Opinion Quarterly* entitled "Is Gunnar Myrdal on the Right Track?" Noting that Myrdal's "landmark" study seemed destined to become "the supreme authority upon the American Negro problem," Crespi expressed concern that Myrdal's conception of the issue as a moral problem might lead Americans in the wrong direction as they sought to combat racial prejudice. He feared that Myrdal's approach would suggest "treating the individual to eliminate Negro prejudice—with the remedies of ethical exhortation—whereas society is more properly the patient, and the remedies are social and economic planning which will remove the gain from prejudice." Crespi argued that if the economic condition of whites were improved, they would "cease to heap upon the back of the Negro scapegoats the burden of their economic frustrations." While Reuter, Davie, and Kimball Young had faulted Myrdal for overemphasizing social engineering, Crespi thought that he had proposed too little. But if Crespi overlooked Myrdal's chapters on the economic condition of blacks and his suggestions for economic planning, he nonetheless pointed to an important aspect of the reception of *An American Dilemma*: readers were focusing primarily on Myrdal's opening chapters on the race issue as a moral problem, and many of them were concluding that education, rather than economic reform, was the primary strategy for reducing prejudice and discrimination.[91]

The Marxist sociologist Oliver Cox indicted *An American Dilemma* as a "mystical" approach to the race issue in a review essay in the *Journal of Negro Education* in 1945. An Afro-American from Trinidad who studied ethnicity and class in comparative perspective, Cox objected to Myrdal's use of the term *caste* to characterize race relations in a dynamic, urban society. He maintained that *An American Dilemma* rested upon a fundamental misconception that racial prejudice was an idea or attitude that could be eradicated through education. Cox held that racial discrimination was the result of an economic system in which the ruling class was able to divide and rule workers by invoking the race issue. He reserved his greatest scorn for Myrdal's contention that upper-class whites were less hostile than white workers to blacks, and he argued that the "aristocracy" only used more "respectable weapons" of racial domination, tactics that were "infinitely more powerful and effective." Cox insisted that the only viable strategy for ending white supremacy lay in "teaching the white masses to understand and to recognize the ruling-class function of [racist] beliefs and their effect as instruments in the exploitation of the white as well as the black masses."[92]

In 1946 the historian Herbert Aptheker, a leading intellectual of the Communist party, lambasted Myrdal in a short book entitled *The Negro People in America: A Critique of Gunnar Myrdal's "An American Dilemma."* Aptheker's book featured an introduction by Doxey Wilkerson, Myrdal's former collaborator, who portrayed *An American Dilemma* as a "corporation-financed," "pseudo-scientific" attempt to come up with a "safe" line on the race question. "The rulers of our society," he charged, "have found it necessary to invent an elaborate network of myths, stereotypes, and ideologies designed to obscure the real driving power behind the oppression of the Negro people" by focusing on "some unexplained 'moral' defect in the personalities of individual white Americans." This "safe" view ignored the economic causes of race prejudice and offered as a "solution" only the "long, gradual, never-ending process of 'education.'" Wilkerson neglected to mention his own role in the Carnegie-Myrdal study, as he commended to his readers Aptheker's analysis of Myrdal's "ideological monstrosity."[93]

Aptheker pointed to a number of weaknesses in Myrdal's historical analyses, particularly the Swedish scholar's tendency to overestimate the influence of the

American creed on southern whites in the nineteenth century. As a confirmed materialist, Aptheker labeled Myrdal a philosophical idealist (a term Myrdal would have rejected) because of his conception of the race issue as a moral dilemma or "problem in the heart of the American." The young historian reiterated Cox's argument that Myrdal had obscured the economic causes of race prejudice and deflected progressive Americans from the struggle against capitalism, the true cause of segregation and discrimination.[94] Aptheker linked Myrdal to the former Communist Richard Wright and suggested that both underestimated the degree of resistance to racial oppression among the masses of black people. Disputing Myrdal's portrayal of the masses as politically passive, he suggested that evidence to the contrary could be found in Afro-American songs, poetry, and folktales and in the struggle of such black heroes as Nat Turner and Frederick Douglass. Aptheker was one of the few reviewers in the 1940s to criticize Myrdal for his exaggeration of the damage done to black Americans and his failure to detect greater resistance among the masses of poor blacks. But this criticism was delivered in a tract so full of polemical tirades that few scholars noticed it. Not content to criticize Myrdal's methodology and conclusions, Aptheker attributed malicious motives as well and concluded his critique by finding "Myrdal's philosophy to be superficial and erroneous, his historiography demonstrably false, his ethics vicious and, therefore, his analysis weak, mystical, and dangerous."[95]

Gunnar Myrdal, who was deeply engaged in Swedish politics at the time, did not answer any of his critics, nor did he follow the scholarly debates on American race relations. Arnold Rose decided to answer Crespi's criticisms in the *Public Opinion Quarterly*, which he considered a "respectable" journal, but he shrugged off Aptheker's hectoring as more of a nuisance than a threat and wrote Myrdal that "since only the Communists read Aptheker, it would not be wise to answer the Pamphlet."[96]

Horace Cayton, a socialist scholar who was not affiliated with any political organization, took umbrage at Aptheker's claim that Myrdal, Wright, Cayton, and St. Clair Drake formed a "liberal" school of thought on race relations that expressed "in somewhat elevated language, the same basic ideas as those of Allen Tate, Donald Davidson, David Cohn—and Bilbo and Rankin." In an angry retort in the *New Masses*, Cayton blasted the Communist party for its wartime policy of advising blacks to pursue their civil rights goals with "caution" and "patience" so as not to harm the war effort. He quoted Richard Wright's assertion that the Communists, as well as the "political Right," were trying "to change the Negro problem into something they can control." In response to Aptheker's critique, Cayton defended Myrdal's moral dilemma approach as a viable strategy for convincing white Americans to undertake structural reforms:

> The only justification for writing about the Negro question is to help individuals resolve their dilemmas in action. So writers (including Aptheker and Wright, Myrdal, Drake and Cayton) shame them, enrage them, encour-

age them, and appeal to patriotism, class solidarity, idealism, etc. They even try to terrify them by pointing out the certain doom that awaits the social order unless we act now to change it. We force individuals to choose between the actual discomfort of a guilty conscience and the feared discomfort of inconvenience, and often danger, of taking a firm stand for social justice. . . . The difference between an indoctrinated Nazi and an average American is that the latter has been taught to believe that "All Men are Created Equal" and he is consciously or unconsciously disturbed at the conflict between this doctrine and reality.

Cayton rejected the notion of a dichotomy between moral suasion and structural change and argued that appealing to morality at that moment in history was not incompatible with a larger strategy for economic and political transformation. "To say that economic and political forces are decisive in the long run" he observed, "is not at all inconsistent with saying that *individuals* face the Negro problem as a moral dilemma." Reaching for the ultimate put-down, Cayton declared that "only what Engels called 'vulgar' Marxists would deny that 'superstructure' influences day-by-day behavior, or that 'ideology' (i.e. the moral factor) is not extremely important."[97]

The strident tone of Aptheker's book reflected a sense of desperation about the decline of the Communist party's appeal to Afro-Americans and the waning influence of the Left generally. In the 1930s, the Communists had been far ahead of all other large, predominantly white political organizations in their militance on the race question, and for a time they had made civil rights one of their major issues. The Communist party's work on the Scottsboro case, unemployed councils, and labor organizing had appealed to many blacks, and the Communists had also given opportunities to black intellectuals at a time when white liberals ignored them. The Popular Front period of 1935–39 had marked the apex of Communist influence on Afro-Americans, as many black intellectuals had been active in Popular Front organizations, especially the National Negro Congress. There had been a sense of intellectual ferment on the Left, and many black scholars had hoped that a mass socialist movement would unite the poor of both races. But prominent socialists such as A. Philip Randolph and Ralph Bunche had resigned from the National Negro Congress by 1940 because of their opposition to Communist tactics. The Nazi-Soviet Pact of 1939 and the Communist policy of deemphasizing civil rights during World War II had further alienated many black intellectuals, including Richard Wright who left the party in 1942. No other socialist organization attracted a critical mass of black intellectuals during World War II, and the ensuing Cold War would lead to unprecedented repression of the Left.

When Gunnar Myrdal began his work in 1938, relatively few white intellectuals were seriously interested in race relations, and several of the brightest young scholars in the field were blacks who were influenced by Marxism. By 1946, many white liberals were acknowledging civil rights as an important issue, many white intellectuals and journalists were writing about blacks, and the Left was in considerable disarray. Aptheker feared that the Marxist perspective was simply being swamped by the outpouring of liberal rhetoric about racial discrimination; he considered Myrdal's moralistic appeals and elite-directed social engineering to be an ineffective strategy for opposing racism; and he recognized that *An American Dilemma* was the key book in shaping a new liberal consensus on the race issue.

The Emerging Orthodoxy and Neglected Alternatives

Since several social scientists and historians, on both the Right and the Left, raised serious objections to Myrdal's moral dilemma thesis and doubted the effectiveness of Myrdal's moralism and liberal social engineering in changing American race relations, why did *An American Dilemma* remain the leading work in the field for another twenty years? To answer this question, one must consider the status of Myrdal's critics, the absence of criticism from major figures in the field, the politics of the social sciences, and the changing politics of the race issue nationally.

To most observers in the 1940s, Myrdal's critics appeared to be only a few discordant voices amid a general chorus of approbation. Neither Couch, Reuter, Davie, Kimball Young, Cox, nor Aptheker were major intellectual figures, and none of them stimulated a significant scholarly controversy in the first two years after the publication of *An American Dilemma*. Howard Odum, a past president of the American Sociological Society, was the only senior figure in the social sciences to write a negative review, and he had conceded that Myrdal's study was "the best thing that has been done on the Negro and is likely to be the best for a considerable time to come." The most likely centers of opposition—the southern liberals, the black Left, and the Chicago school—failed to mount a concerted assault.

As we have seen, such distinguished scholars as Lynd, Du Bois, and Frazier praised the book. In addition, there were many prominent scholars and political reformers listed in Myrdal's preface as collaborators or consultants who did not review the book. Though they may have had private misgivings, their participation in the study was interpreted by many readers as a general endorsement of Myrdal's findings. In sociology, the list included Robert Park (who died in 1943), John Dollard, Charles S. Johnson, Guy B. Johnson, William F. Ogburn, Arthur Raper, Ira DeA. Reid, Edward Shils, Bernhard Stern, Samuel Stouffer, Dorothy Swaine Thomas, W. I. Thomas, Louis Wirth, Thomas J. Woofter, Jr., and Donald Young. Franz Boas, who had died in 1942, headed a list of anthropologists that included M. F. Ashley-Montagu, Ruth Benedict, Melville Herskovits, Ralph Linton, and Hortense Powdermaker. The psychologists Kenneth Clark, Allison Davis, Otto Klineberg, and Edward L. Thorndike contributed to the study, as did economists Abram L. Harris, Paul Norgren, and Sterling Spero. Myrdal's collaborators included the political scientist Ralph Bunche, the poet Sterling Brown, the historian Guion G. Johnson, and the philosopher and cultural critic Alain Locke. Edwin Embree of the Julius Rosenwald Fund and Jackson Davis of the General Education Board had offered advice. Finally, Myrdal had thanked New Deal administrators Will Alexander and Clark Foreman, Urban League leaders Eugene Kinckle Jones and L. Hollingswood Wood, and NAACP secretary Walter White. Taken together, the list was a veritable who's who in American social science and racial reform organizations.

Most of the social scientists who had collaborated with Myrdal did not review *An American Dilemma*. Many believed that professional ethics barred them from reviewing a book that emerged from a project in which they had participated. Some liberals were reluctant to focus on the methodological weaknesses of a major study that condemned racial inequality so forcefully and broadcast that message to a wide audience. Others looked upon the Carnegie-Myrdal project as if it were part of the war effort—a large, collaborative enterprise to produce a report for the general public on a sensitive issue bound up with the morale of American troops, the productivity of the war industries, and the ideology of the war against fascism. Several of the younger scholars who had worked with Myrdal were in military or government service in 1944 and 1945 and were unavailable for reviewing. Finally, tact vis-à-vis the foundations doubtless played a role. The Carnegie Corporation had invested its prestige and considerable resources in the project, and neither the GEB nor the Rockefeller Foundation had supported any large investigations of American race relations pending the outcome of Myrdal's investigation. Scholars believed that the Myrdal study would influence the future direction of foundation support for social science research on race relations.

To many American social scientists, Myrdal's advocacy of social engineering seemed less radical in 1944 than it would have ten years earlier. To be sure, many American scholars were not prepared to accept Myrdal's assault on their claims concerning the objectivity of their work, nor were they ready to embrace Myrdal's notion that social engineering was "the supreme task of social science."[98] Yet few were willing to join Reuter in an all-out battle against the Swedish heretic. W. F. Ogburn, that archon of the sociological establishment whom Keppel had enlisted to evaluate the collaborators' manuscripts, privately grumbled that Myrdal had associated too much with radicals but declined to criticize the book publicly.[99] Donald Young, who was then advising the War Department on racial matters, thought that Myrdal had not "made any contribution to the understanding of race relations . . . in a scholarly sense" but did not offer any evaluation in print.[100] Nor did Samuel Stouffer, another prominent empirical sociologist, who had super-vised the Carnegie Negro study during Myrdal's absence in Sweden and was then heading the government-sponsored research to be published as *The American Soldier*. None of these leading positivists had the appetite for a full-scale *metho-denstreit* in the middle of World War II. The war had uprooted these and many other social scientists from their usual posts, thrust them into a closer relationship with the federal government than ever before, and involved them in various forms of social engineering. As the war drew to a close, social scientists realized that the links forged between Washington and the academy would remain strong in the years ahead.

Both liberal and conservative collaborators pulled their punches because of loyalty to Myrdal or the Carnegie Corporation or because they did not want to express in print during wartime their reservations about America's capacity to live up to its ideals on the race issue. Herskovits did not review the book, although Myrdal's conclusions regarding Afro-American culture were diametrically opposed to his own. He wrote Crespi that "on the whole" he agreed with Crespi's critique of the moral dilemma thesis, but added: "the Negro problem as it exists today is so complicated that we cannot understand it unless all possible factors that have made it what it is are taken into full account."[101] Edward L. Thorndike, the Columbia psychologist who had been a close friend and advisor to Keppel, did not publicly criticize Myrdal's summary of the environmentalist position on inherited genetic differences between the races, but he continued to believe that genetic factors contributed to the differences between the races in intelligence test scores. "Of course I do not agree with your estimate of the negro genes," he wrote Myrdal, "but it may be that it is better to plan for negro welfare on the hypothesis that genetic differences are negligible. Someone else can work out what modifications of your plans are desirable on any defined hypothesis as to the genetic differences."[102] Howard Odum confided to a foundation official that he had mitigated his criticisms in his review.[103] Jackson Davis, the GEB staff member who had been Myrdal's first tour guide in the South, wrote a privately circulated, unpublished critique that faulted Myrdal for excessive optimism with regard to racial change.[104]

Myrdal's collaborators, who had interrupted their own research or teaching in 1939–40 to frantically patch together memoranda for the "Swedish Simon Legree," naturally hoped that their labors would lead to foundation grants for their own work. Most were destined to be disappointed. One of the effects of the Myrdal project was to dry up foundation money for major studies of race relations and of Afro-American communities and culture for the next twenty years. Myrdal never intended this and, in fact, made many suggestions throughout the book for further studies.[105] Nor was it the intent of Keppel, who died in 1943 while the book was in press. But in January 1944, as *An American Dilemma* appeared in print, Donald Young—ever active behind the scenes—circulated a memo to the foundations in which he argued against support for major new research on race relations. Young's memo was prompted by a desire to help foundations develop a strategy for allocating their resources to combat an anticipated increase in racial conflict after the war. He noted great concern about this issue on the part of federal, state, and local governments, industry, religious groups, and social agencies, but he reported a lack of consensus on strategies for bringing racial practices into line with the American creed. Young pointed to an array of tactics advocated by reformers: moral exhortation, education, new civil rights laws, and direct action by pressure groups. He expressed concern that so many reformers "want all or nothing at all right now" and lamented that people like himself, "who believe that the process of adjustment requires the careful and perhaps slow utilization of all possible opportunities and devices which present themselves," are "called opportunists, gradualists, tories, fascists, and worse for their pains." Young suggested that the key questions for the postwar period were why prejudice and discriminatory behavior exist and what kinds of programs might be devised to reduce or eliminate such behavior. He doubted that the social scientists specializing in race relations, particularly the "warhorses" who had been working in the field for some time, had anything new to say. Rather than support new theoretical research in the field, Young recommended that the foundations encourage work that focused on the actual "point of contact between groups, such as at the factory, in the store, at school, in the city street, or on the bus." The people best qualified to do this research, he added, were not the race relations specialists but the economists, educators, and others who knew most about these specific points of contact. He suggested that the black press, which had been a thorn in the side of the Roosevelt administration, might be improved if four or five black journalists a year were sent to Harvard as Nieman Fellows. Young thus discouraged new theoretical research on race relations, sidestepped the question of how segregation might be ended, and proposed a program of reducing "inter-group tensions" within existing institutions. His memo represented a more cautious alternative to Myrdal's moralistic immediatism, globalist liberalism, and advocacy of ambitious social engineering.[106]

Young seems to have had his finger on the pulse of the foundations, and he accurately assessed the direction in which social science research was moving as well. The Carnegie Corporation chose not to support new research on race relations during the postwar era, though it received many applications from scholars in the field. Walter Jessup, who succeeded Keppel as president, had always been skeptical of Myrdal's racial liberalism, remarking privately that "human nature is always discriminatory" and "you don't want, for instance, to have your chauffeur to dine with you." In the annual report of 1944, Jessup stated that the corporation had no special programs for blacks. In a memorandum surveying Carnegie aid to blacks in the aftermath of the Myrdal study, Robert M. Lester recommended that the foundation concentrate on a few large grants to black universities rather than disperse "funds in small grants to many agencies of varying purpose and degrees of effectiveness." Though one of the purposes of the Myrdal study had been to guide the foundation in making grants to groups concerned with race relations in the North, Lester's memo ironically reaffirmed the Carnegie Corporation's traditional policy of aiding a few black universities in the South. Subsequent presidents did not, however, follow Keppel's practice of doling out small amounts of money to "exceptional men" in the field such as Du Bois, Herskovits, Locke, and E. E. Just. When Guy B. Johnson, Arthur Raper, and other former collaborators of Myrdal applied to the Carnegie Corporation for research funds, they were turned down, though Louis Wirth did manage to win some support for the program in Education, Training, and Research in Race Relations at the University of Chicago.[107] In 1967 a Carnegie Task Force on the Disadvantaged reported that the foundation had neglected the disadvantaged until 1963, when "suddenly . . . the Corporation awoke to the impact that the desegregation decision and the civil rights movement were having on negro education." In an interview in 1967 a Carnegie official acknowledged that the foundation had overlooked research on blacks for two decades following the Myrdal study.[108]

Both the Carnegie Corporation and the GEB turned down applications from social scientists working on race relations while the Myrdal study was in progress. In 1941, Du Bois had abandoned his Encyclopedia of the Negro project, citing the Carnegie commitment to the Myrdal study as one of the reasons that the encyclopedia had not secured funding. When the GEB declined to act favorably on an application by Franklin Frazier in 1943, Jackson Davis wrote Frazier that the GEB was awaiting the publication of Myrdal's book to get an idea of which fields needed further investigation. But even after *An American Dilemma* was out, the GEB concentrated on aiding southern education and generally avoided support-ing research on controversial issues.[109]

No other foundation took the lead in sponsoring research on Afro-Americans during the 1950s. The Julius Rosenwald Fund, which had played an innovative role in the interracial field, ceased operations in 1948. Foundations generally proceeded with caution during the McCarthy period because of congressional investigations into foundation support of "subversives." Alternative sources of funding steered research away from theoretical explorations of black culture and communities toward new concerns. Religious groups sponsored studies of preju-dice and intercultural education. As the desegregation process got under way, agencies of local, state, and federal government requested policy-oriented re-search. St. Clair Drake observed:

> After the war, arguments about how to conceptualize race relations didn't really interest anybody anymore. People were interested in evaluation stud-ies: Are blacks actually getting more jobs in industry? Is discrimination really going out in the Armed Forces? You had this kind of research. And that's where the money was. Nobody was going to give anybody any money to do a *Deep South*. I call Myrdal the study to end all studies. Once Carnegie put a quarter of a million into that, I think the feeling was that that ends an epoch.[110]

An American Dilemma occupied a curious place in American social science during the postwar era. It was the leading work in a field in which little new theoretical research was being done. Myrdal did not participate actively in schol-arly discussions of American race relations, nor did he institutionalize a research tradition at an American university nor train a group of graduate students committed to liberal social engineering. No strong institutional center of social science research on race and ethnicity developed after the war. During the 1920s and early 1930s, Robert Park had made the study of race and ethnicity a major focus of the nation's leading sociology department. But Park's successors turned to other issues, and by the end of World War II, the Chicago school was no longer a cohesive group that set the terms of the debate among sociologists of race and ethnicity. Leadership in sociology shifted from Chicago to Harvard and Columbia, departments with no tradition of research in the field of race and ethnicity.[111]

Guy B. Johnson would continue Odum's tradition of working for regional economic development, improving black education, and combating racial violence as a professor of sociology at the University of North Carolina at Chapel Hill and as president of the Southern Regional Council, the organization that succeeded the Commission on Interracial Cooperation. A southern racial moderate and something of a gradualist, Johnson never embraced the moralistic immediatism of Myrdal, yet he would be vilified by extreme segregationists after *Brown* for his role as deputy director of the Myrdal study. After Odum's death in 1955, the Chapel Hill sociology department and the Institute for Research in Social Science turned away from regionalism toward new concerns. Though research on southern issues would continue, the rise of behavioralism and the addition of new faculty with a broad range of national and international interests led to greater intellectual diversity, a deemphasis on social problems research, and a declining attention to the race question.[112]

From his post at Northwestern University, Herskovits continued to encourage the development of Afro-American studies as an interdisciplinary enterprise with a comparative perspective. He supervised several doctoral dissertations on black peoples in the Caribbean and Latin America and started a short-lived journal, *Afro-America*. In 1939, when it had become apparent that he would have little influence over the Myrdal study, Herskovits had made another attempt to gain control over the development of the field. As the historian Robert L. Harris has noted, Herskovits was the chairman and the driving force behind the American Council of Learned Societies' (ACLS) Committee on Negro Studies, which he launched with a conference at Howard University in 1940. The Northwestern anthropologist packed the committee with scholars "whose studies are from a long term point of view rather than pointed toward immediate solution of the race problem" and pressed the group to survey research in the field, "so that we would have the field entirely canvassed and be prepared to make recommendations in light of any report that would be turned in by Myrdal."[113] The irrepressible Herskovits sought to expand the scope of this empire by creating a joint committee on African and Negro studies that would be an official clearinghouse for the SSRC and the National Research Council as well as the ACLS. Such a committee, as Harris observes, "would have given Herskovits as chairman a virtual barony over all research projects in the United States on the Negro." When the SSRC refused to go along with this plan, the ACLS committee limited its objectives to the study of the history of blacks in the Americas and their African antecedents and the analysis of New World Negro art, literature, and language.[114]

Herskovits's views on the significance of African influences on the culture of blacks in the United States were fundamentally at odds with the reigning liberal orthodoxy that Myrdal had done so much to shape, and the ACLS committee never enjoyed much support from the foundations. Despite his determined efforts, Herskovits was unable to attract the funding necessary to develop Afro-American studies as an interdisciplinary field nationally or as a program at Northwestern. When some of the black members of the ACLS committee sought to organize a conference that would highlight discrimination against blacks by professional organizations, journals, and research institutions, Herskovits demurred. By 1950, the committee gave way before the assimilationist assumptions of the age. "Ideally," the committee concluded, "Negro history is 'history,' Negro music is 'music,' and Negro art is 'art.'" The committee recommended that it be disbanded and that its functions be taken over by other ACLS standing committees.[115]

Herskovits's original interest had been in African studies, and he had made numerous unsuccessful appeals to the foundations before the war to fund research in that field. During World War II he had advised the State Department on African affairs, and after the war the foundations finally recognized the strategic importance of Africa. With a grant from the Carnegie Corporation, Herskovits launched the nation's first African studies program at Northwestern in 1947. From that point until his death in 1963, Herskovits devoted most of his attention to African, rather than Afro-American, studies.[116]

Carter G. Woodson, the "father of Negro history," who had been frozen out of the Myrdal study, died in 1950. His Association for the Study of Negro Life and History continued to publish the *Journal of Negro History*, to hold an annual scholarly meeting, and to sponsor observances of Negro History Week in public schools. In an era when most white historians still ignored Afro-American history, the association played a crucial role in encouraging new research in the field and disseminating information about black history to the black community. But black historians still lacked an institutional base for training Ph.D.'s. A small number of black graduate students continued to attend predominantly white universities in the North, where Afro-American history was a marginal concern.[117]

Black universities had always experienced great difficulties in attracting funds to develop social science research, but in the 1950s they faced not only traditional racism but also an assumption by many liberals that integration would lead to assimilation and the eventual disappearance of black institutions. Charles S. Johnson remained the most successful black social scientist in terms of fund raising and institution building. He brought distinguished visiting faculty to Fisk, trained a cadre of young sociologists in his M.A. program, and even founded a separate department of race relations in 1942. During the 1940s, in addition to writing *Patterns of Negro Segregation* for the Carnegie-Myrdal project, Johnson wrote a book on the personality development of black youth and compiled a statistical atlas of southern counties.[118] As racial tensions mounted during the war, Johnson turned his attention to applied social research designed to prevent race riots and to prepare communities for improvements in the status of blacks and eventual desegregation. With support from the Julius Rosenwald Fund and the American Missionary Association, Johnson and his staff conducted studies of communities that were experiencing racial conflict. The results were published in *To Stem This Tide* (1943), which surveyed racial discrimination and antiblack violence and recommended public and private cooperation to provide jobs for blacks after the war, economic planning, and educational campaigns against prejudice.[119] A companion volume, *Into the Mainstream* (1947), surveyed the "best practices" in interracial relations in the South in such fields as housing, employment, education, health, and religion.[120] In addition, Johnson published *The Monthly Summary*, a digest of news about race relations, and developed the Fisk Community Self-Survey in Race Relations, a self-study program that cities such as Minneapolis and San Francisco adopted to analyze their race relations.[121] Johnson's work after the war was fundamentally in accord with Myrdal's ideas and focused on educational campaigns and practical remedies within existing institutions. In view of the obstacles facing black scholars in southern black universities, Johnson and his team produced an extraordinary range of social investigations. Yet Fisk did not command the resources to establish a doctoral program in sociology, and after Johnson's death in 1956, his successors lacked the national reputation and skills at grantsmanship to sustain the momentum of Johnson's research program.[122]

E. Franklin Frazier was the most brilliant sociologist of the black experience writing in the period from World War II to his death in 1962. He followed his famous book on the black family with a comparative analysis of race and culture, a controversial analysis of the black bourgeoisie, a study of the black church, and many essays.[123] In 1949, when Frazier published *The Negro in the United States*, a broad-ranging analysis of Afro-Americans, he wrapped himself in the mantle of Myrdal in the preface, stressing his role in the Myrdal study. So great was the prestige of *An American Dilemma* in the postwar era that Frazier felt it necessary to explain why he had written another long book on black Americans so soon after Myrdal's "monumental study." The focus of his book, Frazier explained, was not social policy but "the processes by which the Negro has acquired American culture and has emerged as a racial minority or ethnic group, and the extent to which he is being integrated into American society."[124] Frazier, who had strongly influenced Myrdal's conception of Afro-American culture, emerged as a major exponent of integration and assimilation in the postwar period and continued to emphasize the damage done to blacks as a part of his critique of American racism. Frazier was a man of feisty temperament who lacked Johnson's capacity for interracial diplomacy, grantsmanship, and institution building. He was not especially noted as a teacher, and, as a committed champion of integration and an acerbic critic of the "mediocrity" of black institutions, he declined to support a doctoral program in sociology at Howard because it would have been a segregated program. Though he was elected president of the American Sociological Association, the highest honor of his profession, Frazier was never offered tenure at a major, predominantly white university. He was unable to institutionalize a research program at Howard, and he failed to train a cohort of young sociologists of race and ethnicity.[125]

Though Frazier had been a socialist in the 1930s and remained sympathetic to the Left in the 1940s and 1950s, his public position was that of scholarly critic of American racism, rather than that of advocate of particular radical or reform programs. Such a shift was also apparent among other members of the circle of young black leftists at Howard whom Myrdal had met at the end of the 1930s. The economist Abram Harris, who had once been a socialist, accepted a position at the University of Chicago, where he worked within the tradition of institutional economics. Ralph Bunche, who had stimulated Myrdal by offering a socialist critique of the NAACP and other liberal reform organizations, worked for the State Department during World War II and rose to become a high-ranking diplomat with the United Nations and a Nobel laureate after the war.

While many black intellectuals were abandoning Marxism, W. E. B. Du Bois continued to offer vigorous criticisms of United States foreign policy as well as a Marxist interpretation of domestic racism. When Du Bois returned to Atlanta University in 1934 after resigning from the NAACP, he sought to revive the old Atlanta University conferences that he had begun at the turn of the century and to build a cooperative movement among southern black colleges and universities to support social science research on Afro-Americans. With a small grant from Keppel, he held a conference of black leaders in 1941 to plan these investigations. The following year, the presidents of the southern Negro land-grant colleges endorsed Du Bois's proposal for a cooperative program of social science research. This movement was abruptly terminated in 1944, when the president of Atlanta University, troubled by Du Bois's radicalism, forced him to retire.[126] Returning to New York at age seventy-six, Du Bois immersed himself in political activity on many fronts. Hounded by the Justice Department during the McCarthy period, he joined the Communist party and in 1961 moved to Ghana, where he died two years later.

Looking back on the collapse of the cooperative research program in his *Autobiography*, Du Bois wrote, "Up to this time the Negro himself had led in the study and interpretation of the condition of his race in the United States. Beginning with 1944, with accelerated speed the study of the Negro passed into the hands of whites and increasingly southern whites."[127] This statement contains some exaggeration, especially regarding the significance of southern whites in postwar research on Afro-Americans. Yet it is true that in the 1930s when Du Bois had planned his encyclopedia, the study of the Negro was a relatively small field in which black investigators played prominent roles and several of the leading scholars were black Marxists. Myrdal had taken this rather isolated area of social scientific and historical research and related it to central issues of American politics and culture. In doing so, he brought the issue of racial discrimination to the attention of many whites who had ignored the work of Du Bois and other black investigators and helped to shape a new racial liberalism among whites that would be increasingly important as the civil rights movement got under way. Myrdal had pointed to the study of prejudice and to educational campaigns against prejudice as key areas for future work, and much of the activity in these fields would be carried out by young white scholars. By defining the "Negro problem" as a white problem, Myrdal had put the focus of his study squarely on white prejudice and discrimination, but his assimilationist vision contained a blind spot on the subject of Afro-American communities and culture. Like Frazier, he assumed that Afro-American communities were notable as repositories for social pathologies, and he thought that Afro-American culture was a damaged variant of white American culture. Since Myrdal assumed that the ghettos would be broken up and that blacks would increasingly move into the mainstream of American culture, he held that the study of Afro-American communities and culture was less important than the study of white prejudice and discrimination. Most American intellectuals, social scientists, religious leaders, and foundation officers would share these views in the postwar era. The widespread acceptance of a liberal orthodoxy in favor of integration and assimilation by white social scientists was an important step in the assault on legalized Jim Crow, but it carried with it certain costs. Research on Afro-American communities and culture enjoyed little prestige, and black universities received scant funds for investigations of these subjects.

Although Charles Hamilton Houston had made the Howard Law School an important training ground for civil rights lawyers as early as the 1930s, no black university emerged as a center of social scientific research between World War II and the 1960s. Despite the unparalleled prosperity of the era and the generally high prestige of the social sciences, no black university commanded the resources to establish a doctoral program in any of the social science disciplines. This development resulted from institutionalized patterns of discrimination in foundations and in agencies of local, state, and federal government; inadequate endowments, libraries, and faculty salaries; and the insensitivity and hostility of accrediting associations in the South. Of the many black scholars who collaborated with Myrdal, only two would train a significant number of doctoral students: Allison Davis in education at the University of Chicago and Kenneth Clark in psychology at the City College of New York. This dearth of black Ph.D's would be keenly felt in the 1960s when an explosion of interest in black life would lead to a demand for Afro-American studies programs.

Few white scholars in the late 1940s and 1950s would notice that the black universities were not sharing in the era's prosperity and rapid expansion of the academic enterprise. It was a time of optimism and confidence in American institutions, and Gunnar Myrdal had appealed to the hopeful spirit of that era when he predicted that the American creed would enable Americans to overcome their "greatest scandal." As the "American Century" commenced, the Swedish prophet contended that, with an ambitious program of social engineering and education, Americans could demolish the Jim Crow system, reduce white prejudice, and integrate black people into the mainstream of American life. This new immediatist liberal orthodoxy stood in sharp contrast to the pessimism and gradualism of many social scientists and reformers of the 1930s. As black protest attained a new militance and visibility, *An American Dilemma* would provide a handy guidebook for elite whites. It would take another twenty years of agitation by blacks to force Congress to pass a strong civil rights bill, but the idea of civil rights had more legitimacy by the end of World War II than ever before. The limits of Myrdal's liberal orthodoxy would not become apparent to most American intellectuals for another generation.

7

The Rise and Fall of
a Liberal Orthodoxy

For twenty years after its publication, *An American Dilemma* remained the leading work of social science concerning Afro-Americans. Myrdal's strategy of moral exhortation and social engineering won converts among scholars in many fields, and his program of civil rights, integration, assimilation, and equal economic opportunity became a liberal orthodoxy among American intellectuals. The Swedish visitor had placed the American race issue in a global context, predicted a reinterpretation of the Fourteenth Amendment by the Supreme Court, forecast an upsurge in black militancy, and anticipated the breakdown of the Jim Crow system in the South. Above all, he had portrayed the race issue as a conflict in the minds of individual whites and appealed to the American conscience to end racial inequality. These ideas were bold and outside the mainstream when Myrdal drafted *An American Dilemma* in 1941 and 1942, but in the ensuing twenty years they would move to the center of American political discourse as Supreme Court justices and presidents embraced this liberal orthodoxy in their rhetoric, if not in their actions.

An American Dilemma stimulated much new research on prejudice and encouraged educational campaigns designed to change white attitudes. It also led to a renewed interest in the damage that racism inflicted on the personality of Afro-Americans. But the conservative political climate of the late 1940s and 1950s discouraged the ambitious programs of social engineering that Myrdal had advocated, and few economists pursued Myrdal's suggestions for further institutional studies of discrimination by corporations and unions. Myrdal remained a creative and iconoclastic scholar in the 1950s and 1960s, generating new ideas about Third World poverty and Western welfare states, but he chose not to apply his critical intellect and extraordinary energy to the American race issue during those years. Living outside the United States during that period, he declined to participate in debates about American race relations, leaving to others the task of interpreting and building on *An American Dilemma*. The book thus became a monument standing on the American landscape, to which liberal activists pointed with assurance as proof of the scientific validity of their beliefs. But Myrdal was not reformulating or extending his ideas in response to the accelerating black struggle. Social scientists gradually chipped away at the moral dilemma thesis even as the stature of the book grew among the public as a whole. The ideas of *An*

American Dilemma thus underwent a process of ossification and by the mid-1960s would seem irrelevant to many intellectuals.

The Growing Legitimacy of Civil Rights

As the United States demobilized after World War II, Afro-American leaders were encouraged by the upsurge of white liberal rhetoric on civil rights, but they recognized that they faced a long battle to wrest from the federal government guarantees of civil rights, desegregation, and equal employment opportunity. Many feared a recurrence of the race riots and lynchings that had followed the First World War. Yet civil rights leaders pressed ahead with renewed confidence. They had won victories in the establishment of the wartime FEPC; in the Supreme Court's *Gaines v. Missouri* decision (1938), which ordered a black man admitted to the University of Missouri law school; and in the *Smith v. Allwright* decision (1944), which outlawed the white primary. Black leaders knew that Afro-Americans were an important voting bloc in several northern industrial states, and they believed that blacks might hold the balance of power in the 1948 presidential election. As Myrdal had observed, the expansion of the federal government under the New Deal gave Afro-Americans a "broader and more variegated front to defend and from which to push forward."[1] During the Truman administration, civil rights groups lobbied for a permanent FEPC, desegregation of the military, fair housing legislation, and the abolition of the poll tax. The NAACP Legal Defense Fund initiated lawsuits to challenge the doctrine of "separate but equal" in public education. At the state and local levels, blacks campaigned for fair employment and fair housing legislation.

To readers of the mainstream white press in the postwar era, black leaders spoke with remarkable unity about the goals of the race. From the end of World War II to the beginning of the 1960s, the average white American discerned no major controversies among black leaders comparable to the Du Bois-Washington debate, the uproar over the Garvey movement, or the bitter ideological battles between the NAACP and the Communist party during the 1930s. The appearance of unity resulted in part from government repression of black Communists and from the decline of Afro-American nationalism, so that ideas from those quarters rarely reached the mainstream press. Civil rights leaders such as Walter White, Roy Wilkins, Lester Granger, A. Philip Randolph, and Martin Luther King, despite personal rivalries and tactical differences, spoke with a notably unified public voice about "what the Negro wants," emphasizing the right to vote; desegregation of schools, transportation, and public accommodations; equal opportunity in the private economy; and the desire of blacks to be a part of the mainstream American culture, not a separate, inferior unit. These issues that black leaders highlighted for white Americans corresponded in large measure to Myrdal's liberal orthodoxy.

Afro-Americans made only limited progress toward these goals during the

Truman administration, and most black people in the South saw little improvement in their status. But the cause of civil rights continued to gain moral legitimacy and political support at the national level. Blacks were not as marginal politically as they had been in the 1930s. Their allies included the CIO and urban liberal Democrats in the North. Some Republicans appealed for black votes and supported civil rights legislation. Jewish groups often joined with the NAACP in filing suits to end discrimination in housing and employment, and Protestant and Catholic leaders also spoke out in support of civil rights.

During the Truman years, as the historian Alonzo Hamby has observed, "civil rights became a central component of liberalism."[2] With the conservative coalition in control of Congress, there was no mandate for New Deal–style programs to help the poor or for structural reform of the economy, and liberals turned to Keynesian economics in an effort to ensure prosperity and full employment. While New Dealers had avoided raising the race issue directly, preferring to concentrate on programs that helped the poor of both races, white liberals of the postwar era endorsed a range of civil rights measures. A new sense of urgency pervaded the rhetoric of the liberals. In the wake of the Nazi holocaust, many Americans saw prejudice as a virus that might spread until it infected the whole body politic. Just as Hitler's persecution of the small Jewish minority in Germany had been a prelude to his assault on other peoples, so, liberals thought, prejudice against blacks might lead to greater intolerance and ultimately to some form of domestic fascism. In an era when the GI bill opened the doors of higher education to unprecedented numbers of Americans, liberals looked to education as a way of reducing prejudice and providing opportunities to previously disadvantaged groups. And as the Cold War mentality gripped the country after 1947, many liberals also argued that the United States had to set its own house in order on civil rights to insure the victory of the Free World over international communism.

When Harry Truman assumed the presidency in 1945, he was not closely identified with the cause of civil rights, though he had supported antilynching legislation in the Senate. In response to pressures from blacks and from white liberals, however, Truman ultimately would become the first president to develop a broad legislative program for the protection of civil rights. During his first year in office, he was preoccupied with the war, foreign policy, and planning for postwar reconversion, and he devoted little time to black issues. Shortly after taking office, Truman endorsed a permanent FEPC but was unable to get it through Congress. Then, in 1946, as the United States demobilized, a series of racial incidents and lynchings in the South attracted national attention. A white mob in Columbia, Tennessee, murdered two black prisoners in the local jail and rampaged through the black section of town, vandalizing and looting black homes. A white policeman in Aiken, South Carolina, gouged out the eyes of Sergeant Isaac Woodard shortly after Woodard's return to civilian life. Two black men and two black women were murdered in a lynching outside Monroe, Georgia. These atrocities sparked a wave of protest and demands for federal antilynching and civil rights legislation. The National Emergency Committee Against Mob Violence, which included representatives of civil rights, labor, religious, professional, and veterans' organizations, turned out fifteen thousand people for a protest meeting in New York and another fifteen thousand for a rally in Washington. Walter White warned that "a dread epidemic is sweeping across our country."[3] As Myrdal had predicted, the NAACP began preparing a long petition which documented violations of civil rights for presentation to the United Nations Human Rights Commission.[4]

In response to the upsurge of racial incidents and to the protests by blacks and white liberals, Truman established the President's Committee on Civil Rights to determine how law enforcement measures might be strengthened to protect civil rights. This idea of a presidential committee had been proposed during the Roosevelt administration after the race riots of 1943 but was rejected by FDR. Truman chose Charles E. Wilson, the president of General Electric, to head this panel of prominent citizens, which also included Charles Luckman, president of Lever Brothers; AFL economist Boris Shiskin; and James B. Carey of the CIO. The president named two white southern liberals, President Frank P. Graham of the University of North Carolina and Dorothy Tilly, who had been active in the Commission on Interracial Cooperation, as well as two black members, Channing Tobias of the Phelps-Stokes Fund and Sadie T. Alexander, an attorney. A Catholic bishop, Francis J. Haas, served along with Henry Knox Sherill, the presiding Episcopal bishop, and Rabbi Roland P. Gittleson. John S. Dickey, president of Dartmouth; civil liberties attorney Morris L. Ernst; attorney Francis P. Matthews; and Franklin D. Roosevelt, Jr., rounded out the list.

The committee presented its report, entitled *To Secure These Rights*, to President Truman in October 1947. The report was a bold statement of the new liberal orthodoxy and a benchmark of how far many prominent Americans had moved on the issue of civil rights, which FDR had refused to touch only three years earlier. Myrdal's conceptualization of the race issue as a conflict between American ideals and racial practices lay at the heart of the committee's report. The authors placed their discussion of civil rights in the context of "the American heritage of freedom and equality" as expressed in the Declaration of Independence and the Bill of Rights, then proceeded to analyze how the nation had fallen short of fulfilling its goals. They provided graphic descriptions of violence against blacks and bluntly termed lynching a "terrorist device" designed to impress upon all blacks their inferior status. To build as broad a consensus as possible, the authors defined discrimination and prejudice as problems that adversely affected a number of other minorities, including Catholics, Jews, Indians, Mexican-Americans, and Japanese-Americans. They surveyed the effects of discrimination in employment, justice, the military, housing, education, and government services, and carefully built their case that "separate but equal" was a myth that masked a system of racial inequality.

The authors delivered a concise, popular statement of many of the key ideas of postwar racial liberalism. They cited social science studies of interracial contact in the army, the merchant marine, and a housing project to support the assertion that contact among the races led to a reduction of prejudice. They assumed that moral exhortation and education would reduce ethnic hostility because "most prejudice can not survive real understanding of the great variations among people in any one group; or of the scientific findings which establish the equality of groups, and disprove racist nonsense; or of the fact that in a democratic common-wealth, prejudice is an immoral outlaw attitude."[5] The authors constructed a Keynesian argument that the nation's chief economic problem was "achieving maximum production and continued prosperity," a goal threatened by discrimina-tion against minority groups, which deprived the country of needed purchasing power and domestic markets. They quoted a former president of the U.S. Cham-ber of Commerce, who lectured businessmen, "You can't sell an electric refrigera-tor to a family that can't afford electricity. Perpetuating poverty for some merely guarantees stagnation for all. True economic progress demands that the whole nation move forward at the same time. . . . Intolerance is destructive; prejudice produces no wealth; discrimination is a fool's economy."[6]

In addition to the financial cost of discrimination, the committee cited the cost in "damaged, thwarted personalities." The authors quoted Myrdal's statement that "not only occasional acts of violence [by blacks], but most laziness, carelessness, unreliability, petty stealing and lying are undoubtedly to be explained as con-cealed aggression."[7]

To Secure These Rights was most indebted to Myrdal in its conception of the race question as a moral conflict. "We need no further justification for a broad and immediate [civil rights] program," the authors stated, "than the need to reaffirm our faith in traditional American morality." They found that "the pervasive gap between our aims and what we actually do is creating a kind of moral dry rot which eats away at the emotional and rational bases of democratic beliefs." Ameri-ca's "civil rights transgressions," they insisted, caused "moral damage" not only to the "victimized" but to "those who are responsible for these violations as well."[8]

The committee framed its racial liberalism in a global context, but it was a different type of globalism from Myrdal's. Coming in the year of the Greek-Turkish aid crisis and the Truman Doctrine, the report reflected the hardening Cold War position of the administration and warned that American lynchings provided "excellent propaganda ammunition for Communist agents." If the United States did not take action on civil rights, the authors feared that the "democratic ideal" might lose in the global struggle with the totalitarian adversary. After linking the civil rights struggle to the fate of the Free World, the committee outlined its policy proposals, which were remarkably liberal in the context of congressional politics of the Truman years. The recommendations included an antilynching law, an FEPC, abolition of the poll tax, legislation against discrimina-tion in voter registration, an end to segregation in the armed forces, legislation against segregation in interstate transportation, and a cutoff of federal funds to any public or private agency practicing discrimination or segregation. The committee made it clear that these proposals were only a beginning, and the authors advocated the "elimination of segregation, based on race, color, creed, or national origin, from American life."[9]

To Secure These Rights received substantial press attention and won high praise in liberal and black newspapers and journals. The book and pamphlets summarizing its contents reached hundreds of thousands of readers. Civic and church forums and study groups discussed and debated the committee's recommendations. President Truman called it a "charter of human rights for our time."[10]

In February 1948 Truman announced his administration's civil rights program in a special message to Congress. Building on the report of his committee, the president requested antilynching legislation, a permanent FEPC, prohibition of discrimination in interstate transportation, an anti-poll-tax law, and the creation of a civil rights division in the Justice Department. In addition, he promised an executive order to end discrimination in the civil service and announced that he would eliminate "the remaining instances of discrimination in the armed services." With a Myrdalian flourish, the president reminded Congress of the Founding Fathers' belief that all men were created equal and declared: "There is a serious gap between our ideals and some of our practices. This gap must be closed." Truman's dramatic proposal was designed to enhance his appeal to black citizens, who voted in increasing numbers in crucial industrial states in the North. He sought to blunt the appeal of Henry Wallace's Progressive party candidacy and to forestall a threatened campaign of civil disobedience to the draft that A. Philip Randolph was organizing. But Truman had seriously underestimated the magnitude of the opposition from white southerners. In March, the Southern Governors Conference passed a resolution opposing Truman's nomination and recommending that presidential electors refuse to vote for any candidate who supported civil rights legislation. Truman accordingly backpedaled and delayed action on his civil rights program until after the Democratic convention. He did, however, link the cause of civil rights to anti-communism in a major speech in Chicago. When citizens "are arbitrarily denied the right to vote or deprived of other basic rights, and nothing is done about it," he warned, "that is an invitation to communism."[11]

Pressure from black leaders and their white liberal allies continued to mount. Randolph stepped up his advocacy of civil disobedience to the draft, in spite of allegations that he was guilty of treason. One poll of black college students indicated that 71 percent supported the use of that tactic as a means of protesting segregation in the armed forces.[12] Walter White disavowed civil disobedience but vigorously prodded the administration to implement its civil rights program and pointedly reminded Democrats of the significance of the black vote. During the spring and summer, Democratic liberals, chiefly members of the Americans for Democratic Action (ADA), quietly made plans to fight for a strong civil rights plank in the party's platform. Truman sought to defuse the crisis by securing the adoption of a vague civil rights plank by the platform committee, but liberals carried the fight to the convention floor. Led by Minneapolis's young mayor, Hubert Humphrey, liberal, labor, and civil rights forces won an unexpected victory by gaining the convention's approval of a civil rights plank that included all the major recommendations of the President's Committee on Civil Rights.[13]

Truman campaigned on the civil rights plank and issued executive orders providing for gradual desegregation of the armed forces and a Fair Employment Board in the Civil Service Commission. In the November election, South Carolina governor Strom Thurmond carried four southern states as the candidate of the States Rights party, and Henry Wallace drew votes from some liberals in northern industrial states. But Truman preserved enough of the New Deal coalition to win an upset victory over Republican Thomas E. Dewey. Truman won a greater percentage of black votes than Roosevelt had in any of his four presidential elections, and Truman's margin of victory among black voters in California, Illinois, and Ohio gave him an electoral college majority.[14] As civil rights leaders had argued, blacks did indeed hold the balance of power in a close presidential election. Black electoral power had compelled a president to propose a legislative program of civil rights measures and to issue an executive order ending segregation in the nation's armed forces.

Yet blacks had not won these victories by fighting alone. A new racial liberalism had grown rapidly among significant groups of white Americans in the North. Afro-Americans found important allies in the labor movement, in liberal groups such as the ADA, and among clergy, journalists, and educators. In the late 1930s and early 1940s, as the historian Harvard Sitkoff has noted, northern white liberals in Congress had been willing to vote for antilynching and anti-poll-tax legislation but not to "battle all-out for it."[15] But by 1948, Democratic liberals were ready to risk splitting the party to secure the adoption of a strong civil rights plank in the party platform. Civil rights had come to occupy a high place on the national public policy agenda, and support for civil rights by leaders in so many areas of American life gave the cause a moral authority in the eyes of many whites that it had not had before the war.

The intensification of the Cold War after 1947 provided a global context in which the protection of civil rights was seen as an integral part of America's democratic system, which was thought to be under siege by Soviet totalitarianism. The Cold War also helped to shape the character of the civil rights movement. As congressional committees began investigating ties between civil rights organizations and communist groups, mainstream leaders such as Walter White and Roy Wilkins of the NAACP and Lester Granger of the Urban League spurned alliances with black Marxists such as Paul Robeson and Du Bois and assured white elites that the Negro was firmly opposed to communism. When the Cold War turned hot in Korea in 1950, civil rights leaders realized that they had won much more cooperation from Truman than they ever had from Roosevelt and that, therefore, they had more to lose if they did not support the war. Fearing that they might become a target for Senator Joseph McCarthy and other witch-hunters, they declined to use the leverage of the war to press for black advances, as they had in the Double-V campaign of World War II.[16] With the Korean War in progress, Truman needed the support of southerners in Congress, and he did not press vigorously for his legislative program on civil rights. His FEPC, antilynching, and anti-poll-tax bills languished in the Senate where the threat of a southern filibuster effectively killed them. When he ended his term in January 1953, Truman could point to the desegregation of the military as his most important civil rights achievement, but the determined opposition of southern members of Congress would delay the enactment of meaningful civil rights legislation for another eleven years.

Intercultural Education, Prejudice, and Damage

Though the spotlight of national attention was focused on battles over civil rights at the federal level, citizens organized campaigns against discrimination at the state and local levels as well. Between 1945 and 1951, eleven states and twenty-eight cities passed FEPC laws, while eighteen states banned discrimination in public accommodations.[17] To be sure, effective enforcement of these laws varied, but their passage gave civil rights advocates a sense of momentum while southern filibusters stalled civil rights legislation in Congress. Outside the South, public censure of racial prejudice and discrimination increased notably after the war. This upsurge of liberal activism at the local level also included a wave of educational campaigns designed to reduce prejudice and improve the public's knowledge about minorities and their role in American life. Social scientists played a key role in defining the nature of prejudice and in articulating the goals of groups that combated racial and religious intolerance.

As Roy Wilkins had predicted, *An American Dilemma* served as a bible for Americans concerned about racial injustice, and the reputation of Myrdal's book grew steadily after World War II. Though he had intended to encourage research on a number of different fronts, Myrdal, by defining the "Negro problem" as a conflict in the minds of white Americans, helped to focus postwar research on psychological issues at the expense of social structural and economic analysis. In surveying the history of social scientific writing about black-white relations, the social psychologist Thomas F. Pettigrew has noted, "The postwar years were characterized by the dominance of psychological analysis of race relations with emphasis upon 'prejudice.'"[18]

The battle against prejudice had its roots in the 1920s, when citizens had formed groups such as the National Conference of Christians and Jews to foster greater tolerance in the wake of the race riots, the revival of the Ku Klux Klan, and the nativist hysteria that followed World War I. In reaction to Nazi racism, the Progressive Education Association had established in 1937 a Commission on Intercultural Education, which sponsored an Education for Democracy program that heralded the contributions of immigrants to American life. Activities such as these had mushroomed during World War II, as liberals sought to celebrate America's tolerance of ethnic diversity while stressing the nation's consensus on political institutions and the universalist values of the American creed.[19] During the war, concerned social scientists, clergy, and educators began planning educational programs to reduce intergroup hostility in the hope of averting race riots and anti-Semitic and anti-Catholic incidents once the complex process of postwar reconversion began. One article of faith for the men and women who campaigned against prejudice was the Keynesian view that economic abundance was an essential precondition of greater ethnic tolerance. Though the political climate was hostile to redistributionist measures, liberals hoped that they could persuade white Protestant Americans that no group lost by ending discrimination, that the whole pie was getting bigger in the expanding economy of postwar America.[20]

A second article of faith in this movement was that education was the basic means of gaining leverage in the fight against racial and religious bigotry. Education was the form of social engineering that had the greatest legitimacy in the United States, and Americans had long looked to public education to provide opportunities for social mobility and cultural assimilation of immigrants. The GI bill opened the nation's colleges and universities to the largest and most socially diverse group of students in American history. Though black students were still heavily concentrated in black colleges, record numbers of Catholic and Jewish students and professors entered public and private universities. Revulsion from Nazi racism and the holocaust, together with anxiety about America's future, convinced many civic, religious, and educational leaders that the national interest required greater tolerance of ethnic diversity and acceptance of citizens from different ethnic groups.

Postwar liberals turned to the social sciences, especially psychology, to develop more sophisticated techniques for educating Americans about how to think clearly about their fellow citizens who came from different backgrounds. Research on racial attitudes, which had begun in the 1920s, generated a sizable literature by the 1940s, and the concept of ethnic prejudice came into wide usage outside the academy.[21] As psychologists defined them, prejudices were attitudes that developed as a result of ignorance about and limited contact with people of other ethnic or religious groups.[22] It therefore followed that education designed to change these attitudes and programs aimed at increasing intergroup contact were the key elements in a strategy that would lead to changes in behavior and ultimately to the acceptance of minority-group members throughout American society. The Columbia sociologist Robert MacIver, a leader in the intercultural education movement, succinctly summarized this view: "Always, in so far as I have spoken about group relations, I have tried to insist that the primary thing is the attitude back of our behavior; that the first need is to cultivate right attitudes; that our attitudes are based on understanding of our society; and that we carry, then, these attitudes through into wholesome practice."[23]

As a result of this movement, millions of Americans began to hear about the concept of prejudice. The number of organizations across the country working to fight ethnic hostility and to champion the American creed jumped from roughly 300 in 1945 to more than 1,350 by the end of the decade.[24] Perhaps the most common means of battling prejudice were resolutions condemning racial and religious bigotry passed by civic, professional, and religious organizations. In 1946, for example, the Federal Council of Churches, which included most of the major Protestant denominations, issued a statement renouncing segregation as "unnecessary and undesirable and a violation of the Gospel of love and human brotherhood." The council pledged to work for a "non-segregated Church and a non-segregated society."[25] The resolution came as the result of two years of study by a special commission within the organization headed by Will Alexander, who wrote Myrdal that "the earnestness with which the Council adopted this new policy is due in no small degree to the new atmosphere that has been created among all thoughtful people in America by your two volumes on the *American Dilemma*." An activist in interracial matters since World War I, Alexander informed Myrdal that he had "never known a study of any social problem that had such a definite effect as this study of yours. You have really given us a new start."[26]

Though moral exhortation was the most common tactic in the war against prejudice, the battle was waged by other means as well. Intercultural educators developed public school programs, teacher education courses, adult education forums, pamphlets, religious programs, discussion groups for businesses and unions, films, radio programs, dramatic productions, comic books, arts and craft shows, folk dancing, poetry readings, encounter groups with role playing and psychodrama, interracial Boy Scout troops, multiethnic luncheon clubs, and brotherhood dinners. Seeking to write ethnic tolerance into the American creed, the Governor's Inter-Racial Commission urged all Minnesotans to incant the following pledge: "I will never by rumor or careless conversation indict a whole race or religious group by reasons of the delinquency of a few members. I will daily deal with every man in business, social, and political relations solely on the basis of his individual work."[27]

The movement for intercultural education and better human relations spawned a host of influential studies of prejudice, as religious and civic groups as well as foundations sponsored social science research. Charles E. Hendry, director of the American Jewish Congress's Commission on Community Interrelations, acknowledged the heightened prestige of the social sciences in his introduction to a popular book on intercultural education. "During World War II," he recalled, "the social scientist took his place, with dignity, alongside the medical and physical scientist" in helping to plan and evaluate the "vast, synchronized, scientific operation" of modern warfare. Social scientists now faced the challenge of supplying a "strategic guide to the war against prejudice," he contended. Hendry saw "group tensions and hostilities" as "the symptoms of a disturbed, distorted, and diseased group life." "To bring such under control," he continued, "requires . . . rigorous research and a realistic therapy." Conceiving of "hate" as a "contagious disease" that called for "community diagnosis and treatment," Hendry concluded that "what now is involved is the conquest of conflict itself." He admonished Americans that "before man can control the atom he must learn to control himself."[28]

While Hendry's comments express the innocence of many of the intercultural educators, his organization sponsored some of the most sophisticated research on intergroup relations, notably the work of the social psychologist Kurt Lewin. A Jewish refugee from Nazi Germany, Lewin had come to the United States in 1933 and had held research positions at the School of Home Economics at Cornell and at the Iowa Child Welfare Research Station before founding the Research Center for Group Dynamics at the Massachusetts Institute of Technology in 1944. Though initially an outsider in American academic life, Lewin enjoyed support from the Rockefeller Foundation and quickly won the respect of many American social scientists for his work on such topics as conflict resolution and "authoritarian" versus "democratic" leadership. In the 1930s, he had founded the Society for the Psychological Study of Social Issues as an activist alternative to the American Psychological Association. Lewin advocated "action research" designed to break down prejudice and to help people to change. Sharing Myrdal's scorn for do-nothing social science, he adopted the motto: "No action without research, no research without action." If a democratic society were to survive, Lewin insisted, concerned citizens had to mobilize the resources of the social sciences to foster better intergroup relations. Accordingly, he assembled a team of young social psychologists who worked with community groups to plan community self-studies, diagnose problems, and recommend remedial measures. One of his greatest concerns was raising the self-esteem of members of minority groups by encouraging a sense of pride in belonging to the group, and he proposed to strengthen the "we-feeling" of American Jews through programs of Jewish education. Though a meliorist who believed, like Myrdal, that prejudice could be reduced, Lewin did not think that assimilation was the answer. His studies of Jews in Germany and America convinced him that members of minority groups paid a psychic price in assimilating to the larger culture. Lewin died in 1947 at the age of fifty-seven and did not have the opportunity to apply his ideas about strengthening minority group self-esteem to Afro-Americans. After his death, the Commission on Community Interrelations sponsored the work of a number of young social psychologists such as Stuart Cook, Isidor Chein, Kenneth Clark, and John Harding, who carried on "action research."[29]

The American Jewish Committee's Department of Scientific Research also initiated research in this field and sponsored several important books in a series entitled "Studies in Prejudice." The most famous of these was *The Authoritarian Personality* by T. W. Adorno, Else Frenkel-Brunswik, Daniel J. Levinson, and R. Nevitt Sanford. Bruno Bettelheim and Morris Janowitz contributed a study of prejudice among American veterans, while Nathan W. Ackermann and Marie Jahoda wrote a psychoanalytic study, *Anti-Semitism and Emotional Disorder*.[30]

Protestant groups sponsored work on intercultural relations as well. In the early 1930s, the Society of Friends had conducted summer institutes on race relations, which brought prominent social scientists together at Swarthmore College. During World War II, the American Missionary Association of the Congregational Christian Church established a Department of Race Relations at Fisk University, headed by Charles S. Johnson, which supported research on intergroup relations, proposed action programs for community groups, and published a bulletin entitled *A Monthly Summary of Events and Trends in Race Relations*.[31]

In addition to these religious organizations, the SSRC established in September 1945 a Committee on Techniques for Reducing Group Hostility consisting of Charles Dollard of the Carnegie Corporation, Carl I. Hovland of Yale University, and Leonard S. Cottrell, Jr., of Cornell University. With support from the Rockefeller Foundation, the SSRC committee surveyed techniques used by "action agencies" to reduce tensions and conflicts among "racial, cultural, and class groups"; proposed research to evaluate these techniques; and investigated how social psychological theory might be applied to lessen hostility and resolve conflict.[32]

Taken together, these initiatives by religious groups and foundations helped to make social psychology an exciting subject after the war, as a cohort of young veterans entered the field and worked with émigré scholars as well as Americans of the older generation to develop new theories and methods in an effort to reduce ethnic and religious hostility and conflict. The Studies in Prejudice series also stimulated American psychology by applying sophisticated psychoanalytic perspectives to the problems of anti-Semitism and intolerance. One important consequence of this sponsorship, however, was the steering of social science research on race and ethnicity toward the study of intergroup contact and the psychodynamics of prejudice at the expense of analyses of how ethnic discrimination was rooted in institutions, social structure, and the economic system. Thomas F. Pettigrew exaggerated only slightly when he claimed that, in an era when federal government support for research was almost nonexistent, the "human relations" or intercultural education movement was "virtually 'the only game in town'" for social psychologists who wanted to test hypotheses about intergroup behavior.[33]

Prominent sociologists such as Louis Wirth, Charles S. Johnson, and Robert MacIver also took leading roles in the intergroup relations movement and in campaigns against prejudice. The evolution of Wirth's concerns in the five years after the war strikingly illustrates the movement toward the psychological and social psychological emphasis in studies of race and ethnicity. In a 1945 article, "The Problem of Minority Groups," Wirth cast his discussion in a cultural-pluralist framework and—in a burst of wartime solidarity—suggested that the Soviet Union, rather than the United States, offered the rest of the world a model of ethnic pluralism and respect for minority languages and cultures.[34] A year later, in an essay called "The Unfinished Business of American Democracy," Wirth took a position very similar to the last chapter of *An American Dilemma*, which he praised. Emphasizing that America's position in the world depended upon its treatment of minorities at home, Wirth presented a more specific agenda of political reform than Myrdal had offered: full employment, a permanent fair employment practices commission with "vigorous enforcement," fair housing legislation, equalization of public services for all, a national housing act, a national health act, a comprehensive social security act, and federal aid to education to lessen disparities in educational opportunities. He conceded that achieving "a democratic public policy . . . will not automatically erase private prejudices," but argued that it would "go a long way to minimize the adverse effects of such prejudices." Wirth asserted that prejudices could be overcome only through a lengthy process of education that would modify "attitudes which for the most part have nonrational foundations."[35]

In a survey entitled "Research in Racial and Cultural Relations" in 1948, Wirth noted the proliferation of groups working for the "improvement of race relations" but fretted about the "impatience" of these reformers, who often did not understand the complexity of the issues they were dealing with or the limits of social scientific knowledge. "They want practical results and they want the research workers to deliver them now," he complained. Nevertheless, he acknowledged that "we know that *all* the facts will never be in, and meanwhile we must act on the basis of such knowledge and wisdom as we have." Accordingly, Wirth outlined the work of his Committee on Education, Training, and Research on Race Relations at the University of Chicago, funded by the Rockefeller and Carnegie corporations, which was designed to evaluate the effectiveness of various strategies and programs for improving intergroup relations. He dismissed most of the tactics used by the intergroup relations movement to reduce ethnic hostility as "shot-gun approaches rather than weapons designed to deal specifically with highly differentiated problems," and he called upon social scientists to "invent new and better techniques."[36]

By 1950 Wirth had adopted a remarkably Myrdalian approach to race relations, referring to the United States as a "dynamic, powerful, national society striving to live by the democratic creed." Myrdal's emphasis upon the importance of analyzing valuations in conflict accorded well with Wirth's longstanding interest in studying the ways in which attitudes and values shaped behavior. Wirth argued that *An American Dilemma* was leading American social scientists to focus their research on issues of prejudice and attitude formation: "By calling attention to the central fact that the 'American Creed' has shaped the consciousness and the conscience of the American public—White as well as Negro—and has thus shaped the definition of the problems of race relations in the United States, [Myrdal's] work has given fresh impetus to the social-psychological approach to the wider issues of racial and cultural relations." In the conservative political climate of the day, Wirth replaced his New Dealish list of legislative reforms with more general goals which he claimed to be "linked with the dominant values of American society." These included "(1) the reduction of intergroup prejudice;

(2) the minimization of discrimination and segregation; (3) the lessening of inter-group tensions and conflicts and (4) the minimization of the adverse conse-quences of prejudice, discrimination, segregation, tension and conflict." American social scientists, Wirth noted, had come up with four general directions of re-search in pursuit of these objectives: "(1) Studies concerning the nature, genesis and modifiability of attitudes; (2) studies of personality; (3) studies of situational factors and (4) studies of norms, values, and social sanctions." While Wirth commended citizens who fought inequalities through "legislation, litigation, and community organization," his own efforts were largely centered on the intergroup relations movement through his involvement with the American Council on Race Relations and the Committee on Education, Training, and Research on Race Relations of the University of Chicago.[37]

The shift toward a psychological and social psychological orientation in re-search on race relations thus stemmed from several factors: the direction offered by Myrdal, the infusion of new ideas from European émigrés, the priorities of funding agencies, and the political climate at the national level, which ruled out a federal assault on poverty and ambitious programs of social engineering. The priorities of the social scientists themselves were also important: In the late 1940s and 1950s many psychologists and some sociologists were ready to move into action in response to public concern about intolerance, while few economists were interested in following up Myrdal's investigations of discrimination by busi-ness and unions. Institutional studies of the sort that Myrdal advocated were not fashionable among the vast majority of American economists.[38]

Both social scientists and funding agencies in the late 1940s and 1950s gener-ally assumed that studying prejudice was a more fundamental issue than studying Afro-American social behavior, institutions, communities, and culture. Prejudice was thought to be the result of individual personality disorder, economic depriva-tion, or social strain. Since a prejudiced person was usually hostile to many out-groups and might turn his or her hostility from blacks to another scapegoat, social scientists considered it more important to study the source of the hostility rather than the target group. Besides, if prosperity and tolerance prevailed, in another generation there would be no black communities or institutions, so why study them? White intercultural educators ironically devoted little attention to Afro-American culture and assumed that blacks had no distinctive culture. While white liberals generally acknowledged that many Catholics and Jews wished to preserve a distinctive identity within American society, they assumed, like Myrdal, that blacks wished to break down all social barriers and assimilate to the dominant culture as rapidly as possible.[39]

In 1947 Robin M. Williams, Jr., a young social psychologist at Cornell Univer-sity, synthesized much of the emerging literature on prejudice and intergroup relations in *The Reduction of Intergroup Tensions*. Sponsored by the SSRC Commit-tee on Techniques for Reducing Group Hostility, Williams's book was an impor-tant statement of the new activist social science and would remain an influential work in social psychology for a generation. A student of Talcott Parsons, Williams began his study by citing the "incompatibility" between widespread ethnic and religious conflict and the universal values of "what Myrdal has called the American Creed." Though he recognized that "temporary intensification of conflict" had sometimes led to gains for blacks, the overall thrust of his book was to focus on techniques for reducing hostility and conflict between ethnic groups and for educating white Protestant Americans about prejudices against blacks, Catholics, Jews, and other minorities. In this period of wavering commitment to civil rights at the federal level, Williams made no national policy proposals on minority affairs but instead offered advice to local "action programs," which he believed could "exert an appreciable degree of control over intergroup behavior."[40]

In his analysis of intergroup prejudice, Williams sought to integrate certain concepts from Freudian psychology with a functionalist view of the social system—an approach that led him to somewhat less optimistic conclusions than Myrdal. He conceded, for example, that prejudices were often learned in early childhood, a stage at which it was almost impossible for action programs to intervene. Williams suggested, moreover, that all individuals harbor a certain amount of "free-floating aggression" resulting from resentments rooted in childhood socialization and later deprivations and frustrations. This hostility could focus on minority groups as a result of personal insecurity, economic deprivation, or competition for wealth or status. Aggression was such a fundamental part of human nature that "insofar as education and propaganda reduces hostility toward any specific group or towards out-groups in general, it does so largely by re-channelizing aggressive impulses rather than removing them." Since prejudice could be so deeply rooted in an individual's personality, Williams warned that direct moral appeals to prejudiced people (such as Myrdal's attempt to stir the guilty consciences of whites) could have a "boomerang effect" and make certain individuals feel under attack and hence unwilling to change.[41] Williams therefore recommended a strategy of indirect approaches to intercultural education, such as focusing on common goals and common social problems that contending groups faced, as well as inserting positive information about minorities into the "ordinary action" of an organization in its day-to-day work, rather than holding special meetings about prejudice or minority affairs. In addition, he questioned the prevailing assumption that more contact among ethnic groups would lead to greater tolerance and indicated that the class and status of the individuals, the situations in which they came into contact, and the intimacy and duration of the contact all affected whether contact lessened or reinforced prejudice.[42]

For the most part, Williams avoided macrosociological analysis and recommended new research on psychological issues, but he did give a qualified endorsement to Myrdal's principle of cumulation, the idea that it is possible to break the "vicious circle" of discrimination and poverty by intervening at any one of several strategic points. In Williams's Parsonian conception of the social system, society was more stable and contained more checks on innovation than Myrdal had allowed. Williams warned, "Social systems are not indefinitely plastic but have inherent (although rather wide) functional limits to variation." This meant that "the cumulation of effects is checked by broad functional limits, e.g., need for a certain amount of order, beyond which a given system can not go without disruption." Seizing on Myrdal's suggestion that raising the educational level of southern blacks might be the crucial factor for reversing the vicious circle, Williams surmised that such a move might succeed up to a point until it seemed to threaten the "caste-like system," whereupon white hostility would intensify.[43]

The young social psychologist accepted other elements of the Myrdalian orthodoxy without cavil, especially the notion that economic security was crucial to intergroup tolerance and the view that upper-income groups were more tolerant than lower-income groups. Though he paid homage to the concept of cultural pluralism as a middle way between the ideals of the melting pot and the ethnic mosaic, the overall thrust of Williams's approach was in keeping with the assimilationism of the era. He asserted, "Dispersion of minorities as individuals or small groups (*not* as communities) throughout a wide area and in various positions in the social structure tends to diffuse hostility and in the long run to reduce it." He also recommended the following steps by which a "vulnerable minority" could help to reduce hostility toward it from the "dominant group":

(a) educating its members to an understanding of the dominant group's reaction to the minority's values and behavior

(b) careful study of the behaviors of its own members which are regarded as objectionable by other groups

(c) minimizing conspicuous display of traits of marked negative-symbol value

(d) participating *as individuals* in wider community activities which are widely regarded as necessary in the common welfare.[44]

Williams's synthesis represented a more cautious version of Myrdal's racial liberalism, yet he accepted all the essential arguments of *An American Dilemma*. Recognizing many subtle difficulties in changing the attitudes of the white majority, Williams nonetheless saw education as the key point of leverage in reducing ethnic hostility and devoted himself to refining techniques for intercultural education and contact programs. Williams, who lived in the northeastern section of the country and focused on prejudice against Catholics and Jews as well as blacks, assumed that strategic programs aimed at specific groups of citizens could lessen prejudice and allow the democratic consensus and universalist norms in the society to expand opportunities for minorities. His strategy did not really come to grips with the situation of southern blacks, who were excluded from participating in the democratic process and for whom civil rights would come, as Myrdal had suggested, only after protracted conflict. Williams and most other American social scientists of the late 1940s and early 1950s failed to follow up Myrdal's analysis of the institutions that practiced racial discrimination and played a large role in generating and sustaining the prejudice that Williams sought to diminish.[45]

In 1950 Theodor Adorno and his associates published *The Authoritarian Personality*, a massive study of nearly one thousand pages based on in-depth clinical observation of prejudiced individuals and employing a variety of psychological tests. The authors presented a psychoanalytic interpretation that linked repressive child-rearing practices to the development of prejudice against out-groups and authoritarian political attitudes. They devised the famous F-scale (with F standing for fascist) to measure authoritarian attitudes. Though the authors' own political perspectives ranged from socialist to liberal, the implications of their findings were disheartening to liberal activists in the intercultural education or human relations movement. Prejudice, they contended, was so deeply rooted in the personality that it would not yield easily in response to moral suasion, educational efforts, or intergroup contact. The authors considered it pointless to focus on discrimination against a particular minority group because if educators succeeded in diverting hostility from one group, the hostility would simply be turned against another group. This approach precluded a careful analysis of the unique economic, cultural, and institutional causes of prejudice and discrimination against blacks. Instead, Adorno and company centered their analysis on such psychological mechanisms of the prejudiced person as "stereotypy, emotional coldness, identification with power, and general destructiveness." They warned liberal activists that "rational arguments cannot be expected to have deep or lasting effects upon a phenomenon that is irrational in its essential nature." Yet the authors insisted that organizations fighting for social justice should not slacken their efforts, and they held out the hope that prejudiced individuals who were "submissive toward authority" would obey antidiscrimination laws. For the long term, Adorno and his colleagues glimpsed the possibility that more liberal child-rearing techniques would increase tolerance in the society.[46]

The Authoritarian Personality stirred a lively debate among social scientists in the early 1950s. Scholars raised a host of methodological objections and cast doubt on the authors' claim to predict political behavior on the basis of personality type. In particular, critics argued that the authors focused on personality development to such an extent that they ignored or minimized economic, social, and situational causes of prejudice.[47] Arnold Rose, Myrdal's protégé who had become a prominent sociologist of race and ethnicity, dismissed their psychoanalytic arguments and suggested that "there are about as many 'authoritarian personalities' today among the fighters against discrimination as among the fighters for it."[48]

On the eve of the *Brown* decision in 1954, the Harvard psychologist Gordon W. Allport published his influential study *The Nature of Prejudice*, which would remain the most important book on the subject and a popular textbook for many years. Then fifty-seven years old, Allport was a senior figure in American psychology, respected for his work on personality theory as well as social psychology.

In contrast to some of the more pessimistic writers on the subject, Allport proclaimed himself an unabashed meliorist and insisted that it was possible to reduce discrimination by changing public policy and to lessen prejudice through a variety of educational strategies. In his advocacy of desegregation and equality of opportunity, in his placing of the issue of tolerance in a global context, in his assimilationist view of Afro-American culture, and in his willingness to appeal to the conscience of white Americans, Allport delivered a powerful affirmation of Myrdal's liberal orthodoxy.

Allport rejected what he termed "closed system" analyses of prejudice—whether it be the psychological closed system that saw prejudice purely as a function of personality disorder or the economic determinism or social structural determinism that considered it futile to try to change the attitudes of individuals. He contended that prejudice stemmed from multiple causes and must be analyzed in terms of the interaction of personality and society. Like Myrdal and Williams, Allport conceived of American society as being in a state of dynamic equilibrium; therefore, the liberal activist might intervene at any one of a number of strategic points, reverse the vicious circle, and move the system in a progressive direction through the principle of cumulation. Marshaling his scientific evidence, Allport declared that there was "considerable agreement that it is wiser to attack segregation and discrimination than to attack prejudice directly."[49] Antidiscrimination laws, once on the books, might not change the attitudes of the "compulsive bigot," but they would affect the behavior of the "middle range of mortals who need them as a mentor in molding their habits." "When discrimination is ended," he insisted, "prejudice . . . tends to lessen." Allport conceded that laws controlled only "the outward expression of intolerance," but he added that psychological research had shown that "outward action . . . has an effect upon inner habits of thought and feeling." Decisive public action against discrimination would pull along wavering citizens because most Americans "deep inside their consciences do approve civil rights and antidiscrimination legislation." Allport thought Myrdal's rank order of discrimination a sensible guide for setting priorities for changes in public policy and recommended focusing on job discrimination as the issue most important to blacks and least offensive to whites.[50]

The Harvard psychologist regarded intercultural education as a useful supplement to legislative attacks on segregation and discrimination, and he devoted considerable attention to analyzing some of the most promising techniques that had been developed since the war. Like Myrdal, he believed that education could gradually break down the rationalizations that bigots used to defend their prejudices. He admitted that occasionally educational efforts met with a "boomerang effect" but contended that making a person uncomfortable about his prejudices was a necessary stage in the process of change. "Investigation shows," he claimed, "that people who are aware of, and ashamed of, their prejudices are well on the road to eliminating them." Allport was unclear on what role blacks should play in the process of intercultural education. He discussed the idea of cultural pluralism but asserted that it was problematical in regard to black people because they "can scarcely be said to have a distinctive culture."[51]

As a senior figure in the field writing a book for educated lay readers as well as for students, Allport put an optimistic interpretation on the findings of social science research about the power of state action to end discrimination and eventually change attitudes. He concluded his study by quoting Myrdal's statement, "We cannot plead that we must wait 'until all the facts are in,' because we know full well that all the facts never will be in. Nor can we argue that 'the facts speak for themselves' and leave it 'to the politician and the citizen to draw the practical conclusions.'" Allport affirmed Myrdal's view that it was up to the social scientist to make sense of the findings of social investigations and recommend courses of action. In addition, he emphasized the central importance in a democratic society of fostering tolerance. Observing that the triumph of democratic values was not inevitable, Allport expressed concern about both McCarthyism at home and totalitarianism abroad. "Democracy" he wrote, "places a heavy burden upon the personality" and demands a capacity to "think rationally" about other groups and to tolerate diversity. Allport, like Myrdal, ended his book with a moral challenge to Americans: would the nation, he asked, continue to make "progress toward tolerance" or would a "fatal retrogression . . . set in?" He declared, "The whole world watches to see whether the democratic ideal in human relationships is viable."[52]

The Nature of Prejudice was a masterful synthesis of the literature on intergroup relations and the psychodynamics of prejudice as well as a compelling brief for desegregation and civil rights. Allport, like Myrdal, was less afraid of intergroup conflict than many intercultural educators, and he avoided their heavy-handed language about achieving control over behavior. He differed from many American social scientists of his own generation, which came of age before World War II, in his willingness to appeal to the consciences of Americans and use social science to influence public policy, but his work, together with Myrdal's, inspired a younger generation of activist scholars. Kenneth Clark observed that "Allport and Myrdal personify the insistence that thoughtful, moral, rationalistic social scientists must be the contemporary custodians of such enduring human values as justice—and that trained human intelligence is an important weapon in the ongoing struggle against ignorance, superstition, and injustice."[53] This liberal credo continued to exert a powerful influence on discussions of race and ethnicity for at least ten years following the *Brown* decision, as prominent social scientists, whatever their methodological disagreements, reached a remarkable degree of consensus in support of desegregation and civil rights legislation.

Although social psychologists studied white racial attitudes in the 1940s and 1950s, they compiled very little information about black attitudes. As Paul Sheatsley, a pioneer in research on white attitudes in that era, noted: "It never occurred to us when we wrote questions in the Forties and Fifties to ask them of blacks because Myrdal's dilemma was a white dilemma and it was white attitudes that demanded study."[54] When social scientists did look at the effects of prejudice on blacks, they focused on the damage that racial hostility inflicted on Afro-Americans. Myrdal, as we have seen, had drawn on a social science literature that charted the deleterious effects of segregation and discrimination on black institutions, family life, personality, and culture. While no serious student of Afro-American life could afford to ignore the manifold injuries of racism, Myrdal, in his discussion of the Negro community, had overemphasized social pathologies and had neglected the mechanisms, strategies, beliefs, symbols, and institutions that gave coherence and meaning to Afro-American communities and enabled blacks to resist oppression. In the aftermath of the Myrdal study, many liberal social scientists, eager to shock white Americans into an awareness of the consequences of prejudice and discrimination, focused on the damage done to blacks.

Foremost among the students of damage was Frazier, whose clinical dissections of black pathologies were now divorced from the eschatology of socialist transformation. The Howard sociologist followed his landmark study of the black family with an investigation entitled *Negro Youth at the Crossways* (1940), in which he analyzed the ways that discrimination contributed to low self-esteem among black youth, especially of the urban lower class. Frazier examined the history and current condition of the black community in *The Negro in the United States* (1949), a major work that examined both the damage of slavery and racism and the ways in which Afro-Americans had accommodated themselves to American society. In *Black Bourgeoisie* (1957), he made it clear that social pathologies were by no means limited to the lower class. Drawing on his own experiences as a participant-observer, Frazier argued that middle-class blacks lived in a "world of make-believe" behind the walls of segregation, losing themselves in a milieu of superficial social activities instead of leading the struggle for racial equality.[55] His expositions of damage did not lead Frazier to despair, however. Like Myrdal, he maintained that the rise of African, Asian, and Latin American nations to world prominence created a pressure on white Americans to honor their principles of human freedom and human equality, and he prophesied that an alliance of Negroes, white minority groups, and the labor movement would lead to an eventual reorganization of American life in support of racial equality.[56]

The psychiatrists Abram Kardiner and Lionel Ovesey contributed an influential analysis of the damage of white supremacy in *The Mark of Oppression: Explorations in the Personality of the American Negro* (1950). Based on twenty-five life history interviews with black subjects, this psychoanalytic work built on the research of Myrdal, John Dollard, and Frazier but focused on the impact of discrimination on the personalities of black people. Economic discrimination, the authors concluded, caused the black man to fail in his "patriarchal" role as "great provider and source of all bounties within the family." When this happened, the man's "magical powers no longer exist and his wife and children are exposed to anxieties of survival." If the wife has a job and the husband is unemployed, "the father takes his place as one of the siblings" and loses "parental authority." With the family thus eroded as a "place of refuge against the hostile world," the lower-class Negro was caught in a Myrdalian vicious circle of gambling, drinking, drugs, crime, and a religion of escape into fantasy. Kardiner and Ovesey stressed that blacks were not to blame for their victimization, nor could they be expected to climb out of their situation through education. The authors echoed Myrdal in arguing that only a transformation in white attitudes and behavior and changes in public policy could stop the oppression and put an end to its tragic consequences.[57]

In 1951 the NAACP Legal Defense Fund decided to mobilize the growing social science literature on damage in its legal campaign to desegregate public schools. In preparing the South Carolina case of *Briggs v. Elliott*, NAACP attorney Thurgood Marshall told his staff that "we had to try this case just like any other one in which you would try to prove damages to your client. If your car ran over my client, you'd have to pay up, and my function as an attorney would be to put experts on the stand to testify to how much damage was done."[58] Accordingly, Marshall and his staff approached various prominent social scientists about appearing in court on behalf of the NAACP. When several of the big names in the field proved unwilling or too busy to testify, Marshall turned to a young black psychologist who had been a research assistant on the Myrdal study. Kenneth B. Clark, together with his wife Mamie Clark, had written several articles and a book that explored the ways in which segregation and discrimination damaged the self-esteem of black children. The most dramatic evidence he offered was his doll tests, in which three- to seven-year-old black children were shown two white dolls and two brown dolls. They were asked to "give me the doll you like to play with" and to "give me the doll that is a nice color." The majority of black children tested chose the white dolls.[59] Clark and several other social scientists took the stand and testified that segregation damaged the mental and emotional development of black children. In preparing its defense in the *Briggs* case, the state of South Carolina was unable to find a prominent social scientist who would testify in favor of segregation—an indication of the extent to which the Myrdalian liberal orthodoxy had triumphed among social scientists. Though Howard Odum and other prominent white southern liberals privately doubted that the South was ready to accept, without violence, an immediate end to segregation of public schools, they declined to say so under oath.[60]

Thurgood Marshall's use of social science evidence was an unorthodox and risky strategy when he put Clark and others on the stand in the early 1950s, but it would become commonplace in the twenty years following the *Brown* decision. As more and more social scientists testified in school desegregation cases, they increasingly focused their research on the damage that racism did to black Americans. This liberal, activist social science played a significant role in influencing public policy and in persuading many educated white Americans that segregation was harmful to blacks and to the public interest. The days in which social scientists vied with each other to establish their objectivity by distancing themselves from public controversy were clearly over. Yet the new, liberal orthodoxy focused on prejudice while ignoring the economic, social structural, and institutional sources of racism and emphasized damage at the expense of structures of resistance in the black community.

Racial Liberalism from *Brown* to the Voting Rights Act

When the Supreme Court handed down its decision in the case of *Brown v. Board of Education of Topeka, Kansas* on May 17, 1954, Chief Justice Earl Warren cited the work of Myrdal, Clark, Frazier, and other social scientists in support of the assertion that segregated schools damaged the educational motivation and mental development of black children. Warren drew on these social science authorities in order to counter the dubious psychology of the 1896 *Plessy v. Ferguson* decision, which denied that segregation "stamps the colored race with a badge of inferiority."[61] Social science evidence was not at the core of legal reasoning in the *Brown* decision, which built on earlier decisions in which the Court had found that segregated graduate schools and law schools denied to blacks the Fourteenth Amendment's guarantee of equal protection of the laws. Nor was the use of social science evidence an innovation: the Supreme Court had taken account of similar types of expert testimony in many cases since the Progressive Era. But the citation of Myrdal, Clark, Frazier, and others provoked a storm of criticism that greatly exceeded earlier debates about social science evidence and thrust *An American Dilemma* into the center of public controversy.[62]

The Supreme Court, in a gesture of conciliation to the white South, issued a vague implementation ruling on May 31, 1955, which declared that desegregation should proceed "with all deliberate speed" but declined to set deadlines. Each local school district in the South would set its own timetable for desegregation, and each federal district judge would oversee compliance with *Brown*. When President Dwight Eisenhower refused to speak out in support of compliance, the stage was set for southern defiance.[63] Southern politicians began a campaign of massive resistance aimed at blocking implementation of the Supreme Court decision.[64] In the wake of *Brown*, segregationists assailed Myrdal with rhetoric tinged with McCarthyism and xenophobia. In 1955, Senator James Eastland of Mississippi denounced him as a "Swedish Socialist" who had employed Communists and subversives on his study. Other southern politicians joined in the assault, and the Citizens' Council, a segregationist organization, regularly condemned Myrdal in its literature. Editorial writers throughout the South linked Myrdal to an international Communist conspiracy to undermine the United States Constitution.[65] The Supreme Court, so the argument went, had been duped by this foreign socialist and his Communist co-conspirators into basing their decision on sociology rather than the Constitution. Robert Welch, founder and president of the John Birch Society, gave the Communists credit for "forcing through the anti-segregation decision of the Supreme Court, which [they] certainly planned as far back as when [they] had Gunnar Myrdal brought over here to write his mammoth book."[66] Carleton Putnam, a retired airline executive and author of *Race and Reason*, a tract widely circulated by the Citizens' Council, deplored Myrdal's "highly socialistic" bias and indicted him for purveying the doctrines of Franz Boas, "a foreign-born Columbia University professor . . . who was himself a member of a racial minority group."[67]

Yet the liberal orthodoxy had triumphed so completely in the social sciences that massive resistance was deprived of scientific legitimacy in the eyes of most educated Americans, North and South. To be sure, a handful of social scientists protested the *Brown* decision and continued to support discredited theories of the innate racial inferiority of blacks. But these scientific racists had no impact on the larger community of social scientists. The American Anthropological Association, Society for the Psychological Study of Social Issues, and the Society for the Study of Social Problems all passed resolutions reaffirming that science offered no support for the theory of inherent racial differences in intelligence.[68] Few southern intellectuals of significant stature joined the campaign against the Supreme Court decision. Howard Odum and Guy Johnson called on their fellow southerners to obey the Supreme Court ruling. Leading southern journalists such as Jonathan Daniels and Ralph McGill, whatever their private misgivings about the quickening pace of change, publicly opposed massive resistance.[69]

The attacks of segregationists merely enhanced the status of *An American Dilemma* in other quarters. A year after *Brown*, the Chicago sociologist Ernest W. Burgess declared that Myrdal's book had been of "first importance" in recent "epoch-making advances in the field of race relations." He considered *An American Dilemma* "the most powerful instrument of action in the field of race relations since Harriet Beecher Stowe's *Uncle Tom's Cabin*." The historian Oscar Handlin agreed that "few serious studies of American society have been more widely read than Gunnar Myrdal's social-science classic." He termed the book "a magnet to scholars and a catalyst to political groups" and observed that "its recommendations have helped shape the strategy of every organization interested in legislation and in judicial interpretations."[70]

Myrdal's moral challenge to Americans resonated through the early years of the civil rights struggle. While many whites were surprised by the sudden outbreak of a mass movement among southern blacks in 1960, Myrdal had forecast it, though he had not foreseen the critical role of the black church and of college students within the movement. When reporters asked black college students in Greensboro, North Carolina, what ideas had contributed to their decision to undertake the first sit-in demonstration in February 1960, they responded that they were influenced by Myrdal as well as by Gandhi and the novelist Lillian Smith.[71]

No one expressed the tenets of moralistic liberalism more eloquently than Martin Luther King, and no black leader had a surer grasp of how to appeal to the conscience of white America. In his 1963 "I Have a Dream" speech, King called on the nation to "live out the true meaning of its creed—we hold these truths to be self-evident, that all men are created equal." King embraced Myrdal's central argument in his last book, *Where Do We Go from Here: Chaos or Community?* "Ever since the birth of our nation," he wrote, "white America has had a schizophrenic personality on the question of race. She has been torn between selves—a self in which she proudly professed the great principles of democracy and a self in which she sadly practiced the antithesis of democracy."[72]

Presidents Kennedy and Johnson haltingly took up the rhetoric of racial liberalism in response to accelerating black protest across the South. During his years in the House and Senate, John F. Kennedy had never been in the forefront of the movement for civil rights legislation. Regarding himself as a tough-minded pragmatist, he distanced himself from crusading liberals and sought to set a domestic agenda of carefully managed change. But when he was elected president by a slim majority in 1960, Kennedy realized that he would need both the black vote and white southern support to win reelection in 1964. He therefore sought to contain the civil rights movement by limiting the federal government to filing suits on behalf of black voting rights and to quietly seeking voluntary pledges from private industry not to discriminate in employment policy. But the direct-action tactics of civil rights groups in the South forced Kennedy to act. When white mobs attacked freedom riders in Alabama in 1961, the president reluctantly sent four hundred federal marshals to protect them after the governor of Alabama refused to guarantee their safety. The following year, Kennedy dispatched troops to Oxford, Mississippi, to protect James Meredith, the first black to enroll at the University of Mississippi. The decisive event compelling Kennedy to change course was the series of civil rights marches in Birmingham led by Martin Luther King in the spring of 1963. When nonviolent demonstrators were bitten by police dogs and knocked down by high-pressure fire hoses, the international outcry was exceedingly embarrassing to the United States government.[73]

Faced with the failure of his gradualist civil rights strategy, Kennedy went on national television and announced that he was sending to Congress a strong civil rights bill. Improvising upon a speech written by Theodore Sorensen, he declared:

> We are confronted primarily with a moral issue. It is as old as the scriptures and is as clear as the American Constitution.
>
> The heart of the question is whether all Americans are to be afforded equal rights and equal opportunities, whether we are going to treat our fellow Americans as we want to be treated. If an American, because his skin is dark, cannot eat lunch in a restaurant open to the public, if he cannot send his children to the best public school available, if he cannot vote for the public officials who represent him, if, in short, he cannot enjoy the full and free life which all of us want, then who among us would be content to have the color of his skin changed and stand in his place? Who among us would then be content with the counsels of patience and delay?[74]

The president made it clear that the issue required immediate attention if violence were to be averted. Civil rights legislation was necessary to "move this problem from the streets to the courts." Citing statistics compiled by social scientists, Kennedy observed that "the Negro baby born in America today . . . has about one-half as much chance of completing high school as a white baby born in the same place on the same day, one-third as much chance of completing college, one-third as much chance of becoming a professional man, twice as much chance of becoming unemployed, about one-seventh as much chance of earning $10,000 a year, a life expectancy which is 7 years shorter, and the prospects of earning only half as much." Pointing to the international implications of the issue, the president inquired: "We preach freedom around the world, and we mean it, and we cherish our freedom here at home, but are we to say to the world, and much more importantly, to each other that this is a land of the free except for the Negroes; that we have no second-class citizens except Negroes; that we have no class or caste system, no ghettoes, no master race except with respect to Negroes?"

In his framing of the civil rights issue as a moral question, in his conception of the black struggle as a demand for individual civil rights, in his emphasis upon the doctrine of equality of opportunity, and in his assumption that skin color, rather than culture, was the only thing that separated black from white Americans, Kennedy faithfully reiterated the liberal orthodoxy that Myrdal had helped to put in place among American intellectuals twenty years earlier. His use of quantitative evidence and reference to the class and caste system revealed the extent to which social science ideas had penetrated the consciousness of educated Americans. The president's warnings of violence if nothing were done, his emphasis upon the international implications of domestic racial inequality, and his reference to the Nazi "master race" theory all recalled the conclusion of *An American Dilemma*.

After Kennedy's assassination, his successor, Lyndon B. Johnson, pushed the civil rights bill through Congress in 1964 as a memorial to the slain president, subduing in a few months the southern opposition that had killed or weakened civil rights legislation for decades. When Martin Luther King dramatized to the nation the continuing violence with which white authorities responded to blacks who attempted to register to vote in Selma, Alabama, Johnson went before a joint session of Congress on prime-time television on March 15, 1965, and called for voting rights legislation designed to send federal registrars into the counties of the South in which few blacks voted. Calling on all Americans to "overcome the crippling legacy of bigotry and injustice," the Texan resolved that "we . . . shall . . . overcome."[75]

The endorsement of civil rights legislation by presidents Kennedy and Johnson gave to racial liberalism a degree of public legitimacy that would have been inconceivable to all but the most optimistic observers in the late 1930s when Myrdal first tackled the "Negro problem." It had taken beatings, jailings, terror, and murder to shock white Americans into taking steps to guarantee to southern blacks their rights under the Constitution. Yet never before had the United States seen a president and a Congress so committed to federal intervention on the civil rights issue. And Johnson did not propose to stop there. Enjoying the support of large Democratic majorities in both houses of Congress, the president declared war on poverty and proposed the most ambitious program of social engineering since the New Deal. With the most visible forms of segregation crumbling in the urban South, as restaurants, theaters, and motels accommodated blacks in the wake of the Civil Rights Act, liberals triumphantly concluded that stateways could indeed change folkways.[76] Now they turned to the task of improving black job opportunities and addressing the needs of Afro-Americans in the urban ghettos in the North.

On June 4, 1965, with the voting rights bill on its way toward passage, Johnson spoke at Howard University about the unfinished agenda for black Americans. In a text that had been approved in advance by Martin Luther King, Whitney Young, and Roy Wilkins, the president proclaimed that the administration sought to achieve not just equality of opportunity for blacks, but "equality as a fact": "But freedom is not enough. You do not wipe away the scars of centuries by saying: Now you are free to go where you want, do as you desire, and choose the leaders you please.

"You do not take a person who, for years, has been hobbled by chains and liberate him, bring him up to the starting line of a race and then say, 'you are free to compete with all the others,' and still justly believe that you have been completely fair."

Drawing upon a then-unpublished report on the black family by Assistant Secretary of Labor Daniel Patrick Moynihan, Johnson suggested that family disorganization was a leading cause of the social problems of the urban black poor. Pledging a strong antipoverty program, he announced that he was calling a conference of scholars and black leaders at the White House to draw up a blueprint for the campaign to create "equality as a fact and equality as a result."[77]

The chances of finding a consensus among social science experts and black leaders were quickly disappearing, however. The civil rights movement was beginning to fragment, and the liberal orthodoxy that had helped to give the movement such legitimacy among whites was on the verge of collapse. The causes of the decline of the liberal orthodoxy stemmed, for the most part, from the politics of the black protest rather than from disputes within the academic world. The young black activists within the Student Nonviolent Coordinating Committee (SNCC) had been alienated from the Kennedy administration as early as 1961 over the administration's failure to protect civil rights workers from white violence in the South. SNCC's emphasis upon grass-roots organization and participatory democracy had always been at odds with the technocratic liberalism and social engineering advocated by mainstream liberals. The SNCC activists' suspicion of the federal government and of liberal Democrats had deepened after Lyndon Johnson and his lieutenants offered the Mississippi Freedom Democrats only token representation at the 1964 Democratic National Convention. Yet SNCC leaders had not sought to emphasize these differences before the national media during the struggles for the Civil Rights Act and Voting Rights Act. In the wake of the Voting Rights Act, however, SNCC militants focused on increasing black political and economic power in the South through all-black political organizations and cooperatives. Differing from Martin Luther King and most other black leaders, they argued that the black movement needed to be freed from white influence. The young black activists who had endured countless beatings, jailings, and the omnipresent threat of death advocated self-defense instead of nonviolence, and they were in no mood to tolerate the paternalism that they often encountered in white liberals.[78]

The implications of the new militance among young black activists were felt in all fields of intellectual expression as Afro-American writers, artists, and scholars emphasized their independence from white political and cultural authority and sought to attain the important but elusive goal of self-determination. James Baldwin, in his best-selling book, *The Fire Next Time* (1963), had charged that "white Americans find it as difficult as white people elsewhere do to divest themselves of the notion that they are in possession of some intrinsic value that black people need, or want." Portraying white American culture as intrinsically racist and emotionally sterile, he asked: "Do I really want to be integrated into a burning house?" Baldwin admonished white Americans that "the Negroes of this country may never be able to rise to power, but they are very well placed indeed to precipitate chaos and ring down the curtain on the American dream."[79] Malcolm X's resolute independence and the eerie calm with which he referred to whites as "devils" and prophesied their demise in appearances on TV talk shows exhilarated and amused many blacks who did not embrace his Muslim faith or agree with his advocacy of retaliatory violence. The Afro-centrism of the Muslims and of LeRoi Jones's (Imamu Amiri Baraka's) *Blues People* (1963) anticipated the trend toward Afro-American nationalism that would flourish on college campuses and in ghettos across the nation after the advent of the Black Power movement in 1966.[80] In the early and mid-sixties, however, the tone of heightened militance, the warnings of violence, and the specter of separatism were seen by most white liberal intellectuals as portents of an impending nightmare if black Americans did not get a piece of the American dream.

As black intellectuals publicly voiced their lack of faith in the conscience of white America, white liberals groped for a response and began to reconsider their commitment to the standard program of civil rights, integration, equal opportunity, and assimilation of blacks into white culture. Some of the tensions within liberalism were apparent in a roundtable discussion, "Liberalism and the Negro," at New York's Town Hall, a transcript of which was published in *Commentary* magazine in March 1964. At this dramatic encounter, moderated by *Commentary* editor Norman Podhoretz, Baldwin faced three white liberals: the sociologist Nathan Glazer, the philosopher Sidney Hook, and Gunnar Myrdal. For the previous twenty years, Myrdal had not answered criticisms of *An American Dilemma*, had not participated in scholarly debates about American race relations, and had rarely spoken publicly in the United States about the race question.

The terms of the debate were set by Baldwin, who declared that black people were not humbly petitioning whites to let them integrate one by one into American institutions. The whole system, in his view, needed a radical restructuring. Baldwin invoked Myrdal's observation that "before one can really talk about the Negro problem in this country, one has got to talk about the white people's problem." But the novelist, unlike Myrdal, insisted that the United States was "essentially *not* ethical." Baldwin dismissed the American creed, commenting, "If I had believed, if any Negro on my block had really believed what the American Republic said about itself, he would have ended up in Bellevue [a mental hospital]. If you are a Negro, you understand that somehow you have to operate outside the system and beat these people at their own game—which means that your real education essentially occurs outside of books." When Podhoretz asked Baldwin if it were "conceivable . . . that the Negroes will within the next five or ten or twenty years take their rightful place as one of the competing groups in the American pluralistic pattern," Baldwin rejected the terms of the question. He was not so sure, he said, that blacks wanted a piece of that pie. "From . . . my personal point of view," he exclaimed, "there is much in that American pie that isn't worth eating."[81]

Myrdal, addressing the question of whether the American system was "ethical," reaffirmed his belief that "this country succeeds in living a very sinful life without being deeply cynical. That is the difference between Europe and America, and it signifies that ethics *means* something here." Myrdal judged that there had been significant changes in white racial attitudes during the previous twenty years, but he continued to insist that "no upper class ever gave up its monopoly or its privileges out of ethical principles; the submerged group needs power to force its way in, and it is this that makes the ethical principles prevail. . . . So power is important, but attitudes and ethical principles count also."[82]

Noting that the civil rights movement was gaining legitimacy, Myrdal expressed confidence that racial distinctions would soon be removed from American law, but he worried about the situation of the poor of both races. He had recently published an economic study, *Challenge to Affluence* (1963), in which he had argued that the only way for the United States to overcome its problem with economic stagnation was to develop programs to educate, train, and provide jobs for the unemployed. Borrowing an old Swedish term for the lower class, *underklassen*, he had written about the problems of a growing "under-class" of poor people of various ethnic groups who were not sharing in the affluence of American life.[83] In the *Commentary* roundtable debate, Myrdal insisted that a massive national effort to lift the multiracial underclass out of poverty was the crucial next step for the United States, and he agreed with Baldwin that it would mean "remaking American society." He thought it politically impossible to help only blacks, however, and recommended an antipoverty program designed to assist the poor of all ethnic groups. Myrdal opposed preferential treatment for blacks on the grounds that it would "tend to make firmer and more lasting the differences among groups." Still a staunch assimilationist, Myrdal proclaimed that he looked forward "to a society which is color blind" and claimed that he had visited "a few university campuses . . . where people already move around together and don't notice who is Negro and who is white."[84]

Baldwin provoked loud protests from the white American members of the roundtable by terming white liberals an "affliction" and deploring their "missionary complex" and attitude that "they must help me into the light." Myrdal acknowledged that white liberals often "need you to give them a push," but he lectured Baldwin that "you will have to rely upon the liberals because . . . it's not the conservatives who are going to fight for the bigger reforms . . . to eradicate poverty . . . , to create a fully mobile society where everyone can get ahead through education and hard work, to liberate the *whole* submerged group." Myrdal hoped that blacks "will help the liberals to get into power and do the job that has to be done."[85]

Kenneth Clark, a member of the audience, rose to support Baldwin for "helping some of the rest of us cope with this difficult problem of facing the American liberal with the fact that in relation to the Negro he has never been as liberal as he likes to profess." Clark pointed out that he had been identified with American liberalism throughout most of his adult life, but he added that "I must confess bluntly that I now see white American liberalism primarily in terms of the adjective 'white.'" He warned that blacks now had to "learn how they can deal with a curious and insidious adversary—much more insidious than the out-and-out bigot." Turning to his mentor, he continued: "With all due respect to my friend and former colleague and boss, Professor Myrdal, I have come to the conclusion that so far as the Negro is concerned, the ethical aspect of American liberalism or the American Creed is primarily verbal. There is a peculiar kind of ambivalence in American liberalism, a persistent verbal liberalism that is never capable of overcoming an equally persistent illiberalism of action."[86]

The *Commentary* roundtable exposed some profound fissures in the civil rights coalition. Myrdal, though emphasizing a war on poverty more than the appeal to American ideals, still offered essentially the same liberal vision of civil rights, integration, assimilation, and equal economic opportunity. Baldwin's comments, though offered with the hyperbole of a man of letters, anticipated the kinds of criticisms of the liberal orthodoxy that black intellectuals would make with growing frequency and heightened intensity in the years ahead.[87]

Kenneth Clark's claim that the words of the American creed were often belied by an "illiberalism of action" reflected the views of an increasing number of social scientists. As the civil rights battle raged across the South, social scientists grappled with Myrdal's moral dilemma thesis and its optimistic conclusion that white Americans would bring their racial practices into line with their ideals. A social science critique of Myrdal's central argument had been building for two decades, even though the book enjoyed enormous prestige as the leading interpretation of American race relations. In the late 1940s and 1950s, several social scientists had disputed Myrdal's moral dilemma thesis and criticized his optimism about the prospect of lessening racial prejudice. Though this critique had quietly gained momentum by the early 1960s, it had not dislodged *An American Dilemma* from its position of primacy in the field, in part because the critics found much to agree with in the book even as they questioned its central thesis, and in part because no new synthesis was at hand to take its place. In 1949 the Columbia sociologist Robert Merton had suggested that adherence to the American creed was "unevenly distributed throughout the society, being institutionalized as an integral part of local culture in some regions and rejected in others." Merton argued that a strongly prejudiced person did not feel a conflict between his ideals and his behavior. Such a person's ideals "proclaim the right, even the duty, of discrimination." According to Merton, social science investigations indicated that college-educated people were as likely to practice discrimination as people with less education. A person might declare himself free of prejudice, profess allegiance to the generalized norms of the American creed," and still practice discrimination in specific situations, Merton observed. The Columbia sociologist also maintained that campaigns against prejudice disseminated through the mass media did not reduce ethnic hostility among strongly prejudiced people, who either evaded the propaganda or "selectively assimilated" the propaganda into their "prejudice-system."[88]

Drawing on recent research in social psychology and sociology, Nahum Medalia offered a reevaluation of Myrdal's moral dilemma argument in a 1962 article in *Social Forces*. "Myrdal's thesis has become so well institutionalized among sociologists," he wrote, "that its assumptions have never been systematically examined." Medalia challenged Myrdal's assumption that a unified national creed was necessary for the social integration of a complex urban society. Citing David Riesman and Karl Mannheim, he claimed that mass society tends to produce a variety of different value systems and that individuals hold "diverse and . . . incompatible values" within their own consciousness.[89] Instead of a simple conflict between the American creed and racial prejudice, Medalia saw a process in which whites "repress their generalized feelings and attitudes" toward blacks in specific situations. He pointed to a study of whites in Chicago who "1) resided in a neighborhood strongly opposed to the acceptance of Negroes, 2) belonged to a union which implemented a policy of Negro-white equality, 3) shopped mainly in stores which served Negroes on the basis of complete equality." Whites adapted their behavior to each of these situations.[90] Turning to massive resistance in the South, Medalia reiterated Merton's argument that segregation "may well assume the status of a creed, rather than an aberration of one," but suggested that the southern insistence on "no social equality" was rooted in a "rural-folk" society which did not recognize a social distance between the world of work and the home. As the

South became more urbanized and industrialized, he predicted that the "processes of role differentiation, and psychic segregation between different social contexts" would "together operate to restructure and delimit segregation between the races in the South." Medalia doubted that the American creed would triumph in all spheres of life. He predicted that white southerners, like their northern counterparts, would learn to treat blacks "universalistically" as "customers, voters, employees, litigants, riders on public transportation, or students in public schools" but they would continue to discriminate in spheres closer to home.[91]

Medalia's critique, coded as it was in sociologese, reached few readers outside the academy, but in 1964, the white liberal journalist Charles E. Silberman pointed out the weaknesses of Myrdal's moral dilemma argument in his best-selling book, *Crisis in Black and White*. "The tragedy of race relations in the United States," Silberman wrote, "is that there is no American Dilemma." He sadly concluded that "white Americans are not torn and tortured by the conflict between their devotion to the American creed and their actual behavior." What upset them about the civil rights movement was that "their peace is being shattered and their business interrupted."[92]

Liberalism in Crisis

It was not just Myrdal's moral dilemma thesis that was in jeopardy by the mid-1960s. His whole strategy of appealing to the conscience of whites, which had been brilliantly executed by Martin Luther King, was giving way to an emphasis upon black political power.[93] His conception of the black struggle in terms of individual rights was yielding to a framework that emphasized group rights.[94] The other elements of the liberal orthodoxy would soon come under assault as well. Responding to a more militant and radical black movement, scholars questioned prevailing assumptions about the nature of Afro-American culture, the desirability of top-down social engineering by the federal government, and the doctrine of equal opportunity. The event that triggered this debunking of remnants of the liberal orthodoxy was the publication of Moynihan's report on the black family, which Lyndon Johnson had hoped to use as the basis for a White House conference in which social science experts and black leaders would reach a consensus on how to achieve "equality of results."

Moynihan, a political scientist who had worked on a variety of public policy issues concerning ethnicity and urban affairs, wrote his report for a small audience of top policymakers in the Johnson administration. He oversimplified the complex situation of lower-class black families in the hope of stimulating government officials to take immediate action on the issue.[95] Invoking Myrdal in his preface, Moynihan warned that the nation was "approaching a new crisis in race relations." "The fundamental problem," he announced, "is that of family structure." Social science evidence indicated that "the Negro family in the urban ghettos is crumbling." Unless the government developed a new set of policies aimed at "the establishment of a stable Negro family structure," the "cycle of poverty and disadvantage would continue to repeat itself." To support these assertions, Moynihan offered a distillation of the conventional wisdom among liberal social scientists on the black family. Citing Frazier and the sociologist Nathan Glazer, he outlined the damage to Afro-American family structure from enslavement to urbanization. Moynihan argued that Negro youth, crippled by a "matriarchal" family structure in a "patriarchal" society, were caught in a "tangle of pathology" that was difficult to overcome—even in an era of heightened support for civil rights. He assumed, like Frazier and Myrdal, that Afro-American culture was an imperfectly assimilated version of white culture, and that differences between black and white culture could be explained in terms of black deficiencies caused by racism.[96]

The assistant secretary did differ from Frazier and Myrdal, however, in contending that lower-class black family structure was the *fundamental* issue in the crisis in race relations. Frazier, writing in 1939, had seen the "breakdown" and "pathology" of urban black families as part of a larger cycle of change in race relations, resulting from the breakdown of Negro "peasant" culture under the impact of urbanization and 50 percent unemployment rates during the Depression. Instead of viewing family structure as the fundamental issue, Frazier had expected that the "social disorganization" of the black family would lead to a "reorganization" in which blacks would become part of an insurgent working class pressing for a socialist transformation of society.[97] Myrdal, as we have seen, considered black family structure such a minor part of the larger picture of race relations tha the delegated the writing of the chapter concerning the black family and culture to Arnold Rose after he returned to Sweden. Nor did Myrdal embrace such an avowedly patriarchal model of family life as Moynihan. Frazier and Myrdal did, however, emphasize the social pathologies of black culture, and Moynihan argued that the tangle of pathology had seriously worsened in the years since World War II.

Although he wrote the report to prod policymakers to adopt measures designed to alleviate black poverty, Moynihan omitted his policy recommendations from the report because he wanted government officials to focus first on the problem itself and he feared that premature discussions of budget estimates might detract from the sense of urgency he sought to convey to the president and his advisors. Moynihan favored a standard liberal agenda of jobs, income maintenance programs, housing, and birth control for the urban poor. He did, however, believe that all government programs should be evaluated in terms of their effect on black family structure, and he thought that further studies were needed to determine if Aid to Families with Dependent Children policies caused black men to leave home. Since he did not share these policy ideas with his readers, Moynihan ended the report on an ambiguous note that some readers interpreted as implying a strategy of black self-help or an emphasis by the government on therapeutic programs of family counseling rather than jobs or the enhancement of black political power.[98] The Moynihan report did not have the pervasive moral language of *An American Dilemma*, but it did contain the same faith in social engineering and the conviction that the state had the responsibility to intervene to "strengthen" families.

The Moynihan report set off one of the most turbulent public controversies ever generated by a social science document. Civil rights leaders issued stinging rebukes. Floyd McKissick, the director of CORE, attacked Moynihan for assuming "that middle class American values are the correct ones for everyone in America." Bayard Rustin concurred, suggesting that "what may seem to be a disease to the white middle class may be a healthy adaptation to the Negro lower class."[99] McKissick's and Rustin's cultural relativist argument contrasted with the rhetorical strategy that most black leaders had used in the early stages of the civil rights struggle, when they had emphasized the cultural similarity between whites and blacks as an argument in favor of desegregation. James Farmer, while agreeing that Moynihan approached the subject with a white middle-class bias, shied away from the cultural relativist argument and maintained instead that black sexual behavior was not so different from white, but that blacks lacked access to information about contraception, illegal abortions, and divorce. Whitney Young, the moderate leader of the Urban League, was willing to accept Moynihan's definition of lower-class ghetto family patterns as pathological, but insisted that lower-class whites exhibited similar pathologies and that Moynihan had stigmatized all blacks when only a minority exhibited these behavior patterns.[100]

The deepest concern of black leaders, however, was that the Moynihan report would be used by government officials to blame blacks for their poverty and thereby provide an excuse for government inaction in the war on poverty and in enforcement of civil rights legislation.[101] McKissick charged that "Moynihan . . . emphasizes . . . negative aspects of the Negroes and then seems to say that it's the individual's fault when it's the damn system that really needs changing." Farmer sounded the alarm, asserting that the report "provides the fuel for a new racism. . . . It succeeds in taking the real tragedy of black poverty and serving it up as an essentially salacious 'discovery' suggesting that Negro mental health should be the first order of business in a civil rights revolution."[102]

Several social scientists questioned the assumptions, methods, and conclusions of Moynihan. The sociologist Herbert Gans made the cultural relativist argument that "however much the picture of family life painted in that report may grate on middle-class moral sensibilities, it may well be that instability, illegitimacy, and matriarchy are the most positive adaptations possible to the conditions which Negroes must endure."[103] The anthropologist Charles Valentine extended this argument and indicted Frazier, Glazer, and Moynihan for establishing a "pejorative tradition" of writing about lower-class black life.[104] William Ryan, a psychologist, contended that Moynihan saw the "unstable Negro family" as the cause of racial inequality rather than the result.[105] Finally, the sociologist Christopher

Jencks, while dismissing the accusations of many of Moynihan's critics as "paranoid," offered the following criticism from a socialist perspective: "The guiding assumption [of the Moynihan report] is that social pathology is caused less by basic defects in the social system than by defects in particular individuals and groups which prevent their adjusting to the system. The prescription is therefore to change the deviants, not the system."[106]

Why did Moynihan's rendition of the liberal orthodoxy set off such a donnybrook? Lee Rainwater and William Yancey note that Moynihan's omission of his policy recommendations made him vulnerable to unfair charges that he was "blaming the victim," and they point out that the press played up "sensational" aspects of the report in the weeks before it was made public.[107] But, more fundamentally, the civil rights movement was at a moment of transition. It had succeeded in winning legislation that dismantled many of the legal Jim Crow barriers in the South, and the nation was poised, many believed, for a historic assault on black poverty and powerlessness in the urban ghettos. Many black leaders and white critics feared that this report by an official in the Johnson administration would deflect the government from job programs and efforts to strengthen black political power by focusing attention on family questions. A growing number of radicals thought that the problem lay in the economic system, which produced wide disparities of income, required a certain amount of unemployment to keep wages low, and used unemployed black men as a reserve labor force. Many Afro-American intellectuals were tired of seeing blacks portrayed as victims. A type of social scientific analysis that had been a crucial part of the liberal indictment of racial inequality since Frazier's *Negro Family* and Myrdal's *An American Dilemma* now seemed demeaning. The civil rights movement had stimulated black pride, as two presidents had been forced to respond to organized black protest with substantive legislative changes. Blacks reacted viscerally against the image of themselves as patients surrounded by social scientists taking their pulse and probing their pathologies. Finally, veterans of the civil rights movement had come to feel a deep suspicion of the federal government, stemming from the hesitation that the Kennedy and Johnson administrations had shown in embracing civil rights and the reluctance of both presidents to protect civil rights workers from white violence in the South. Black leaders would continue to fight for programs that delivered jobs and political power to black communities, but the ambitious vision of social engineering by the federal government that had seemed so liberating to Gunnar Myrdal was beginning to look coercive to many Afro-American activists.

When the White House held a planning session for its civil rights conference in November 1965, the conferees failed to achieve consensus on a program of economic and political advancement for blacks. The full conference was held in June 1966, and the delegates, carefully picked by the Johnson administration, gave the president a standing ovation, supported the policies of the administration, and defeated resolutions condemning the war in Vietnam.[108] The following year, Talcott Parsons attempted to prop up the faltering liberal orthodoxy in his introduction to a collection of essays that he edited with Kenneth Clark entitled *The Negro American*. Though Parsons avoided taking up Myrdal's moral dilemma thesis, he contended that the success of the civil rights movement could be explained by its strong "*moral* resonance" for Americans. The movement had brought together "elements of both races in a *common* moral cause" and contributed to "the current moral 'reenergizing' of American society." Parsons feared, however, the possibility of a "polarization" between the "radicals" in the movement and their opponents. He hoped that a process of polarization would be held in check by "the pluralistic institutional frameworks of the society" and the "moral values characterized by Myrdal as the American creed." For Parsons, therefore, race was still preeminently a moral issue and the American creed was a means of keeping the civil rights movement within the bounds of peaceful, gradual reform.[109]

Events were quickly lurching out of control, however, and other liberals were moving beyond the Myrdalian framework. While Myrdal's work continued to be respected, there was no Myrdal school in American social science that controlled key journals and departments and whose members were prepared to leap to the defense of the master any time his ideas were criticized. At the American Academy of Arts and Sciences conference that led to the volume Parsons edited, Myrdal's name rarely came up during the discussions. Liberal social scientists discussed a host of social engineering proposals, such as busing, compensatory education programs, preferential hiring, and job training for the "hard core unemployed," but they devoted little attention to the moral dilemma or the problem of changing white attitudes. Thomas F. Pettigrew suggested that "one of the great fallacies we have in the field of race relations for many, many decades has been to worry about attitudes rather than about conditions. It is a crude but, I think, generally correct statement to say that attitudes are more often a result than a cause of most of our race-relation situations. We have to worry about the more basic issues which until recently were never even considered as part of race-relation concerns."[110] Robin Williams, in his book *Strangers Next Door* (1964) also insisted that "*real societies are not made up of homogenized aggregates of interchangeable and unattached psychological molecules*" and emphasized the study of the social structures in which ethnic prejudices developed.[111]

Kenneth Clark, in his introductory essay to *The Negro American*, went further and declared that "the new American Dilemma is one of power." Though acknowledging the significance of appeals to morality, he contended that "ideals, at best, are part of a constellation of practical power imperatives and sometimes have sufficient strength to require at least the verbal commitment to change in their direction." The black psychologist knew that the rage of Afro-Americans would find more public expression as black people sought a stance that offered dignity and independence. Clark stressed the inevitability of conflict and the possibility of a retrogression in the status of blacks. "The Negro must be aware," he asserted, "that no fundamental change in his status can come about through deference to or patronage from whites." He conceded that Afro-Americans were a minority but argued that blacks had to accept the risks of confronting the white power structure rather than allow their fate to be determined by the "ideological consensus of the white majority." But while Clark sounded a note of political militance, he continued to agree with Myrdal's liberal vision of integration, assimilation, and economic reform within the framework of capitalism, and he ended the essay by citing Myrdal's claim, in *Challenge to Affluence*, that the way out of economic stagnation in the United States was to provide equality of economic opportunity to the poor. "Ideals alone," Clark concluded, "do not bring justice. Ideals, combined with necessity, may."[112]

While Clark sought to advance a more tough-minded liberalism—one focused on increasing black political and economic power—other Afro-American intellectuals broke more decisively with the liberal orthodoxy that had reigned supreme for the previous twenty years. A major challenge to Myrdal's interpretation of Afro-American culture had appeared in 1964 with the publication of Ralph Ellison's review of *An American Dilemma* in his collection of essays entitled *Shadow and Act*. Ellison's review, written in 1944, had remained unpublished for twenty years, but it would become an influential critique of Myrdal in the late 1960s in the wake of the controversy over the Moynihan report. The black novelist argued that Myrdal and other liberals, in their study of black social pathologies, had underestimated the capacity of black Americans to shape a rich and distinctive culture. Ellison quoted Myrdal's claim that "the Negro's entire life and, consequently, also his opinions on the Negro problem are, in the main, to be considered as secondary reactions to more primary pressures from the side of the dominant white majority." "But can a people," Ellison asked, "live and develop for over three hundred years simply by reacting? Are American Negroes simply the creation of white men, or have they at least helped to create themselves out of what they found around them? Men have made a life in caves and upon cliffs, why cannot Negroes have made a life upon the horns of the white man's dilemma?" Ellison concluded with a cultural pluralist argument that "in Negro culture there is much of value for America as a whole."[113]

Intellectuals in many fields sharply criticized the excessive emphasis that Myrdal and the postwar generation of social scientists and historians had put upon the damage done to black culture by racism. The controversies over Stanley Elkins's historical study, *Slavery* (1959), and William Styron's novel, *The Confessions of Nat Turner* (1967), both turned on the ways in which those authors portrayed the damage of slavery and underemphasized the resistance of slaves.[114] From the mid-1960s into the 1970s, anthropologists and sociologists developed new approaches to Afro-American culture that focused on the strengths of the black family and kinship networks, the cohesiveness of black communities, and the distinctiveness and resilience of Afro-American culture.[115] Instead of studying the experience of traumatized individuals, historians of slavery wrote about the ways in which slaves created a "slave community" and analyzed black folklore to understand slave resistance.[116]

In turning to these new concerns, scholars were responding, in part, to the new strains of Afro-American nationalism that captured a great deal of public attention after the election of Stokely Carmichael as SNCC chairman in 1966 and the adoption of a new battle cry, "Black Power!" On college campuses and in ghettos across the nation in the late 1960s, young blacks adopted natural hairstyles, gave clenched-fist salutes, and excluded whites from the black struggle as they sought to define an Afro-American political strategy and cultural identity. In the best-known political statement of nationalism, Stokely Carmichael and Charles V. Hamilton's *Black Power: The Politics of Liberation in America* (1967), the authors advocated community control of schools, all-black political movements, black cooperatives, and black business. Disdaining appeals to the white conscience, they asserted that "there is no 'American dilemma' because black people in this country form a colony, and it is not in the interest of the colonial power to liberate them." Carmichael and Hamilton directed attention to "institutional racism," the processes through which blacks were kept in a subordinate position despite civil rights laws and the end of de jure segregation.[117] Though nationalist political movements failed to develop a strong political base among black Americans, the nationalist interest in Afro-American culture and the concept of "black is beautiful" would have a lasting impact. As a result of black nationalism, the renewed interest in Afro-American culture, and the critique of the damage model, some black intellectuals questioned whether white scholars were capable of understanding the Afro-American experience. The majority of social scientists and historians who wrote about black Americans in the 1940s, 1950s, and 1960s were white, and many black scholars and students struggled for the establishment of black studies programs that would enable blacks to assert control over the study of black issues.[118]

Not everyone was pleased with black militance, however. Evidence of a white backlash against the civil rights movement had appeared in the North as early as 1964, when George Wallace, Alabama's segregationist governor, won protest votes in northern Democratic primaries against President Johnson by appealing to the fears of urban white Americans who worried about a black "invasion" of their neighborhoods and schools and were anxious about black competition for their jobs. A series of race riots in major American cities from 1965 to 1968 claimed the lives of scores of blacks and some whites and destroyed millions of dollars' worth of property. Stokely Carmichael and his successor as SNCC chairman, H. Rap Brown, attracted much media attention with violent rhetoric that deepened white anxieties. The Vietnam War also divided Americans and further undermined Johnson's liberal coalition. The war drained funds from the war on poverty, thereby dashing the hopes that Johnson had aroused by promising equality as a fact to black Americans. The assassination of Martin Luther King in April 1968 deprived the nation of the one civil rights leader capable of leading a broad interracial coalition committed to nonviolence, and Robert Kennedy's assassination, two months later, removed the one liberal political leader who was popular both with blacks and with blue-collar whites. That same year, the National Advisory Commission on Civil Disorders, investigating the causes of race riots, concluded that white racism was the source of the conflict and warned that the United States was "moving toward two societies, one black, one white—separate and unequal." With America deeply divided by the war and the race issue, Richard Nixon won the White House in 1968 in a campaign that appealed to the white backlash, stressed law and order, and pursued a "southern strategy" aimed at stalling the drive toward civil rights.[119]

With the civil rights movement divided and broken, the white student Left turning increasingly toward self-destructive violence, and the liberals out of power, the possibilities for achieving a consensus in support of a liberal policy on race relations were exhausted. The hopes of the early 1960s had been crushed as the war continued and the federal government failed to respond decisively to the economic needs of black Americans. Most intellectuals were deeply pessimistic, and Gunnar Myrdal's optimistic and idealistic approach to racial reform found far fewer adherents by the end of the decade. While liberal scholars had softened their criticisms of Myrdal during the height of the civil rights movement when the liberal orthodoxy had seemed an essential component of the struggle for racial equality, many candidly admitted in the late sixties that the book was deeply flawed. In a 1969 article in the *New York Times Magazine*, "Where Myrdal Went Wrong," the historian Carl Degler articulated for a general audience the social science critique of Myrdal's central argument. A white liberal whose interest in the history of black-white relations had been greatly stimulated by his reading of *An American Dilemma* twenty-five years earlier, Degler was broadly sympathetic to Myrdal's view of the race question as a moral issue, but he found Myrdal's optimism to be the book's greatest weakness. He observed that improvement in the status of blacks triggered greater hostility from many whites, not greater tolerance as Myrdal had predicted in his principle of cumulation. Degler argued that Myrdal had relied too heavily on education as the primary means of diminishing prejudice.[120] As northern ghettos erupted in riots and a virulent white backlash spread in all parts of the country, Myrdal's concept of the race issue as a moral dilemma, a "problem in the heart of the American," appeared naive and strangely antiquated. *An American Dilemma* offered few answers to such problems as the enduring poverty of the black urban underclass, the absence of black political power, and institutional racism.

A younger generation of radical scholars was not as reticent as the postwar generation in pointing out the flaws in Myrdal's work, which they saw as an "official orthodoxy within the sociological establishment." These scholars questioned the assumption that racism was a carryover from the past that was dying out as it came into contact with modern American values in an urban-industrial setting. Many were skeptical that the doctrine of equal opportunity within the capitalist economic system would raise the standard of living of the lowest class of poor blacks. Instead of viewing the race issue as a moral dilemma in the minds of white Americans, they held that racism was "integral in American society" and "central to the culture and interests of the white majority." They argued that the granting of civil rights to blacks would not alter existing power arrangements unless measures were taken to increase black political and economic power. According to this view, the elimination of racism would require serious social conflict and fundamental institutional change.[121]

An American Dilemma exerted a powerful influence on American intellectuals, the educated reading public, and policymakers for twenty years after its publication. Myrdal's book played a key role in the campaign against disfranchisement and segregation in the South; it convinced many whites that modern social science supported racial equality; it framed the question as a moral issue; and it helped to build some support for social engineering to lift the mass of blacks out of poverty. By the end of the sixties, however, many scholars concluded that Myrdal had been excessively optimistic about the power of education to reduce prejudice and that he had overlooked the many psychological strategies that whites could use to adhere formally to the general principles of the American creed and still practice many forms of racial discrimination. Most scholars rejected Myrdal's formulations about the pathologies of black culture as inadequate for understanding the complex social and cultural life of poor blacks. Myrdal's assimilationist assumptions clashed with the desire of many blacks to define a distinctive Afro-American cultural identity. Liberals had moved beyond Myrdal's idea of equality of opportunity to advocate new forms of social engineering designed to produce equality of results, while radicals argued that the whole system had to be changed.

The liberal orthodoxy had fallen, but no new orthodoxy had arisen to replace it. Social scientists were as divided as other intellectuals on the issue of race at the end of the 1960s. On the Left, black nationalists quarreled with Marxists in framing an analysis of American racism. In the center, liberal advocates of integration and assimilation differed from those who favored a model of consensual pluralism.[122] And on the Right, a variety of neoconservatives recoiled from expensive welfare programs and questioned the methods that liberals had used in the programs designed to eradicate poverty and achieve equality as a fact in race relations.[123]

If social scientists at the end of the sixties saw *An American Dilemma* as a work mainly of historic interest, that was not the view of Gunnar Myrdal. With rare exceptions, such as the 1964 *Commentary* roundtable, Myrdal had declined to participate in scholarly controversies about American race relations because he was living in Europe and India and writing about a variety of other issues. But he was not temperamentally inclined to sit on the sidelines or to allow his name to be invoked in connection with a dead orthodoxy. In the early 1970s, Myrdal would return to the United States, resume his struggle for a viable policy of racial liberalism, and attempt to call Americans back to the tenets of their creed.

8

Dreamer, Planner, and Fighter

An American Dilemma in Perspective

Gunnar Myrdal's influential study of American race relations was the work of a man who had long been committed to social engineering and to social science as a moral enterprise. *An American Dilemma* emerged, however, from a complex process of interaction between this politically minded intellectual and a foundation, a community of American social scientists, and broader currents of political, social, and economic change.

The "Negro problem" had not been a major political or intellectual issue nationally in 1935 when Newton Baker grew concerned about the unemployment and social problems of blacks in northern cities. Yet fundamental changes in black-white relations were under way, as the Depression drove thousands of southern blacks from rural areas to the cities of the North and South, where many appeared doomed to the status of long-term relief clients. The New Deal raised the hopes of Afro-Americans through relief and job programs and a rhetoric of concern for the poor, but the Roosevelt administration was not prepared to respond effectively to the emerging crisis in race relations. Refusing to touch the politically explosive civil rights issue, Roosevelt sanctioned segregation in many New Deal agencies and hoped that programs of economic aid for the poor of both races would gradually reduce racial hostility. The black protest movement grew more militant in the 1930s, but it was not united.

When Frederick Keppel took up Baker's suggestion for a Negro study, he knew little about Afro-Americans. He was aware, though, from dealing with the NAACP, the Urban League, the Encyclopedia of the Negro project, and with individual black scholars that no consensus existed among blacks on the proper approach to the race issue, and he encountered a wide range of opinions among white scholars as well. Keppel decided that the situation called for a sensitive diplomatic mission by a European with experience in public affairs—someone like Lord Hailey—who would make a dispassionate report on American race relations. When Melville Herskovits and Donald Young convinced him that blacks would not accept a study by a man from an imperial country as unbiased, he turned to Gunnar Myrdal as a Scandinavian scholar with experience in government and a strong reputation with former Rockefeller Foundation officers. In choosing Myrdal, Keppel made a leap in the dark, but he did manage to take the initiative in race relations research away from the American social scientists, who mostly wrote for specialized scholarly audiences, and hand it to an experienced, pragmatic problem solver who promised to come up with a fresh approach in a book aimed at a broad audience of educated Americans. The whole process of setting up the study was pervaded by a colonial mindset, a paternalistic attitude toward blacks, and by what scholars of a later generation would term institutional racism. The Carnegie Corporation never awarded large sums of money to black social scientists, and Keppel declined to fund Du Bois's proposed Encyclopedia of the Negro. Yet Keppel was to demonstrate a capacity for growth and change as he learned more about the race issue. He was a nineteenth-century liberal who did not believe in interfering with research: once he had found his "exceptional man," he was willing to let him have his say.

In Gunnar Myrdal, Keppel found a man with a unique combination of talents, experience, and commitment to social engineering and moral reform. Born into an egalitarian, rural society in Dalarna, Myrdal had watched his father leave that milieu to become a successful entrepreneur in Stockholm while retaining much of the religious and folk culture of his native region. As a gymnasium and university student in Stockholm, Myrdal had gradually rejected the piety of his upbringing and embraced instead the rationalism of the Enlightenment and the vision of using reason to enable humankind to plan for a more stable, prosperous, and peaceful world. An "intellectual aristocrat" during his undergraduate years, Myrdal had scorned the masses as ignorant and had briefly advocated a "party of the intelligent," consisting of bright men from all classes, who would reach a consensus on public policy and steer Sweden through the dangerous waters of parliamentary democracy. Largely apolitical during the 1920s, he had forged a brilliant career as an economist in the neoclassical tradition. In response to the Depression, he plunged into political life in Sweden, encouraged by Alva Myrdal, a Social Democratic feminist, and inspired in part by the broad-ranging vision of interdisciplinary research and social engineering he had encountered in the United States as a Rockefeller Fellow in 1929–30.

Myrdal's immersion in Social Democratic politics had resolved some of the tensions he had felt in moving through so many different worlds. His efforts to combat unemployment, poverty, and substandard housing drew on the egalitarianism and moral values of his childhood, and his work in economic planning and the formulation of social welfare policy carried forth the vision of the Enlightenment. Yet there remained in his thought a tension between his commitment to equality and his infatuation with an elitist conception of social engineering. He tried to resolve the tension by drawing the "instrumental norm" for his research from the valuations of the population being studied. As a member of royal commissions and parliamentary committees, Myrdal also worked with representatives of various interest groups to broker compromises, helping to steer Sweden along its middle way of Social Democratic reform that avoided the extremes of fascism and communism. Though nominally a socialist, he was relatively uninterested in stimulating greater political participation by workers and farmers at the grass-roots level. Myrdal brought to his study of American race relations an extraordinary range of experience with such issues as unemployment, banking, agriculture, housing, and population. Most significantly—and in contrast to most American scholars—he brought a conception of social science as a process of moral inquiry and a belief that social engineering was the "supreme task of an accomplished social science."

After his arrival in the United States in 1938, Myrdal set out to put the issues of civil rights and black poverty on the policy agenda of the federal government. Approaching his task with supreme self-assurance, he perceived his invitation from the Carnegie Corporation as a quasi-official commission to produce a major investigation that would shape public policy on a crucial issue. Adroitly manipulating Keppel's admiration for European scholars, Myrdal used the power, financial resources, and political and educational contacts of the Carnegie Corporation to create a large, collaborative study with social scientists and activists representing a broad spectrum of centrist, liberal, and radical opinions. Drawing upon his experience with royal commissions and parliamentary committees, Myrdal sought to create a consensus behind a liberal analysis of American race relations. He was especially careful to include as many young black scholars as possible in his study—a notable departure from the usual practice in American social science—but neither black nor white collaborators were given any control over the final report, which was to be written by Myrdal alone. This procedure set off a battle among American social scientists to influence the future direction of foundation grants in the area of race relations and Negro studies, as social scientists and political activists scrambled to get their ideas before the Swedish visitor. Not content to rely on the reports of his collaborators, Myrdal set out to see much of America for himself. In his travels with Ralph Bunche along the back roads of the South and in his visits to urban ghettos, Myrdal encountered poverty and human suffering on a scale that exceeded anything he had ever seen. And yet he also discerned among many Americans a will to do something about it and a moral earnestness and optimism that he found lacking among most Europeans.

Myrdal's experience in Sweden during 1940–41 convinced him that ideas did matter, that a democratic political ideology did profoundly affect a people's ability to resist fascism. Disturbed by the restrictions on freedom of the press, by the self-censorship of Swedish journalists, and by the extent of official accommodation to Nazi Germany, Gunnar and Alva Myrdal concluded that Swedes needed something like the American creed to guide them in maintaining democratic principles and procedures in the face of German diplomatic pressure and the threat of invasion. In *Kontakt med Amerika* they argued that Swedish intellectuals faced a "moral dilemma": if they criticized Nazi Germany too severely, they might provoke an invasion by their powerful neighbor, but if they remained silent, they contributed to a moral defeatism in which the nation forgot the principles that it stood for. Gunnar Myrdal's action in interrupting his study of American race relations to return home was, in many ways, a quixotic gesture, since there was very little that he or any other intellectual could do that would make a difference in the fate of a small neutral country that was surrounded by German armies. He felt anguish over the fact that friends in Germany and in German-occupied countries had been imprisoned or killed for resisting Nazism, and he felt guilty that he, as a citizen of a neutral nation, was not directly fighting Hitler. Nevertheless, Myrdal believed that it was important for a Swedish intellectual to struggle against fascism in spite of the odds. It was up to the intellectuals to articulate the principles that the nation stood for, to help the Swedish people maintain a spirit of resistance, to set an example of refusing to give in to defeatism, and to carry on their own work of planning for a better world after the war. Optimism, he realized, would not guarantee a democratic Sweden, but pessimism would ensure a defeat of the principles of the Enlightenment. Addressing American race relations in *Kontakt med Amerika*, Gunnar Myrdal reconceptualized the problem as a "moral dilemma," a conflict in the mind of the American between the principles of the American creed and the practice of racial discrimination. However vague and nebulous the American creed would seem to a later generation of critics, it appeared to Gunnar Myrdal to be a palpable, functioning set of values that was vital to the struggle against Nazism and a potential source of leverage against racial discrimination in the United States.

Resuming his work in the United States in March 1941, Myrdal found the opportunity to take the decisive stand against fascism that he had been unable to take in Sweden. He fashioned a powerful interpretation of American race relations that flattered Americans about their culture and political principles even as it challenged them to live up to their creed. In emphasizing the importance of the American creed in the minds of ordinary Americans, Myrdal was responding to the heightened interest of American intellectuals of the late 1930s and early 1940s in defining the national identity in terms of democratic values of the national tradition—what the historian Ralph Gabriel called the "American democratic faith." Myrdal seriously exaggerated the influence of these values on behavior in everyday life, but in doing so, he was ascribing to the American people the concerns of its intellectuals.

Myrdal reinjected a moral language into social science discussions of race relations after a generation of scientific naturalism. In challenging Americans to live up to their ideals, he was using a rhetorical strategy that reformers from Frederick Douglass to Walter White had employed for over a century but that had not been prominent in the social science literature on race and ethnicity in the 1920s and 1930s. Myrdal did not, however, simply point out a discrepancy between ideals and practice; he argued that white Americans experienced the contradiction as a psychological and moral conflict—one that would grow more acute as black Americans pressed their grievances to the forefront of political debate. Since the moral dilemma thesis developed out of Myrdal's conversations with Americans and was formulated in Sweden, it was not an initial hypothesis for the study, and therefore it did not rest on any empirical testing of the attitudes of white Americans.

The conflict between the American creed and racial inequality was not merely a psychological issue, in Myrdal's view. It had institutional, economic, and social structural dimensions as well. Encouraged by the New Deal's interest in planning and concern for the poor, Myrdal put aside his doubts about the ability of the federal government to plan for full employment after the war and suggested that the trends toward federal regulation of the labor market and unionization would lead to greater equality of opportunity for blacks. He saw the black vote in the North as a strategic factor that would compel both political parties to address the civil rights issue, and he prophesied that the Supreme Court would continue to broaden the scope of its rulings, demanding compliance with the Fourteenth and Fifteenth Amendments in areas such as voting rights, jury selection, and higher education.

Myrdal's analysis of Afro-American institutions and culture constituted the weakest part of the book. Though he was familiar with their work, he largely ignored the attention that Du Bois, Woodson, Charles S. Johnson, and Herskovits had given to the strengths of black culture. Strongly influenced by Bunche and Frazier, he saw blacks as "shut in by caste": barred from participating in the broader society, they turned their anger inward and escaped into otherworldly religion, "trivial" social clubs, or ideologies of race chauvinism. Like Bunche and Frazier, Myrdal portrayed most black institutions as the fiefdoms of a black petit bourgeois elite that used appeals to race solidarity as a way of securing the allegiance of the black masses. Building on the work of Frazier, Myrdal portrayed Afro-American culture as rife with social pathologies caused by racial oppression, poverty, and social isolation. But while Frazier had seen the social disorganization of the black poor in the cities as a prelude to the development of a new interracial working-class culture, Myrdal was more dubious about such a development and viewed social engineering by the federal government and black adjustment to the norms of white middle-class society as the only cures for these pathologies.

In his conclusion, Myrdal predicted a convergence of trends that would force the issue of black equality before the white public: the increasingly militant tactics of the black movement, the legal campaign against segregation and discrimination, the growing significance of the black vote, and the rising importance of blacks within the labor movement. From his perspective as a foreign observer, he described the ideological terrain of the war against Nazi racism, prophesied the increasing power of colored peoples in the world after the war, and warned of the embarrassment that segregation and discrimination would cause the United States. Whatever his private doubts, Myrdal wrote with a fervent optimism about the power of the American creed to vanquish racial inequality. Anything less, in his view, would have been defeatism. Though he had made a number of gradualist suggestions in the book about enfranchising blacks in stages and approaching desegregation from graduate schools down, the rhetoric of the last chapter was so pervaded by a moral immediatism that many readers interpreted the book as a call for immediate enfranchisement of southern blacks, desegregation of all public institutions, and the elimination of the color line from American life.

In writing *An American Dilemma*, Gunnar Myrdal drew on the values that had sustained his life and thought. Though he had rebelled against his religious upbringing, he concluded the book with a jeremiad offering Americans a choice between following their creed or succumbing to the protracted conflict of a nation at war with itself. Like earlier American Jeremiahs, Myrdal was confident that, in the end, the democratic creed would win out over the false god of racism. He deliberately concluded the book with the word *Enlightenment*, the intellectual movement that had been the touchstone for his thought since his gymnasium years, the source of the modern ideas of human rights for both liberals and social democrats. *An American Dilemma* also contained, in many passages, the language of elite reform that Myrdal had learned as a gymnasium and university student, practiced by writing speeches for his father, and developed by arguing for prophylactic reforms in parliamentary debates of the 1930s. The book combines liberal and social democratic ideas in a social welfare ideology that he had called for in the early 1930s as an alternative to both fascism and Stalinist communism. Myrdal assumed, in *Kontakt med Amerika*, *An American Dilemma*, and *Amerika mitt i världen* that New Deal liberalism would evolve into a social democratic movement, with business leaders accepting greater government regulation and workers, farmers, and black Americans becoming better organized into unions and protest organizations. It was not until he did the research for *Varning för fredsoptimism* in 1943 that he perceived that American politics were moving to the right, leading to a reaction against "big government" at home and suspicion of the Soviet Union abroad. To be sure, *An American Dilemma* was optimistic, but it was an optimism founded upon a structural analysis of the American economic and political system and an assumption that poorer Americans would become better organized to fight for their rights. It was not based upon a naive belief that education and moral suasion alone would bring change. Yet by stressing the moral dilemma argument in his early chapters and in the conclusion, Myrdal helped to popularize a psychological and moral interpretation of the race issue. Though the book contained structural analysis and policy recommendations, it was most frequently read as a call for greater education against prejudice.

In *An American Dilemma*, Myrdal did not simply summarize the views of American social scientists. Most of the senior white scholars, such as Robert Park, Donald Young, John Dollard, and Melville Herskovits, avoided the discussion of policy questions in their research and shunned overt appeals to morality. Though nearly all black social scientists were activists, prominent blacks such as Charles S. Johnson and Frazier usually followed the canons of the profession during the 1930s and omitted policy questions from their scholarly articles, reserving such issues for articles in liberal, left, or civil rights magazines. When Myrdal began his work in 1938, there was no consensus among social scientists and reformers as to the proper strategy for black advancement. Most New Dealers and white southern liberals argued that the most effective approach was to work toward improving the economic security, health, and education of both whites and blacks but to avoid attacking segregation directly. Many young black intellectuals believed that the only hope of defeating racial inequality lay in an interracial working-class alliance. Myrdal rejected both of these alternatives and contributed to the development of a new racial liberalism that appealed to the conscience of whites while insisting that the federal government must assault discrimination and segregation directly through legislation, economic planning, and social engineering. This massive book, researched from 1938 to 1940, reconceptualized in Sweden in 1940–41, and completed by September 1942, helped mightily to shape postwar liberal thought on race relations.

Appearing at a time when American intellectuals were profoundly concerned with defining American values and when many social scientists were engaged in wartime social engineering projects, Myrdal's interpretation resonated powerfully with his American audience. It also offered to many whites a persuasive interpretation of the race issue at a critical juncture in Afro-American history, coming soon after Randolph's March on Washington movement, the Double-V campaign, and the Detroit race riot. White liberals in both political parties were beginning to conclude that the civil rights issue could no longer be ignored or dealt with indirectly through economic relief programs. It was a moral issue, and one that required rhetorical support if not a high place on the legislative agenda. Yet liberal rhetoric on the race issue was often vague and inchoate, and *An American Dilemma* helped to focus the attention of many white Americans on race relations and provided an education on the scope and complexity of racial discrimination.

It would take another generation of Afro-American protest to force Congress to pass a strong civil rights law, but Myrdal's book helped to give to elite white Americans a symbolic framework that enabled them to make concessions to blacks once the civil rights movement got under way. The impact of *An American Dilemma* rested on its timing, its blend of searching criticism and optimism about American culture, and its adroit juxtaposition of the American creed with Nazi racism. The book also combined the putative detachment of a foreign scholar with the implied endorsement of a roster of America's leading social scientists and the imprimatur of a prominent foundation.

After the war, the influence of *An American Dilemma* was a factor directing social science research toward the study of prejudice and educational solutions to the problem of racial inequality at the expense of studies of Afro-American communities and culture and investigations of the economic and institutional causes of racial inequality. This was not, as some have argued, because the Carnegie Corporation planned the Myrdal study as a "safe," reformist line on the race question. *An American Dilemma* turned out quite differently from Newton Baker's original idea for a conventional social science survey of blacks in northern cities. The Swedish

Tocqueville was in no sense a captive of the foundation. He was driven, by temperament and conviction, to rebel against authority, to find new solutions to social problems, and to plan for the elimination of poverty and injustice. In the context of World War II, Myrdal was far more concerned with strengthening American democracy for the war against Hitler and for America's postwar responsibilities than with gaining favor with the foundations. Though he regarded Keppel as a mentor, he did not hesitate to move beyond him, as he had with earlier mentors such as Cassel, Wohlin, and Wigforss. Indeed the foreign observer provided Frederick Keppel with quite an education on the scope of racial oppression and black poverty: the Carnegie president, who had originally planned to invite a colonial administrator to investigate the American "Negro problem," eventually concluded that white southerners had a "blow coming to them" that was "long overdue." But if Myrdal greatly influenced Keppel, Keppel also influenced Myrdal in one important respect: he epitomized for Myrdal the educated white American who would take action on the civil rights issue if he just knew the facts. And Myrdal, who had enjoyed extraordinary access to elite Americans since his first visit to the United States as a Rockefeller Fellow in 1929–30, was excessively optimistic about the power of educational efforts and moral appeals to induce elite white Americans to make substantive changes in the economic and social status of blacks. Though Myrdal tackled problems of economic, political, and legal change in race relations, he argued that the underlying problem was a moral dilemma in the minds of Americans, and An American Dilemma, together with other intellectual and institutional trends, led to a focusing of postwar research on changing the minds of individual whites.

Frederick Keppel's interest in supporting research on blacks was not shared by most foundation officials. Although Myrdal recruited many black scholars for his staff and learned a great deal from Bunche and Frazier, black social scientists generally failed to attract support from the foundations during the postwar period. In the struggle for scarce dollars to conduct social science research, black investigators operated from a weaker institutional base in the black colleges. Too often they were excluded from elite networks within the various disciplines. In the atmosphere of heightened anticommunism after the war, many of the black radicals faced an additional barrier as well. Though white social scientists, in unprecedented numbers, set out to battle prejudice, there was not a corresponding increase in the number of black scholars. Before the war, Negro studies had been a relatively small field, but black intellectuals had played a prominent role in it. After the war, the study of intergroup relations was a rapidly growing field, but the place of blacks within it was increasingly marginal.

An American Dilemma had its greatest influence beyond the academy, where it helped to create a new racial liberalism that influenced political leaders, judges, civil rights activists, and thousands of educated white Americans. Myrdal's study was the key text in shaping a liberal orthodoxy in support of civil rights, desegregation, equal opportunity, and the assimilation of blacks into mainstream American culture. These ideas proved to be remarkably durable for twenty years after the publication of *An American Dilemma*—an extraordinarily long life in the turbulent world of racial politics—and the orthodoxy took on a life independent of its author, who was living outside the United States and writing about the European economy and the Third World. But while Myrdal's book persuaded many whites that both their conscience and political necessity required them to support civil rights for blacks, it offered fewer guidelines for the next phase of the black struggle after the passage of the 1964 Civil Rights Act and 1965 Voting Rights Act. Myrdal himself moved beyond the orthodoxy in *Challenge to Affluence* (1963), arguing that the next step was to create a number of public policies to bring the underclass into the American economy and break the vicious circle of poverty. Liberals of both races grappled with the problems of how the political and economic system could be compelled to yield equality as a fact in addition to equality of opportunity. They struggled to determine how black political power was to be increased in the face of racial polarization and the white backlash, how de facto segregation in urban school systems was to be ended, and how the poverty of the urban black underclass was to be eliminated. Afro-American intellectuals faced the questions of how the desire for black control over black institutions and communities could be reconciled with the goal of desegregation and whether a system of group pluralism could be compatible with social justice in a system in which blacks had so few resources with which to compete. Gunnar Myrdal would confront these issues and other problems when he returned to the United States at the age of seventy-four to write "An American Dilemma Revisited."

The Cold War and McCarthyism

The years from 1944, when *An American Dilemma* was published, to 1973, when he began work on a sequel, were filled with an extraordinary range of intellectual and political achievements for both Gunnar and Alva Myrdal. After years of heading economic and social investigations in both Sweden and America, Gunnar was finally given positions of executive authority, both in Sweden and in the United Nations. The global perspective that he had developed in writing *An American Dilemma* would be broadened further in studies of the European economy and of poverty in the Third World. Though Myrdal did not write about American race relations during these years, he did not hesitate to make vigorous criticisms of American foreign policy and economic policy. His advocacy of East-West trade during the height of the Cold War and his vehement criticism of American policy in Vietnam strained his relations with the United States government but eventually won him the respect of many Americans. To all of his activities during the 1940s, 1950s, and 1960s, Myrdal brought an enormous energy, an iconoclastic spirit, and a moral intensity.

In 1943, the voters of Dalarna reelected Gunnar Myrdal to the upper house of the Swedish parliament, and he served as the driving force on the commission that planned Sweden's postwar economy. In 1945, he was appointed minister of commerce in the first postwar Social Democratic government. Myrdal's two years in the Swedish cabinet were marked by turbulent conflict. Like most Swedish economists and business leaders, he expected that the United States and most of the Western European countries would experience a serious depression after the war. Both Ernst Wigforss, the finance minister, and Bertil Ohlin, Myrdal's predecessor as minister of trade in the wartime coalition government, favored a trade agreement with the Soviet Union designed to secure a market for Swedish exports and to promote peaceful relations with their most powerful neighbor. It fell to Myrdal to negotiate the trade and credit agreement, which was approved by the Swedish parliament in the fall of 1946. Under the agreement, Sweden sold to the Soviets on credit 200 million kronor a year of precision equipment and machinery for five years. The Soviets were to repay the loan after fifteen years. But, contrary to expectations, the West prospered after the war, and Sweden's robust economy— undamaged by the war—had no shortage of markets abroad, making the deal with the Soviet Union less attractive economically. Myrdal was blamed for carrying out a policy that had enjoyed broad support. The United States government officially protested the Swedish-Soviet trade agreement, and Myrdal's former friend, the liberal political scientist Herbert Tingsten, bitterly attacked the deal in a series of editorials in *Dagens Nyheter*, a major Stockholm newspaper. In addition to this public controversy, Myrdal alienated some of his Social Democratic colleagues in the cabinet by his abrasive manner. Per Albin Hansson had died in 1946, and Myrdal's relations with Tage Erlander, the new prime minister, were not close. Though Myrdal had been active in politics for fifteen years, he found it excruciatingly painful to subordinate his own independent viewpoint to the policy of the party—especially on matters of economic policy on which he was an expert. By the end of 1946, it was clear that he would have to resign as minister of trade, and his future in Swedish politics looked very dim. Gunnar Myrdal had never before failed at a major public assignment, and he would complain bitterly for the rest of his life about the "campaign of persecution" in the Swedish press.[1]

After his work on *An American Dilemma*, Sweden seemed too small an arena for a long-range planner with a global perspective, and in 1947 Myrdal accepted an appointment as secretary-general of the United Nations Economic Commission for Europe (ECE), a post he would hold for a decade. The idea for the ECE had been proposed in February 1946 by the American economist and State Department official Walt W. Rostow, who saw the need for a continental organization, operating under the United Nations charter, that would seek a comprehensive approach to the reconstruction of war-torn Europe and counteract the forces that were splitting Europe into two blocs. The UN General Assembly approved the ECE a year later, and in April 1947, Secretary-General Trygvie Lie appointed Myrdal the first director of the fledgling organization. From the outset, Gunnar Myrdal knew that he had taken on an enormous challenge. As early as 1943 he

Gunnar Myrdal, *right*, as minister of trade, with Prime Minister Tage Erlander, 1946
(courtesy Arbetarrörelsens Arkiv, Stockholm)

had predicted serious postwar conflict between the United States and the Soviet
Union. But, in the wake of his failure in Swedish politics, he was determined to
give his utmost effort to the ECE as part of his desire to further the vision of
"democratic internationalism" that he had advanced during the war. He and Alva
sold their futuristic house in Stockholm and used all the proceeds to buy furniture
for their official residence, Les Feuillantines, in Geneva. Looking back in later
years on his decision to leave Sweden for the risky enterprise of the ECE, Gunnar
observed, "My sane judgement was that more probably than not this whole thing
would explode . . . but [the ECE] should not explode because I did not put in
everything I could of my brains, of my money. . . . Everything of me should be at
the disposal of this adventure."[2]

As Gunnar Myrdal had foreseen, it was an extraordinarily difficult time to
launch an international organization. On March 12, 1947, President Truman had
asked Congress for $400 million in economic and military aid to the governments
of Greece and Turkey, and on June 5, Secretary of State George Marshall announced that the United States would launch its own program of economic
assistance to war-torn Europe. Myrdal lobbied energetically with American, Brit-

ish, French, and Soviet diplomats to establish an aid program for the whole of Europe, administered by the ECE, but his efforts met with resistance on several fronts. Over the next few years, the Marshall Plan would operate independent of the ECE and would have the aim of developing Western Europe as a bulwark against Communism and as a market for American exports. On the other side, the Soviet Union was suspicious of the ECE, fearful of being outvoted by non-Communist member states and reluctant to release economic data to the international organization. The early sessions of the ECE were largely taken up by propagandistic speeches from both sides, and the Soviets and their allies boycotted many of the ECE committees. But Gunnar Myrdal was not discouraged by this difficult beginning. He encouraged participation in the ECE by all governments in the region and took care to involve governments of both Eastern and Western Europe, as well as representatives of both zones of Germany. Under his leadership, the ECE created a network of subsidiary bodies to deal with concrete problems and to draw up policy recommendations. Myrdal established an independent Secretariat in Geneva that took initiatives on European problems, with considerable independence from UN Headquarters in New York. At the Geneva Secretariat, he built up a body of international civil servants, selected for their abilities, who were responsible to the Secretariat rather than to their home countries. This staff included a number of brilliant young economists whom Myrdal recruited from different nations. He tracked down Walt W. Rostow in 1947 while Rostow was honeymooning in Paris and persuaded the young American economist to resign from his position as associate professor at Harvard and join the research staff of the ECE. Myrdal added to his team the Danish couple Mogens and Esther Boserup, the British economist Nicholas Kaldor, and the Swede Ingvar Svennilson. As always, Myrdal drove himself to the limit and expected much from his staff. In frequent staff meetings, he directed their research projects and long-term planning of economic growth and built an esprit de corps and loyalty to the United Nations. Myrdal energetically defended one young American during a loyalty inquest in the United States and stood up for several staff members from the East bloc who had problems with their home governments. The reports of the ECE staff won the respect of diplomats and economists from many countries for their high level of technical sophistication and fairness to the various member states.[3]

Myrdal's greatest contributions during his decade at the ECE were his effort to encourage East-West trade and his attempt to promote détente before it was fashionable in Washington and Moscow. Many of his plans were blocked during the early years of the ECE by Western trade embargoes designed to deny the East bloc industrial products and materials that might aid in the expansion of its industrial and military power. Tensions rose during the Korean War, and both sides obstructed various plans put forth by Myrdal and the ECE Secretariat. With the end of the Korean War boom, however, Western business leaders in need of new markets began to look toward the East bloc, and the Western governments reduced their "strategic trade" controls. By 1954, East-West trade increased substantially, and the Soviet Union and the Eastern European countries began participating more fully in ECE committees. The structure that Myrdal developed at the ECE was to prove useful as the superpowers gradually replaced brinkmanship with détente. With the relaxation of tensions during the 1970s and the dramatic changes in the Soviet Union and in Eastern Europe in the Gorbachev era of the late 1980s, Myrdal's dream of European cooperation would come much closer to realization.[4]

Gunnar Myrdal's endeavors to reconcile East and West inevitably brought him into conflict with the government of the nation that he considered his second homeland, the United States. When his appointment as secretary-general of the ECE was announced, Matthew Wohl, the conservative vice-president of the American Federation of Labor, wrote to Secretary of State George Marshall complaining that Myrdal was pro-Soviet. The FBI, which had cleared Myrdal of charges of being pro-Nazi four years earlier, combed its files and reported that he had predicted, in *An American Dilemma*, that American Negroes would take their case before an international tribunal after the war, and that the NAACP had, in fact, sent an observer to the International Security Council meeting in San Francisco. The bureau found no evidence of Communist sympathies on Myrdal's part, however. U.S. Army intelligence filed a report on Myrdal in January 1948 that termed him "very friendly to the Soviet bloc" and cited his proposals for channeling U.S. economic aid through the ECE. On March 3, 1948, the State Department drew up a confidential biographical report on Myrdal that contended that "he seems to favor the Soviet Union and its point of view to an unwarranted degree" and that he "has opposed the Marshall Plan since its announcement, charging that it seeks to supplant the all-European ECE with a frankly Western and anti-Soviet bloc." In addition, the report noted, "He has . . . been called an empire-builder of colossal ego, convinced that no one is so admirably qualified as he to solve the world's problems." This biographical report provoked a letter of protest from Paul R. Porter, a liberal Democrat who served as deputy United States representative to the ECE. Porter accepted some of the critique, writing that Myrdal "is extremely naive, and should the Soviets set out to dupe him, they could probably be successful for a time, at least." But he insisted that Myrdal had no sympathy for Communism and that he was no "fellow traveler." Porter found the ECE director to be "generous, impulsive and talkative, often indiscreet and generally tactless, . . . almost childlike in his enthusiasms, . . . [and sometimes] irrationally stubborn." He concluded, however, that the Swede often referred to himself as "half-American," that he was "genuinely an admirer of the United States," and that he "has a large circle of friends in the American Government and in academic life." When the Committee of 100, a group of citizens in New York, headed by Carl Van Doren, invited Myrdal to a banquet honoring him for *An American Dilemma* in 1948, Myrdal cleared the invitation with Porter, who had the FBI check out the group to make sure that they were "non-Communist liberals."[5]

Never one to underestimate his abilities, Gunnar Myrdal aspired to the post of secretary-general of the United Nations, but he was destined to be disappointed. Secretary-General Trygvie Lie managed to alienate both American and Soviet diplomats, and by mid-1949 there were private discussions among Western diplomats about a possible successor when Lie's term expired in February 1951. Dean Rusk told a Canadian official that the prospect of Myrdal as secretary-general gave the State Department "cold shivers."[6] The following year, Lie hinted to the press that he would not be a candidate for another term, setting off a flurry of rumors that Myrdal was the only person who might be acceptable to both the United States and the Soviet Union. However, the American Embassy in Stockholm compiled a list of unfavorable clippings from the nonsocialist press that raised the issue of the Swedish-Soviet trade agreement, portrayed Myrdal as the candidate of the Soviet bloc and suggested that he had been a failure in Swedish politics. The issue was moot in 1951 as Lie chose to serve another year, but when Lie did step down in the fall of 1952, Gunnar Myrdal was not a serious candidate. Representatives of various countries saw him as more of an intellectual than a diplomat, and the UN chose another Swede, Dag Hammarskjöld, who aroused less hostility from the United States government. It was a bitter disappointment for Myrdal, who regarded Hammarskjöld as something of a rival, though they enjoyed a working relationship. A younger member of the Stockholm school of economics, Hammarskjöld had clashed with Myrdal over economic policy during Myrdal's term as minister of trade. Myrdal had also been critical of Hammarskjöld's positions as deputy foreign minister in Sweden as "very pro-Western" at a time when Myrdal was trying to work out an "all-European" solution to the problem of economic reconstruction. Nor did Myrdal feel personally comfortable with this fastidious, upper-class intellectual with a poetic and mystical temperament. Once in office as secretary-general, however, Hammarskjöld was to surprise both Myrdal and the U.S. State Department by developing an independent role for the secretary-general and vigorously pursuing peace between the superpowers. This soft-spoken Swede, thought to be a dull technocrat, emerged as an eloquent champion of the ideal of international cooperation. Though he and Gunnar sometimes disagreed on UN policies, Hammarskjöld would prove his friendship to the Myrdals when Alva encountered the rising tide of McCarthyism in the United States.[7]

Alva Myrdal's route to a career in international diplomacy was an unusual one, strewn with obstacles which she surmounted with ingenuity, tact, and persistence. During the 1940s, she had gradually emerged from under the shadow of her famous husband and achieved prominence in Sweden as an expert on education. In a chapter that she had written in *Kontakt med Amerika*, she had introduced Swedes to John Dewey's ideas about progressive education, and she became known as a leading critic of authoritarian methods of teaching and as a champion of a more active, creative role for students. She also advocated democratizing education so that all children had an equal opportunity and the schools did not simply reflect the class system. In 1946, she had served as a Social Democratic member of the national school commission headed by Tage Erlander, where she fought for these ideals as well as for raising standards in public schools. Alva was also active on many committees within the Social Democratic party and in many civic groups.[8]

The Myrdals' home life had been less happy in the late 1940s, as Gunnar had seemed to turn ever more away from his family and toward work, and the tensions of his political career reverberated on the home front. During Gunnar's two years in the Swedish cabinet, the family had lived under the pressure of unrelenting publicity. Gunnar had quarreled frequently with Jan, who inherited much of the strong will of his father as well as Gunnar's rebellious temperament. A precocious youth who read voraciously and followed the political events of the time, Jan was eager to live his own life and was uncomfortable with the stress of being a public official's son. He dropped out of school at seventeen, left home, went to work for a labor newspaper, and took an active part in the Communist youth movement. To Alva, Gunnar seemed to have less of the playful, humorous spirit that had attracted her to him as a young man. Nevertheless, in 1947, Alva resigned as principal of her teacher training institute, interrupted her political activities, and left her many friends in Stockholm in order to accompany Gunnar to Geneva, where she held no official position. The next two years were difficult as she tried to cheer up her husband, who was still depressed over the collapse of his political career in Sweden. Alva remained active in UNESCO and the International Labor Organization, and she continued to write on educational, population, social welfare, and women's issues. She also served as a hostess for parties for UN diplomats and raised her two teenaged daughters. To the Myrdals' friends and to the public, Alva appeared the loyal wife. When Gunnar celebrated his fiftieth birthday in December 1948, his old friend, the economist Egon Glesinger, prepared a short unpublished biographical sketch that celebrated Gunnar's many achievements. Glesinger wrote that Alva "gradually understood that one big person was as much as a balanced family could have and therefore decided to be Gunnar's indispensable support, rather than to concentrate on her own career." "She must have made this decision," Glesinger concluded, "because she knew how much he needed her."[9]

Even as Glesinger wrote, however, Alva was making plans to change this state of affairs and to break out of the unhappiness that she felt in Geneva. In 1949, Secretary-General Trygvie Lie appointed her head of the United Nations' Department of Social Welfare. She moved to New York, leaving her daughters in Geneva in the care of Gunnar and a housekeeper. Looking back on this momentous step in later years, she wrote, "Now I see clearly that I first became a free person in 1949. And so *happy* in New York, in Paris, in New Delhi." Alva came to realize her talent as a diplomat and to recognize that her happiness lay in that sphere rather than that of child psychologist, educational expert, or subordinated wife of a great man. Two years later, she accepted an appointment as head of the UNESCO's

Department of Social Science in Paris, which enabled her to be closer to her family. The relationship with Gunnar continued at a distance, as each visited the other in Paris or Geneva, and they discussed whether their marriage would continue. Eventually they reconciled, but their marriage would never again be on the same unequal terms as before.[10] In 1956, Alva Myrdal published, with Viola Klein, *Women's Two Roles: Home and Work*, a sociological study that drew on insights from Alva's thirty-year struggle to combine career and family. Though striking a more moderate note than she had in the 1930s, Alva Myrdal argued vigorously that greater longevity, a declining birthrate, an increasing divorce rate, and technological changes in housework would combine to push a larger percentage of women into the work force for a longer period of their lives. She explored the psychological tensions that women felt between their roles as wives and mothers and their roles as workers, and she argued that society did not adequately prepare women for their responsibilities in the workplace and as citizens. Alva Myrdal advocated a host of policy and social changes, including changes in women's education and socialization, education of men to assume a better partnership in the home, extended maternity leaves, job retraining programs for women over forty, and "rationalization" of housework. In the conservative 1950s, *Women's Two Roles* was one of the strongest statements of feminism published in English.[11]

If Gunnar and Alva had difficulties in their marriage, they nonetheless remained committed to the same ideals, and their work in different branches of the United Nations brought them together on issues of common concern, such as European reconstruction, disarmament, and development in Africa, Asia, and Latin America. They also faced some of the same obstacles during the height of the Cold War. When Trygvie Lie named Alva Myrdal to head UNESCO's Department of Social Sciences, the American undersecretary of state Dean Acheson suggested "caution" because of Gunnar Myrdal's attitudes at the ECE and requested an evaluation from the U.S. embassy in Stockholm. An embassy official cabled the secretary of state that Alva was "too egotistical, a busybody, given to fickle enthusiasms and dislikes, unstable and radical." The official declared her a "danger from standpoint US interests, a stormy petrel and a disruptive influence" who might "fill Social Science Department with fellow-travelling types." Meanwhile, an anonymous informant wrote the FBI, calling for an investigation of Alva Myrdal for allegedly pro-Communist views and alerting them to the fact that her son was a Communist. A year later, the U.S. embassy in Stockholm cleared Alva of the charge of Communist sympathies but noted that Jan was "a young fellow traveling intellectual who . . . recently attended the Berlin Youth Festival." Alva's appointment to UNESCO went through despite these objections, and neither she nor Gunnar had any public conflict with the United States government during the remainder of the Truman administration, though the FBI continued to gather information on both of them.[12]

On March 19, 1953, Alva Myrdal arrived in New York's Idlewild Airport on a commercial flight from Paris. She was on official business for UNESCO, with plans to attend various meetings at UN headquarters, and she had a U.S. visa that had been issued in Bern. To her astonishment, U.S. immigration agents denied her lawful entry into the United States and forced her to sign a parole agreement which prevented her from traveling outside the New York area without State Department approval. She was not given any reason for the restriction. Though Alva did not herself seek to publicize this episode, it quickly became a minor international incident and was one of the first crises that Dag Hammarskjöld had to address in his new role as secretary-general. Apparently a zealous immigration official, with access to FBI records on the Myrdals' possibly subversive activities, decided to put Alva on parole. With Senator Joseph McCarthy still leading investigations of Communists, higher officials were reluctant to overrule the parole agreement and appear "soft on Communism." A. M. Rosenthal broke the story in the *New York Times*, quoting an anonymous U.S. government official who said that Alva was barred under the McCarran Act, which prohibited the entry of aliens who sought to "engage in subversive acts or to join subversive organizations." *L'Observateur* of Paris carried an article with the headline "Madame Myrdal Victime du MacCarthysme [sic]," which speculated that *le clan McCarran* had done this because they were enraged over Gunnar Myrdal's efforts to promote East-West trade. *Dagens Nyheter* had a different theory. Their reporter in New York claimed that the immigration authorities suspected Alva Myrdal of subversive activities because of Jan's Communist affiliations. *Aftonbladet*, another Swedish newspaper, interviewed Jan Myrdal by telephone in Bucharest, where he was helping to organize a Communist festival. The young radical expressed his regret if it were true that "mamma is persecuted for my sake." He declared, "My parents are honorable people . . . I esteem and respect them, and I know that they both also respect my viewpoint, despite differences." Richard Sterner, Gunnar's close friend and collaborator on *An American Dilemma*, officially protested the incident before the United Nations Economic and Social Council, to which he was Sweden's delegate.[13]

As officials of the United Nations, neither Alva nor Gunnar Myrdal thought it appropriate to speak directly to the press on the matter, but they both protested vigorously through private communications. Alva circulated to UN officials a thirty-one-page memo, with ten appendixes, in which she outlined her political beliefs in detail, discussed her political differences with her son, and denied any subversive activity. Gunnar was outraged that his wife should be treated like a criminal by the country whose creed he so admired, and he wrote to various friends in the United States, asking them to intervene. In a letter to Walter Lippmann, he expressed his incredulity that anyone could suspect that Alva was engaged in subversive activity, since she was "so near an angel as a human being can be." He admitted that his son was a Communist but explained that "Jan has always been a problem child" and suggested that "his Communism is, of course, a psychologic protest against his parents." Gunnar insisted that his son was entitled to his own opinions, "though we have tried to convert him," and that "our door will never be closed" to him. "As a matter of fact," he quipped, "the boy is a good human being, except that, as a poet, he does not earn any money." Gunnar expressed his hope that Jan's "Communism will be a passing ailment."[14]

While Alva Myrdal became a cause célèbre in the European press, Dag Hammarskjöld patiently negotiated with Henry Cabot Lodge, the U.S. ambassador to the UN, regarding the U.S. government's right to restrict UN officials from traveling in the country. For Hammarskjöld, a matter of principle was involved: the Myrdal case was only the latest of many incidents of harassment of UN civil servants by the State Department, the FBI, and by House and Senate investigating committees. In 1949, Trygvie Lie had violated the UN charter by making a clandestine agreement with the U.S. State Department that allowed the FBI to screen, without their knowledge, applicants for UN positions and members of the UN staff. This agreement was aimed at American citizens who worked for the UN, but the surveillance came to include citizens of other nations as well as the staff of UN agencies abroad, such as UNESCO. Lie had allowed the FBI to set up a fingerprinting operation in the basement of UN Headquarters and had provided the bureau with an office on the third floor for interrogating UN civil servants. A number of UN employees had resigned or been fired as a result of these loyalty investigations, and Lie had completely lost the confidence of the UN staff.[15] After months of negotiations, Hammarskjöld obtained a set of agreements with the U.S. government designed to safeguard the independence of the Secretariat and to offer more protection to UN employees. Though Hammarskjöld made a number of concessions to the U.S. authorities, who continued to screen American applicants for UN jobs, he did manage to get the FBI out of UN Headquarters, and the intensity of the witch-hunting gradually diminished. Secretary of State John Foster Dulles was reluctant, at first, to overturn the ruling on Alva Myrdal, claiming that it was based upon "substantial and serious allegations which United States Government has under investigation." But on August 18, 1953, the State Department declared Alva Myrdal "persona grata to the United States authorities" and granted her "unimpeded access" to the United States.[16]

Though Alva was cleared of the charge of "subversive activities," it was not the end of the Myrdal family's problems with American anti-Communists. While Hammarskjöld was negotiating with the State Department over Alva's visa dispute, the State Department announced in June, 1953, that it had removed more than three hundred books from U.S. libraries abroad, under a new directive designed to rid the shelves of books by Communist, pro-Communist, and "controversial" writers. This was not enough for Senator Joseph McCarthy, who demanded in a televised Senate hearing in July that the State Department remove all books by authors who had invoked the Constitutional right against self-incrimination, the so-called Fifth Amendment Communists. That same month, Swedish newspapers carried reports that *An American Dilemma* was on the list of controversial books purged from the shelves of American libraries abroad. Gunnar Myrdal complained to a friend at the State Department, and an official of the United States

Information Administration denied that *An American Dilemma* had been banned.[17] When he heard that Alva had been vindicated and that *An American Dilemma* was still on the shelves, Charles Dollard, then president of the Carnegie Corporation, wrote Gunnar that he was "relieved and pleased to know . . . that all is well again between the Myrdals and the land of the free and the home of the brave." Dollard conceded that "the whole business of which this was a part was pretty unpleasant," but he expressed his hope that "it has served the purpose of slowing up some of our domestic fascists." However, the following year, Dollard was subpoenaed by the House of Representatives Special Committee to Investigate Tax Exempt Foundations to answer charges that *An American Dilemma* was the work of a foreign socialist who criticized the United States Constitution. Though Dollard was not called to testify, he submitted a sworn memorandum on July 7, 1954, in which he defended Myrdal against the charges and declared that "*An American Dilemma* stands and will stand as one of the great social documents of the century, and Dr. Myrdal will continue to be admired here and abroad as an objective and completely honest scholar."[18]

The climate of fear and hysteria about Communist subversion in the United States began to subside after the Senate censured McCarthy in November 1954, but the Myrdals continued to feel occasional wisps of suspicion. In September 1955, Gunnar complained to his friend Richard Wright that American diplomats were suspicious of him because his son was a Communist. He insisted that he was proud of Jan, who had published his first book the year before, and he asked Wright, then living in Paris, to find a French publisher for Jan's book. Gunnar also sought his friend's advice on how to improve his relationship with his son. Wright, who had written bitterly about his own father in his autobiography and forgiven him in later years, took Jan to lunch in Paris and found him "terribly reasonable and rational." "Indeed," Wright remarked, "he is so sensible that I wonder just how long will the beloved comrades want him around." "I'm in 1000% agreement with you," the novelist had written Gunnar, "never turn your back on Jan no matter what hostile governments say. Blood is thicker than ideology and life is stronger than passing governmental policies."[19]

If Wright and Myrdal could perceive the Cold War as transitory, that was not the view of the FBI, which looked with suspicion on Gunnar Myrdal's work on behalf of East-West trade. In the aftermath of the *Brown* decision, southern members of Congress and right-wing activists in other parts of the country regularly portrayed *An American Dilemma* as a Communist-inspired work. When a Mrs. J. B. Matthews made such charges in 1957 in the fortnightly journal *Christian Economics*, J. Edgar Hoover ordered an investigation. The New York office of the FBI compiled a list of forty-one people mentioned in the preface and observed that "many of the individuals listed by the author are or were members of the CP, CP sympathizers or members of front organizations." James E. Jackson, who had been a research assistant, had been convicted under the Smith Act, and Doxey Wilkerson had been in the party. Most of the other allegations of Communist affiliations were ludicrous: Ruth Benedict was said to be a member of the New York Committee for Democracy and Intellectual Freedom and Guy B. Johnson had once written a book review for the journal *Pacific Affairs*. The coming of the civil rights movement in the 1960s brought a renewal of attacks on Myrdal by southern segregationists. When a senator asked the bureau about Gunnar Myrdal shortly after passage of the Voting Rights Act in 1965, Cartha D. "Deke" DeLoach, the assistant director for crime records who kept tabs on the movement, pulled out public source records which portrayed Gunnar as "a sociologist of extreme left-wing views" and repeated the allegation that Alva was "unstable and radical."[20]

As a great admirer of American civilization, Gunnar Myrdal was saddened by the myopic nationalism and anti-Communist hysteria of the late 1940s and 1950s. In 1956, at the end of his term at the ECE, he observed that Americans had once felt "secure" behind two oceans and had long displayed a quality of "great open-mindedness." Now, he feared, the United States was in danger of becoming "touchy and narrowly nationalistic," of giving way to its streak of puritan "self-righteousness." The sympathetic critic who had contrasted the American creed with Nazi racism now charged that in the United States the "good citizen" was afraid to stand up for his ideals for fear of "being branded as Communist by the people who are using the opportunity of our ideological ailment to enforce *Gleichschaltung*."[21]

As an intellectual who loved a good argument and who treasured his independent viewpoint, Gunnar Myrdal had to exercise extraordinary self-control during his ten years as secretary-general of the ECE. That he managed to set a structure in place for planning European economic recovery and promoting intergovernmental cooperation at the height of the Cold War was a remarkable achievement. Though the experience took a toll on him and on his family, he remained resolutely determined "to act as a negotiator and impartial broker between violently disagreeing countries." If he was often exasperated by the hard-liners in both the United States and the Soviet Union, he still hoped that both countries would relax their ideological rigidity, liberalize their political systems, and find a basis for greater international cooperation. To Hammarskjöld, he joked that if "a group of fundamentalist American clergymen from the interior of the USA" visited Russia, they might find much to admire in this Spartan country with "puritan morals" and "devotion to work," a culture much like Max Weber's portrait of early capitalism. After the end of the Korean War, the death of Stalin, and the ebbing of McCarthyism, Myrdal saw the beginning of a "political relaxation" in both of the superpowers, and he believed that the ECE was sufficiently established as an institution to continue without him. He wrote Hammarskjöld that he was "available for some major negotiation or arbitration job, if it arises on the horizon and if you should like to entrust it to me."[22] The call never came, however, and Gunnar Myrdal was to spend the last thirty years of his life as a scholar, free to speak out unceasingly on the issues of peace, Third World poverty, and racial equality. In a reversal of roles from their earlier years, it was Alva Myrdal who would serve as a public official, both in Sweden and abroad.

The Challenge of Third World Poverty

Both Alva and Gunnar Myrdal had long shared an interest in the nations of Asia and Africa, and their respective positions in the United Nations led to a deepening of those interests in the early 1950s. Alva visited India in 1952 in her role as director of the Social Science Division of UNESCO, and Gunnar toured the nations of South and Southeast Asia a year later. When they talked about places in the world where they would both like to live, New Delhi emerged as a possibility. In 1955 Alva accepted an appointment as Sweden's ambassador to India, a post she would hold until 1961. Gunnar resigned as director of the ECE early in 1957 and took up residence at the Swedish ambassador's quarters in New Delhi, ending an eight-year period in which the two had not lived together regularly. Official duties would continue to draw the couple apart for weeks or months at a time, but they would live together for most of each year for the rest of their lives. With their children grown, much of the old comradeship of their early marriage returned, and the two enjoyed long talk-fests as in their youth. Gunnar had suffered a serious automobile accident in 1952. He could now walk only with a cane, and he was not able to lead as active a life as before. But his energy level was still extraordinary. Determined not to give in to his infirmity or to grow old prematurely, he plunged into an ambitious new study of poverty in South Asia.[23]

Before his move to India, Gunnar Myrdal had already published two books that challenged conventional free-market thinking about the developing world. In *An International Economy* (1956), Myrdal revisited a theme he had broached in the last chapter of *An American Dilemma*, warning of potential conflict between the white nations and the peoples of color in the world. He argued that the gap between the prosperity of the Western countries and the poverty of the nations of Africa, Asia, and Latin America was growing greater and threatening a "political catastrophe." In another generation, he suggested, the "advanced" countries would become small, wealthy islands engulfed by a vast "external proletariat." Myrdal acknowledged that most of the "poor" nations needed internal reforms designed to redistribute land, income, and power from tiny elites to the masses. But he addressed most of his remarks to the "rich" nations of the West, especially the United States. Resuming his role as Jeremiah, Myrdal argued that international trade was hampered by restrictions, that the investment of rich nations in poor nations was minuscule, and that technical assistance and humanitarian aid were woefully inadequate. Taking a bold, if not utopian, position at that point in the Cold War, he insisted that the nations of the world must work toward an integrated world economy based on rapid industrialization of the poor countries and on policies of aid and assistance leading toward an equalization of the world's economic resources. Myrdal bluntly told Americans that aid programs would not work if they were based on Cold War strategic priorities, that "*the world cannot be run as a company town*—at least, not if we want it to be a democratic world." Applying the thesis of *An American Dilemma* to the whole world, he contended that the developed nations faced a "moral dilemma" of whether they would extend their concepts of equality of opportunity and universal human rights to the rest of the world. Technological change, population growth, and the potential for proliferation of nuclear weapons all made it imperative that men and women look beyond their immediate parochial concerns and think of the future of humanity. Hearkening back to the Enlightenment, he declared that "not merely to save the world, but primarily to save our own souls, there should again be dreamers, planners, and fighters."[24] The book received a chilly response from mainstream economists, who complained about the author's lack of rigor in substantiating his technical arguments and derided his "neo-mercantilist" solutions. Kenneth Boulding, on the other hand, hailed Myrdal as the "world's top social scientist," compared the book to Adam Smith's *Wealth of Nations* in its "breadth of vision," and urged Americans to heed the advice of the Swedish prophet.[25]

In a series of lectures before the Bank of Egypt in Cairo in 1956, published as *Development and Under-Development*, Myrdal presented an extended critique of the equilibrium model of international trade offered by classical economists, which, he contended, failed to explain why the rich nations were growing richer and the poor poorer.[26] Conventional economics taught that every disturbance of international trade provoked a reaction that led back to stable equilibrium. But Myrdal reintroduced his principle of circular and cumulative causation that he had derived from Wicksell and broadened in his analysis of race relations in *An American Dilemma*. This held that economic and social forces interlocked to produce vicious circles that spiraled downward unless planners intervened but that, conversely, a process of cumulative improvement could be stimulated. Myrdal also made an institutionalist critique of traditional economics, which artificially restricted analysis to economic factors and excluded non-economic causes of behavior. Such analysis was invalid even in the West, he suggested, and was particularly inappropriate in evaluating complex patterns of social life in non-Western societies. In an era in which most economists defined "development" as economic growth, as measured by increases in per capita GNP, Myrdal conceived of development in broader terms, including improvements in education, health, welfare, and political participation.[27]

While Myrdal envisaged an eventual international world economic order based on cooperation among nations, he recognized that the present order was completely unequal and counseled a short-term strategy of economic nationalism for the poor countries. In contrast to most Western economists, he advanced the unorthodox notion that the governments of the poor nations themselves should assume most of the responsibility for planning their own development rather than imitating the pattern of capitalist development that Western Europe and the United States had followed in the nineteenth century. Each of the underdeveloped countries needed to prepare a national economic plan that would put its own interests ahead of those of the Western countries, and the governments of the "backward" countries would have to take over many functions that were left to private business in the West.

Myrdal then made one of the most radical suggestions of his career, that the underdeveloped nations should organize themselves to extract better terms from the wealthy nations. "By joining hands and pooling what they have of bargaining power," he suggested, "the underdeveloped countries can together gain for them-selves considerations which they would not have got individually." Myrdal made it clear that this proposal, which in many ways anticipated the strategy of the Organization of Petroleum Exporting Countries in the 1970s, was only one stage on the road toward a world economy. After the underdeveloped "majority" orga-nized itself, the richer nations gradually would "join, by careful steps the majority, which is becoming powerful, in common policies for common goals." In this scenario, the underdeveloped nations would lead the rest of the world toward a "world state."[28] Throughout his career, Myrdal conceived of reforms occurring through a combination of organized pressure from below and enlightened self-interest from above. But in speaking before this Egyptian audience, he stressed the need for the poor nations to be the driving force for change:

> No society has ever substantially reformed itself by a movement from above: by a simple voluntary decision of an upper class, springing from its social conscience, to become equal with the lower classes and give them free entrance to the class monopolies. Ideals and the social conscience do play their very considerable role, which should not be forgotten, but they are weak as self-propelled forces, originating reforms on a large scale: they need the pull of demands being raised and pressed for. When power has been assembled by those who have grievances, and the storm is gathering, then is the time when ideals and the social conscience can become effective.[29]

Myrdal's debut as an economist of development was thus marked by a combina-tion of tough-minded counsel to poor nations and a bold vision of international cooperation in the future.

When Gunnar Myrdal moved to New Dehli in 1957, he found India in a state of ferment, idealism, and hope ten years after independence. Both Gunnar and Alva Myrdal admired Prime Minister Jawaharlal Nehru and identified passionately with his optimistic vision of democratic socialism; human rights; rapid development; reduction of ancient inequalities of caste, class, and gender; and leadership in the struggle for world peace through the movement of nonaligned nations. Born to a Brahmin family in Allahabad in 1889, Nehru had been educated at Harrow and Cambridge, and he brought to the Indian struggle for independence a devotion to the Western ideals of scientific and technological progress as well as a commitment to democratic procedures. As leader of the Indian National Congress in the late 1920s and 1930s, he had advanced a socialist program, but as the nation's first prime minister after independence, he pursued an economic strategy aimed at increasing production and raising per capita income through national economic plans that left most private ownership of industry and land intact. Like the Fabians in Britain and the Swedish Social Democrats, Nehru rejected neoclassical and Marxist orthodoxies and sought a planned economy that would evolve gradually toward a welfare state on the "socialist pattern."[30]

A charismatic intellectual who traveled constantly throughout India and spoke before mass audiences, Nehru was a powerful symbol of national unity. Like the Myrdals, he was a strong universalist who had championed a secular constitution and sought to promote unity among India's many religious, linguistic, regional, and social groups. Nehru secured passage of laws that opened opportunities for the nation's Untouchables and improved the status of women. The Western-oriented prime minister preached efficiency and the work ethic to his people and promoted a "scientific" approach to human problem-solving. He also built support for his program through moral exhortation, calling the middle and upper classes to an ethic of public service and urging the peasantry to unite behind a program of rural development based on self-help and cooperative agriculture. Gunnar Myrdal found Nehru "one of the most perfect human beings" he had known, one of the few "absolutely honest men" he had ever met, a "noble man" who was "working hard in the interests of the common man because he was a democrat and an egalitarian." Alva Myrdal, who developed a close friendship with the prime minister, said that Nehru was "truly speaking, one of the very, very few who can stand the test of the Gandhian idea, that is of living according to the principle of truth."[31] In many long conversations, Nehru and Alva discussed his years with Gandhi, the principle of nonviolence, and his efforts to promote peace through the movement of nonaligned nations. He remained an inspiration for Alva, who devoted the last decades of her life to the issues of nuclear disarmament, education, health, and welfare in the Third World. She would cherish a large photograph of Nehru for the rest of her life, even carrying it to her last hospital room.[32]

At Nehru's invitation, Gunnar Myrdal addressed the Indian parliament on April 22, 1958, and expressed his support for the nation's experiments in economic planning. India's first priority, in his view, was raising agricultural production, but he noted that improvements in the standard of living could only come through greater industrial development. Echoing Nehru, Myrdal emphasized the importance of improving the productivity of workers and strengthening the work ethic. One means to this end, he noted, would be a program of compulsory national service for all young men and women. In an era when Americans worried about the threat of Communism to other Asian countries, Myrdal declared that the real challenge posed by Communism was not a military threat or subversion but the question of whether a democracy like India could summon the "minimum of

Ambassador Alva Myrdal with India's prime minister, Jawaharlal Nehru
(courtesy Arbetarrörelsens Arkiv, Stockholm)

national discipline" necessary for rapid economic development "while preserving political freedom and full civil liberties." Though some of his American friends feared that India had embarked on too radical a course, Myrdal worried that the nation was advancing too slowly toward Nehru's stated goal of establishing a "socialist pattern of society." Predicting that the newly enfranchised masses would demand a higher standard of living, he warned that rapid development and greater equality in the distribution of resources were imperative if Indian democracy was to survive.[33]

Gunnar Myrdal originally intended to spend three years writing a study of poverty in South Asia that would be a contribution to policy debates about planning for economic development in those countries. Ever since *An American Dilemma*, he had wanted to write another big book that would reshape ideas about a major human problem. South Asia offered an extraordinary challenge to the social engineer, as well as an opportunity to join with Asian leaders, economists, and other social scientists in planning for economic growth and human welfare. As Myrdal delved into his research, however, he soon discovered that he had taken on an even more daunting task than the American race issue. The scale of poverty in India was immense. Despite progress during Nehru's first five-year plan, per capita income in 1956 was a mere $59. Population continued to increase in this nation of nearly 400 million, and a majority of the people remained illiterate. Although Nehru inspired millions with his vision of social transformation, he failed to carry out an effective program of land reform, failed to curb corruption in the Congress party, and failed to make the government bureaucracy work effectively. Perhaps the most disturbing obstacles to development, in Myrdal's view, were the ancient customs that inhibited social and geographical mobility, kept productivity low, and stood in the way of an effective strategy of modernization. Myrdal confided to his friend and collaborator Paul Streeten that, while he had been able fully to identify with American ideals in his work on *An American Dilemma*, he found Indian culture strange and disorienting. "When I saw those half-naked brown bodies in an Indian textile family," he said, "they seemed to me like animals; I could not find anything in common with them."[34] Yet he would struggle—not always successfully—to overcome his ethnocentrism, to identify his own biases as well as the value premises that underlay Western modernization theory.

If the culture of India and the mind of the masses remained an enigma to Myrdal, he nonetheless found kindred spirits among the Western-oriented elite of planners and intellectuals. They, like Nehru, represented the future of India to Myrdal, and he was determined to join with them in the struggle against poverty. The misery of the poor in India and other Third World countries became an obsession for Myrdal, and he spent the next fifteen years attempting to devise an effective strategy for combating poverty with the help of a team of researchers and coauthors, financed by the Twentieth Century Fund. He confessed to friends that he would sometimes wake up in the middle of the night in despair over the scope of the task that he had taken on, depressed by the fear that he would never finish it. But Alva would reassure him: "Gunnar, you have to go on, you have to give whatever is in you."[35]

Myrdal had always been an individualist with a unique and original perspective on most of the problems that he tackled. His formidable ego, brilliance, and toughness had enabled him to withstand enormous pressure from powerful interests and to propose bold reforms in Sweden, America, and within the United Nations. But Myrdal's early and mid-career had also been marked by a certain pragmatism and ability to gauge the spectrum of opinions within a particular country or institution or community of thinkers and to propose policies that were timely or that were just emerging on the horizon of possibility. He was now in his late fifties and sixties, no longer closely involved in the political life of Sweden or the UN, and not really part of a community of thinkers in any country. Lacking these anchors, Myrdal's egocentricity became all the more pronounced. The young outsider from Dalarna who had burst onto the Stockholm scene as an enfant terrible was still an outsider, an angry prophet warning the world of disaster if something were not done about the catastrophic problem of hunger and poverty in the Third World, and he missed no opportunity to lecture Americans and Western Europeans about the remedies that were needed. Myrdal became increasingly convinced of the correctness of his views, and he frequently did not listen carefully to what other scholars in the field were saying. Even his admirers admitted that a conversation with Myrdal was difficult, that one had to be persistent and assertive to get one's ideas across to him. He had become, in Paul Streeten's words, an "*enfant terrible* emeritus."[36]

The results of Gunnar Myrdal's ten years of research on South Asia were published in 1968 in *Asian Drama: An Inquiry into the Poverty of Nations*, a three-volume work of 2,221 pages.[37] In this study, he reached far more pessimistic conclusions than he had in *An American Dilemma*. By the 1960s, it was clear that both native elites and Western modernization theorists had erred in their belief that India and its neighbors could quickly reach an industrial "take-off" through a crash program of industrialization; the development of technologically advanced, capitalist agriculture; the accumulation of savings; and an infusion of foreign capital. Myrdal found that both modernizing elites in South Asia and Western economists had underestimated the persistence of traditional attitudes and institutions that inhibited the growth of a productive capitalist economic system and a strong state capable of delivering social welfare benefits to its people. He struggled to find an alternative set of policies that fostered economic growth in a fashion that was compatible with political democracy.

In *Asian Drama*, Myrdal continued the critique of classical economic doctrines with respect to problems of development that he had begun in *An International Economy*, arguing that conventional Western economic concepts such as capital, employment, unemployment, income, and savings did not effectively describe the complex social and economic realities of traditional societies. Both classical economics and orthodox Marxist economics, according to Myrdal, described an "economic man" that did not exist in South Asia. After exposing how previous Western economists were influenced by hidden biases and reiterating his view that no form of social analysis was value-free, he sought to lay out, in his usual fashion, the value premises upon which the study was based. Here Myrdal candidly admitted that his own valuations stemmed from the Enlightenment and that he sought to turn the nations of South Asia into modern welfare states based upon the principles of economic and social equality, freedom of social and spatial mobility, national integration, and the pursuit of a higher standard of living for all. He looked forward to social changes that would encourage Asians to be efficient, hardworking, frugal, enterprising, honest, and tolerant, and he sought to foster a scientific worldview free of "superstitious beliefs and prejudices." There was no place in Myrdal's scheme of things for traditional religion, mysticism, or an organic sense of community. Acknowledging that his valuations were Western in origin, Myrdal nonetheless insisted that this type of modernization was advocated by the indigenous elites that had led the national liberation movements and now served (in India) as the elected political leaders. He quoted Nehru's remark, "You can't get hold of a modern tool and have an ancient mind. It won't work."[38] The problem, for the Swedish social engineer, was how to spread these values among the masses of people and to muster the political will to engage in the type of economic planning necessary to avert catastrophe. For Myrdal, the drama of South Asia was in this clash between traditional cultures laden with a high degree of "irrationality" and the forces of modernization. For him, the suspense of the uncompleted plot rested on whether the values of the Enlightenment could win out before it was too late.

The list of social and economic problems that Myrdal compiled was staggering. South Asia's natural resources were poor and its climates enervating. Population, already dense, was increasing at a rate of 2 to 3 percent a year. Earnings from exports were declining. Foreign aid from the wealthy countries had been ineffective because its distribution had been largely guided by strategic and political considerations. Vietnam, for example, had received more foreign aid than India. In several countries, aid had strengthened reactionary elites, and in most of the South Asian countries it had fostered rapid industrialization at the expense of agriculture, health, and education. Surveying the region that contained one-fourth of the world's people, Myrdal saw little evidence that it was poised for an economic take-off.

The economic and social problems of South Asia were compounded, according to Myrdal, by a political phenomenon he called "soft states." The governments of most of these countries proclaimed their allegiance to the goals of modernization, but they were unable or unwilling to demand the social discipline among their people necessary to carry out their declared policy goals. Myrdal's critique of "soft states" was in no sense a call for authoritarian government but rather a demand for effective democratic regimes. Thus, in Myrdal's view, a government might be coercive in its treatment of oppressed minorities and still "soft" in its unwillingness to press for an effective program of birth control, to combat a caste system, to fight corruption in the civil service, or to tax adequately its wealthy citizens. In India, the largest nation in the region and the focus of *Asian Drama*, Myrdal charged that the hopes engendered by independence were foundering four years after the death of Nehru, as inequality increased, "superstitious" practices seemed to grow stronger, cosmopolitan elites appeared to be losing out to reactionary provincials, and linguistic and ethnic differences threatened to tear the nation apart. Just as he had pointed to American hypocrisy on the race issue a generation earlier, Myrdal portrayed the Indian elite as hypocritical—professing modern, egalitarian values, but acquiescing in reactionary, traditional practices.

Given these seemingly intractable problems, Myrdal was pessimistic that any set of policies could reverse the pattern of economic stagnation, population explosion, political incompetence, and the persistence of traditional cultures. Yet he ventured to offer a few policy proposals, advocating a "Third World of planning" that entailed neither the state coercion of the Soviet model nor the laissez-

faire ethic of capitalism. Myrdal attacked the assumption of modernization theorists that commercialized agriculture should be allowed to drive millions of
redundant agricultural workers off the land and into the cities, where they would
form a reserve labor force that would propel an industrial boom. Such a policy, in
his view, would only add to the misery in the cities, where industrialization could
not be expected to absorb the uprooted peasants. Instead, Myrdal insisted that
short-term efforts had to be focused on improving agricultural productivity,
primarily by changing attitudes toward work, caste, and religion. New ways had to
be found to use the vast amounts of idle labor time in the rural areas and to create
a stronger work ethic. Land reform and a reduction of inequalities, he argued,
were a necessary part of modernization. Aid agencies should introduce better
varieties of wheat and rice into cultivation, and governments should rapidly
disseminate new technologies of birth control.

Reviews of *Asian Drama* were decidedly less favorable than those that had
greeted Myrdal's earlier masterpiece. The initial round of reviews in American
magazines was positive, and many readers compared the massive tome to *An
American Dilemma* and termed it a monumental work of scholarship.[39] But a
mischievous (and anonymous) reviewer for London's *Times Literary Supplement*
suggested that "if greatness could be conferred on a book by the time and
resources consumed in its composition," it would be on a plane with Smith's *The
Wealth of Nations*. Noting the lavish financing by an American foundation and the
distinguished team Myrdal had assembled, the *Times* critic wrote: "The reader
tends to approach *Asian Drama* with the kind of awe with which the serious and
well-informed tourist approaches York Minster or the Taj Mahal. It has a monumental quality. One must nevertheless cast aside one's instinctive reverence and
ask whether this is Myrdal's monument or Myrdal's folly." The reviewer applauded
the contribution that Myrdal had made since the mid-1950s in criticizing Western
models of economic development and modernization theory but suggested that
Asian Drama was more a critique of a generation of scholarship than a bold
opening in a new direction. The "final impact of *Asian Drama*," he judged, "is one
of deep discouragement" because the Asian governments lacked the capacity to
implement Myrdal's proposals. "If there is no real possibility of building a bridge
between the 'must' and the 'can,'" he concluded, "it is futile to draw up plans for
such a structure."[40]

The conservative economist P. T. Bauer pounded *Asian Drama* in the pages of
the *Spectator*. The only merit Bauer saw in the book was Myrdal's "grudging"
recognition that "what holds back the underdeveloped (i.e. poor) countries is the
people living there." In other respects, the book "reveals what happens when
ostensibly scholarly reasoning is subordinated to political purposes, when the
economist sees his task as the remaking of man and society rather than as the
illumination of the scene by observation and analysis." Bauer saw nothing wrong
with inequality if some people worked harder than others, argued that central
planning would not raise the standard of living, opposed land reform, and criti-

cized Myrdal's attempt to explain underdevelopment by factors external to the region.[41]

The reception in India was also mixed. The economist P. C. Mahalanobis, the former head of planning under Nehru, energetically defended Myrdal as "a very great man who has written a great book with the highest sense of intellectual integrity and with intense sympathy and anguish for the poverty and stagnation of one-fourth of the world's population who live in the countries of South Asia." Though he differed from Myrdal on some points, Mahalanobis agreed that India needed egalitarian reforms and modernization to overcome a "mediaeval and authoritarian" social structure, political corruption, and certain "superstitions and ritualistic religious practices devoid of spiritual values."[42]. A number of reviewers, however, complained about Myrdal's failure to overcome his own ethnocentrism despite his ponderous critique of the biases of previous economic theorists and modernizers. Krishna Prakash Gupta charged that "under the veneer of academic detachment . . . , Myrdal's monumental study mixes jargon, common sense and a missionary desperation, to communicate a sense of unrelieved pessimism." The Indian scholar objected to Myrdal's headlong assault on traditional Asian values and faulted him for ignoring recent work by social scientists that contended that "Asian institutional forms are in fact highly adaptable to development." If Myrdal had studied Japan, Gupta claimed, "he would have found that kinship ties, paternalism and many other 'obstacles' are not necessarily inimical to economic development."[43]

The anthropologist Clifford Geertz developed this line of criticism in a long review essay in *Encounter*. Myrdal's portrayal of India, he declared, was "completely stereotypic . . . , astonishingly abstract, . . . unnuanced and unparticularized." "It would seem impossible," Geertz asserted, "to write nearly a million words on a country with so rich a history, so profound a culture, and so complex a social system and fail to convey the force of its originality and the vitality of its spirit somewhere; but Professor Myrdal has accomplished it." While applauding Myrdal's criticisms of the concept of rapid industrialization, he insisted that Myrdal's plans for agricultural reform were "utopian." Though he had no program of his own to offer, Geertz was certain that the world required a "less Western centered, and less moralistic analysis of what is really happening in India . . . [and] a sociology which is more than broad generalisations derived from 'staple general reasonings' and 'the values of the Enlightenment as expressed in the welfare state.'"[44]

Undisturbed by these criticisms, Myrdal broadened the scope of his analysis to the entire Third World in *The Challenge of World Poverty: A World Anti-Poverty Program in Outline* (1970). Originally delivered as a series of lectures at Johns Hopkins University, the book summarized Myrdal's policy recommendations and represented the culmination of fifteen years of work on the issue of Third World poverty. *The Challenge of World Poverty* consisted of two sermons: one for the nations of the Third World, the other for the industrialized West.[45] Though pessimistic about the prospects for change, Myrdal nevertheless passionately urged both the Western nations and the Third World states to change their ways in order to cope with this colossal problem. As a citizen of a small country that was neutral in the Cold War and that had no history of colonialism, Myrdal was more blunt than many other Western scholars in pointing out the shortcomings of Third World governments. For three decades, he noted, leaders of Third World nations had paid lip service to the ideal of equality but had not instituted the programs necessary to achieve it. Extending his concept of "soft states" to include Latin America as well as the countries of South Asia, Myrdal argued that public administration was weak, corruption was rampant, and governments often failed to collect taxes from their wealthiest citizens. He insisted that the Third World nations must assume responsibility for improving their governments, planning their own development, establishing effective programs of birth control, and instituting greater social and economic equality. Land reform, in his view, was essential to increasing agricultural productivity, and educational systems should be redesigned so that they reached the masses and not just an educated elite.

To the industrialized West, Myrdal recommended prophylactic reforms based on enlightened self-interest, noting that world poverty led inevitably to disorder and perhaps to systems of government hostile to the West. He criticized aid policies that required recipient nations to purchase goods from the granting nation. Myrdal asserted that industrialized nations should not only eliminate tariffs and quotas that inhibit imports from Third World countries; they should adopt policies that discriminate in favor of imports from the Third World. Aid should be tied to programs of land reform and mass education. Finally, he declared that the United States would only provide effective aid to the poor in Third World nations when it did so out of a sense of moral responsibility, rather than as part of anti-Communist strategy or an attempt to further the interests of American corporations.[46]

In his work on Third World poverty, as in his advocacy of the Swedish welfare state and in *An American Dilemma*, Myrdal argued to elites that the morally right thing to do was also politically expedient. He evinced the same willingness to criticize bluntly those in positions of political power as well as those who were leading movements that challenged power. A passionate concern to relieve suffering led him to lay out in grim detail the damage that the powerful inflicted on the poor, as well as the habits which, in his view, the poor had to change to improve their status. Deeply committed to the universal values of the Enlightenment, Myrdal displayed a remarkable insensitivity to the dynamics of different cultures. As his friend and collaborator Paul Streeten acknowledged, Myrdal's models for economic and social change did not allow for cultural variation, and he did not attempt to incorporate traditional values into the process of modernization. In approaching the problems of India and the Third World, he had little use for small-scale and decentralized forms of organization and no sympathy at all for those who placed the maintenance of traditional cultures ahead of material advance. Yet Myrdal's ideas about development had undergone considerable transition from 1955 to 1970. Originally an advocate of the "big push" for industrialization, with extensive centralized planning of the economies of underdeveloped countries, he had become skeptical of the capacity of corrupt, inefficient bureaucracies to plan effectively and had shifted much of the emphasis of his development strategy to agriculture and to the need for internal reforms in underdeveloped countries.[47]

While his fundamental values remained much the same, Myrdal found himself growing more pessimistic as he began the eighth decade of his life. By 1970, the vision he had cherished of a world based on reason, freedom, and equality seemed farther away than ever. Yet Myrdal proclaimed himself a "cheerful pessimist."[48] Even if the chances of overcoming a problem were one in a hundred, he affirmed that he was willing to struggle for his ideals. In the early 1930s, he had defied the conventional wisdom of neoclassical economics in order to plan for Sweden's welfare state. In 1938 and 1939 he had set out to plan a new public policy on civil rights for blacks when the issue was still on the periphery of American politics. In 1940, as Hitler's army occupied Norway and Denmark and threatened to invade Sweden, he and Alva had dared to urge Swedes to look forward to playing a leading role in planning for postwar reconstruction in Europe and for development aid to the nations of Africa and Asia. During the Cold War he had ignored pressures from both sides and worked to establish a planning structure for European cooperation and East-West trade. And so in 1970 he mapped out a set of bold and idealistic policy recommendations on Third World poverty, even though there was little chance that either the United States government, the Soviets, or Third World states would heed them. He would continue to speak out on development issues into the early 1980s, arguing that most Western aid policies merely propped up reactionary elites and military dictatorships in the Third World.[49]

If Myrdal's ambitions were truly global, so too was the scope of the problems he had taken on, and his ideas were severely criticized by scholars across the political spectrum. His books on the economics of development constituted an important critique of modernization theory but did not really point the way to a new consensus among scholars of Third World development, nor did they have much impact on the policies of the wealthy nations. In the late 1960s and 1970s, social scientists specializing in the Third World were increasingly polarized. A neo-Marxist interpretation of development, most prominently associated with Andre Gunder Frank, gained many adherents for a time among younger scholars in Latin America, Europe, and the United States. Mainstream economists, on the other hand, regarded both Myrdal and the neo-Marxists as ideologues whose work lacked technical rigor, and the trend in American economics in the 1980s was toward skepticism about the effectiveness of government planning in less developed countries. During the 1970s, there was much discussion within international organizations of the idea of redirecting aid programs to focus on the "basic needs" of the poor and of the need for redistribution reforms within Third World nations. Third World elites frequently blocked such strategies, however; American aid policies remained strongly tied to Cold War strategic thinking, and Myrdal's vision of international cooperation seemed to recede farther from realization.[50]

America's Critic and Friend

During the 1960s, while working on the issue of Third World poverty, Gunnar Myrdal frequently visited the United States. Though disagreeing with much of American foreign and domestic policy, he and Alva viewed the United States as a kind of second home where they had many friends as well as a daughter, the philosopher Sissela Bok, who lived in Cambridge, Massachusetts, and later became a professor at Brandeis University. "For my hormonal balance," Gunnar joked, "I need to be in the United States some 4–5 times a year, usually giving some lecture or being available in a college or university."[51] On his visits to the U.S., Gunnar Myrdal testified before congressional committees, received honorary degrees, gave interviews to the press, and appeared on television talk shows, where he was an explosive presence—chain-smoking, interrupting his hosts with his thickly accented English, and still brimming with ideas on a range of issues. The young Rockefeller Fellow from Sweden who had quickly grown accustomed to going around America "like a light from Nazareth with opinions ready on everything possible" still found Americans eager to listen to what he had to say. Myrdal's brashness, his boastfulness, his impatience, and his love of argument had gotten him into trouble in Swedish politics, but Americans expected such qualities in celebrities. In Sweden, Alva was now a prominent figure in Social Democratic politics, while Gunnar was less well known among younger Swedes, since he had not held office in his native land since 1947, and he complained that Swedes did not appreciate his contributions to scholarship.[52] Gunnar told the journalist Stephen Rosenfeld that in America, "I'm a wise guy, an elder statesman. In Sweden I'm nobody. I like to be treated with irreverence." But adulation was what he often received in the United States, even as he criticized American foreign policy and economic and social welfare policy. To a man raised on the frugal ethic of Dalarna, the sheer extravagance of American celebrity worship was astonishing and seductive. In 1968 he cheerfully submitted to a fourteen-hour interview with *Look* for a short article and allowed their photographers to spend a whole morning taking pictures of him, knowing they would use only one.[53]

Although Gunnar Myrdal's trips to the United States offered a good deal of ego gratification, he continued to use his status as a leading foreign observer to challenge Americans to live up to their ideals, and his talks to Americans increasingly came to resemble sermons. The jet-setting Jeremiah certainly did not regard himself as a saint—he knew that his own personal morality had not been impeccable and that he had sometimes brought pain to those closest to him. But Myrdal's doubts about his own self-worth drove him to ever more intense efforts to spur Americans to a higher standard of public morality. He thought that his experience as a social investigator had given him perspective on the good as well as the evil in human nature. He still believed that the average person's consciousness contained a mass of contradictory valuations, that behavior was a compromise among all those valuations, and that a person's conscience or moral valuations were an important part of the total field of his mental life. "For Lord's sake," he exclaimed in an interview, "human behavior is always a compromise. If we would sit down of an evening and think over how we are living our daily lives, we would know very well what compromises we are making. If you scrutinize yourself, you'll say, 'What in hell sort of humbug and hypocrite am I?' We all live in compromises where every value has a certain importance." He kept stressing that the average person struggled with his conscience and was therefore open to the kind of moral appeals that Myrdal liked to make.[54]

In *Beyond the Welfare State* (1960) and *Challenge to Affluence* (1963), Gunnar Myrdal ventured major criticisms of American economic and social policies. The first of these books grew out of a series of lectures he delivered at Yale University in 1958. As one of the creators of the Swedish welfare state, Myrdal attempted to redress one of the failings of his earlier work by taking up the question of how to increase popular participation in modern democracies. Heretofore, he had generally been an advocate of social engineering from the top down, relatively indifferent to the problem of popular participation. But with poverty virtually eliminated in Sweden, he believed that the next priority was to reduce the role of the bureaucracy and encourage the citizen to take a more active role at the grass roots. In pointing Sweden (and eventually the United States) toward this next stage, he drew upon the ideas of John Dewey and argued that it was necessary to reconstruct modern societies so that individuals played a greater role in shaping the institutions and policies that affect their lives. Once the policies of the welfare state were in place, many governmental functions could be decentralized to allow for greater participatory democracy at the local level.[55]

While Myrdal pointed to this vision of participatory democracy as a long-term goal for the United States, he insisted that America still required the social engineer to engage in economic planning and to attack the problem of poverty. In *Challenge to Affluence*, he asserted that the United States' sluggish economy was "the most important problem in the world today." Americans had become "defeatist" about their economy and settled for too low a rate of economic growth. If the United States did not solve the problem of economic growth, he warned, it would decline as a world power. More was needed, according to Myrdal, than the Kennedy administration's Keynesian policy of tax cuts and tinkering with the money supply. One of the major obstacles to economic growth was "structural unemployment." Technological change created a need for skilled and educated workers, yet there was a large class of unemployed and underemployed people living in the inner cities and in rural areas who were not trained for the jobs that were available.[56] Myrdal termed this group of poor Americans an "under-class" and argued that its existence threatened "the very tenets of American society." With every year that went by, he averred, it would become more and more difficult to integrate these poor Americans into the modern, technologically advanced economy because they would become more apathetic and demoralized and their problems would deepen in a vicious circle. Myrdal observed that the "class line becomes demarcated almost as a caste line, since the children in this class tend to become as poorly endowed as their parents." Though a majority of the underclass was white, blacks were disproportionately represented in the group, and racial prejudice was a major factor in preventing the current generation of poor Americans from moving up, as Southern and Eastern European immigrants had done a generation before. Since these people were poorly educated and untrained, Myrdal noted, they were a hindrance to economic expansion, and since they lacked the means to consume very many goods, they constituted an untapped market for American industry.[57] The way out of this problem, he suggested, was through greater economic planning, education, vocational training programs, improvements in Social Security and health care, and public works projects. In addition, there was a need for "large-scale distributional reforms" to "build a more solid foundation in aggregate demand for expansion of production." If inflation resulted from deficit spending and measures to lower unemployment, Myrdal did not hesitate to advocate wage and price controls. In sum, he argued, with his usual combination of moral exhortation and prophylactic reform, that aiding the poor to find good jobs was both morally right and economically necessary.[58]

If Myrdal continued to address his argument to elites, he nonetheless insisted that much of the pressure for these reforms would have to come from the poor themselves. He pointed out that the United States had "the least revolutionary proletariat in the world," and he regretted that poor people often did not vote, did not belong to unions, and had little influence on either political party. Myrdal declared that "it is fatal for democracy, and not only demoralizing for the individual members of the under-class, that they are so mute and without initiative and that they are not becoming organized to fight for their interests." "For its own health and even preservation," he insisted, "an effective, full-fledged democracy needs movements of protest on the part of the underprivileged."[59] Picking up a theme from *Beyond the Welfare State*, Myrdal admitted that long-range planning and major reforms would require some "big government" measures but insisted that planning did not mean "detailed controls" over everyday life. He preferred decentralization of many government functions so that much regulation was carried out by state and local governments with greater possibilities for citizen participation. "It is a very long time," he reflected, "since I looked with any glee or exhilaration to the prospect that technological change and other fundamental changes in our national communities and in the world would force us to plan and control our economic life ever more intensely through the means of government."

Responding to the mass insurgency of blacks in the South, he declared that "if the masses of people can be induced to participate more intensely in the molding of their nation's and their own destiny, . . . I foresee a good, indeed extraordinarily good, future for America."[60]

Challenge to Affluence remains Gunnar Myrdal's second most important book about the United States. It represented an attempt to address some of the major economic and social problems that were closely intertwined with race, just as the youthful president was seeking to stimulate the sluggish economy and as the black revolt was sweeping across the South. The book contains prophetic statements about America in the 1960s. Myrdal warned that if the president and Congress started a boom without appropriating enough money to educate and train the underclass, American prosperity would be based on a shaky foundation. In his discussion of foreign policy, Myrdal called for trade with the Soviet bloc and normalization of relations with China and objected to the United States' unhealthy dependence upon military spending. "I shudder to think," he wrote, "of all the serious and extremely dangerous mistakes an America, frustrated by a sense of losing out in the economic race, may commit."[61]

Most American reviewers failed to appreciate the originality and breadth of vision of *Challenge to Affluence*. Some lamented its "utopianism," while others deplored Myrdal's failure to provide detailed economic analyses in support of his assertions.[62] But many American intellectuals by now had begun to see Myrdal more as a prophet and social critic than a technical economist. His defenders sought to broaden the scope of political discourse about economic policy in mainstream journals so as to insure that Myrdal received a hearing. Ben B. Seligman, in *Commentary*, urged readers not to "dismiss Myrdal's profound strictures as so much gab from a Dutch uncle and assert that change of this magnitude is too difficult to accomplish."[63] Henry David, in the *Saturday Review*, called the book "a sermon delivered by a political economist . . . whose knowledge of and affection for the United States and its people have been amply demonstrated." "As a devoted friend of the United States, Myrdal is prepared to speak frankly and bluntly," David noted. "But this should make him no less valuable a friend."[64]

Gunnar Myrdal thus enjoyed a unique status in establishment circles as a privileged critic of the United States in the 1960s and 1970s. He was the one European Social Democrat who had proved his friendship for the United States a generation earlier by his "wise" and "farsighted" counsel on the race issue. Myrdal thus was able to command respectful attention in the mainstream journals for proposals about economic and social justice among classes and among nations that were "socialistic" and beyond the pale of ordinary political discourse in America. Thus *Time* magazine, in a garbled review of *Challenge to Affluence*, began by reciting Myrdal's pedigree as the successor to Tocqueville and Bryce and author of a "definitive study of the American Negro" that influenced the *Brown* decision. After discussing Myrdal's prescriptions for America's ills, the review concluded that his proposals were "too far to the left for most Americans" but suggested that "it is refreshing to find a member of the European Left who is not grousing about American power in the world."[65]

That review appeared before Myrdal's opposition to the Vietnam War, but even afterwards, the mantle of Tocqueville still rested on Myrdal's shoulders. And in occasional interviews and essays in the 1960s and 1970s, he commented on the changes in American race relations since the publication of *An American Dilemma* a generation earlier. Though Myrdal continued to view the race question as a moral and psychological issue, he was not entirely comfortable with the way in which liberals had emphasized only one aspect of *An American Dilemma* in the late 1940s and 1950s to focus on educational campaigns to reduce prejudice and change the minds of individual whites. That was certainly important, in Myrdal's view, but he thought that the United States also needed to make structural changes in the economy and to use social engineering to guarantee to its citizens the rights that Swedes enjoyed under their welfare state. Though he thought that Lyndon Johnson's war on poverty was a rather feeble effort, it was at least a beginning toward the program Myrdal had outlined in *Challenge to Affluence*.

Myrdal greatly admired Martin Luther King, whom he and Alva had entertained in Stockholm in 1964 when the civil rights leader stopped by on his way home from receiving the Nobel Peace Prize in Oslo. When King had asked his advice during that visit on whether to speak out against the Vietnam War, Myrdal had urged him to "follow your conscience," which the young Nobel laureate subsequently did, with Myrdal's full support.[66] Since *Kontakt med Amerika*, Myrdal had hoped for the development of a social democratic movement in the United States that would unite the poor of both races, though he recognized the immense obstacles in the path of such a development. *Challenge to Affluence* had included a call for such a movement at a time when few thought it likely. In a 1967 interview, Myrdal praised Martin Luther King's struggle to lead a poor people's movement designed to unite the poor into a political force that would demand economic justice. Though he continued to insist that there was no "natural solidarity" among the poor of different races, Myrdal hoped that poor Americans would come to recognize that their interests required united action. Thus he envisioned a scenario in which economic and welfare reforms might come in response to organized pressure from below together with enlightened self-interest on the part of educated, middle-class liberals.[67]

After King's assassination and Nixon's election, Myrdal acknowledged that the task of securing full employment and decent housing, education, and medical care for the poor would be far more difficult. Instead of a united poor people's movement forming, racial divisions among the poor seemed to be deepening. With King's death, Myrdal felt that whites as well as blacks had lost a great leader. On his occasional visits to the United States, he got a glimpse of the Black Power movement and found it disturbing. "They see every white as a pig," he complained. "They are most against the liberals on their side. But they don't represent the majority and they are self-defeating, because they cannot win without the help of the majority of Americans who are white."[68] Myrdal preferred, however, to concentrate his criticism on the white power structure rather than on black radicals. In *Against the Stream* he indicted the United States as "that country among the rich countries that has the most and the worst slums, the highest rate of unemployed and unemployables, and the least developed health services, and that is the most niggardly toward its old people and its poor children who are so many, as well as being the country that leads the whole Western world in violence, crime, and corruption in high places."[69] Myrdal tried to shock Americans by suggesting that "you are in the same situation as any underdeveloped country." "You need changes in everything," he thundered, "education, social development, transportation, rebuilding the cities. Over a generation it will cost you a trillion dollars."[70]

Myrdal was a vigorous critic of the United States' policy in Vietnam, arguing to Americans in the mid-1960s that they should negotiate with the Vietnamese Communists. His own research on Southeast Asia led him to the conclusion that President Johnson was poorly advised about the nature of the conflict in Vietnam, and he questioned the competence of his former colleague from the ECE, Walt W. Rostow, as an expert on Asia.[71] On December 8, 1966, Myrdal addressed a peace rally at Madison Square Garden on "The Vietnam War and the Political and Moral Isolation of America." He did not hesitate to put his prestige on the line and tell Americans that the war was contrary to American ideals and that the United States had already lost the battle for world opinion. Myrdal traced the history of the war from the U.S. support for the French colonial regime to the establishment of a succession of juntas in South Vietnam, explained the toll that American bombing was taking on the civilian population, and argued that Americans—but no one else in the world—had been taken in by the propaganda of the United States government.[72] "If this escalating continues," he warned Americans in 1967, "you will isolate yourselves morally and politically in the world. If you rely on financial and military power to run the world, everything you stand for could be lost."[73]

In Sweden, Myrdal served as chairman of the Swedish Vietnam Committee, which sent humanitarian aid to North Vietnam, supported the peace movement in the United States, and welcomed American draft resisters and deserters to Sweden. The committee also sought to mobilize Swedish public opinion against the war, opposed diplomatic relations between Sweden and the South Vietnamese junta, and called for an end to the U.S. bombing. On February 21, 1968, Myrdal addressed a mass demonstration outside the United States embassy in Stockholm denouncing the Johnson administration for breaking international law, using inhuman methods of war, and escalating the war to the point that it threatened a "world catastrophe." All the nations of the world must oppose the war, he declared, and Sweden, as a nonaligned state, must take a leading role in the world antiwar movement. Myrdal also served as cochairman of the International Commission of Inquiry into U.S. War Crimes in Indochina. He complained that the American press gave little coverage to the hearings he had chaired in Stockholm

Gunnar Myrdal, *center*, with Olof Palme, *left*, and Ngyen Tho Chyan, North Vietnam's ambassador to the Soviet Union, demonstrating against the Vietnam War outside the U.S. embassy in Stockholm, 1968 (courtesy Reportagebild, Stockholm)

concerning U.S. war crimes, that Americans were exercising a protective self-censorship and trying to insulate themselves from the growing criticism of American foreign policy in the rest of the world.[74]

In an essay published in the collection *Against the Stream* (1973), Myrdal sought to make Americans aware of the international outrage that many around the world felt over the terror bombing of Hanoi at Christmas 1972. It was not enough, he insisted, for Americans to view Vietnam as a strategic mistake and to withdraw because the war could not be won. "The largest possible number of Americans," Myrdal urged, "must also go through an intellectual and moral catharsis and recognize that the war has been immoral, illegal, cruel, even hideously criminal in the eyes of international law." "Otherwise," he contended, "the United States will not regain the confidence and trust of good people everywhere in the world." After reproving Americans for allowing their government to wage an immoral war, Myrdal proclaimed that he was not a "defeatist" and did not "despair about America." "Among the nations I have come to know," he declared, "none is more prepared and accustomed to revise and change its views and policies." Americans had shown a capacity for "radical conversions," he insisted. The nation had abandoned isolationism after Pearl Harbor, the public had repudiated McCarthy after seeing his bullying tactics on television, and the United States had outlawed segregation and disfranchisement of blacks in the South. If he could just get through to the American conscience, Myrdal believed that he could precipitate another conversion on the Vietnam War. He affirmed that he still "love[d] and admire[d] America next to my own country" and earnestly hoped that it would return to its Enlightenment ideals.[75]

Gunnar Myrdal also confronted Americans on the issue of nuclear disarmament, a goal to which he and Alva shared a deep commitment. Alva Myrdal emerged during the 1960s as a leading spokesperson for the international movement for nuclear disarmament. She had been elected to the upper house of the Swedish parliament in 1962, a year after the Myrdals moved back to Stockholm from New Delhi. From 1962 to 1973, Alva Myrdal headed Sweden's delegation to the United Nations talks on disarmament in Geneva. She also appeared frequently before the United Nations General Assembly in New York, where she appealed to other non-aligned nations to organize nuclear-free zones and to pressure both of the superpowers to end the arms race. In her book *The Game of Disarmament* (1976), she would argue that neither of the superpowers was seriously negotiating for reduction of nuclear weapons. Alva Myrdal brought to the issue a lifetime of political experience in many different fields, and she sought to plan for disarmament from the ground up, urging schoolchildren to visualize a world without nuclear weapons, to write to politicians demanding change, and to organize for peace. Enormously well read, self-disciplined, tactful, and energetic, she was an effective diplomat who could build support for her positions. One of few women in senior diplomatic positions at the United Nations, she was a striking figure: attractive, always fashionably dressed, with a sense of humor and a host of friends from her years of work in Europe, America, and Asia. Alva Myrdal's combination of idealism and common sense won her a broad public following in Sweden, where she came to symbolize the disarmament movement and served in the cabinet as minister for disarmament from 1967 to 1973.[76]

On the nuclear disarmament issue, Gunnar Myrdal strongly supported his wife's work, which he frequently cited in articles, lectures, and interviews in the United States. Alva's resilient faith in humanity's capacity for reason and enlightened self-interest on the disarmament issue helped to keep alive Gunnar's hopes that the world would yet see the kind of international cooperation that the Myrdals had long advocated. In 1964 Gunnar and Alva Myrdal were instrumental in founding the Stockholm International Peace Research Institute (SIPRI), and each of them served terms as chairperson of this center, supported by the Swedish government, which compiles information on the international arms trade. In

1970 the Myrdals jointly received the peace prize of the West German Book Publishers' Association for their work on behalf of nuclear disarmament and equality.[77]

Though Gunnar Myrdal had written and spoken out on many issues, he was always remembered in the United States as the author of *An American Dilemma*, a book that had influenced policymakers and sold over one hundred thousand copies. While many American journalists "tuned out" when he spoke about nuclear disarmament or the need for social welfare reforms and a movement of poor people, they still remembered him as the great expert on the race issue. And so, when Alva stepped down as minister for disarmament and sought time to write a book about the arms race, the Myrdals agreed to return to the United States as visiting scholars so that Gunnar could write a sequel to his masterpiece. As he contemplated writing "An American Dilemma Revisited," Gunnar Myrdal faced some difficult decisions. He had the ear of the establishment press, though not the White House. What would he say? Would the author be Myrdal the pragmatist or Myrdal the utopian? Myrdal the prophet or Myrdal the economic planner? Would he build on *An American Dilemma* and aim to reconstruct a liberal consensus on American race relations, or would he be more daring and provocative, as he had been in *Beyond the Welfare State*, *Challenge to Affluence*, and in his writings on Third World poverty?

The Dilemma Revisited

While many distinguished intellectuals and public figures would choose to spend their seventies writing their memoirs and enjoying their grandchildren, Gunnar Myrdal was determined not to grow old gracefully. He continued to do what he loved most—analyzing social problems and exhorting people to take measures to avert the disasters that threatened to overwhelm humanity in the 1970s and 1980s. "I detest the idea of getting old," he told a Swedish reporter as he and Alva prepared to depart for the United States. "We shall never retire."[78] And so the redoubtable social engineer returned to his "second homeland" in the fall of 1973 to commence work on "An American Dilemma Revisited" as a Fellow of the Center for the Study of Democratic Institutions at Santa Barbara, California. Alva was also a Fellow at the Center, engaged in writing her book on disarmament, and Gunnar was happy to be with her twenty-four hours a day after so many years in which public duties had taken up so much of their time.[79]

The America that Gunnar Myrdal encountered in the early and mid-1970s was a less hopeful country than the one he had known in the late 1930s and early 1940s. He had looked on with dismay as the liberal coalition that had supported the Civil Rights and Voting Rights acts had collapsed in the late 1960s amid race riots, white backlash, and a resurgent conservatism. By the early 1970s, the Nixon administration had dismantled what remained of Johnson's war on poverty. Even more disturbing to him was the fact that, after the assassination of Martin Luther King, there was no strong movement of the poor to demand jobs, housing, decent education, and health care—things that Swedes had taken for granted for thirty years. In the era of Watergate, Americans also seemed to be experiencing a crisis of confidence. Polls indicated that citizens distrusted politicians, viewed their government with increasing cynicism, and thought the nation was entering a period of decline.

Gunnar Myrdal believed that American intellectuals were not providing the kind of leadership that the nation required at this juncture in its history. They were not, in his view, affirming a belief in the ideals of the American creed or offering the kind of constructive planning that was needed to implement the goal of equality for the poor and for minorities. Myrdal was disturbed, on the one hand, by the rise of the neoconservative movement, with its pessimism about the ability of government to create a more egalitarian society. On the other hand, he felt that academic Marxists were not much help in the process of constructing a viable policy that would result in greater equality. In Myrdal's eyes, they were much like the radicals he had met on his first visit to America in 1929–30—shrill and dogmatic precisely because they were so impotent.[80]

In listening to American intellectuals discuss the race issue, Myrdal found himself a dissenter from the concept of cultural pluralism, which was in vogue in the 1970s. He realized, of course, that cultural pluralism was not a new idea in the United States. Intellectuals such as Randolph Bourne, Horace Kallen, Louis Adamic, and Will Herberg had made it a respectable, though not dominant, ideology for sixty years. But it reached a new peak in the 1970s, as the assimilationism that had carried the nation through World War II and the civil rights movement no longer seemed to satisfy either blacks or whites. The Black Power and Black is Beautiful movements of the late 1960s helped to spark an ethnic revival among many European-American ethnic groups as the celebration of ethnic roots gained a new legitimacy. In response to these trends, most social scientists of the 1970s came to see ethnicity as a more enduring feature of American life than it had appeared to Gunnar Myrdal thirty years earlier. Yet few scholars offered a clear program for applying a theory of cultural pluralism to a large continental nation with power and resources unevenly distributed among many groups.[81]

Myrdal fired a salvo against the cultural pluralists in an article, "The Case against Romantic Ethnicity," in 1974. He shrewdly avoided singling out black nationalism for criticism and focused his assault on the ethnic revival movement among whites, which he characterized as "upper-class intellectual romanticism." The real problem of the mass of "ethnics," according to Myrdal, was not a "craving for historical identity," but poverty. The poor needed to overcome ethnic particularism and unite across ethnic lines to better their situation. Since the masses in the United States were traditionally passive, intellectuals had a responsibility to provide leadership. "They must try to instruct and mobilize the passive masses," he urged. "The task of social scientists is to identify and analyze these difficulties and then develop a social engineering that will overcome them." Myrdal seemed unaware of the extent to which many European ethnics had moved into the middle class in the thirty years since the end of World War II. His arguments in many ways recapitulated the views that Ralph Bunche and Franklin Frazier had held during the 1930s. Myrdal concluded that "like all romanticisms," [the ethnic revival movement] "serves conservative and, in fact, reactionary interests because it is innocent and innocuous. . . . Since it does not raise the crucial problems of power and money, it does not really disturb the conservatives."[82]

During his year in Santa Barbara, Myrdal came to realize that he could not do all the research for "An American Dilemma Revisited" alone and that, in the political climate of the 1970s, it would be prudent to ask a black scholar to join him as coauthor. Accordingly, he invited his old friend Kenneth Clark to share in the authorship of the book. Myrdal told Clark that he respected his work and admired him for remaining a steadfast advocate of integration, even as the "black segregationists" gained ground in academic circles in the late 1960s and 1970s. Clark, as a graduate student at Columbia, had been a research assistant on the original Carnegie-Myrdal project thirty years earlier. He had been impressed then by Myrdal's fairness and by the way that Myrdal had treated him as a colleague despite his lowly academic status, taking him out to lunch and arguing vigorously about the most effective strategies in the struggle for racial equality. Now, with a grant from the Carnegie Corporation, the two men planned a major study that would involve the collaboration of a staff of social scientists to survey the vast social science literature on various aspects of black-white relations and address policy questions in such areas as unemployment, welfare, housing, health, education, and crime. With America's bicentennial in progress, it seemed like an appropriate time to assess the United States' success in living up to its Enlightenment ideals on the race issue and to survey the progress in the securing of civil rights since the publication of An American Dilemma as well as to examine the problems that remained.[83]

The partnership between Myrdal and Clark was not to last, however. Even though their views were similar on most major issues, the two old friends found themselves in a personality conflict. Myrdal's health was beginning to fail, as Parkinson's disease added to the pain he still felt from the auto accident twenty years earlier. He knew that there was much to say about the many dimensions of American racial and economic inequality, and he knew that he might not live to finish the project. Myrdal spoke to Clark and to other psychologists about his fear of death, and asked for their advice on how to face it; Clark gave him books and articles by psychologists on death and dying. According to Clark, his friend compensated for his failing health by becoming somewhat dictatorial with respect to the project. Clark, accustomed to directing his own research projects, was temperamentally unable to bear this situation and withdrew from the collaboration, while reassuring Myrdal of his great respect, friendship, and good wishes for

Kenneth Clark, *left*, briefly collaborated with Gunnar Myrdal on "An American Dilemma Revisited." He is shown here with Alva and Gunnar at a reception in New York City, 1975. (courtesy Arbetarrörelsens Arkiv, Stockholm)

the study.[84] Myrdal admitted that he really wanted to write the book alone as his final statement on the American race issue. He had found it disorienting to share the direction with Clark, who had so many other commitments, and to deal with a staff in Washington while he was living in New York and spending part of the year in Stockholm. At age seventy-six, he feared becoming a mere figurehead in a study that might take several years to complete.[85]

Gunnar Myrdal continued to work on "An American Dilemma Revisited" as a visitor at several American universities in the late 1970s, but he and Alva continued to live part of each year in Sweden. When a Swedish reporter asked him why he kept returning to the United States, he replied that "the doctor must devote himself to the seriously ill."[86] But with his own health failing, and lacking a stable institutional base and a research staff, Myrdal was unable to keep abreast of the scholarly literature on race and ethnicity to produce the kind of ambitious, interdisciplinary social science study that he was accustomed to writing. More and more, the project became one man's reflections on America's successes and failures in living up to its ideals with respect to its black citizens.

In a lecture at Columbia University on October 28, 1976, Myrdal presented some of his initial findings on "Race and Class in a Welfare State." Part of an American bicentennial symposium, "The National Purpose Reexamined," the occasion was tailor-made for him. He posed the question of why white Americans accepted, and in some cases actively supported, the Civil Rights Act of 1964 and the Voting Rights Act of 1965. Myrdal asserted that they did not do so out of fear but because their consciences had been "stamped" with Enlightenment ideals of the American Revolution, which had become "an active social force." The Swedish observer marveled at the changes that had come to the South in the previous fifteen years, as public facilities were desegregated, blacks voted freely, and politicians abandoned white supremacist rhetoric. He cited opinion research that indicated dramatic reversals in white attitudes toward blacks, and he noted that affirmative action programs were helping some blacks to enter the middle class, though these programs did little for the underclass.[87]

Turning to black attitudes and ideologies, Myrdal conceded that "a forceful confirmation that 'black is beautiful' is a healthy reaction, and so is the resistance against giving up all cultural traits that have emerged in their somewhat special history." But he counseled against "self-segregation" by blacks, such as all-black dormitories on college campuses or all-black programs of black studies. What was needed was more integration, more awareness by all Americans of "black history, economy, and culture." "In a fully integrated American nation there would be little reason for black nationalism," he concluded.[88]

Myrdal lectured his audience that the United States, unlike most Western European countries, utterly lacked a conception of social reform as an investment in people, a "prophylactic" measure designed to prevent crime, disorder, and inefficiency. Everywhere in America he encountered a "defeatist" attitude toward the poor, as even experts concluded that the answer was to "lock them up" and bring back capital punishment. The Swedish critic declared that medical care for the poor was "underdeveloped" in the United States and that a vast gap existed in the quality of schools for rich and poor children. He charged that the welfare system was "generally acknowledged to be muddled, relatively expensive, humiliating and unfair, and to produce many unfortunate effects on the welfare clientele." Surveying the period since World War II, Myrdal traced the retreat of the U.S. government from a commitment to full employment, as the "acceptable" level of unemployment rose from 3 to 4 to 6 percent. Meanwhile, the masses remained politically apathetic, and voter participation hovered at 50 percent, compared with over 90 percent in many European countries. In view of the problem of "mass passivity," Myrdal suggested that it was up to educated middle-class Americans to exert the moral leadership needed to overcome the United States' political and social problems.[89]

America, Myrdal concluded, faced a "multifaceted" crisis so severe that one had to ask if it even made sense to measure the nation's performance against the ideals of the American creed. His answer to this rhetorical question was "definitely yes." America's problems were fundamentally a "moral crisis." "I cannot believe," he affirmed, "that America has come to the end of its long march to become a more perfect union."[90] But Myrdal made no specific policy proposals in the speech. Nor did he develop specific policy ideas in the various drafts of "An American Dilemma

Revisited" that he would write in the late 1970s and early 1980s. Though he thought that the United States needed to spend a trillion dollars on a domestic Marshall Plan for its cities and its poor, he realized that he lacked the expertise, the staff, and the health to present the kind of detailed policy proposals that he had offered in his work on Third World development.

In his work on "An American Dilemma Revisited," Myrdal was prepared to offer stinging indictments of American racism and economic inequality, but he did not come up with the kind of daring policy proposals that he had made to various governments on the issue of development. In a sense, he remained a captive of the liberal orthodoxy he had created thirty years earlier. Myrdal seemed incapable of moving very far beyond it, except to connect in a general way his version of moralistic American liberalism to the goals of the welfare state. He often said with pride that in the United States, he talked to Americans as if he were an American, saw problems "from an American viewpoint," and did not resort to foreign "isms" or try to impose a Swedish model on a very different social and political system.[91] While this was in some ways a strength, it could also be a weakness. One of the striking things in his work on the sequel was his failure to apply any new concepts from his work on the Third World or to build on his ideas in *Beyond the Welfare State* and *Challenge to Affluence* about strengthening political participation and decentralizing bureaucracy. Nor did he have any new ideas about how Afro-Americans or the poor could organize themselves to maximize their power in a difficult period. On his early visits to the United States, Myrdal had learned not to talk about socialism in America, a lesson reinforced by his experiences during the McCarthy period. While he would have welcomed a powerful movement from below to change the nation's politics and bring about greater equality, such a movement was not in the offing in the 1970s. When he looked upon the United States' "underdeveloped" systems of welfare, education, health care, housing, and transportation, he saw little hope for massive structural changes unless he could somehow get through to the conscience of middle-class Americans and shock them into working for change. At age seventy-seven, he found his most effective role to be that of moral critic rather than social engineer.

In a speech to the annual meeting of the Lutheran Council of America during the United States' bicentennial year, Myrdal delivered a valedictory address to his second homeland, as well as an ironic jeremiad aimed at the churchgoing nation that threatened to blow up the world with nuclear weapons while ignoring the poor in its cities and the hungry in the Third World. If he sounded a bit shrill, it was because he could not help feeling frustrated with Americans, who showered honorary degrees and celebrity interviews on him and bought his books in sufficient quantities to give him a sizable income but refused to listen to his advice about foreign policy or domestic reforms. Since his boyhood visits to the mission house in Solvarbo, Myrdal had been skeptical of most forms of organized religion, and he had consistently underestimated the importance of religion as an influence on social and political behavior. Never a churchgoer in his adult life, his private conversation was usually laced with profanity, which he used to shock his listeners into an awareness of social and moral problems. Yet in looking back on his life, Myrdal concluded that "in insisting that social science is a moral science and that economics is political economy, I express my Lutheran heritage." He had been fortunate, he recounted, to grow up in an era of optimism, when the heritage of the Enlightenment blended with the Lutheran moral vision to produce a faith in the improvability of humankind. Since Sweden had been spared the horrible carnage of World War I, his generation had not lost faith in the possibility of human progress. Myrdal confessed that he and his generation had "play[ed] with certain romantic feelings for Napoleon . . . and . . . indulge[d] in the pessimism of a Schopenhauer [and] in the aggressive egocentricity of a Nietzsche." But these were passing fancies, he claimed, less important to his intellectual development than the philosophers of the Enlightenment and the "French and English utopian socialists who, unlike Marx, were planners in the great tradition of the Enlightenment philosophy." Though the philosophes of the eighteenth century had lambasted the "superstition" and "priestcraft" of Christianity, from Myrdal's vantage point in the 1970s, both intellectual traditions were similar in offering hope for human improvement. The Enlightenment and Christianity "both recognized evil but saw the prospect of the amelioration of personal and social life—in religious terms, of 'conversion.'" "This is the spiritual heritage I have preserved," he affirmed, "and it has become deeply rooted in my way of feeling and thinking."[92]

Myrdal reassured his audience that he still believed that "America is not going to give up its essential national personality" in dealing with the race issue. Ironically invoking Martin Luther, he declared: "Here I stick to my basic optimism from the Roosevelt era and, further back, to my devotion to [the] Enlightenment and to the influence of my Lutheran heritage." But Americans, he insisted, must face the fact that the nation was in a moral crisis. "What is at stake in the present many-faceted crisis in America is nothing less than the nation's soul." Myrdal then ticked off a list of the United States' deepest failings. "The Vietnam War," he charged, "was not only a gross miscalculation, politically and militarily, but a moral wrong inflicted by a massive use of cruel weapons forbidden by international law, mostly against poor and innocent civilians." Myrdal chastised Americans for trying to forget about the nation's mistakes in Vietnam. "Americans must honestly face what for a long time they have permitted their government to do," he asserted. "Otherwise they will not be cured of the evil."[93]

The Swedish moralist deplored the United States' policies toward underdeveloped countries, which, he said, were motivated by self-interest and strategic considerations, not concern for the poor. He reminded his audience that Americans gave a smaller percentage of their wealth to poor nations than other advanced countries, and he noted that the gap between rich nations and poor nations was growing greater. During the oil crisis of the early 1970s, he charged, "America was niggardly with its food aid, and its government was pleased that the high food prices improved its balance of trade. Meanwhile hundreds of millions in underdeveloped countries went hungry and tens of millions starved." At the same time that the United States ignored the hungry, he complained, it continued to contribute to the spiraling arms race. Myrdal pointed out that the cost of armaments equaled "the total production and income of the poorer half of humankind." Citing Alva Myrdal's *The Game of Disarmament*, Gunnar protested the superpowers' "strange 'cooperation'" in "stalling" disarmament negotiations. "The underlying idea of the nuclear arms race—that the superpowers need to 'balance' each other—is totally irrational for both of them," he exclaimed.[94]

Looking back on his youth, Myrdal recalled, "It was the firm conviction of secular philosophy as well as religious teaching . . . that morals and rational reasoning lead to the same conclusions, and this was the basis of the trust in progress I was brought up with." For fifty years, he had been writing books in which he had argued that the correct moral choice was also the politically neces- sary course of action, but he worried that "I am growing old and nearing the end of my life in a situation rapidly approaching disaster." Myrdal insisted, however, that his ideals remained unchanged and that he was "not prepared to be a defeatist," even when "a realistic analysis produces a gloomy picture." He adjured his Lu- theran audience to stand up against the arms race and to fight poverty and injustice. Praising the ecumenical movement, Myrdal proclaimed that "questions about dogma or even faith shrink to insignificance in a world where there is uncertainty whether any human beings will be left at the turn of the century." With a humorous touch, he warned the Lutheran clergy not to yield to the "temptation" to "play down the social gospel and to focus one's teaching on the salvation of the individual." The old skeptic suggested that if humankind were to survive into the twenty-first century, pastors would have to inspire their flock "to care intelligently about broader national and international moral problems." Myrdal concluded his address by admitting that he had taken a lot of criticism from social scientists for making moral arguments in his research, but he insisted that "when social scien- tists, in their efforts to remain simply 'objective,' forget that people have a con- science to which they plead, they are in my opinion unrealistic and are not doing their duty as scientists."[95]

The Last Years

After delivering these impassioned speeches in an effort to call Americans back to their ideals, Gunnar Myrdal returned to Stockholm to complete "An American Dilemma Revisited." He and Alva lived in an apartment in a seventeenth-century house on a cobblestone street in the heart of Stockholm with a view that looked out over the gabled rooftops of city's Old Town district. They still worked at the large desk specially made for them that allowed them to face each other while writing. Gunnar Myrdal had received honorary degrees from more than thirty universities around the world and had been awarded the Nobel Prize in economics in 1974. Though he had scoffed at Nobel prizes in economics as "silly" and grumbled about having to share his with the conservative Austrian economist Friedrich von Hayek, Gunnar nonetheless had donned his tuxedo and accepted the prize from King Carl XVI Gustaf. The young man who had dreamed of forming a "party of intelligence" could look back on a career that had brought him into contact with such extraordinary figures as Gustav Cassel, W. I. and Dorothy Thomas, Ernst Wigforss, Ralph Bunche, Louis Wirth, Franklin Frazier, Dag Hammarskjöld, Jawaharlal Nehru, and, of course, Alva, as he had engaged in economic planning, social engineering, and political analysis in Europe, America, and South Asia. Gunnar could still joke to a Swedish colleague that if he and his friend John Kenneth Galbraith were together on a mountain in Switzerland with a staff of assistants, they could solve all the problems of the world. In reality, though, he knew that the problems of the arms race, world hunger, and environmental mismanagement threatened to overwhelm all of the experts in the world, and in later years he supplemented his advocacy of planning with recommendations for decentralization of certain governmental functions and greater citizen participation.

Alva Myrdal was awarded the Nobel Peace Prize in 1982 for her work on disarmament, making the Myrdals the only married couple to win Nobel prizes independently in different fields. In her late seventies, Alva remained an active public figure in Sweden, a prominent Social Democrat, a symbol of the disarmament movement, and a role model for many women. Year after year in public opinion polls, Swedes named her the nation's most admired woman. Between them, the Myrdals had worked on nearly every important political and social issue of the twentieth century: the welfare state, economic planning, birth control, feminism, child care, public housing, agricultural policy, antifascism, race relations, educational reform, European reconstruction, East-West détente, opposition to the Vietnam War, nuclear disarmament, the global environment, and Third World poverty.

As children of the Enlightenment, the Myrdals had always sought to live their lives according to rational principles, to incorporate current psychological theories into their own family life, and to open their lives to a certain amount of public scrutiny. Gunnar in particular felt that it was important for people to understand the valuations that social scientists brought to their work. Accordingly, they gave their vast collection of professional correspondence to the Archive of the Labor Movement in Stockholm and opened their papers to scholars during their lifetime. In a "Self-declaration" written in 1982, Gunnar reminisced about his life and values and acknowledged that his royalty income and prizes had made him rich, causing his conscience to work overtime trying to figure out how to give the money away and leading him to scrutinize his expenditures to see if he was spending too much on his lifestyle. With a touch of self-deprecating humor, he confessed to a few "moral compromises," notably his summer house in the resort town of Mariefred, but he hoped that he was not as bad as Thomas Jefferson, who

Gunnar Myrdal, *left*, receives the Nobel Prize for economics from King Carl XVI Gustaf, 1974. Afterward, Myrdal commented, "I don't like ceremonies." (courtesy Reportagebild, Stockholm)

had kept his slaves because he needed them to maintain Monticello.[96] In his later years, Gunnar also admitted to a problem with immodesty, even going so far as to apologize to his friend John Kenneth Galbraith for being "egocentric" and talking too much at a session of the American Economic Association.[97]

In a joint interview in 1980, Gunnar and Alva reflected on their long relationship that had begun with the bicycle trip in 1919. Asked how their marriage endured all the long separations when professional responsibilities drew them to different parts of the globe, Alva replied diplomatically, "Even when duty makes us sail apart, we're still consort battleships." When asked about hobbies, Alva responded, "We enjoy talking together more than anything else," to which Gunnar added, "Alva is my hobby." He declared, "People don't realize the great happiness there is in living to be very old and together all the time. The older we get, the closer we are."[98] Gunnar was fully aware of the vital and multifaceted role that Alva had played in his life and career. "I have never believed in God," he remarked to his Indian friend Tarlok Singh, "but there must be a God, or Alva would not have come to me."[99]

Despite all their accomplishments and their efforts to enjoy their old age together, the last years would be painful for both Alva and Gunnar Myrdal. Their

Gunnar and Alva in their apartment in Stockholm's Old Town, 1978
(courtesy Reportagebild, Stockholm)

peace was shattered in 1982 when their son, Jan, a fifty-five-year-old, radical Swedish writer, published the first volume of a literary autobiography, which covered his life to the age of ten. Jan had had a difficult childhood. The experience of being left with his grandparents for a year in 1929–30 when he was two years old, while Gunnar and Alva traveled to the United States as Rockefeller Fellows, had left emotional scars. Labeled a "problem child" by his parents, he had grown into a rebellious teenager who quarreled with Gunnar and Alva and left home before finishing gymnasium. Though Jan continued to disagree with his parents about politics, he lived with them in Geneva and New Delhi for short periods in the 1950s. As a literary critic, journalist, and political commentator in Swedish newspapers, he became an important and controversial figure in Swedish letters and achieved international recognition for his books *Report from a Chinese Village* and *Confessions of a Disloyal European.* Gunnar had been particularly proud of his son's work on the Third World, though they often disagreed, and he gave copies of Jan's books to his friends. The relationship between Jan and his parents had ruptured in the winter of 1967–68 over the Vietnam War, however. All of the Myrdals had been against American policy, of course, but Jan belonged to a more radical group within the Vietnam movement in Sweden, and he had believed that Prime Minister Tage Erlander's Social Democratic government, in which Alva served as a minister, was not really doing anything to aid the National Liberation Front. When Jan got into a scuffle with the Stockholm police during a demonstration, he blamed the Social Democratic government for the police's actions in breaking up the demonstration. Gunnar told him to stop embarrassing his mother. After a tumultuous argument with his parents, Jan broke off communication with Gunnar and Alva in 1968 and never spoke to them again.[100]

Instead he crafted his book *Barndom*, the title of which was a pun that could be read as meaning both "childhood" and "child's verdict." A painful portrait of an unhappy childhood, the book portrayed his parents as ambitious, driven people who had little interest in nurturing children. Gunnar, in this account, was explosive, egotistical, and domineering; Alva was cold, manipulative, and lacking in spontaneity. Their rhetoric about equality and morality was a pose that masked their own personal ambitions. In Jan's eyes, his parents, like most Social Democratic leaders, were not really concerned about the poor; they wanted an upper-class lifestyle and the power to manipulate people. In his view, Gunnar and Alva's public image was a lie, covering up a failed marriage, a disastrous relationship with their son, and phony politics. Jan read his book over Swedish radio on Saturday mornings, as the nation listened with amazement to this account of the turmoil and conflict within a family that many Swedes had viewed with respect and admiration. Gunnar and Alva, at the ages of eighty-three and eighty, suddenly found their family problems played out in a Strindbergesque drama before the Swedish media. Television and radio covered the family quarrel, intellectuals offered psychological analysis in newspaper columns, and the tabloid press reported on the Myrdals in a sensational manner. Though Sissela Bok and Kaj Fölster loyally supported their parents during this crisis, both lived outside of Sweden, and the Swedish press focused its coverage on Jan, who was a major figure in Swedish intellectual life. The media uproar over Jan's book cast a shadow over Alva's career during the year in which she won the Nobel Peace Prize. Some reviewers hailed *Barndom* as a masterpiece of modern Swedish literature and compared it to Rousseau's *Confessions* while others saw it as cruel and vindictive. Jan said that the book should be seen as imaginative literature, not as a strictly literal account of every event mentioned in the book.[101] He insisted that his intent was not to create a scandal but to write an honest book that captured the emotions of an unhappy childhood.

For Gunnar and Alva Myrdal, who had risen to fame in Sweden forty years earlier as champions of welfare reforms designed to enable people to have a happier family life, it was a bitter wound to bear in their old age. As young reformers in the 1930s, both had believed that frank and open discussions of family issues were essential to a more rational approach to family life. In middle age, Gunnar and Alva had acknowledged to each other that their marriage was troubled, but they had reconciled and resumed their close, interdependent relationship. Jan's book was the first glimpse that the public had into the conflict that had accompanied their extraordinary marriage and family life. Never one to take

Alva Myrdal, Sweden's most admired woman, diplomat, feminist, and champion of disarmament, 1980 (courtesy Arbetarrörelsens Arkiv, Stockholm)

criticism lying down, Gunnar fumed, in a newspaper article, that his son had written a "hateful" book, full of lies, and he proceeded to offer a point-by-point refutation of several anecdotes in *Barndom*. Gunnar regarded himself as a social scientist who had pursued truth fearlessly, often putting himself at odds with governments and established opinion, and he was outraged at Jan's portrait of him as a man whose public pronouncements of egalitarian values were belied by private sentiments of elitism and condescension. But what most infuriated him was Jan's attack on Alva and the implication that she had not been a good mother. The old and ailing man raged against his ungrateful child before the press. "He has spit on us," Gunnar exclaimed. "When I am dead, people will know the truth," he declared, noting that he was dictating his memories of Jan's childhood into a tape recorder and promising that his and Alva's personal letters and diaries would eventually be opened to a curious public.[102] Jan replied with two more volumes, carrying the story through his crisis of puberty, with more tales of his father's tyrannical behavior and his mother's coldly rational aloofness.[103]

Alva Myrdal had suffered from aphasia for some time, as a brain tumor caused excruciating headaches and left her speechless for hours or days. In 1984 she and Gunnar moved to a nursing home in a suburb of Stockholm, and shortly thereafter, Alva underwent neurosurgery, which failed to improve her condition. She remained in the hospital, in a coma. Burdened with grief and loneliness, Gunnar called her doctors every morning to inquire about her condition, which grew no better. She died on February 1, 1986.[104]

A memorial service for Alva, televised throughout Sweden, was held in the Storkyrkan, a large cathedral in Stockholm. The diplomatic corps, including the American and Soviet ambassadors, members of Parliament, and leaders of the women's, peace, and trade union movements, all took part in the ceremony. Prime Minister Olof Palme eulogized his colleague in one of his last speeches before his assassination, reminding Swedes that Alva Myrdal had been an early champion of women's liberation and a practical reformer who had struggled for equality and human rights for all peoples. She never doubted that reason would overcome the madness of the nuclear arms race, he declared. She had never given up, despite the heightening of tension between the superpowers during the last years of her life. Palme remembered her as a generous and loving person, a light for Swedish Social Democrats and for the world. For Gunnar Myrdal, it was the end of a remarkable relationship that had begun sixty-seven years earlier and endured through many personal, professional, and political challenges in Europe, America, and Asia. Alva had deepened his concern for social justice, sharpened his understanding of psychological and social issues, and offered extraordinary understanding and support. Gunnar listened silently to the eulogies and laid a wreath in honor of his wife. At the close of the service, supported by grandsons on either arm, he walked out of the church, surrounded by a procession of two thousand people carrying candles into the dark winter night and singing, "We shall overcome."[105]

Gunnar, *left*, with daughter Sissela Bok and Bishop Krister Stendahl, at memorial service for Alva, Stockholm, 1986 (courtesy Reportagebild, Stockholm)

Gunnar Myrdal had kept up a rigorous schedule of writing in the midst of all this pain. He refused to write an autobiography, regarding such an enterprise as a misuse of his talents when he could still make a contribution to the fight against war, racism, and inequality. He did take time out from his work on American race relations to write a book on how Sweden is governed, in which he included autobiographical material on Swedish politics in the 1930s and 1940s as well as some acerbic comments on the bureaucracy in the 1970s.[106] But the major task of his last years was "An American Dilemma Revisited." He had written several chapters during his visits to the United States in the 1970s, in which he had sketched out the changes in American race relations during the 1950s and 1960s. Back in Sweden, however, he lacked the resources, staff, and libraries to write the kind of comprehensive analysis of contemporary black-white relations that his Columbia University address had promised. Increasingly "An American Dilemma Revisited" became more of a reminiscence about the original Myrdal study and an attempt to restore a sharp moral focus to the issue of racial inequality, which many white Americans had managed to forget in the years since the civil rights movement. Myrdal struggled to keep up his optimism about America's capacity to combat racism and poverty. The election of Ronald Reagan in 1980 was a severe shock. But Myrdal wrote in 1982 that the new president's economic policies were "idiotic," and he prophesied that Reagan would be "a short episode in America's development."[107]

In a last attempt to save "The American Dilemma Revisited," the Carnegie Corporation dispatched the American political scientist and civil rights activist Leslie Dunbar to Sweden to work with Gunnar Myrdal as a coauthor. A southern liberal who had been closely involved with the civil rights movement, Dunbar visited Myrdal in the nursing home in 1984, read over his chapters, and taped interviews, trying to evoke Myrdal's ideas about the history of the black revolt in the South and his observations about black-white relations in the 1980s. But it was too late.[108]

After Alva was hospitalized in 1984, Gunnar lived alone in a small room in the nursing home with only a narrow bed, a desk, a chair, a radio, and a paperback edition of *An American Dilemma*. For a man whose identity was bound up with his intellectual work and who read voraciously in several languages, Parkinson's disease and the infirmities of old age were a cruel punishment. Myrdal experienced tremors in his hands and feet, making it difficult to write or walk. He was virtually blind and suffered a severe loss of memory. As his world grew darker around him, Gunnar Myrdal fought to retain his faith in human reason and struggled fiercely to continue his work, dictating into a tape recorder. In 1985 he appended the following note to a draft of the sequel:

> I am now 86 years of age. My trouble is that I, who have never been ill, have got a more and more serious bout of Parkinson's Disease. It has to the extent been going above my neck that I am now unable to write legibly enough to read my own handwriting. My eyesight has deteriorated and is deteriorating. I can see only with one eye.
>
> Because of these disabilities I have not been able to travel to America or even to visit a Swedish library which in any case would be very poorly stocked with relevant material. My only printed source has been a copy of *An American Dilemma* which I read ten years ago and which has many annotations in the margin.[109]

Alva's death in 1986 brought a further deterioration in Gunnar's health. In the spring of 1987, Gunnar Myrdal was moved to a Stockholm hospital, where his daughters, Sissela Bok and Kaj Fölster, and his grandsons, Stefan Fölster and Janken Myrdal, visited him regularly. Gunnar Myrdal died on May 17, 1987, the thirty-third anniversary of the United States Supreme Court's *Brown v. Board of Education* decision.

Legacy

A famous story, told by Gunnar Myrdal's friends and authenticated by Alva, concerns his relations with the older generation of Swedish economists in the late 1920s. After the brash young turk had managed to offend several of the older scholars by his irreverent criticisms of their work, David Davidson, one of the senior figures, had taken him aside and warned him to be more careful not to hurt their feelings because he would need their support to get promoted. With the impetuousness of youth, Gunnar had replied, "Ah, but you forget. It is we *young-sters* who will the have the last word: for it is we who will write your obituaries."[110] It never occurred to Gunnar Myrdal at the time that someday his own obituary would be written by his son, but it was an opportunity that Jan was not prepared to pass up. In a long essay published in a Swedish newspaper, Jan acknowledged that his father had been an original thinker and one of the century's great economists and social scientists, whose books were part of a tradition that included Adam Smith, Marx, and Keynes. Gunnar Myrdal's 1956 Cairo lectures, *Development and Underdevelopment*, had influenced Castro, Nehru, and other Third World leaders and had "opened an epoch of debate on development and underdevelopment." Jan discounted the influence of American liberalism on his father's thought and contended that Gunnar Myrdal had remained an advocate of the strong nation-state from his youthful enthusiasm for Rudolf Kjellén through his advocacy of the Swedish welfare state to his critique of "soft states" in the Third World. Reviewing various family crises that he had discussed in his writings and that his sister Sissela Bok had described in her biography of Alva Myrdal, Jan argued that his parents' marriage had been a folie à deux. He insisted that his father had an aristocratic conception of himself, expected deference from those around him, and interpreted criticism as a personal affront. It was a good thing, Jan concluded, that the Social Democrats had not allowed Gunnar to become prime minister, or this "Nietzsche-reading student" who had grown into a man with "imperial notions" would have had the power of the state to use against his critics.[111]

Jan's obituary, which overlooked his father's contributions to the American civil rights struggle, misinterpreted his concept of the "soft state," and minimized his father's concern with issues of equality, was scarcely the last word on Gunnar Myrdal's career. Although Gunnar, as a man who disliked ceremony, had directed that there should be no large funeral or public memorial service after his death, a small number of friends and family members, but not Jan, gathered for a memorial meeting in Stockholm. Lars Ingelstam, a friend and younger colleague, remarked that Gunnar Myrdal was a "paradoxical man": "behind the facade of academic aristocrat burned eyes alert with intellectual curiosity." He remembered Gunnar as "always straining after new thoughts, after stimulation in a clash of opinions, after weak points in his own or others' reasoning." Ingelstam observed that there was in Gunnar Myrdal "an unbending desire to bring about change, an insistence that the world could be arranged in a more rational manner." Therefore

Myrdal had never succumbed to the cynicism so common to intellectuals, even though he was profoundly critical of the actions of governments around the world. To the end, he had fought a battle "against cynicism and for hope." His struggle to use human reason to combat injustice was inspirational for those who knew him, even if they disagreed with him on particular issues.[112]

From many parts of the earth, men and women assessed the remarkable life and multifaceted contributions of Gunnar Myrdal. Prime Minister Ingvar Carlsson called him a mentor to a generation of Social Democrats, and a Swedish newspaper termed him "The Conscience of the Whole World."[113] In Geneva, Melvin Fagen, a United Nations official who had served his apprenticeship under Myrdal at the ECE, observed, "No other social scientist of our times has had a more profound and pervasive influence on the world today than Gunnar Myrdal," noting his work on race, underdevelopment, détente, the arms race, and the welfare state.[114] The American economist Charles Kindleberger wrote that Myrdal had been "enormously creative in technical economics" but that his greatest contributions were in calling attention to the hidden value premises of economists and in extending the scope of economic investigations to include political, social, and psychological factors.[115] In India, Tarlok Singh remembered Myrdal's "personal identification with India and with the goals set by Mahatma Gandhi and Jawaharlal Nehru and his fervent wish that we in India must strive to the utmost to fulfil them." When Myrdal had spoken out against corruption and inefficiency in the Indian government, Singh observed, the Swedish critic had tried to live up "to Abraham Lincoln's maxim that hung in his room, 'To sin by silence when they should protest makes cowards of men.'"[116]

In the United States, Coretta Scott King wrote of Gunnar Myrdal's legacy for Americans. She remembered how much she and Martin Luther King valued the "friendship and wisdom" of Gunnar and Alva. After noting the impact of *An American Dilemma* on American thought and the *Brown* decision, she observed:

> Dr. Myrdal understood that we could never build a sound economy in America or elsewhere around poverty. He also had great admiration and expectation for America and like Martin did not hesitate to say that America on the issue of the Vietnam war was wrong. Dr. Myrdal shared Martin's dream that the conflict between American idealism and the reality of racism would be resolved. . . . He will be remembered as a statesman, reformer, dissenter, pacifist, foe of inequality and most important a dreamer who actively pursued the realization of his dream for all humankind.[117]

In the manuscript "An American Dilemma Revisited" that he dictated during those last painful years, Gunnar Myrdal relived the experiences that had begun fifty years earlier when he had received Keppel's amazing invitation to travel to the United States to conduct an "unbiased" study of the American race issue. Though he had struggled with many other issues during his long life, none had engaged his moral concerns so deeply. Looking back on those days, Myrdal remembered his gradual discovery of the enormity of the problem he had taken on as Jackson Davis drove him and Sterner through the South in an old Buick in the fall of 1938. He recalled his travels with Ralph Bunche and their risky defiance of the color line in the South, and he reminisced about his interviews with sheriffs, plantation owners, sharecroppers, prisoners on chain gangs, and high officials in Washington. Gunnar relived his and Alva's dangerous passage back to Sweden in May 1940 aboard the *Mathilda Thordén* and recalled the frantic pace at which he, Sterner, and Rose had labored on their "war work" at Princeton. But Gunnar Myrdal sought to write more than a book of memories. He was distressed that the optimism of that era in American history had given way to cynicism and despair. He found it hard to believe that the wealthiest nation on earth tolerated 50 percent rates of unemployment among black youth in its poor neighborhoods, that it had allowed its central cities to deteriorate into wretched slums, and that it viewed its poor people as an unemployable underclass to be written off as hopeless. And so Myrdal spent many of the last lucid moments of his life in an attempt to reawaken America's conscience to the moral challenge posed by racism and economic injustice.[118]

With the passing of Gunnar Myrdal, the United States lost a unique figure, a foreign critic who declared that he loved Americans but hated the injustice that the nation tolerates at home and abroad. As a young man, he had drawn inspiration from the intellectual legacy of America's Progressive movement, with its optimistic faith in social engineering and moral exhortation. He and Alva had felt energized and stimulated by American culture and intellectual life even as they criticized the nation's political conservatism and economic inequality. The New Deal had raised Myrdal's hopes for the United States, and during World War II he had been able to reach Americans with his appeal to the nation's conscience, his invocation of the universal values of the Enlightenment, and his vision of social engineering. *An American Dilemma* had caught the optimistic spirit of the war years and appealed to the belief in American exceptionalism—the idea that the United States had been founded on the ideals of democracy, liberty, and equality and that it held itself to higher standards of public behavior than other nations. The liberal orthodoxy that Myrdal created endured for twenty years, withstanding the onslaught of segregationists after the *Brown* decision and offering powerful support to the civil rights movement. A later generation of scholars pointed to Myrdal's lack of empirical verification of the moral dilemma thesis, his exaggeration of the pathological elements in black culture, and his inadequate treatment of the economic causes of racism. They noted that Myrdal's stark assimilationism did not comprehend the complex social fabric of a multicultural society and that his social engineering often disregarded the importance of political participation by people of all social classes. Yet *An American Dilemma* has had an enduring power because of Myrdal's insistence that Americans live up to their creed and accord political and economic justice to all citizens.

During the 1960s and 1970s, Gunnar Myrdal was the only European Social

Democrat who was both willing to make frank criticisms of American policies and able to command a broad audience in the American press over a considerable period of time. In speeches, articles, and interviews, in *Challenge to Affluence* and in his work on "An American Dilemma Revisited," he sought to push Americans to do something about the scandal of poverty in a society of abundance. Myrdal's combination of moral exhortation and optimism about American culture and institutions, and his distinguished record of intellectual achievement, sometimes enabled him to penetrate the defenses that Americans usually put up against censure from outsiders. Yet Americans in the 1980s seemed unwilling to summon the political will to act decisively on the issues of racism and poverty that Myrdal entreated them to face. Gunnar Myrdal did not live to sketch out in detail policy alternatives for combating institutional racism and poverty among the underclass, but he did call on Americans to build on the successes of the civil rights movement by insuring a decent standard of living for all citizens. To the end of his life, he continued to challenge Americans to take their ideals seriously and to look within themselves for the moral strength to eliminate racism and poverty from American society.

Notes

Abbreviations

AMP   Alva Myrdal Papers, Arbetarrörelsens Arkiv, Stockholm
CCA   Carnegie Corporation Archives, New York, N.Y.
FBI   Federal Bureau of Investigation Headquarters, Washington, D.C.
GEB   General Education Board
GMP   Gunnar Myrdal Papers, Arbetarrörelsens Arkiv, Stockholm
NA   National Archives, Washington, D.C.
NSGC   Negro Study General Correspondence, Carnegie Corporation Archives, New York, N.Y.

Preface

1. Gunnar Myrdal, with the assistance of Richard Sterner and Arnold Rose, *An American Dilemma: The Negro Problem and Modern Democracy* (New York: Harper & Brothers, 1944). On the influence of the book, John Higham has written that *An American Dilemma* "dominated the study of the American Negro for the next twenty years." *Send These to Me: Jews and Other Immigrants in Urban America* (New York: Atheneum, 1975), p. 217. Nell Irvin Painter has called *An American Dilemma* "the most influential book on Afro-Americans of the century." *The Narrative of Hosea Hudson* (Cambridge, Mass.: Harvard University Press, 1979), p. 392. David Southern's *Gunnar Myrdal and Black-White Relations: The Use and Abuse of "An American Dilemma," 1944–1969* (Baton Rouge: Louisiana State University Press, 1987) is an excellent study of the reception of Myrdal's classic. See also Richard Kluger, *Simple Justice: The History of Brown v. Board of Education and Black America's Struggle for Equality* (New York: Knopf, 1975), pp. 890–92. L. Paul Metzger's article, "American Sociology and Black Assimilation: Conflicting Perspectives," in *American Journal of Sociology* 76 (1971): 627–47, uses the term "orthodoxy" in referring to Myrdal's influence on sociologists, but I have used the term to refer to a broader influence on American thought.

2. Gunnar Myrdal, *An American Dilemma*, p. xlvii.

3. Ibid., pp. 997–1024.

4. Ibid., pp. 69–70.

5. Ibid., pp. 928–29.

6. Robert S. Lynd, "Prison for American Genius," *Saturday Review*, April 22, 1944.

7. W. E. B. Du Bois, "The American Dilemma," *Phylon* 5 (1944): 118–24; E. Franklin Frazier, "Race: An American Dilemma," *The Crisis* 51:105–6, 129.

8. See especially Howard W. Odum, "Problem and Method in *An American Dilemma*," *Social Forces* 23 (October 1944): 94–98.

9. Gunnar Myrdal, *An American Dilemma*, pp. v–viii.

10. John Madge, *The Origins of Scientific Sociology* (Glencoe, Ill.: Free Press, 1962), pp. 255–60; Victor S. Navasky, "In Cold Print: American Dilemmas," *New York Times Book Review*, May 18, 1975, p. 3; John M. Russell, *Giving and Taking across the Foundation Desk* (New York: Teacher's College Press, 1977), pp. 27–30.

11. Herbert Aptheker, *The Negro People in America: A Critique of Gunnar Myrdal's "An American Dilemma"* (New York: International Publishers, 1946); Ralph Ellison, *Shadow and Act* (New York: Random House, 1964), p. 313; John H. Stanfield, *Philanthropy and Jim Crow in American Social Science* (Westport, Conn.: Greenwood Press, 1985), pp. 139–84.

12. George Fredrickson, *The Black Image in the White Mind* (New York: Harper & Row, 1971), p. 330; Harvard Sitkoff, *A New Deal for Blacks: The Emergence of Civil Rights as a National Issue; The Depression Decade* (New York: Oxford University Press, 1978), p. 202; August Meier and Elliot Rudwick, *Black History and the Historical Profession, 1915–1980* (Urbana: University of Illinois Press, 1986), p. 122.

13. Gunnar Myrdal, like many American progressives, defined the term *social engineering* broadly to include a wide range of educational and welfare activities, economic and social planning, and eugenics.

14. The Works Progress Administration funded research for St. Clair Drake and Horace Cayton, *Black Metropolis: A Study of Negro Life in a Northern City* (New York: Harcourt, Brace, 1945) and supported the collection of slave narratives and oral interviews with southern blacks.

15. Southern, *Gunnar Myrdal and Black-White Relations*.

Introduction

1. Harvard Sitkoff, *A New Deal for Blacks: The Emergence of Civil Rights as a National Issue; The Depression Decade* (New York: Oxford University Press, 1978), p. 36.

2. Paul Mertz, *New Deal Policy and Southern Rural Poverty* (Baton Rouge: Louisiana State University Press, 1978), pp. 3, 6; Charles S. Johnson, Edwin R. Embree, and Will W. Alexander, *The Collapse of Cotton Tenancy: A Summary of Field Studies and Statistical Surveys, 1933–1935* (Chapel Hill: University of North Carolina Press, 1935), pp. 4–5.

3. Gavin Wright, *Old South, New South: Revolutions in Southern Agriculture* (New York: Basic Books, 1986), p. 203.

4. Mertz, *New Deal Policy and Southern Rural Poverty*, pp. 5, 13.

5. Ibid., p. 14.

6. Arthur F. Raper, *Preface to Peasantry* (Chapel Hill: University of North Carolina Press, 1936), p. 36.

7. Mertz, *New Deal Policy and Southern Rural Poverty*, p. 11.

8. Sitkoff, *A New Deal for Blacks*, pp. 50–51.

9. John A. Salmond, "The Civilian Conservation Corps and the Negro," *Journal of American History* 52 (June 1965): 75–88.

10. John B. Kirby, *Black Americans in the Roosevelt Era: Liberalism and Race* (Knoxville: University of Tennessee Press, 1980), p. 149.

11. James T. Patterson, *America's Struggle against Poverty, 1900–1980* (Cambridge, Mass.: Harvard University Press, 1981), pp. 56–71.

12. Raymond Wolters, "The New Deal and the Negro," in *The New Deal: The National Level*, ed. John Braeman, Robert H. Bremner, and David Brody (Columbus: Ohio State University Press, 1975), p. 189; Richard Sterner, *The Negro's Share: A Study of Consumption, Housing and Public Assistance* (New York: Harper & Brothers, 1943), p. 364.

13. St. Clair Drake and Horace Cayton, *Black Metropolis: A Study of Negro Life in a Northern City* (New York: Harcourt, Brace, 1945), p. 88.

14. Sterner, *The Negro's Share*, pp. 228–29.

15. Patterson, *America's Struggle against Poverty*, p. 51.

16. Pete Daniel, *Breaking the Land: The Transformation of Cotton, Tobacco, and Rice Cultures since 1880* (Urbana: University of Illinois Press, 1985), p. 169.

17. Donald H. Grubbs, *Cry from the Cotton: The Southern Tenant Farmers' Union and the New Deal* (Chapel Hill: University of North Carolina Press, 1971), pp. 145–46; Daniel, *Breaking the Land*, p. 182.

18. George B. Tindall, *The Emergence of the New South, 1913–1945* (Baton Rouge: Louisiana State University Press, 1967), pp. 423–26.

19. Gavin Wright, *Old South, New South*, p. 232.

20. Wolters, "The New Deal and the Negro," pp. 174, 176.

21. Gavin Wright, *Old South, New South*, p. 237.

22. Ibid., p. 225.

23. Sitkoff, *A New Deal for Blacks*, p. 90.

24. U.S. National Emergency Council, *Report to the President on the Economic Conditions of the South* (Washington, D.C.: NEC, 1938), pp. 61, 64.

25. Ibid., pp. 20, 25.

26. Patterson, *America's Struggle against Poverty*, pp. 60–61.

27. Sitkoff, *A New Deal for Blacks*, pp. 40–41.

28. Ibid., p. 74.

29. John Salmond, *A Southern Rebel: The Life and Times of Aubrey Willis Williams, 1890–1965* (Chapel Hill: University of North Carolina Press, 1983), pp. 121–78.

30. Kirby, *Black Americans in the Roosevelt Era*, p. 32; Morton Sosna, *In Search of the Silent South* (New York: Columbia University Press, 1978), pp. 63–74; Peter J. Kellogg, "Northern Liberals and Black America: A History of White Attitudes, 1935–1952" (Ph.D. diss., Northwestern University, 1971), pp. 1–84; John T. Kneebone, *Southern Liberal Journalists and the Issue of Race, 1920–1944* (Chapel Hill: University of North Carolina Press, 1985), pp. 95–96.

31. Nancy J. Weiss, *Farewell to the Party of Lincoln* (Princeton: Princeton University Press, 1983); Sitkoff, *A New Deal for Blacks*, pp. 89, 95.

32. Sitkoff, *A New Deal for Blacks*, p. 202.

33. Raymond Wolters, *Negroes and the Great Depression* (Westport, Conn.: Greenwood Press, 1970), pp. 341–42; Sitkoff, *A New Deal for Blacks*, pp. 256–57.

34. Walter White, *A Man Called White* (New York: Viking, 1948; New York: Arno Press, 1969), pp. 169–70.

35. Robert Zangrando, *The NAACP Crusade against Lynching, 1909–1950* (Philadelphia: Temple University Press, 1980), pp. 139–53.

36. Wolters, *Negroes and the Great Depression*, pp. 353–76.

37. Sitkoff, *A New Deal for Blacks*, pp. 170, 175–86.

38. James T. Patterson, *Congressional Conservatism and the New Deal* (Lexington: University of Kentucky Press, 1967); Sitkoff, *A New Deal for Blacks*, pp. 112–13, 118–20.

Chapter 1: Finding a Tocqueville

1. On the growth of foundations and their role in planning, see Barry D. Karl, "Philanthropy, Policy Planning and the Bureaucratization of the Democratic Ideal," *Daedalus* 105 (1976): 129–49; Barry D. Karl and Stanley N. Katz, "The American Private Philanthropic Foundation and the Public Sphere, 1890–1930," *Minerva* (1981): 236–70; and Ellen

Condliffe Lagemann, *Private Power for the Public Good: A History of the Carnegie Foundation for the Advancement of Teaching* (Middletown, Conn.: Wesleyan University Press, 1983).

2. See James D. Anderson's discussion of the industrial philanthropists in *The Education of Blacks in the South* (Chapel Hill: University of North Carolina Press, 1988), pp. 245–78. On the concept of institutional racism, structural discrimination that exists even when individuals believe that they are not discriminating, see Joe R. Feagin and Clairece Booher Feagin, *Discrimination American Style: Institutional Racism and Sexism* (Englewood Cliffs, N.J.: Prentice Hall, 1978), and Louis L. Knowles and Kenneth Prewitt, eds., *Institutional Racism in America* (Englewood Cliffs, N.J.: Prentice Hall, 1969).

3. Andrew Carnegie, "Wealth," *North American Review* 148 (June 1889): 653–64, and 149 (December 1889): 682–98. For a discussion of the essay, see Joseph Wall, *Andrew Carnegie* (New York: Oxford University Press, 1970), pp. 804–8.

4. Burton J. Hendrick, *The Life of Andrew Carnegie* (Garden City, N.Y.: Doubleday, 1932), 2:297–322, 334–36.

5. Ibid., 1:421–42.

6. Carnegie to Trustees of Carnegie Corporation, November 11, 1911, quoted in Hendrick, *Life of Andrew Carnegie*, 2:350–51.

7. Hendrick, *Life of Andrew Carnegie*, 2:353.

8. Joseph C. Kiger, "Frederick Paul Keppel," *Dictionary of American Biography*, 3d suppl. (New York: Scribners, 1973), pp. 415–17; Harry J. Carman et al., *Appreciations of Frederick Paul Keppel by Some of His Friends* (New York: Columbia University Press, 1951), pp. xi–xiii, 72.

9. Henry James, "President of the Carnegie Corporation," in Carman et al., *Appreciations of Frederick Paul Keppel*, p. 51.

10. Keppel to Newton D. Baker, February 20, 1931, Keppel Papers, Columbia University Library, New York, N.Y.; Keppel to John C. Merriam, October 31, 1935, Merriam Papers, Box 106, Library of Congress, Washington, D.C.; Francis Keppel, interview with author, April 18, 1978, Cambridge, Mass.

11. Frederick Keppel, *The Foundation* (New York: Macmillan, 1930), pp. 43–44, 51–52, and "American Philanthropy and the Advancement of Learning," *Brown University Papers* 11 (1934): 9–10; John M. Russell, *Giving and Taking across the Foundation Desk* (New York: Teachers College Press, 1977), pp. 27–30.

12. Frederick Keppel, "Andrew Carnegie as Founder," in *Andrew Carnegie Centenary, 1835–1935* (New York: Carnegie Corporation of New York, 1935), p. 66.

13. Francis Keppel, interview with author.

14. Keppel's wish to keep the foundation out of political controversies was in part a reaction to the investigation of foundations conducted by the congressionally appointed Commission on Industrial Relations in 1915. The commission had held hearings to investigate charges that foundations were instruments by which men of great wealth hoped to control government. It summoned Andrew Carnegie, John D. Rockefeller, Sr., John D. Rockefeller, Jr., and other witnesses. Although the commission's final report recommended legislation giving Congress strict control over foundations, no such legislation was enacted. See Barbara Howe, "The Emergence of Scientific Philanthropy, 1900–1920: Origins, Issues, and Outcomes," in *Philanthropy and Cultural Imperialism: The Foundations at Home and Abroad*, ed. Robert F. Arnove (Boston: G. K. Hall, 1980), pp. 25–54.

15. James, "President of the Carnegie Corporation," pp. 48–51.

16. On the expansion of the Rockefeller philanthropies, see Raymond B. Fosdick, *The Story of the Rockefeller Foundation* (New York: Harper & Row, 1952).

17. John M. Russell, "Inside FPK," in Carman et al., *Appreciations of Frederick Paul Keppel*, p. 90. Keppel's approach contrasted with that of Henry Pritchett, president of the Carnegie Foundation for the Advancement of Teaching, who emphasized expertise, efficiency, and the scientific approach to social issues. See Lagemann, *Private Power*, pp. 21–36.

18. James, "President of the Carnegie Corporation," pp. 58–59, 61.

19. "London Conference of Advisors, Held at Chatham House, April 14, 1937," memo enclosed in Keppel to John Merriam, June 7, 1937, Merriam Papers, Box 106; Russell Leffingwell, "A Postscript," in Carman et al., *Appreciations of Frederick Paul Keppel*, p. 117; Keppel, "American Philanthropy and the Advancement of Learning," p. 10.

20. Russell, "Inside FPK," pp. 84–85. In a letter to John Merriam, Keppel recommended Nicholas Kelley, Frederick Osborn, and L. D. Coffman for vacancies on the board of trustees, mentioned their respective professional achievements, and added, "They are cooperative people who understand the importance of team play." Keppel to Merriam, October 31, 1935, Merriam Papers, Box 106.

21. Leffingwell, "A Postscript," p. 122.

22. Gunnar Myrdal, interview with author, August 18, 1980, Stockholm.

23. Thomas Jesse Jones to Keppel, June 19, 1935, Phelps-Stokes Fund Papers, Schomburg Center for Research in Black Culture, New York, N.Y.

24. Carnegie Corporation of New York, *Report of the President* (New York: Carnegie Corporation, 1935), pp. 38–39.

25. Carnegie Corporation of New York, *Report of the President* (New York: Carnegie Corporation, 1937), p. 49.

26. Minutes, Board of Trustees, XIII, 29 (October 24, 1935), CCA; Russell, *Giving and Taking across the Foundation Desk*, pp. 7–8; John M. Russell, interview, Columbia Oral History Project, 1967, Columbia University, New York, N.Y., pp. 145–48; Robert M. Lester, interview, Columbia Oral History Project, 1967, pp. 302–4.

27. C. H. Cramer, *Newton D. Baker: A Biography* (Cleveland: World Publishing Company, 1961), pp. 14, 23–30, 34–63.

28. Newton D. Baker to Emmett Scott, November 30, 1917, Records of the Secretary of War, cited in Daniel R. Beaver, *Newton D. Baker and the American War Effort, 1917–1919* (Lincoln: University of Nebraska Press, 1966), p. 228.

29. Beaver, *Newton D. Baker and the American War Effort*, pp. 224–31.

30. Cramer, *Newton D. Baker*, pp. 174, 188, 209–34.

31. Elliot A. Rosen, *Hoover, Roosevelt, and the Brains Trust* (New York: Columbia University Press, 1977), pp. 100–101, 259.

32. Arthur M. Schlesinger, Jr., *The Politics of Upheaval* (Boston: Houghton, Mifflin, 1960), p. 364; Cramer, *Newton D. Baker*, p. 260.

33. Newton D. Baker, "The Decay of Self-Reliance," *Atlantic Monthly*, December 1934, p. 732.

34. Baker to Henry James, October 24, 1936, Baker Papers, Box 132, Library of Congress, Washington, D.C.

35. Newton D. Baker, "Homeless Wanderers Create a New Problem for America," *New York Times*, December 11, 1932.

36. Minutes of Meeting, American Youth Commission, October 12–13, 1936, and May 10–11, 1937; Homer P. Rainey to Baker, December 9, 1937, Baker Papers, Box 30. The books in the series included Charles S. Johnson, *Growing Up in the Black Belt: Negro Youth in the Rural South* (Washington, D.C.: American Council on Education, 1941); E. Franklin Frazier, *Negro Youth at the Crossways: Their Personality Development in the Middle States*

(Washington, D.C.: American Council on Education, 1940); W. Lloyd Warner, Buford H. Junker, and Walter A. Adams, *Color and Human Nature: Negro Personality Development in a Northern City* (Washington, D.C.: American Council on Education, 1940); Allison Davis and John Dollard, *Children of Bondage: The Personality Development of Negro Youth in the Urban South* (Washington, D.C.: American Council on Education, 1940); and Ira DeA. Reid, *In a Minor Key: Negro Youth in Story and Fact* (Washington, D.C.: American Council on Education, 1940).

37. Cramer, *Newton D. Baker*, p. 189.

38. Newton D. Baker, "Our Times," in *The American Way*, ed. Newton D. Baker, Carlton J. H. Hayes, and Roger W. Straus (Chicago: Willett, Clark, 1936), pp. 9–10.

39. Ira DeA. Reid, "Current Aspects of the Negro Situation in the United States," in Stenographic Proceedings, Williamstown Institute of Human Relations, Williams College, Williamstown, Mass., August 25–30, 1935, pp. 152–54 (copy in Baker Papers, Box 170). Reid did not attend the conference and his paper was read by Arthur L. Swift.

40. Stenographic Proceedings, Williamstown Institute of Human Relations, pp. 156–58.

41. Baker et al., *The American Way*, pp. 39, 82.

42. Baker to Robert M. Lester, December 26, 1934, Baker Papers, Box 53, Carnegie Corporation file.

43. U.S. Office of Education, *Fundamentals in the Education of Negroes*, ed. Ambrose Caliver (Washington, D.C.: United States Government Printing Office, 1935), pp. 1–2.

44. Baker to Keppel, December 23, 1935, Baker Papers, Box 53, Carnegie Corporation file. Although Baker attributed the term "the wisdom of life" to the Chinese, it resembles the motto of Hampton Institute, "education for life." He refers to a popular historical novel that deals with the slave trade, Hervey Allen, *Anthony Adverse* (New York: Farrar & Rinehart, 1933).

45. Baker to Keppel, April 22, 1936, Baker Papers, Box 53, Carnegie Corporation file.

46. James, "President of the Carnegie Corporation," p. 57.

47. For an overview of the Carnegie Corporation's grants to black organizations, see Keppel's memo, "For Discussion with Professor Myrdal," May 11, 1938, NSGC. See also Keppel, foreword to Gunnar Myrdal, *An American Dilemma: The Negro Problem and Modern Democracy* (New York: Harper & Brothers, 1944), pp. v–vi; Gunnar Myrdal, interview, Columbia Oral History Project, 1967, p. 7; Nancy J. Weiss, *The National Urban League, 1910–1940* (New York: Oxford University Press, 1974), p. 243. During the depression, Keppel managed to give the black biologist E. E. Just a grant of $10,000 to enable him to complete his book *The Biology of the Cell Surface*. See Kenneth Manning, *Black Apollo of Science: The Life of E. E. Just* (New York: Oxford, 1983), pp. 251, 318.

48. John M. Russell to Eugene Kinckle Jones, May 18, 1934, CCA, quoted in Nancy J. Weiss, *National Urban League*, p. 243.

49. Walter White to Keppel, August 8, 1935, NAACP file, CCA.

50. For a sympathetic history of the GEB by its former president, see Raymond B. Fosdick, *Adventure in Giving: The Story of the General Education Board* (New York: Harper & Row, 1962). Critical accounts emphasizing the GEB's support for segregation include Louis R. Harlan, *Separate and Unequal: Public School Campaigns in the Southern Seaboard States, 1901–1915* (New York: Atheneum, 1968); Henry Allen Bullock, *A History of Negro Education in the United States* (Cambridge, Mass.: Harvard University Press, 1967); and James D. Anderson, "Philanthropic Control Over Private Black Higher Education," in *Philanthropy and Cultural Imperialism*, ed. Arnove, pp. 147–77. The best general study of foundations and southern black education is Anderson, *The Education of Blacks in the South*. On

Mississippi governor James K. Vardaman's attempt to close black schools, see Albert Kirwan, *The Revolt of the Rednecks* (Lexington: University of Kentucky Press, 1951), p. 162.

51. Quoted in Fosdick, *Adventure in Giving*, p. 11.

52. Ibid., pp. 334, 335.

53. For a view of Davis's network and his attitudes toward black organizations, see Jackson Davis Diary, GEB Papers, 586.1, Rockefeller Archive Center, Tarrytown, N.Y. Another Rockefeller philanthropy had played a somewhat more liberal role in the field of race relations during the 1920s. The Laura Spelman Rockefeller Memorial, headed by Beardsley Ruml from 1923 to 1929, aided black universities in the hope of training more black social scientists and professionals. In his *Final Report of the Laura Spelman Rockefeller Memorial* (New York: Laura Spelman Rockefeller Memorial, 1933), Ruml made no effort to pay homage to the Tuskegee ideal or to stress the memorial's commitment to the education of southern whites. Instead he emphasized that the memorial's program had been based on the idea of increasing the number of Negro leaders and professionals and stated that "the absence of scientific knowledge concerning the Negro's position in American life" could only be remedied through the education of "competent Negro investigators." The memorial, therefore, had sought to build up three principal university centers for blacks at Fisk, Howard, and Atlanta that would have strong programs in the social sciences and in the professions of law, business, social work, and public administration. After the demise of the Laura Spelman Rockefeller Memorial, the Rockefeller Foundation de-emphasized support for the social sciences. Foundation support in the social sciences was concentrated in "high-grade university centers" in the United States and abroad. Responsibility for black universities and for the training of black scholars was transferred from the memorial to the GEB. Thus the preliminary linkage which Ruml had achieved between the development of the social sciences and black universities was lost in the new division of labor in which the Rockefeller Foundation concentrated on supporting the social sciences at elite white universities and the GEB focused on fostering "Negro education." Although the GEB funded the research for Howard Odum's *Southern Regions of the United States* (Chapel Hill: University of North Carolina Press, 1936), neither the GEB nor the Rockefeller Foundation played an innovative role during the thirties in the social science study of blacks. See Fosdick, *Adventure in Giving*, p. 267, and Waldemar Nielsen, *The Big Foundations* (New York: Columbia University Press, 1972), p. 59.

54. Edwin R. Embree and Julia Waxman, *Investment in People: The Story of the Rosenwald Fund* (New York: Harper & Brothers, 1949), pp. 180–82, 201–2.

55. A. Gilbert Belles, "The Julius Rosenwald Fund: Efforts in Race Relations, 1928–1949" (Ph.D. diss., Vanderbilt University, 1972), pp. 149–58.

56. Kenneth King, *Pan-Africanism and Education: A Study of Race Philanthropy and Education in the Southern States of America and East Africa* (Oxford: Clarendon Press, 1971), pp. 40–41.

57. W. E. B. Du Bois, "Thomas Jesse Jones," *The Crisis* 22 (October 1921): 254.

58. Keppel to Franklin F. Hopper, June 1, 1932, NAACP file, CCA. The Carnegie Corporation did make a grant of $2,500 to the NAACP in 1933. See Carnegie Corporation of New York, *Report of the President and of the Treasurer* (New York: Carnegie Corporation, 1933).

59. Keppel to Du Bois, March 16 and November 28, 1934, Du Bois file, CCA. The grant to Du Bois came from Keppel's fund, "Administration General Expenses, Publication and Distribution," and may not have required formal approval of the board.

60. Carnegie Corporation, "Memorandum for Counsel: Notes on Carnegie Files Regard-

ing W. E. B. Du Bois" [for Cox Committee Congressional Investigation], August 27, 1952, CCA. Du Bois applied again for a trip to South Africa in 1939. Gunnar Myrdal endorsed the idea, but Senator J. D. Rheinallt Jones, a South African advisor to the corporation, objected, and Du Bois's request was again denied. See Jones to J. M. Russell, July 31, 1939, and Keppel to Du Bois, August 29, 1939, Du Bois file, CCA.

61. Anson Phelps Stokes to Keppel, October 19, 1931; Carter G. Woodson to Benjamin Brawley, November 28, 1931 (copy); Robert M. Lester, memo, "Encyclopedia of the Negro: RML at Washington Meeting," January 9, 1932; Anson Phelps Stokes to Keppel, April 21, 1934; Alvin Johnson to Keppel, April 28, 1934; Waldo Leland to Keppel, May 21, 1934; "AHA and Dr. R. T. Crane," memo, June 9, 1936; Lester to Keppel, memo re Negro Encyclopedia, n.d.; Woodson to Carnegie Corporation, June 26, 1936; Keppel, memo, "FPK and Donald Young," June 10, 1937; all in Encyclopedia of the Negro file, CCA. See also August Meier and Elliott Rudwick, *Black History and the Historical Profession, 1915–1980* (Urbana: University of Illinois Press, 1986), pp. 63–66, 288–90.

62. Keppel, "Andrew Carnegie as Founder," in *Andrew Carnegie Centenary*, p. 75. In calling for a "talented tenth" of educated blacks, W. E. B. Du Bois used the same term: "Progress in human affairs is more often a pull than a push, a surging forward of the exceptional man, and the lifting of his duller brethren slowly and painfully to his vantage-ground." *The Souls of Black Folk* (1903; reprint, New York: New American Library, 1969), p. 127.

63. Melville Herskovits to Keppel, April 8, 1936, and "E.G." to Keppel, staff memo, December 1, 1936, Northwestern U—Research in Field of Negro Cultures (Melville J. Herskovits) file (hereafter, Northwestern U-Herskovits file), CCA; Keppel, memo, "Negro Study, Personnel Suggestions through July 15, 1937," NSGC. This last memo is reprinted in John H. Stanfield, *Philanthropy and Jim Crow in American Social Science* (Westport, Conn.: Greenwood Press, 1985), pp. 142–48. Thorndike thought that "intelligence" was linked to race and that genetic factors explained the lower average scores of blacks on I.Q. tests. It is curious that he recommended Herskovits, a man who did not hold these views and who was, in addition, quite liberal on civil rights issues. Thorndike was, however, a leading exponent of quantification in social science research, and his admiration for Herskovits was based on Herskovits's anthropometric studies, especially *The American Negro* (New York: Knopf, 1928). For a critical study of Thorndike, see Russell Marks, "Legitimating Industrial Capitalism: Philanthropy and Individual Differences," in *Philanthropy and Cultural Imperialism*, ed. Arnove, pp. 87–122. See also Geraldine Joncich, *The Sane Positivist: A Biography of Edward L. Thorndike* (Middletown, Conn.: Wesleyan University Press, 1968).

64. Bertram Schrieke, *Alien Americans* (New York: Viking, 1936).

65. Keppel to Baker, April 20, 1936, Baker Papers, Box 54, Carnegie Corporation file. Ironically, Myrdal would poke fun at Schrieke's idea that the South "offers a unique opportunity for the development of the new peasant" who would practice self-sufficient agriculture while enjoying the advantage of radios, automobiles, movies, and telephones. Myrdal pointed out that world agricultural prices would have to improve considerably before southern "peasants" could maintain a decent standard of living, much less buy the gadgets that Schrieke envisioned. *An American Dilemma*, p. 1251.

66. Melville Herskovits, "Through Alien Eyes," *The Nation* 142 (June 27, 1936): 850–51.

67. Guy Stanton Ford to W. C. Dougall, February 25, 1925, Laura Spelman Rockefeller Memorial Papers, III, 8, 98, f. 1016, Rockefeller Archive Center; Kenneth King, *Pan-Africanism and Education*, pp. 121–39, 145, 152–53, 179–81, 252–59. See also Edward Berman, "Educational Colonialism in Africa: The Role of American Foundation, 1910–

1945," in *Philanthropy and Cultural Imperialism*, ed. Arnove, pp. 179–201. Herskovits criticized the foundations' practice of sending British colonial administrators to study Negro education in the South. See Charles Dollard, memo, "C. D. and Melville Herskovits," September 1, 1938, Northwestern U-Herskovits file, CCA.

68. Kenneth King, *Pan-Africanism and Education*, pp. 165, 172–74, 205, 210; Berman, "Educational Colonialism in Africa," pp. 189–90; Robert Lester to Newton D. Baker, April 2, 1936, Baker Papers, Box 54, Carnegie Corporation file.

69. Another model for the Negro study was the diplomatic mission of Charles P. Howland, who "supervised the repatriation of Greeks in Asia Minor after the close of the first World War." See Keppel, foreword to Gunnar Myrdal, *An American Dilemma*, p. vi; Keppel to Myrdal, August 16, 1939, NSGC; Lord Hailey, *An African Survey: A Study of Problems Arising in Africa South of the Sahara* (London: Oxford University Press, 1938); Penelope Hetherington, *British Paternalism and Africa, 1900–1920* (London: Frank Cass, 1978), pp. 7–8, 99–103, 139–40; J. M. Lee, *Colonial Development and Good Government* (Oxford: Clarendon Press, 1967), pp. 3–4, 9, 31–32, 41–44, 87.

70. Keppel to J. T. Moll, November 12, 1936, NSGC.

71. J. T. Moll to Hendrik Mouw, copy enclosed in Moll to Keppel, November 2, 1936, NSGC.

72. Keppel to Moll, November 12, 1936, NSGC.

73. Baker to Keppel, November 17, 1936, and Keppel to Baker, November 19, 1936, Baker Papers, Box 54, Carnegie Corporation file.

74. Keppel, memo, "Negro Study Personnel Suggestions through July 15, 1937," Keppel to J. Huizinga, February 1, 1937, and Huizinga to Keppel, February 14, 1937, NSGC.

75. Keppel, memo, "FPK and Melville J. Herskovits," Chicago, December 4, 1936, Northwestern U-Herskovits file, CCA.

76. Herskovits to Donald Young, January 2, 1937, Herskovits Papers, Myrdal file, Northwestern University, Evanston, Ill.; Keppel memo, "FPK and Melville J. Herskovits," Chicago, December 4, 1936, Northwestern U-Herskovits file, CCA.

77. Donald Young to Keppel, January 30, 1937, copy enclosed in Young to Herskovits, January 30, 1937, Herskovits Papers, Myrdal file.

78. Herskovits to Young, January 2, 1937; Young to Herskovits, January 30, 1937; Herskovits to Young, February 1, 1937, Herskovits Papers, Myrdal file.

79. Young to Herskovits, December 23, 1936, Herskovits Papers, SSRC National (Donald Young) file.

80. Herskovits to Young, January 2, 1937, Herskovits Papers, Myrdal file.

81. Young to Keppel, January 30, 1937, Herskovits Papers, Myrdal file.

82. Young to Herskovits, March 31, 1937, Herskovits Papers.

83. Keppel to Young, February 4, 1937, quoted in Young to Herskovits, February 4, 1937, Herskovits Papers, Myrdal file.

84. James Bryce to Keppel, September 24, 1904, Keppel Papers.

85. Rappard had longstanding ties to the Rockefeller Foundation, and Harrod had been recommended by Ivison S. Macadam, one of Keppel's British advisors. See Keppel, memo, "Negro Study Personnel Suggestions through July 15, 1937"; Malcolm W. Davis to Keppel, March 8, 1937; Raymond B. Fosdick to Keppel, May 11, 1937, NSGC.

86. Keppel, memo, "Negro Study Personnel Suggestions through July 15, 1937," NSGC; Keppel to Raymond Fosdick, June 8, 1938, GEB Papers, 586.1, Box 270.

87. Ruml's career is treated in Alva Johnston, "The National Idea Man," *New Yorker*, February 10, 1945, pp. 28–35; February 17, 1945, pp. 26–34; and February 24, 1945, pp.

30–39; C. Hartley Grattan, "Beardsley Ruml and His Ideas," *Harpers*, May 1952, pp. 78–86; "Beardsley Ruml," *Fortune*, March 1945, pp. 135–38, 170–80; *Current Biography Yearbook, 1943* (New York, 1944), pp. 647–50. For Ruml's economic ideas, see Robert M. Collins, "Positive Business Responses to the New Deal: The Roots of the Committee for Economic Development, 1933–1942," *Business History Review* 52, no. 3 (Autumn 1978): 380–84, and Collins, *The Business Response to Keynes* (New York: Columbia University Press, 1981), pp. 67–71, 137–39.

88. John Van Sickle to Sydnor H. Walker, December 11, 1933, and Edmund E. Day to Selskar M. Gunn, June 21, 1932, Rockefeller Foundation Archives 800S, Myrdal (Social Sciences), Rockefeller Archive Center, Tarrytown, N.Y. On Myrdal's role as an advisor to the Rockefeller Foundation, see Myrdal to Van Sickle, July 18, 1932; Tracy B. Kittredge to Myrdal, June 25, 1934; Myrdal to Kittredge, September 29, 1934; Myrdal to Kittredge, March 28, 1935, Rockefeller Foundation file, GMP.

89. Tracy B. Kittredge to John Van Sickle, January 18, 1935, Rockefeller Foundation Archives, 800 S: U Stockholm Social Science Institute, Rockefeller Archive Center.

90. Keppel, memo of conversation with Dora Chernstrom (secretary to Lawrence K. Frank), July 13, 1937, and Keppel, memo, "Negro Study, Personnel Suggestions through July 15, 1937," NSGC.

91. Keppel to G. Myrdal, August 12, 1937, NSGC. Ruml represented a freewheeling, risk-taking approach to the social sciences which had fallen into disfavor at the Rockefeller Foundation by the mid-1930s. In 1967, Gunnar Myrdal recalled that most of the officials of the Rockefeller Foundation had warned Keppel against the idea of importing a foreign scholar to study American blacks. Gunnar Myrdal, interview, Columbia Oral History Project, pp. 5, 44.

92. Keppel did not consult Newton Baker regarding Myrdal because Baker was in poor health throughout most of 1937 and died in December of that year. Keppel informed Baker of the negotiations with Myrdal after an offer had been made. See Keppel to Baker, September 20, 1937, Baker Papers, Box 54, Carnegie Corporation file.

93. Keppel had very limited knowledge of Swedish affairs. There is no indication in the correspondence, for example, that he had read Marquis Childs's *Sweden: The Middle Way* (New Haven, Conn.: Yale University Press, 1936), although it had been a bestseller the previous year. Donald Young later said that neither he nor the Carnegie Corporation knew that Myrdal was nominally a socialist when Myrdal was selected. See Young, interview, Columbia Oral History Project, p. 41.

94. Keppel to G. Myrdal, August 12, 1937, NSGC.

95. G. Myrdal to Keppel, August 30, 1937, NSGC.

96. G. Myrdal to Keppel, October 7, 1937, NSGC. Myrdal's statement on racial differences is generally compatible with the writings of the Boas school in the 1930s. See Franz Boas, *Race, Language, and Culture* (New York: Macmillan, 1940), pp. 10–14.

97. In a report to the trustees in 1937, Keppel budgeted $100,000 for the Negro study for the years 1937–42 (see Keppel to Newton Baker, June 28, 1937, Baker Papers). The following year, Keppel estimated to the trustees that the total cost of the Negro study would not exceed $75,000 (see "Comprehensive Study of the Negro—Preliminary Survey," January 20, 1938, NSGC). Actual appropriations during the research phase of the Myrdal study were as follows: January 1938, $25,000; January 1939, $40,000; September 1939, $15,000; November 1939, $165,000. *Minutes*, Board of Trustees, CCA. The cost of the Myrdal study was exceeded by at least one previous social science research project. The

Rockefeller Foundation had appropriated $560,000 for the volume *Recent Social Trends in the United States* (1933). See Barry D. Karl, "Presidential Planning and Social Science Research: Mr. Hoover's Experts," *Perspectives in American History* 3 (1969): 377.

98. Russell Leffingwell to Keppel, October 17, 1941, Keppel Papers.

Chapter 2: Social Engineering

1. Gunnar Myrdal, "Gunnar heter jag," *Aftontidningen*, August 16, 1943.
2. Olle Veirulf, ed., *Dalarna: ett vida berömt landskap* (Stockholm: Svensk Litteratur, 1951); K. E. Edwards, ed., *Sweden: Dalarna Studies* (London: Le Play Society, 1940), pp. 24–50; Sven Sjöberg, *Vår by: Gammalt och nytt om Solvarbo* (Borlänge: Borlänge Bokhandel, 1957).
3. Parish records, Gustafs.
4. Gunnar Myrdal, "Gunnar heter jag;" Anna Sofia Pettersson, letter written on Gunnar Myrdal's fiftieth birthday, and Gunnar Myrdal, oral history memoir, quoted in Stellan Andersson, "Gunnar Myrdal: Barn—och ungdomsår: Några minnesbilder och dokument," July 1989, Arbetarrörelsens Arkiv, Stockholm.
5. Gunnar Myrdal, *Hur styrs landet?* (Stockholm: Rabén & Sjögren, 1982), p. 11 nn. 4 and 5, p. 23. In "Gunnar heter jag," he wrote that "I have always felt that my most honest identification is with this impudent, individualistic, traditional, stable, old democratic valley village."
6. Gunnar Myrdal, "Gunnar heter jag."
7. Sissela Bok, *Alva: Ett kvinnoliv* (Stockholm: Bonniers, 1987), pp. 62–64. For a portrait of Carl Adolf Pettersson in a book that its author describes as "imaginative literature," see Jan Myrdal, *Barndom* (Stockholm: P. A. Norstedt, 1982), pp. 98–100.
8. Bok, *Alva*, p. 168. Gunnar Myrdal, oral history memoir, in Andersson, "Gunnar Myrdal: Barn—och ungdomsår," pp. 11–12.
9. Bok, *Alva*, pp. 61–69.
10. Document, Kongelige Ecklesiastik-Departementet, 1914, GMP; Gunnar Myrdal, *Hur styrs landet?* p. 11 n. 5.
11. John Lindqvist to G. Myrdal, December 4, 1927, GMP.
12. Gunnar Myrdal, "Den s.k. Upplysningen" (1917), GMP.
13. Gunnar Myrdal, "Dalfolket" (1917), GMP.
14. Ibid.
15. Ibid.
16. Gunnar Myrdal, oral history memoir, in Andersson, "Gunnar Myrdal: Barn—och ungdomsår," p. 7.
17. Gunnar Myrdal, "Historisk I: Föredrag om Darwins 'Naturliga urvalet' . . . ," (1918?), GMP.
18. On Kjellén's influence, see Andersson, "Gunnar Myrdal: Barn—och Ungdomsår," pp. 19–21.
19. Gunnar Myrdal, "Små nationens insats i världshistorien," (1917), GMP.
20. Carl-Göran Andrae, "The Swedish Labor Movement and the 1917–18 Revolution," in Steven Koblik, ed., *Sweden's Development from Poverty to Affluence*, pp. 232–53.
21. Gustaf Näsström, "'En idéspruta . . .' Makarna Myrdals nya bok *Kontakt med Amerika*," pamphlet (Stockholm: Bonniers, 1941), p. 2; Gunnar Myrdal, "Modern student-

kultur: Stockholms studenter och de idealla intressena," *Svenska Dagbladet*, May 6, 1919; cf. Fritz Thorén, "Studentkulturens dekadans," *Svenska Dagbladet*, May 7, 1919; Andersson, "Gunnar Myrdal: Barn—och ungdomsår," pp. 21–22.

22. On the "revolt of youth" in various European countries before the First World War, see Robert Wohl, *The Generation of 1914* (Cambridge, Mass.: Harvard University Press, 1979), especially chapters 2 and 6. It should be noted, though, that Gunnar Myrdal did not feel any attraction to militarism or fascism during his youth.

23. Gunnar Myrdal, "Massan och intelligensen," GMP. In the 1970s, Gunnar Myrdal dated the essay 1918. The archivist Stellan Andersson believes that it was written in the spring of 1919.

24. Ibid.

25. Ibid.

26. Ibid.

27. Ibid.

28. Gunnar Myrdal, "Socialpolitikens dilemma" *Spektrum* 2, nos. 3 and 4 (1932): 1–31; see also Gunnar Myrdal, *Against the Stream: Critical Essays on Economics* (New York: Pantheon, 1973), p. 41.

29. While Myrdal's arguments were conservative, they did reflect a widespread fear of universal suffrage among the educated middle class. The young Social Democrat Gustav Möller wrote an article for *Tiden* calling for a two-chamber parliament with an upper house for experts representing universities, technical institutes, doctors, and trade unions. See Möller, "Ett demokratiskt problem," *Tiden* 7 (1915): 9–12.

30. C. A. Pettersson, "Några politiska funderingar," *Strangnäs Tidning*, June 2, 1925; C. A. Pettersson, "Högerns lokalorganisationer på landsbygden," *Strangnäs Tidning*, June 12, 1925, copies in Pettersson scrapbook, GMP.

31. "C. A. Pettersson, Gesta, 50 År," *Sörmlandsposten*, April 3, 1926; Obituary, *Eskilstuna Kuriren*, January 22, 1934; Obituary, *Säters Tidning*, January 26, 1934.

32. G. Myrdal to C. A. and Sophie Pettersson, June 5, 1919, GMP; Bok, *Alva*, pp. 54–60; Lars G. Lindskog, *Alva Myrdal* (Stockholm: Sveriges Radios Förlag, 1981), p. 15; Ulrich Herz, *Alva och Gunnar Myrdal i fredens tjänst* (Stockholm: Rabén & Sjögren, 1971), p. 13; Gunnar Myrdal, oral history memoir, March 1985, GMP.

33. Annette Kullenberg, "Jag ville städa samhället," in *Det gäller vårt liv* (Stockholm: Kulturhuset, 1976), p. 13.

34. Bok, *Alva*, p. 37; Kullenberg, "Jag ville städa samhället," p. 13; Lindskog, *Alva Myrdal*, p. 11.

35. Lindskog, *Alva Myrdal*, pp. 10–14; Bok, *Alva*, p. 69.

36. Gunnar Myrdal, "A Worried America," *Current* 202 (April 1978): 47–48.

37. Gunnar Myrdal, *Hur styrs landet?* p. 274; Gunnar Myrdal, interview with author, August 19, 1980, Stockholm; Gunnar Myrdal, "Gunnar heter jag"; Richard Swedberg, introduction to Gunnar Myrdal, *The Political Element in the Development of Economic Theory*, unpublished manuscript in author's possession.

38. Gustav Cassel, *I förnuftets tjänst: En ekonomisk självbiografi*, 2 vols. (Stockholm: Natur och Kultur, 1940); Eric Englund, "Gustav Cassel's Autobiography," *Quarterly Journal of Economics* 57 (May 1943): 466–68, 471–72, 489; Björn Hansson, "The Swedish Tradition: Wicksell and Cassel," in *Neoclassical Economics*, ed. Warren Samuels (Boston: Kluver Academic Publishers, forthcoming).

39. Allan C. Carlson, "The Roles of Alva and Gunnar Myrdal in the Development of a

Social Democratic Response to Europe's 'Population Crisis' 1929–1938" (Ph.D. diss., Ohio University, 1978), p. 126.

40. Gunnar Myrdal, "Gustav Cassel in Memoriam," *Bulletin of the Institute of Economics and Statistics*, Oxford 25 (February 1963): 1–10; on the "intellectual aristocrats," see the original review in Swedish *Ekonomisk revy* 2 (1945): 3–13; on the "healthy realism," see Gunnar Myrdal, "Postscript," in *Value in Social Theory* (London: Routledge & Kegan Paul, 1958), p. 242; Carlson, "Roles of Alva and Gunnar Myrdal," p. 126.

41. Gunnar Myrdal, *Prisbildningsproblemet och föränderligheten* (Uppsala: Almqvist & Wicksell, 1927); Carlson, "Roles of Alva and Gunnar Myrdal," p. 127.

42. Carlson, "Roles of Alva and Gunnar Myrdal," p. 128.

43. Alf Johansson, "Minnesbilder," in *Det gäller vårt liv* (Stockholm: Kulturhuset, 1976), p. 17.

44. Bok, *Alva*, pp. 76–78.

45. Lindskog, *Alva Myrdal*, p. 21.

46. Johansson, "Minnesbilder," p. 17.

47. Bertil Ohlin, *Memoarer: ung man blir politiker* (Stockholm: Bonniers, 1972), pp. 158–59.

48. Gunnar Myrdal, *Vetenskap och politik i nationalekonomien* (Stockholm: Kooperativa förbundets bokförlag, 1930). Quotations and page references are from the English edition, *The Political Element in the Development of Economic Theory* (Cambridge, Mass.: Harvard University Press, 1961), pp. x, xii–xiii.

49. Axel Hägerström, *Social teleologi i Marxismen* (Uppsala: Akademiska boktryckeriet, E. Berling, 1909), pp. 59–70; Hägerström, *Om moraliska förestallningars sanning* (Uppsala: 1911); Hägerström, *Till frågan om den objektiva rättens begrepp* (Uppsala: Akademiska bokhandeln, 1917); Hägerström, *Der römische Obligations-begriff im Lichte der allgemeinen römischen Rechtsanschauung* (Uppsala: Almqvist & Wiksell, 1927); A. Wedberg, "Axel Hägerström," in *The Encyclopedia of Philosophy*, ed. Paul Edwards (New York: Macmillan, 1967), 3:402–4; on Weber and Hägerström, see Gunnar Myrdal, *Political Element*, pp. 12–13.

50. Gunnar Myrdal, *Political Element*, p. 194.

51. Ibid., p. 196.

52. Ibid., p. 199.

53. Ibid., p. 203.

54. Ibid., pp. 203–4, 206.

55. Ibid., p. 205.

56. Gunnar Myrdal, "Förord till den svenska upplagen," *Vetenskap och politik i nationalekonomien* (Stockholm: Rabén & Sjögren, 1972), pp. 10–11, quoted by Swedberg, introduction to Gunnar Myrdal, *Political Element*.

57. Gunnar Myrdal, oral history memoir, quoted in Andersson, "Gunnar Myrdal: Barn—och ungdomsår," p. 41.

58. Irving Fisher to G. Myrdal, 1927, GMP.

59. Gunnar Myrdal, *The Cost of Living in Sweden, 1830–1930* (London: P. S. King & Son, 1933); "Stor Rockefellerdonation till Socialvetanskapliga Institutet vid Högskolan," *Svenska Dagbladet*, March 28, 1926; "Veckans porträtt: Gösta Bagge," *Nya Dagligt Allehanda*, November 8, 1931.

60. Bok, *Alva*, pp. 83–84.

61. Alva Myrdal, "Report on the Year 13.6.1929–13.6.1930, Spent in England and

America as a Rockefeller Fellow," AMP.

62. Gunnar Myrdal, *An American Dilemma: The Negro Problem and Modern Democracy* (New York: Harper & Brothers, 1944), pp. 21–22.

63. G. Myrdal to Cassel, October 29, 1929, GMP.

64. G. Myrdal to Cassel, January 18, 1930, GMP.

65. A. Myrdal to Else-Merete and Alf Ross, December 20, 1929, AMP.

66. G. Myrdal to Cassel, January 18, 1930, GMP.

67. G. Myrdal to Cassel, October 29, 1929, GMP.

68. Gunnar Myrdal, *Against the Stream: Critical Essays on Economics* (New York: Pantheon, 1973), p. 6; Gunnar Myrdal, "Institutional Economics," *Journal of Economic Issues* 12 (September 1978): 771–72.

69. G. Myrdal to Cassel, October 29, 1929 (translation by Allan Carlson in "Roles of Alva and Gunnar Myrdal," p. 140.

70. G. Myrdal to Gösta Bagge, February 8, 1930, GMP.

71. Bok, *Alva*, p. 84.

72. G. Myrdal to Cassel, March 24, 1930, GMP.

73. Gunnar Myrdal, *Political Element*, p. 205. This quotation and the one that follows appeared in the last chapter of the book, which Myrdal completed in Washington, D.C., in December 1929. Although the main ideas of the chapter had been developed in Sweden, he did add these examples which he drew from his experiences in the United States.

74. Ibid., p. 200; cf. Gunnar Myrdal, *Vetenskap och politik*, p. 287.

75. G. Myrdal to Cassel, March 24, 1930, GMP.

76. G. Myrdal to Bagge, April 7, 1930, GMP.

77. G. Myrdal to Cassel, March 24, 1930, GMP.

78. G. Myrdal to Bagge, April 7, 1930, GMP.

79. G. Myrdal to Cassel, March 24, 1930, GMP.

80. G. Myrdal to Cassel, January 30, 1930, GMP.

81. G. Myrdal to Bagge, February 3, 1930, and G. Myrdal to Cassel, March 30, 1930, GMP.

82. G. Myrdal to Cassel, January 18, 1930, GMP.

83. Gunnar and Alva Myrdal, interview in Herz, *Alva och Gunnar Myrdal i fredens tjänst*, pp. 109–10.

84. Gunnar Myrdal, interview with author, August 19, 1980, Stockholm; Carlson, "Roles of Alva and Gunnar Myrdal," p. 142.

85. G. Myrdal to Cassel, January 18, 1930, GMP.

86. Herz, *Alva och Gunnar Myrdal i fredens tjänst*, pp. 109–10.

87. G. Myrdal to Cassel, January 18, 1930, GMP.

88. Egon Glesinger, "Gunnar Myrdal," unpublished biographical sketch, enclosed in Glesinger to G. Myrdal, January 3, 1949, pp. 1–3; G. Myrdal to Gösta Bagge, February 27, 1931; G. Myrdal to Ernst Wigforss, May 10, 1931; all in GMP.

89. Gunnar Myrdal, "Socialism eller kapitalism i framtidens Amerika?" *Tiden* 23 (1931): 205–6.

90. Ibid., pp. 205–6.

91. Ibid., pp. 207–8.

92. Ibid., pp. 208–9.

93. Ibid. pp. 210–11; cf. Werner Sombart, *Why Is There No Socialism in the United States?* (White Plains, N.Y.: International Arts and Sciences Press, 1976), original German edition,

Warum gibt es in den Vereinigten Staaten keinen Sozialismus? (Tübingen: Verlag von J. C. B. Mohr, 1906).

94. Gunnar Myrdal, "Socialism eller kapitalism," pp. 211–12.

95. Ibid., p. 218.

96. Ibid., pp. 212, 218–19.

97. Ibid., p. 218.

98. Ibid., pp. 226–27.

99. Ibid., p. 230.

100. Herbert Tingsten, *The Swedish Social Democrats: Their Ideological Development* (Totawa, N.J.: Bedminster Press, 1973), p. 285.

101. Gunnar Myrdal, "Socialpolitikens Dilemma."

102. Ibid., pp. 14–20.

103. Ibid., pp. 25–31.

104. Timothy Tilton, "Ideologins roll i socialdemokratisk politik," in *Socialdemokratins samhälle: SAP och Sverige under 100 år*, ed. Klaus Misgeld, Karl Molin, and Klas Åmark (Stockholm: Tiden, 1988), pp. 369–89; Steven Koblik, ed., *Sweden's Development from Poverty to Affluence*, p. 254.

105. Tingsten, *The Swedish Social Democrats*, pp. 279, 312; Franklin Scott, *Sweden: The Nation's History* (Cambridge, Mass.: Harvard University Press), p. 496.

106. Leif Lewin, in *Sweden's Development*, ed. Koblik, p. 285.

107. Nils Unga, *Socialdemokratin och arbetslöshetsfrågan, 1912–1934* (Kristianstad: 1976), pp. 223–25.

108. Carl G. Uhr, "The Emergence of the 'New Economics' in Sweden: A Review of a Study by Otto Steiger," *History of Political Economy* 5, no. 1 (Spring 1973): 243–49.

109. Ibid., p. 250.

110. C. G. Uhr, "Economists and Policymaking 1930–1936: Sweden's Experience," *History of Political Economy* 9, no. 1 (Spring 1977): 97–101.

111. Gunnar Myrdal, *Konjunkturer och offentlig hushållning*, Bilaga III till Statsverksproposition 1933, Stockholm, January 2, 1933, pp. 1–45. My discussion of this article is drawn from the interpretation given in Uhr, "Economists and Policymaking," pp. 102–7.

112. Uhr, "Economists and Policymaking," pp. 116–17.

113. Gunnar and Alva Myrdal to John Van Sickle, July 20, 1933, Rockefeller Foundation file, GMP.

114. Gunnar Myrdal, *Monetary Equilibrium* (London: Hodge, 1939), original Swedish edition, "Om penningteoretisk jämvikt: En studie över den 'normala räntan' i Wicksells penninglära," *Ekonomisk Tidskrift* 33 (1931): 191–302; Paul Streeten, "Gunnar Myrdal," in *The New Palgrave: A Dictionary of Economics*, ed. John Eatwell, Murray Milgate, and Peter Newman (New York: Schocken, 1987), p. 581.

115. Carlson, "Roles of Alva and Gunnar Myrdal," p. 143. I am indebted to Rudolph Haerle for the information about the Thomases. On the model for the Thomases' Scandinavian work, see W. I. Thomas, *The Polish Peasant in Europe and America*, 5 vols. (Chicago: University of Chicago Press, 1918–20).

116. Gustav Cassel, *I förnuftets tjänst*, 2:374, 383. Egon Glesinger, "Gunnar Myrdal," p. 5; Gunnar Myrdal, interview with author, August 18, 1980, Stockholm. According to one account, Myrdal actually urged Cassel to retire so that he could have the job! See Swedberg, introduction to *Political Element*, p. 38.

117. Carlson, "Roles of Alva and Gunnar Myrdal," p. 147.

118. Gunnar Myrdal, *Bostadsfrågan såsom socialt planläggningsproblem* (Stockholm: Finansdepartementet, 1933).

119. Carlson, "Roles of Alva and Gunnar Myrdal," pp. 179–84. My discussion of *Kris i befolkiningsfrågan* and its influence draws heavily on Carlson's work.

120. Alva Myrdal and Gunnar Myrdal, *Kris i befolkningsfrågan* (Stockholm: Bonniers, 1934), pp. 7–14

121. Ibid., p. 173.

122. Ibid., pp. 66–78.

123. Ibid., p. 76.

124. Ibid., pp. 105–11.

125. Ibid., pp. 226–29.

126. Ibid., p. 112; Carlson, "Roles of Alva and Gunnar Myrdal," pp. 200–201.

127. Alva Myrdal and Gunnar Myrdal, *Kris i befolkningsfrågan*, p. 218.

128. Ibid., pp. 220–21.

129. The last two quotations are from the English edition of the book, Alva Myrdal, *Nation and Family: The Swedish Experiment in Democratic Family and Population Policy* (New York: Harper & Brothers, 1941), pp. 116, 213.

130. Alva Myrdal and Gunnar Myrdal, *Kris i befolkningsfrågan*, pp. 263, 265–67, 278–79.

131. Ibid., p. 295.

132. Ibid., p. 321.

133. Ibid., p. 319.

134. Ibid., pp. 321–25.

135. Carlson, "Roles of Alva and Gunnar Myrdal," pp. 265–71; "Lugnare for både barn och foräldrar i 'Myrdalshusen,'" *Svenska Morgonbladet*, June 10, 1938.

136. Glesinger, "Gunnar Myrdal."

137. Carlson, "Roles of Alva and Gunnar Myrdal," pp. 234–35, 249–50, 257–59, 282–85.

138. Ibid., pp. 296–98. See also Ann-Katrin Hatje, *Befolkningsfrågan och välfärden* (Stockholm: Allmänna förlaget, 1974), p. 28.

139. Carlson, "Roles of Alva and Gunnar Myrdal," pp. 381, 386, 388–91, 395–96.

140. Gunnar Myrdal, *Jordbrukspolitiken under omläggning* (Stockholm: Kooperativa Förbundets Bokförlag, 1938), p. 38.

141. Ernst Wigforss, *Minnen III, 1932–1949* (Stockholm: Tidens Förlag, 1954), pp. 361–64; G. Myrdal to W. I. Thomas, February 10, 1931, GMP.

142. Glesinger, "Gunnar Myrdal," GMP; Tore Browaldh, *Gesällvandring* (Stockholm: Norstedt, 1976), p. 53.

143. Bok, *Alva*, pp. 167–68.

144. See David Hollinger, "Ethnic Diversity, Cosmopolitanism, and the Emergence of the American Liberal Intelligentsia," in *In the American Province* (Bloomington: Indiana University Press, 1985), pp. 56–73.

145. Gunnar Myrdal, *An American Dilemma*, p. 711.

146. Bok, *Alva*, p. 168.

147. Tore Browaldh, interview with author, May 17, 1989, Stockholm; Browaldh, *Gesällvandring*, pp. 17–18.

148. Bok, *Alva.*, pp. 166–70.

149. Ibid., pp. 170–72.

150. "Myrdalska idealhemmet, byggt for barn och hemliv," *Eskilstuna Kuriren*, December 10, 1938; Gunnar Myrdal, *Hur styrs landet?* p. 281; Bok, *Alva*, p. 109.

151. Gunnar Myrdal, interview with author, August 18, 1980, Stockholm; G. Myrdal to Jacob Viner, February 14, 1938, GMP; Milton Viorst, "Gunnar Myrdal," *Washington Post*, June 9, 1968.

152. G. Myrdal to Keppel, November 12, 1937, Negro Study General Correspondence, CCA.

153. G. Myrdal to Dorothy S. Thomas, March 1, 1938, GMP.

Chapter 3: Encountering the "Negro Problem"

1. G. Myrdal to Cassel, January 2, 1939, Cassel Papers, Royal Library, Stockholm; G. Myrdal to Siegfrid Hansson, February 25, 1939, GMP; Marquis Childs, "How Fares Democracy?" *St. Louis Post-Dispatch*, June 25, 1939, copy in Myrdal clipping collection, GMP.

2. G. Myrdal to Keppel, October 7, 1937; Keppel, memo, "For Discussion with Professor Myrdal," May 11, 1938, Negro Study General Correspondence, CCA; Gunnar Myrdal, interview with author, August 18, 1980, Stockholm. Myrdal gives an account of the organization of the study in the author's preface to *An American Dilemma: The Negro Problem and Modern Democracy* (New York: Harper & Brothers, 1944), pp. ix–xx.

3. G. Myrdal to Stockholms Stadsrullföringsområde, December 22, 1939, GMP.

4. Jackson Davis, Diary, October 3–20, 1938, GEB Papers, 586.1, Rockefeller Archive Center, Tarrytown, N.Y.; Gunnar Myrdal, author's preface to *An American Dilemma*, pp. ix–x; Gunnar Myrdal, interview, Columbia Oral History Project, Columbia University, New York, N.Y., November 27, 1967, p. 25.

5. G. Myrdal to Cassel, September 9, 1938, Cassel Papers.

6. G. Myrdal to Cassel, January 2, 1939, Cassel Papers.

7. *Birmingham News*, November 1938, copy in clipping file, GMP.

8. Barbro Alving, "Striden i USA, hård som sovjets," *Dagens Nyheter*, June 20, 1939.

9. Donald Young, interview, Columbia Oral History Project, p. 44; Guy B. Johnson, interview, Columbia Oral History Project, p. 50.

10. Gunnar Myrdal, interview with author, August 19, 1980, Stockholm.

11. Ibid.; Childs, "How Fares Democracy?"

12. Jackson Davis, Record of conversation with Charles Dollard and R. M. Lester, November 7, 1938, GEB Papers, 586.1, Box 270, f. 2787.

13. Gunnar Myrdal, author's preface to *An American Dilemma*, p. xviii. Myrdal later stated that the social scientists he proposed for this committee were Donald Young, Charles S. Johnson, and T. J. Woofter, Jr. Interview with author, August 19, 1980, Stockholm.

14. On Myrdal's use of the royal commission model, see "Sweden's Technique of Democracy Outlined to Inter-Racial Delegates," *Atlanta Constitution*, May 25, 1939, copy in clipping collection, GMP, and T. J. Woofter, Jr., to G. Myrdal, April 27, 1940, GMP.

15. Gunnar Myrdal, interview with author, August 19, 1980.

16. G. Myrdal to Keppel, August 14, 1939, and Keppel to G. Myrdal, August 16, 1939, NSGC; Gunnar Myrdal, interview, Columbia Oral History Project, 1967, p. 107.

17. Gunnar Myrdal, interview with author, August 19, 1980.

18. Keppel, memo, "FPK and E. L. Thorndike," May 22, 1939; G. Myrdal, memo,

"Conference with Dr. Keppel, Sunday, March 13, 1939; Keppel to Howard Odum, June 1, 1939; Samuel Stouffer to G. Myrdal, December 9, 1941; Charles Dollard to Chairman, Local Draft Board No. 27, Chicago, Illinois, March 10, 1942; all in NSGC.

19. G. Myrdal to Siegfried Hansson, February 25, 1939, GMP.

20. G. Myrdal to Einar Tegen, March 4, 1939, GMP.

21. Fred H. Matthews, *Quest for an American Sociology: Robert E. Park and the Chicago School* (Montreal: McGill-Queen's University Press, 1977).

22. Ibid., pp. 184–89.

23. Edward Shils, "Tradition, Ecology, and Institution in the History of Sociology," *Daedalus* (Fall 1970): 793–94.

24. Quoted in Anthony Oberschall, *The Establishment of Empirical Sociology: Studies in Continuity, Discontinuity, and Institutionalization* (New York: Harper & Row, 1972), pp. 242–43.

25. This overview of social scientists and race relations in the 1930s cannot do justice to the complex issue of objectivity and the many divergent positions within the social sciences. On sociology, see Robert C. Bannister, *Sociology and Scientism: The American Quest for Objectivity, 1880–1940* (Chapel Hill: University of North Carolina Press, 1987).

26. E. Franklin Frazier to Charles S. Johnson, October 27, 1928; Johnson to Frazier, February 26, 1929; Johnson to Frazier, May 21, 1929; all in Frazier Papers, Howard University, Washington, D.C.

27. Donald Young, *American Minority Peoples: A Study in Racial and Cultural Conflicts in the United States* (New York: Harper & Brothers, 1932).

28. Odum's classic statement of regional sociology is *Southern Regions of the United States* (Chapel Hill: University of North Carolina Press, 1936). My interpretation closely follows that of Morton Sosna, *In Search of the Silent South* (New York: Columbia University Press, 1977), pp. 42–59.

29. John Dollard, *Caste and Class in a Southern Town* (New Haven, Conn.: Yale University Press, 1937), p. 1.

30. Ibid, p. 15.

31. Ibid., pp. 173–87.

32. Ibid., p. 170.

33. Ibid., pp. 365–66.

34. Ibid., pp. 393, 426–32.

35. Ibid., pp. 171, 208.

36. W. Lloyd Warner, "American Caste and Class," *American Journal of Sociology* 42 (1937): 234–37; St. Clair Drake and Horace Cayton, *Black Metropolis: A Study of Negro Life in a Northern City* (New York: Harcourt, Brace, 1945); Allison Davis and John Dollard, *Children of Bondage: The Personality Development of Negro Youth in the Urban South* (Washington, D.C.: American Council on Education, 1940).

37. W. E. B. Du Bois, "The Relation of Negroes to the Whites in the South," *Annals of the American Academy of Political and Social Science* 18 (1901): 121–40; W. I. Thomas, "The Psychology of Race-Prejudice," *American Journal of Sociology* 9 (1904): 593–611; Emory S. Bogardus, "Measuring Social Distance," *Journal of Applied Sociology* 9 (1925): 299–308; Bogardus, *Immigration and Race Attitudes* (Boston: Heath, 1928); Bruno Lasker, *Race Attitudes in Children* (New York: Henry Holt, 1929), pp. 368–84. On the development of the concept of prejudice, see Franz Samelson, "From 'Race Psychology' to 'Studies in Prejudice': Some Observations on the Thematic Reversal in Social Psychology," *Journal of the History of*

the Behavioral Sciences 14 (1978): 265–78; and Donald Fleming, "Attitude: The History of a Concept," *Perspectives in American History* 1 (1967): 341–47.

38. Daniel Katz and Kenneth Braly, "Racial Stereotypes of One Hundred College Students," *Journal of Abnormal and Social Psychology* 28 (1933): 280–90; Katz and Braly, "Racial Prejudice and Racial Stereotypes," *Journal of Abnormal and Social Psychology* 30 (1935): 175–93; Eugene L. Horowitz, "The Development of Attitude toward the Negro," *Archives of Psychology* 28 (1936): 5–36.

39. Paul Lewinson, *Race, Class, and Party: A History of Negro Suffrage and White Politics in the South* (London: Oxford University Press, 1931); Harold Gosnell, *Negro Politicians: The Rise of Negro Politics in Chicago* (Chicago: University of Chicago Press, 1935).

40. Sterling Spero and Abram Harris, *The Black Worker: The Negro and the Labor Movement* (New York: Columbia University Press, 1931); Abram Harris, *The Negro as Capitalist: A Study of Banking and Business among American Negroes* (Philadelphia: The American Academy of Political and Social Science, 1936); Horace Cayton and George S. Mitchell, *Black Workers and the New Unions* (Chapel Hill: The University of North Carolina Press, 1939).

41. For an overview of Herskovits's views prior to the Myrdal study, see Herskovits, "The Negro in the New World," *American Anthropologist* 32 (1930): 145–55; and Walter A. Jackson, "Melville Herskovits and the Search for Afro-American Culture," in *Malinowski, Benedict, Rivers, and Others: Essays on Culture and Personality, History of Anthropology* 4 (1986): 95–126, ed. George W. Stocking, Jr.

42. See Chapter 1 on Herskovits's letter-writing campaign against Du Bois's Encyclopedia of the Negro project. E. Franklin Frazier, though respecting Du Bois's contribution to the civil rights struggle, pointedly referred to himself as a professional sociologist, not a "Negro leader." In a letter to Howard Odum, he wrote that "I have studiously avoided what has appeared to me to be a pitfall which lies in the path of most educated Negroes, namely: being forced into the role of a Negro leader." Frazier to Odum, November 29, 1949, Frazier Papers, Box 54, f. 17.

43. W. E. B. Du Bois, "A Negro Nation within the Nation," *Current History* 42 (June 1935). See also Raymond Wolters, *Negroes and the Great Depression* (Westport, Conn.: Greenwood Press, 1970), pp. 230–58. On the critique of Du Bois's program by young black radicals, see James O. Young, *Black Writers of the Thirties* (Baton Rouge: Louisiana State University Press, 1973), p. 29.

44. W. E. B. Du Bois, *The Negro* (New York: Henry Holt, 1915), pp. 110–14.

45. See Jacqueline A. Goggin, "Carter G. Woodson and the Movement to Promote Black History" (Ph.D. diss., University of Rochester, 1984); Patricia W. Romero, "Carter G. Woodson: A Biography" (Ph.D. diss., Ohio State University, 1971); and August Meier and Elliott Rudwick, *Black History and the Historical Profession, 1915–1980* (Urbana: University of Illinois Press, 1986), pp. 1–71.

46. Richard Robbins, "Charles S. Johnson," in *Black Sociologists: Historical and Contemporary Perspectives*, ed. James E. Blackwell and Morris Janowitz (Chicago: University of Chicago Press, 1974), pp. 56–81; see also Patrick Gilpin, "Charles S. Johnson: An Intellectual Biography" (Ph.D. diss., Vanderbilt University, 1973).

47. Charles S. Johnson, *Shadow of the Plantation* (Chicago: University of Chicago Press, 1934), pp. 208–12, 50.

48. On Harris and Bunche, this discussion follows closely the interpretation in James O. Young, *Black Writers of the Thirties*, pp. 35–63; see also Walter A. Jackson, "Politics and

Culture in the Thought of E. Franklin Frazier," paper read at American Historical Association Meeting, Washington, D.C., December 28, 1987.

49. Ralph Bunche, "Education in Black and White," *Journal of Negro Education* 5 (July 1936): 353–54.

50. E. Franklin Frazier, *The Negro Family in the United States* (Chicago: University of Chicago Press, 1939).

51. See Mark Calvin Smith, "Knowledge for What: Social Science and the Debate over Its Role in 1930s America" (Ph.D. diss., University of Texas, 1980), pp. 3, 8–10. On social engineering in the Progressive Era, see John F. McClymer, *War and Welfare: Social Engineering in America, 1890–1925* (Westport, Conn.: Greenwood, 1980), and on the 1920s, see Guy B. Alchon, *The Invisible Hand of Planning: Capitalism, Social Science, and the State in the 1920s* (Princeton: Princeton University Press, 1985).

52. Robert S. Lynd, *Knowledge for What?* (Princeton: Princeton University Press, 1939). The social science reaction against scientific naturalism is discussed in Edward Purcell's *The Crisis of Democratic Theory: Scientific Naturalism and the Problem of Value* (Lexington: University of Kentucky Press, 1973), pp. 179–96.

53. Louis Wirth, preface to Karl Mannheim, *Ideology and Utopia* (New York: Harcourt, Brace, 1936), pp. ix–xxx.

54. John Dewey, *Freedom and Culture* (New York: Putnam, 1939), p. 162.

55. G. Myrdal, memorandum to Keppel, January 28, 1939, copy in Herskovits Papers, Myrdal file. Myrdal's memorandum to his staff of February 8, 1940, reaffirmed this practical, problem-solving orientation of the study. Copy in Herskovits Papers, Myrdal file.

56. G. Myrdal, memorandum to Keppel, January 28, 1939, Herskovits Papers, Myrdal file, p. 8.

57. Ibid., pp. 11, 33–34, 40; on the visit to Father Divine's Kingdom, see Jan Myrdal, *En annan värld* (Stockholm: Norstedt, 1984), p. 237.

58. G. Myrdal, memorandum to Keppel, January 28, 1939, Herskovits Papers, Myrdal file, pp. 36–37.

59. Ibid., pp. 46–51.

60. Gunnar Myrdal, author's preface to *An American Dilemma*, p. x.

61. Bunche to W. Z. Park, December 5, 1938, Bunche Papers, Box 1, University of California, Los Angeles.

62. Bunche to Herskovits, February 17, 1939, Herskovits Papers.

63. Herskovits to Bunche, March 24, 1939, Herskovits Papers.

64. W. E. B. Du Bois to Ira Reid, April 14, 1939, in *The Correspondence of W. E. B. Du Bois*, ed. Herbert Aptheker (Amherst: University of Massachusetts Press, 1973–78), 2:190–91.

65. Ralph McGill, "One Word More," *Atlanta Constitution*, n.d., enclosure, Odum to Keppel, May 27, 1939, NSGC.

66. Bunche to W. Z. Park, December 5, 1938, Bunche Papers.

67. Gunnar Myrdal, author's preface to *An American Dilemma*, p. x; "Interview with Donald Young," February 12, 1939, Carnegie Corporation memorandum, unsigned, NSGC. After Myrdal's arrival in the United States, Young apparently did not attempt to influence the conclusion of Myrdal's study. See Gunnar Myrdal, interview, Columbia Oral History Project, p. 70.

68. Guy B. Johnson, interview, Columbia Oral History Project, pp. 30–31, 61; Gunnar Myrdal, interview with author, August 19, 1980, Stockholm.

69. Charles Dollard, notes of conversation with G. Myrdal, March 7, 1939, NSGC; G.

Myrdal to Keppel, March 8, 1939 (copy in Arnold Rose Papers, University of Minnesota, Minneapolis, Minn.); Gunnar Myrdal, author's preface to *An American Dilemma*, p. xi.

70. A complete list of all research memoranda written for the Myrdal project is given in Gunnar Myrdal, author's preface to *An American Dilemma*, pp. xii–xiv. Copies of the memoranda are at the Schomburg Library, New York, N.Y.

71. Charles Dollard, interview with G. Myrdal, March 7, 1939, NSGC.

72. Ibid.; Guy B. Johnson, interview with author, April 21, 1977, Chapel Hill, N.C. Before Myrdal arrived in the country, Keppel had promised Herskovits that Myrdal would discuss the Negro study with him. Keppel, memo, "FPK and M. J. Herskovits," September 1, 1938, Herskovits file, CCA. Myrdal had also heard very favorable remarks about Herskovits from his friend, the Swedish anthropologist Gunnar Dahlberg. See G. Myrdal to Dahlberg, March 4, 1939, GMP.

73. G. Myrdal to Guy B. Johnson, May 5, 1939, copy in NSGC.

74. Charles Dollard, interview with G. Myrdal, March 7, 1939.

75. G. Myrdal to Keppel, March 8, 1939, copy in Arnold Rose Papers.

76. Unsigned interview with Donald Young, February 12, 1939, NSGC.

77. G. Myrdal to Keppel, April 28, 1939, copy in Arnold Rose Papers. Myrdal invited Abram Harris to write a monograph on "The Negro in Non-Agricultural Pursuits." Harris declined. Several other young black scholars, including Kenneth B. Clark, were employed as research assistants.

78. Gunnar Myrdal, interview with author, August 19, 1980, Stockholm.

79. St. Clair Drake, interview with author, December 31, 1978, Palo Alto, Calif.

80. S. A. Stouffer to Charles Dollard, Shelby M. Harrison, William F. Ogburn, and Donald R. Young, March 18, 1941, GMP, American Dilemma file.

81. G. Myrdal to Charles Dollard, March 30, 1941, GMP American Dilemma file. In later years, Myrdal stressed that his primary interest had been in recruiting competent researchers, not in their political affiliation: "I did not think very much in terms of whether they were rightists or leftists. . . . I thought about their competence." On Doxey Wilkerson, "I had looked upon him as a young intellectual. I didn't care whether he was a Communist or not. I never cared about that." Gunnar Myrdal, interview with author, August 19, 1980, Stockholm.

82. G. Myrdal, memo, "Conference with Dr. Keppel, Sunday, March 12, 1939," NSGC.

83. See G. Myrdal to Keppel, January 28, 1939, copy in Herskovits Papers. For an overview of the growing literature on Afro-American history which Myrdal ignored, see Meier and Rudwick, *Black History*, pp. 73–122.

84. Herskovits to Lydia Parrish, July 26, 1940, Herskovits Papers.

85. Alain Locke to Herskovits [n.d.], filed June 1939, Herskovits Papers, Locke file.

86. Bunche to Herskovits, May 23, 1939, Herskovits Papers.

87. Keppel memo, "For Discussion with Professor Myrdal," May 11, 1938, NSGC.

88. Walter White to Bunche, September 25, 1939, "Myrdal Study, 1939," NAACP Papers, Group II, Series L, Box 20, Library of Congress, Washington, D.C.; Robert M. Lester to White, May 5, 1941, NAACP Papers, Group II, Box A165.

89. Charles Dollard, memo, "CD and Eugene Kinckle Jones," January 2, 1940, NSGC.

90. Wilkins to White, October 21, 1939, NAACP Papers, Group II, Box A164, Carnegie Myrdal Study General file.

91. Wilkins to White, March 28, 1940, NAACP Papers, Group II, Box A164.

92. G. Myrdal to Keppel, August 22, 1940, American Dilemma file, GMP.

93. Guy B. Johnson, interview with author, April 22, 1977, Chapel Hill, N.C.

94. G. Myrdal to Keppel, April 28, 1939, quoted in Gunnar Myrdal, *An American Dilemma*, pp. x–xi.

95. G. Myrdal, "Appendix 1B, Memorandum on the Disposition of the Study," September 10, 1939, p. 5, copy in Herskovits Papers. Myrdal had previously developed the argument that political economists should derive their instrumental norms from an analysis of the valuations of interested groups in the society being studied in "Ends and Means in Political Economy," originally published in *Zeitschrift für Nationalökonomie* 4 (1933), reprinted in *Value in Social Theory*, ed. Paul Streeten (London: Routledge & Kegan Paul, 1958), pp. 206–30. Myrdal discusses his methodology in appendices 1, 2, and 3 of *An American Dilemma*, pp. 1027–70.

96. G. Myrdal, "Appendix 1C—Positive Methodological Discussion, Memorandum on the Disposition of the Study," September 10, 1939, p. 8.

97. G. Myrdal, "Memo on the Disposition," pp. 10–11, 13.

98. Gunnar Myrdal, "Socialism eller kapitalism i framtidens Amerika?" *Tiden* 23 (1931): 207–8; Gunnar Myrdal, *The Political Element in the Development of Economic Theory* (Cambridge, Mass.: Harvard University Press, 1961), p. 205. See Chapter 2.

99. G. Myrdal, "Memo on the Disposition," p. 187.

100. Barbro Alving, "Striden i USA"; Gunnar Myrdal, foreword to Arnold M. Rose, *The Negro in America* (Boston: Beacon, 1948), p. xiii.

101. Doxey Wilkerson, interview with author, February 2, 1978, South Norwalk, Conn.; Donald Young, interview, Columbia Oral History Project, p. 54; Arnold Rose, "Myrdal: The American Dilemma," oral history memoir, p. 5, Arnold Rose Papers.

102. Charles Dollard, interview, Columbia Oral History Project, p. 86.

103. Guy B. Johnson, interview, Columbia Oral History Project, April 19, 1967, p. 15; G. Myrdal to Guy B. Johnson, August 27, 1940, GMP; Guion Johnson, interview with author, April 21, 1977, Chapel Hill, N.C.; Doxey Wilkerson, interview with author, February 2, 1978, South Norwalk, Conn.

104. Bunche to Herskovits, April 2, 1940, Herskovits Papers, Myrdal file; Bunche to Herskovits, October 29, 1940, Herskovits Papers, ACLS-Conference on Negro Studies file.

105. Charles Dollard, memo, "CD, Dr. Myrdal, and Donald Young," n.d. [spring 1940], GMP.

106. G. Myrdal to Guy Johnson, August 27, 1940, GMP.

107. G. Myrdal to Staff Members and Collaborators, February 8, 1940, copy in Herskovits Papers, Myrdal file.

108. Gunnar Myrdal, *An American Dilemma*, p. 1023. On American writers' travelogues, see William Stott, *Documentary Expression and Thirties America* (Chicago: University of Chicago Press, 1973), and Richard Pells, *Radical Visions and American Dreams* (New York: Harper & Row, 1973), pp. 194–201.

109. Arthur Raper, interview with author, April 13, 1977, Oakton, Va.; Raper, interview with Morton Sosna, April 23, 1971, Southern Oral History Collection, University of North Carolina, Chapel Hill, p. 54; Arnold Rose, "The American Dilemma" oral history memoir, p. 47, Arnold Rose Papers; Guy B. Johnson, interview with author, April 22, 1977, Chapel Hill, N.C.

110. "Dr. Gunnar Myrdal's interview with Senator Theodore G. Bilbo, April 8, 1940," Bunche Papers, Box 85.

111. Ibid., pp. 3, 5–6.

112. Ibid., p. 5.

113. Ibid., pp. 8–11.

114. See Alva Myrdal and Gunnar Myrdal, *Kontakt med Amerika* (Stockholm: Bonniers, 1941), p. 53, on Gunnar Myrdal's interview with a Dr. Evans of the Ku Klux Klan. See also Arnold Rose, "Myrdal: The American Dilemma," oral history memoir, n.d., pp. 46–47, Arnold Rose Papers; and Ralph Bunche, "Field Notes, Southern Trip," Book III, pp. 36–37, Bunche Papers.

115. E. Franklin Frazier, review of *An American Dilemma* in *American Journal of Sociology* 50 (May 1945): 557.

116. Kenneth Clark, quoted in obituary of Gunnar Myrdal, *New York Times*, May 18, 1987, p. 19.

117. Kenneth Clark, interview with author, October 1986, Hastings-on-Hudson, New York.

118. White to Myrdal, August 4, 1942, NSGC.

119. Walter White to Alva Myrdal, November 15, 1939, NAACP file, AMP; A. Myrdal to Eva Nyblom, November 16, 1938, Idun file, AMP; A. Myrdal to Brita Åkerman, November 16, 1938, AMP.

120. Bunche to Ira W. Williams, December 11, 1939, Bunche Papers, Box 85.

121. Gunnar Myrdal, interview with author, August 19, 1980, Stockholm.

122. Arthur Raper, "Lest I Forget," November 11, 1949, Raper Papers, Box 5, Folder 172, Southern Historical Collection, University of North Carolina Library, Chapel Hill; Gunnar Myrdal, interview with author, August 19, 1980, Stockholm; Arthur Raper, interview with author, April 13, 1977, Oakton, Va.; G. Myrdal to Bunche, November 21, 1939, and Bunche to Myrdal, May 1, 1940, NSGC; Guy B. Johnson, interview with author, April 22, 1977, Chapel Hill, N.C.

123. Richard Babb Whitten, "Report No.1: A Day of Escape," November 15, 1939, pp. 3–10, Arnold Rose Papers.

124. Whitten, "A Day of Escape," pp. 11–22.

125. Bunche to Willard Z. Park, December 19, 1939, Bunche Papers, Box 1.

126. Bunche, "Interview with Mr. Justice Hugo Black, Supreme Court Building, February 13, 1940," Bunche Papers, Box 85.

127. Bunche, "Memo on Interview with Mrs. Franklin D. Roosevelt at the White House, May 15, 1940," Bunche Papers, Box 82.

128. Donald Young, interview, Columbia Oral History Project, p. 44.

129. Gunnar Myrdal, *An American Dilemma*, pp. 1031–34; Gunnar Myrdal, interview, Columbia Oral History Project.

130. Gunnar Myrdal, interview, Columbia Oral History Project, p. 61. Bunche's memoranda are cited extensively in *An American Dilemma*, especially chapters 22, "Political Practices Today"; 37, "Compromise Leadership"; and 39, "Negro Improvement and Protest Organizations." Bunche's close contact with Myrdal was emphasized by Arthur Raper, Guy B. Johnson, and Doxey Wilkerson in their interviews with the author.

131. Ralph Bunche, "Conceptions and Ideologies of the Negro Problem," memorandum, p. 135, Bunche Papers; copy also in the Schomburg Library.

132. James Jackson, "Field Notes," Wilhelmina Jackson, "Student-Worker Conference" (Durham, N.C.), Bunche Papers, Box 85; Ralph J. Bunche, *The Political Status of the Negro in the Age of FDR* (Chicago: University of Chicago Press, 1973), pp. 492, 554, 563.

133. Bunche, "Conceptions and Ideologies," p. 168.

134. Bunche, "The Programs, Ideologies, Tactics, and Achievements of Negro Betterment and Interracial Organizations," p. 788, Bunche Papers; copy also in the Schomburg Library.

135. Bunche, "Conceptions and Ideologies," p. 130.

136. Ibid., p. 170.

137. Ibid., pp. 3–4.

138. Gunnar Myrdal, *Political Element*, pp. 200–201.

139. G. Myrdal to Keppel, February 13, 1940, NSGC.

140. For Myrdal's critique of the NAACP, see *An American Dilemma*, pp. 831–36. On the need for different kinds of Negro protest organizations, see pp. 855–57.

141. Gunnar Myrdal, *An American Dilemma*, p. 73.

142. Ibid., pp. 69–70.

143. Bunche, "Conceptions and Ideologies," pp. 11–12.

144. Ibid., p. 93.

145. Ibid., p. 37.

146. Allison Davis, "Negro Churches and Associations in the Lower South," and St. Clair Drake, "Negro Churches and Associations in Chicago," unpublished manuscripts, Carnegie-Myrdal Study, Schomburg Library.

147. See "Myrdal's interview with Mr. Horace Cayton on the afternoon of January 3, 1940, Interview No. II," Bunche Papers, Box 85; see also David Southern, *Gunnar Myrdal and Black-White Relations: The Use and Abuse of "An American Dilemma"* (Baton Rouge: Louisiana State University Press, 1987), p. 23.

148. Alain Locke to Myrdal, February 23, 1939, Locke Papers, Box 84, Howard University Library, Washington, D.C.

149. Alain Locke, "Who and What Is 'Negro'?" *Opportunity* 20: 83–84.

150. Tore Browaldh, *Gesällvandring* (Stockholm: Norstedt, 1976).

151. Sterling Brown, "The Negro in American Culture," unpublished manuscript, Carnegie-Myrdal Study, Schomburg Library.

152. Alva Myrdal and Gunnar Myrdal, *Kontakt*, p. 104.

Chapter 4: My War Work

1. G. Myrdal to Keppel, April 22, 1940, Negro Study General Correspondence, CCA; Gunnar Myrdal, interview with author, August 19, 1980, Stockholm.

2. G. Myrdal to Siegfried Hansson, February 25, 1939, GMP.

3. G. Myrdal to Ernst Wigforss, September 2, 1939, GMP.

4. Lars G. Lindskog, *Alva Myrdal* (Stockholm: Sveriges Radios Förlag, 1981), pp. 68–69; G. Myrdal to Professor Ilm. Kovero, December 22, 1939, and G. Myrdal to Torsten Gårdlund, February 2, 1940, GMP.

5. Herbert Tingsten to G. Myrdal, December 8, 1939, GMP; Tingsten, *Mitt liv: Mellan trettio och femtio*, 2d ed. (Stockholm: Norstedt, 1962), pp. 309–13.

6. G. Myrdal to Tingsten, January 12, 1940, GMP.

7. G. Myrdal to Elliott D. Smith, April 16, 1940, GMP.

8. G. Myrdal to Fredrik Ström, April 2, 1940, GMP.

9. Gunnar Myrdal, "With Dictators as Neighbors," *Survey Graphic* (May 1939): 309–33, 351–57; Myrdal, "The Defenses of Democracy," *Survey Graphic* (June 1939): 385–88, 409–15.

10. Marquis Childs, "How Fares Democracy?" *St. Louis Post-Dispatch*, June 25, 1939, copy in clipping collection, GMP.

11. G. Myrdal to Gustav Cassel, August 3, 1939, Cassel Papers, Royal Library, Stockholm.

12. Alva Myrdal, "Education for Democracy in Sweden," in *Education for Democracy: The Proceedings of the Congress on Education for Democracy, Teachers College, Columbia University, August 15–17, 1939* (New York: Teachers College, 1939), pp. 169–80.

13. John R. Childs to Alva Myrdal, August 21, 1939, AMP.

14. Alva Myrdal, "På andra sidan syndafloden," *Vecko-journalen*, November 19, 1939, pp. 13–15, 40.

15. Alva Myrdal, "USA's präster, kriget Europas, freden vår," *Vecko-journalen*, no. 47 (1939): 14–15, 40.

16. Alva Myrdal, "Nya världens nyårstankar om den gamla," *Vecko-journalen*, December 31, 1939, pp. 12–13, 33.

17. G. Myrdal to Cassel, March 5, 1940, Cassel Papers.

18. Alva Myrdal and Gunnar Myrdal, *Kontakt med Amerika* (Stockholm: Bonniers, 1941), pp. 21–22.

19. G. Myrdal to Elliott Smith, April 16, 1940, GMP.

20. Alva Myrdal to Disa Västberg, February 26, 1940; A. Myrdal to Karin Koch, February 26, 1940; A. Myrdal to Eva von Zweigbergk, March 13, 1940; all in AMP. See also G. Myrdal to Herskovits, April 29, 1940, GMP.

21. G. Myrdal to Keppel, April 22, 1940, American Dilemma file, GMP.

22. Keppel to Guy Johnson, April 30, 1940, NSGC.

23. Bunche to G. Myrdal, May 1, 1940, GMP. See also G. Myrdal to Sterling Brown, April 29, 1940, GMP.

24. Lindskog, *Alva Myrdal*, p. 69; Gunnar Myrdal, interview with author, August 19, 1980, Stockholm; Herskovits to G. Myrdal, May 2, 1940, Herskovits Papers, Myrdal file, Northwestern University Library, Evanston Ill.

25. The Myrdals were founding members of Kulturfront, an antifascist organization started in 1935 in Stockholm. Alva Myrdal served on the board of directors the following year. See Louise Drangel, *Den kämpande demokratin: En studie in antinazistisk opinionsrörelse, 1935–1945* (Stockholm: Liber, 1976), pp. 14–15, 229. The Myrdals also aided refugees from Nazi Germany who fled to Sweden in the 1930s. Myrdal attempted to aid refugee intellectuals in finding jobs, both in Sweden and in America. See Myrdal, Oskar Lange, Jacob Viner to Bertil Ohlin, n.d., filed February 1940, GMP.

26. G. Myrdal to Arthur R. Burns, May 8, 1940, GMP.

27. G. Myrdal to Frederick Osborn, May 6, 1940, and G. Myrdal to Burns, May 8, 1940, GMP; Alva Myrdal and Gunnar Myrdal, *Kontakt*, p. 28.

28. Alva Myrdal and Gunnar Myrdal, *Kontakt*, pp. 21–23; Sissela Bok, *Alva: Ett kvinnoliv* (Stockholm: Bonniers, 1987), p. 133.

29. "Myrdals hemma: 'U.S.A. kommer med,'" *Dagens Nyheter*, May 28, 1940.

30. Alva Myrdal to Evelyn and Arthur R. Burns, July 21, 1940, Madesin Phillips file, AMP.

31. Alva Myrdal and Gunnar Myrdal, *Kontakt*, p. 27.

32. Wilhelm M. Carlgren, *Swedish Foreign Policy during the Second World War* (New York: St. Martin's Press, 1977), pp. 54–68.

33. Ibid., pp. 68–72, 83; Richard Petrow, *The Bitter Years: The Invasion and Occupation of Denmark and Norway, April 1940–May 1945* (New York: William Morrow, 1970), p. 94.

34. Ibid., pp. 61, 82–86.

35. Thorsten Nybom, *Motstånd—anpassning—uppslutning: linjer i svensk debatt om utrikespolitik och internationell politik, 1940–1943* (Stockholm: Liber, 1978), pp. 129–84.

36. G. Myrdal to Richard Sterner, June 25, 1940, and G. Myrdal to Samuel Stouffer et al., August 26, 1940, GMP.

37. *Dagens Nyheter*, June 23, 1940.

38. Quoted in Bok, *Alva*, p. 60.

39. G. Myrdal to Keppel, June 26, 1940, GMP.

40. G. Myrdal to Sterner, June 25, 1940, GMP.

41. G. Myrdal to Stouffer et al., August 26, 1940, GMP.

42. Alf W. Johansson, *Per Albin och kriget: Samlingsregeringen och utrikespolitiken under andra världskriget* (Stockholm: Tidens Förlag, 1984), pp. 191, 435; Gunnar Myrdal, *Hur styrs landet?* (Stockholm: Rabén & Sjögren, 1982), p. 286.

43. "Svensk självstyrelse: Ord om demokratin vid ett bordssamtal," *Vi*, December 21–28, 1940, p. 12.

44. Drangel, *Den kämpande demokratin*, pp. 215–17.

45. G. Myrdal to Wigforss, June 19, 1940, GMP. Myrdal discussed the complicated issue of neutrality in an article published at the end of the war. See Gunnar Myrdal, "Neutralitet och vårt samvete," *Tiden* 37 (May 1945): pp. 257–70.

46. G. Myrdal to Åke Hassler, September 25, 1940, Stockholms Högskola file, GMP.

47. Lindskog, *Alva Myrdal*, p. 60.

48. Jean-Paul Sartre, "La République du silence," in *Situations* (Paris: Gallimard, 1949), 3:11 (quoted in James D. Wilkinson, *The Intellectual Resistance in Europe* (Cambridge, Mass.: Harvard University Press, 1981), p. 264.

49. Alva Myrdal, "Amerikas sociala försvar," *Morgonbris*, no. 7 (July 1940): 8–9, 25.

50. ——— Möller to Alva Myrdal, June 27, 1940, AMP.

51. In writing *Kontakt*, the Myrdals drew upon the following articles: Alva Myrdal, "Ny vetenskap i åsiktsmåtning," *Vecko-journalen*, January 8, 1939; Alva Myrdal, "På andra sidan syndafloden"; Alva Myrdal, "USA's präster, kriget Europas, freden vår"; Alva Myrdal, "Nya världens nyårstankar om den gamla"; Alva Myrdal, "Överfallet på Norden, Amerikas vändpunkt," *Vecko-journalen*, April 28, 1940; Alva Myrdal, "Amerika med—om man hinner," *Vecko-journalen*, June 9, 1940, pp. 14–15, 32; Alva Myrdal, "Amerikas sociala försvar"; Alva Myrdal, "5 för Roosevelt, 4 för Willkie," *Vi*, November 3, 1940, pp. 32–34; Gunnar Myrdal, "Vad får vi veta och vad är sant i nyheterna från utlandet?" *Vi*, November 23, 1940, pp. 3, 14; Gunnar Myrdal, "Återseende med den svenska pressen," *Publicistklubbens Årsbok 1941*, no. 23, February 15, 1941, pp. 72–86.

52. Alva Myrdal and Gunnar Myrdal, *Kontakt*, p. 24.

53. Ibid., pp. 27–31.

54. Ibid., pp. 32–33.

55. Ibid., p. 52.

56. Ibid.

57. Ibid. I assume that both authors were responsible for the arguments presented in this jointly written book. I attribute to Gunnar Myrdal, however, the portions of the book concerning the race issue in America and its relationship to the American creed and American social science, especially pages 52–56. Indeed, he used the first person singular in recounting experiences in the South in that portion of the book.

58. Ibid., p. 53; cf. "Dr. Gunnar Myrdal's Interview with Senator Theodore G. Bilbo,

April 8, 1940," Ralph Bunche Papers, Box 32, University of California, Los Angeles.

59. Alva Myrdal and Gunnar Myrdal, *Kontakt*, p. 54.

60. Ibid., p. 55.

61. Ibid., pp. 50, 56.

62. William Stott, *Documentary Expression and Thirties America* (Chicago: University of Chicago Press, 1973), pp. 171–89.

63. Richard Pells, *Radical Visions and American Dreams* (New York: Harper & Row, 1973), pp. 292–99.

64. In *An American Dilemma: The Negro Problem and Modern Democracy* (New York: Harper & Brothers, 1944), p. 1182 ff., G. Myrdal cited Ernest Bates, *American Faith: Its Religious, Political, and Economic Foundations* (New York: Norton, 1940). See also Lewis Mumford, *Faith for Living* (New York: Harcourt, Brace, 1940); Charles C. Alexander, *Nationalism in American Thought, 1930–1945* (Chicago: Rand McNally, 1969), pp. 164–89; and Edward Purcell, *The Crisis of Democratic Theory: Scientific Naturalism and the Problem of Value* (Lexington: University of Kentucky Press, 1973).

65. *Kontakt*, pp. 89–90.

66. Ibid., pp. 92, 95, 101, 110–11, 132.

67. Ibid., pp. 133–34.

68. Ibid., p. 135.

69. Ibid., p. 243.

70. Ibid., p. 245.

71. Ibid., p. 152.

72. Ibid., pp. 243–44.

73. Ibid., p. 246.

74. Ibid., pp. 246–47.

75. Ibid., p. 274.

76. Ibid., pp. 279, 282–83.

77. Ibid., p. 180.

78. Ibid., p. 186.

79. Ibid., p. 283.

80. Ibid., p. 303.

81. Ibid., pp. 304–5.

82. Ibid., p. 308.

83. Ibid., p. 309.

84. Ibid., p. 312.

85. Ibid., p. 342.

86. Ibid., p. 350.

87. Ibid., pp. 352–58.

88. Ibid., p. 355.

89. Ibid., p. 370.

90. Ibid., p. 372.

91. Ibid., p. 373. Looking back on *Kontakt* in later years, both Alva and Gunnar Myrdal stressed that they had written the book as a "preparedness" or "resistance" book, not as a scholarly volume. Both admitted that their discussion of the United States had not been as critical as it might have been in other circumstances. Lindskog, *Alva Myrdal*, p. 70; Gunnar Myrdal, interview with author, August 19, 1980, Stockholm.

92. G. Myrdal to Charles Dollard, July 7, 1942, NSGC; Gunnar Myrdal, interview with

author, August 19, 1980, Stockholm.

93. Gunnar Myrdal, "Socialism eller kapitalism i framtidens Amerika?" *Tiden* 23 (1931): 205–11.

94. Richard Pells, *Radical Visions and American Dreams*, pp. 362–64.

95. Richard Sterner to G. Myrdal, July 15, 1940; Sterner to G. Myrdal, October 6, 1940; Sterner to G. Myrdal, November 27, 1940; Sterner to Myrdal, December 21, 1940; all in GMP. In an interview, Myrdal credited Sterner with persuading him to return to America to complete the Negro study. Gunnar Myrdal, interview with author, August 19, 1980, Stockholm.

96. Sterner to G. Myrdal, October 6, 1940, GMP.

97. Sterner to G. Myrdal, October 6, 1940, GMP

98. G. Myrdal to Stouffer et al., August 26, 1940, GMP.

99. Samuel Stouffer to G. Myrdal, April 28, 1940, NSGC; Arnold Rose, oral history memoir, "The American Dilemma," Arnold Rose Papers, University of Minnesota Library, Minneapolis, Minn.

100. G. Myrdal to Dollard, July 22, 1942, GMP.

101. G. Myrdal to Keppel, November 5, 1940, NSGC.

102. F. A. Sterling to Secretary of State Cordell Hull, January 29, 1941, document no. 032/1463, National Archives, Washington, D.C.; Egon Glesinger, "Gunnar Myrdal," unpublished biographical sketch, enclosed in Glesinger to G. Myrdal, January 3, 1949, pp. 8–9, GMP. Two authors have suggested that Dankwort was secretly sympathetic to the German military and political leaders who were plotting against Hitler. See Christopher Sykes, *Tormented Loyalty: The Story of a German Aristocrat Who Defied Hitler* (New York: Harper & Row, 1969), pp. 402–3, and Ingeborg Fleischauer, *Die Chance des Sonderfriedens: Deutsch-Sowjetsche Geheimgespräche 1941–1945* (Berlin: Siedler Verlag, 1986), p. 57.

103. Gunnar Myrdal, *Hur styrs landet?* p. 287; G. Myrdal to Keppel, November 5, 1940, NSGC; Glesinger, "Gunnar Myrdal," pp. 8–9; Gunnar Myrdal, interview with author, August 19, 1980, Stockholm; Lindskog, *Alva Myrdal*, p. 70.

104. Gunnar Myrdal, speech reprinted in *The American Swedish Monthly* (April 1941): 5, 27–28; see also *New York Times*, March 26, 1941.

105. Gunnar Myrdal, *Varning för fredsoptimism* (Stockholm: Bonniers, 1944), p. 51; cf. Gunnar Myrdal, *Amerika mitt i världen* (Stockholm: Kooperativa förbundets bokförlag, 1943), pp. 43–52.

106. G. Myrdal to Dollard, July 22, 1942, GMP; Myrdal, interview with author, August 19, 1980, Stockholm; Arnold Rose, "Myrdal: The American Dilemma," oral history transcript, Arnold Rose Papers.

107. Sterner wrote drafts of the nine chapters concerning economic problems in part 4 of *An American Dilemma*, wrote appendix 6 on "Pre-War Conditions of the Negro Wage Earner in Selected Industries and Occupations," and criticized other sections of the book. Rose prepared drafts for chapters 5, 6, 7, and 8 concerning race and population, chapter 22 on politics, chapters 41 and 42 on the black church and black education, appendix 4 on the "Meaning of Regional Terms as Used in This Book," appendix 7 on "Distribution of Negro Residences in Selected Cities," and appendix 8 on "Research on Caste and Class in a Negro Community." Rose also wrote part 10, "The Negro Community," after Myrdal returned to Sweden. See Myrdal, author's preface to *An American Dilemma*, pp. xv–xvi. Myrdal insisted that both Rose and Sterner should have their names on the title page of the book. G. Myrdal to Dollard, September 2, 1942, NSGC.

108. G. Myrdal to Sven Tunberg, August 13, 1941, GMP.

109. G. Myrdal to Keppel, September 4, 1941, NSGC.

110. Glesinger, "Gunnar Myrdal," p. 10.

111. Alva Myrdal, letter, n.d., quoted in Bok, *Alva*, p. 139.

112. G. Myrdal to Charles Johnson, June 21, 1941, Negro Study-Stouffer file, CCA.

113. G. Myrdal to Keppel, July 7, 1941, and G. Myrdal to Keppel, September 4, 1941, NSGC; Francis Keppel, interview with author, April 18, 1978, Cambridge, Mass.; Lindskog, *Alva Myrdal*, pp. 71–72; Bok, *Alva*, p. 139.

114. Gunnar Myrdal, interview with author, August 19, 1980, Stockholm. Although the beginning and concluding chapters of *An American Dilemma* placed the American race problem in the context of the war, Myrdal and his assistants did not do any new research on the status of blacks during the war. Edward Shils wrote a short memo for Myrdal on "Negro Organizations and the War," but the book is based primarily on research done by Myrdal and his collaborators from 1938 to 1940. Shils's memo is in the Negro Study-Guy B. Johnson file, CCA.

115. Gunnar Myrdal, "The Negro and America's Uneasy Conscience," *Free World*, November 6, 1943, pp. 412–22; Gunnar Myrdal, "Neutralitet och vårt samvete," pp. 257–70.

116. Federal Bureau of Investigation, File no. 100-2893, "Gunnar Myrdal or Myrdal Gunnar" 9/19/41; File no. 100-4910, "Gunnar Myrdal," 10/14/41; File no. 100-15527, "Karl Gunnar Myrdal, with alias Gunnar Myrdal," 7/7/42; File no. 100-16381, "Gunnar Myrdal, Alva Myrdal," 10/31/42; all in FBI Headquarters, Washington, D.C.

117. Keppel to Walter Jessup, July 27, 1942, NSGC.

118. G. Myrdal to Keppel, July 7, 1941, NSGC.

119. Charles Dollard, memo, "FPK, DY, Dr. Stouffer and CD (dinner meeting at Coffee House) October 4, 1940," NSGC.

120. Keppel, "Memorandum on the Status of the Negro Study," July 9, 1941, NSGC.

121. Ellsworth Faris to Samuel Stouffer, August 23, 1940, NSGC. Morse Cartwright to Stouffer, August 26, 1940; Alain Locke, "Memorandum on Stern Report," September 30, 1940; Paul Lazarsfeld to Stouffer, n.d.; Richard Sterner to Stouffer, August 27, 1940; Louis Wirth to Stouffer, n.d.; memo on Stern ms.; T. J. Woofter, Jr., to Charles Dollard, October 18, 1940; Newton Edwards to Stouffer, October 29, 1940; Louis R. Wilson to Stouffer, n.d.; all in Negro Study Correspondence, Reel 2, Wilkerson file, CCA.

122. Jackson Davis, memo on Wilkerson's "The Negro in American Education," n.d.; Horace Mann Bond to Stouffer, August 15, 1940; Guion Griffis Johnson to Stouffer, August 20, 1940; Charles H. Thompson to Stouffer, August 20, 1940; Merle Curti to Stouffer, September 27, 1940; Newton Edwards to Stouffer, September 14, 1940; Louis R. Wilson to Stouffer, n.d.; all in Negro Study Correspondence, Reel 2, Wilkerson file, CCA. See also "Negro Study—Staff Lists" on Wilkerson and Stern, February 23, 1943; Walter Jessup to Dollard, March 3, 1941; Stouffer to Dollard, Harrison, Ogburn, and Young, March 10, 1941 ("Report of Committee Meeting, March 8, 1941"); Stouffer to Dollard, Harrison, Ogburn, and Young, March 18, 1941; all in NSGC. Interestingly, the committee did not consider Ralph Bunche to be biased and appropriated $250 for stenographic assistance to aid Bunche in completing his manuscript, a courtesy they did not extend to other authors, but Bunche still did not finish the manuscript by their deadline. See Stouffer to Bunche, March 24, 1941, NSGC.

123. Keppel, "Memorandum on the Status of the Negro Study," July 9, 1941, NSGC.

124. Myrdal had great respect for Wirth as a scholar, and Wirth was one of the few senior American sociologists sympathetic to Myrdal's methodological ideas on the problem of objectivity. Myrdal also asked officials of the NAACP, National Urban League, and Commis-

sion on Interracial Cooperation to comment on the sections of the manuscript dealing with those groups. He received comments from Walter White, L. Hollingsworth Wood, and Howard Odum. See White to G. Myrdal, August 4, 1942, Roy Wilkins to G. Myrdal, August 11, 1942; Odum to G. Myrdal, August 12, 1942; all in NSGC.

125. G. Myrdal to Keppel, March 17, 1942, GMP.

126. G. Myrdal to Dollard, June 22, 1942, NSGC.

127. Gunnar Myrdal, interview with author, August 19, 1980, Stockholm.

128. David S. Wyman, *The Abandonment of the Jews: America and the Holocaust, 1941–1945* (New York: Pantheon, 1984), pp. 124–29.

129. Russell Leffingwell to Keppel, March 2, 1943, Keppel Papers, Columbia University Library, New York, N.Y.

130. Wyman, *The Abandonment of the Jews*, pp. 129–31.

131. Gunnar Myrdal, interview with author, August 19, 1980, Stockholm; Charles Dollard to G. Myrdal, November 28, 1941, NSGC; Keppel to G. Myrdal, July 13, 1942, copy in Arnold Rose Papers.

132. G. Myrdal to Dollard, June 22, 1942, NSGC.

133. Myrdal to Dollard, June 22, 1942, and Keppel to Walter Jessup, July 27, 1942, NSGC.

134. Keppel to Walter Jessup (identified as WAJ), July 27, 1942, NSGC.

135. G. Myrdal to Keppel, September 2, 1942, copy in Arnold Rose Papers.

136. G. Myrdal to Dollard, June 22, 1942, NSGC; G. Myrdal to Keppel, September 2, 1942, copy in Arnold Rose Papers.

137. Keppel to Jessup, July 27, 1942, NSGC.

138. G. Myrdal to Keppel, March 17, 1942, GMP.

139. G. Myrdal to Frazier, August 18, 1943, Frazier Papers, Box 27, f. 16, Howard University, Washington, D.C.

140. Frazier to Myrdal, June 24, 1942, NSGC.

141. Frazier to G. Myrdal, September 9, 1942, NSGC.

142. G. Myrdal to Keppel, September 2, 1942, copy in Arnold Rose Papers; see Gunnar Myrdal, *An American Dilemma*, pp. 858–924.

143. G. Myrdal to Keppel, September 2, 1942, copy in Arnold Rose Papers. Myrdal left Rose some notes and an outline for the section. A version of Myrdal's remarks quoted here appears in *An American Dilemma*, p. 929.

144. Frazier to Rose, December 14, 1942, NSGC; Frazier to Rose (n.d.), 1943, Arnold Rose Papers.

145. Keppel to Wirth, December 23, 1942, NSGC.

146. Wirth to Keppel, January 5, 1943, Wirth Papers, University of Chicago, Chicago, Ill.

147. G. Myrdal to Dollard, September 2, 1942, NSGC; Rose to G. Myrdal, December 1, 1942, GMP.

148. G. Myrdal to C. Dollard, August 24, 1942, and G. Myrdal to C. Dollard, September 4, 1942, NSGC.

149. G. Myrdal to Dollard, September 2, 1942, NSGC.

150. G. Myrdal to Dollard, July 22, 1942, GMP.

151. Keppel to G. Myrdal, September 4, 1942, copy in American Dilemma file, GMP.

152. Keppel to Ordway Tead, April 16, 1943, and Charles Dollard to Keppel, September 15, 1942, NSGC.

153. G. Myrdal to Ruth Moulik, October 14, 1942, and G. Myrdal to Moulik, Arnold and Caroline Rose, February 3, 1943, GMP.

154. G. Myrdal to Siegfried Hansson, February 25, 1939, and G. Myrdal, Oskar Lange, and Jacob Viner to Bertil Ohlin, n.d., filed February 1940, under "L," GMP.

155. Helmut Mussener, *Exil in Schweden; Politische und kulturelle Emigration nach 1933* (Munich: Carl Hanser, 1974), pp. 80, 207–10.

156. Klaus Misgeld, *Die "Internationale Gruppe demokratischer Sozialisten" in Stockholm 1942–1945* (Uppsala: Almqvist & Wiksell, 1976), pp. 48–61.

157. Willy Brandt, *Links und frei: Mein Weg 1930–1950* (Hamburg: Hoffmann und Campe, 1982), pp. 332–33; Bruno Kreisky, *Zwischen den Zeiten: Erinnerungen aus fünf Jahrzehnten* (Berlin: Siedler, 1986), pp. 374–78.

158. Misgeld, *Die "Internationale Gruppe demokratischer Sozialisten,"* pp. 167–78; Brandt, *Links und frei,* pp. 336–46.

159. Gunnar Myrdal, *Amerika mitt i världen,* pp. 7–16, 20–21, 88.

160. Ibid., pp. 101–4.

161. Ibid., pp. 105–28.

162. Ibid., pp. 69–70, 73–78.

163. Gunnar Myrdal, "Anmärkningar om Amerikas inre politik, ekonomiska läge och utrikespolitik senhösten 1943," report to the Swedish Foreign Ministry, GMP; Tore Browaldh, *Gesällvandring* (Stockholm: Norstedt, 1976), pp. 19, 26, 45; Tore Browaldh, interview with author, May 17, 1989, Stockholm.

164. Browaldh, *Gesällvandring,* p. 37; Browaldh, interview with author, May 17, 1989, Stockholm; Gunnar Myrdal, *Varning för fredsoptimism,* pp. 42–50, 56, 70–72.

165. Gunnar Myrdal, *An American Dilemma,* p. 214.

166. Gunnar Myrdal, "Anmärkningar om Amerikas inre politik."

167. Gunnar Myrdal, "Economic Developments and Prospects in America," unpublished address before the National Economic Society of Sweden, March 9, 1944, copy in Baker Library, Harvard Business School, Cambridge, Mass.

168. Gunnar Myrdal, "Economic Developments and Prospects in America," pp. 1–9, 25.

169. Ibid., pp. 9, 11, 21.

170. Ibid., pp. 25–27.

171. Gunnar Myrdal, *Varning för fredsoptimism;* Gunnar Myrdal, "Is American Business Deluding Itself?" *Atlantic Monthly,* November 1944, pp. 51–58.

172. John Scott, *Europe in Revolution* (Boston: Houghton Mifflin, 1945), p. 93.

173. G. Myrdal to Charles Dollard, July 7, 1942, NSGC.

174. R. Taylor Cole, interview with author, June 26, 1989, Durham, N.C.

175. On Kollontai's career, see Barbara Evans Clements, *Bolshevik Feminist: The Life of Aleksandra Kollontai* (Bloomington: Indiana University Press, 1979), and Kollontai, *The Autobiography of a Sexually Emancipated Communist Woman* (New York: Schocken, 1975).

176. Henry O. Malone, *Adam von Trott zu Solz: Werdegang eines Verschwörers, 1909–1938* (Berlin: Siedler, 1986); Malone, "Adam von Trott zu Solz" (Ph.D. diss., University of Texas, 1980); Sykes, *Tormented Loyalty;* Marie Vassiltchikov, *Berlin Diaries, 1940–1945* (New York: Knopf, 1987).

177. Peter Hoffmann, *German Resistance to Hitler* (Cambridge, Mass.: Harvard University Press, 1988); Hoffmann, *Widerstand, Staatsstreich, Attentat: Der Kampf der Opposition gegen Hitler* (Munich: R. Piper, 1969), pp. 279–85; Malone, *Adam von Trott zu Solz,* pp. 221–25; Sykes, *Tormented Loyalty,* p. 423.

178. Gunnar Myrdal, *Amerika mitt i världen*, pp. 34–35.

179. John Scott, *Behind the Urals: An American Worker in Russia's City of Steel* (Boston: Houghton Mifflin, 1942; Bloomington: Indiana University Press, 1973).

180. Gunnar Myrdal, calendar, June 22–23, 1944, GMP; Herschel Johnson to the Secretary of State, June 26, 1944, *Foreign Relations* 1 (1944): 523–25; R. Taylor Cole, *The Recollections of R. Taylor Cole: Educator, Emissary, Development Planner* (Durham, N.C.: Duke University Press, 1983), pp. 80–84; R. Taylor Cole, interview with author, June 26, 1989, Durham, N.C.; Malone, *Adam von Trott zu Solz*, pp. 225–26; Hoffmann, *Widerstand*, pp. 285–86; John Scott, *Europe in Revolution*, pp. 178–80.

181. Herschel Johnson to Secretary of State, June 26, 1944, *Foreign Relations* 1 (1944): 523–25; Cole, *Recollections of R. Taylor Cole*, pp. 81–83; R. Taylor Cole, interview with author, June 26, 1989, Durham, N.C.

182. Brandt, *Links und frei*, pp. 368–70; Malone, *Adam von Trott zu Solz*, pp. 225–26. Malone notes that Trott went to Holland in early July and attempted to send a message to British Intelligence through the Dutch Resistance.

183. Quoted in Hoffmann, *German Resistance to Hitler*, p. 135.

184. Malone, *Adam von Trott zu Solz*, pp. 226–28; Sykes, *Tormented Loyalty*, pp. 323, 449–50.

185. G. Myrdal to Allen Dulles, August 8, 1947, GMP.

186. Willy Brandt, *My Road to Berlin* (Garden City, N.Y.: Doubleday, 1960), p. 143.

Chapter 5: *An American Dilemma*

1. G. Myrdal to Charles Dollard, July 22, 1942, Negro Study General Correspondence, CCA.

2. Gunnar Myrdal, *An American Dilemma: The Negro Problem and Modern Democracy* (New York: Harper & Brothers, 1944), p. 1024.

3. Ibid., p. liii.

4. See David Howard-Pitney, "The Jeremiads of Frederick Douglass, Booker T. Washington, and W. E. B. Du Bois and Changing Patterns of Black Messianic Rhetoric, 1841–1920," *Journal of American Ethnic History* 6 (Fall 1986): 47–61.

5. On South-baiting, see George B. Tindall, "The Benighted South: Origins of a Modern Image," *Virginia Quarterly Review* 40 (1964): 281–94.

6. Frederick Keppel, foreword to Gunnar Myrdal, *An American Dilemma*, p. v.

7. Ibid., pp. v–viii.

8. Gunnar Myrdal, *An American Dilemma*, pp. x–xiv.

9. Ibid., pp. xviii–xix.

10. Ibid., pp. xlvii–xlviii.

11. Ibid., p. xlix.

12. Ibid., p. li.

13. See Chapter 7.

14. See the discussion of the reviews of Robert S. Lynd, E. Franklin Frazier, Horace Cayton, Richard Wright, and W. E. B. Du Bois in Chapter 6.

15. Gunnar Myrdal, *An American Dilemma*, p. lxxii.

16. W. E. B. Du Bois, *The Souls of Black Folk* (1903; reprint, New York: New American Library, 1969), pp. 52, 207–8.

17. Alain Locke, ed., *The New Negro* (New York: Boni, 1925), p. 13.

18. Gunnar Myrdal, *An American Dilemma*, pp. l, lvi.

19. See Chapter 2.

20. Gunnar Myrdal, *An American Dilemma*, p. 3; cf. Alva Myrdal and Gunnar Myrdal, *Kontakt med Amerika* (Stockholm: Bonniers, 1941), pp. 32–33.

21. Gunnar Myrdal, *An American Dilemma*, p. 6.

22. Ibid., pp. 8–12.

23. Ralph Gabriel, *The Course of American Democratic Thought: An Intellectual History since 1815* (New York: Ronald Press, 1940), pp. 373–87.

24. Gunnar Myrdal, *An American Dilemma*, pp. 14–21.

25. See Chapter 4 and Alva Myrdal and Gunnar Myrdal, *Kontakt*, p. 54.

26. Gunnar Myrdal, *An American Dilemma*, pp. 19–21. John Dewey made the argument that a contradiction between ideals and actions may produce psychological discomfort and lead to change. See John Dewey, *Freedom and Culture* (New York: Putnam, 1939), pp. 47–48.

27. Gunnar Myrdal, *An American Dilemma*, p. 24.

28. William Fielding Ogburn, *Social Change with Respect to Culture and Original Nature* (New York: Viking, 1922), pp. 256–65.

29. Warren Susman, "The Culture of the Thirties," in his *Culture as History: The Transformation of American Society in the Twentieth Century* (New York: Pantheon, 1984), pp. 150–83.

30. Gunnar Myrdal, *An American Dilemma*, pp. 1027–34.

31. Ibid., pp. 32–40; cf. Ray Stannard Baker, *Following the Color Line: American Negro Citizenship in the Progressive Era* (New York: Doubleday, 1908). Arnold Rose remembered that Myrdal wrote the first two chapters by himself, basing them largely on his personal observations. Rose, "The American Dilemma," oral history memoir, p. 36. Arnold Rose Papers, University of Minnesota Library, Minneapolis, Minn.

32. Gunnar Myrdal, *An American Dilemma*, pp. 40–42, 46.

33. Ibid., pp. 48–49; cf. Carl Becker, "Some Generalities That Still Glitter," *Yale Review* 29 (June 1940): 649–67. Myrdal knew Lippmann and Arnold personally but did not refer to Lippmann's *Public Opinion* (New York: Harcourt, Brace, 1922), Arnold's *The Folklore of Capitalism* (New Haven, Conn.: Yale University Press, 1937), or Harold Lasswell's *Psychopathology and Politics* (Chicago: University of Chicago Press, 1934).

34. John Madge, *The Origins of Scientific Sociology* (Glencoe, Ill.: Free Press, 1962), p. 274.

35. Gunnar Myrdal, *An American Dilemma*, pp. 60–61.

36. Ibid., pp. 67–70.

37. Ibid., p. 73.

38. Ibid., p. 69.

39. Ibid., p. 78.

40. Ibid., p. 74.

41. Charles S. Johnson used the term *vicious circle* in a more narrow sense to refer to the relationship between blacks and labor unions in "The New Frontage on American Life," in *The New Negro*, ed. Locke, p. 293.

42. Gunnar Myrdal, *An American Dilemma*, p. 75–76.

43. Quotation from Paul Streeten, "Gunnar Myrdal: The Cheerful Pessimist," *New Society* 5 (December 1974). Streeten cites Wicksell's *Interest and Prices* (1898). See also appendix 3 of *An American Dilemma*, pp. 1065–70.

44. Gunnar Myrdal, *An American Dilemma*, p. 77.

45. Ibid., p. 80.

46. Ibid., pp. 83–84.

47. Ibid., p. 89.

48. Ibid., p. 91.

49. Eugene L. Horowitz, "'Race' Attitudes," in *Characteristics of the American Negro*, ed. Otto Klineberg (New York: Harper & Brothers, 1944), pp. 244–47; Gunnar Myrdal, interview with author, August 19, 1981, Stockholm.

50. Gunnar Myrdal, *An American Dilemma*, p. 97.

51. Ibid., p. 102.

52. Ibid., p. 109.

53. Ibid.

54. Ibid., pp. 110–12.

55. Ibid., p. 115.

56. Ibid., p. 117.

57. Klineberg, ed., *Characteristics of the American Negro*.

58. Gunnar Myrdal, *An American Dilemma*, pp. 147–49.

59. Ibid., pp. 175–76.

60. Ibid., p. 177.

61. Ibid., p. 201.

62. Ibid., p. 205.

63. Ibid., p. 208.

64. Ibid., p. 209.

65. Ibid., pp. 209, 212.

66. Ibid., p. 214.

67. Ibid., p. 219.

68. Rupert Vance, *Human Geography of the South* (Chapel Hill: University of North Carolina Press, 1932); T. J. Woofter, Jr., and Associates, *Landlord and Tenant on the Cotton Plantation* (Washington, D.C.: Works Progress Administration, 1936); Woofter, "The Negro and Agricultural Policy," unpublished manuscript prepared for the Myrdal project, 1940.

69. Charles S. Johnson, Edwin R. Embree, and Will W. Alexander, *The Collapse of Cotton Tenancy: A Summary of Field Studies and Statistical Studies, 1933–1935* (Chapel Hill: University of North Carolina Press, 1935).

70. Gunnar Myrdal, *An American Dilemma*, pp. 220–21.

71. Ibid., pp. 222–24.

72. Ibid., pp. 227–29. In making his point about extralegal violence, Myrdal cites Arthur Raper, "Race and Class Pressures," unpublished manuscript prepared for the Myrdal project, Schomburg Library, New York, N.Y.

73. Gunnar Myrdal, *An American Dilemma*, pp. 232–34.

74. Ibid., p. 240.

75. Ibid., p. 249.

76. Ibid., p. 252.

77. Ibid., pp. 254–55, 260, 251.

78. Ibid., p. 266.

79. Ibid., p. 278.

80. Ibid., p. 264.

81. Ibid., p. 279.

82. Ibid., pp. 295–303.

83. Ibid., pp. 1079–1124.

84. Ibid., p. 307.

85. Ibid., p. 313; Myrdal cited Abram Harris, *The Negro as Capitalist: A Study of Banking and Business among American Negroes* (Philadelphia: The American Academy of Political and Social Science, 1936), and Ira DeA. Reid, "The Negro in the American Economic System," unpublished manuscript prepared for Myrdal study (1940), Schomburg Library.

86. Gunnar Myrdal, *An American Dilemma*, pp. 342–43.

87. Ibid., pp. 351–52.

88. Ibid., pp. 353–54.

89. Ibid., p. 358.

90. Ibid., pp. 364–82.

91. Ibid., p. 383.

92. Ibid., pp. 384–85.

93. Ibid., pp. 407–8.

94. Ibid., pp. 386–88, 395.

95. Ibid., pp. 409–14.

96. Ibid., pp. 415, 422.

97. Ibid., pp. 424, 426.

98. Myrdal introduced the term *underclass* into economic and sociological analysis in *Challenge to Affluence* (New York: Pantheon, 1962), p. 14.

99. Gunnar Myrdal, *Against the Stream: Critical Essays on Economics* (New York: Pantheon, 1973), p. 295.

100. Gunnar Myrdal, *An American Dilemma*, p. 430. On this point Myrdal cited Willis D. Weatherford and Charles S. Johnson, *Race Relations* (Boston: D. C. Heath, 1934), and T. J. Woofter, Jr., *The Basis of Racial Adjustment* (Boston: Ginn and Company, 1925). He also relied on Paul Lewinson, *Race, Class, and Party* (New York: Oxford University Press, 1932).

101. Gunnar Myrdal, *An American Dilemma*, pp. 432–37.

102. Ibid., p. 440.

103. Ibid., pp. 486–90; cf. Ralph Bunche, *The Political Status of the Negro in the Age of FDR* (Chicago: University of Chicago Press, 1973).

104. Gunnar Myrdal, *An American Dilemma*, p. 441.

105. Ibid., pp. 449–51. Myrdal cited Rupert Vance, *Human Geography of the South*, and W. J. Cash, *The Mind of the South* (New York: Knopf, 1941).

106. Gunnar Myrdal, *An American Dilemma*, pp. 454–55; Myrdal cited Paul Lewinson, *Race, Class, and Party* (1932).

107. Gunnar Myrdal, *An American Dilemma*, pp. 458–60.

108. Ibid. p. 462.

109. Ibid., p. 456

110. Ibid., pp. 470–71.

111. Ibid., p. 473.

112. Arthur Raper, interview with author, April 13, 1977, Oakton, Virginia.

113. Gunnar Myrdal, *An American Dilemma*, pp. 484–86; Myrdal cited Bunche, "The Political Status of the Negro," and Raper, "Race and Class Pressures," both unpublished manuscripts prepared for the Myrdal study, Schomburg Library, as well as Lewinson, *Race, Class, and Party*, chap. 6.

114. Gunnar Myrdal, *An American Dilemma*, p. 510.

115. Ibid., p. 520.

116. See Myrdal's discussion of coordinated change in his *Against the Stream*, p. 306.

117. Gunnar Myrdal, *An American Dilemma*, p. 530.

118. Ibid., pp. 532–33, 558.

119. Ibid., pp. 523–24, 535.

120. Ibid., pp. 535–45.

121. Ibid., pp. 546, 556.

122. Ibid., pp. 556, 568.

123. See Chapter 4.

124. Gunnar Myrdal, *An American Dilemma*, p. 683.

125. Ibid., p. 603.

126. Ibid., p. 574; cf. Dewey, *Freedom and Culture*.

127. Gunnar Myrdal, *An American Dilemma*, pp. 625–27.

128. Ibid., p. 672.

129. Ibid., p. 680. Myrdal cited W. E. B. Du Bois, *Dusk of Dawn* (1940), pp. 130–31.

130. Gunnar Myrdal, *An American Dilemma*, p. 674.

131. Ibid., p. 676.

132. Ibid., pp. 713–17. Cf. Gunnar Myrdal, "Socialism eller kapitalism in framtidens Amerika," *Tiden* 23 (1931): 205–30.

133. Gunnar Myrdal, *An American Dilemma*, p. 720.

134. Ibid., pp. 721, 729–32.

135. Ibid., pp. 768–74.

136. Ibid., pp. 757, 759, 771, 781–86.

137. Ralph Bunche, "The Programs, Ideologies, Tactics, and Achievements of Negro Betterment and Interracial Organizations," unpublished manuscript prepared for Myrdal study, quoted in Gunnar Myrdal, *An American Dilemma*, p. 748.

138. Gunnar Myrdal, *An American Dilemma*, pp. 791–94.

139. Ibid., pp. 852–57.

140. Ibid., p. 836.

141. Ibid., pp. 837–50.

142. Ibid. pp. 852–57.

143. See Chapter 3.

144. Gunnar Myrdal, *Against the Stream*, pp. 299–300.

145. See Chapter 3.

146. Guy and Guion Johnson, "The Church and the Race Problem in the United States," unpublished manuscript for Myrdal study; Carter G. Woodson, *The History of the Negro Church* (Washington, D.C.: Associated Publishers, 1921); W. E. B. Du Bois, *The Negro Church: Report of a Social Study Made under the Direction of Atlanta University* (Atlanta: Atlanta University Press, 1903).

147. St. Clair Drake, "Negro Churches and Associations in Chicago" (1940), and Allison Davis, "Negro Churches and Associations in the Lower South" (1940), unpublished manuscripts written for Myrdal study, Schomburg Library; Benjamin Mays and J. W. Nicholson, *The Negro's Church* (New York: Institute of Social and Religious Research, 1933).

148. Gunnar Myrdal, *An American Dilemma*, pp. 873, 732, 875.

149. Ibid., p. 878.

150. Ibid., pp. 879, 882–86, 903–7.

151. Ibid., pp. 908, 917, 921, 923–24.

152. Myrdal to Keppel, September 2, 1942, copy in Arnold Rose Papers.

153. Gunnar Myrdal, *An American Dilemma*, p. 927.

154. Ibid., pp. 911–12, 1394.

155. Ibid., pp. 928–29.

156. Alva Myrdal and Gunnar Myrdal, *Kris i befolkningsfrågan* (Stockholm: Bonniers, 1934), pp. 303, 317–25 (translation from Allan C. Carlson, "The Roles of Alva and Gunnar Myrdal in the Development of a Social Democratic Response to Europe's 'Population Crisis' 1929–1938" [Ph.D. diss., Ohio University, 1978], pp. 227–29).

157. Gunnar Myrdal, *An American Dilemma*, pp. l–li.

158. Ibid., pp. 930–35.

159. Ibid., pp. 952–55. This argument anticipates Frazier's description of the "world of make-believe" in his *Black Bourgeoisie* (Glencoe, Ill.: Free Press, 1957), pp. 162–75. It was a standard criticism of the black middle class among the younger generation of radical black intellectuals of the 1930s.

160. Gunnar Myrdal, *An American Dilemma*, p. 956.

161. Ibid., p. 966.

162. Ibid., p. 994. See Sterling Brown, "The Negro in American Culture," unpublished manuscript prepared for Myrdal study, Schomburg Library.

163. Gunnar Myrdal, *An American Dilemma*, pp. 998–1004, 1013–14.

164. Ibid., p. 1004.

165. Ibid., pp. 1017–18.

166. Ibid., p. 1019.

167. Ibid., pp. 1021–22.

168. Ibid., pp. 1023–24.

169. Ibid., p. 904.

Chapter 6: The Study to End All Studies

1. *Time*, January 3, 1944, pp. 15–22; James MacGregor Burns, *Roosevelt: The Soldier of Freedom* (New York: Harcourt, Brace, Jovanovich, 1970), pp. 443–45; William Manchester, *The Glory and the Dream* (Boston: Little, Brown, 1974), pp. 279–80.

2. Burns, *Roosevelt*, pp. 387–88.

3. Ibid., p. 130.

4. Ibid., pp. 379–81.

5. Wendell Willkie, *One World* (New York: Simon and Schuster, 1943), p. 190.

6. Henry Wallace, "The Price of Free World Victory," address before the Free World Association, New York City, May 8, 1942, reprinted in Wallace, *Democracy Reborn* (New York: Reynal and Hitchcock, 1944), pp. 190–96.

7. Henry Wallace, "Our Second Chance," address before the Foreign Policy Association, New York City, April 8, 1941, reprinted in Wallace, *Democracy Reborn*, pp. 176–79.

8. Henry Wallace, "America Tomorrow," in Wallace, *Democracy Reborn*, p. 240.

9. Burns, *Roosevelt*, pp. 424–25.

10. John Morton Blum, *V Was for Victory* (New York: Harcourt, Brace, 1976), pp. 234–39, 249–50; Burns, *Roosevelt*, p. 362.

11. Richard Polenberg, *War and Society: The United States, 1941–1945* (New York: J. P. Lippincott, 1972), pp. 89–94; Blum, *V Was for Victory*, p. 328.

12. Polenberg, *War and Society*, pp. 94–98.

13. Robert Park, "Racial Ideologies," in *American Society in Wartime*, ed. William Fielding Ogburn (Chicago: University of Chicago Press, 1943), p. 174.

14. Blum, *V Was for Victory*, pp. 184–85.

15. *Time*, December 27, 1943.

16. Harvard Sitkoff, "Racial Militancy and Interracial Violence in the Second World War," *Journal of American History* 58 (1971): 661–81.

17. Roy Wilkins to Walter White, March 24, 1942, Stephen J. Spingarn Papers, Harry S. Truman Library, Independence, Missouri (cited in Richard Dalfiume, *Desegregation of the U.S. Armed Forces: Fighting on Two Fronts, 1939–1953* (Columbia: University of Missouri Press, 1969), p. 107.

18. "Memorandum of Will Alexander, Charles S. Johnson, and Edwin Embree on the Rosenwald Fund's Program in Race Relations," June 27, 1942, attached to Embree to Alexander, July 1, 1942, Rosenwald Fund Papers, Amistad Research Center, Tulane University, New Orleans. Quoted in Patrick Gilpin, "Charles S. Johnson: An Intellectual Biography" (Ph.D. diss., Vanderbilt University, 1973), p. 488.

19. Howard Odum, *Race and Rumors of Race* (Chapel Hill: University of North Carolina Press, 1943), p. 167.

20. Dalfiume, *Desegregation of the U.S. Armed Forces*, p. 123.

21. Morton Sosna, *In Search of the Silent South* (New York: Columbia University Press, 1978), pp. 116–18.

22. Odum, *Race and Rumors of Race*, p. 171.

23. Ibid., pp. 6, 145–46.

24. Polenberg, *War and Society*, pp. 97–98; cf. Allen J. Matusow, *The Unraveling of America: A History of Liberalism in the 1960s* (New York: Harper & Row, 1984), p. 64.

25. Gavin Wright, *Old South, New South: Revolutions in the Southern Economy Since the Civil War* (New York: Basic Books, 1986) pp. 239–49; George Tindall, *The Emergence of the New South, 1913–1945* (Baton Rouge: Louisiana State University Press, 1967), pp. 696–700, 703.

26. Morton Sosna, "The GI's South and the North-South Dialogue During World War II," unpublished paper in author's possession.

27. Jonathan Daniels to Howard Odum, August 24, 1942, Daniels Papers, Southern Historical Collection, University of North Carolina, Chapel Hill, cited in Sosna, *In Search of the Silent South*, p. 107.

28. Virginius Dabney, "Nearer and Nearer the Precipice," *Atlantic Monthly* January 1943, pp. 94–100; Sosna, *In Search of the Silent South*, pp. 131–33.

29. Blum, *V Was for Victory*, p. 204; Polenberg, *War and Society*, pp. 127–28.

30. Dalfiume, *Desegregation of the U.S. Armed Forces*, p. 130; Sosna, *In Search of the Silent South*, p. 108.

31. Keppel to Ordway Tead, April 16, 1943, NSGC.

32. Arnold Rose to G. Myrdal, April 6, 1944, GMP; Carnegie Corporation memo, "KF and Mr. Ordway Tead," December 30, 1943, NSGC.

33. Franklin D. Roosevelt, Message to Congress, January 6, 1943, quoted in Harper & Brothers brochure, "The Negro in American Life Series," NSGC.

34. *New York Herald Tribune*, January 26, 1944.

35. *Time*, February 7, 1944.

36. *New Republic*, March 20, 1944, pp. 384–86; *Survey Graphic*, March 1944, p. 183.

37. *New York Times Book Review*, April 2, 1944.

38. *Book of the Month Club News*, April 1944.

39. Arnold Rose to G. Myrdal, April 6, 1944, GMP.

40. Harry Hansen, "Unfinished Business of Democracy," *Survey Graphic*, March 1944, pp. 183–84.

41. Albert Deutsch, "The Great American Dilemma—Democracy and the Negro," *P.M.*, September 1, 1944.

42. *New York News*, August 3, 1944.

43. Robert S. Lynd, "Prison for American Genius," *Saturday Review*, April 22, 1944, pp. 5–7, 27.

44. Reinhold Niebuhr, review of *An American Dilemma* in *Christianity and Society* 9 (Summer 1944): 42; Niebuhr, "Editorial Notes," *Christianity and Crisis* 4 (September 18, 1944): 2.

45. Mordecai Grossman, "Caste or Democracy? An American Dilemma," *Contemporary Jewish Record* 7 (1944): 475–86.

46. Henry Steele Commager, "The Negro Problem in Our Democracy," *American Mercury*, June 1945, pp. 751–56.

47. J. Saunders Redding, "The Negro: America's Dilemma," *New Republic*, March 20, 1944.

48. "Negro Rights: They Will Come When the White South's Fear Is Divided into Rational Parts," *Life*, April 24, 1944.

49. W. E. B. Du Bois, "The American Dilemma," *Phylon* 5 (second quarter, 1944): 118–24.

50. E. Franklin Frazier, review of *An American Dilemma* in *American Journal of Sociology* 50 (May 1945): 555–57.

51. E. Franklin Frazier, "Race: An American Dilemma," *The Crisis*, 51:105–6, 129.

52. Horace Cayton, "Fear and Hunger in Black America," Chicago *Sun*, March 14, 1945.

53. "Richard Wright Suggests," *New York Post*, November 30, 1944.

54. Richard Wright, introduction to St. Clair Drake and Horace Cayton, *Black Metropolis: A Study of Negro Life in a Northern City* (New York: Harcourt, Brace, 1945), p. xxix.

55. Quoted in Michel Fabre, *The Unfinished Quest of Richard Wright* (New York: William Morrow, 1973), p. 586.

56. Henry Steele Commager, "The Negro Problem in Our Democracy"; Herbert Aptheker, *The Negro People in America: A Critique of Gunnar Myrdal's "An American Dilemma"* (New York: International Publishers, 1946), pp. 62–63.

57. L. D. Reddick, "A Wise Man Writes a Frank Book," *Opportunity* (Summer 1944): 124–25.

58. L. D. Reddick, "Scholarship and Candor," *Journal of Negro Education* 13 (Spring 1944): 192–94.

59. L. D. Reddick, review of *An American Dilemma* in *Science and Society* 8 (Summer 1944): 283–86.

60. George Schuyler, "Free and Equal," *Politics* 1 (July 1944): 181–82.

61. Carter G. Woodson, review of *Characteristics of the American Negro*, ed. Otto Klineberg, in *Journal of Negro History* 29 (1944): 234; Woodson, "Notes," *Journal of Negro History* 29 (1944): 494; August Meier and Elliott Rudwick, *Black History and the Historical Profession, 1915–1980* (Urbana: University of Illinois Press, 1986), pp. 67–68; David Southern, *Gunnar Myrdal and Black-White Relations: The Use and Abuse of "An American Dilemma," 1944–1969* (Baton Rouge: Louisiana State University Press, 1987), pp. 93–94; Ralph Ellison, *Shadow and Act* (New York: Random House, 1964), pp. 303–17.

62. New Orleans *Informer*, September 30, 1944; Dallas *Express*, September 16, 1944; Washington, D.C., *Afro-American*, September 23, 1944.

63. Washington, D.C., *Afro-American*, January 22, 1944.

64. Ben Burns, "Carnegie Study on Race," *Chicago Defender*, January 29, 1944.

65. P. L. Prattis, "The Horizon," *Pittsburgh Courier*, n.d. (filed 1944), GMP.

66. Richmond *Times-Dispatch*, March 6, 1944; Richmond *News Leader*, February 18, 1944. For an overview of the southern liberals' reaction, see David W. Southern, "*An American Dilemma* Revisited: Myrdalism and White Southern Liberals," *South Atlantic Quarterly*, 75 (Spring 1976): 182–97.

67. Birmingham *Age Herald*, August 30, 1944.

68. Gerald W. Johnson, "Problem of the American Negro," *New York Herald Tribune Weekly Book Review*, August 13, 1944.

69. Howard W. Odum, "Problem and Method in *An American Dilemma*," *Social Forces* 23 (October 1944): 94–98.

70. Rupert B. Vance, "Tragic Dilemma: The Negro and the American Dream," *Virginia Quarterly Review* 20 (Summer 1944): 440–44.

71. Daniel J. Singal, *The War Within: From Victorian to Modernist Thought in the South, 1919–1945* (Chapel Hill: University of North Carolina Press, 1982), pp. 275–78, 296–99.

72. W. T. Couch, publisher's introduction to Rayford W. Logan, ed., *What the Negro Wants* (Chapel Hill: University of North Carolina Press, 1944), pp. ix–xxiii.

73. Singal, *The War Within*, pp. 300–301.

74. Theodore G. Bilbo, *Take Your Choice: Separation or Mongrelization* (Poplarville, Miss.: Dream House Publishing Company, 1947), pp. 170–72.

75. Gunnar Myrdal, interview with author, August 19, 1980, Stockholm.

76. Frank Tannenbaum, *Darker Phases of the South* (New York: Putnam, 1924).

77. Frank Tannenbaum, *Slave and Citizen: The Negro in the Americas* (New York: Knopf, 1946).

78. Frank Tannenbaum, review of *An American Dilemma* in *Political Science Quarterly* 59 (September 1944): 321–40.

79. Ibid., pp. 334–35, 338–40.

80. D. W. Brogan, "The American Negro Problem," *The Economic History Review* 15 (1945): 73–78.

81. Harold Gosnell, review of *An American Dilemma* in *American Political Science Review* 38 (October 1944): 995–96.

82. E. B. Reuter, "Racial Theory," *American Journal of Sociology* 50 (May 1945): 452–61.

83. E. B. Reuter, "The American Dilemma," *Phylon* 5 (1944): 114–18.

84. On Sumner's influence, see Davie's introduction to *Essays of William Graham Sumner*, ed. Albert Galloway Keller and Maurice Davie (New Haven, Conn.: Yale University Press, 1934), 1:xv–xix.

85. Maurice Davie, *A Constructive Immigration Policy* (New Haven, Conn.: Yale University Press, 1923), pp. 6–7.

86. Maurice Davie, *World Immigration* (New York: Macmillan, 1936), p. 382.

87. Maurice Davie, review of *An American Dilemma* in *Annals of the American Academy of Political and Social Science* 233 (May 1944): 253–54.

88. Kimball Young, review of *An American Dilemma* in *American Sociological Review* 9 (June 1944): 327–30.

89. Gwynne Nettler, "A Note on Myrdal's 'Notes on Facts and Valuations,'" *American Sociological Review* 9 (1944): 686–88; George A. Lundberg, "The Proximate Future of American Sociology: The Growth of Scientific Method," *American Journal of Sociology* 50 (1945): 502–13; Robert C. Bannister, *Sociology and Scientism: The American Quest for*

Objectivity, 1880–1940 (Chapel Hill: University of North Carolina Press, 1987), pp. 152–54.

90. Gunnar Myrdal, *An American Dilemma: The Negro Problem and Modern Democracy* (New York: Harper & Brothers, 1944), p. 69.

91. Leo Crespi, "Is Gunnar Myrdal on the Right Track?" *Public Opinion Quarterly* 9 (Summer 1945): 201–12.

92. Oliver C. Cox, "An American Dilemma: A Mystical Approach to the Study of Race Relations," *Journal of Negro Education* 14 (Spring 1945): 132–48.

93. Doxey Wilkerson, introduction to Aptheker, *The Negro People in America.*

94. Aptheker, *The Negro People in America*, pp. 62–63.

95. Ibid. p. 66.

96. Arnold Rose to G. Myrdal, July 3, 1946, and Rose to Myrdal, February 20, 1947, GMP.

97. Horace Cayton, "Whose Dilemma?" *New Masses*, July 23, 1946, pp. 8–10. Cayton's article criticized an article in which Aptheker summarized his critique of Myrdal that appeared later that year in his book. See Aptheker, "A Liberal Dilemma," *New Masses*, May 14, 1946. For an interesting critique of Aptheker by another Marxist writer, see Ernest Kaiser, "Racial Dialectics: The Aptheker-Myrdal School Controversy," *Phylon* 9 (1948): 295–302.

98. Gunnar Myrdal, *An American Dilemma*, p. 1024.

99. W. F. Ogburn to Charles Dollard, July 20, 1942, NSGC.

100. Donald Young, interview, Columbia Oral History Project, Columbia University, New York, N.Y., p. 58.

101. Melville Herskovits to Leo Crespi, October 23, 1945, Crespi to Herskovits, n.d. (filed 1945), Herskovits Papers, Northwestern University, Evanston, Ill.

102. Edward L. Thorndike to G. Myrdal, January 12, 1944, GMP.

103. Howard Odum to A. R. Mann, August 8, 1944, GEB Papers, 586.1, Box 270, f.2789, Rockefeller Archive Center, Tarrytown, N.Y.

104. Jackson Davis, "Book Review, *An American Dilemma*," unpublished manuscript, copy in American Dilemma file, GMP.

105. Gunnar Myrdal, *Against the Stream: Critical Essays on Economics* (New York: Pantheon, 1973), p. 297.

106. Donald Young, memo, "Possible New Activity in the Field of Race Relations," January 16, 1944, Herskovits Papers, Myrdal folder.

107. On the Carnegie Corporation's policies toward research on blacks after the Myrdal study, see Waldemar Nielsen, *The Big Foundations* (New York: Columbia University Press, 1972), p. 40; Osborn-Jessup interview, n.d., CCA, quoted in Charles William Bourne, "The Origins of *An American Dilemma*," M.A. essay, Department of History, Columbia University, 1985; Robert Lester, memo "Education and Welfare of the Negro," enclosure in Lester to G. Myrdal, December 26, 1944, GMP. See also Arthur Raper to Charles Dollard, February 25, 1956; G. Myrdal to Charles Dollard, April 2, 1956; Charles Dollard to G. Myrdal, April 9, 1956; all in GMP; Guy B. Johnson, interview with author, April 22, 1977; Arthur Raper, interview with author, April 13, 1977; Louis Wirth, "Research in Racial and Cultural Relations," *Proceedings of the American Philosophical Society* 92 (1948): 382.

108. "How Can Carnegie Corporation Attack Poverty? A Report from the Task Force on the Disadvantaged," submitted by Stephen H. Stackpole, Margaret E. Mahoney, Frederic A. Mosher, Barbara D. Finberg, Eli Evans, October 16, 1967, CCA, quoted in Ellen Lagemann,

Private Power for the Public Good: A History of the Carnegie Foundation for the Advancement of Teaching (Middletown, Conn.: Wesleyan University Press, 1983), p. 191; Florence Anderson, interview, Columbia Oral History Project, 1967, p. 71; Gunnar Myrdal, interview with author, August 19, 1980, Stockholm.

109. W. E. B. Du Bois to Board of Editors of the Encyclopedia of the Negro, May 29, 1941, Du Bois Papers, Reel 53, University of Massachusetts, Amherst. Du Bois and Guy B. Johnson did publish a bibliographic volume, *Encyclopedia of the Negro: Preparatory Volume with Reference Lists and Reports* (New York: Phelps-Stokes Fund, 1946). On the GEB and Frazier, see Jackson Davis to Frazier, June 18, 1943, Frazier Papers, Howard University, Washington, D.C.

110. St. Clair Drake, interview with author, December 31, 1978, Palo Alto, Calif. On the paucity of foundation support for research on race relations during the 1950s, see Thomas F. Pettigrew, *Racially Separate or Together?* (New York: McGraw Hill, 1971), p. 106, and Pettigrew, *The Sociology of Race Relations: Reflection and Reform* (New York: Free Press, 1980), p. 193. Few such community studies were done in the period between 1945 and 1960, an exception being Hylan Lewis's *Blackways of Kent* (Chapel Hill: University of North Carolina Press, 1955).

111. Edward Shils, "Tradition, Ecology and Institution in the History of Sociology," *Daedalus* (Fall 1970): 808–9.

112. Guy Benton Johnson and Guion Griffis Johnson, *Research in Service to Society: The First Fifty Years of the Institute for Research in Social Science at the University of North Carolina* (Chapel Hill: University of North Carolina Press, 1980); Guy Johnson, interview with author, April 22, 1977, Chapel Hill, N.C.

113. Melville Herskovits to Waldo Leland, January 10, 1939, and Herskovits to Mortimer Graves, December 1, 1939, Herskovits Papers, quoted in Robert L. Harris, Jr., "Segregation and Scholarship: The American Council of Learned Societies' Committee on Negro Studies, 1941–1950," *Journal of Black Studies* 12 (March 1982): 318–19.

114. Harris, "Segregation and Scholarship," pp. 322–23.

115. *ACLS Bulletin* (1951): 41–42; quoted in Harris, "Segregation and Scholarship," p. 329.

116. Walter A. Jackson, "Melville Herskovits and the Search for Afro-American Culture," in *Malinowski, Rivers, Benedict, and Others: Essays on Culture and Personality, History of Anthropology* 4 (1986): 95–126, ed. George W. Stocking, Jr.

117. Meier and Rudwick, *Black History and the Historical Profession*, pp. 115–36.

118. Charles S. Johnson, *Patterns of Negro Segregation* (New York: Harper & Brothers, 1943); Johnson, *Growing Up in the Black Belt: Negro Youth in the Rural South* (Washington, D.C.: American Council on Education, 1941); Johnson and Associates, *Statistical Atlas of Southern Counties* (Chapel Hill: University of North Carolina Press, 1941).

119. Charles S. Johnson, *To Stem This Tide: A Survey of Racial Tension Areas in the United States* (Boston: Pilgrim Press, 1943).

120. Charles S. Johnson, *Into the Mainstream: A Survey of Best Practices in Race Relations in the South* (Chapel Hill: University of North Carolina Press, 1947).

121. Gilpin, "Charles S. Johnson," pp. 501–21.

122. Ibid., p. 486.

123. E. Franklin Frazier, *Race and Culture Contacts in the Modern World* (New York: Knopf, 1957); Frazier, *Black Bourgeoisie* (Glencoe, Ill.: Free Press, 1957); Frazier, *The Negro Church in America* (Liverpool: Liverpool University Press, 1961).

124. E. Franklin Frazier, *The Negro in the United States* (New York: Macmillan, 1949).

125. On Frazier's objections to Howard and other black universities, see G. Franklin Edwards, "E. Franklin Frazier: Race, Education, and Community," in *Sociological Traditions from Generation to Generation*, ed. Robert K. Merton and Matilda W. Riley (Norwood, N.J.: Ablex Publishing Company, 1980), pp. 122–28.

126. W. E. B. Du Bois, *The Autobiography of W. E. B. Du Bois* (New York: International Publishers, 1968), pp. 308–23.

127. Ibid., p. 323.

Chapter 7: A Liberal Orthodoxy

1. Gunnar Myrdal, *An American Dilemma: The Negro Problem and Modern Democracy* (New York: Harper & Brothers, 1944), p. 74.

2. Alonzo Hamby, *Beyond the New Deal: Harry S. Truman and American Liberalism* (New York: Columbia University Press, 1973), p. xviii.

3. This account follows closely Donald R. McCoy and Richard T. Ruetten, *Quest and Response: Minority Rights in the Truman Administration* (Lawrence: University Press of Kansas, 1973).

4. Ibid., p. 67; Barton J. Bernstein, "The Ambiguous Legacy: The Truman Administration and Civil Rights," in *Politics and Policies of the Truman Administration*, ed. Bernstein (Chicago: Quadrangle Books, 1970), p. 279.

5. President's Committee on Civil Rights, *To Secure These Rights* (Washington, D.C.: Government Printing Office, 1947), pp. 82–83, 85, 134. On the report's debt to Myrdal, see David W. Southern, *Gunnar Myrdal and Black-White Relations: The Use and Abuse of "An American Dilemma," 1944–1969* (Baton Rouge: Louisiana State University Press, 1987), pp. 113–18.

6. President's Committee on Civil Rights, *To Secure These Rights*, pp. 143–44.

7. Ibid., pp. 145–46.

8. Ibid., pp. 139–41.

9. Ibid., p. 166.

10. McCoy and Ruetten, *Quest and Response*, pp. 92–95.

11. Harry S. Truman, *Public Papers* 1948 (Washington, D.C.: U.S. Government Printing Office, 1963), pp. 287–90, quoted in Ruetten and McCoy, *Quest and Response*, p. 120.

12. Bernstein, "The Ambiguous Legacy," p. 286.

13. Hamby, *Beyond the New Deal*, pp. 243–44; Steven Gillon, *Politics and Vision: The ADA and American Liberalism, 1947–1985* (New York: Oxford University Press, 1987), pp. 47–50.

14. Harvard Sitkoff, "Harry Truman and the Election of 1948: The Coming of Age of Civil Rights in American Politics," *Journal of Southern History* 37 (1971): 587–616.

15. Harvard Sitkoff, *A New Deal for Blacks: The Emergence of Civil Rights as a National Issue; The Depression Decade* (New York: Oxford University Press, 1978), p. 136.

16. Harvard Sitkoff, *The Struggle for Black Equality, 1954–1980* (New York: Hill and Wang, 1981), p. 18.

17. Louis Ruchames, *Race, Jobs, and Politics: The Story of FEPC* (New York: Columbia University Press, 1953), p. 165; McCoy and Ruetten, *Quest and Response*, p. 158.

18. Thomas F. Pettigrew, *The Sociology of Race Relations: Reflection and Reform* (New York: Free Press, 1980), p. 133.

19. Philip Gleason, "Americans All: World War II and the Shaping of American Identity," *Review of Politics* 43 (January 1981): 499–503.

20. Louis Finkelstein, "Three Paths to the Common Good," in *Unity and Difference in American Life*, ed. Robert MacIver (New York: Harper, 1947), pp. 6–7; Ruchames, *Race, Jobs, and Politics*, pp. 193–96.

21. Gleason, "Americans All," p. 497.

22. Thomas F. Pettigrew, "The Intergroup Contact Hypothesis Reconsidered," in *Contact and Conflict in Intergroup Encounters*, ed. Miles Hewstone and Rupert Brown (London: Basil Blackwell, 1986), pp. 172–75.

23. Robert MacIver, "What We All Can Do," in *Unity and Difference in American Life*, ed. MacIver (New York: Harper & Brothers, 1947), p. 154.

24. Julius Rosenwald Fund, *Directory of Agencies in Race Relations, National, State and Local* (Chicago: Julius Rosenwald Fund, 1945); Gordon Allport, *The Nature of Prejudice* (Reading, Mass.: Addison-Wesley, 1954), p. xvii.

25. Frank S. Loescher, *The Protestant Church and the Negro* (New York: Associated Press, 1948), p. 42.

26. Will W. Alexander to Myrdal, March 11, 1946, GMP.

27. Goodwin Watson, *Action for Unity* (New York: Harper & Brothers, 1947), pp. 26, 31–42, 46, 49–51, 64.

28. Charles E. Hendry, foreword to Watson, *Action for Unity*, pp. ix–x.

29. Kurt Lewin, *Resolving Social Conflicts* (New York: Harper & Brothers, 1948); Alfred Marrow, *The Practical Theorist: The Life and Work of Kurt Lewin* (New York: Basic Books, 1969), pp. 191–200; Mitchell G. Ash, "Psychology in the 'Intellectual Migration': The Case of Kurt Lewin," unpublished paper, International Congress for History of Science, Berkeley, Calif., 1985.

30. T. W. Adorno, Else Frenkel-Brunswik, Daniel J. Levinson, and R. Nevitt Sanford, *The Authoritarian Personality* (New York: Harper & Brothers, 1950); Bruno Bettelheim and Morris Janowitz, *Dynamics of Prejudice: A Psychological and Sociological Study of Veterans* (New York: Harper & Brothers, 1950); Nathan W. Ackermann and Marie Jahoda, *Anti-Semitism and Emotional Disorder: A Psychoanalytic Interpretation* (New York: Harper & Brothers, 1950).

31. David M. Reimers, *White Protestantism and the Negro* (New York: Oxford University Press, 1965), pp. 117–18.

32. Charles Dollard, Carl I. Hovland, and Leonard S. Cottrell, Jr., foreword to Robin M. Williams, Jr., *The Reduction of Intergroup Tensions: A Survey of Research on Problems of Ethnic, Racial, and Religious Group Relations* (New York: SSRC, 1947), pp. vii–x; see also SSRC *Annual Report, 1944–45*, p. 45.

33. Pettigrew, "Intergroup Contact Hypothesis," p. 174; Pettigrew, *The Sociology of Race Relations*, p. 183.

34. Louis Wirth, "The Problem of Minority Groups," in *The Science of Man in the World Crisis*, ed. Ralph Linton (New York: Columbia University Press, 1945), pp. 346–72.

35. Louis Wirth, "The Unfinished Business of American Democracy," *Annals of the American Academy of Political and Social Science*, 244 (March 1946): 7–9.

36. Louis Wirth, "Research in Racial and Cultural Relations," *Proceedings of the American Philosophical Society* 92 (1948): 381–86.

37. Louis Wirth, "Problems and Orientations of Research in Race Relations in the United States," *British Journal of Sociology* 1 (1950): 117–25. Wirth cited the work of Robert MacIver, Arnold Rose, Kurt Lewin, Bruno Bettelheim and Morris Janowitz. See also Wirth, "Research in Racial and Cultural Relations," pp. 382, 386.

38. A few studies analyzed blacks in the economy. See Herbert R. Northrup, *Organized Labor and the Negro* (New York: Harper & Brothers, 1944); Robert Weaver, *Negro Labor: A National Problem* (New York: Harcourt, Brace, 1946); Weaver, *The Negro Ghetto* (New York: Harcourt, Brace, 1948); Gary S. Becker, *The Economics of Discrimination* (Chicago: University of Chicago Press, 1957); and Paul H. Norgren, *Employing the Negro in American Industry: A Study of Management Practices* (New York: Industrial Relations Counsellors, 1959).

39. Watson, *Action for Unity*, p. 73; Allport, *Nature of Prejudice*, p. 517; Marrow, *Practical Theorist*, p. 195.

40. Williams, *Reduction of Intergroup Tensions*, pp. 2, 10.

41. Ibid., pp. 51–55, 65. As early as 1945, Talcott Parsons had warned of the "boomerang effect" in discussing Myrdal's proposal for an educational campaign. See Parsons, "Racial and Religious Differences as Factors in Group Tensions," in *Approaches to National Unity*, ed. Lyman Bryson, Louis Finkelstein, Robert MacIver (New York: Harper & Brothers, 1945), pp. 196–97.

42. Ibid., pp. 58–59, 65, 69–71.

43. Ibid., p. 45.

44. Ibid., pp. 59–60, 77.

45. Pettigrew, "Intergroup Contact Hypothesis," pp. 172–73.

46. Adorno et al., *Authoritarian Personality*, pp. 973–76.

47. See the essays in Richard Christie and Marie Jahoda, eds., *Studies in the Scope and Method of "The Authoritarian Personality"* (Glencoe, Ill.: Free Press, 1954), especially Christie's "Authoritarianism Reexamined," p. 194. See also John P. Kirscht and Ronald C. Dillehay, *Dimensions of Authoritarianism: A Review of Research and Theory* (Lexington: University of Kentucky Press, 1967); George E. Simpson and J. Milton Yinger, *Racial and Cultural Minorities: An Analysis of Prejudice and Discrimination* (New York: Harper & Brothers, 1953), pp. 94–96, 691; and Franz Samelson, "Authoritarianism from Berlin to Berkeley: On Social Psychology and History," *Journal of Social Issues* 42 (1986): 191–208.

48. Arnold M. Rose, *The Negro in America* (Boston: Beacon, 1956), p. xxvii. For Rose's own approach, see Arnold M. Rose, *Studies in the Reduction of Prejudice*, 2d ed. (Chicago: American Council on Race Relations, 1948), and Arnold and Caroline Rose, *America Divided: Minority Groups in the United States* (New York: Knopf, 1948).

49. Allport, *Nature of Prejudice*, pp. 506–7, 509.

50. Ibid., pp. 472, 467.

51. Ibid., pp. 508, 517.

52. Ibid., pp. 503, 518.

53. Kenneth B. Clark, introduction to Gordon Allport, *The Nature of Prejudice*, 25th anniv. ed. (Reading, Mass.: Addison-Wesley, 1979), pp. ix–x.

54. Paul Sheatsley, quoted in Howard Schuman, Charlotte Steeh, and Lawrence Bobo, *Racial Attitudes in America: Trends and Interpretations* (Cambridge, Mass.: Harvard University Press, 1985), p. 139.

55. E. Franklin Frazier, *Negro Youth at the Crossways: Their Personality Development in the Middle States* (Washington, D.C.: American Council on Education, 1940); Frazier, *The Negro in the United States* (New York: Macmillan, 1949); Frazier, *Black Bourgeoisie* (Glencoe, Ill.: Free Press, 1957).

56. Frazier, *Negro in the United States*, pp. 704–5.

57. Abram Kardiner and Lionel Ovesey, *The Mark of Oppression: Explorations in the*

Personality of the American Negro (Cleveland: World Publishing Company, 1951), pp. 381–87.

58. Richard Kluger, *Simple Justice: The History of Brown v. Board of Education and Black America's Struggle for Equality* (New York: Knopf, 1975), p. 397.

59. Ibid., p. 399; see also Kenneth B. Clark and Mamie K. Clark, "The Development of Consciousness of Self and the Emergence of Racial Identification in Negro Preschool Children," *The Journal of Social Psychology* 10 (1939): 591–99; and Clark and Clark, "Skin Color as a Factor in Racial Identification of Negro Preschool Children," *The Journal of Social Psychology* 11 (1940): 159–69.

60. Kluger, *Simple Justice*, p. 432.

61. Ibid., p. 891.

62. Albert P. Blaustein and Clarence Clyde Ferguson, Jr., *Desegregation and the Law: The Meaning and Effect of the School Segregation Cases* (New Brunswick, N.J.: Rutgers University Press, 1957), pp. 126–37; Frank T. Read, "Judicial Evolution of the Law of School Integration since *Brown v. Board of Education*," in *The Courts, Social Science, and School Desegregation*, ed. Betsy Levin and Willis D. Hawley (New Brunswick, N.J.: Transaction Books, 1977), p. 9.

63. Robert Fredrick Burk, *The Eisenhower Administration and Black Civil Rights* (Knoxville: University of Tennessee Press, 1984), pp. 150–73.

64. Numan V. Bartley, *The Rise of Massive Resistance: Race and Politics in the South during the 1950s* (Baton Rouge: Louisiana State University Press, 1969); Francis M. Wilhoit, *The Politics of Massive Resistance* (New York: George Braziller, 1973), pp. 92–99.

65. See David Southern's excellent discussion of the segregationist response to Myrdal in Southern, *Gunnar Myrdal and Black-White Relations*, pp. 172–85.

66. Robert Welch, *The Politician* (Belmont, Mass.: privately printed, 1963), p. 65, quoted in Idus A. Newby, *Challenge to the Court: Social Scientists and the Defense of Segregation, 1954–66* (Baton Rouge: Louisiana State University Press, 1967), p. 224.

67. Carleton Putnam, *Race and Reason: A Yankee View* (Washington, D.C.: Public Affairs Press, 1961), p. 23.

68. Newby lists the leading scientific racists of the late 1950s and early 1960s as Henry E. Garrett, Frank C. J. McGurk, Audrey Shuey, Robert T. Osborne, and Wesley Critz George. Newby, *Challenge to the Court*, pp. 89–90.

69. Guy B. Johnson, "A Sociologist Looks at Racial Desegregation in the South," *Social Forces* 33 (October 1954): 1–10; John T. Kneebone, *Southern Liberal Journalists and the Issue of Race, 1920–1944* (Chapel Hill: University of North Carolina Press, 1985), pp. 222–25.

70. Ernest W. Burgess, "Social Planning and Race Relations," in *Race Relations, Problems and Theory: Essays in Honor of Robert E. Park*, ed. Jitsuichi Masuoka and Preston Valien (Chapel Hill: University of North Carolina Press, 1961), pp. 20–21; Oscar Handlin, review of *An American Dilemma* (20th anniv. ed.), *New York Times Book Review*, April 21, 1963, p. 1.

71. Pat Watters, *Down to Now: Reflections on the Southern Civil Rights Movement* (New York: Pantheon, 1971), p. 73.

72. Martin Luther King, Jr., "I Have a Dream," in *A Testament of Hope: The Essential Writings of Martin Luther King, Jr.*, ed. James M. Washington (New York: Harper & Row, 1986), p. 219; Martin Luther King, Jr., *Where Do We Go from Here: Chaos or Community?* (Boston: Beacon Press, 1967), p. 68.

73. Carl M. Brauer, *John F. Kennedy and the Second Reconstruction* (New York: Columbia

University Press, 1977); Allen J. Matusow, *The Unraveling of America: A History of Liberalism in the 1960s* (New York: Harper & Row, 1984), pp. 62–70.

74. Quoted in Brauer, *John F. Kennedy and the Second Reconstruction*, pp. 260–62.

75. Doris Kearns, *Lyndon Johnson and the American Dream* (New York: Harper & Row, 1976), pp. 229–30; Matusow, *The Unraveling of America*, pp. 184–85.

76. Matusow, *The Unraveling of America*, p. 187.

77. The text of Johnson's speech is reprinted in Lee Rainwater and William L. Yancey, *The Moynihan Report and the Politics of Controversy* (Cambridge, Mass.: MIT Press, 1967), pp. 125–32.

78. Clayborne Carson, *In Struggle: SNCC and the Black Awakening of the 1960s* (Cambridge, Mass.: Harvard University Press, 1981), pp. 191–211.

79. James Baldwin, *The Fire Next Time* (New York: Dial Press, 1963), pp. 102, 108.

80. LeRoi Jones (Imamu Amiri Baraka), *Blues People: Negro Music in White America* (New York: William Morrow, 1963).

81. "Liberalism and the Negro: A Round-Table Discussion," *Commentary* 37 (March 1964): 32, 35.

82. Ibid., p. 33.

83. Gunnar Myrdal, *Challenge to Affluence* (New York: Pantheon, 1962).

84. "Liberalism and the Negro," p. 30.

85. Ibid., p. 42.

86. Ibid., p. 39.

87. The black nationalist writer Harold Cruse had little sympathy for Baldwin's view of white liberals, however. He termed Baldwin's performance "childish" and a "futile rhetorical exercise." Cruse, *The Crisis of the Negro Intellectual* (New York: William Morrow, 1967), pp. 194–95.

88. Robert K. Merton, "Discrimination and the American Creed," in *Discrimination and the National Welfare*, ed. Robert M. MacIver (New York: Harper & Brothers, 1949), pp. 99–126.

89. Nahum Medalia, "Myrdal's Assumptions on Race Relations: A Conceptual Commentary," *Social Forces* 40 (March 1962): 223–27. Medalia cited David Riesman, *The Lonely Crowd* (New York: Doubleday, 1955).

90. Medalia, "Myrdal's Assumptions," p. 226; Medalia cited Joseph Lohman and F. Reitzes, "Note on Race Relations in Mass Society," *American Journal of Sociology* 58 (November 1952): pp. 240–46.

91. Frank M. Westie reached an ambivalent conclusion in his article, "The American Dilemma: An Empirical Test," *Social Forces* 43 (August 1965): 527–38. Westie's sample of whites in Indianapolis agreed, almost unanimously, with the generalized principles of the American creed, but the majority declined to accept a black family living next door or to invite blacks into their homes for a dinner party. When challenged by the interviewer to explain the conflict, most resolved it in favor of the American creed, allowing Westie to conclude that "Myrdal's optimism was not unjustified." His experiment made no effort to discern how these attitudes affected actual behavior, however.

92. Charles Silberman, *Crisis in Black and White* (New York: Random House, 1964).

93. See Kenneth B. Clark, "Introduction: The Dilemma of Power," in *The Negro American*, ed. Talcott Parsons and Kenneth B. Clark (Boston: Beacon Press, 1967), pp. xi–xviii.

94. The issue of group rights and preferential treatment was debated at the roundtable on "Liberalism and the Negro," pp. 25–30. See also Stokely Carmichael and Charles V.

Hamilton, *Black Power: The Politics of Liberation in America* (New York: Random House, 1967).

95. Lee Rainwater and William L. Yancey, *The Moynihan Report and the Politics of Controversy* (Cambridge, Mass.: MIT Press, 1967), p. 26.

96. Daniel Patrick Moynihan, *The Negro Family: The Case for National Action* (Washington, D.C., 1965), reprinted in Rainwater and Yancey, *The Moynihan Report*, pp. 39–124.

97. Walter A. Jackson, "Politics and Culture in the Thought of E. Franklin Frazier," paper presented at the American Historical Association meeting, Washington, D.C., December 28, 1987; Herbert Gutman, letter to the editor, *The Nation*, February 2, 1980, p. 116; G. Franklin Edwards, "E. Franklin Frazier," in *Black Sociologists: Historical and Contemporary Perspectives*, ed. James E. Blackwell and Morris Janowitz (Chicago: University of Chicago Press, 1974), p. 100.

98. Rainwater and Yancey, *The Moynihan Report*, pp. 29, 94, 135.

99. Ibid., p. 200.

100. Ibid., pp. 412–13, 202.

101. Ibid., p. 197.

102. Ibid., pp. 200, 410.

103. Ibid., p. 450.

104. Charles Valentine, *Culture and Poverty: Critique and Counter-Proposals* (Chicago: University of Chicago Press, 1968), pp. 20–42.

105. Rainwater and Yancey, *The Moynihan Report*, p. 463.

106. Ibid., p. 443.

107. Ibid., pp. 28, 153.

108. Matusow, *The Unraveling of America*, pp. 197–98.

109. Talcott Parsons, "Introduction: Why 'Freedom Now,' Not Yesterday?" in *The Negro American*, ed. Parsons and Clark, pp. xix–xxviii.

110. "Conference Transcript," *Daedalus* 95 (Winter 1966): 312.

111. Robin M. Williams, Jr., *Strangers Next Door: Ethnic Relations in American Communities* (Englewood Cliffs, N.J.: Prentice-Hall, 1964), p. 361.

112. Kenneth B. Clark, "Introduction: The Dilemma of Power," in *The Negro American*, ed. Parsons and Clark, pp. xi–xviii.

113. Ralph Ellison, *Shadow and Act* (New York: Random House, 1964), pp. 315–16.

114. Although Elkins's *Slavery: A Problem in American Institutional and Intellectual Life* (Chicago: University of Chicago Press) was published in 1959, it did not ignite a major scholarly controversy until the mid-1960s. See Ann J. Lane, ed., *The Debate over Slavery: Stanley Elkins and His Critics* (Urbana: University of Illinois Press, 1971), and August Meier and Elliott Rudwick, *Black History and the Historical Profession, 1915–1980* (Urbana: University of Illinois Press, 1986), p. 253. For the controversy over Styron's portrayal of the historical Nat Turner, see William Styron, *The Confessions of Nat Turner* (New York: Random House, 1967), and John Henrik Clarke, ed., *William Styron's Nat Turner: Ten Black Writers Respond* (Boston: Beacon Press, 1968).

115. Charles Keil, *Urban Blues* (Chicago: University of Chicago Press, 1966); Charles Horton, "Time and Cool People," *Transaction* 4 (April 1967); Robert Blauner, "Black Culture: Lower-Class Result or Ethnic Creation?" in *Afro-American Anthropology*, ed. Norman E. Whitten and John F. Szwed (New York: Free Press, 1970); Carol B. Stack, *All Our Kin* (New York: Harper and Row, 1974).

116. Sterling Stuckey, "Through the Prism of Folklore," *Massachusetts Review* 9 (Summer 1968); Lawrence Levine, *Black Culture and Black Consciousness* (New York: Oxford Univer-

sity Press, 1977); Peter Wood, *Black Majority* (New York: Norton, 1974); Herbert Gutman, *The Black Family in Slavery and Freedom* (New York: Pantheon, 1976); John Blassingame, *The Slave Community* (New York: Oxford University Press, 1972); Eugene Genovese, *Roll, Jordan, Roll: The World the Slaves Made* (New York: Pantheon, 1974).

117. Carmichael and Hamilton, *Black Power*, p. 5.

118. See Meier and Rudwick, *Black History*, pp. 277–308, and the debates in Armstead L. Robinson, Craig C. Foster, and Donald H. Ogilvie, eds., *Black Studies in the University: A Symposium* (New Haven, Conn.: Yale University Press, 1969).

119. *Report of the National Advisory Commission on Civil Disorders* (New York: Bantam, 1968); William H. Chafe, *The Unfinished Journey: America since World War II* (New York: Oxford, 1986), pp. 365–80.

120. Carl N. Degler, "The Negro in America—Where Myrdal Went Wrong," *New York Times Magazine*, December 7, 1969. Degler, who was then researching a book comparing U.S. and Brazilian race relations, also faulted Myrdal for not casting his analysis in comparative perspective.

121. L. Paul Metzger summarized the critique of Myrdal by sociologists who emphasize conflict in his article on "American Sociology and Black Assimilation: Conflicting Perspectives," *American Journal of Sociology* 76 (1971): 627–47. See also Pierre L. van den Berghe, *Race and Racism: A Comparative Perspective* (New York: Wiley, 1967), pp. 78, 126; John Horton, "Order and Conflict Theories of Social Problems as Competing Ideologies," *American Journal of Sociology* 71 (1966): 701–13; and Stanford Lyman, *The Black American in Sociological Thought* (New York: Capricorn, 1972), pp. 99–120.

122. As noted in Chapter 5, cultural pluralist ideas had a long history in America, going back to Du Bois, Bourne, and Kallen at the beginning of the century and continuing through such thinkers as Will Herberg in the 1950s. The black struggle of the 1960s gave a new life to cultural pluralism. See John Higham, "Ethnic Pluralism in Modern American Thought," in his *Send These to Me: Jews and Other Immigrants in Urban America* (New York: Atheneum, 1975), pp. 196–230. See also Milton Gordon, *Assimilation in American Life: The Role of Race, Religion, and National Origins* (New York: Oxford University Press, 1964), pp. 132–59, and Williams, *Strangers Next Door*, pp. 364–65.

123. Peter Steinfels, *The Neoconservatives: The Men Who are Changing America's Politics* (New York: Simon & Schuster, 1979).

Chapter 8: Dreamer, Planner, and Fighter

1. Gunnar Myrdal gave his account of his time in government in *Hur styrs landet?* (Stockholm: Rabén & Sjögren, 1982), pp. 224–48. See also Ernst Wigforss, *Ur mina minnen* (Stockholm: Prisma, 1964), pp. 387–89; Tage Erlander, *Tage Erlander, 1940–1949* (Stockholm: Tidens Förlag, 1974), pp. 273–78; Nicholas W. Balabkins, "Gunnar Myrdal (1898–1987): A Memorial Tribute," *Eastern Economic Journal* 14 (1988): 101–2.

2. Václav Kostelecký, *The United Nations Economic Commission for Europe: The Beginning of a History* (Göteborg: Graphic Systems AB, 1989), pp. 20–24, 37, 54; Walt W. Rostow, *The Division of Europe after World War II: 1946* (Austin: University of Texas Press, 1981), pp. 51–75, 108–10.

3. Kostelecký, *United Nations Economic Commission for Europe*, pp. 87–109; Walt W. Rostow, "The Economic Commission for Europe," *International Organization* 3 (1949): 254–68; David Wightman, *Economic Co-Operation in Europe: A Study of the Economic*

Commission for Europe (New York: Praeger, 1956), pp. 38–48, 255–56; Melvin M. Fagen, "Gunnar Myrdal and the Shaping of the United Nations' Economic Commission for Europe," *Coexistence* 25 (1988): 427–35.

4. Fagen, "Gunnar Myrdal and the Shaping of the United Nations' Economic Commission for Europe," pp. 434–35; Wightman, *Economic Co-Operation in Europe*, pp. 202–25, 255–56; *Foreign Relations of the United States* 4 (1950): 34, 233; and 1 (1951): 1222–23.

5. Matthew Wohl to Secretary of State Paul R. Porter to Secretary of State George C. Marshall, May 2, 1947, Document no. 840.5043/5-27, NA; Assistant Secretary Willard Thorp to Wohl, May 26, 1947, Doc. no. 840.5043/5-247, NA; Director, FBI to Attorney General, August 18, 1947, item no. 100-294500-132, and Karl Gunnar Myrdal Summary, February 8, 1955, item no. 100-7660-4458, Gunnar Myrdal file, FBI; Paul R. Porter to Secretary of State, December 15, 1948, Doc. no. 111.20A/12-1548, NA; Paul R. Porter to Secretary of State, April 7, 1948, copy in Gunnar Myrdal file, FBI.

6. John W. Holmes, Memorandum for the Deputy Under-Secretary of State for External Affairs, July 26, 1949, File 5475-I-40, Archives Division, Department of External Affairs, Ottawa, cited in James Barros, "The Importance of Secretaries-General of the United Nations," in *Dag Hammarskjöld Revisited: The UN Secretary-General as a Force in World Politics*, ed. Robert S. Jordan (Durham, N.C.: Carolina Academic Press, 1983), p. 31.

7. Hugh S. Cummings, Jr., to Department of State, January 10, 1950, Doc. no. 315/1-1050, NA; Brian Urquhart, *Hammarskjöld* (New York: Harper & Row, 1972), pp. 3–16; Brian Urquhart to author, July 21, 1989; Gunnar Myrdal, *Hur styrs landet?* pp. 226–32; Kostelecký, *United Nations Economic Commission for Europe*, p. 49 n. 37.

8. Lars G. Lindskog, *Alva Myrdal* (Stockholm: Sveriges Radios Förlag, 1981), pp. 77–82.

9. Egon Glesinger, "Gunnar Myrdal," unpublished manuscript enclosed in Glesinger to G. Myrdal, January 3, 1949, and G. Myrdal to Arnold and Caroline Rose, February 26, 1945, GMP; Sissela Bok, *Alva: Ett kvinnoliv* (Stockholm: Bonniers, 1987), pp. 176–94.

10. Bok, *Alva*, p. 195; Lindskog, *Alva Myrdal*, pp. 83–93.

11. Alva Myrdal and Viola Klein, *Women's Two Roles: Home and Work* (London: Routledge & Kegan Paul, 1956).

12. Dean Acheson telegram, February 15, 1950, U.S. State Department, Doc. no. 398.43 UNESCO/2-1550, NA; ——— Mathews to Secretary of State, February 17, 1950, Doc. no. 100.43310-25, copy in Alva Myrdal file, FBI; Anonymous to J. Edgar Hoover, February 7, 1950, Alva Myrdal file, FBI; W. Walton Butterworth to Department of State, Washington, D.C., May 4, 1953, copy in Alva Myrdal file, FBI.

13. United States Immigration and Naturalization Service, "Parole Agreement," March 19, 1953, copy in AMP; Dag Hammarskjöld to Alva Myrdal, June 19, 1953, AMP; A. M. Rosenthal, "Noted Sociologist Paroled into U.S.," *New York Times*, April 30, 1953; "Madame Myrdal victime du MacCarthysme," *L'Observateur*, May 7, 1953; "Jan Myrdal beklager att mamman trakasseras," *Dagens Nyheter*, May 5, 1953; Minutes, United Nations Economic and Social Council, 15th Session, 686th Meeting, April 15, 1953, Headquarters, New York, copy in AMP; Richard Sterner, "Alva Myrdal's Journey to the United Nations," translated article from *Morgon-Tidningen*, May 5, 1953, enclosed in W. Walton Butterworth to Department of State, Washington, D.C., copy in Alva Myrdal file, FBI.

14. A. Myrdal to Acting Director-General, UNESCO, June 4, 1953, AMP; G. Myrdal to Walter Lippmann, May 8, 1953, copy in AMP.

15. Julian Behrstock, *The Eighth Case: Troubled Times at the United Nations* (Lanham, Md.: University Press of America, 1987), pp. 7–38; Shirley Hazzard, *Defeat of an Ideal: A Study of*

the Self-Destruction of the United Nations (Boston: Little, Brown, 1973), p. 15; Hazzard, "Reflections: Breaking Faith—1," *New Yorker*, September 25, 1989, pp. 63–75.

16. "Text of Note from the Secretary General of the United Nations to Ambassador Lodge concerning Alva Myrdal," enclosed in Donald B. Laurie to Attorney General Herbert Brownell, April 9, 1953, State Department Records, document no. 398.43UNESCO/4-853, NA; Brian Urquhart, *Hammarskjöld*, pp. 58–70. For a critical discussion of Hammarskjöld and McCarthyism, see Conor Cruise O'Brien, "Conflicting Concepts of the United Nations," The Twenty-First Montague Burton Lecture on International Relations (Leeds: Leeds University Press, 1964), and Hazzard, *Defeat of an Ideal*, pp. 52–69. On Alva Myrdal's case, see John Foster Dulles to U.S. Consul, Geneva, July 8, 1953, copy in Alva Myrdal file, FBI, and Charles A. Thompson to John W. Taylor, August 18, 1953, copy in AMP.

17. Walter H. Waggoner, "U.S. Bans 300 Titles Abroad," *New York Times*, June 26, 1953; Harold B. Hinton, "McCarthy Disputes Senators and Bedell Smith on Books," *New York Times*, July 25, 1953. Also G. Myrdal to Joseph Greenwald, July 13, 1953, T. W. Simpson to G. Myrdal, n.d., received August 7, 1953; Charles Dollard to G. Myrdal, September 1, 1953; all in GMP.

18. Charles Dollard to G. Myrdal, September 1, 1954, GMP; "Statements of Carnegie Corporation of New York, Submitted to Special Committee to Investigate Tax Exempt Foundations, July, 1954," copy in GMP; "Foundation Head Defends 5 Studies," *New York Times*, July 12, 1954.

19. Richard Wright to G. Myrdal, September 7, 1955, GMP.

20. "Gunnar Myrdal's Visit to Moscow Seen Spur to East-West Trade," *Daily Worker*, March 12, 1954; J. Edgar Hoover to E. Tomlin Bailey, Department of State, April 10, 1957; Mrs. J. B. Matthews, "The Strange Case of Myrdal," *Christian Economics*, March 19, 1957; "Karl Gunnar Myrdal, Alva Myrdal—Internal Security Report," June 25, 1957; M. A. Jones to DeLoach, memo, "Re: Inquiry You Received from Senator Robert Byrd for Information Concerning Gunnar Myrdal," September 21, 1965; all in Gunnar and Alva Myrdal file, FBI. Senator Byrd, the Majority Whip, supported the Voting Rights Act. On Cartha DeLoach's role in surveillance of the civil rights movement, see Kenneth O'Reilly, *"Racial Matters": The FBI's Secret File on Black America, 1960–1972* (New York: Free Press, 1989), pp. 50, 144–47, 186–89, 207–11.

21. Gunnar Myrdal, *An International Economy: Problems and Prospects* (New York: Harper & Brothers, 1956), p. 304.

22. G. Myrdal to Hammarskjöld, January 28, 1954, GMP.

23. Bok, *Alva*, pp. 211–12, 220–21.

24. Gunnar Myrdal, *An International Economy*, pp. 180, 318–30.

25. Raymond F. Mikesell, "International Economics," *American Economic Review* 46 (December 1956): 1011–16; K. E. Boulding, "Warning to Nineveh," *Christian Century* 73 (September 12, 1956): 1053–54.

26. Gunnar Myrdal, *Development and Underdevelopment* (Cairo: National Bank of Egypt, 1956).

27. H. W. Arndt, *Economic Development: The History of an Idea* (Chicago: University of Chicago Press, 1987), pp. 50–51.

28. Gunnar Myrdal, *Development and Underdevelopment*, pp. 59–61.

29. Ibid., p. 62.

30. Michael Brecher, *Nehru: A Political Biography* (London: Oxford University Press, 1959), pp. 510–53; Sarvepalli Gopal, *Jawaharlal Nehru: A Biography; Volume III: 1956–1964*

(Cambridge, Mass.: Harvard University Press, 1984), pp. 13–20. Gopal notes that Nehru was influenced by Myrdal's *Economic Theory and Under-developed Regions.*

31. Tarlok Singh, "For the Well-being of All Mankind: Gunnar and Alva Myrdal," Indian Association of Social Science Institutions *Quarterly Newsletter* 6 (June 1987): 10.

32. Bok, *Alva,* p. 210.

33. Gunnar Myrdal, "Aims of Planning" (1958), reprinted in Indian Association of Social Science Institutions *Quarterly Newsletter* 6 (1987): 1–7.

34. Paul Streeten, "Gunnar Myrdal," unpublished manuscript in author's possession; cf. Streeten, "Gunnar Myrdal: The Cheerful Pessimist," *New Society,* December 5, 1974.

35. Singh, "For the Well-being of Mankind," p. 11.

36. Ulrich Herz, *Alva och Gunnar Myrdal i fredens tjänst* (Stockholm: Rabén & Sjögren, 1971), p. 47; Streeten, "Gunnar Myrdal," unpublished manuscript.

37. Gunnar Myrdal, *Asian Drama: An Inquiry into the Poverty of Nations* (New York: Twentieth Century Fund, 1968). I have drawn on Streeten, "Cheerful Pessimist," in my summary of *Asian Drama.*

38. Gunnar Myrdal, *Asian Drama,* 1:130.

39. Manning Nash, review of *Asian Drama* in *Atlantic* 211 (April 1968): 132; Kenneth E. Boulding, "Asia: Soft States and Hard Facts," *New Republic,* May 4, 1968, pp. 25–28; Thomas Balogh, "The Scrutable East," *New York Times Book Review,* March 24, 1968, pp. 1, 44–46; George E. Taylor, "A Monumental Study," *Virginia Quarterly Review* 44 (Summer 1968): 474–77; Naomi Bliven, "Nowhere to Go But Up," *New Yorker,* February 15, 1969, pp. 116–20.

40. "Modernize or Perish," *Times Literary Supplement,* November 21, 1968, p. 1297.

41. P. T. Bauer, "Million-Word Pamphlet," *Spectator,* January 11, 1969.

42. P. C. Mahalanobis, "The Asian Drama: An Indian View," *Economic and Political Weekly* (Bombay), July 1969, pp. 1119–32.

43. Krishna Prakash Gupta, review of *Asian Drama* in *Commonweal* 89 (October 4, 1968): 35–36. For other criticisms of Myrdal's ethnocentrism, see S. S. Wagle, "An Inquiry into the Poverty of Nations," *United Asia* 20 (August 1968): 202–9; Romesh Thapar, "Poverty of Nations or Notions?" *Yojana,* May 12, 1968, pp. 2–6, 31; Rohit Dave, "Unfolding Saga of Asian Development," *Commerce,* July 20, 1968, pp. 146–47; K. S. Krishnaswamy, "Some Thoughts on a Drama," *Indian Journal of Social Research* 10 (April 1969): 71–78; S. Shukla, "Planning and Educational Development," *Indian Education Review* 5 (July 1970): 156–65.

44. Clifford Geertz, "Myrdal's Mythology: 'Modernism' and the Third World," *Encounter* 33 (January 1, 1969): 26–34.

45. See Robert Lekachman, review of *The Challenge of World Poverty* in *Saturday Review,* October 3, 1970, pp. 35–37.

46. See the discussion in Charles W. Bergquist, *Alternative Approaches to the Problem of Development: A Selected and Annotated Bibliography* (Durham, N.C.: Carolina Academic Press, 1979), item no. 213.

47. See Streeten, "Cheerful Pessimist."

48. Gunnar Myrdal, interview with author, August 19, 1980, Stockholm; Streeten, "Cheerful Pessimist."

49. Gunnar Myrdal, "Need for Reforms in Underdeveloped Countries," in *The World Economic Order: Past and Prospects,* ed. S. Grassman and E. Lundberg (London: Macmillan, 1981).

50. Aidan Foster-Carter, "From Rostow to Gunder Frank: Conflicting Paradigms in the

Analysis of Underdevelopment," *World Development* 4, no. 3 (March 1976): 167–80; Bergquist, introduction to *Alternative Approaches to the Problem of Development*, pp. vii–xvii; Arndt, *Economic Development*, pp. 115–77; Andre Gunder Frank, *Capitalism and Underdevelopment in Latin America: Historical Studies of Chile and Brazil* (New York: Monthly Review Press, 1967); Frances Moore Lappe, Joseph Collins, and David Kinley, *Aid as Obstacle: Twenty Questions about Our Foreign Aid and the Hungry* (San Francisco: Institute for Food and Development Policy, 1980); P. T. Bauer, *Dissent on Development* (Cambridge, Mass.: Harvard University Press, 1976).

51. G. Myrdal to Richard Fulton, January 30, 1967, GMP.

52. Gunnar Myrdal, *Hur styrs landet?* p. 261.

53. Stephen S. Rosenfeld, "Gunnar Myrdal: A Realist Who Believes in Future of U.S.," *Washington Post*, December 23, 1968.

54. Frank L. Keegan, "The American Dilemma Revisited," *Current*, September 1972, pp. 36–37.

55. Gunnar Myrdal, *Beyond the Welfare State: Economic Planning and Its International Implications* (New Haven, Conn.: Yale University Press, 1960), pp. 92–102.

56. Gunnar Myrdal, *Challenge to Affluence* (New York: Pantheon, 1962), pp. 10–12, 14, 18–20.

57. Ibid., pp. 22, 24, 26, 30–31, 38, 99.

58. Ibid., pp. 29, 58, 64–65.

59. Ibid., pp. 39, 43.

60. Ibid., pp. 92–95, 101.

61. Ibid., pp. 30–31, 108, 115, 125–26.

62. Seymour L. Harris, review of *Challenge to Affluence* in *New York Times Book Review*, October 3, 1963; Peter L. Bernstein, "Myrdal's Long Look at Us," *New Republic*, November 2, 1963, pp. 23–24; Bertram F. Levin, "Justice, Poverty, and Affluence," *Virginia Quarterly Review* 80 (Winter 1964): 144–46; Edwin L. Dale, Jr., "Myrdal on American Affluence," *American Scholar* 33 (Winter 1964): 145–47.

63. Ben B. Seligman, "The Underclass," *Commentary* 39 (February 1964): 91–92.

64. Henry David, "Problems of Prosperity," *Saturday Review*, January 11, 1964, pp. 58–59.

65. *Time*, October 18, 1963, p. 120.

66. Gunnar Myrdal, interview with author, August 19, 1980, Stockholm.

67. Donald McDonald, "The American Dilemma 1967: An Interview with Gunnar Myrdal," *Center Magazine* 1, no. 1 (October/November, 1967).

68. Rosenfeld, "Gunnar Myrdal: A Realist Who Believes in Future of U.S."

69. Gunnar Myrdal, *Against the Stream: Critical Essays on Economics* (New York: Pantheon, 1973), p. 284.

70. Keegan, "The American Dilemma Revisited," p. 42.

71. "Gunnar Myrdal: International Prophet," *Nonaligned Third World Annual*, 1970, p. 20.

72. Gunnar Myrdal, "The Vietnam War and the Political and Moral Isolation of America," December 8, 1966, GMP.

73. McDonald, "The American Dilemma 1967," p. 33.

74. Protokoll, Svenska Kommitten för Vietnam, January 24, 1968, October 17–18, 1970; Gunnar Myrdal's remarks to Vietnam demonstration, February 21, 1968; G. Myrdal to Eugene McCarthy, September 23, 1970; G. Myrdal to J. William Fulbright, October 23, 1969; all in GMP.

75. Gunnar Myrdal, *Against the Stream*, pp. 271–78, 291–92; cf. Keegan, "The American Dilemma Revisited," pp. 35–43.

76. Lindskog, *Alva Myrdal*, pp. 115–54.

77. Gunnar Myrdal, *Against the Stream*, pp. 228–29, 281–82, 289; Gunnar Myrdal, "A Worried America," *Current* 202 (April 1978): 54–55; Lindskog, *Alva Myrdal*, p. 136; Herz, *Alva och Gunnar Myrdal i fredens tjänst*, pp. 11, 47–48.

78. Ken Olofsson, "'Jag avskyr att bli gammal,'" *Aftonbladet*, May 18, 1987.

79. Viveka Vogel, "24 timmar om dygnet med Alva," *Vecko-journalen*, June 1974.

80. Gunnar Myrdal, interview with author, August 19, 1980, Stockholm.

81. John Higham, "Ethnic Pluralism in Modern American Thought," in his *Send These To Me: Jews and Other Immigrants in Urban America* (New York: Atheneum, 1975), pp. 196–230.

82. Gunnar Myrdal, "The Case against Romantic Ethnicity," *Center Magazine* 7, no. 4 (July/August 1974): 26–30.

83. Kenneth Clark, interview with author, October 21, 1986, Hastings-on-Hudson, N.Y.; G. Myrdal to Clark, December 26, 1973, and G. Myrdal and Clark, "Proposal for the Writing of An American Dilemma Revisited," February 22, 1974, GMP. Also Clark to G. Myrdal, January 2, 1974; Clark to Alan Pifer, February 25, 1974; Clark to Dorothy K. Newman, June 18, 1974; all in Clark Papers, Library of Congress, Washington, D.C.

84. Kenneth Clark, interview with author, October 21, 1986; Otto Klineberg, interview with author, October 20, 1986, New York; Clark to G. Myrdal, January 7, 1975, and G. Myrdal to Alan Pifer, February 11, 1975, Clark Papers.

85. G. Myrdal to Alan Pifer, December 18, 1974, copy in Clark Papers; G. Myrdal to David Hamburg, December 7, 1983, copy in possession of Leslie Dunbar, Durham, N.C.

86. Lars Weiss, "Därför reser Gunnar Myrdal tillbaka till USA: Doktorn måste ägne sig at de allvårlig sjuka," *Aftonbladet*, September 29, 1974.

87. Gunnar Myrdal, "Race and Class in a Welfare State," unpublished lecture to a symposium on "The National Purpose Reconsidered: 1776–1976," Columbia University, October 28, 1976, copy in possession of author, pp. 14–15, 27, 29, 31.

88. Ibid., pp. 19–20.

89. Ibid., pp. 33–36, 39–40, 44.

90. Ibid., p. 54.

91. Gunnar Myrdal, *Hur styrs landet?* p. 259.

92. Gunnar Myrdal, "A Worried America," *Current* 202 (April 1978): 47–48. The original speech was given at the annual meeting of the Lutheran Council in the USA, Philadelphia, March 11, 1976.

93. Ibid., pp. 51, 53.

94. Ibid., pp. 53–55.

95. Ibid., pp. 56–57.

96. Gunnar Myrdal, *Hur styrs landet?* pp. 256–64.

97. G. Myrdal to John Kenneth Galbraith, February 2, 1972, GMP.

98. Mary Johnson, "Alva and Gunnar Myrdal Know 'The Great Happiness of Living to be Very Old and Together,'" *People* (1980), pp. 51–52, 57.

99. Singh, "For the Well-being of Mankind," pp. 10–13.

100. Ole Schierbeck, "Åbent opgør i berømt familie," *Politiken*, August 22, 1982; Jan Myrdal, "Eftermäle," *Expressen*, June 3, 1987.

101. Peter Curman, "Ett masterverk!" *Aftonbladet*, June 11, 1984; Nordal Åkerman, "Jan Myrdals 'Barndom,'" *Dagens Nyheter*, November 22, 1982; Leif Carlsson, review of *Barn-*

dom in *Svenska Dagbladet*, November 22, 1982; Sven-Eric Leidman, review of *Barndom* in *SDS*, November 22, 1982.

102. Gunnar Myrdal, "Han talar osanning," *Dagens Nyheter*, December 9, 1982; Ken Olofsson, "'När jag är död ska folk få veta sanningen,'" *Aftonbladet*, January 24, 1986.

103. Jan Myrdal, *En annan värld* (Stockholm: P. A. Norstedt, 1984); Jan Myrdal, *Ord och avsikt* (Stockholm: P. A. Norstedt, 1986).

104. Sissela Bok, "Alva Myrdal," *Yale Review* 76 (Spring 1987): 300.

105. *Aftonbladet*, February 17, 1986.

106. Gunnar Myrdal, *Hur styrs landet?*

107. Ibid., pp. 76–77.

108. Avery Russell, memo to David Hamburg et al., December 23, 1983; Andre Schiffrin to G. Myrdal, January 17, 1984; David Hamburg to G. Myrdal, February 21, 1984; Avery Russell to Hamburg, May 14, 1984; Hamburg to G. Myrdal, May 31, 1984; G. Myrdal to Leslie Dunbar, June 26, 1984; Dunbar to Russell, August 3, 1984; Dunbar to G. Myrdal, August 10, 1984; Schiffrin to Russell, August 8, 1985; all copies in possession of Leslie Dunbar, Durham, N.C.; interview with Leslie Dunbar, August 25, 1989, Durham, N.C.

109. Gunnar Myrdal, draft, "An American Dilemma Revisited" (1985), GMP.

110. Robert K. Merton, "Remarks on the Occasion of the First Honor Award by South Asian Sociologists, 12 April 1975, to Gunnar Myrdal," Clark Papers, Box 14.

111. Jan Myrdal, "Eftermäle," pp. 30–33.

112. Lars Ingelstam, "Kampen mot cynismen; Minnesord om Gunnar Myrdal," June 2, 1987, copy in author's possession.

113. Ingvar Carlsson, "Inspirade de unga i s," *Svenska Dagbladet*, May 18, 1987; "Han var samvete for en hel värld," *Aftonbladet*, May 18, 1987.

114. Melvin M. Fagen, "Gunnar Myrdal in Retrospect," *Coexistence* 25 (1988): 423–25.

115. Charles Kindleberger, "Gunnar Myrdal, 1898–1987," *Scandinavian Journal of Economics* 89 (1987): 393–403.

116. Singh, "For the Well-being of Mankind," p. 13.

117. Coretta Scott King to Sissela Bok, May 19, 1987, copy in author's possession, furnished by Professor Bok.

118. Gunnar Myrdal, draft, "An American Dilemma Revisited" (1985), GMP.

Essay on Sources

The starting point for any investigation into Gunnar Myrdal's career is the Arbetarrörelsens Arkiv (Archive of the Labor Movement) in Stockholm. Most of Myrdal's correspondence is organized in a letter collection indexed by correspondent and arranged by decade. There is also a file marked "American Dilemma," which includes correspondence with Myrdal's collaborators and with Carnegie Corporation officials. Although most of Myrdal's correspondence is in Swedish, much of his international correspondence concerning the social sciences is in English, and a smaller amount is in German. Gunnar Myrdal's clipping file is a valuable source of newspaper and magazine articles about him and of reviews of *An American Dilemma*. Alva Myrdal's letter collection contains much information about her intellectual and political development, and her clipping file includes many of her articles about Swedish politics, education, family policies, and women's issues. Gunnar and Alva Myrdal's family correspondence remains closed until the year 2000. The Gustav Cassel papers at the Royal Library include several important letters from Gunnar Myrdal to his mentor.

The Carnegie Corporation of New York has preserved two reels of microfilmed correspondence and memoranda concerning the Myrdal study. (Copies of the microfilm are also available at the Arbetarrörelsens Arkiv.) Researchers do not have access to an index of the Corporation's files, but they may request files on particular persons or institutions. The files of W. E. B. Du Bois, Melville Herskovits, the National Association for the Advancement of Colored People, and the Encyclopedia of the Negro were pertinent to my research. The Newton D. Baker papers at the Library of Congress provide valuable insight into a trustee's involvement in inaugurating the Myrdal study, and papers of John C. Merriam, also at the Library of Congress, contain reports concerning Carnegie Corporation policies. The small collection of Frederick Keppel's personal papers at the Columbia University Library is disappointing, but the correspondence gives some insight into his networks and political views. The Rockefeller Archive Center in Tarrytown, New York, has correspondence and memoranda concerning Myrdal's long relationship with the Rockefeller Foundation. In the General Education Board files, there are letters and memoranda by Jackson Davis concerning Myrdal and a diary of Davis's trip through the South with Myrdal and Richard Sterner. The Phelps-Stokes Fund papers at the Schomburg Library in New York include extensive materials on Du Bois's proposed Encyclopedia of the Negro, a project that failed to win foundation support partly because of the resources committed to the Myrdal study.

Myrdal's collaborators produced a number of scholarly memoranda, which have been deposited at the Schomburg Library in New York and are also available on microfilm at several other libraries in the United States. Of the memoranda that remain unpublished, the most interesting are Ralph Bunche's "Conceptions and Ideologies of the Negro Problem" and Arthur Raper's "Race and Class Pressures." The latter includes much evidence of extralegal violence against blacks and labor union organizers in the South. The Arnold Rose papers at the University of Minnesota Library contain correspondence concerning the Myrdal study, a draft of the first part of *An American Dilemma* that is marked "very first draft," and an oral history memoir by Rose. The Melville Herskovits papers at the Northwestern University Library include correspondence with virtually every major figure in the social science study of black Americans in the 1930s as well as correspondence with foundation officials. Ralph Bunche's papers at the University of California, Los Angeles, contain correspondence concerning the Myrdal project as well as extensive field notes on Bunche's travels with Myrdal in the South. The Franklin Frazier papers at Howard University include Frazier's comments on the manuscript of *An American Dilemma*, while the Alain Locke papers, also at Howard, contain a small amount of correspondence with Myrdal. Louis Wirth's comments on the manuscript of *An American Dilemma* are available in the Wirth papers at the University of Chicago. The Howard Odum papers at the Southern Historical Collection, University of North Carolina at Chapel Hill, offer important insights into Odum's relations with the foundations, social scientists, and interracial reformers as well as his private reaction to Myrdal's book.

Several participants in the Myrdal study generously granted me interviews. Gunnar Myrdal met with me for several lengthy sessions in Stockholm in 1980, 1981, and 1985 and offered detailed comments about his work. The late Arthur Raper invited me to his farm at Oakton, Virginia, in 1977 and described his experiences traveling with Myrdal in the South. Guy B. Johnson and the late Guion G. Johnson discussed their roles in the project in interviews in Chapel Hill in 1977. Doxey Wilkerson reviewed his conflicts with Myrdal in an interview at his home in South Norwalk, Connecticut, in 1978. St. Clair Drake described the politics of the study and the attitudes of young black scholars of the 1930s in an interview at Stanford University in 1978. Kenneth Clark analyzed his efforts to collaborate with Myrdal in an interview in Hastings-on-Hudson, New York, in 1986. In 1967 the Carnegie Corporation underwrote an oral history of its activities, conducted by the Columbia Oral History Project. The Columbia University Library has a lengthy interview with Gunnar Myrdal as well as interviews with Guy B. Johnson and Guion G. Johnson. Interviews with Donald Young, Charles Dollard, and Florence Anderson touch upon the Myrdal project. The Arbetarrörelsens Arkiv has collected tapes of several oral history interviews with Gunnar Myrdal, but these have not yet been transcribed.

Harvard Sitkoff, in *A New Deal for Blacks: The Emergence of Civil Rights as a National Issue; The Depression Decade* (New York: Oxford University Press, 1978), offers the most comprehensive discussion of the social, political, economic, and intellectual status of Afro-Americans in the 1930s. Though he overstates the extent to which civil rights emerged as a national issue during the 1930s, Sitkoff provides an invaluable portrait of black-white relations on the eve of the Myrdal study. Nancy Weiss, in *Farewell to the Party of Lincoln* (Princeton: Princeton University Press, 1983), and John B. Kirby, in *Black Americans in the Roosevelt Era: Liberalism and Race* (Knoxville: University of Tennessee Press, 1980), stress the limits of the New Deal's commitment to civil rights while noting the emergence of Afro-Americans as an important interest group within the Democratic party. In *The Emergence of the New South, 1913–1945* (Baton Rouge: Louisiana State University Press, 1967) George B. Tindall examines the myriad ways in which the New Deal and the Second World War set in motion fundamental changes in southern race relations. Paul Mertz, in *New Deal Policy and Southern Rural Poverty* (Baton Rouge: Louisiana State University Press, 1978), and Pete Daniel, in *Breaking the Land: The Transformation of Cotton, Tobacco, and Rice Cultures since 1880* (Urbana: University of Illinois Press, 1985), note the effects of New Deal agricultural policy in uprooting southern black tenant farmers, and Gavin Wright, in *Old South, New South: Revolutions in Southern Agriculture* (New York: Basic Books, 1986), observes that no new manufacturing jobs for blacks were being created in the South during the 1930s. Wright also stresses the transformations in the southern economy wrought by defense industries during World War II. James T. Patterson, in *America's Struggle against Poverty, 1900–1980* (Cambridge, Mass.: Harvard University Press, 1981) analyzes the haphazard creation of a national welfare apparatus but says little about how it affected blacks. On black protest movements during the 1930s, Dan T. Carter's *Scottsboro: A Tragedy of the American South* (Baton Rouge: Louisiana State University Press, 1979) remains a valuable source on the rivalry between the National Association for the Advancement of Colored People and the Communist party. Mark Naison's *Communists in Harlem during the Depression* (Urbana: University of Illinois Press, 1983) provides a detailed examination of the relationship between a local Communist party and the national party leadership, while Robin D. G. Kelley, in "Hammer 'n Hoe: Black Radicalism and the Communist Party in Alabama, 1929–1941," Ph.D. dissertation, University of California, Los Angeles, 1987, examines black traditions of resistance to planters in the black belt. In *The NAACP Crusade against Lynching, 1909–1950*, Robert A. Zangrando investigates the struggle for antilynching legislation in the 1930s.

Scholars have presented sharply divergent interpretations of the history of philanthropic foundations and their relationship to black Americans. Rockefeller official Raymond B. Fosdick offers a sympathetic history of the General Education Board in *Adventure in Giving: The Story of the General Education Board* (New York: Harper & Row, 1962). Critical accounts appear in Louis R. Harlan's *Separate and Unequal: Public School Campaigns in the Southern Seaboard States, 1901–1915* (New York: Atheneum, 1968) and Henry Allen Bullock's *A History of Negro Education in the South* (Cambridge: Harvard University Press, 1967). A more radical interpretation is offered in James D. Anderson's "Philanthropic Control over Private Black Higher Education," in *Philanthropy and Cultural Imperialism: The Foundations at Home and Abroad*, edited by Robert F. Arnove, pp. 147–77 (Boston: G. K. Hall, 1980). James D. Anderson, in *The Education of Blacks in the South* (Chapel Hill: University of North Carolina Press, 1988), explores these issues in a broader context. In *The Big Foundations* (New York: Columbia University Press, 1972) Waldemar Nielsen offers some valuable, though poorly documented, observations on foundation programs for blacks. Ellen Condliffe Lagemann's *Private Power for the Public Good* (Middletown, Conn.: Wesleyan University Press, 1983), though not directly concerned with the race issue, provides a valuable critique of the strategies of elite reform in one of Andrew Carnegie's other foundations. Lagemann's *The Politics of Knowledge: The Carnegie Corporation, Philanthropy, and Public Policy* (Middletown, Conn.: Wesleyan University Press, 1989), appeared after this book had gone to press.

Most authors who have discussed the institutional origins of the Myrdal study have accepted uncritically the account given by Frederick Keppel in his foreword to *An American Dilemma*. John Madge, for example, in his chapter on Myrdal in *The Origins of Scientific Sociology* (Glencoe, Ill.: Free Press, 1962), merely repeats Keppel's version. Charles W. Bourne's unpublished M.A. essay, "The Origins of *An American Dilemma*," Department of History, Columbia University, 1985, breaks with this tradition and offers a detailed account of the decision making within the foundation. Herbert Aptheker initiated a Marxist line of interpretation in his scathing book, *The Negro People in America: A Critique of Gunnar Myrdal's "An American Dilemma"* (New York: International Publishers, 1946). While Aptheker makes some good criticisms of Myrdal's discussions of Afro-American history and culture, he presents a simplistic analysis of the Swedish Social Democrat as a tool of American corporate interests. Ralph Ellison's radical review essay in *Shadow and Act* (New York: Random House, 1964), pp. 303–17, is brilliant in its critique of Myrdal's discussion of Afro-American culture and raises an important question about the origins of the Myrdal study. Ellison surmises that the study resulted from corporate elites feeling "a need . . . for a new ideological approach to the Negro problem." To support this claim, however, he offers only a vague and undocumented theory that the Myrdal project was a response to the New Deal's desire to boost employment and consumption in the South. Ellison underestimates the racism of Carnegie trustee Newton Baker and misreads the intentions of Keppel when he suggests that "*An American Dilemma is the blueprint for a more effective exploitation of the South's natural, industrial, and human resources.*" John H. Stanfield's *Philanthropy and Jim Crow in American Social Science* (Westport, Conn.: Greenwood Press, 1985) is a more recent Marxist interpretation of the relationship between foundations and social science studies of Afro-Americans. Stanfield has done extensive research in foundation archives and presents a veritable battery of "smoking guns" that document the paternalistic attitudes of foundation officers who conceived of themselves as mentors of black scholars and vigilant watchdogs ready to steer black protest into moderate channels. Unfortunately, Stanfield's discussion of the Myrdal study contains numerous factual errors. He exaggerates Jackson Davis's influence on Myrdal and overestimates the Swedish scholar's dependence upon the work of his American collaborators. Stanfield fails to investigate Myrdal's political views stemming from his work in Sweden and thus portrays him as a captive of the Carnegie Corporation rather than as the creator of a decisively new interpretation of American race relations. Stanfield's study also neglects to discuss the sizable social science literature that Du Bois and other black radicals managed to produce in spite of foundation pressures in the opposite direction.

Harald Bohrn and Kerstin Assarsson-Rizzi's *Gunnar Myrdal: A Bibliography, 1919–1981* (New York: Garland Press, 1981) is the most comprehensive bibliography of Gunnar Myrdal's writings. Gunnar Myrdal never found time to write an autobiography, but he did produce a short article, "Gunnar heter jag," in *Aftontidningen*, August 16, 1943, as well as biographical notes in *Against the Stream* (New York: Pantheon, 1973) and *Hur styrs landet?* (Stockholm: Rabén & Sjögren, 1982). An excellent study of the Myrdals and the population issue, which includes an account of Alva and Gunnar Myrdal's careers until 1938, is provided by Allan C. Carlson in "The Roles of Alva and Gunnar Myrdal in the Development of a Social Democratic Response to Europe's 'Population Crisis' 1929–1938," Ph.D. dissertation, Ohio University, 1978. Ulrich Herz's *Alva och Gunnar Myrdal i fredens tjänst* (Stockholm: Rabén & Sjögren, 1971) consists mainly of interviews with the Myrdals and with several of their associates and friends. Annette Kullenberg's interview with Alva Myrdal, "Jag villa stada samhället" in *Det gäller vårt liv* (Stockholm: Kulturhuset, 1976) is revealing on Alva's childhood. Lars G. Lindskog, in *Alva Myrdal* (Stockholm: Sveriges Radios Förlag, 1981), discusses Alva Myrdal's intellectual and political career. Lindskog's book is based largely on interviews with Alva Myrdal for a series of programs on Swedish radio, supplemented with work in the Arbetarrörelsens Arkiv. Per Thullberg's article on Alva Myrdal in the *Svenskt biographiskt lexikon* 127 (1987): 161–78, includes a comprehensive discussion of her career and an extensive bibliography of her published works. A forthcoming volume edited by Laurent Lepage, *Gunnar Myrdal et son oeuvre* (Montreal: University of Montreal Press), should offer new perspectives on Gunnar Myrdal's economic thought.

Jan Myrdal's autobiographical works, *Barndom* (Stockholm: P. A. Norstedt, 1982), *En annan värld* (Stockholm: P. A. Norstedt, 1984), and the autobiographical essays in *Ord och avsikt* (Stockholm: P. A. Norstedt, 1984) pose a difficult interpretive challenge for the historian interested in Jan's parents. The first two works are essentially literary autobiography, and Jan Myrdal has insisted that they are imaginative literature and should not be seen as an attempt at historical writing. *Barndom* and *En annan värld* tell the story of Jan Myrdal's childhood from the child's point of view and are based almost entirely on Jan's recollections with only occasional reference to other sources. The focus is thus on the child's emotions and perceptions from age two to age thirteen, and there is no attempt to discuss the parents' own perceptions of their lives or to explain how events in their careers affected their behavior at home. Jan Myrdal's portrayal of Gunnar's father, Carl Adolf Pettersson, is rather romanticized, and his discussion of Alva fails to come to grips with the difficult choices faced by women of her generation who sought to have both careers and families. Nevertheless, Jan Myrdal's books do provide vivid portraits of Gunnar's parents, and Jan's stark portrait of his father's role in the home cannot be ignored. Jan Myrdal's "Eftermäle," *Expressen*, June 3, 1987, pp. 30–33, is useful in calling attention to Gunnar Myrdal's youthful conservatism, though Jan underestimates his father's commitment to human rights and understates Gunnar's interest in issues of equality. Sissela Bok's *Alva: Ett kninnoliv* (Stockholm: Bonniers, 1987) is an attempt to offer a more sympathetic portrait of Alva Myrdal than that offered by her brother. Bok, the only author to have access to the Myrdal family correspondence, presents a compelling biographical portrait of Alva based on many different sources as well as her own memories of their home life. In explaining the pressures on Alva Myrdal at home, Bok confirms some of the negative impressions of Gunnar Myrdal as a parent that emerge from a reading of Jan Myrdal's volumes.

Harvard Sitkoff provides an able summary of the social science literature on the concept of race in the 1930s in *A New Deal for Blacks*, pp. 190–215; but his account portrays the social science community as more activist than it was, and he overstates the degree of consensus in the social and cultural study of black Americans. George W. Stocking, in *Race, Culture, and Evolution: Essays in the History of Anthropology* (New York: Free Press, 1968), discusses the development of Boasian anthropology in the early part of the twentieth century. In "Ideas and Institutions in American Anthropology: Thoughts toward a History of the Interwar Years" in *Selected Papers from the American Anthropologist, 1921–45* (Washington, D.C., 1976), Stocking analyzes the discipline during the 1930s. A discussion of the major anthropologist that Myrdal confronted is provided in Walter A. Jackson, "Melville Herskovits and the Search for Afro-American Culture," in Stocking, ed. *Malinowski, Rivers, Benedict and Others: Essays on Culture and Personality* (History of Anthropology, Vol. 4) (Madison: University of Wisconsin Press, 1986): 95–126. Fred H. Matthews's *Quest for an American Sociology: Robert E. Park and the Chicago School* (Montreal: McGill-Queen's University Press, 1977) is an excellent biography of the senior sociologist of race and ethnicity in the 1930s. The essays by Richard Robbins on Charles S. Johnson and by G. Franklin Edwards on E. Franklin Frazier in *Black Sociologists: Historical and Contemporary Perspectives*, edited by James E. Blackwell and Morris Janowitz (Chicago: University of Chicago Press, 1974), are both insightful. For a more critical discussion of Johnson, see August Meier, "Black Sociologists in White America," *Social Forces* 56, no. 1 (September 1977): 259–70. Patrick Gilpin's "Charles S. Johnson: An Intellectual Biography," Ph.D. dissertation, Vanderbilt, 1973, is also useful. G. Franklin Edwards's article, "E. Franklin Frazier: Race, Education, and Community," in *Sociological Traditions from Generation to Generation*, edited by Robert K. Merton and Matilda W. Riley (Norwood, N.J.: Ablex Publishing Company, 1980), is good on the institutional context in which Frazier worked. James O. Young's *Black Writers of the Thirties* (Baton Rouge: Louisiana State University Press, 1973) contains an excellent discussion of Frazier, Ralph Bunche, and Abram Harris at Howard University.

Wayne Brazil's "Howard W. Odum, the Building Years, 1884–1930," Ph.D. dissertation, Harvard University, 1975, covers Howard Odum's career until 1930. Morton Sosna's *In Search of the Silent South: Southern Liberals and the Race Issue* (New York: Columbia University Press, 1977) is a perceptive study of Odum and other southern liberals. Daniel J.

Singal, in *The War Within: From Victorian to Modernist Thought in the South, 1919–1945* (Chapel Hill: University of North Carolina Press, 1982), provides a valuable discussion of Odum, Guy B. Johnson, Arthur Raper, and W. T. Couch. John T. Kneebone's *Southern Liberal Journalists and the Issue of Race, 1920–1944* (Chapel Hill: University of North Carolina Press, 1985) places southern liberal ideas about race relations in the context of World War II. On northern white liberals, see Peter J. Kellogg's "Northern Liberals and Black America: A History of White Attitudes, 1936–1952," Ph.D. dissertation, Northwestern University, 1971, in which he examines articles in the *Nation* and the *New Republic*.

David W. Southern's *Gunnar Myrdal and Black-White Relations: The Use and Abuse of "An American Dilemma," 1944–1969* (Baton Rouge: Louisiana State University Press, 1987) is an excellent study of the reception of Myrdal's classic work. L. Paul Metzger, in "American Sociology and Black Assimilation: Conflicting Perspectives," *American Journal of Sociology*, 76 (January 1971): 627–47, discusses the influence of Myrdal's assimilationist ideas on American sociology but overstates the affinity between Myrdal's theory of society and Talcott Parsons's. John Higham's "Ethnic Pluralism in Modern American Thought," in his collection of essays, *Send These to Me* (New York: Atheneum, 1975), pp. 196–230, contrasts Myrdal's views with those of American cultural pluralist thinkers.

Index

65; memorial service for, 365–66

Myrdal, Gunnar: selected by Carnegie Corporation to head Negro study, xiii–xiv, 31–35, 312–13; early political and social ideas, xiv, 41–50, 384 (nn. 22, 23, 29); and objectivity question, xvi, 56–58, 114–15, 313, 394 (n. 95); builds research team, xvi–xvii, 92–94, 106–17, 314; intellectual influence of Alva on Gunnar, xv, 54–55; encounters institutional economics, xv, 60–62; ideas about welfare state, xv–xvi, 69–71, 313; and Swedish neutrality policy, xvii–xviii, 137, 142–49, 154–58, 160–61, 177–78, 181, 184–85; works on "An American Dilemma Revisited," xix, 352–57, 366–67, 369–71; childhood, 36–40, 383 (n. 5); marriage to Alva Reimer, 50–53, 82–86; study with Gustav Cassel, 53–54; writes *The Political Element in the Development of Economic Theory*, 56–58, 386 (n. 73); children of, 59, 79, 81–84, 162, 172; Rockefeller Fellow, 59–64; turns toward interdisciplinary social scientific research, 61–64; reacts to stock market crash, 63–64; as visiting professor in Geneva, 64–65; criticizes American labor movement, 65–68; joins Social Democratic party, 68–69; and Stockholm school of economics, 72–75; appointed to chair in economics at University of Stockholm, 75, 387 (n. 116); research on population in Sweden, 75–81; calls for housing reform, 76, 84; supports women's rights, 77–79; advocates eugenic policies, 78; research on agriculture in Sweden, 81; decides to undertake Carnegie Negro study, 81–87; first impressions of American race issue, 62, 67–68; begins Carnegie Negro study, 89; first research trip to the South, 90–92; friendship with Ralph Bunche, 110–11, 121–34; relations with black intellectuals, 110–13, 121–32, 393 (n. 81); as interviewer, 117–21; and outbreak of World War II, 135–36; and Swedish restrictions on press freedom, 146–47, 154–55, 160–

61; writes *Kontakt med Amerika*, 147–58, 314–15; writes *An American Dilemma*, 161–64, 315–17; plans for postwar Europe, 173–81; involvement with July 20, 1944, plot to kill Hitler, 181–85; text of *An American Dilemma*, 186–230; declines to answer critics, 259, 272, 310–11; and civil rights movement, 298–300, 348–49; serves as minister of commerce, 321–22; heads Economic Commission for Europe, 321–24, 331; marital conflict, 326–27; encounters McCarthyism, 327–31; studies poverty in Third World, 332–44; advocates reforms of welfare states, 345; calls for antipoverty program in United States, 345–49; criticizes American policy in Vietnam, 349–51; and disarmament, 351–52; wins Nobel Prize, 359–61; conflict with Jan, 361–65; death, 367; eulogies of, 368–69. *See also* American creed; *American Dilemma, An*; Moral dilemma argument; Myrdal, Alva Reimer; Prophylactic reform; Social democracy; Social Democratic party: in Sweden; Social engineering; Welfare state

Myrdal, Jan, 55, 59, 83, 85, 162, 326–29, 361–65, 368

Myrdal, Janken, 367

NAACP, xiii, 5–8, 20, 23–25, 89, 97, 102–3, 112–13, 115, 122, 127, 129, 208, 216–17, 219, 222, 224, 236, 239, 246, 262, 269, 273–74, 278, 292, 312

Napoleon Bonaparte, 52, 358

Nässtrom, Gustaf, 46

National Conference of Jews and Christians, 19

National Emergency Council, 4

Nationalism: Afro-American, 130–31, 353–54, 356; Swedish, 158; German, 183

National Negro Congress, 7–8, 127, 260

National Recovery Administration, 18

National Research Council, 266

National Resource Committee, 32

National Resources Planning Board, 234

National Urban League, 23, 24, 89, 102,